Managing the modern organization

Managing the modern organization

Third edition

Theo Haimann
Saint Louis University

William G. Scott
University of Washington

Patrick E. Connor
Oregon State University

Houghton Mifflin Company   Boston
Dallas   Geneva, Illinois   Hopewell, New Jersey
Palo Alto   London

Originally published as *Management in the Modern Organization*.

Copyright © 1978 by Houghton Mifflin Company. All rights reserved. No part of this work may be reproduced or transmitted in any form or by any means, electronic or mechanical, including photocopying and recording, or by any information storage or retrieval system, without permission in writing from the publisher.

Printed in the U.S.A.
Library of Congress Catalog Card Number: 77-75879
ISBN: 0-395-25512-0

Contents

Preface xxi

Chapter 1 Managing 1
    Where it happens 1
    Who makes it happen 2
    Focusing on managing 2
    Systems theory
    Contingency approach
    Human values
    What managing is about 8
    What happens: The process of management 9
    Managers' skills
    Management functions 11
    Planning
    Organizing
    Staffing
    Influencing
    Controlling
    Fundamental linking processes 13
    Decision making
    Communicating
    Basic managerial purpose 14
    Organizational effectiveness
    Interrelationships of functions, processes, and purposes
    Summary 15
    Discussion questions 15
    Supplementary readings 16

Part I The managerial perspective 17

Chapter 2 Landmarks in management history 20
Management in preindustrial times 20
The Industrial Revolution 23
The scientific management movement 24
The start of scientific management and the ASME
Frederick W. Taylor
The mental revolution of scientific management
The classical period 28
The management process
The human relations movement
Organization theory
Transition 32
Summary 33
Discussion questions 34
Supplementary readings 34

Chapter 3 Modern management: Systems, science, and emerging issues 35
Management principles, systems, and contingencies 35
The systems approach
The contingency approach
Technological change 38
Work force changes
Complex organizations
Organizational interdependence
Science and management 41
The behavioral sciences
Science and quantitative methods
Science and communication
Emerging issues in management 45
Energy
Capital generation
The physical environment
Summary 48
Discussion questions 48
Supplementary readings 48

Part II Planning 49

Chapter 4 Objectives, policies, and contingencies 51
A model for examining objectives 52
Research on business objectives
Grand strategy

Strategy
Balancing objectives
Changing objectives
Policies 60
Characteristics
Origin
Communication
Periodic policy review
Procedures 64
Methods and rules 66
Summary 66
Discussion questions 67
Supplementary readings 67

Chapter 5   The nature of planning 68

Planning as an intellectual process and a primary function 69
Relationship to the other managerial functions
Control and feedback
The manager plans 70
Time span
Planning participation
Characteristics of planning 71
The planning period
Commitments
The trend toward long-range planning
Integration of short- and long-range plans
The good plan
Dissemination
Summary 75
Discussion questions 75
Supplementary readings 76

Chapter 6   Information for planning: Forecasting 77

The place of forecasting in modern organizations 77
Economic variables and control
Organization for forecasting
Forecasts as planning premises
External planning premises and forecasts 81
The general business climate
Industry climate
Availability of information
Techniques
Internal planning premises and forecasts 88
The sales forecast
Other internal planning premises
Forecasts in general 93
Shortcomings

Length of the forecast period
Expense
Summary 94
Discussion questions 95
Supplementary readings 95

Chapter 7 **Planning: The action phase** 96
Strategy and long-range planning 97
A systems concept
Strategy compared with tactics
New long-range planning processes
The role of the planning staff
Short-range planning 101
Revenue and expense forecast
Cash forecast
Pro forma statements
Budgets
PERT
Limitations of planning 110
Internal limitations
External limitations
Summary 114
Discussion questions 114
Supplementary readings 115

Cases for Part II 117

Case II/1   **The Mohawk Shoe Company** 118

Case II/2   **The Central Lumber Company** 119

Case II/3   **The good citizen** 120

Case II/4   **The Optico Company** 121

Case II/5   **The closing of Middletown** 123

Case II/6   **The Elbert Manufacturing Company** 125

Part III   Organizing 127

Chapter 8   Introduction to organizing: Two underlying concepts 130
An ageless concept: Span of management 131
Span and organizational levels

Determining the proper span
Span: How large?
The trade-off problem
A second concept: Authority 139
The source and nature of authority
Formal-authority theory
Acceptance theory
The organizational character of authority 144
Bases of authority
Types of authority
Interaction of the sources of authority
Summary 149
Discussion questions 150
Supplementary readings 150

Chapter 9   Structuring the organization: Departmentalization 152
Evolution of the division of labor 152
Specialization and efficiency
Steps in the division of labor
Departmentalization 154
Departmentalizing by function
Departmentalizing by product
Departmentalizing by territory
Departmentalizing by customer
Departmentalizing by process and equipment
Departmentalizing by time
A composite organizational structure 164
Summary 164
Discussion questions 166
Supplementary readings 166

Chapter 10   Structuring the organization: Managing through authority 167
Delegating authority 168
The scalar chain
Unity of command
The process of delegation
Decentralizing authority 176
Centralization
Decentralization
When to decentralize
How much to decentralize
Decentralization in the various functions
Recent trends
Summary 188
Discussion questions 188
Supplementary readings 188

Chapter 11 Structuring the organization: Line-staff relationships 189

Line and staff 189
Historical evolution of staff
Evolution of staff in organizations
Role and authority of staff
Functional authority
The relation of staff to line 197
Levels of staff participation in the organization
Staff growth patterns
Human problems of line-staff relations
Other specialized organizational functions 201
"Assistant-to"
Liaison
The traditional organizational structure 202
Summary 204
Discussion questions 205
Supplementary readings 205

Appendix A Preparing formal organization charts and manuals 206

Organization charts 206
Advantages
Limitations
Responsibility for charting
Types of charts
Additional charting considerations
Organization manuals 213
Content
Preparation and revision

Chapter 12 Managing the structure: Coordinating 217

The meaning of coordination 218
Definitions and interpretations
Coordination and cooperation
Self-coordination
Achieving coordination 220
The difficulties of coordinating
Contingencies in coordinating
Types of coordinating
The principles of Mary Parker Follett
Coordination and the five managerial functions
Liaison people
External coordination
Summary 229
Discussion questions 230
Supplementary readings 230

Appendix B Problems with traditional structures 231
   Problems for people 231
   Attitudes
   Behavior
   Problems for the organization 232
   Rules
   Delegation
   Conclusion 236
   References 237

Chapter 13 Committees 238
   Types of committees 239
   Function and level
   Line and staff committees
   Temporary or standing committees
   Committees: Some assets 240
   Combined opinion
   Coordination and cooperation
   Development of executives
   Representation of interest groups
   Committees: Some liabilities 242
   High costs
   Effectiveness limited to certain situations
   Divided responsibility
   Danger of weak compromise decisions
   Strain on interpersonal relations
   Effective operation of the committee 245
   Clear definitions of function, scope, and degree of authority
   Selection of appropriate members
   Reasonable number of members
   Thorough preparation for meetings
   Committee procedures
   The right chairperson
   Group interaction
   Follow-up of committee action
   Evaluation of committee work
   Summary 249
   Discussion questions 251
   Supplementary readings 251

Chapter 14 Designing organizations 252
   Design characteristics 252
   Differentiation
   Formalization
   Centralization
   Situational management 254

Organizational goals 255
Design constraints 255
External environment
Organizational technology
People
A design example 258
Two situations
Two designs
A contemporary design: The matrix organization 261
The matrix idea
Purpose
An example
Conclusion
Summary 267
Discussion questions 267
Supplementary readings 267

Cases for Part III 269

Case III/1   The A. B. Electronics Company 270

Case III/2   The concerned boss 272

Case III/3   The frustrated engineer 274

Case III/4   The Fabric Outlet Stores 275

Case III/5   The manager's dilemma 276

Case III/6   The Good Samaritan Hospital 278

Part IV   Staffing 281

Chapter 15   The staffing process 283

The scope of the human resource system 283
The general nature of staffing 285
A line function
Staffing policies
Sequence of steps in staffing
Special problems of staffing 289
The problem of measurement
The small number of staffers
Nonstandardized positions

Summary 290
Discussion questions 290
Supplementary readings 291

Chapter 16 Forecasting executive needs 292

External factors in the demand for executives 292
Work force issues
Industry issues
Legislative issues
Economic issues
Internal factors in the demand for executives 295
Determining the types of executive needed 297
Position descriptions
Skills
Determining the number of managers needed 300
Executive inventories
Replacement tables
Summary 302
Discussion questions 302
Supplementary readings 303

Chapter 17 Performance appraisal of managers 304

An appraisal system 305
The appraisal process 307
Who should appraise?
Regularity of appraisal
How far down?
Review of the appraisal
Implementing the appraisal program
Difficulties in appraising
The assessment center approach 312
The management by objectives approach 315
MBO as a system
An appraisal of MBO
Summary 319
Discussion questions 319
Supplementary readings 319

Chapter 18 Executive change and development 321

Executive obsolescence 322
Expanding managerial horizons 323
Executive development in the appraisal system 323
In-organization executive development programs 324
Planned progression systems
Lateral transfers
Special projects

Temporary assignments
Assistant-to positions
Coaching and counseling
Out-organization executive development programs 328
College and university programs
Special institutes
Use of consultants
Trends in executive development 330
Summary 330
Discussion questions 331
Supplementary readings 331

Chapter 19 Selecting and training new managers 332
Recruitment and selection 333
Public policy issues in recruitment
Initial screening
Interviewing, testing, and final selection
Training 336
Assessing training needs
Training objectives
Principles of learning
Training programs 338
Presupervisory work
Additional presupervisory training
Assignment to managerial positions
Additional training devices 341
Committees
Junior boards
Training outside the firm
Evaluation of training programs 343
Summary 344
Discussion questions 344
Supplementary readings 344

Chapter 20 Executive compensation 345
Salary determinants 346
Internal consistency and external competitiveness 347
Internal evaluation of management positions
External compensation alignment
Other forms of direct financial compensation 349
Incentive and bonus systems
Stock options
Profit sharing
Pension plans
Indirect financial compensation 355
Compensation contingencies 356
Communication

Participation
Disclosure
Summary 357
Discussion questions 357
Supplementary readings 358

Cases for Part IV 359

Case IV/1   **The likely candidate** 360

Case IV/2   **The hatchet man** 362

Case IV/3   **The board's dilemma** 363

Case IV/4   **The informal promotion** 364

Case IV/5   **The appraisal interview** 365

Case IV/6   **Simmons Retail Chain Store: Selection of an auditor** 366

Part V   **Influencing** 369

Chapter 21   **The influencing process** 372
    Authority 372
    Bases of authority
    Types of authority
    Compliance
    Power 374
    Sources
    Outcomes
    Authority, power, and influence 375
    Contingency factors in influencing 377
    Summary 378
    Discussion questions 378
    Supplementary readings 378

Chapter 22   **The individual in the organization** 380
    Perception 380
    Frame of reference
    Selective perception
    Managerial implications
    Values and attitudes 385
    Values and attitudes and behavior
    Values, attitudes, and managing

Needs 388
A hierarchy of needs
Final comment 389
Summary 389
Discussion questions 390
Supplementary readings 390

Chapter 23 Informal relationships 391

Why people form groups 392
Attraction to specific groups
Benefits from group participation
Work group effectiveness 395
Group problem solving: Some assets
Group problem solving: Some liabilities
Conclusion
Nature of informal relationships 397
Structure
Behavior
Leadership
Relationships between formal and informal organizations
Informal working relationships 401
Summary 402
Discussion questions 402
Supplementary readings 403

Chapter 24 Motivation and leadership 404

The nature of human motivation 404
Motivation models 405
Individual motives
Motive classification
Choice-process models
Motivation by managers: The leadership process 410
The diversity of leadership roles
Leadership theories
Leadership style
Leadership style and effective influence
Summary 416
Discussion questions 416
Supplementary readings 416

Chapter 25 Organizational climate and change 417

Organizational climate theories 418
Theory X and Theory Y
Likert's theory
The current consensus
Organizational design
Morale and satisfaction 422

The components of morale
Morale contingencies
The outcomes of morale and job satisfaction
Changing organizations 425
Job change
Changing decision roles
Changing organizational processes
Summary 428
Discussion questions 428
Supplementary readings 428

Cases for Part V 431

Case V/1　The punctual president 432

Case V/2　The zealous graduate student 433

Case V/3　The new directive 434

Case V/4　Juanita and her department 436

Case V/5　The chemical laboratory 438

Case V/6　The administrative assistant 440

Part VI　Controlling 443

Chapter 26　The control process 446
A general model of control 447
The human aspects of control systems 449
Behavior and control
Design of an effective control system 451
Understandability
Rapid reporting of deviations
Flexibility
Economic criteria
Indication of corrective action
Basic steps in the control process 453
Setting standards
Strategic control points
Checking on performance
Corrective action
Summary 458
Discussion questions 458
Supplementary readings 459

Chapter 27 The budget: Control aspects 460
       Budgeting and budgetary control 460
       Comprehensive and partial budgeting
       Numerical expression
       Managerial budget preparation 462
       A line function
       Staff or committee assistance
       Approval by the board
       Administration of a budgetary program 464
       Sales budget
       Budgeted income statements (operating budget)
       The budgeted balance sheet
       Flexibility of the budgetary program 468
       Length of the budget period
       Alternative budgets
       Variable expense budgets
       Supplemental monthly budget plan
       Budget review or budget revision
       The relationship of budgeting to other managerial activities 471
       Budgets: Planning and control
       Budgets and accounting
       Budgets and organization
       Budgets as an aid for coordination
       Budgets and human problems
       Summary 474
       Discussion questions 475
       Supplementary readings 475

Chapter 28 Controlling overall performance 476
       Break-even point analysis 477
       Break-even chart
       Profit-and-loss control 479
       Control through return on investment 482
       Internal auditing control 483
       Meaning and scope
       Position within the organization
       The control unit 484
       Need
       Purpose
       Position within the organization
       External auditing control 486
       Summary 487
       Discussion questions 488
       Supplementary readings 488

Cases for Part VI 489

Case VI/1 Willard's controller 490

Case VI/2   **The pricing dispute** 491

Case VI/3   **The copying machine** 493

Case VI/4   **The administrator's problem** 494

Case VI/5   **The Elysée Manufacturing Company** 496

Case VI/6   **The fledgling company** 497

Part VII   The linking processes 499

Chapter 29   Linking process 1: Decision making 501
    Elements of the decision process 502
    Conditions for making decisions 503
    Making decisions under certainty
    Making decisions under risk
    States of nature
    Making decisions under uncertainty
    Problems with the rational model 510
    Boundaries of rationality
    Boundaries of bounded rationality
    Decision making and organization design 513
    Operations research 515
    Methods
    Presentation of alternative solutions
    Models
    Techniques of operations research 518
    Probability theory
    Game theory
    Queuing theory
    Linear programming
    Summary 519
    Discussion questions 519
    Supplementary readings 520

Chapter 30   Linking process 2: Communicating 521
    The nature of communicating 523
    Channels of communication 523
    Formal channels
    Informal channels: The grapevine
    The communication media 527
    Written communication
    Oral communication
    Barriers to communication 529
    Organizational structure

xx   Contents

    Status and position
    Language
    Resistance to change
    Other barriers
    Means for overcoming barriers to communication 532
    Feedback
    Sensitivity to the receivers' world
    Effective listening
    Actions speak louder than words
    The importance of being an expert
    Summary 535
    Discussion questions 536
    Supplementary readings 536

Conclusion 537

Chapter 31   Organizational effectiveness 538
    Measures of organizational effectiveness: A contingency problem 538
    The traditional approach to determining effectiveness 540
    Application of efficiency rules
    Organizational design and effectiveness
    Organizational complexity and effectiveness
    Management audits
    Social responsibility as an effectiveness contingency 545
    The arena of social responsibility
    The social audit and human-assets accounting
    Summary 550
    Discussion questions 550
    Supplementary readings 551

Comprehensive cases 553

Case 1   Case of the questionable communiqués 554

Case 2   The case of the borderline black 565

Case 3   Crisis in conscience at Quasar 572

Case 4   Lennert Company Limited 585

Case 5   J. R. Sanford Corporation (A) 591

Index 599

Preface

Systems, processes, functions, and contingencies are the backbone of modern management theory and practice. Previous editions of this book were built around these concepts, and the new edition continues the orientation. Our objective is still to integrate the proven, traditional, functional approach to managing with current developments in the contingency approach, systems theory, and the behavioral sciences. This framework permits us to discuss managing in systems terms, with regard to the external environment that influences the nature of organizational inputs and outputs. The relationship between the planning and controlling functions is one example of the use of this kind of analysis in our book. Another example is the interrelationship of goal setting, planning, and organizational design.

We consider managing a facilitating activity that allocates and utilizes resources, influences human action, and plans change in order effectively to accomplish rationally conceived goals. Managing consists, therefore, not of simply one activity, but of several distinct, though interrelated processes—planning, organizing, staffing, influencing, and controlling. The systems approach helps the student to understand the intricate relationships among these five processes and thus to visualize managing as a dynamic, unified activity. In addition, the contingency approach highlights the importance that situational factors have in determining effective managerial performance.

Our point of view enables us to incorporate in this book current developments in managing and in the behavioral sciences. Attention is given to sociology and psychology as they bear upon managing human resources. Thus leadership, group dynamics, and motivation are all appropriate subjects to treat within the framework we have selected. Moreover, quantitative tools and techniques can be included. We discuss such quantitative subjects as operations research, PERT, rational decision making, and financial controls. The level of our treatment is introductory, however, requiring a minimum of mathematical preparation.

This edition of *Managing the Modern Organization* retains its emphasis on the five basic managerial functions. These functions represent the essential elements of managing; they are what managers do. By weaving the functional approach into a systems framework and buttressing it with contingency analysis, we strive to make management pertinent to the student of the late 1970s and early 1980s. One overwhelming fact of our society is that it is dominated by professional managers in such organizations as business firms, universities, hospitals, government departments, and social agencies. Our book therefore portrays management as a critical discipline and underscores the professional nature of the management field.

Many important changes have been made in this third edition of *Managing the Modern Organization*. First, we have integrated the concepts of systems and contingencies more thoroughly with the text material. We use these ideas as common themes throughout the wide span of subject matter covered in the text. Second, we try to present our subject in a dynamic mode. Therefore, we write about manag*ing* to convey the idea of people actively engaged in the critical job of running an organization. In order to emphasize the last point, we have written a new Chapter 1 called "Managing" to set the stage for the discussion of functions that follows. Third, a comprehensive revision and updating of all the existing chapters in the book has been accomplished. Major improvements over the previous edition have been achieved by adding material on organization design, performance appraisal, MBO, planned change, individual and small-group behavior, motivation and leadership, executive development, and organizational effectiveness. Included in the revision are new introductory and concluding chapters, and new chapters in the "Organizing" and "Influencing" Parts. Fourth, chapters on decision making and communicating have been separated from the managerial functions Parts in order to highlight their particular roles as significant linking activities. Fifth, every effort has been made to depict managing as an integrated process involving a logical progression of functions and objectives. This point of view is expressed as a diagram, repeated at each Part introduction, which shows readers where they have been, where they are now, and where they are going.

These and other improvements have been made to ensure that this book is an effective teaching and learning instrument. Our objective is to give beginning business and administration students the foundation necessary for advanced work in management, and for courses like marketing, finance, accounting, and public administration, which sometimes rely on a management orientation.

Theory, concepts, and illustrative examples of practice are fine starting points for building an understanding of managing. But they do not reflect the everyday organizational world entirely. Organizations have ways of taking turns and jumps that cannot be foreseen through abstractions alone. Very likely the sharpest insights into the challenges managers face come from the analysis of case studies based on organizational experiences.

This edition has many new cases. At the end of each discussion of a process is a number of short cases that enable students to apply to real situations the concepts covered in each Part of the book. Concluding the book is a number of comprehensive cases describing complex situations and showing the interaction of all the managerial functions.

The cases reveal the interdisciplinary nature of management. In them are many contributions from the behavioral sciences, as well as many of the theoretical concepts discussed in the book. Close analysis of the case studies will demonstrate both the relevance and the limitations of theory. It will also reaffirm the importance of the human factor in managing and reemphasize the need for managers to utilize human resources effectively.

Two problems of language that we faced when writing the first two editions continued to bother us as we prepared this one. Throughout the text we use the term *subordinate* to designate a person who is below a manager in an organization's hierarchy. We make no qualitative judgment by our use of this word and certainly are not disparaging nonmanagerial people. The term should be understood to denote position, not worth. The other problem results from the lack of a pronoun in English that unambiguously refers to men and women together, making awkward "his or her" and "he or she" locutions unnecessary. Current authoritative publications, including those issued by the federal government, use the masculine pronoun even when a reference is to men and women. Nonetheless, we have for the most part attempted to avoid such language wherever possible.

A book of readings and a study guide are available for use with this third edition of *Managing the Modern Organization*. Patrick E. Connor has compiled and introduced a collection of articles drawn from current literature on management. The anthology *Dimensions in Modern Management* (2d edition) is coordinated chapter by chapter with this textbook. Douglas B. Simpson of California State University, Fresno, has prepared the Study Guide, which summarizes the key points of each chapter of *Managing the Modern Organization,* provides objective questions for review, and suggests discussion questions for individual and class use. The aim of the Study Guide is to maximize students' comprehension of and involvement in the subject of the textbook. *Dimensions in Modern Management* and the Study Guide, used in conjunction with *Managing the Modern Organization,* comprise a set of complementary materials designed to enhance the teaching and learning effectiveness of our book.

For instructors, Professor Simpson has also prepared an excellent instructor's manual which should be gratefully received by busy instructors and those new to the teaching of management. Professor Simpson has worked closely with us to provide a helpful and informative manual.

Our revision of the text has benefited from suggestions made by many individuals. Detailed analyses and reviews of the manuscript were prepared by Gabor Abou El Enein (Mankata State University, Minnesota), LaRue Hubbard (Glendale Community College, Arizona), and Michael J. Jedel (Georgia State University). Some users of the second edition kindly took the time to suggest ways to improve the third edition. They are George S. Abshier (Indiana State University), P. H. Anderson (University of Minnesota), Phil Anderson (Bowling Green University, Ohio), John C. Athanassiades

(Georgia State University), Richard E. Baldwin (Cedarville College, Ohio), Hrach Bedrosian (New York University), Bruce C. Brunfield (Jackson State University, Mississippi), M. F. Cairol (The College of Insurance, New York), Howard M. Carlisle (Utah State University), G. N. Clawson (California State College, Dominguez Hills), Charles C. Dean (Dublin, Virginia), John Deeney (Delaware State College), Charles Drake (Piedmont Technical College, South Carolina), Leo A. Giles (Community College of Denver), Sister Paulette Gladis (Avila College, Missouri), Allen K. Gulezian (Central Washington State College), F. James Hahn (Western State College, Connecticut), Raymond Hilgert (Washington University, Missouri), William J. Jedlicks (William Rainey Harper Company, Palatine, Illinois), William J. Kearney (University of Cincinnati), Alan MacDonald (Park College, Missouri), Jack McDonnell (California State College, San Bernardino), J. B. Orris (Butler University, Indiana), Margaret A. Paranilam (Loyola University, Louisiana), H. Dean Ryder (Gloucester County College, New Jersey), John E. Seitz (Oakton Community College, Illinois), Donald R. Shaul (California State University, Fullerton), Harvey Shore (University of Connecticut), C. J. Walters (Menlo College, California), Fred Ware, Jr. (Valdosta State College, Georgia), and Warren C. Weber (California State Polytechnic University). The ideas and comments of all these people helped us to prepare this book.

Finally, all of us wish to acknowledge the contributions made by others to the writing of this book, especially the assistance we received from our editors at Houghton Mifflin. In addition to the considerable tolerance shown by his family, and the invaluable assistance of Elizabeth M. Smith, Patrick Connor appreciates the contribution given to his peace of mind by a Portland FM radio station.

T. H.
W. G. S.
P. E. C.

Chapter 1

Managing

Objectives of the chapter

1 To introduce the activity known as *managing* and to provide a focus for its study.
2 To identify the reasons why society requires this activity.
3 To describe two approaches that help managers make sense of their task: systems and contingency.
4 To describe the activity of managing, that is, to summarize managers' functions.
5 To provide a framework for relating the various managerial functions to each other.

In June 1977, the United States had a population of some 215 million people. How do all these people acquire their food, automobiles, health care, shoes, Rose Bowl tickets, unemployment checks, Dylan tapes, and fire protection? How are human and material resources combined to produce all these goods and services? The answer: the organization.

Where it happens

The organization is an extremely common yet critical social invention. Organizations seem to be everywhere and to provide the means for doing everything. A sociologist, Amitai Etzioni, has said it well:

We are born in organizations, educated by organizations, and most of us spend much of our lives working for organizations. We spend much of our leisure time paying, playing, and praying in organizations. Most of us will die in an organization and when the time comes for burial, the largest organization of all—the state—must grant official permission.[1]

There are, of course, many types of organizations. These range from small mom-and-pop businesses to large bureaucracies, communities, and nations. All are important to developing, distributing, and using human and material resources. We are mainly concerned however, with that type known as the *complex organization,* which includes manufacturing firms, hospitals, colleges, automobile plants, police departments, professional football clubs, and penitentiaries. These are the organizations from which we acquire the goods and services our society requires.

Who makes it happen

The organization is the place where resources come together. Who is responsible for making sure that these resources come together in a sensible way? The answer: managers. Managers are responsible for acquiring, organizing, and combining resources to accomplish goals. *Managing*—the process by which managers fulfill their responsibilities—involves a set of activities called *functions.* Loosely, managing applies to virtually every aspect of life, individually and collectively. We manage our studies, we manage our homes, we even manage our diversions and our hobbies. Whenever we attempt to conduct our affairs with rational forethought, logical distribution of time, and planned allocation of resources, we can say that we are managing.

In this book however, our focus on management must be more narrow. As a first step, we shall consider management to be the body of knowledge and discipline that is practiced in the kinds of public and private organization that were mentioned earlier. As a second step, let us consider these organizations—each with independent legal and social status—to be complex and *interacting,* dominating the society in which we live. The key word here is *interacting,* because the management of a legally independent organization must try to achieve the numerous goals that are imposed on it externally.

Focusing on managing

Two current approaches, called *systems* and *contingency,* help managers find their way through the maze of organizational interrelationships that they encounter. Both approaches focus on the different factors, variables, forces, and demands with which managers must cope as an inevitable part of their jobs.

[1] Amitai Etzioni, *Modern Organizations* (Englewood Cliffs, N.J.: Prentice-Hall, 1964), p. 1.

Who are the managers in America?

Managers are hospital administrators, generals, college deans, heads of government agencies, chiefs of subdivisions, school superintendents, labor leaders, bishops, charity fund administrators, and business executives. The administrative, or managerial, group is composed not only of top-level men and women but also of subordinate executives. All are managers.

Social background
In early years, business leaders tended to come from wealthy families of independent business executives. There is little doubt that today's executives are drawn from wider socioeconomic classes than ever before. The reason for this democratization is education. The greater relative availability of education makes it possible for individuals of all classes to qualify for employment in large organizations. This opportunity, together with the stress on science in higher education, has increased upward mobility, regardless of employees' social backgrounds.

Mobility
A successful managerial career depends on more than education. Managers tend to come from big cities rather than from small towns or farms. They frequently move around the country during their careers, often transferring within their companies but changing companies as well. Geographic mobility appears to be related directly to a successful business career. Generally, large companies seem to offer more opportunity for rapid advancement than do smaller companies. However, small firms that create and produce space-age products often provide unusual opportunities, and scientists with an administrative bent and managers with a science background frequently find that these small firms provide an excellent setting for a career. For example, Route 128, which circles Boston, is lined with many small, science-oriented businesses that employ bright young scientists and administrators.

    For those in the middle and lower managerial levels the opportunities also seem great. Individuals who lack connections, who came from small towns, who grew up in laboring and farm families, who have not attended prestigious schools, frequently find careers in management. Young men and women can expect to equal or exceed their parents' social and economic status through advancement in management.

Systems theory

The systems approach deals with interdependencies among the elements that comprise managers' environments. There is an old saying that "nothing happens by itself" — if one part of a system is changed, other parts will change as well. For instance, a management decision to relocate a factory has rippling effects throughout the community in which it is located and the community to which it intends to move. Obviously, relocating a plant will affect the people within the organization, as well as those outside it. Systems theory, then, can be applied to the inside and the outside of an organization as a way of understanding and anticipating the consequences of a management decision.[2]

Basically, the systems approach says that organizations acquire resources from the external environment, transform these input resources into output goods and services, and dispose of the outputs in such a way as to allow the organizations continually to acquire additional inputs. This process is illustrated in Figure 1-1. As an example of the process, let us consider a shoe manufacturing firm. The company acquires people (labor), equipment, leather, other raw materials, financing, and so forth. These input resources are turned into shoes and the shoes are then sold at a profit, part of which is used to purchase additional labor, equipment, and so on. And the cycle repeats itself. This systems view may be elaborated, as shown in Figure 1-2.

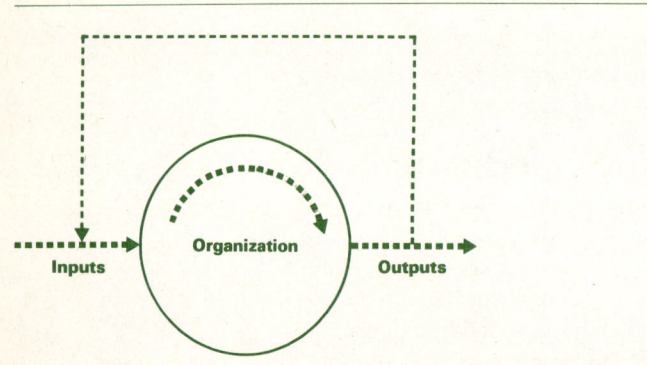

Figure 1-1 Systems view of the organization (a)
Source: Adapted from Patrick E. Connor and Boris W. Becker, "Values and the Organization: Suggestions for Research," *Academy of Management Journal* 18 (September 1975):553.

The environment of management

As suggested by Figure 1-2, an organization operates within a larger framework. The *task environment* is that part of the world, outside an organization, with which the organization comes into frequent operating contact. Customers, suppliers, competitors, the labor and financial markets, governmental regulating agencies—these groups represent the types of people and institutions that comprise the task environment.

The organization also operates in a larger context, called the *societal/cultural environment*. Managing two shoe factories that are alike in all technical respects still will be significantly different if one factory is located in

---

[2] Strictly speaking, this approach is commonly referred to as the *open-systems* approach, suggesting that the system is open to its external environment. A *closed* system, by contrast, is shut off from its environment. Since no system, including the organization, can long survive without interacting with its environment, we are concerned in this book with open systems.

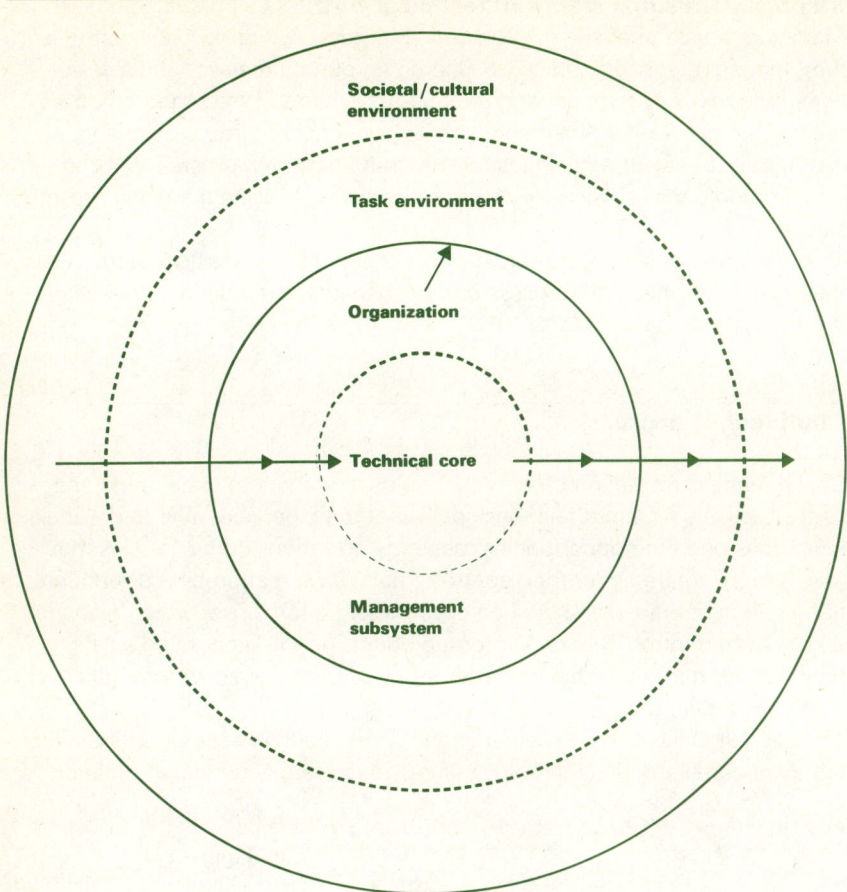

Figure 1-2 Systems view of the organization (b)
Source: Adapted from Patrick E. Connor and Boris W. Becker, "Values and the Organization: Suggestions for Research," *Academy of Management Journal* 18 (September 1975):553.

New Jersey and the other, in Tokyo. Customs, traditions, cultural values, and norms—all affect the practice of management.

There are several systems within these subenvironments. Among the more important are the economic system, the political system, the productive and distributive systems, and the resource system. Each of these systems has ends toward which it is directed, and often these ends are in conflict. For example, the economic system has the goal of full employment with a moderate rate of inflation. To achieve this goal, the productive and distributive systems must work efficiently. The problem, however, is that these systems also consume resources and energy at an enormous rate. This drains the resource system, with the net effect of raising prices and increasing unemployment. In turn, the political system encourages managers to achieve greater productivity, thus accelerating the drain on the resource system. And the cycle goes on. A problem such as this demonstrates that managers are involved in a very complicated set of relationships with their organizations' environments.

Management subsystem and technical core

Managers must cope with environmental factors. As Figure 1-2 illustrates, the "management subsystem" is located (in our mind's eye, at least) between the task environment and the operating heart of the organization—at the "technical core." When competitive or economic pressures change, it is not up to, say, the machinist or the draftsman to make sure that the organization copes successfully with that change; it is the manager's responsibility.

As we shall see, managers have a number of tools to help them meet their responsibilities. The *process of management,* introduced in this chapter, consists of these tools.

Contingency approach

Contingency is the second theory that helps managers to understand and deal effectively with interrelationships. What managers are able to do, their limitations and their opportunities, depends on various contingencies that may or may not be under their control. Public laws that prohibit discrimination in hiring are an example of an environmental force over which managers do not have control. The market for a product, on the other hand, is a contingency that managers can attempt to influence directly, through advertising or product design.

In a significant way, the contingency approach is a method for analyzing managerial problems. It helps managers to identify factors that affect

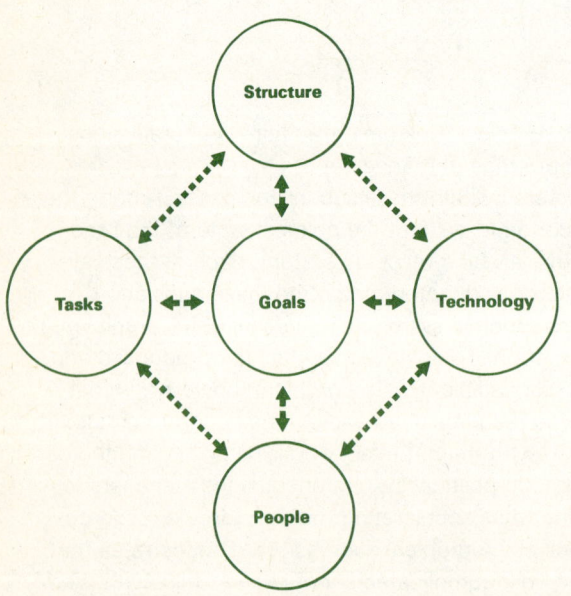

Figure 1-3 Internal organizational variables
Source: Adapted from H. J. Leavitt, "Applied Organization Change in Industry: Structural, Technological and Humanistic Approaches," in *Handbook of Organizations,* ed. J. G. March (Chicago: Rand McNally, 1965), p. 1145.

managerial decision making. In essence, the contingency approach borrows from systems theory, enabling managers to recognize the major factors with which they must deal. Internal to the organization are several critical variables: organizational goals, people, technology, tasks, and structure. These variables are all interrelated, as shown in Figure 1-3, and the manager is responsible for managing these interrelationships.

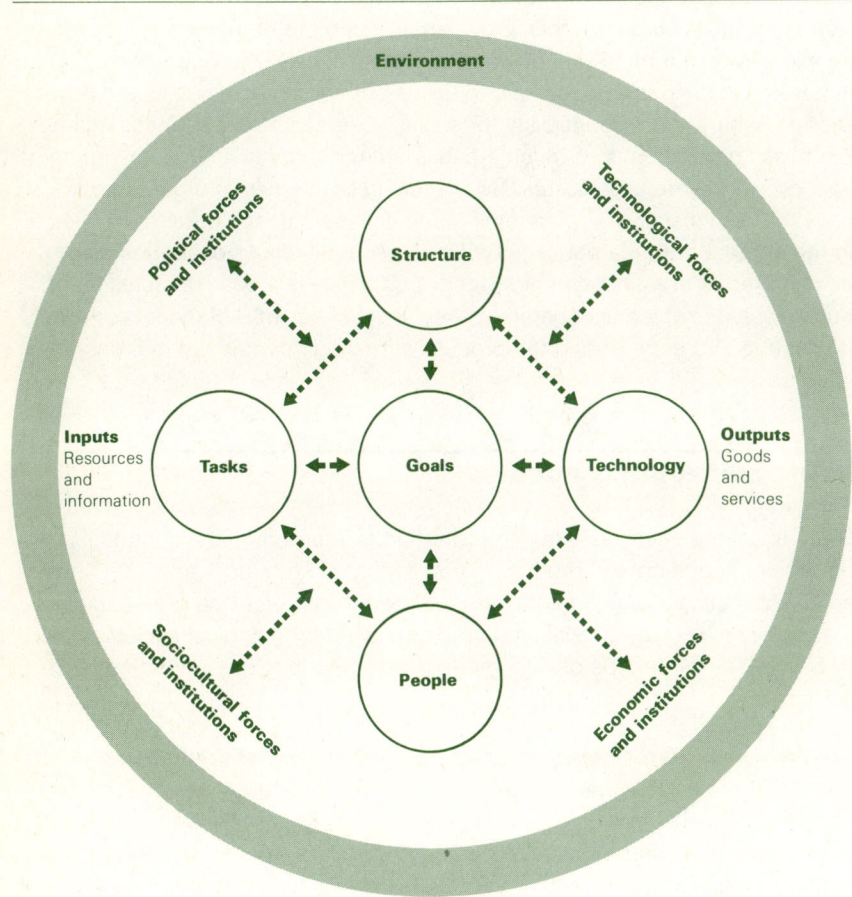

Figure 1-4 Internal and external variables dealt with by managers
Source: Adapted from H. M. Carlisle, *Situational Management* (New York: American Management Association, 1973), p. 29.

We have seen that in addition to internal organizational factors, managers must cope with forces and demands from outside the organization. The environmental systems mentioned earlier—the economic system, the political system, the productive and distributive systems, and the resource system—all exert pressure on the organization. Managers must continually find a way (usually, various ways) to manage these pressures. The range of internal as well as external variables is illustrated in Figure 1-4.

Human values

Coincident with the major themes of systems and contingency, a third idea contributes to our focus on managing. It is the most difficult of all to express because it involves human values. People have certain expectations that they try to fulfill by working in organizations or by supporting organizations in other ways. Managers must be sensitive to these expectations, not only in terms of providing jobs, products, and economic rewards, but also with regard to broader social obligations. This awareness often is called *social responsibility*. As organizations grow larger and more numerous, affecting people's lives in a multitude of ways, social responsibility becomes more important. It is no longer realistic to divide our society into public and private sectors, where the responsibility for social welfare is neatly defined. A large business corporation is as much a public organization as a large government agency is a private organization. Managers in both types of organizations have the responsibility of maintaining and advancing each other's well-being in the interest of the larger society. Of course, just what constitutes well-being in terms of management strategy and policy is a political question of human values, which is debated at every level of society. Managers are not immune to this debate, and the process of management is not immune to its effects.

What managing is about

Given this state of affairs—large organizations interacting in a continual process of acquiring and producing the resources required—a unique human endeavor, called management, has appeared to serve as one of the chief means for solving the puzzles and problems of a technological society. Peter F. Drucker describes the development of management as a potent force in our society:

The emergence of management as an essential, a distinct and a leading institution is a pivotal event in social history. Rarely, if ever, has a new basic institution, a new leading group, emerged as fast as has management since the turn of this century. Rarely in human history has a new institution proven indispensable so quickly; and even less often has a new institution arrived with so little opposition, so little disturbance, so little controversy.[3]

Just how critical management has become in our world is emphasized by a biophysicist, John Platt, who warns that if managers fail to solve our society's problems, a crisis will develop second only to that of nuclear destruction.[4]

---

[3] Peter F. Drucker, *The Practice of Management* (New York: Harper & Row, 1954), pp. 3–4.
[4] John Platt, "What We Must Do," *Science* 166 (November 28, 1969): 1115–1121.

This enormous responsibility, which exists on a global scale, is almost unparalleled in human history. What is it about management that makes it different from other human endeavors, such as politics, for example? A simplified answer: rationality. In its essence, management is a process that includes elements of technical, organizational, and political rationality (usually found in that order of importance in organizations).

Technical rationality is reflected in the efficiency-type decisions that managers must make. The general form of technical rationality is expressed by the equation $E = O/I$, where E is efficiency, O is output, and I is input. The object of technical rationality is to increase E by varying the ratio of O and I. Obviously, technical rationality is important. It is a critical measure of management performance that is reflected in a number of economic yardsticks, such as costs, prices, profits, and competitive status in markets. Both Dent[5] and England[6] found, in studies conducted years apart, that the business executives surveyed assigned the highest priority to decisions pertaining to technically rational problems.

The purpose of *organizational rationality* is to achieve and maintain systems of organizational coordination. Coordination is critical to the health of any organization; also, it is essential to the satisfaction people gain from participating in an organization. Thus, organizational rationality includes management decisions that are directed toward maintaining the organization as a system of coordination.

Finally, *political rationality* is reflected in those decisions that managers make to maintain their organizational positions. It is the means that managers use to obtain acceptance of their decisions and policies. Political rationality is obviously translated frequently into highly personal terms: managers do things to protect their jobs and to increase their power. Therefore, it is their notion of personal enhancement through political means that differentiates political rationality from organizational rationality.

What happens: The process of management

The rationality that underlies the management process is reflected in its goal-seeking nature. Specifically, *management is a social and technical process that utilizes resources, influences human action, and facilitates changes in order to accomplish an organization's goals.*

In essence, where those goals come from and how managers pursue them is what this book is about. Basically, managers design, engage in, and oversee a variety of organizational tasks and processes that are necessary for goal accomplishment. There are, of course, many ways to depict the management process. By and large, however, writers in the field of business

[5] James K. Dent, "Organizational Correlates of the Goals of Business Management," *Personnel Psychology* 12 (Autumn 1959):365–394.
[6] George W. England, "Personal Value Systems of Managers and Administrators," *Academy of Management Proceedings,* 33d Annual Meeting (Boston, 1974), pp. 81–88.

administration agree with the following.[7] First, managers formulate plans for reaching goals; they recruit, organize, and motivate people in accordance with these plans; and they monitor the effectiveness with which these goals are pursued. Second, to accomplish these tasks, managers must develop useful information and allocate resources. Developing and acquiring information involves the managerial process known as *communicating*; allocating resources is what *decision making* means. Third, and here we come to the bottom line: the success with which the managerial functions and processes are conducted determines how effectively the organization operates.

The various managerial tasks and their relationships are illustrated in Figure 1-5. The process shown in the figure reflects the essence of organization and management. *The organization is an instrument that has been established to perform a set of tasks; the manager's job is to wield that instrument as effectively as possible.* We have designed this book around the model in Figure 1-5. Each management function and the two fundamental linking processes constitute separate Parts of this volume. The basic managerial purpose, organizational effectiveness, is treated in the concluding chapter.

Managers' skills

Regardless of their level of authority, managers need human, conceptual, specialized, and general skills. They must be able to motivate people to accomplish organizational objectives while at the same time creating a climate for the satisfaction of individual needs. Conceptual skills permit executives to generalize solutions to business problems and to apply them to specific situations. Specialized and general managerial skills vary according to executives' positions in organizations. Most managers at low levels use specialized skills extensively in their work. At higher levels, specialized techniques become less important and the application of general skills grows. There is a saying that, in any position in an organization, everyone who is above a given individual seems to be a generalist, and everyone below, a specialist.

Clearly, chief executives exercise fewer technical skills than do their subordinates. However, generalists must know what specialized talents are needed by the organization. When specialties have been determined according to the requirements of the tasks to be performed, the generalist's job becomes one of coordinating activities.

Technology shapes the role of management and the structure of the

---

[7] See, for example, Howard M. Carlisle, *Management: Concepts and Situations* (Chicago: Science Research Associates, 1976), p. 10; Theo Haimann and William G. Scott, *Management in the Modern Organization* (Boston: Houghton Mifflin, 1970), p. 2; Don Hellriegel and John W. Slocum, Jr., *Management: A Contingency Approach,* 2d ed. (Reading, Mass.: Addison-Wesley, 1978), p. 13; and Harold Koontz and Cyril O'Donnell, *Management,* 6th ed. (New York: McGraw-Hill, 1976), pp. 99–123.

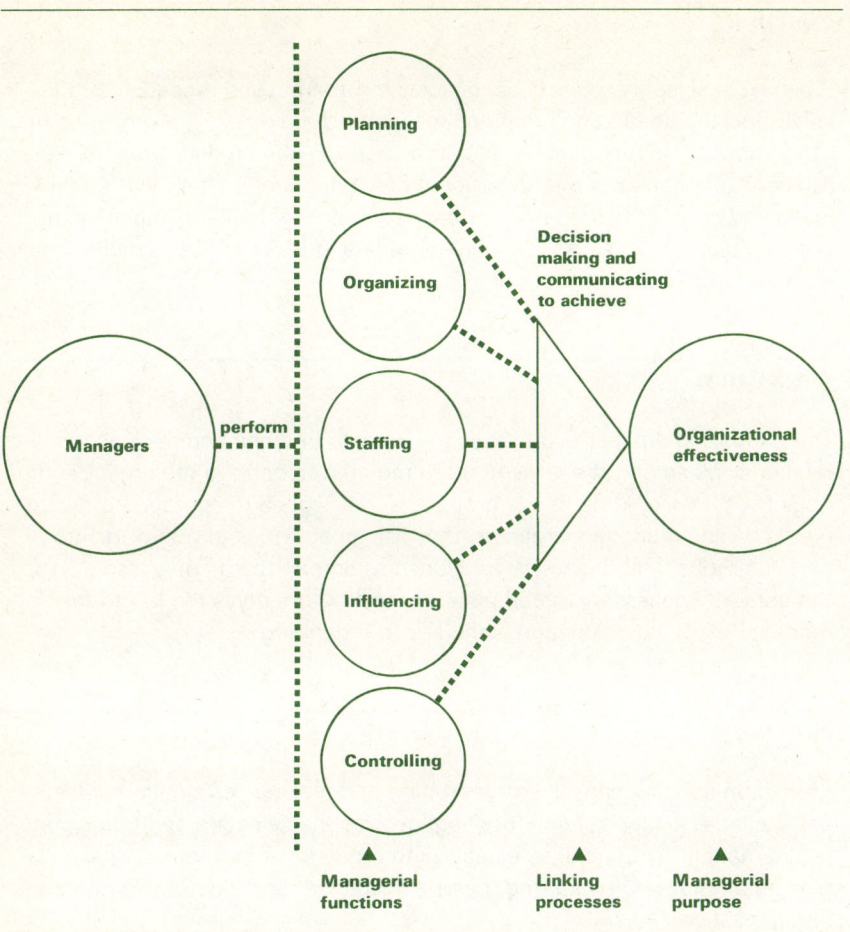

Figure 1-5 The process of management

organization. The nature of the work determines the behavior of people on the job, the relationships among them, and the work they do. For example, work in a gravel pit is unskilled, and the structure of the organization is likely to be rigid. Work in a research laboratory requires considerable education and skill, and the structure of its organization will probably be loose. The managerial generalist should be aware of such differences in task and technology. They affect the design of the organization and management's role in it.

Management functions

Regardless of the complexity of the organization's purpose, its managers perform or administer several basic managerial activities, conventionally called *functions*. The performance of each function moves the organization toward the attainment of its goals.

Planning

Planning is selecting objectives, policies, programs, and procedures. It involves looking ahead and preparing for the future. Logically, it precedes the other managerial functions; at the start, nothing can be done without a plan. As managers carry out their functions, they continue to plan, revising their ideas and choosing alternatives when necessary. Although planning is the primary function, it is also a continuing one and is carried out simultaneously with the other principal functions.

Organizing

The organizing process establishes the work to be done and decides the relationships among the tasks that are required to achieve the organization's objectives. Work elements are grouped and assigned to appropriate departments. When managers organize, they assign activities, divide work into particular jobs, and define the relationships among them. They also delegate the authority necessary to complete the task. Authority is the key to the manager's job; its delegation is the key to organizing.

Staffing

Management is responsible for recruiting and making certain that workers are available to fill positions. Staffing involves the selection and training of future managers. It includes establishing procedures for promoting and replacing employees, appraising their performance, and devising a system of compensation.

Influencing

Influencing is concerned with motivation. It has many dimensions: morale, employee satisfaction and productivity, and leadership. Management's goal is to create a climate the workers find agreeable and that promotes the objectives of the organization. In addition, influencing has important effects on an organization's flexibility and adaptability.

Controlling

The control process involves activities that are essential to ensuring that events proceed as planned. Through control, managers determine whether or not objectives are being achieved (and take corrective action when they are not). Here again, we see the significance of planning as a primary managerial function. A manager could not determine whether work was proceeding properly if there were no plan to check it against.

Management: Art or science?

Management is not a science in the way that the natural and physical sciences are. The experimentation that is characteristic of the latter is impossible in management, which is not able to control all factors. However, managers can define, analyze, and measure phenomena, and they can use some of the techniques that enable scientists to experiment and obtain data.

Frederick W. Taylor, an early major contributor to management theory, directed his attention to science and management. While considering the best way to make a cut of specified dimensions in a piece of metal of a particular size and hardness, he realized that an operation could be repeated but that experiment and proof were less applicable to dealings with people. Nevertheless, he proposed to standardize motivation through financial incentive systems and the selection of employees according to specific job requirements. Taylor applied "scientific" techniques to studies of planning, organization, routing, and costing. He used a scientific approach to derive new techniques for action.

What can be said about management as an art? Art is the systematic application of knowledge and skill to achieve an objective. This definition applies not only to the creation of a painting or a symphony, but also to a managerial undertaking, such as organizing a sales promotion program for a new product. The key word in our definition of art is *application.* Management is an activity that applies knowledge and skill to achieve objectives.

Chester I. Barnard, an eminent contributor to management theory, pointed out that the function of the sciences is to explain the phenomena, the events, the situations of the past. Their aim is not to produce specific events, effects, or situations but rather to produce explanations, which are termed *knowledge*. The arts, on the other hand, function to accomplish concrete ends. These arts must be mastered and applied by the manager, who learns mainly through practice and experience.

Fundamental linking processes

Managers require good information and must allocate resources effectively if they hope to perform the management functions well. Further, the management functions are linked together by processes of resource allocation and information sharing. These linking processes are called *decision making* and *communicating,* respectively.

Decision making

Managerial performance is judged on the basis of how well resources are used to accomplish an organization's objectives. The process by which resources are allocated and distributed is called *decision making*. Managerial decision making is conscious deliberation about alternative ways to use resources. Because resources are limited, the capacity of managers to exploit opportunities is limited. Decisions are made to discriminate rationally among available alternatives. Decision making is a linking process; it ties one function to another. Further, it ties one segment of an organization to the others. The decisions of one manager or organizational unit are never made in isolation. Their implications and outcomes are related to other decisions throughout the organizational system.

Communicating

At its basic level, communication is the process of passing information from one person to another. It entails imparting ideas and making oneself understood by others. Communication, therefore, promotes a way of motivating and influencing people. At a more complex level, communication links the management functions: it is through collecting and sharing information that managers can tie the functions together and evaluate progress toward the organization's goals.

Basic managerial purpose

Organizational effectiveness

The degree to which an organization accomplishes goals is called its *effectiveness*. Effectiveness compares performance with criteria that are composed of past achievements and future expectations. Therefore, effectiveness is always a dependent variable; it can be assessed only in relation to other standards. Since managers pursue a variety of goals, more than just those that relate to profits or costs, organizational effectiveness involves more than just efficiency. It is the degree to which the combination of organizational goals is accomplished.

Interrelationships of functions, processes, and purposes

Managers set standards for controlling in the planning process; staffing is organized and influenced; organizational goals both influence and control staff members. Managerial decisions must be appropriate to the overall organizational task requirements; organizational effectiveness depends on how well these decisions are made and implemented. The interrelationships could be multiplied endlessly. Conceptually, we can separate managerial functions, linking processes, and organizational effectiveness for analysis. Empirically, however, in the manager's day-to-day job, the activities are inseparable.

The management process, then, is a system of interdependent activities. The sequence in which these activities are performed and the amount of time that is spent on each are not the significant issues. Each blends into and affects the performance of the others. The output of one activity provides the input for another.

The view of management as a system of interrelated functions and processes did not emerge suddenly; it evolved over nearly eighty years. Chapter 2 is an examination of that evolution—a consideration of some of the antecedents of contemporary management.

Summary

Organizations are the social instruments by which human tasks are performed in our society. Managers are the people who are charged with the responsibility for wielding these instruments. Modern organizations are enmeshed in an environment that consists of a complex network of interconnected elements. Among these elements are other organizations, the political and economic systems, labor and financial markets, customers, suppliers, and so forth.

Our attention is focused on two analytic managerial tools: open-systems theory and contingency analysis. The systems approach helps managers to recognize the nature of the context within which they must operate. The contingency approach focuses managers' attention on the variables, both inside and outside the organization, that affect their performances.

These analytic tools are reflected in the management process. Specifically, managers perform several interdependent functions: they plan strategies and means to achieve organizational goals; they organize their firm, agency, college, whatever, so that their plans are carried out; they staff various departments with the people whose skills are most appropriate to the organization's tasks; they provide motivation—incentives—for themselves and other organizational members; and they continually monitor the effectiveness with which goals are pursued.

In addition, managers conduct decision-making and communication processes—processes that link the basic management functions and contribute to their interdependent effectiveness.

Finally, though ultimately beyond their responsibility, is something for which managers are accountable: nothing less than the effectiveness with which organizational goals and policies are met. This is the ultimate test of managers' judgment and skills, of the success of their art and science.

Discussion questions

1 In a six-month period, how many professional managers do you come into contact with? When your parents and grandparents were your age, did they have fewer of these contacts? more of these contacts? Explain your answers.
2 In what ways is the management of modern organizations a science? an art?

3 Identify three organizations with which your college interacts on a regular operating basis.
4 In what ways is the organization an instrument?
5 Apply the process shown in Figure 1-5 to an organization with which you are familiar—a travel agency, a McDonald's, the student-union cafeteria. Consider, for example, what kind of planning takes place, how decisions are made, and how effectiveness is measured.

Supplementary readings

American Institute of Management. "What Is Management?" New York: American Institute of Management, 1959, pp. 2—6. Reprinted in *Dimensions in Modern Management,* 2d ed., edited by Patrick E. Connor. Boston: Houghton Mifflin, 1978.

Blau, Peter M., and Scott, W. Richard. "The Concept of Formal Organization." In *Formal Organizations: A Comparative Approach,* pp. 2—8. New York: Intext Educational Publishers, 1962. Reprinted in *Dimensions in Modern Management,* 2d ed., edited by Patrick E. Connor. Boston: Houghton Mifflin, 1978.

Duncan, W. Jack. "Management Theory and Practice." *Business Horizons,* October 1974, pp. 48—52.

Mintzberg, Henry. *The Nature of Managerial Work.* New York: Harper & Row, 1973.

Mooney, James D., and Reiley, Alan C. *Onward Industry!* New York: Harper & Brothers, 1931.

Part I

The managerial perspective

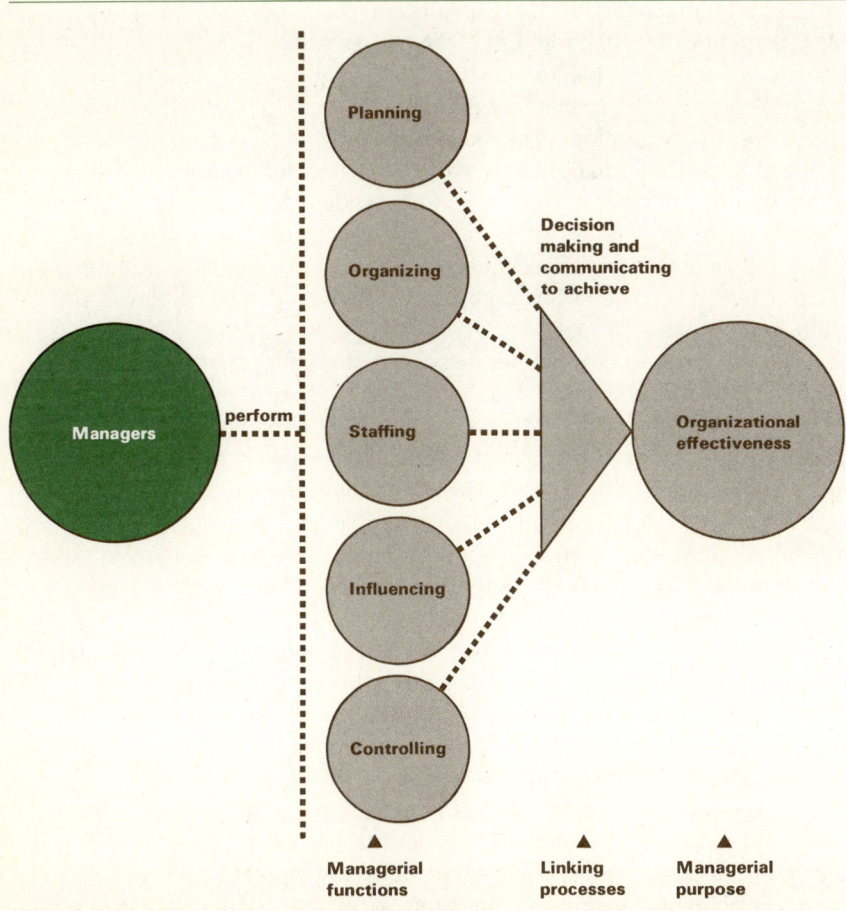

Management evolution Management has changed in techniques and in perspective over the years. However, its dedication to organizational effectiveness has remained unaltered.

The dominant social and economic force in the latter decades of the twentieth century is large, complex organizations and the managers who run them. Insofar as evolutionary matters are concerned, it did not take long for organizations to reach this preeminent position. Our perspective on management goes back only some seventy-five years, roughly to the turn of the century. In this period, America changed from a rural to an industrial society; it became urbanized, creating a melding of technology with administrative systems whose present character is historically unique. Overseeing all this are managers, whose cardinal decisions in positions of economic and governmental power profoundly influence our lives. The purpose of this Part of the book is to trace major developments in management theory and practice.

Traditionally, management has been defined by describing its activities, an approach that is limited by its depersonalization of the process. Management itself is not depersonalized, although it might seem so if we look at it in terms of systems, contingencies, processes, and functions. Management *is* this, and more. It is the human force in organizations. Managers are responsible for activities that affect millions of persons who consume products and services, who work for them, and who have ownership shares in corporations. The modern manager is one of the most strategically placed individuals in society. But this has not always been the case. Management's present status results from modern social and technological changes. In other nations, the dominant class may be capitalist entrepreneurs, politicians, clergy, or soldiers. These groups are still important in our society, but their power is shared by managers who pursue careers in administrative positions.

Of the many forces that are responsible for the appearance of career managers, technology, specialization, and complexity of organization are among the most important. Modern manufacturing methods and an abundance of products are signs of technological advances in applied science and engineering. Increased specialization through the education and experience of employees accompanies technological sophistication. Finally, the growth in the size and complexity of organizations creates a variety of skills and a combination of specialties that are not found in most small enterprises.

Historically, these forces widened management's role. Around the turn of the century, managers were concerned with the coordination of machines, raw materials, and production processes. Employees were not ignored but were considered to be things—economic factors of production. Today they are viewed by management as people with a full range of social and psychological needs. In light of this development, it has become fashionable to talk about sociotechnical systems. These are systems that permit machines, people, groups, tasks, and technology to interact effectively. To design interactional systems that account for all the resource inputs of an organization is one of the most important challenges facing professional management. Effective organizational design is not static; it must include the ability to adapt to change.

Fortunately, the enlarged responsibilities have been met by new techniques. The computer revolution and the applied behavioral sciences help managers to do their jobs. Additionally, information is increasing at an explosive rate. Managers know more; they can, therefore, manage with a surer hand and be in a better position to plan. Improved techniques increase management's confidence that it can wisely shape an organization's destiny. Nevertheless, management still deals with uncertainty. The impression that managers can predict with assurance is false. History tells us that managers are endlessly questing the "one best way," constantly searching for rational and appropriate methods to achieve a particular end and to improve the techniques for organizing, producing, and distributing goods and services.

The burden of modern management is awesome. Managers are responsible for (1) the design of interactions in a sociotechnical system; (2) change and organizational flexibility; (3) the allocation and flow of material and human resources; (4) processes affecting the production, distribution, and financing of goods and services; (5) the relationship of the organizational system to its environment. In short, managers seem to do everything.

The purpose of management theory is to make contact with, and sense out of, this vast reality. The earliest approach was to think in terms of management principles and functions. Then the idea of systems was introduced. Finally, the systems concept was modified with the contingency approach. These ideas represent a quest for models of what managers should do in complex organizations. There is no reason to suppose that this quest has ended. Indeed, the search for better means to achieve organizational effectiveness is probably more imperative now than ever before.

Chapter 2

Landmarks in management history

Objectives of the chapter

1 To trace the development of management from earliest times to 1940.
2 To discuss the contributions to theory and practice by various management movements.
3 To point out the major turning points in management history.
4 To evaluate the significance of various contributions to management.

A need for managerial coordination exists whenever people engage in group effort. In early times, the evidence of management was seen only in the products of organization—the monuments, armies, and governments. There were no ancient books about management, nor were there any systematic attempts to describe what management did then. All of this had to wait until the industrialization of Western Europe, around 1790. Even so, management literature from the 1800s is scarce, and significant attempts to explore management theory and practice were not made until after the turn of the century. (See Figure 2-1.)

But momentum to do this had been building in America. So, when a hole was punched in the dike by Frederick W. Taylor, a flood of management information followed. The result was that the first forty years of this century were the most fruitful for the development of management as a theoretical and practical subject. The people who wrote and worked in management during that time set the direction that has influenced management to the present day.

Management in preindustrial times

The great structures of antiquity must have required a high order of managerial skill. We tend to think that the pyramids of Egypt were constructed by a corps of slaves under the lash of the Pharaoh's overseers. Actually, they were a sort of public-works project, built for the most part by the freemen of villages. The stones in the pyramids were quarried many miles up the Nile River from the construction site and were cut to size so that they could be fitted into place with slight adjustment. Each piece was moved by barge to the place of construction, according to a well-synchronized schedule. Architects and engineers had important jobs to do. Orders and reports had to be passed up and down the line of command so that various activities could be coordinated. Indeed, the Egyptians had to know basic principles of management.

Figure 2-1 Landmarks in management history

Preindustrial
- Public works of artistic and religious significance
- Military formations
- Government bureaucracies, especially of the Roman Empire
- Organization of the Roman Catholic Church
- Commercial trade

Industrial

1790	**Industrial Revolution**
1830	Andrew Ure and Charles Babbage
1886	Henry R. Towne and the ASME
1895	Frederick W. Taylor
	The scientific management movement including Taylor, Gantt, the Gilbreths, Emerson, and Cooke. This period also included the rise of the field of industrial psychology.
1926	**The management process idea** developed by Henri Fayol and Ralph C. Davis
1927	**The human relations movement** emerged under the leadership of Elton Mayo, William J. Dickson, and Fritz Roethlisberger
1930	**Classical organization theory** given definitive treatment by Mooney and Reiley, and Lyndall Urwick
1938	**Transition** from an industrial to a technological and managerial society foreseen by Chester I. Barnard, James Burnham, and Mary Parker Follett
1940	

The Greeks also had managerial knowledge. Socrates, in his discourse with Nicomachides, answers a question about whether one individual could manage a chorus as well as an army. He expresses his understanding and opinion of management: "Over whatever a man may preside, he will, if he knows what he needs and is able to provide it, be a good president, whether he have the direction of a chorus, a family, a city or an army."[1]

---

[1] Plato and Xenophon, *Socratic Discourses,* trans. J. S. Watson (New York: Dutton, 1910), bk. 3, chap. 4, p. 80.

In ancient Rome, it was an unwritten law that soldiers, administrators, and judges had to take counsel before action, even though the advice was not followed. This is one of the first instances of the principle of compulsory staff advice. As the Roman Empire grew, the governmental bureaucracy grew with it. Government agencies proliferated. Official control was felt in important areas of government activity—tax collection, public works, food supply, administration of territories, entertainment, accounting for the fiscal affairs of the state. The chief accountant, in fact, had the title *a rationibus*, denoting the rational management of financial affairs, one of the earliest applications of rationality to administration.[2]

In spite of such indications of managerial efforts, no systematic treatise on management and organizational problems was written in preindustrial times. The government, the military, and the Catholic Church were the major administrative organizations in preindustrial society. They were run in accordance with rules and demanded from the people associated with them a commitment to their goals. The objectives of each were rather uncomplicated. The church and the military used chains of command, coordination, unity of command, and staff.

From the military, in particular, came numerous applications of many of the principles that modern businesses later adopted. The military chain of command originated in the armies of antiquity and medieval times. The scalar principle—the ranking of duties according to the amount of authority and responsibility involved in them—was the backbone of early military organizations and remains important in organizing activities. In the military, the chain is longer than in other organizations, originating with the supreme commander and extending to squad leader. Lengthening the chain of command requires lengthening the chain of delegated authority. This became necessary in Napoleon's time, though the commander in chief was still able to survey the entire field of battle. Later, when the military faced larger and even worldwide battlefields, the conduct of warfare involved no new principles of organization but merely an extension of the old ones. Thus, centralization of command and decentralization of operations evolved.

The staff concept also originated with the military. Use of staff is probably as old as war itself because of an army's ever-present need for quarters. However, the formal function of a quartermaster, who is a staff officer, did not emerge until 1655 in the army of the margrave of Brandenburg, the precursor of the Prussian army. The evolution of a staff and the idea of a general staff were Prussia's contributions to modern military organization, the former beginning in the early part, and the latter being developed toward the end, of the nineteenth century. The Prussian army included in its system of staff training the periodic return of staff officers to line duty. General Scharnhorst, concerned that line and staff officers might become segregated, insisted on the rotation of duties.[3]

---

[2] H. Stuart Jones, "Administration," in *The Legacy of Rome*, ed. Cyril Bailey (Oxford: Clarendon Press, 1923), pp. 98–99.
[3] Walter Goerlitz, *History of the German General Staff* (New York: Praeger, 1959).

In addition to the concepts of line and staff organization, managers have learned other things from the military. The military long has been aware of the necessity of not only telling soldiers what was expected of them but also telling them why. According to James D. Mooney: "It is recorded of Napoleon, the most autocratic of men, that he never gave an order without explaining its purpose, and making sure that this purpose was understood. He knew that blind obedience could never ensure the intelligent execution of any order."[4]

The Industrial Revolution

The Industrial Revolution, which occurred in Europe at the end of the eighteenth century, brought great changes to business life and social structure. Its essential characteristic — the transfer of human skill and energy to machines — had profound consequences for management. Artisans who could not afford to purchase their own machinery were obliged to work on the premises of an artisan who possessed the necessary equipment. For the first time, salaried employees worked in an employer's home or workshop. At the same time, we see the start of the putting-out system. An entrepreneur of means who could not perform the functions of the artisan might purchase machinery and raw material, put them into the homes of artisans or workers, and at regular intervals collect the finished product. Entrepreneurs had to manage workers, materials, and machinery; they had to coordinate the efforts of people toward a common objective.

The use of power, first from water and then from steam, together with concentrations of capital in the form of machinery, brought people together in a central location, from which emerged the city as well as the complex manufacturing organization. Eventually, the "managerial revolution" followed from these beginnings, for it was only natural that with the increase of business activities came a corresponding increase of managerial problems. However, there was a time lag before managerial problems were recognized. Logically, some attempts to produce a science of management should have been undertaken during the Industrial Revolution or shortly thereafter. But such an effort did not materialize. Management was the most neglected element of the Industrial Revolution; it was superseded by mechanical and technological improvements to create a mass-production, mass-consumption economy.

Because the Industrial Revolution did not bring about managerial enlightenment, managers had to meet the demands of a growing economy and the necessity for specialization as best they could, with whatever their knowledge and experience suggested. Some took clues from the military and Church organizations, which had successfully applied principles of management for hundreds of years. These institutions provided "effective examples

---

[4] James D. Mooney, *The Principles of Organization*, rev. ed. (New York: Harper & Row, 1947), p. 131.

of the application of the principles to a single industrial unit for its internal operating necessities."[5]

The scientific management movement

Although Andrew Ure and Charles Babbage,[6] early nineteenth-century British writers, were concerned with management in a limited way, the real beginnings of a science of management did not emerge until nearly a hundred years later. Some remarkable Americans—mostly engineers, such as Frederick Winslow Taylor, Henry Lawrence Gantt, Harrington Emerson, Morris L. Cooke, Frank Bunker Gilbreth, and Lillian Moller Gilbreth—are credited with laying the foundation of the management movement, which became known as *scientific management*. Some credit must also be given to progressive American manufacturers, such as Henry R. Towne and William Sellers, the latter for a long time Taylor's employer.

The start of scientific management and the ASME

Industrialization created both technological and human problems for management. Although neither set of problems could be ignored, management was better prepared to cope with the first than with the second. Virtually nothing had been written about how to coordinate and motivate human effort in a business operation. Furthermore, there was no way for managers who were engaged in the daily running of their businesses and shops to exchange experiences.

In this vacuum Henry R. Towne, in 1886, made an appeal for writings about management theory and practice. He did this mainly through the American Society of Mechanical Engineers (ASME), whose members were in the theoretical and practical sides of mechanical engineering. Among them were managers and owners of businesses, including Towne, who was the founder of the Yale and Towne Lock Company. The ASME provided a kind of professional association for shop managers. When Towne was elected president of the society in 1886, his inaugural address was an appeal to people in management to contribute articles on this subject to *Transactions*, the group's official magazine.

Frederick W. Taylor

At first the response to Towne's appeal was not overwhelming. However, in 1895 an article by Frederick W. Taylor appeared. His contribution was titled

---

[5] *Ibid.*, p. 169.
[6] Andrew Ure, *The Philosophy of Manufacturers* (London: Charles Knight, 1835); and Charles Babbage, *The Economy of Machinery and Manufacturers*, 3d ed. (London: Charles Knight, 1833).

"Piece Work System" and included two revolutionary proposals (shown in Figure 2-2). He first urged the establishment of performance standards based on the scientific determination of how long a job should take. Workers who exceeded the standard were to be paid more than those who did not. The standard speed for a job might be thirty pieces an hour and the rate for each of the first thirty pieces might be $.05. A worker who makes thirty pieces an hour might receive a wage of $1.50. For the thirty-first piece produced, the rate jumps to $.08 and the hourly wage increases to $2.48. The strong financial incentive that this system provides is obvious. The scheme was in line with Taylor's philosophy of rewarding "first-class" men amply and punishing those who did not meet productivity goals. The *differential rate* became the basic ingredient of modern incentive systems.

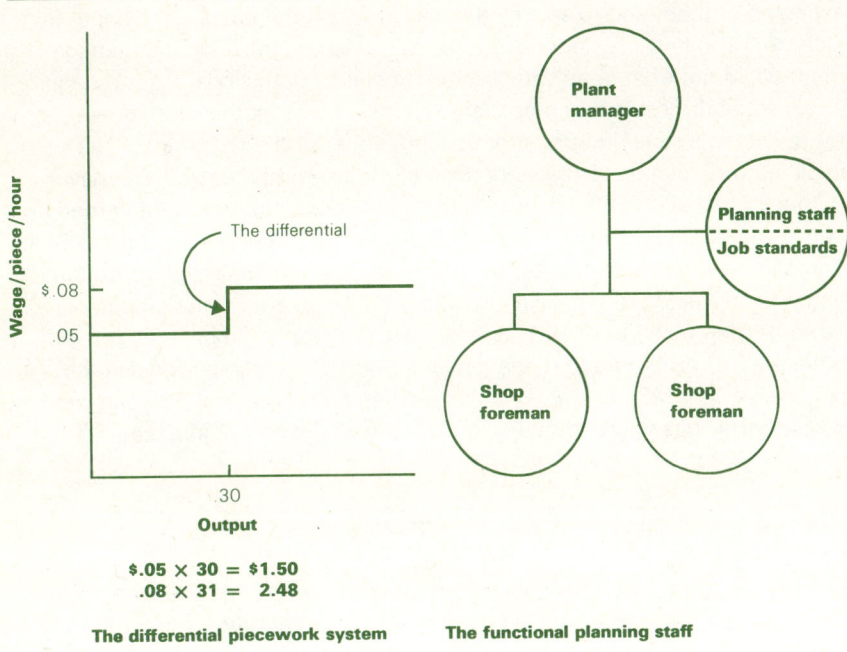

Figure 2-2 Taylor's revolutionary proposals in 1895

Taylor's second proposal was that people who were responsible for making time measurements and setting job standards should concentrate on this task and be removed from those who supervised production activities. The notion of separating "planning from doing," as Taylor called it, was the beginning of the idea of *functional staff* organization. Taylor expanded on the functional concept in later years.

Taylor's article was the first foray into the hitherto uncharted management field. The time was right for his experimentation. An engineer, he was trained in the basic physical sciences and was accustomed to applying the analytical tools of a scientist to problems of all kinds. Taylor founded the scientific management movement, though he did not coin the term *scientific management*.[7]

Before 1895, foremen were responsible for setting job standards. Workers did not know how much management could and should expect of them, and in their concern for their livelihood they tended to make jobs last as long as they could. In various experiments Taylor applied scientific methods to learn how much a worker should do. Not surprisingly, his efforts met with objections. Workers feared that his purpose was to force them to work faster. However, his intention was not only to increase production; it was also to increase rates of pay as workers produced more.

Taylor's efforts marked the first time that scientific principles were applied to the problems of management. Taylor tried to determine how much workers could do, given the proper tools and instruction in their use. He was the first to state that management's duty was to tell workers what is expected of them and to specify the way in which the job is to be done. In all his experiments, Taylor strove to be fair. He thought scientific management could not exist in an establishment unless "both sides . . . recognize as essential the substitution of exact scientific investigation and knowledge for the old individual judgment or opinion, either of the workman or the boss, in all matters relating to the work done in the establishment."[8] Whenever output increased, he raised wages. Most of his experiments were carried on between 1880 and 1890, while he was superintendent at the Midvale Steel Company in Philadelphia. After several years as a management consultant and another period of employment with the Bethlehem Steel Company, Taylor settled down to record his findings and theories. In general, he and other early contributors to management, whose writings appeared in the pages of the ASME *Transactions*, focused on one question: How can we devise better financial incentives to motivate workers to produce more?

The mental revolution of scientific management

Management interests, hesitatingly expressed in the ASME *Transactions* in the late 1800s became the basis of a lively movement after the turn of the century. Exponents of scientific management sought no less than a "mental

---

[7] In 1910 and 1911, following the request of railroads in the East, the Interstate Commerce Commission held hearings to increase freight charges. Shippers opposed to the rate increase hired as their attorney Louis Brandeis, who later became a justice of the U.S. Supreme Court. Brandeis, in turn, engaged the services of general management experts, among them Harrington Emerson, a man with years of experience in improving business and personnel efficiency through scientific methods. During the hearings, Emerson stated that if railroads used modern management techniques they could probably save great amounts of money. In these discussions the expression *scientific management* was used. Taylor adopted the phrase when he published his book *The Principles of Scientific Management* in 1911.

[8] Frederick W. Taylor, "Testimony Before the Special House Committee," *The Principles of Scientific Management* (New York: Harper & Row, 1911), pp. 39–73.

revolution'' on the part of workers and management to change human relationships in industry and to reduce conflict.

The heart of the movement, and the way to industrial peace, was *mutuality of interests*, which in turn was largely dependent on expanding productivity. People reasoned that the objectives of workers and managers were compatible: workers wanted wages, managers wanted profits, and greater wages and profits depended on increasing productivity. Therefore, workers and managers had a mutual interest in making sure productivity increased. Scientific management was supposed to stimulate the mental revolution, causing managers to manage better and workers to work harder in order to improve efficiency.

Taylor looked at management practice primarily from the bottom up, starting at the shop level. He himself had begun at the bottom of the industrial hierarchy and had worked upward. Nevertheless, any evaluation of his contributions must recognize that, to Taylor, scientific management had two levels—one of philosophy and the other of mechanisms. Taylor's philosophical aims were not realized, because his hope that enlightened workers and managers would cooperate as partners in expanding productivity failed to materialize—at least not in the way he had anticipated. The assumption

---

Emerson's twelve principles of efficiency

- *The first principle*   Clearly defined ideals (a definition of objectives).
- *The second principle*   Common sense (take a long-range point of view and consider consequences).
- *The third principle*   Competent council (seek and rely on expert advice).
- *The fourth principle*   Discipline (the need for order coupled with self-reliance).
- *The fifth principle*   The fair deal (reward good performance well).
- *The sixth principle*   Reliable, immediate, and adequate records (records are essential for control of operations).
- *The seventh principle*   Dispatching (communication of work assignments).
- *The eighth principle*   Standards and schedules (relation of performance standards to wage rates).
- *The ninth principle*   Standardized conditions (uniformity in work assignment).
- *The tenth principle*   Standardized operations (uniformity in task performance).
- *The eleventh principle*   Written standard-practice instructions (job descriptions as part of company records).
- *The twelfth principle*   Efficiency reward (the payoffs to workers and managers).

Source: Adapted from Harrington Emerson. *The Twelve Principles of Efficiency* (New York: Engineering Magazine, 1912)

of mutual interest in the successful performance of an organization was not sufficient for the establishment of industrial harmony.

On the level of mechanisms, however, Taylor's scientific management found acceptance and widespread use. Various wage incentives, time study, motion study, work simplification, efficiency systems, and other devices were adopted and applied in business and government organizations. That some of these were misused to exploit employees and deprive them of their share of increased productivity is a matter of record.

Taylor would have deplored the abuses. He felt that the fruits of efficiency had to be distributed equitably for the goals of scientific management to be attained. The scientific management movement failed to achieve this, but it left a legacy from which management continues to benefit. It opened the door to scientific methods and techniques. It freed management from its reliance on tradition and rule-of-thumb methods to solve problems. To this extent, then, management science is a direct outgrowth of Taylor's efforts at scientific management.

In addition to Taylor, other notable individuals gave momentum to the movement. Henry Gantt, a student of Taylor's, is best known for this contribution to the techniques of production control. The Gantt chart is still used to keep track of production schedules in manufacturing firms. Later in his career, Gantt became interested in industrial leadership and the role of scientific management in building national power.

Frank and Lillian Gilbreth also were important to the early movement. Their slogan was the "one best way." To find the best way to do a job, they used motion study, which reduced each task to its component movements. They believed that from motion and time studies more accurate job standards could be developed. Motion studies were also used to eliminate unnecessary movements. Lillian Gilbreth, a pioneer in personnel management, was interested in the scientific selection, placement, and training of personnel. Morris L. Cooke, known for his application of scientific management to public administration, also was active from the turn of the century until 1925.

The classical period

The 1930s were an extremely productive decade for management. During this period, three major movements were established: the management process, human relations, and organization theory. They have influenced management thinking to the present.

The management process

At the time of Taylor's activity in the United States, Henri Fayol, a French mining engineer, was making a great contribution to the science of management in Europe. Born in 1841 and graduated as a mining engineer in 1860, Fayol was employed by a French coal mine combine. He became its chief executive and remained in that position until he retired in 1918 to devote his time to the study of management. From 1918 until his death in 1925, Fayol sought to popularize his theory of administration. He was instrumental in starting a center of administrative studies in Paris, at which weekly meetings were held and from which came a considerable amount of management literature. There, too, a series of lectures, described as "Fayolism at the School of Higher Commercial Studies," was given. In addition to his interest in popularizing his administrative theories, Fayol set himself another goal: "trying to persuade government to pay some attention to principles of administration."[9]

Fayol continuously tried to apply managerial principles to managerial functions. In 1900 and 1908 he delivered two papers indicating his thinking about management. In 1916 his book *Administration Industrielle et Générale* was published. It was not available in English until 1929, and even then only a few hundred copies were distributed. Not until 1949 was an English edition, retitled *General and Industrial Management*, widely distributed in the United States.

In *General and Industrial Management*, Fayol looked at management activities from the point of view of top management. In his preface he stated: "Management plays a very important part in the government of undertakings: of all undertakings, large or small, industrial, commercial, political, religious or any other. I intend to set forth my ideas here on the way in which that part should be played."[10] He proposed to divide his work into four parts. The first dealt with the necessity and possibility of teaching management. The second contained the principles and elements of management. In the third part, Fayol intended to write about his personal observations and experience, and in the fourth he planned to add the lessons of the war. The last two parts, however, were never written. Apparently he was going to present in them the practical application of the principles he set forth in the first two. Lyndall F. Urwick, a British authority on management, pointed out in his foreword to Fayol's book that the essence of Fayol's views could be found in an interview published in 1925.[11]

Dealing with principles and elements of management, Fayol divided activities into six groups: technical, commercial, financial, security, accounting, and managerial. He dwelled on the last group and distinguished between "general principles of management" and "elements of management." Some of what he included in the former category would today be considered policies, rules, and guides. Fayol's "elements of management" are functions, which he divided into five broad categories: planning, organizing, command, coordination, and control.

Many concepts that have since become traditional—universality of management, unity of command, the scalar chain, authority, and responsibility—were originally applied to management by Fayol. His contribution to

---

[9] Lyndall F. Urwick, foreword to Henri Fayol, *General and Industrial Management*. trans. Constance Storrs (London: Pitman, 1949), p. viii.
[10] Fayol, *General and Industrial Management*, p. xxi.
[11] Urwick, foreword to Fayol, *General and Industrial Management*, p. x.

the theory of management is probably the most revolutionary and constructive ever made. His short book is the culmination of an outstandingly effective managerial career.

Ralph C. Davis, in his book *Industrial Organization and Management*, also built his treatment of management around the functional analysis of planning, organizing, and controlling. He described how these functions are related to each other and how they tie into business objectives, business values, and executive leadership. There is hardly a basic management textbook today that does not follow a functional approach. Therefore Davis's influence on the development of management in the 1930s cannot be overestimated, though the influence of Fayol on Davis's work is difficult to assess. Perhaps the functional approach to management was a case of simultaneous discovery.

The human relations movement

A major current of management thought, stemming from the scientific management movement, assumed that people are rational and economically motivated to work. The human relations movement, which added another dimension to the understanding of human motivation at work, began at Harvard University, where a group of scholars, led by the psychologist Elton Mayo, designed a research project to measure the effect on productivity of conditions in the work environment, such as light, noise, and rest periods. The project started as a straightforward series of experiments in industrial psychology, based on the hypothesis of a direct relationship between workers' productivity and the physical conditions of the work environment. The experiments were conducted in 1927 at the Hawthorne plant of the Western Electric Company in Cicero, Illinois. F. J. Roethlisberger and William J. Dickson, with other researchers, were responsible for the field work. The research came to be known as the Hawthorne Studies.[12]

The researchers were not far into their project when they realized something was wrong. They were not obtaining the results they expected. When the light in the experimental room was reduced, for example, productivity went up instead of down. Something was indeed peculiar about the way the experiments were turning out. The researchers suspended activities and reviewed their initial findings, assumptions, and research design. They concluded that their basic assumption was wrong. Much more than the physical surroundings of the work environment affected productivity. Workers reacted to psychological and social conditions by producing at greater or lesser rates. Informal groups affected productivity; so did participation in decision making and recognition of the individual employee, both of which had a favorable effect. Clearly, giving or withholding social and psychological satisfactions could influence employees' morale. It was only a step from this

---

[12] See F. J. Roethlisberger and William J. Dickson, *Management and the Worker* (Cambridge, Mass.: Harvard University Press, 1956).

realization to the deduction that morale and productivity are directly related: high morale leads to high productivity and vice versa.

Experiments that used the behavioral sciences to test these preliminary observations were devised. This was the first time that behavioral sciences, such as sociology and social psychology, were used together, systematically, in the service of management. If the Hawthorne Studies did nothing else, they introduced behavioral sciences to management. Actually, they did much more than this. They demonstrated that workers are motivated by more than the satisfaction of economic needs and that they seek to fulfill social and psychological needs, which cannot be met entirely by money. They showed that an organization is a social system, not just a logical arrangement of work functions. Although tasks are important, so are the interactions of individuals and small groups with the tasks and with each other. The Hawthorne Studies also provided management with tools and skills to run organizations better by taking human factors into account.

With the development of the human relations movement in the 1930s, management theory divided into two main streams: the industrial management approach, following the traditions of scientific management, and the human factors approach, following the lead set by the Hawthorne Studies. This division still exists, and current developments, such as management science and industrial humanism, reflect the quantitative and humanistic aspects of early management theory.

Organization theory

Organization theory was the third management area to be established in the 1930s. It reached a much more advanced stage of development than the other two. In fact, Lyndall Urwick said in 1932 that now that we know all there is to know about the principles of organization, we should turn our attention to creating various techniques for their application.[13]

Organization theory of this time was a theory of formal organizational authority. James D. Mooney and Alan C. Reiley systematized the theory into a body of laws and principles.[14] Central to their approach was the managerial need for coordination, or the *principle of unity of action,* as they called it. The amount of necessary coordination was based on the commitment employees had to the objectives and the policies of a company. The less the employees were committed, the greater the need for formal structures of organizational control.

Since it was the opinion of many writers at this time that most industrial employees would not have a very strong "willingness to serve," the

---

[13] Lyndall F. Urwick, "Organization As a Technical Problem," in *Papers in the Science of Administration,* ed. Luther Gulick and Lyndall F. Urwick (New York: Institute of Public Administration, 1937), p. 49.

[14] James D. Mooney and Alan C. Reiley, *Onward Industry!* (New York: Harper & Brothers, 1931).

more critical the formal chain of command would be in imposing the necessary and desired coordination. Based on the principle of coordination, Mooney and Reiley developed three subordinate principles that dealt with the formal structure of organization:

1. The *scalar principle,* based on delegation that created the chain of command, coupled with unity of command.
2. The *functional principle,* based on specialization of work.
3. *Line and staff,* which introduced the idea of support and advisory activities for the main functions of an organization.

So many, besides Mooney and Reiley, contributed to organization theory that it is impossible to mention them here. However, we must note a book of considerable merit; it is a distinguished collection of articles, edited by Luther Gulick and Lyndall Urwick and published as *Papers in the Science of Administration.*[15] This book does not represent a single model of management; rather, it brings together a number of essays on various topics with emphasis on organization theory. One such article, for example, was written by V. A. Graicunas on the span of control. The span-of-control concept has an important place in classical organization theory. However, other articles went beyond organization theory including the one by Mary Parker Follett, which speculated on future growth and change in the management profession.

Papers in the Science of Administration was a milestone in management thought. It demonstrated the progress management had made in a relatively short time. However, the change in management did not end here. Events were altering management's role in our industrial society, and the full effect of these changes was not to be felt until after World War II. However, such transitional thinkers as Chester I. Barnard and James Burnham had some remarkably accurate insights into the future.

Transition

Chester I. Barnard, who for many years was vice president of the New Jersey Bell Telephone Company, was the most influential management writer of the 1930s. His work anticipated and inspired many of the directions taken by management after World War II.[16] Best known of Barnard's ideas was the *cooperative system,* which was his attempt to bring together, in a single framework, human relations and industrial management practices.

Barnard's connection with the Harvard human relations group was instrumental in developing the idea that managers must create a cooperative

---

[15] Luther Gulick and Lyndall F. Urwick, *Papers in the Science of Administration* (New York: Columbia University Press, 1937).
[16] Chester I. Barnard, *The Functions of the Executive* (Cambridge, Mass.: Harvard University Press, 1938).

system. This system was able to satisfy the personal objectives of employees while meeting the impersonal objectives of organizations. He said that an organization could exist by satisfying one or the other objective, but a cooperative system would meet both. Therefore managers need proficiency in both human and technical skills; there is no inconsistency between these skills when all organizational and human needs are considered.

And Barnard went much further. He foresaw the growing impact of management and organizations on society. He thought that managers in public and private organizations were becoming more and more influential in shaping human values. He discussed executive responsibility in terms of management's obligation to create enlightened values that will allow the human and industrial potentials of America to be fulfilled.

James Burnham was less optimistic. In his book he asked which side was winning the struggle between capitalism and socialism.[17] His answer: neither. An entirely new "ism" was emerging, which he called *managerialism*. The new managerial society was quite different from anything in the past. Managers constituted a new elite class, which had the power to run a society without a basis in property or elected mass support. The power of managers originated in their expertise to run complex administrative systems. Once having acquired this power in the key decision centers of organizations, the managerial elite is virtually irremovable.

A common theme ran through Burnham's and Barnard's works: the blind forces, including the competitive market, that we have relied on to make managers behave in the social interest, were weakening. Their places were being filled by administrative systems run by managers who have the personal power to shape values. Whether these managers would do this benevolently and effectively was an open question, and it still is. Recent polls indicate that people do not think managers are meeting this obligation. The most interesting thing about these polls is that people want what organizations are able to provide, but they are unhappy with the way organizations are run.

In any event, management was at a point of transition when America was on the threshold of World War II. Management had earlier made tremendous strides in practice and theory, and the war effort was a demonstration of this. However, the full significance of management was not to unfold until the 1950s, when management moved from the industrial society into the technological society. These events are discussed in the next chapter.

Summary

Management is a product of the twentieth century. Although management existed in preindustrial times, it took the Industrial Revolution, plus the development of complex business and government organizations, to create a

---

[17] James Burnham, *The Managerial Revolution* (New York: John Day, 1940).

management discipline. The main movements behind the rise of this discipline were scientific management, the management process, human relations, and organization theory. These movements appeared in America in the first forty years of this century. Toward the end of the 1930s, Barnard and Burnham sensed a transition that ultimately would raise professional management to a preeminent status in our society.

Discussion questions

1 The most notable contributions to management theory and practice were made during the 1930s. Briefly discuss three such contributions.
2 What do you consider to be the principal difficulties with the concepts of classical management theory?

Supplementary readings

Barnard, Chester I. *The Functions of the Executive.* Cambridge, Mass.: Harvard University Press, 1938.

Fayol, Henri. *General and Industrial Management.* Translated by Constance Storrs. London: Pitman, 1949.

Koontz, Harold. "The Management Theory Jungle." *Academy of Management Journal,* December 1961, pp. 174–188. Reprinted in *Dimensions in Modern Management,* 2d. ed., edited by Patrick E. Connor. Boston: Houghton Mifflin, 1978.

Mooney, James D. *The Principles of Organization.* New York: Harper & Brothers, 1947.

Chapter 3

Modern management: Systems, science, and emerging issues

Objectives of the chapter

1 To emphasize the problems of organizational complexity and interdependency that confront modern management.
2 To discuss management principles, systems, and contingencies.
3 To indicate the significance of technological change on management.
4 To describe the influence of the behavioral and quantitative sciences on management.
5 To outline some unresolved questions that are affecting management now and that will affect it in the future.

Management has come quite a distance since Henry Gantt wrote: "The greatest problem before engineers and managers today is the economic utilization of labor." If modern management were faced by only this problem, its job would be comparatively easy. Instead, the modern manager is confronted by so many interdependent problems and complexities that to isolate even one or two of them is a dangerous oversimplification.

Management is a changing discipline, first because its environment has changed and second because its techniques and its knowledge base have changed. Behind these developments are three related dynamic forces, which we discuss in this chapter: fundamental change in the concept of the management process, technological change, and the extended use of science in management. All these factors, working simultaneously, have created a theory and a practice that were unanticipated in many aspects twenty-five years ago.

Management principles, systems, and contingencies

Traditional management theory may be compared to a well-charted plain. Its landmarks stand out distinctly against a background of rational assumptions about the business enterprise, its organization, and the managerial behavior appropriate to it. Harold Koontz attributes the following seven features to traditional theory:

1. Management is a process composed of functions. What management is can be deduced by analyzing what managers do.
2. The principles of management have an empirical foundation; they are based on the experience of those who developed and used them and, thus, have value for clarifying and improving management practice.
3. Management principles provide a take-off point for research to prove their validity and improve their applications to practice.
4. Management principles are valuable, practical, a priori elements of managerial theory and stand as universal truths until disproved.
5. The practice of management is an art that relies on principles.
6. Even if, in a given situation, a manager ignores a principle (but incurs an added cost) in achieving an objective, the principle is in no way invalidated.
7. Management encompasses a unique and definable body of knowledge. It is not so broad that it includes everything, nor is it so narrow that it excludes the possibility of making some generalizations.[1]

This list shows the heavy emphasis traditional theory gives to principles (items 2 through 6). The theory says that managers should rely on principles when laying out a course of action, executing functions, and following up on results. From the standpoint of traditional theory, principles are *prescriptive*.

This view has brought much criticism. Critics charge that principles do not generally prescribe good management practice. Rather they describe certain situations and hence do not apply in all cases; indeed, in some cases they may be misleading. Joan Woodward, who has written extensively on the influence of technology on a firm's organizational structure, observes:

One interesting characteristic of classical management theory . . . is that it was developed in a technical setting but independently of technology. In general the formulas are closely linked with the personalities of those who worked and wrote in this field. . . . The expedients they found effective in practice were often given the status of fundamental truths or general laws by those attracted to their ideas.[2]

The principles approach to the management process creates many difficulties. Because it is prescriptive, it is applicable to certain managerial situations and not to others. Therefore, it does not adapt well to the profound changes that have occurred in American management since 1960. Increasing organizational complexity and interdependency have made revision necessary in the manner in which the management process is viewed.

[1] Adapted from Harold Koontz, "The Management Theory Jungle," *Journal of the Academy of Management* 4 (December 1961):174–199.
[2] Joan Woodward, *Industrial Organization: Theory and Practice* (London: Oxford University Press, 1965), p.35.

This change in managerial perspective has been achieved through the systems approach and the contingency approach, which we discussed in Chapter 1. However, these ideas are so important in the evolution of management thought that we reemphasize them here.

The systems approach

The systems approach is one of the most important concepts in modern management because it deals with change and interrelationships in complex organizations. The idea of systems interdependency is critical because it acknowledges that a change in one part of the system has consequences in other parts of the system. For example, a managerial decision to increase outpatient care in a hospital will affect nursing and treatment resources because the nature of patients' needs will change.

The systems approach sees the organization as more than an economic unit that rationally uses people, machines, and materials to increase efficiency and profits. It regards an organization as a fusion of parts, processes, and goals that make a living, changing, human enterprise.

The *parts* consist of people, machines, and material resources, as well as tasks, formal structures of authority and power, and small groups that also possess some authority and power. Depending on and influencing one another, the parts are tied together by *processes,* such as communication and decision making, which in turn link the parts and aim them squarely at organizational *goals*.

The systems concept frees management from a narrow, efficiency view of the organization; it incorporates many variables that affect the system and influence the actions of management. The concept gives the manager more leverage for adjusting the system and a more realistic picture of the manager's place in it and his or her impact on it.

The contingency approach

The contingency approach is a major departure from the principles-of-management model. Where the principles are universal and prescriptive, the contingency approach is situational and nonprescriptive. Although contingency ideas have been around from the time of Fayol, serious attention was not given to them until Joan Woodward's research was published.

Woodward has shown that some traditional ideas on organizational structure pertain to firms with a particular kind of technology and are less relevant for firms with other technologies. The differences between two manufacturing operations illustrate this point. An assembly activity, like that for the mass production of television sets, uses a technology different from that of a continuous-process activity, in which crude oil is refined into a number of consumer and industrial products. Dissimilar technologies, therefore, cause variations in the structure of organizations. For example, firms in mass-production industries tend to have more levels of authority and narrower spans of management. Thus, the structure of an organization is *contingent* on the technology the organization uses.

The contingency approach has not stopped with a concern for technology and organizational structure. Kast and Rosenzweig point out:

The contingency view seeks to understand the interrelationships within and among subsystems as well as between the organization and its environment and to define patterns of relationships or configurations of variables. It emphasizes the multivariate nature of organizations and attempts to understand how organizations operate under varying conditions and in specific circumstances. Contingency views are ultimately directed toward suggesting organizational designs and managerial actions most appropriate for specific situations.[3]

The contingency approach is based on a systems model of complex organizations. It deals with interactions among subsystems within an organization and with interactions between an organization and its environment. But most important of all, the contingency approach focuses on specific kinds of organizational design that are most effective for coping with a wide variety of different managerial situations. It says, basically, that there is no "one best way" of managing and that what is best depends on the circumstances. This point of view places emphasis on research and training to find and to apply knowledge about various relationships of interest to management. Among these interests are leadership, organizational structure, control, and, of course, objectives and policies, which we discuss in the next chapter. However, technological change is one of the chief reasons for the growing importance of the contingency approach.

Technological change

Technology has changed the nature of the work force, increased organizational complexity, and expanded interdependence among organizations. Technology has two minimum requirements: (1) "the systematic application of scientific or other organized knowledge to practical tasks" and (2) a division of labor so that this knowledge can be focused on a well-defined segment of work.[4] *Technological advancement* is the progressive use of applied science and continuous specialization. For example, William Boeing and a few mechanics built their first airplane in a converted shed on the shores of Lake Union in Seattle. It was a crude vehicle in comparison with the modern 747 aircraft. Behind the 747 and other jet-age products are

---

[3] Fremont E. Kast and James E. Rosenzweig, *Contingency Views of Organization and Management* (Chicago: Science Research Associates, 1973), p. 313.
[4] John Kenneth Galbraith, *The New Industrial State* (Boston: Houghton Mifflin, 1967), p. 12.

dramatic changes in aircraft manufacturing techniques that required work specialization of a sort not anticipated in the early days of the Boeing Company.

John Kenneth Galbraith points out that the application of science and specialization generates six additional effects[5] which, when combined, cast industry in its modern technological mold:

1. A lengthening span of time separating the start and finish of a production process.
2. An increase in the amount of capital required for running an enterprise.
3. A tendency toward inflexibility in task performance, meaning that capital invested and time required to make changes slow the rapidity with which a technology can be altered for any particular job.
4. A growth of specialists in the labor force.
5. Increased intensity of organization.
6. The growing importance of planning so as to be sure that the most effective allocation of time, capital, and labor is achieved within the constraints of the current state of the planning art.

Work force changes

In response to these changes the general work force and management have been upgraded. Throughout the labor market higher levels of skill are needed—among white-collar workers, employees in service industries, and manual workers in production jobs. Since 1900, the proportion of the labor force employed in professional and technical jobs has been growing. Figure 3-1 illustrates the changing character of the American work force between 1900 and 1970.

Projections to 1985 indicate growing numbers and percentages of workers in white-collar occupations. Using the twelve-year period from 1960 to 1972 as a base period, one forecast projects that professional, technical, managerial, and clerical occupations will show faster growth rates than the base period. Generally, the number of blue-collar workers, farm workers, and service workers will grow at a slower rate than that during the base period.[6]

Part of these trends are accounted for by the increasing complexity of our technological society. More managers with greater technical skills are needed. As people move into the labor force with higher levels of education, their expectations about work and the work environment will change. Conventional ideas about motivation, leadership, and organizational design will have to vary accordingly. Obviously, specific prescriptions about good management cannot be made for each circumstance that will be encountered. Management's actions to achieve effectiveness will depend on the people employed in and the tasks required of the organization.

[5] Ibid., pp. 13–17.
[6] Neal H. Rosenthal, "Projected Changes in Occupations," *Monthly Labor Review*, December 1973, pp. 18–25.

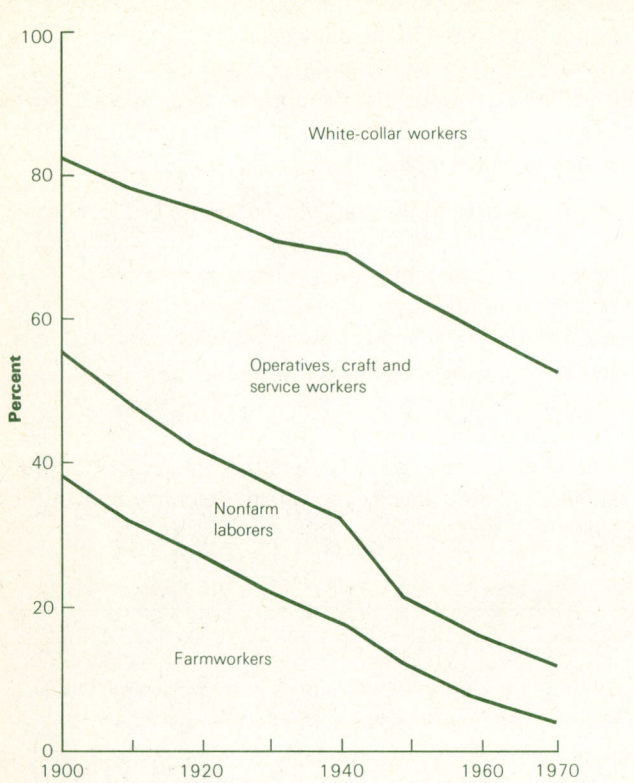

Figure 3-1 The projected increase in the percentage of white-collar workers will continue a long-standing labor force trend *Source:* U.S. Department of Labor and U.S. Department of Commerce. Nonfarm laborers includes private household workers.

Complex organizations

Technological progress often requires complex organizations, because advanced products and processes cannot be accommodated by simple, straightforward line-type organizations. There are many aspects of organizational complexity. From the standpoint of structure, staff departments offer specialized service to the line in such areas as quality control, market research, and personnel. Various support departments are also required in complex organizations. For example, computer-based management information systems fill part of the communication needs of these organizations.

Managers use different structures to achieve coordination in organizations with diverse and specialized activities. Matrix and project organizations, emphasizing lateral communication, are two such structures. Structures of control over work flow, job standards, and performance are other means to coordination. As we illustrate in later chapters, in organizing modern businesses and other administrative systems, managers have had to violate well-established principles that were not adaptable to the needs of complex organizations.

The expanding use of specialists in the design of complex organizations has placed new demands on executive leadership. The general upward movement in the skill level of employees has created a need for a new quality in the work environment. People are less and less content with merely "a place to work." They are more and more interested in personal and professional growth. Managers must try to meet these expectations in the interest of employee productivity and satisfaction.

Organizational interdependence

Technological change also has brought greater interdependence among people and organizations. There is growing concern about managing extensive webs of organizational interrelationships. Most managers know that they deal with a system that is much wider than their own organization. This system includes governmental regulatory agencies, labor unions, subcontractors, consumer groups, and a large number of other independent but related organizations in finance, marketing, and production.

Managers have become interrelationship conscious. But managing these relationships is not the same as managing the internal affairs of an organization. Managing interdependence among organizations is probably the most critical and least understood area of modern management. However, we usually are aware, managers and citizens alike, when a major system of interdependence breaks down. The oil embargo of the OPEC nations is a case in point.

In summary, new management concepts and technological change have been among the sources of dissatisfaction with traditional theory. Events in management, organization, and technology have moved very fast since the end of World War II. Management has had to keep up with these changes; specifically, management has had to adapt its skills and its organizations to accelerated change. Science has assisted management with ideas and techniques to help it to adapt.

Science and management

Modern management needs science more than ever before, and science, for its part, has contributed heavily to the expanding knowledge base of management. Such contributions have come in three main areas: science and human behavior, science and quantitative methods, and science and communication.

The behavioral sciences

People are the most important ingredient in organizations. However, their use and motivation are among the most difficult management problems.

Therefore, it is not surprising that the behavioral sciences have played a major role in the development of management theory and practice. Many contributions of the behavioral sciences have been in applied areas, such as psychological testing, training, leadership, communication, job motivation, and organizational change. But the behavioral sciences also affect the way management thinks about people in organizations. Today we hear a great deal about adapting to change, the work environment, and employee expectations. These factors concern the human and social values that the behavioral sciences address.

Psychology

Of all the behavioral sciences, psychology has been the greatest shaper of management thought. Managers continually influence and motivate people, and they must know how to do it effectively. Tactics such as pay increases and threats of punishment may improve productivity but may also raise costs.

Psychologists have shown that people hope to satisfy a wide range of needs at work—not only economic needs but also social and personal needs. To the extent that people find at least partial fulfillment of their needs in the work environment, they can be influenced to work willingly, productively, and cooperatively. In other words, employees' morale appears to depend on how well the work environment satisfies their needs. One objective of management development is to train managers to create a work climate that provides a wide range of satisfaction for the individual. This can be done through providing opportunities for employees to participate in decision making, communicating with employees so that they know what is going on and how it affects them and their jobs, and giving employees recognition so that they feel a sense of worth and believe they are important to the overall operation of the enterprise. Much organizationally oriented psychology is concerned with how the satisfaction of participation, communication, and recognition needs influences morale and productivity.

Sociology

Two major contributions to management have come from sociology. The first is attention to small groups, which are often treated in the literature as the informal components of organization. Much has been learned and conveyed to management about the behavior of small groups, their influence on members, and their impact on the formal structure. For example, the small group is frequently the focus of team effort in many situations. At one extreme, a biller and a packer may form a two-person group that processes customers' orders in a mail order house. At the other extreme, a team of eight or more scientists may work together on a firm's research and development projects. In an entirely different context, small groups may arise in the work setting for social purposes that have little to do with the tasks of the enterprise. The other major contribution of sociology is its study of complex formal organizations.

In addition, sociology has improved managers' understanding of the roles played by leaders and followers and an organization's patterns of authority, power, and influence. Other contributions of sociology are closely related to psychology and may be classified as products of the rapid growth of social psychology.

Social psychology

Social psychologists study the interactions of individuals and the groups with which they associate. They examine how groups and individuals influence and modify one another's behavior. Significant work in using this approach has been done on communication, leadership, and decision making. Most recently, problems of conflict and its resolution have been examined. Because of its interactional nature, social psychology has many applications in business. In fact, it is difficult to find much current work of importance that does not in some way involve the elements of individual and group behavior.

Other behavioral sciences

Psychology, sociology, and social psychology are the key behavioral sciences that shape management thought and practice today. However, anthropology has also made a significant contribution by revealing the impact of culture on organizations. Culture gives an organization its identity. It provides objectives and the means for achieving them, and it is a unifying force.

Political science has not yet been a major contributor to management. Increasingly, however, students of management are becoming aware that organizations are systems of government. Political science eventually should be able to provide valuable insights in this direction.

Science and quantitative methods

The reorientation of management thought, resulting from interaction with the behavioral sciences, is paralleled by changes brought about by management science. The best-known and most widely accepted branch of management science is *operations research,* a technique that works best in narrow decision areas that can be clearly defined and quantified. Operations research is applied to management problems that can be analyzed by mathematical models.

There are many definitions of operations research. According to one: "In simplest terms, operations research can be defined as research into the relationships and functions of an organized activity. The purpose, when applied to business problems, is generally how to use the resources on hand so as to achieve optimum results.[7] Operations research is thus analytical, experimental, and quantitative. It appraises and evaluates the overall implications of various courses of action and provides managers with an improved basis for their decisions.

[7] *Operations Research: Studies in Business Policy,* no. 82 (New York: National Industrial Conference board, 1957), p. 9.

Operations research has been applied to many organizational problems, but more toward inventory control than any other problem in industry. However, other areas, such as production scheduling, sales policies, the effect of night openings on department store sales, improved rail replacement programs, more effective use of equipment, traffic delay at toll booths, and servicing customers, have also received attention. Operations research may be applied to a specific business problem in this way:

A manufacturer of chemical products, with a wide and varied line, sought more rational or logical bases than the customary percentage of sales for distributing his limited advertising budget among products, some of which were growing, some stable, and others declining. An operations research study showed that advertising effectiveness was related to three simple characteristics, each of which could be estimated from existing sales data with satisfactory reliability: (a) the total market potential; (b) the rate of growth of sales; (c) the customer loss rate. A mathematical formulation of these characteristics provided a rational basis for distributing advertising and promotional effort. [8]

Operations research is composed of quantitative methods and theories that are useful in some managerial decision-making and control situations. But many of the problems that now are solved by these methods could not even have been approached before the development of advanced computer technology.

Science and communication

The first commercial computer was marketed in 1954. This major technological event for management not only permitted the solution of very sophisticated engineering problems, but also ushered in the era of management information systems, essential to complex organizations. The heart of such systems is the computer itself. The computer is supported by a vast array of programs, methods, and supporting electronic devices that feed information into the communication channels of an organization.

Modern electronic technology has greatly expanded the human capacity to communicate. This development has been critical for effective management. However, the technology has had to be integrated into an overall organizational design for its most efficient utilization. The information it provides influences all management functions, providing the data necessary for accounting, finance, manufacturing, and marketing. Without modern information technology, it is unlikely that the complex organizations with which we are familiar could exist.

---

[8] Cyril C. Herrmann and John F. Magee, "Operations Research for Management," *Harvard Business Review* 31 (July–August 1953): 102.

Emerging issues in management

Management's strength lies in its use of resources and technology to achieve organizational growth. Most of the sciences that are helpful to management have been applied mainly to solving internal coordination and control problems. However, critical issues for management—such as energy, financial capital, and the physical environment—are now coming from outside the organization.

Energy

Shortages of energy, stemming from dwindling reserves of crude oil, are well publicized.[9] Proven reserves of oil in the United States are good for only 11.7 years. On March 18, 1976, we imported more crude oil than we produced. The dream of energy self-sufficiency is not likely to be achieved in anything like a realistic time projection, given our present rate of consumption.

These circumstances are enormously significant for management. Energy is the absolutely essential commodity in a technological society. Without an abundance of energy, at relatively modest cost, the rate of industrial activity and the prospects for economic growth must be curtailed. The consequences of energy shortages are inflation, unemployment, and a general lowering of American living standards. Some of these effects have been felt already, albeit mildly, as a result of the OPEC embargo on the export of crude oil in 1973.[10] We have recovered from this event, but the long-term energy forecast—over, say, twenty-five years—is not bright.

Brief chronology of the oil embargo

On October 22, 1973, a number of Middle Eastern oil-producing nations announced that they were suspending shipments of petroleum to the United States, Japan, and several European nations. This embargo formed part of a plan to obtain favorable political treatment in the settlement of disputes arising from the Arab-Israeli war of 1973. While the amount of oil involved was small relative to U.S. consumption, it was not inconsequential. (According to the 1974 International Economic Report of the President, 9 percent of all domestic consumption of petroleum was supplied by Arab countries.) Several weeks were required before oil in transit would arrive, so it seemed unlikely that major effects of the embargo would occur before December.

---

[9] This section and the next, on capital formation, are based on a talk by C. Spencer Clark, "The Management of Decline: Beyond the Bicentennial," Academy of Management, Western Division, April 1976.

[10] See John F. Early, "Effect of the Energy Crisis on Employment," *Monthly Labor Review*, August 1974, pp. 8–16.

Anticipating the effects of the embargo, as well as other indications of tightening fuel supplies, the Federal Government initiated certain actions. In mid-October, 1973, propane gas came under mandatory distribution allocations. In early November, several large airlines eliminated 44 daily flights. In December, a Federal law was passed setting a 55-mile-per-hour speed limit nation-wide. On the first of January the Federal Energy Office ordered reductions of 15 percent in supplies of heating oil for home use, a 25-percent reduction for commercial use, and a 10-percent reduction for industrial use. Also early in January, gasoline station supplies were reduced to 85 percent of the January 1972 level. Daylight-saving time was instituted nationwide on January 6. In mid-January, several States instituted plans in which cars with odd-numbered tags bought gas one day, those with even numbered tags the next in an effort to reduce long lines at gasoline stations. At that time fuel for farmers was given top priority. Then, during the first part of February, the Federal Energy Office instituted a State by State gasoline allocation program. Finally in mid-March the oil embargo was lifted. Although some time would elapse before oil began flowing again, pressure seemed to ease and it was possible to make use of unused reserves.

Source: Monthly Labor Review, August 1974, p. 14.

Some say the answer is to develop alternative energy resources, such as conversion of coal in the vast Montana and Alaska fields into petroleum products. This alternative seems attractive superficially but it has inherent shortcomings.

Capital generation

In considering alternative fuel supplies, capital generation is seldom fully appreciated by the popular press. Although it is technically possible to convert coal to petroleum fuels, the amount of capital that is necessary to do this on a large scale is enormous. As Clark points out:

The manufacture of synthetic liquid fuels from coal and vegetable matter sources will be emphasized, but the very quantities of energy required to maintain anything like the status quo will require so much capital in the time span involved that the economic systems of the Western World are incapable of providing any meaningful portion of the requirements from the private sector. Governments will be equally helpless as the tax base is available only through economic activity.[11]

Therefore, unless the problem of energy is solved within the framework of available resources and financial capability, profound changes in the American lifestyle will occur. The first casualty, Clark predicts, will be individual

[11] Clark, "The Management of Decline," pp. 14—15.

mobility by means of the automobile. Consider the impact of reduced auto use on recreational travel, suburban living, shopping centers, automobile manufacturing, primary industries (which include steel), and support industries that supply service and maintenance. However, the energy issue involves more than resources and capital. It concerns our attitudes toward the physical environment.

The physical environment

In 1967 an executive of a large manufacturing business was requested to address a group of students on the subject of social responsibility. After his talk, a student asked what his firm was doing about air and water pollution. Since his company was allegedly the cause of considerable water and air contamination, the executive became quite upset by this question and answered, "I came here to talk about social responsibility, not pollution." It is hard to imagine an executive of a major corporation publicly expressing such an attitude today. Concern for the environment has grown appreciably since the 1962 publication of Rachel Carson's book *Silent Spring.* As a result of her attack on DDT and insecticides, numerous threats to the quality of the environment have been exposed—nuclear contamination, garbage accumulation, intolerable noise levels in cities, oil pipelines in Alaska, oil spills, industrial waste disposal in the air and water, and automobile exhaust.

Heightened sensitivity to environmental matters has induced private and governmental organizations to seek to regulate and control industry. Management must work with regulatory agencies that promulgate and enforce standards of environmental quality. Air quality standards, for instance, cause many difficulties. A firm may install a condenser to remove pollutants before the exhaust of a manufacturing activity is expelled. The condenser is engineered to conform with existing standards, but the agency suddenly changes them, immediately making the control equipment obsolete. Many similar problems might be cited.

The point that the Sierra Club and the Friends of the Earth constantly make is that nature maintains a delicate ecological balance. Interference with this balance causes nature and people to suffer. Just *how* humanity loses as the result of resource utilization is not a clear-cut issue. Obviously, we have to make some trade-offs between the natural environment and the production-consumption cycle, which is essential to the life of a technological society.

In the late 1960s and early 1970s the momentum of public attitudes and public policy was in the direction of environmental conservation and preservation. Recently, however, because of unemployment, inflation, and shortages of conventional resources, attitudes seem to be shifting away from the environmental militancy of just a few years ago. One thing seems fairly certain: there will be greater administrative regulation of both renewable and nonrenewable resources. This could range from more intensive forest management to the rationing of gasoline.

The problems posed by energy, capital, and the environment may bring management face to face with the most critical issue of the final quarter of this century: the expectation of economic growth may have to be reexamined. Indeed, management may have to replace its growth models with models of stability or perhaps decline. Of all the emerging issues that management has to confront, this one is the most important.

Summary

Modern management relies on a systems model of organization coupled with a contingency approach. These new reference points were made necessary by technological change, which in turn has changed the nature of the work force, has created complex organizations, and has increased the interdependency of organizations and society.

Science has helped management to cope with the increased internal complexity of organizations. Major contributions have been made by the behavioral sciences, the quantitative sciences, and the informational sciences. However, management more and more is feeling the impact of the external environment on organizational affairs. Chief among emerging management issues are energy, capital generation, and the physical environment.

Discussion questions

1 The unifying concepts of the social system have been recognized as the major contribution of the behavioral sciences to management. What are the elements of the social system? What is the value of a systems approach for managers?
2 Bob Dylan has observed that "the times are a-changing." In what ways does his observation reflect a contingency view?

Supplementary readings

Bertalanffy, Ludwig von. "The History and Status of General Systems Theory." *Academy of Management Journal,* December 1972, pp. 407–426.

Galbraith, John Kenneth. *The New Industrial State.* Boston: Houghton Mifflin, 1967.

Kast, Fremont E., and Rosenzweig, James E. *Contingency Views of Organization and Management.* Chicago: Science Research Associates, 1973.

Luthans, Fred. "The Contingency Theory of Management: A Path out of the Jungle." *Business Horizons,* June 1973, pp. 67–72. Reprinted in *Dimensions in Modern Management,* 2d ed., edited by Patrick E. Connor. Boston: Houghton Mifflin, 1978.

Part II

Planning

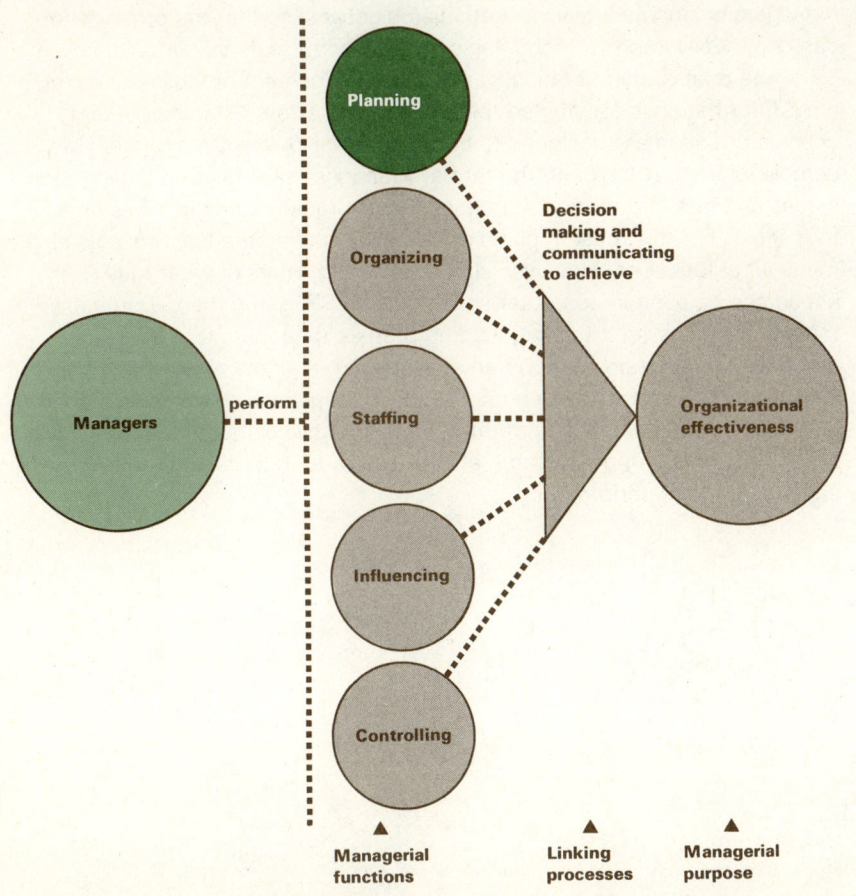

The planning function Planning is a primary managerial task. It precedes, and provides a framework for, all other managerial functions.

Through planning, information-determining objectives and policies are gathered, strategies are laid, and tactics are decided.

In developing plans, managers act in accordance with their organizations' objectives. They are constantly aware of the need to perform efficiently, provide a service, satisfy social obligations, and cater to personal aspirations. Some years ago, debate raged over which of these objectives was of primary importance. More recently, the discussion of objectives has taken a new turn. Managers are influenced by many interest groups—owners, customers, employees, and the public (through the government). How can management balance its objectives so that each group receives an equitable share of the values created by the organization?

The word *values* is crucial. For business management, value is money, and two research studies, presented in Chapter 4, reflect this. Their findings should not be surprising, for the managers of any economic institution should be interested mainly in technological and economic results. However, other values may enter the manager's planning. That is why we ask: How do managers balance all their obligations (objectives) so that the organization can continually improve technologically and increase its value to society?

The relationship of objectives to the management process orients planning. Information is assembled, planning premises are established, and courses of action are designed to fit objectives. However, managers always gamble when they look into the future. Managers have fewer planning techniques and less information than does a horse-racing fan who relies on a tout sheet. For this reason, planning has always been the least reliable of the managerial functions. However, this is changing. Hints of what may lie ahead can be seen in computer simulation, PERT, game theory, probability theory, and behavioral techniques that prepare managers to make better decisions in uncertain environments. Moreover, a whole new area of planning, devoted to forecasting technological change, is also emerging. These developments should make not only planning activities but also the four other managerial functions more effective, providing them with objectives and standards of performance.

Chapter 4

Objectives, policies, and contingencies

Objectives of the chapter

1. To discuss objectives, policies, and the concept of social responsibility.
2. To explore the meaning of profits as a goal of the business enterprise.
3. To identify the multiplicity of legitimate goals that characterize modern organizations.
4. To describe the nature of policies and their relation to managerial action.
5. To emphasize the importance of strategy and tactics in the process of goal formation and implementation.

The management process is based on objectives that provide the basis for planning and the standards for control. Objectives also supply the necessary criteria for designing the organizational structure, staffing it with personnel, and motivating people to work. Beyond this, objectives give an organization its identity, purpose, and direction. They allow people in an organization to have a sense of mission. And, most important of all, objectives are the mirrors of how managers perceive their environment. Objectives are a direct and sensitive reflection of management quality because they are the *value premises* that govern the life of an organization.

For the life of an organization to be healthy, objectives must change. Managers must be able to match their organizations' objectives to the demands of the environment, to guide them through the turbulence of change, and thereby to contribute significantly to their vitality. This requires that managers have the skill to read the environment properly and to take the actions necessary for adapting an organization to change. Objectives provide managers with contingency problems. For example, the original purpose of the March of Dimes was to combat the widespread, crippling disease of poliomyelitis through various programs of medical research, fund raising, and public education. Although the disease was conquered by Salk vaccine, the March of Dimes organization did not shut down; it shifted its objectives to a "war on birth defects."

Change is a fact of managerial life, and it is felt most profoundly in relation to objectives. Managers must have the flexibility to change goals, to redefine missions, and to direct organizations into new avenues of endeavor. An organization's survival depends on its managers' abilities to cope with, adapt to, and influence changing conditions. The management of change requires the skill, insight, and courage to alter objectives.

The contingency approach to objectives is not a one-way street of managers' reacting and adapting to environmental change. Managers try to influence the environment as well. How such influence is exerted depends on the technological, political, economic, social, and labor environment in which managers operate. As these conditions will vary widely, so will the strategies for influencing change. Business lobbyists try to influence the political process to obtain favorable tax legislation; business firms advertise to gain consumer acceptance of their products; government agencies attempt to modify social attitudes on such issues as smoking and employing handicapped workers; labor unions try to enlist public support for their causes, as in the United Farm Workers' effort to boycott nonunion grapes and lettuce. Success or failure in influencing such contingencies (and many others) has major consequences for organizational objectives. If people accept the value premises of an organization, its managers achieve a major victory in organizational survival.

A model for examining objectives

The study of objectives is complex because there are so many of them. They are different for almost every organization, and they differ in levels of importance as well. Some research has been done on objectives; so the best way to introduce the model of objectives is to look at the ways in which managers regard objectives in business enterprises.

Research on business objectives

In one study, James K. Dent[1] asked 145 chief executives in five cities, "What are the aims of top management in your company?" Table 4-1 shows their responses and indicates that the goals most often mentioned by managers were profit, employees' well-being, and public service through good products. These findings are consistent with the objectives most writers, over the years, have attributed to management. However, the most interesting part of Dent's study is the relationship he found between objectives and organizational characteristics.

He observed that managers of large companies express concern for

---

[1] James K. Dent, "Organizational Correlates of the Goals of Business Managements," *Personnel Psychology* 12 (Autumn 1959):365–394.

Table 4-1 Aims of managements in five cities and for three cities separately

Aim	Percentage of managers giving various aims				
	All 5 cities		First 3 aims		
	First aim	First 3 aims	City A	City B	City C
To make money, profits, or a living	36	52	49	75	39
To pay dividends to stockholders	1	9	9	12	2
To grow	12	17	14	5	22
To be efficient, economical	4	12	16	15	—
To meet or stay ahead of competitors	5	13	12	5	15
To operate or develop the organization	9	14	7	15	17
To provide a good product or public service	21	39	47	20	49
To contribute to community relations	—	3	5	—	2
To provide for the welfare of employees: a good living, security, happiness, good working conditions	5	39	51	22	32
Miscellaneous other aims	7	18			
Total	100	a	a	a	a

[a] Adds to more than 100 percent because many executives gave more than one goal.
Source: Adapted from James K. Dent, "Organizational Correlates of the Goals of Business Managements," *Personnel Psychology* 12 (Autumn 1959): 369. Used with permission.

good products and public service more often than do managers of small companies. However, managers of large companies are not uninterested in profits; managers of both large and small firms mention the importance of profits with equal frequency.

The interrelationship of size, unionization, and employee welfare is interesting. Managers of large unionized firms mention employee welfare as an important objective, whereas managers of large nonunionized firms mention this objective much less frequently. This situation is exactly reversed for managers of small unionized and nonunionized firms.

The managers of firms that have a high proportion of white-collar workers list growth as an objective more often than do the managers of firms that have a high percentage of blue-collar workers. The only apparent reason for this is the cultural differences prevailing in the two types of firm. Management emphasis on growth in a predominantly white-collar firm takes on added significance when we recall the changing character of the work force discussed in Chapter 3. It is possible that growth orientation is a response to the increasingly professional character of employees; growth provides opportunities for advancement in the organization.

Top executives of growing businesses also stress good products more strongly than do their counterparts in declining businesses. Finally, Dent observed that management's interest in broad social responsibilities, such as community and employee welfare, does not enhance the growth of a business.

Although Dent found important relationships between certain organizational characteristics and the goals emphasized by management, he stressed that managers mentioned one objective more than any other—profitability. Similarly, George W. England,[2] in a long-running research program, has found a cluster of objectives, which he calls "maximization criteria," as the most influential in shaping managerial action. This cluster includes goals such as organizational efficiency, high productivity, and maximization of profit.

Another cluster of goals, which England found of secondary importance to managers, consists of organizational growth, industry leadership, and organizational stability. These goals are sought not for themselves but as tests for the maximization of alternatives. For example, management may ask what effect an equipment replacement policy will have on capital availability for future expansion.

Employee welfare is of tertiary importance. Although named by a large percentage of managers, it does not compare with either of the first two clusters as a source for the generation or testing of alternatives. This indicates that the welfare of employees does not motivate executive behavior as strongly as do other goals. It is not viewed as a major contribution to organizational success. Likewise, England found the last goal cluster, social welfare or community relations, to be very low as a motivator; few managers see it as either important or necessary to organizational success. However, as problems of community relations assume greater and greater importance in American life, managers might have to give this goal more attention.

The similarities in Dent's and England's studies are striking. Both show high managerial interest in profit and comparatively low interest in employee and social welfare. Between these extremes, customer service, growth, and organizational stability seem to be goals that either stem from or contribute to the first cluster of objectives.

The Dent and England studies show fairly conclusively that business managers rate profit making or efficiency high on their scale of values. However, these studies show that managers formulate other objectives as well. It is also likely that managers in nonbusiness organizations, such as libraries or welfare agencies, will assign different weights to objectives and not consider profit as an appropriate goal.

Therefore, managers not only create objectives and change them, they also have to rank objectives in order of importance. This raises the issue of priorities, which may vary as conditions change. Given all this, it is difficult to present a model of objectives that covers all possible circumstances. However, some generalizations can be made for business organizations, which are illustrated in Figure 4-1. The main elements in this model are grand strategy, primary objectives, strategy, operational objectives, operations, and feedback of results.

---

[2] George W. England, "Personal Value Systems of Managers and Administrators," *Academy of Management Proceedings,* 33d Annual Meeting (Boston, 1974), pp. 81–88.

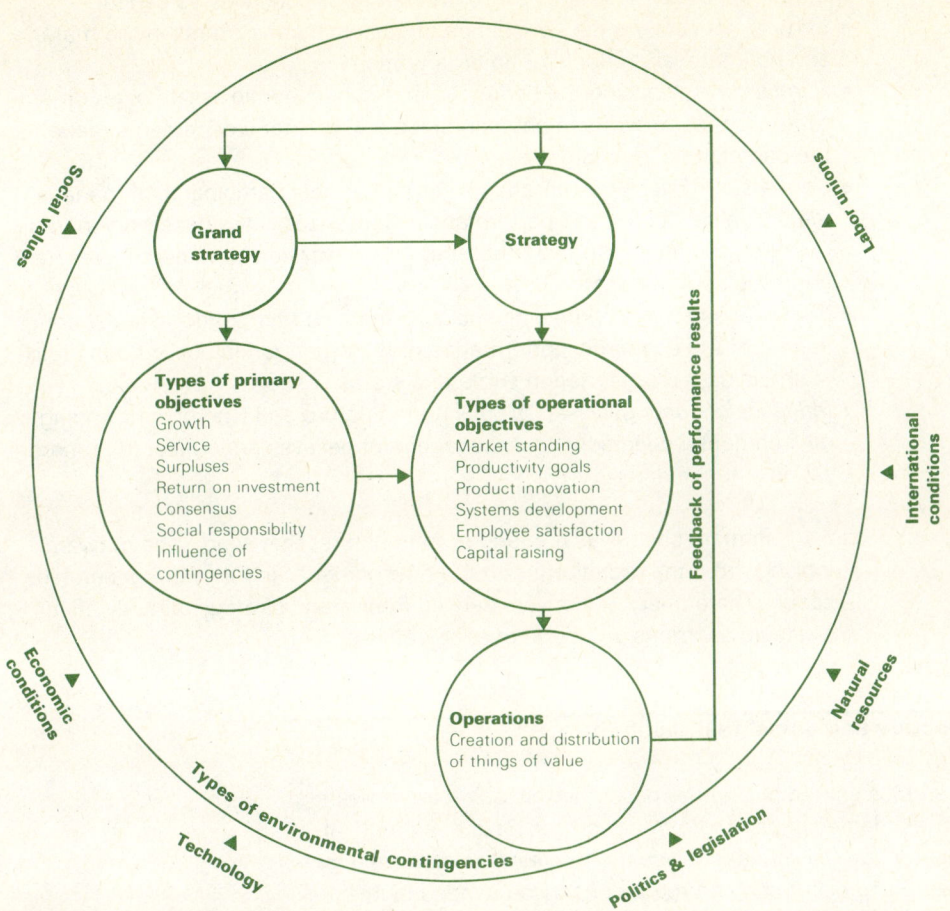

Figure 4-1 Business objectives

Grand strategy

The primary objectives of an organization originate in its grand strategy. This strategy is conducted by people in the top-management segments of an organization. Its orientation is toward combined managerial planning for the purpose of developing integrated, general, overriding goals for an organization. In a military sense, grand strategy always has international political objectives, and it is conducted by a country's political leaders.

The situation is not this clear for a business organization, whose primary objectives involve, although not exclusively, strong interaction with the external environment. Some examples of businesses' grand strategy goals are:

- *Growth*   Expansion of the economic wealth and material power of an enterprise.

- *Return on investment*   Increasing the net return on invested capital.
- *Service*   Enhancing the confidence of customers and clients in the material and nonmaterial products of an organization.
- *Surpluses*   Increasing the economic and noneconomic assets of an organization so that growth can be maintained and greater inducements made to the participants in an organization.
- *Consensus*   Overall acceptance by organizational participants of management's values, aims, and performance. Consensus is the necessary ingredient of organization harmony; therefore, whatever can be done to promote it improves performance.
- *Social responsibility*   Pursuing social obligations that are not directly connected to the economic performance of the organization but are critical to maintaining the organization's role and status in society.
- *Influence of contingencies*   Modifying the nature and type of surrounding environmental conditions that management believes are critical to an organization's health and survival.

Primary objectives are long term in nature; they tend to be outward looking, from the organization to the environment; and they are general in scope. The primary objectives, derived from grand strategy, directly affect strategic decisions on operational objectives.

The profit objective and social responsibility

Profit is the net surplus earned by an enterprise after all legitimate operating costs, fixed charges, depreciation, and other expenses have been met. Although necessary for survival, profit is residual—the result of other endeavors, such as making and distributing a product or service needed by the community. Without profits, a business cannot survive for any length of time.

Even most nonprofit organizations try to operate within their budget of available financial resources. For example, a hospital, school, or welfare agency applies the same logic to its efforts to balance a preestablished budget as does the business manager. Demands for fiscal solvency and even a profit are also often imposed on publicly owned industrial operations, such as utilities.

No fixed rate of profit is generally considered right, just, or socially defensible. Rather, the rate of profit varies greatly from one enterprise to another and from year to year. However, profit making is not the only goal of business; it is at best a limited objective.

There is a feeling among some that the pursuit of profit and organizational efficiency is tainted, that it has less social legitimacy than, say, employing the handicapped, training the hard-core unemployed, eliminating discrimination, or reducing pollution. On the other hand, others believe that business corporations, while remaining efficient, should direct their resources to the relief of social ills. Some call this *the corporate reaction to its social conscience*.

Still others argue strongly against the notion of corporate social responsibility. Milton Friedman, a professor of economics, asks if it is appropriate to give the attributes of a conscience to an entity that is at best an artificial person.

Professional managers are the stewards of property owned by others. Their obligation is to manage this property in the interest of the owner. In a business corporation, this usually means maintaining and increasing corporate earnings, and this, in turn, means maintaining or increasing the value of corporate property.

Friedman points out that if management unilaterally decides to reduce corporate earnings or wealth by contributing to social causes, it is in fact taxing the owners of the corporation. He argues that such a taxation is unjust and that managers who engage in it are not fulfilling their primary obligations—to provide goods and services and make profits in conformance with the basic rules of society.

In practice, conflict often arises between the broader goals of the public at large and the narrower objectives of a business organization. The problem that management faces is balancing these interests in the face of conflicting evidence.

Responsible business behavior is often imposed by the federal government's regulation of interstate commerce. In this century we have seen the concept of interstate commerce extended to provide some form of government regulation in all but a few areas of business activity. The extension has resulted chiefly in the government's perception of the tension between social responsibility and the maximizing behavior of businesses. Consider, for instance, government regulation of automobile safety features. Industry argues that the public is interested mainly in style and power, that safety features do not sell cars. However, the mounting toll of highway accidents indicates that steps must be taken to improve automobile safety in spite of their cost.

Although many more examples could be cited, social responsibility cannot be understood solely on this basis. Ultimately, the values that underlie the various positions have to be considered. Clearly, Friedman supports the inviolability of private property. However, other theoreticians feel that private property is not as sacred as previously supposed, that collective interests are not served by the pursuit of private interests. Their theories lead to government regulation and, at the extreme, nationalization of large segments of the private sector.

Strategy

Strategy is more specific, and it generates operational objectives that are shorter in duration. *Strategy* is the art of using organizational resources to reach the goals defined by grand strategy with minimum risk. It requires marshaling resources for definite missions, planning alternative strategies in anticipation of changing contingencies, and creating flexible conditions in structure and employee attitudes so that positions can be altered advantageously.

Operational objectives are mostly inward looking. They are concerned mainly with maintaining organizational effectiveness. However, they are highly sensitive to environmental changes. Therefore, operational objectives are critical in linking operations and the achievement of primary objectives. There are many types of strategic operational objectives and the following are a few examples:

- *Marketing standing*   Percentage of a given market for a product or service that management aims to capture.
- *Productivity goals*   Efficiency of operations, that is, management's attempt to achieve a favorable ratio of outputs over inputs, expressed as $E = O/I$.
- *Product innovation*   Creation of new and desirable goods and services for customers.
- *Systems development*   Creation of new manufacturing, communication, and distribution technologies to increase the efficiency of the organization.
- *Employee satisfaction*   Development of systems of employee incentives and rewards that will encourage productivity and morale.
- *Capital raising*   Development and exploitation of money markets to supply the resources necessary to finance the plans of an organization.

It is fair to say that managers spend most of their time developing and implementing operational objectives because they are close to the points in an organization where things of value are created and distributed. For example, the long-term potential of a public utility to supply electrical energy to a growing market depends on the ability of its managers to raise capital. The capital needs of this industry are great, and they will become greater as the sources of conventional fossil fuels become harder to find and more expensive to bring into production. Therefore, capital availability and cost are critical growth issues. The question is not so much "Will we grow?" but "Where will the money to grow come from?"

Many electric utility companies predict that future growth will require new energy sources, for example, nuclear fuels. Besides the large amount of capital required to build nuclear-generating plants, there is strong public opposition to them in some areas of the country. The nuclear energy problem forces managers to give serious attention to such grand strategy issues as social responsibility, the influence of public opinion, and the effect of technology on the physical environment. But any solution to these problems has to be translated into specific operational strategies, such as product innovation and system development. Just the disposal of nuclear waste requires a commitment of resources by a firm to scientific and engineering research. Any practical solutions to this problem would be directly implemented into operating procedures.

Balancing objectives

Managers have to satisfy many objectives. Therefore, making trade-offs among objectives is another strategic problem. The ideal solution is to balance objectives so that an organizationally satisfactory system of goals emerges. Sales objectives have to be balanced with productivity objectives; technological innovation has to be balanced with financial capabilities; product diversification has to be balanced with the skills of executives in managing new lines.

Quantifiable values are available for some objectives; for others they are not. Objectives concerning market standing as it compares to market potential can be established. Productivity goals can also be stated relatively clearly, as can the goals concerning physical and financial resources. However, stating objectives in the area of innovation becomes more difficult. The same is true of objectives in the area of profitability. Shall we use profit as a percentage of sales? As a return on invested capital? Or, shall we turn to some other formula? And, of course, there is also: What is a reasonable profit? Other objectives are even less tangible. Workers' performance, morale, and the like are hard to objectify. In addition, it is difficult for a manager to set objectives in such areas as public responsibility and social obligation. Nevertheless, in recent years management has become more aware of its social responsibility to the community, its employees, its stockholders, and the public in general. By striving to incorporate objectives of this nature, the enterprise does not, however, abandon profit to philanthropy. As a matter of fact, conducting a business on the basis of social responsibilities might even be essential to attaining profits.

In balancing various objectives, managers establish what they think is a proper mix between immediate, short-term, and long-term goals. Moreover, they must balance all objectives against one another. They must decide whether to obtain a larger share of the market or to forgo this and improve manufacturing productivity. They must balance lower profitability against more innovation. Emphasizing any objective to the exclusion of the rest will lead to suboptimizing consequences, which jeopardize the effectiveness of total organizational performance.

Changing objectives

The reappraisal and adaptation of objectives are essential to maintaining the health of an organization. The practicality of existing strategies is indicated by information that comes to managers from the external environment and from the feedback of internal operational control information. Feedback information within an organization generally has a direct impact on operational objectives, whereas environmental information affects primary objectives significantly.

The difficulty in all such information, particularly from the environment, is in interpreting its meaning and its lasting importance. Changing styles in the automobile industry are a case in point. The shortage or threat of a gasoline shortage in 1973 stimulated public interest in small cars. The industry shifted its production to accommodate this change in taste. But as the shortage diminished, public demand for larger vehicles grew again. All of this took place in the space of two years. What was initially thought to be a long-term trend toward smaller, more economical cars turned out not to be, as far as 1976 production styles were concerned. This rapid shift in demand caused innumerable problems for short-run operational strategies. However, the long-run forecast of expensive and scarce conventional fuels would seem to suggest not only smaller cars in the future, but also a major curtailing of individual mobility by use of the private automobile. Such a future requires consideration of grand strategy issues by the industry.

Policies

Policies are broad guides to managerial thinking; they set rational limitations to managers' actions. As such, policies are behavioral guidelines that set boundaries on what managers can and cannot do. Generally, policies provide managers with criteria to follow in order to implement operational objectives. However, in some instances, major policies guide the execution of primary objectives as well. As a rule, policies become more specific the further one goes down in the management structure. Ultimately, procedures and methods (discussed later in this chapter) must blend into existing policies.

Major policies are important enough to be made only by the board of directors. The choice of industry, one of the most fundamental of company policies, is written into a firm's charter, but it is the board's prerogative to make policies within that industry's broad limits. For example, the board might decide to seek out the quality market. Every department must then make its plans in accordance with this major policy. The purchasing department would buy only good materials from the most dependable sources; the personnel department would obtain workers capable of producing only quality products; the engineering department would demand close tolerances and fine finishes; the sales department would emphasize quality; and the advertising department would develop a quality appeal.

Characteristics

A certain amount of flexibility is necessary to policy making. Some policy statements have flexibility built in because of such words as *whenever possible, whenever feasible,* and *under usual conditions.* Managers must intelligently adapt the policy to the given set of circumstances. Their flexibility, of course, should not be extreme or inconsistent. If policies are clear and provide a uniform guide for thinking, they will inspire confidence in the plans and goals that they reflect. If they are not clear, sooner or later widespread dissatisfactions and irritations will develop and employees will be less effective than they should be.

The areas of policy formulation are as varied as the activities of an enterprise. One broad group of policies pertains to the management of the company—planning, organizing, staffing, influencing, and controlling. Another is directed toward its functions—sales, finance, production, personnel relations, and public relations. Specifically, a company's policy might be to promote from within, to accept the premise that the customer is always right, to initiate a fixed price, to underprice the competition, to require preventive maintenance of equipment, to decide to buy goods or to make them, to own or to lease capital equipment, to adhere to high moral and ethical standards in performing the business's activities. Policies also govern the scope of research activities, distribution and procurement, and much more.

Origin

Policies are determined by management or, at times, by outside forces. Policies can emerge in several ways. They may be management originated, appealed, or imposed.

Originated policy

The originated, or management-created, policy is no doubt the most significant. Top management is in a position to see the overall policies that are required to guide the thinking of subordinates so that the enterprise's objectives can be achieved. For example, a firm may have a policy that requires division managers to purchase all components of an assembly process from other divisions of the firm. Although there might be a less expensive source of supply, the division manager would realize that the purpose of the policy is to maximize the total profit of the corporation, not merely that of his or her division.

Once broad policy has been created by top management, it becomes the guide for policy making by various managers lower in the managerial hierarchy. Of course, all these lower managerial decisions will implement the broader policy that was originated by top management. Policies, therefore, help further uniformity in decision making throughout the organization.

At times, instead of originating at the top and flowing downward, policy may originate at or near the bottom of an organization and flow upward. "In a sense, policies are sometimes generated at the operating and first-line supervisory levels and imposed upward. If certain matters are not recognized or provided for by the set of policies adopted, or if regularly adopted policies are not enforced, customs may gradually emerge and achieve the generality, permanence, and authority of true policies."[3] The

---

[3] Billy E. Goetz, *Management Planning and Control* (New York: McGraw-Hill, 1949), p. 65.

extent to which this policy contributes to the success of the organization will largely depend on whether or not it operates under the principles of free and democratic supervision and whether or not subordinates can freely express themselves.

At times, policy may also be formulated simultaneously from both directions. Such policy will incorporate top management's point of view but, at the same time, give ample consideration to the opinion of people on lower levels of the organization.

Appealed policy

An appealed policy is most often formulated to cope with some exceptional and (usually) current problem. Managers appeal to their superiors for decisions because the managers do not know how to resolve particular problems or because they disagree with previous decisions and want the questions reviewed. Decisions, handed down by superiors, then set what is known as *appealed policy*. Appealed policies can also occur in a slightly different manner: subordinates might not know if a decision is within their jurisdiction or within the frame of broad policy, and they therefore appeal to their superiors.

There is a danger in having too many policies formulated by appeal, because they are often inconsistent, uncoordinated, and confusing. Therefore, managers who must frequently make policy decisions by appeal had better check into originated policies in the areas where questions are arising. They may find that too wide an area has been left without coverage or that the coverage needs updating or clarification. Additional policies may be required to fill the gaps. In this event, originated policies should predominate.

Imposed policy

A third kind of policy originates externally. Here, policy is imposed on an enterprise by external forces, such as government, labor unions, and trade associations. The word *imposed* indicates that compliance cannot be avoided. Thus, policy formulation is imposed when a federal, state, or local law is passed and, to conform, managers must translate it into company policy. Labor policies resulting from collective bargaining and union contracts are imposed, as are the responsibilities expressed in labor laws and fair employment policies dictated by federal and state laws. Policy may also be imposed by trade associations or other groups that seek to eliminate trade abuses and to protect their members from destructive practices and competition. The legal status of such directives is sometimes difficult to determine.

Communication

Written and unwritten policies

Once formulated, it is essential that policies be carefully and explicitly stated and communicated so that they will be fully understood. This is no easy task.

Since different meanings can be attached to words, it is difficult to avoid ambiguity. However, although there is no guarantee that even the written word will be properly understood, it is desirable that policies be written.

There are several distinct advantages to having written statements of policy. When managers force themselves to sit down and write, the very act of writing probably will reveal discrepancies, conflicts, and omissions. Written policies are beneficial to all managers, whatever their level. Once written, they are readily accessible, their meaning cannot be changed by word of mouth, and the chance that they will be misinterpreted is small. If a misunderstanding occurs, it can be settled by recourse to a few written words. Moreover, written policy statements can readily be sent to all who are affected by them, and new managers can speedily orient and inform themselves by reading them.

A disadvantage of written policies is management's reluctance to change them, even when they are outdated. This is not a disadvantage of the written policy per se. Oral policies can likewise become outdated. In such instances, the thoughtful subordinate should appeal for a revision.

The advantages of having a written policy far outweigh the disadvantages, but many organizations seem to prefer policies that are handed down by word of mouth. Oral policies are flexible and can be adjusted to changed circumstances with ease. However, since their exact interpretation might not be known, oral policies become less desirable than written ones.

Implied policies

Policies that are neither written nor stated are said to be *implied*. They can be ascertained only by watching the behavior of managers. Many organizations, for example, state that they have no upper age limit in their hiring policy. However, examination of the ages of the individuals who are hired during a given year might reveal that no one over fifty was employed. Another implied policy can often be observed in the failure to employ women and members of racial minorities.

At times, managers justify implied policies by pointing out that in some areas policies are too difficult to state. They also say that they do not want to limit employees' freedom too drastically or that the enterprise is too dynamic for policies to be set in certain areas. Although such explanations are expedient, implications often leave large areas open to misinterpretation.

Periodic policy review

Managers may alter organizational strategies because of changing contingencies and operational feedback data. As a result, objectives and statements of policy might need modification and revision. Conditions may be such that the overall thrust of an organization is no longer the same. Therefore, periodic policy review and appraisal is essential. Such a review might uncover practices that are in complete contradiction to stated policies. It might also show that the policies lack integration. In all probability, a periodic review will show the necessity for some changes and adjustments.

To say the least, it is undesirable to keep policies that have become ignored and outdated. As long as they exist, individuals must judge which policies remain current and should be observed and which do not and should not. Such decisions are really management's job. Regardless of how well conceived the policies were when they were originated, the dynamics of the organizational environment make periodic review and adjustment necessary.

Procedures

Procedures are guides to action; therefore, they are more specific than policies.

Procedures, in common with other forms of planning, seek to avoid the chaos of random activity by directing, coordinating, and articulating the operations of an enterprise. They help direct all enterprise activities toward common goals, they help impose consistency across the organization and through time, and they seek economy by enabling management to avoid the costs of recurrent investigations and to delegate authority to subordinates to make decisions within a frame of policies and procedures devised by management.[4]

Policies define a broad field whose area is determined and limited by the objectives of the enterprise. *Procedures* show the sequence of concrete acts. As illustrated in Figure 4-2, procedures chart a path through the area of policy; they present the chronological order of acts to be performed. "Policy always sets an objective or delimits an area of action, while procedures fix a path toward the objective or through the area. Sequence is the *sine qua non* of procedure."[5]

Consider, for example, the statement: "The customer is always right." This is policy. Procedure specifies the steps to be taken to ensure that policy. In a department store, the procedure might be to send a complaining customer to the buyer, then to the department manager or the floor walker, and finally to the adjustment office. Whatever decision these various managers make will be within the broad guideline of thinking that the customer is right. Although the managers might not believe in a particular instance that the customer is justified, the complaint will be handled according to a prescribed procedure derived from the policy of the store.

Preparing a procedure requires analysis and study of the matter in question. Once a procedure is established, it should provide for uniform performance and action. It should also provide managers with a standard for appraising the work done by their subordinates. Inasmuch as a procedure specifies a sequence of action, it reduces the need for further decision

[4] Ibid., p. 83.
[5] Ibid., p. 84.

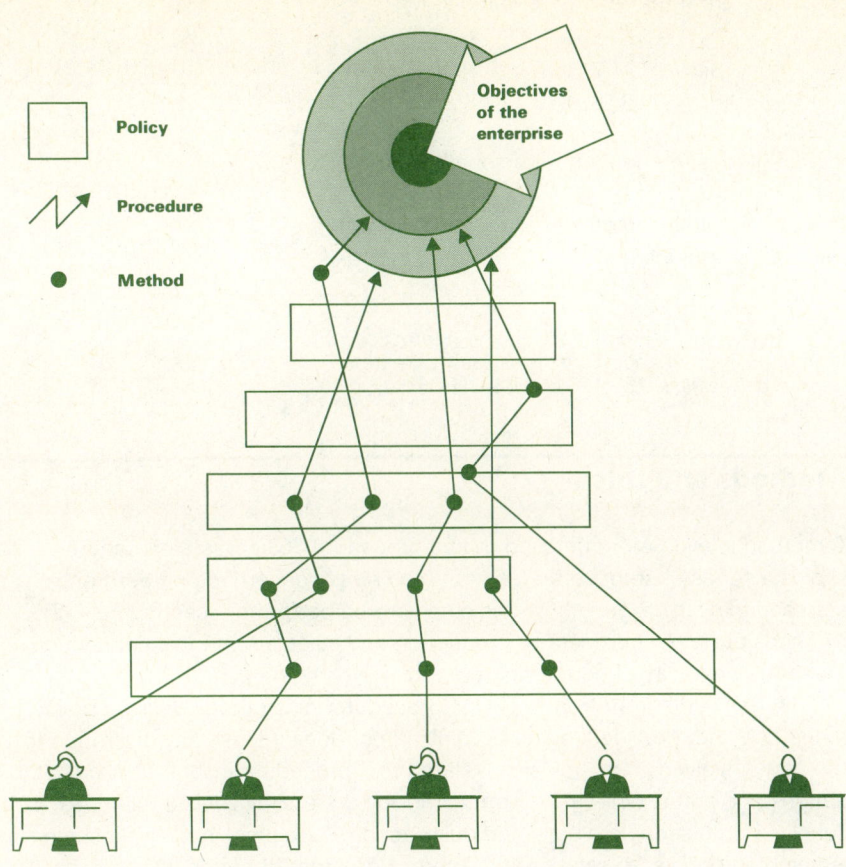

Figure 4-2 The relationship of policies, procedures, and methods

making and, moreover, permits better coordination. There is, however, the danger that a procedure will stifle innovation and development of new ways of doing the work. This disadvantage can be overcome with periodic review of standing procedures.

Values, objectives, and strategy

A hierarchy of generality links such organizational characteristics as objectives, values, procedures, strategies, and so forth. One way to put these matters in a useful form is the following:

- Values provide long-range guides to action.
- Performance objectives provide more detailed goals then do values and a measurement yardstick.
- Strategy defines plans to carry out value and performance objectives; these plans become more specific and detailed, the lower the organizational level.

Underlying these relationships are three recommendations for managers:

1. Organizational objectives and strategies should guide decision-making processes at all levels of the enterprise.
2. Top management should provide guides; it should not personally involve itself in decisions at all levels.
3. Top management should not confuse policy guidelines with implementation methods; methods are subordinate to guidelines.

Source: Adapted from Jackson E. Ramsey, "A Framework for the Interaction of Corporate Value Objectives, Corporate Performance Objectives, and Corporate Strategy," *Journal of Economics and Business* 28 (1976):171–180.

Methods and rules

A method is even more detailed than a procedure. Whereas a procedure shows a series of steps to be taken, a *method* is concerned only with one step and explains exactly how this step is to be performed (see Figure 4-2). Methods are most pertinent to production and sales and, in this connection, mean the best way of performing the job.

A *rule* is different from a policy, procedure, or method. Unlike a policy, a rule does not provide a guide to thinking nor does it leave any discretion to the party involved. It is, however, related to a procedure insofar as it guides actions and states what must or must not be done. However, a rule does not specify a time sequence for a particular action. "No smoking," for instance, is one of a long list of safety rules. There is no order of action involved, as there is with a procedure; "No smoking" pertains whenever and wherever the rule is in effect. Further, a rule is not to be confused with a company's safety policy, which might state, for example, that the company intends to carry on a continuous educational campaign about the danger of smoking. The company's safety policy provides the guidelines for safety rules, but the two are clearly distinguished.

Summary

Objectives are the value premises of an organization. Managers establish objectives to give an organization direction and to give the people in it a sense of mission. Primary objectives are derived from an organization's grand strategy, which sets far-reaching goals and determines the nature and course of strategy, from which operational objectives develop.

Objectives are formulated, balanced, and changed by managers. In these processes, sensitivity to external contingencies, diagnosis of feedback information, and flexibility to new, emerging conditions are critical for an organization's health and survival.

Managers need guidelines for implementing objectives. Policies provide these guidelines for thinking as well as the boundaries to the action people can take in an organization. Policies may be general or specific, becoming more specific at lower levels in an organization. Procedures, methods, and rules are guides to action within the overall framework of established policies.

Discussion questions

1 Identify two or three recent demands for organizational social responsibility that you have read about in your local newspaper. For each, how do you think the managers in question should respond?
2 Many organizations have a policy of equal pay for equal work. What objective do you think this policy is trying to achieve? Where do you think this policy originated? Which procedures, methods, and rules are appropriate for the implementation of this policy?

Supplementary readings

Dent, James K. "Organizational Correlates of the Goals of Business Managements." *Personnel Psychology,* 12 (Autumn 1959):365–394.

England, George W., "Personal Value Systems of Managers and Administrators." *Academy of Management Proceedings,* 33d Annual Meeting (Boston, 1974), pp. 81–88.

Ramsey, Jackson E. "A Framework for the Interaction of Corporate Value Objectives, Corporate Performance Objectives, and Corporate Strategy." *Journal of Economics and Business* 28 (1976): 171–180.

Tosi, Henry L.; Rizzo, John R.; and Carroll, Stephen J. "Setting Goals in Management by Objectives." *California Management Review* 12, no. 4 (1970): 70–78. Reprinted in *Dimensions in Modern Management,* 2d ed., edited by Patrick E. Connor. Boston: Houghton Mifflin, 1978.

Chapter 5

The nature of planning

Objectives of the chapter

1 To describe managerial planning.
2 To identify the role of planning in relation to the other managerial processes.
3 To describe the characteristics of planning.
4 To identify the elements of effective plans.

Management planners chart a course of action for the future. Their aim is to achieve a consistent, coordinated set of operations relating action to objectives. Yet, plans alone are not enough; they must be acted on.[1]

In the early 1900s, Fayol, remarking that planning was manifested on many occasions and in a variety of ways, called the plan of action the chief evidence of planning effort. "The plan of action," he said, "is, at one and the same time, the result envisaged, the line of action to be followed, the stages to go through, and methods to use. It is a kind of future picture wherein proximate events are outlined with some distinctness, whilst remote events appear progressively less distinct, and it entails the running of the business as foreseen and provided against over a definite period."[2]

Without being planned, activities are random. Managers must plan continually in order to anticipate problems, to analyze them, to foresee their probable effect on the activities of the enterprise, and to decide on action that will lead to a desired result. As Ross Webber points out, "The critical aspect of planning is knowing where you want to be and how you want the future to turn out."[3] His statement underscores the necessity of managers' defining goals and objectives before they begin the planning activity.

---

[1] Billy E. Goetz, *Management Planning and Control* (New York: McGraw-Hill, 1949), p. 63.
[2] Henri Fayol, *General and Industrial Management,* trans. Constance Storrs (London: Pitman, 1949), p. 43.
[3] Ross A. Webber, *Time and Management* (New York: Van Nostrand Reinhold, 1972), p. 127.

Planning as an intellectual process and a primary function

Planning is a process that requires a mental predisposition to think before acting, to act in the light of fact rather than supposition, and to order events logically. It requires the manipulation of abstract ideas and the anticipation of the impact of the many possible outcomes on the enterprise as a whole. There is no substitute for the intellectual exercise that planning demands. Planning is not the work of a theorist who is locked up in an office and hands out blueprints through a crack in the door. "It is planning that makes it possible for [the manager] effectively to combine knowledge with power in order to achieve the objectives of his enterprise."[4]

Relationship to the other managerial functions

Planning is the primary function. How could managers effectively set up an organization without having a plan in mind? How could they staff and influence subordinates? How could they possibly control? After all, one of the main consequences of planning is setting the standards by which control is accomplished and results are checked. Managers, then, must plan before they can intelligently perform any other function.

This does not mean that planning is a one-time function. Although managers must plan before they can organize, staff, influence, or control, additional planning (of details) and revising of plans will take place continually. Planning must be complete, however, before any other function can be finished (see Figure 5-1).

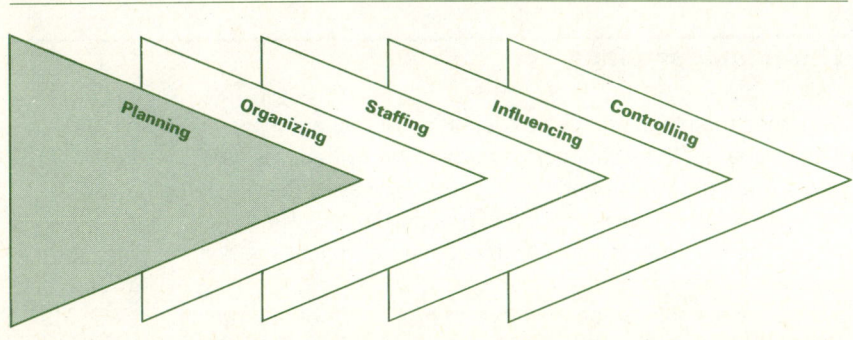

Figure 5-1 Primary importance of the planning function

---

[4] Marshall E. Dimock, *The Executive in Action* (New York: Harper & Row, 1945), p. 123.

Control and feedback

In practice, planning is a bit more complicated than theory would indicate. The controlling functions, in particular, continually create planning problems. These problems could force managers to change plans, and the change might necessitate alternative organizing, staffing, and influencing decisions. After having made their adjustments, managers should again turn to controlling to learn whether the results have occurred as planned. If they did not, it may become necessary to return to the planning stage. In other words, as shown in Figure 5-2, feedback from the controlling process indicates whether changes in plans are needed and whether such changes are effective. Because of the systems character of managerial functions, many adjustments are often required before objectives are realized. For example, if it appears that an annual sales quota may not be met, a firm will have to readjust its plans and take necessary steps in organization, staff, and motivation to stimulate performance or, if the situation dictates, cut back altogether.

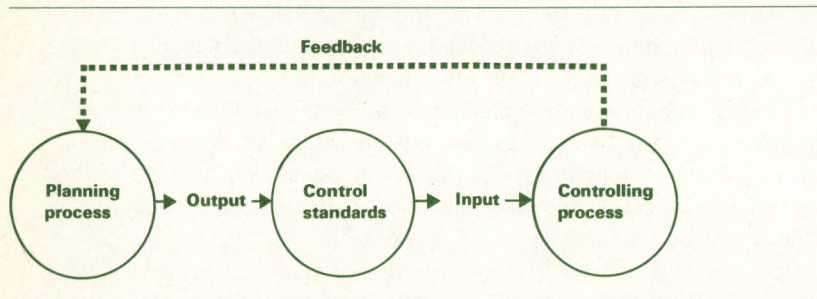

Figure 5-2 The relationship of planning and controlling

The manager plans

Who does the planning? By our definition of management: the manager. Every manager—the chairperson of the board, the president of the company, or the first-line supervisor—plans. However, the magnitude of planning varies with the level on which it is performed. The scope tends to decrease in lower levels of management and near the point of plan execution.

Compare this situation with that of a group of mountain climbers. At the base of the trail, all they can see are the trees around them. After an hour's climb, they may reach a clearing and can look off into the distance and study the countryside. Finally, when they reach the summit, they command a panoramic view of the landscape and can see details many miles off. The analogy is clear: all managers plan, but the higher the managerial scale, the broader the planning responsibility.

Time span

George Orwell, in his book *Animal Farm,* wrote: "All animals are equal, but some are more equal than others." Similarly, though all managers plan, some managers plan more, and for longer periods, than others. The time span of managerial planning is also linked to managerial level. Top executives may plan as long as five years or much longer, whereas supervisors plan on a daily or weekly basis.

The nature of intermediate and long-range planning introduces great uncertainty into the top executive's role. Consequently, planning resources are concentrated at this level. It is here that maximum staff support is required to gather information and intelligence so that strategies for the future can be laid.

Planning participation

Research in the behavioral sciences indicates that as many managers as possible should participate in planning.[5] The more involved managers are, the more enthusiastic they will be in carrying out the various plans and the better will be the quality of those plans. In addition, managers often can contribute their intimate knowledge of operating conditions to the planning process. Also, extensive participation in planning will frequently reveal those individuals in the enterprise who have good judgment, initiative, and originality.

Executives often request staff assistance in their planning responsibilities. They may feel that certain areas call for special knowledge; they may wish to evolve consistent policies in all-pervasive areas, such as personnel and financial procedures. Thus, staff members can greatly help managers in their planning tasks.

Another means of achieving participation in planning is through planning committees. Although there is much to be said for and against the use of such committees,[6] they can generally be helpful if they are properly utilized. Managers at all levels participate in the planning process through regularly scheduled meetings, such as supervisory conferences and management clubs. Top management also stimulates participation by having lower-level managers submit plans. Some degree of joint participation is so beneficial and vital to sound planning that it has become a policy in many organizations.

Characteristics of planning

Planning is rational in that it helps allocate resources. Because planning is concerned with the future, it is never completely finished. In some

---

[5] Rensis Likert, *New Patterns of Management* (New York: McGraw-Hill, 1961).
[6] See Chapter 13.

organizations, however, the future is more discernible than it is in others. Also, the future for a certain product or service can be predicted more reliably at certain times than it can at others. The manufacture of buggy whips is an example. With the advent of the automobile, the future of the buggy whip could easily be foreseen, and plans were made accordingly. Another example is the industry that produces wooden crossties for railroads. In 1900, when railroads were the major means of mass transportation, approximately 100 million crossties were needed; in recent years, only about 20 million crossties are laid annually. Although this decrease was partially caused by now-stabilized factors, such as improvements in the treatment of lumber, the relationship of decreasing rail mileage to tie use can easily be seen. Hence, managers must make plans to seek new products, new outlets, new things to do; they must plan for diversification.

The planning period

Short-run planning covers a period of six to twelve months. Long-term planning usually involves a considerably longer interval. In recent years, there has been a trend toward planning ahead for five, ten, or even twenty years. One- to five-year plans now are considered intermediate-range plans; from five years upward now is considered a long-range plan.

How long should the planning period be? Organizations vary considerably in the length of the period for which they plan. The type of enterprise, the kind of industry, the production cycle, the quality of managerial practice, and many other factors figure in the decision. In general, the more long range the plan, the less flexible the organization will be in adapting to change.[7]

Commitments

The length of the planning cycle should be linked to a firm's commitments. For example, a mail order house commits itself for approximately six months when it sends out a catalog. If commitments have been made in buildings and machinery, planning periods should extend far enough into the future to enable the recovery of the capital outlay. Considerations of this sort justify long-range planning of from ten to twenty years.

The nature of the organization also has a bearing on the length of the planning period. If a firm manufactures a product whose cycle of production takes twelve months, it cannot plan for less than that period of time. If, however, the production cycle is shorter, planning can easily be done for six months or less. In an enterprise that produces high-style fashions, a three- to

[7] "Industry Plans for the Future," *Conference Board Business Record* 9, no. 8 (August 1952):325; and "In Business Everyone's Looking Ahead," *Business Week* (January 5, 1957), pp. 113–118.

six-month plan might be considered long range. In other cases, for example building a large generator that might take several years to complete, three to five years is short range. Paper-making companies plant trees today in order to be able to harvest them in fifty years.

It does not follow that small enterprises usually make short-term plans and that only large enterprises make long-range ones. Many small enterprises have become larger only because they had long-range plans. However, long-range plans seem to predominate in large organizations. Frequently, the larger the organization, the more control it has over its environment. By having at its disposal the means to exert economic, political, and social dominance, it often can make its plans become self-fulfilling prophecies.

The trend toward long-range planning

Although long-range planning is heralded as one of the significant management developments of this century, it is interesting to note that Fayol spoke of it as "the precious managerial instrument" and devised for his firm a master plan made up of a series of yearly, ten-year, and special "forecasts."[8] In the larger economic setting there is an increased need today for long-range planning. David W. Ewing has presented testimony on this need.[9] In his book *Long-Range Planning for Management,* representative heads of leading corporations discuss their methods for long-range planning and the ensuing benefits. As Ewing points out, long-range planning means many things to many people: "Some will find it visionary and impractical. Some who latch on to it will find they have a 'bear by the tail.' Others will make a fad out of it. But it should become for most companies—and for the economy—one of the really significant business developments of the century."[10]

The concept of long-range planning has far-reaching implications for the practice of management because it necessitates looking analytically at a company's operations. Long-range planning produces a vast network of plans that connect the many functions of the enterprise. Therefore, managers need increased conceptual skills "as opposed to technical and human relations skills" to find their way through the maze. In long-range planning, top management takes into consideration the perpetual nature of the organization, the need to build institutions for generations to come. This approach often influences management to forgo short-term profits if they interfere with long-range plans. Long-range planning puts a premium on research and development, expansion and diversification, executive training programs, and many other items that represent a current expense but constitute an investment in the future.

---

[8] Fayol, *General and Industrial Management,* pp. 43—52.
[9] David W. Ewing, *Long-Range Planning for Management* (New York: Harper & Row, 1958).
[10] Ibid., pp. 3—4.

Integration of short- and long-range plans

Long-range and short-range planning must be integrated and coordinated. It is misleading to view long-range planning as an activity separate from and independent of short-range planning. No short-run plan should be made unless it contributes to the goals set out in the long-range plan. Therefore, top management must ensure that all other managers understand the long-range plans and objectives of the company; they also must ascertain whether the short-range plans conform to long-range plans. Doing this is initially less difficult than correcting inconsistencies later on. Some organizations help facilitate integration by establishing major planning departments at high managerial levels.

The good plan

Managers have long known that every good plan should have certain basic characteristics.[11] The plan must be based on a *clearly defined objective*, stated in a clear, concise, and accurate manner. Objectives should be quantified as much as possible so that accomplishments can be compared with goals. A good plan also requires *operational clarity* and should cover all action required for satisfactory fulfillment of the objective. There is usually a hierarchy of plans, each suited to a level of authority and conforming to a portion of the plan's time span. Naturally, the various plans must fit into a *consistent pattern*. The parts of the plan—its purpose, nature, and timing—must also be integrated so that coordination results. Furthermore, plans should be reasonably *economical* and should consider the resources available.

Another important characteristic of a good plan is *flexibility*. A flexible plan can be adjusted smoothly and without delay or serious loss of economy or effectiveness to the requirements of changing conditions. To permit such adjustment, a plan must be broad, containing alternative courses of action to meet possible changes as they arise. Managers must check the feasibility of plans regularly. Planning does not freeze action; at least it should not. If managers learn that a plan does not lead to the required objective or that underlying conditions have changed, they have to select an alternative plan. It is much wiser to be right than to be consistent.

Dissemination

It is essential that plans be properly communicated to the managers who are concerned with their implementation. This, of course, is not necessary if those managers have participated in the planning. Where such participation

---

[11] Lyndall F. Urwick, in *The Elements of Administration* (New York: Harper & Row, 1943), p. 34, cites a number of these characteristics.

is not possible, however, it is the duty of top management to communicate the plans properly. An uninformed manager is an ineffective manager. The better informed managers are, the better they will do their job.

Often there is a gap in knowledge of plans between top-level and second-level managers. This is frequently excused by the claim that many plans are confidential. Practitioners, however, know that little can be kept secret in any organization. Therefore, internal security cannot generally be used as an excuse. Managers, of course, appreciate the fact that there are limitations on the communication of plans; nonetheless, they must be well informed about the plans that will influence their particular activities.

The essence of planning, as we have said, is informed anticipation of the future. Plans are made against a background of information, premises, and assumptions regarding all conditions that will have a bearing on the organization. In addition to purely economic concerns, planning must take into account social, political, and technological change.

Summary

In essence, managerial planners chart a course of future organizational action. The overall purpose of planning is to establish a set of operations that is consistent at all levels with the organization's purpose. Though naturally preceding the other managerial functions, planning is related to them through continual feedback.

Planning occurs at all managerial levels. Participation by managers is helpful in that it tends to improve both planning and implementation. In general, the higher the level, the longer the planning time span. Time spans range from less than a year (short-range planning) to five years (intermediate-range planning) to beyond (long-range planning). The length of the span depends on such contingencies as environmental factors, the nature of the organization's output, technology, and so forth. In general, the length of the planning cycle should be comparable to the length for which resources are committed.

Plans should be based on clear goals and should include the actions necessary for successful goal accomplishment. Plans at various organizational levels should be consistent with one another. Finally, plans should not be mysteries; they should be as widely disseminated as possible. If people are to follow a planned set of actions, they need to know what that set of actions is.

Discussion questions

1 It is popular today to speak of "planning for the year 2000." In light of this statement, consider the following quotation: "Long-range planning produces long-range commitments that reduce the flexibility of the organization."
2 Consider one of your personal objectives. Are you able to identify strategies and plans to support that objective?

Supplementary readings

Ackoff, Russell L. *A Concept of Corporate Planning.* New York: Wiley, 1970.
Drucker, Peter F. *Management: Tasks, Responsibilities, Practices.* New York: Harper & Row, 1974.
Hekimian, James S., and Mintzberg, Henry. "The Planning Dilemma: There Is a Way Out." *Management Review,* May 1968.
Zoglin, Richard. "Does GE Really Plan Better?" *MBA,* November 1975, pp. 42–46. Reprinted in *Dimensions in Modern Management,* 2d ed. edited by Patrick E. Connor. Boston: Houghton Mifflin, 1978.

Chapter 6

Information for planning: Forecasting

Objectives of the chapter

1 To describe the managerial role of forecasting.
2 To relate forecasting to planning.
3 To illustrate the types and techniques of forecasting.
4 To identify the nature and sources of planning premises.

Planning is deciding what is to be done in the future. It can be performed only on the basis of sound information—information that includes knowledgeable estimates of future conditions. Although the future is uncertain, managers must make certain assumptions about it in order to plan properly. These assumptions are based on forecasts.

The place of forecasting in modern organizations

Forecasting as a major source of planning information is in its infancy, but it is growing rapidly. An interesting example of relatively advanced forecasting techniques is demonstrated in *The Year 2000*,[1] a book based on data developed by the Hudson Institute, one of the better-known think tanks in the United States. In his introduction to this book, Daniel Bell writes: "Machiavelli argued that half of men's actions are ruled by chance, the other half are governed by men themselves. This volume, and the work of the Commission of the Year 2000, is an effort to change that balance." Bell's observation is appropriate to the entire planning area. Planning information and forecasts help managers to move from chance and the uncontrollable to prediction and improved control.

---

[1] Herman Kahn and Anthony J. Wiener, *The Year 2000* (New York: Macmillan, 1967).

Forecasting is involved, to some extent, in every conceivable organization decision. Lyndall Urwick has written: "The man who starts a business is making an assessment of a future demand for its products. The man who determines a production programme for the next six months or twelve months is usually also basing it on some calculation of future demand. The man who engages staff, and particularly young staff, usually has an eye to future organizational requirements."[2]

An appraisal of future prospects is inherent in all planning. In fact, the success of a business depends, in large measure, on the skill of managers in foreseeing and preparing for future conditions. This truth has not been lost on one highly visible type of manager, the NFL coach. Most coaches build teams that are a mixture of experienced players (for today) and younger recruits (for tomorrow). Some coaches frequently prefer one or the other extreme. For example, George Allen, head coach of the Washington Redskins, is well known for selecting experienced players only. His is a straightforward planning philosophy: "The future is now."

Economic variables and control

Regardless of a manager's planning philosophy, preparation for the future involves adjusting to four basic economic variables: the international climate, the national climate, industry conditions, and the status of the enterprise itself. An organization would seem to have little control over the first two (barring the military-industrial complex). The extent of control over the third variable seems to depend on the size of the organization. For example, General Motors has more control over events in the automobile industry than, say, a dressmaker has in the ladies' garment industry. Of course, a firm has greatest control in its home territory—that is, within its own enterprise. To achieve this control, however, its managers must be informed; they must be able to recognize industrial, national, and, sometimes, international economic trends. In short, managers must be able to forecast conditions.

The use of forecasting did not become widespread until the depression of the 1930s. At that time, managers became acutely aware of business cycles. More and more organizations began to analyze business conditions in order to anticipate economic trends and to estimate trends' probable effect on their operations.

By forecasting, managers formulate plans so that their enterprise may obtain maximum benefits from an expanding economy and minimize adverse effects when activity slackens. A management group that forecasts becomes aware of the difficulty of bucking the trend of general business conditions, especially as the company grows larger. Management forecasters also realize the possibility of serious losses when economic factors are not given sufficient weight. Evaluating those factors and basing forecasts on them has

---

[2] Lyndall F. Urwick, *The Elements of Administration* (New York: Harper & Row, 1943), p. 21.

been facilitated by the availability of reliable and detailed information about the nation's economy.

Organization for forecasting

The practice of forecasting varies among organizations, from the reading of newspapers to the use of staff experts to interpret and analyze the relationship of current and future conditions to company operations. In all organizations, executives are expected to keep abreast of current economic developments through reading, contacts, and discussions. It is common practice for organizations to place staff forecasters close to top management. In some firms, one executive is responsible for the preparation of forecasts, and the staff of trained forecasting specialists usually works with that individual.[3] General Electric, for example, in 1970 established a formal organizational group called the Strategic Business Unit.[4] Its chief purpose has been to make forecasts regarding the corporation and its relationships with the market, government, and society at large. Its importance—as well as the importance and difficulty of forecasting in general—was noted by the unit's director: "The crunch situation is that *all your knowledge is about the past and all your decisions are about the future.*"[5]

The American Management Association (AMA) reports that most business firms that have their own forecasting staffs separate overall economic forecasting from specialized sales forecasting. If an organization does not employ its own forecasting staff, it will frequently hire economic consultants to analyze and interpret economic developments and forecasts. Some managers feel that in this way they can obtain expert advice at a lower cost than that of maintaining their own staff of specialists. Sometimes a company that has its own staff of forecasters will also employ the services of outside research consultants in order to check on its own staff's predictions as well as to obtain other viewpoints. This, of course, helps to improve the quality of the forecasts.

Some executives encourage discussion of the rationale, assumptions, and implications of their organization's forecasts, regardless of whether a company forecasting staff exists. In certain instances, periodic economic reports are circulated to familiarize managers with the outlook for business. It is of great importance that they be understood by all managers; these forecasts form the basis for planning and other managerial functions.

Forecasts as planning premises

When assumptions about the future are used in a planning context, they are called *planning premises*. These premises, or the assumptions from which

---

[3] *Company Organization for Economic Forecasting,* Research Report No. 28 (New York: American Management Association, 1957), p. 21.
[4] "Does GE Really Plan Better?" *MBA,* November 1975, pp. 42–44.
[5] Ibid., p. 43 (emphasis added).

they are derived, form the foundation of planning. Forecasts are the prerequisites for the entire planning structure; they are the quarry rock from which the planner's foundation stones are cut.

It is possible to forecast in a multitude of areas. Managers select and use, as planning premises or assumptions, only those forecasts that are strategically important and have material bearing on their organization. Forecasts that are important to one enterprise might not be of any significance to another; over time, managers learn which forecasts bear on their planning and which can be neglected. Some assumptions that were once important may become insignificant and can be eliminated; others will be added as time goes on. Therefore, managers must be fully aware of the shifting requirements for their strategic assumptions.[6]

Customer distance

Findings of the AMA indicate that the type of industry in which the enterprise is engaged influences the amount of effort devoted to forecasting. In general, the more an organization is removed from the ultimate consumer, the more difficult forecasting becomes. Therefore, manufacturers of heavy industrial equipment and producers of primary products (such as steel) are likely to make widespread use of forecasting departments in order to overcome this difficulty.

Foreseeability

Likewise, not all events—acts of God, wars, or strikes, for instance—can be foreseen and incorporated into planning premises. In the short run it might be possible to anticipate them, but in the longer run these occurrences cannot be predicted with any exactitude. We therefore have to distinguish between foreseeable and unforeseeable premises.

Controllability

Another way to differentiate planning premises is to look at them from the point of view of controllability. Certain factors are controllable, others are semicontrollable, and still others are noncontrollable. *Controllable* planning premises might include policies, programs, and activities that are entirely regulated by management. *Semicontrollable* premises can be partially regulated; an organization's share of the market is a semicontrollable premise. Managers can do their part to obtain as much of the industry's total as possible, but the activities of competitors are a limiting factor. Of the premises that are *noncontrollable,* the most important is the general business cycle. All firms are affected by it, but there is relatively little an individual firm can do to stave off its effects. However, acknowledging the business cycle and gearing organizational activities to a similar cycle can be a great

---

[6] One of the reasons why requirements shift is the changing developmental stages of the enterprise; different stages have different planning requirements. See Milton Leontiades, "Planning: A Re-examination of Fundamentals," *Journal of Economics and Business* 28 (1976): 189–194.

help to management. Like the business cycle, population trends are based on factors that are beyond the control of management. Government action is frequently another noncontrollable factor. Nevertheless, although the events themselves are noncontrollable, their effects on the firm may be foreseeable.

External planning premises and forecasts

Perhaps the best way to identify planning premises is to distinguish between those that are external to the enterprise and those that are internal. *External premises* primarily refer to the general business climate and to industry conditions; *internal premises* refer to the firm's own climate.

The general business climate

Many managerial actions are affected by the general business climate, but some are affected more than others. Plans for growth and expansion are particularly closely related to business conditions, as are plans for capital equipment purchases. Budgets, production scheduling, inventory levels, financial programming, market expansion, product design, and investments are also closely allied.

Of course, managers cannot blindly assume that the general business climate will always be supportive of expansion. There is a great deal of speculation, based on hard-to-ignore evidence, that the 1970s and 1980s will provide managers with a new and contrary experience. In general, it seems that resource scarcities will require intelligent management of decline, not growth.[7]

The scope of these activities emphasizes the importance of acknowledging the general business climate in forecasts and planning premises. Let us now look at some components of this climate and how they affect particular areas of managerial planning.

Government policies

The job of forecasting general economic conditions and formulating external planning premises has, in some respects, become more difficult and, in others, simpler because of the influence of government policies on economic conditions.

Fiscal policy Managers must make assumptions about the direction of governmental fiscal policy, regardless of how difficult this may be. They must know what to expect in regard to taxation. Managerial planning strongly depends on assumptions about the rate of corporate income taxes and will change if forecasts indicate that the approximately 50 percent corporation

---

[7] See William G. Scott, "The Management of Decline," *Conference Board Record* 13 (June 1976):56–59.

income tax will remain stable or will be raised or lowered. Excess-profit tax rates also affect managerial planning; if rates are high, managers are likely to increase advertising and publicity budgets. Another impact of taxes on planning results form the possibility of accelerated amortization. If this occurs, management should invest in new plants and equipment, one of its prime planning areas.

Taxation is not the only area in which government fiscal policies form the basis for necessary planning assumptions. Another important area is federal government spending, which runs into billions of dollars and takes a large portion of the U.S. gross national product (GNP). An increase or decrease in such expenditures will certainly have a considerable impact on the economy. Managers, therefore, must forecast what future government expenditures will be. Because of the indirect impact of government spending, such a forecast is necessary not only for enterprises for whom the government is an important customer but also for those that do little or no government business.

Monetary policy Managers must also forecast the monetary policy of the Federal Reserve Board—whether it will pursue a policy of loose or tight money and whether that policy will continue over a short or long period of time. If top management thinks that money rates will remain high in the short run, it will probably assume that in the long run there will be periods during which the rates of interest will be lower, and it will postpone floating certificates of indebtedness.

Antitrust policy Planning must take into account the enforcement of antitrust laws. Managers need to appraise whether or not the Anti-Trust Division of the Justice Department intends to enforce the antimonopoly laws vigorously. Forecasts of this nature are particularly important when an organization is considering expansion by merger and consolidation. If the assumption is that the Justice Department will not look kindly on a merger, expansion plans will probably be directed into other channels. If, however, enforcement has not been vigorous, top management will feel freer to pursue expansion plans.

Other government controls Naturally, organizations are influenced by other government controls and restrictions—tariffs, capital inflows and outflows, licensing. Sometimes planners can forecast the nature of controls by knowing a factor such as the political party in power. But whatever the foundation for its assumptions, management's planning will reflect its forecast of the trend in government controls. These factors are of special concern to industries over which regulatory agencies, such as the Federal Communications Commission and the Federal Aviation Administration, are important.

Space, communication, and defense policies Government influence on fiscal, monetary, and antitrust matters has been substantial for many years.

However, government influence in space, communication, and defense—a result of cold war tensions—has added a new dimension to government-business relationships. Space exploration, communication satellites, and missile defense systems are examples of technological achievements that would never have been realized without government sponsorship. Private enterprise is intimately involved in these projects through research, development, and (often) operations.

As contractors and subcontractors on such projects, business firms are subject to many additional regulations. Some of these are obvious; for example, a firm that is contracting to develop and manufacture a specialized missile system for the air force must meet air force specifications for design, performance, and capability. But government contracts frequently regulate more than the character of the finished product. Some contracts require that management employ such techniques as cost effectiveness, PERT, and zero defects. Additionally, contracts specify that a firm must offer equal-opportunity employment to overcome racial bias. These are just a few examples of the regulatory influence that has emerged as the government has become one of industry's main customers.

Population trends

Recent reversal of the birthrate has caused the downward revision of overall population growth projections. The impact of the declining birthrate has already been felt in education, which was formerly geared to a policy of expansion and growth. Few organizations are unaffected by population trends; therefore, estimates of future population must become a planning premise. The trend of the population is a major determinant of the production of products and services. Specifically, organizations that cater to markets for the young will have to change their strategies. Figure 6-1 shows that recent population projections for the United States to the year 2025 depend on fertility assumptions about the average number of births per woman. Table 6-1 summarizes these population projections on the basis of the three assumptions.

Economic activities

Managers also use planning premises in general economic activity—employment, productivity, price levels, and national income. Through the development of comprehensive and accurate statistics, we are now able to analyze the composition and distribution of national income, one of the most widely used indicators of general business health. Basically, one must view the workings of the national economy as a sort of giant double-entry bookkeeping system. One side of the ledger indicates the income; the other side the expenditures.

The GNP is the essential element of this national accounting system. The expenditure side of the GNP consists of three major accounts: personal consumption expenditures (consumer spending), private investment expenditures (business spending), and government purchases of goods and services. It represents the total value at market prices of all goods and services

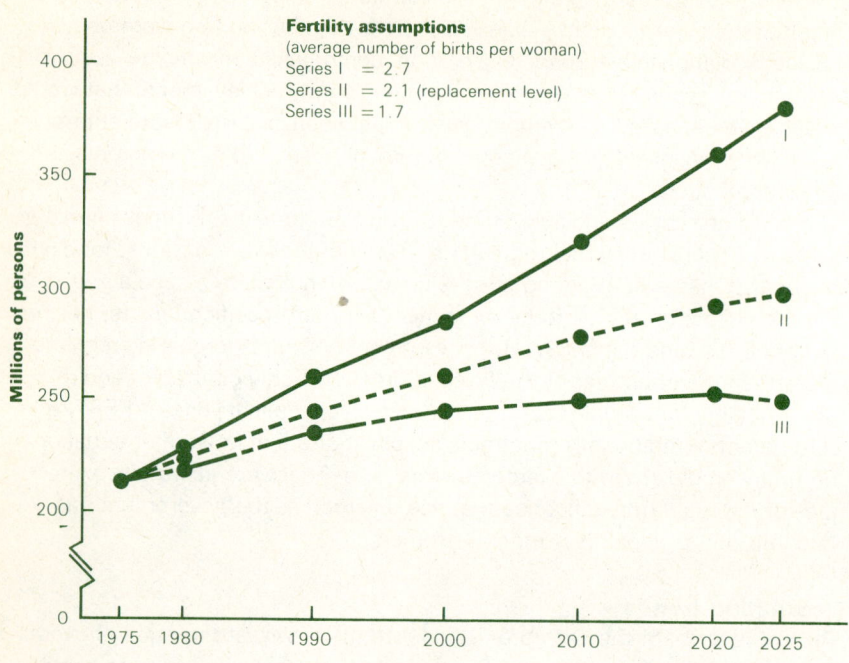

Figure 6-1 Projections of total population, 1975–2025 *Source:* U.S. Department of Commerce, Social and Economic Statistics Administration, Bureau of the Census, *Population Estimates and Projections,* Current Population Reports, Series P-25, no. 541, February 1975.

Year	Series I	Series II	Series III
Estimates			
1970		204,875	
1974		211,909	
Projections			
1975	213,641	213,450	213,323
1980	225,705	222,769	220,356
1985	241,274	234,068	228,355
1990	257,663	245,075	235,581
1995	272,685	254,495	241,198
2000	287,007	262,494	245,098
2005	303,144	270,377	247,926
2010	322,049	278,754	250,193
2015	342,340	286,960	251,693
2020	362,348	294,046	251,884
2025	382,011	299,713	250,421

Table 6-1 Estimates and projections of total population, 1970 to 2025 (Numbers in thousands as of July 1. Includes armed forces abroad.)

Source: U.S. Department of Commerce, Social and Economic Statistics Administration, Bureau of the Census, *Population Estimates and Projections,* Current Population Reports, Series P-25, No. 541, (February 1975).

produced by the nation's economy in a given period. Each of these accounts can be broken down into finer detail. Personal consumption expenditures, for instance, consist of expenditures for durable goods, for nondurable goods, and for services. Data for the various components of these subdivisions are also available.

The income side of the GNP ledger shows the net value of all final goods and services at factor cost of production rather than at market prices. From this side we can draw conclusions and assumptions about the trend of income, savings, and so on. These data, of course, are related to the data on employment and working hours.

Forecasts on productivity and price levels—more realistically, the inflationary trend—also serve as valuable planning premises for management. History shows the erosion of the purchasing value of the dollar and management cannot fully plan for the future without making assumptions about the rate of further erosion.

Technological changes

The activities of many organizations are so closely related to rapid changes in technology that a need for technological forecasting has arisen.[8] In many enterprises, the goods and services that are produced today were unknown a few years ago. Therefore, managers must make efforts to forecast technological developments and to set a timetable for when blue-sky ideas will become realities.

Technological forecasting, however, is still in its early stages, and many years will pass before its techniques are as reliable as those of general economic forecasting. Economists are testing a number of different methods, but three main forecasting approaches stand out. The first is *graphical charting*, which is widely used in aerospace, electronics, and computer industries. It is based on the principle that most engineering developments, as an example, increasing the speed of an aircraft, tend to follow a straight line when plotted on a logarithmic scale. As confirmation, speeds of new aircraft have fallen on this line, as anticipated, and so will those of the supersonic transports. Another approach to technological forecasting was developed by the Rand Corporation and is known as the *Delphi method*. Here, anonymous questionnaires are issued to experts in a field and, from them, individual forecasts are compiled. These are then passed around for written criticism by other participants until a consensus on development and timing is reached. Some companies apply variations of the Delphi method and give them different names. The third major approach to technological forecasting is the *matrix method*. It lists technological developments down one side of a chart and product functions up the other side. The time factor

---

[8] This section is based on "New Products, Setting a Timetable," *Business Week*, May 27, 1967, pp. 52–61. Also see Harper Q. North and Donald L. Pyke, "'Probes' of the Technological Future," *Harvard Business Review* 47 (May–June 1969): 68–82.

can be added to the matrix as a third dimension. There is little doubt that these approaches leave much to be desired. With time and experience, the techniques will change and accuracy will be improved.

Industry climate

After having made planning assumptions regarding the general business climate, managers need a set of assumptions that refer to the climate of the industry in which the enterprise is engaged. Two of the most important assumptions are based on forecasts of the total volumes of domestic industry and foreign imports. If the enterprise is in an industry that has had to face increasing foreign competition, assumptions about future imports will be significant. They will help to indicate whether management should plan to establish branches in foreign countries and thereby import its own products. Other planning premises, specific for the industry, also are needed for assumptions on the industry's expansion or contraction, on the extent of research and development, and on the significance of new technology.

In projecting sales, the automobile industry, for example, is concerned with general assumptions regarding GNP, industrial production, personal income, wholesale prices, consumer prices, and other matters. It also is concerned with numerous specific industry factors for which special assumptions must be made. Some of these are the level of automobile prices in relation to industrial prices, used car prices versus new car prices, new car registrations as a percentage of cars on the road, installment debt repayments as a percentage of disposable income, and the make-up of the car-buying population. Similarly, each industry will have its own set of specific factors for which it will want to obtain future forecasts.

Availability of information

Information and data are readily available on the many subjects for which forecasts and external planning premises are needed. Beginning with the National Recovery Administration in 1933, numerous agencies of the federal government have collected great quantities of basic economic information. Private industry, in addition, has gradually become more willing to make available to government and various research agencies company data that might aid competitors. Moreover, World War II gave added impetus to the collection of economic data.

Current and expected business trends are subjects of considerable interest and study. A constant flow of articles, reports, analyses, and forecasts is circulated not only by government agencies but also by trade associations, consultants, banks, brokerage houses, and research firms. Managers can obtain a wide variety of estimates and information by merely reading the publications of these sources (many of which are free). Much also can be gleaned from newspapers and business weeklies. Although this is an easy way of gauging general business sentiment and of comparing management thinking with other opinions, readers are usually unable to check the accuracy of the information. Sometimes the forecasts that appear in the business or mass media are merely propaganda. Furthermore, readers may find serious conflict between various published reports, and the reports might not appear at a time when they need them most.

Wanted: Helpful information

Aviation experts agree that starting about 1981, the world's airline companies will have to begin replacing their aircraft. How are the managers of the aircraft manufacturers planning for this eventuality? The first thing they need, of course, is information that will help them know what to plan for. It seems that the manufacturers are facing a difficult choice: develop brand new models, or modify existing ones.

The first choice has the obvious advantage of enabling the manufacturers to avoid many of airplanes' current problems, especially their noise and waste of fuel. On the other hand, what are development costs likely to be? Modifying existing designs will clearly save development costs, but will accompanying technological modifications, such as to engines, be feasible?

Finally, and most important, how are the new fleets to be financed? No one company—seller or customer—can afford to undertake all the costs. So the industry needs valid information regarding governmental financing: type of funds, interest, timing, and so forth. In short, the industry's major planning task for the remainder of the 1970's requires information about a variety of economic and technological factors in the 1980's.

Source: Richard Within, "Aircraft Industry Must Make 1980's Decisions Very Soon," *Sunday Oregonian*, September 5, 1976, p. F7 (New York Times News Service).

As we have noted, government agencies and trade associations publish many statistical surveys and interpretations. The U.S. Department of Commerce *Survey of Current Business* is one of the most widely used of the thousands of publications available. Other publications, to cite only a few, are *Economic Indicators,* prepared for the Joint Economic Committee by the Council of Economic Advisers; the *Federal Reserve Bulletin;* and reports by the National Industrial Conference Board. The advantage of the statistical information in such publications is that it represents facts rather than opinions. It gives managers a basis for evaluating outside opinion on the economic outlook before establishing their planning premises.

Techniques

Much has been written about the techniques for forecasting general business and industry trends. *Business Week* has classified them as "loaded deck," "oaks from acorns," and "test tube" techniques.[9]

In the first technique, forecasters work from known data—inside information. They know what has happened and what *is* happening before anyone else finds out. The second technique reasons that the future grows out of the present, though it is not identical with the past. The third strategy refers to theoretical economic models.

Abramson and Mack identify four different groups of forecasting techniques.[10] The first technique is purely mechanical. In it, recurrent cycles, lead series, and data are classified and conclusions are drawn on the basis of past experience, without any examination of past and current causal forces. A second technique is labeled *plans for future action*. The underlying idea of this technique is that at any moment there are plans at various stages of completion, and if these plans can be uncovered in the early stages it is possible to predict what will happen in later ones. The third approach uses the opinions and expectations of others. In this technique the forecast is based on what executives expect their sales to be, on what consumers expect to spend, or, even, on what other forecasters believe will happen. This approach involves neither cause nor history. Abramson and Mack's fourth group of forecasting techniques is called *causal*. In this technique an attempt is made to determine the causes of fluctuations in the series to be forecast and, then, these causes are measured and evaluated.

In an actual forecast it is conceivable and even probable that a number of techniques may be combined.[11] "The identification of specific methods does not mean they should or must be used alone. In fact . . . it is sometimes difficult to separate one method from another, and there are numerous conceivable classifications."[12]

Internal planning premises and forecasts

The sales forecast

Of the various internal planning premises that are used by a firm, we shall devote a large part of our attention to the most important one: the sales

---

[9] "Business Forecasting," *Business Week*, September 24, 1955, pp. 90—122.
[10] Adolph G. Abramson and Russell H. Mack, *Business Forecasting in Practice* (New York: Wiley, 1966).
[11] For those who are interested in learning how one large concern forecasts the general business activity, we call attention to the very interesting article by Donald J. Watson in Abramson and Mack, *Business Forecasting in Practice* (pp. 224—269). At the time the article was written, Mr. Watson held the position of economist, Economic Research and Forecasting Operation, General Electric Company, at its headquarters in Schenectady, N.Y.
[12] Abramson and Mack, *Business Forecasting in Practice*, p. 45.

forecast. The sales forecast is basic to internal planning, serving as both a forecast and a guide. The sales forecast is a projection of expected sales—an estimate of anticipated sales volume extending into the future for six months, a year, or an even longer period. It is also a forecast of the revenue side of the income statement. In making a sales forecast, managers are concerned with the expectations of a single enterprise within an industry, after having determined the outlook for the entire industry. A sales forecast is narrower in scope than is a general business or an industry forecast, although those two often provide important elements in developing it.

In most cases, sales forecasts are rather difficult to make. It is possible, for instance, to make better forecasts of industry volume than of company volume, since the individual company's share of industry production is constantly shifting. In forecasting sales, managers must work with one influential variable that is usually uncontrollable: competition from the other members of the industry. In the past, for example, aggressive expansion by one automobile competitor has easily depressed the volume and competitive shares of all the other firms in that industry.

Methods

A report of the National Industrial Conference Board, *Forecasting in Industry*, concludes that no single forecasting method presently known gives uniformly accurate results.[13] One of the surest aids to sound sales forecasting is to approach the same goal by several methods, with each forecasting method acting as a check on the others. Four different methods of sales forecasting are primarily used: the jury of executive opinion; sales force composite; users' expectation; and statistical.[14]

Jury of executive opinion   This is probably the oldest and simplest method of making sales forecasts. As its name implies, it assembles and averages the opinions of the top management of various divisions in order to obtain a sounder forecast than could be made by a single estimator. Undoubtedly, one advantage of this approach is that it is quick—it does not require elaborate statistics. However, this method also has serious drawbacks. It is based entirely on opinion rather than on facts and analyses. Furthermore, averaging opinions reduces and disperses the responsibility for accuracy.

Sales force composite   This widely used method combines the views of sales managers and members of the sales force concerning expectations of future sales. Members of the sales force estimate the future sales in their individual territories. Each estimate is usually reviewed by regional sales managers, and then by the general sales manager. One obvious advantage is that those closest to the sales—those with a specialized knowledge of the

---

[13] *Forecasting in Industry*, Studies in Business Policy No. 77 (New York: National Industrial Conference Board, 1956).
[14] All these methods except the users' expectation method are cited ibid. The users expectation method is discussed in *Forecasting Sales*, Studies in Business Policy No. 106 (New York: National Industrial Conference Board, 1963), pp. 30—32.

market—do the forecasting. In turn, of course, they are the ones who have to make good on their forecasts.

Yet, this method has many disadvantages. Although their proximity to the market enables those who do the selling to forecast for the immediate future, such people are usually not good long-term forecasters. Some tend to be too optimistic; others play it safe, thereby inviting underachievement. Partly because of such disadvantages, there seems to be a trend away from the use of the sales organization as an integral part of the sales forecasting process.

Users' expectations Some companies ask their customers how much they expect to buy from them and base their sales forecast directly on this information. This method is especially meaningful if the manufacturer serves an industry consisting of few companies. Another advantage of this method is that the cost of obtaining the information—by mail, phone, or personal interview—is negligible, thus enabling a small company with limited resources to make reliable forecasts. Furthermore, the users' expectations method generally provides more current and more complete information than is available from published sources. It is particularly useful in making a forecast on a new industrial product for which there is no previous experience or data.

However, the forecasts obtained by this method are based on expectations subject to change; that is, they rely on estimates of needs, not on commitments. In addition, making these forecasts requires considerable time and effort.

Statistical Many organizations rely on several different statistical approaches to supplement personal judgment and increase sales forecasting accuracy. Correlation analysis and trend-and-cycle projections are the most frequently used statistical methods. They are applied by trained specialists who are usually attached to the staff of the market research department.

Correlation analysis is a method of measuring the relationship between two or more factors. In a sales forecasting context, it is used to discover whether a relationship exists between the company's sales and some other measurable series, then to determine what this relationship is and its reliability. By using correlation analysis, the statistician is able to forecast the company's own sales on the basis of other series whose fluctuations precede those in sales, or to supplement judgment by relating the firm's sales to a well-known series that is being forecast by many others. The National Industrial Conference Board summarizes the advantages and disadvantages of correlation analysis:

It describes in measurable objective terms the relationships influencing the course of sales. It indicates the degree of reliability which can be attached to such relationships; it forces the forecaster to qualify the assumptions underlying his estimates, making it easier for management to check his results. The great disadvantage is the danger of relying too heavily upon such relationships and of abandoning independent appraisal of future events. Even the best correlations are subject to chance variations and one serious variation may be enough to bring severe losses to a company.[15]

Trend-and-cycle analysis defines and measures three basic factors that influence a firm's sales: long-term growth trends, cyclical business fluctuations, and seasonal variations. For most industries this method is useful only in the long-range forecasting of their sales.

In addition to these two methods, some organizations have developed mathematical models and computer simulation techniques in order to forecast sales.[16] Such models can be constructed when the sale of the product depends on several factors, each having a certain known effect on the sale. Thus, the tire industry, for instance, has been able to develop a mathematical model based on the demand for tires being affected by new car production, the number of cars in operation, the tires' wearing qualities, and the amount of service tires receive.[17]

Use

It is interesting to note that the sales forecast is used for a wide variety of purposes. Indeed, a survey of sales forecasting practices made by the AMA indicated that most companies have, on the average, five or six specific uses for their sales forecasts. Of the 297 representative companies surveyed, nearly all listed production planning as the single most general application. Almost the same number also used the sales forecast for budget preparation. Other specific uses included earnings forecasting, equipment and facilities planning, determining sales quotas, manpower planning, raw material stockpiling, promotion planning, inventory planning, and estimating cash requirements. Consumer goods industries use the sales forecast primarily to set sales quotas; service organizations use it primarily for budget preparation.

Time span

Most sales forecasts cover a period of at least one year, but many companies supplement them with additional forecasts both of shorter and longer duration. Four out of five companies review and adjust their forecasts at regular intervals, typically every three months. Logically, the larger the company, the more likely it is to try to see far ahead; conversely, the smaller the company, the more it emphasizes short-range forecasts. Though almost all firms make annual sales forecasts, the vast majority of those that also undertake long-range forecasts project their sales five years ahead. These

---

[15] *Forecasting in Industry,* p. 1.
[16] John R. McNamara, "A Linear Programming Model for Long-Range Capacity Planning in an Electric Utility." *Journal of Economics and Business* 28 (1976): 227–235.
[17] *Forecasting in Industry,* pp. 33–35.

five-year forecasts are usually prepared every year and the annual forecasts are then adjusted every three months.

Forecasting: A contingency process

As with virtually everything else the manager does, forecasting is a contingency process. The forecasting techniques that are used depend on the purpose of the forecast and the way in which it is to be used. For example, different stages of a product's life cycle require different techniques.*

	Stage of life cycle			
	Product development	**Market testing and early introduction**	**Rapid growth**	**Steady state**
Forecasting techniques	Delphi method Historical analysis of comparable products Input-output analysis	Consumer surveys Tracking and warning systems Market tests	Statistical techniques for identifying turning points Tracking and warning systems Market surveys	Time series analysis and projection Causal and econometric models Market surveys Life cycle analysis

* Adapted from John C. Chambers, Satinder K. Mullick, and Donald D. Smith, "How to Choose the Right Forecasting Technique," *Harvard Business Review* 49 (July–August 1971): 45–74. Copyright © 1971 by the President and Fellows of Harvard College; all rights reserved.

Accuracy

The degree of accuracy achieved by the sales forecast tends to increase with the duration of the company's forecasting program. This, in fact, applies to all types of forecasts. Thus, although the first forecast may be in error, a review of the sources of error will lead to increased accuracy in subsequent sales forecasts.

The AMA's survey gives us some indication of how accurate a forecast can be. For the 248 companies included in the survey, the deviation between the sales forecast and actual performance averaged 8 percent. It is interesting to note that producers of consumer nondurable goods came within 4.2 percent, producers of accessory equipment for industry within 5.9 percent, whereas manufacturers of industrial components used as parts of finished products reported the greatest deviation—11 percent. This is not too surprising; this group has to forecast from a point two or three times removed from its final customer.[18]

Other internal planning premises

In addition to the sales forecast, organizations have many other internal planning premises. For instance, the capital to be invested in the enterprise is an internal planning premise, and decisions and assumptions regarding it have significant bearing on future plans. Capital invested in fixed assets will be a particularly important factor in a firm's future direction.

The various basic managerial policies regarding products, prices, labor, financing, and such also involve internal planning premises. They constitute limitations to effective planning in the enterprise and define its nature and character. If needed, policies can be changed; nevertheless, management must include them in its forecasts and planning premises.

Forecasts in general

Shortcomings

At the base of all forecasts lie certain assumptions, approximations, and averages that must conform to existing conditions. Managers may become so entranced with the mechanism of the forecasting system that they fail to question its logic. Or, they may become so intrigued with the forecasting system's record of accuracy, proved perhaps on a trial application of the formula to past operations, that they are not prepared for the unexpected and large deviations that sometimes suddenly appear. There is also a danger that the process of formulating ideas concerning the future outlook may produce an inbred conformity of opinion. Some of the forecasts that emanate from informed sources may not represent the sources' real prediction of the future but may have been uttered to achieve desired effects.

Nevertheless, this critical examination should not discourage forecasting attempts. No manager can afford not to forecast. However, forecasting is an art and not a science; there is no infallible way of predicting the future. Forecasting accuracy increases with experience; good results can rarely be achieved immediately after introducing a formal forecasting system. The original method of forecasting is invariably subjected to continuous refinements necessitated by the particular characteristics of the organization.

---

[18] *Sales Forecasting: Uses, Techniques, and Trends,* Special Report No. 16 (New York: American Management Association, 1956), p. 149. For an interesting description of how the Corning Glass Works prepares and coordinates its sales forecasts, see the article by Richard L. Patey in *Sales Forecasting,* p. 111.

Length of the forecast period

The length of the forecast period is of significance in assessing accuracy. Short-term forecasts are generally more accurate than longer-term ones. Old, established product lines can, of course, be forecast more accurately than can new products with little or no sales history. Overall company forecasts also tend to be more accurate than do forecasts of a specific product or territory.

Expense

Managers—especially those in smaller organizations that have less money to spend on staff activities—often plead that they cannot afford the expense of forecasting. At best, theirs is a narrow point of view. Quite a bit of forecasting information is available just for the asking. It should be possible, at little or no cost, for even the smallest firm to utilize some of the economic data readily available from external sources—data also used by the largest firms. Managers of small enterprises should bear in mind that a dollar saved or earned through forecasting usually means more to them than it does to a large enterprise.

In deciding the amount to be spent for forecasting, managers should consider such factors as production schedules and the stability and complexity of their markets. If, for instance, their firm is engaged in a cyclical or seasonal industry, it will need forecasts especially designed for its circumstances. Firms producing goods that take a long time from production order to the point of sales will also be more vitally concerned with forecasting and more willing to incur additional forecasting expense. Moreover, suppliers selling small quantities to large numbers of customers have a more difficult and, probably, more expensive forecasting problem than do industrial suppliers selling to only a few large customers.

The cost of forecasting, then, varies greatly from industry to industry and from enterprise to enterprise. But no matter what the cost, utilization of forecasting information is vital to the enterprise's success. To paraphrase a familiar advertisement: the future is a moving target—forecasting can improve your aim.

Summary

To perform their planning function effectively, managers need a knowledgeable estimate of the future. Forecasting is the process by which they acquire this estimate.

Forecasts take into account many variables, including general economic conditions in the society, industry conditions, and the nature of the enterprise's product life cycles. In essence, forecasts provide the assumptions, called *premises*, on which managerial planning is based. Premises are contingent on a number of factors: distance of the organization from the ultimate consumer of its product, foreseeability and controllability of future events, government policies, and technological changes.

A large variety of forecasting techniques is available to the modern manager. These range from educated guesses by experienced personnel to sophisticated computer models. Although forecasting is sometimes a tedious activity, whose benefits often are not immediately recognizable, it is essential to effective planning.

Discussion questions

1. Bob Dylan has written: "You don't need a weatherman to know which way the wind blows." In the context of this chapter's discussion, do you agree? disagree? Why?
2. One recent trend in large business has been the movement toward conglomerates. Discuss how this will affect the data that top management needs for forecasting. Do you suppose that the conglomerate movement makes forecasting more difficult? less difficult?
3. What criteria should be used to determine the effectiveness of a particular forecasting process?

Supplementary readings

Chambers, John C.; Mullick, Satinder K.; and Smith, Donald D. "How to Choose the Right Forecasting Technique." *Harvard Business Review* 49 (July–August 1971):45–74.

Leontiades, Milton. "Planning: A Re-examination of Fundamentals." *Journal of Economics and Business* 28 (1976):189–194.

Redfield, James W. "Elements of Forecasting." *Harvard Business Review* 29 (November–December 1951):81–91. Reprinted in *Dimensions in Modern Management,* 2d. ed., edited by Patrick E. Connor. Boston: Houghton Mifflin, 1978.

Roman, Daniel D. "Technological Forecasting in the Decision Process." *Academy of Management Journal* 13 (June 1970):127–138.

Chapter 7

Planning: The action phase

Objectives of the chapter

1 To describe the translation of planning concepts into planning action.
2 To discuss various types of planning.
3 To illustrate the relation of specific forecasting activities to planning.
4 To describe the essentials of Program Evaluation and Review Techniques (PERT) as a planning tool.
5 To point out the limitations of planning.

The ancient Chinese military writer Sun Tzu was the earliest to recognize the nature of strategy and to deal with it systematically: "What is of supreme importance in war is to attack the enemy's strategy."[1] A marvelous passage in his book reflects his view:

In the later Han, K'ou Hsün surrounded Kao Chun. Chun sent his Planning Officer, Huang-fu Wen, to parley. Huang-fu Wen was stubborn and rude and K'ou Hsün beheaded him, and informed Kao Chun: "Your staff officer was without propriety. I have beheaded him. If you wish to submit, do so immediately. Otherwise defend yourself." On the same day Chun threw open his fortifications and surrendered.

All K'ou Hsün's generals said, "May we ask, you killed his envoy, but yet forced him to surrender his city. How is this?"

K'ou Hsün said: "Huang-fu Wen was Kao Chun's heart and guts, his intimate counsellor. If I had spared Huang-fu Wen's life, he would have accomplished his schemes, but when I killed him, Kao Chun lost his guts. It is said: 'The supreme excellence in war is to attack the enemy's plans.'"

All the generals said: "This is beyond our comprehension."[2]

---

[1] Sun Tzu, *The Art of War*, trans. Samuel B. Griffith (New York: Oxford University Press, 1963), p. 77.
[2] Ibid., pp. 77–78.

In this incident Kao Chun's staff officer was the center of intelligence and the source of strategy. That he was also rude, stubborn, and without propriety indicates that staff has not changed much in twenty-five hundred years. Undoubtedly many modern line executives share K'ou Hsün's sentiments about staff decapitation. Nonetheless, Sun Tzu shows us that strategy is the key element in the implementation of plans.

Strategy and long-range planning

The concept of strategy has more than military application. Strategy is the means for carrying out any policy. Its primary concern is effect.[3] What plan will produce the effect of achieving policy? From this definition we can see that objectives and policies must always precede strategy as we pointed out in Chapter 4.

A number of years ago, a major distiller embarked on a program of diversification, moving into areas quite apart from the liquor business. Its policy was to diversify activities, to obtain a wider base of operation and a better opportunity for growth. Corporate management's *strategy* included identifying those industries in which to acquire firms. Its *tactics* included actual acquisition. In other words, high-level strategy became "policy in action."[4]

A systems concept

Long-range planning requires that managers apply a systems approach to the organization. By developing strategies based on plans, managers are forced to account for as many organizational elements and inputs as possible. Beyond this, planning and strategy force top management to visualize the implication of the interrelationships that exist among the elements of an organization. In this respect we emphasize the dictum of the systems approach: nothing happens alone; every act affects every other act in a system of interrelationships. Planning "does not deal with each separate element of the business alone, by itself, but rather permits the manager to see things as parts of a whole."[5] Planning to build new buildings in an urban-renewal program is not in itself sufficient. Thought must be given to the impact of these buildings on community services, shopping, schools, even the cultural values of the people living in them. Some city managers have learned, to their dismay, that new high-rise apartments generate more social problems than existed in the substandard housing they replaced. Thus, the long-range plans to renew the central areas of cities and their resulting strategies must

---

[3] B. H. Liddell Hart, *Strategy* (New York: Praeger, 1954), pp. 333–335.
[4] Ibid., p. 335.
[5] George A. Steiner, *Top Management Planning* (New York: Macmillan, 1969), p. 66.

Strategy compared with tactics

If a department store has a policy of competing on the basis of price, its strategy is to avoid being undersold. This strategy pervades all its tactical devices—determining mark-up and profit margins, and obtaining intelligence information on the pricing activities of competitors. Notice that basic policy and strategy are formulated and implemented on higher managerial levels; the tactics of carrying out the policy occur on the lower levels and include salesperson and customer interaction.

As the foregoing indicates, strategy implies the formulation of plans with longer-range implications than those of tactics. The relationships of strategy, tactics, planning span, and management levels are shown in Figure 7-1.

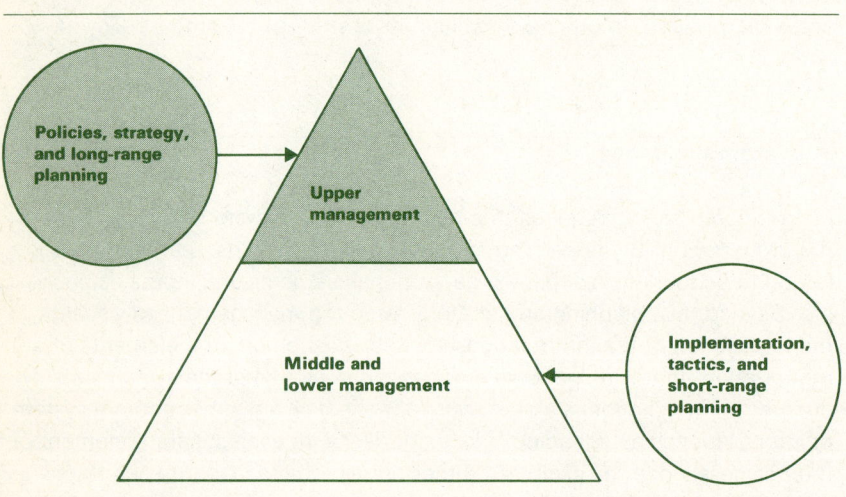

Figure 7-1 The relationship of strategy, tactics, and time span of planning to management levels

Although vital to managing, long-range planning is not nearly as susceptible to scientific treatment as short-range planning is. Intimately connected with policy and strategy, long-range planning derives its data as much from hunch, intuition, and values as from concrete information. Part of the problem rests, of course, in the imprecision of forecasting and planning information. But a further part rests in the irrationality of the motives of the planners themselves. How, for example, does one quantify the power needs of executives or their feelings of social responsibility?

Contingency: Planning, managing, and the environment

As we have seen, managing the enterprise is a contingency process. Specifically, how managers manage depends on what they are managing for, which in turn is constrained by the environment in which they operate. The relevance of this overall relationship for planning is suggested by the following:*

Managing	= f (Strategic choice)	= f (Environment)
Allocating resources	Policies	Markets
Reward systems	Goals and objectives	Uncertainties
Organizing	Actions	Human needs
		Production technology
		Competition

* Adapted from John L. Ward, "The Opportunity to Measure Strategic Variables: An Attempt to Quantify Product-Market Diversity," *Journal of Economics and Business* 28 (1976): 219–226.

New long-range planning processes

Despite the difficulty of quantification, managers do make long-range plans. Eugene Benge notes five steps in their planning process:[6]

1. Realistically appraise the present strengths and weaknesses of the company.
2. Involve the company's key personnel in planning.
3. Base the plan on the consumer; give it a marketing orientation.
4. Establish a five-year plan, subdivide it, and delegate responsibilities.
5. Set up a schedule for key events and try to keep to it.

The long-range plan, if executed properly, will produce guidelines for lower-level, short-range planning. Points 4 and 5 in the list suggest this. For instance, the division of a five-year plan into areas of separate responsibility, such as research, marketing, and manufacturing, objectifies the plan so that managers can clearly see the elements for which they must be concerned. Along with this must go the necessary delegation of authority to enable the subordinate managers to carry out their short-range planning activities. Scheduling of key events ties the accomplishment of goals to a time dimension. This allows the long-range plan to be tested during shorter time periods.

Fremont Kast points out a major dilemma in long-range planning.[7] On the one hand, managers must commit resources over a long planning

[6] Eugene J. Benge, "The Common Sense of Long-Range Planning," *Advanced Management* 24 (1959).
[7] Fremont E. Kast, "A Dynamic Planning Model," *Business Horizons* 11 (June 1968):63–64.

period. On the other hand, faced with changing technologies and market conditions, they may find that during the planning period a better allocation of resources can be made. How can an organization commit its resources rationally over a long period of time while acknowledging increasing uncertainty in the environment? Part of the answer lies in working organizational flexibility into long-range plans. Essentially this amounts to designing organizations and developing managerial attitudes that stress adaptation rather than rigidity.

The role of the planning staff

Around 1800 the Prussian military created the modern concept and the organization of the "general staff."[8] Basically, the staff had two major responsibilities: the creation of military plans and strategies and the coordination of field units in ways consistent with the implementation of those plans and strategies. The German general staff became a highly refined and effective military instrument, and it became, in a sense, a model for planning staffs in nonmilitary organizations.

Very early in management history, Frederick W. Taylor noted that planning must be separated from doing. He reasoned that specialized planning staffs should be used to support the line organization in generating information, providing alternate strategies, and facilitating top management's coordination of operations. He believed that this staff work required considerable skill and specialized knowledge, and that it should be centralized in order to obtain maximum efficiency.

Taylor, perhaps, was ahead of his time. It was not until organizations grew moderately large and began to utilize more complex technologies that planning staffs began to be widely used by management. Steiner lists a staff's major responsibilities:[9]

1 Developing long-range objectives in conjunction with top management.
2 Coordinating plans at various levels of the organization.
3 Assisting departmental and divisional segments of the organization with planning.
4 Reviewing and evaluating plans submitted by subunits of the organization.
5 Preparing specific studies on subjects of interest to top management.
6 Aiding management in planning for diversification, new product research, and new market development.

As we see from this list, a planning staff provides an information service for managers; it collects data, analyzes information, and provides reports. In some instances, a centralized planning staff may also play an important role in coordinating the plans and activities of segments of an organization.

[8] Walter Goerlitz, *History of the German General Staff* (New York: Praeger, 1959).
[9] Steiner, *Top Management Planning*, pp. 116–121.

Short-range planning

Lower-level managers are concerned with implementing the policies and objectives that result from long-range planning. Their activities require shorter planning periods and necessitate an understanding of technique and procedure.

During this phase of the planning process, plans must be translated into more specific financial or numerical terms, if possible. Some plans, however, cannot and need not be translated into such terms, for instance, the initial structuring of an organization. Instead, this type of organizational planning requires delineating, defining, and grouping the different activities of the enterprise in such a way that they may be most logically assigned and effectively executed. It also is concerned with the establishment of authority relationships.

In other cases, however, finances play an important role in business planning. At the end of the fiscal year, the balance sheet, the profit-and-loss statement, and many other records are reviewed by the chief executive, the board of directors, the stockholders, the owners, and, possibly, the public at large.

Revenue and expense forecast

The revenue and expense forecast is one short-range plan that can be translated into dollars and cents. To do so, managers estimate the future revenues and expenses of the organization during a stated planning period of, say, one year. It is relatively simple to forecast financial revenues. Managers need only base their figures on sales forecasts and multiply the units to be sold by the price at which they will be sold. This naturally becomes more complicated when different products are involved.

On the expense side, management will have to anticipate the various costs involved in the creation and distribution of a good or service. In anticipating these costs, management is fully aware that it is looking into the future and that it will have to base its various estimates on prior planning premises. If one such premise assumes further wage increases, management accordingly must figure its costs to be higher. If a planning premise anticipates higher interest rates, the expenses for interest must likewise be figured higher. This is where various intermediate forecasts will help to establish a realistic picture of the expense side of the revenue and expense forecast. Comparing both sides of the forecast, then, managers quickly can see the estimated profit or loss of operations during the planning period.

Cash forecast

Another significant short-range financial plan is commonly known as a *cash forecast*. Everyone knows how important it is to have enough ready cash available to meet obligations. Failing to provide adequate amounts of cash at the proper times will, to say the least, interfere with the smooth flow of an enterprise's operations. A cash forecast shows whether or not there will be an adequate supply of cash on hand when it is needed to pay operating expenses and other liabilities.

Of course, in most enterprises cash inflow is closely related to the volume of sales. Cash outflow requirements also relate closely to the volume of sales. However, a manager cannot forecast a year's inflows and outflows of cash from the anticipated level of sales; such a forecast would tell little about sales timing. Cash inflows and outflows must be coordinated, and it is not enough that the annual total cash receipts exceed the annual total cash disbursements. Thus, the cash forecast must normally relate to monthly operations within a yearly period. This will enable management to judge rather closely how much cash will be coming in and going out from month to month. Based on this forecast, management can anticipate a need to borrow during some period or periods when cash inflow will be insufficient to meet cash requirements. Such a situation is likely to occur in a business that needs to build up its inventories during the first six months of the year and does not begin to sell its goods until the latter part of the year. The cash forecast will enable management to determine how much cash will be available during the months of inventory buildup.

Pro forma statements

Many firms also translate their short-term planning into pro forma balance sheets, or future income statements, based on the information contained in sales, materials, direct labor, and other operating plans. These detailed projections give a manager additional financial information for the planning period. *Pro forma statements,* as they are called, have significant use. Whereas a cash forecast for the coming year may show that the cash balance at the end of the year will be larger than the opening balance, a pro forma statement of profit and loss may indicate that if the planned operations are carried through, a net loss will result. The prospect of such a loss might lead to considerable change in operating plans.

Budgets

A budget is a detailed plan covering some phase of activity in some future period. Budgets are prepared and expressed in numerical terms—usually in financial terms. Financial forecasts often become the basis for budget planning. For instance, the cash forecast can easily become the cash budget and the revenue and expense forecast can often furnish the basis for the revenue and expense budget. However, these forecasts can become the basis of budgets only if they are properly prepared, if they are estimates of what is reasonably attainable—not of what could be obtained under the best possible conditions.

At times some managerial practices result in more liberal financial forecasts than budgets. In order to enhance its chances for obtaining a bank loan, for example, corporate management might be somewhat more optimistic in predicting its cash forecasts than it has a right to be. However, its budgets must still be based on a much tighter plan and are more conservative. But this divergence is not advisable; the financial forecast should be as realistic as the budget given to the various managers of the organization. If a variation does exist, it will soon become known and managers will be guided accordingly. They will feel that top management does not expect them to come up to the budget figures or to stay within them, whichever the case may be. If the divergence continues for any length of time, managers will know that budgets are unrealistic and that they are not bound by them. This, of course, defeats the purpose of a budget. Sound financial plans should be drawn up so realistically that they can automatically become the basis for budgets.

PERT

Up to this point we have discussed primarily the short-range planning of financial matters. However, there are also techniques for planning short-range activities. One of these is called *PERT*. This technique is so important in some modern planning efforts that we devote much of the remainder of this chapter to it.

PERT (Program Evaluation and Review Technique) is a technique that was developed in 1958 through the combined efforts of the U.S. Navy Special Projects Office and Booz-Allen and Hamilton, a management consulting firm. The objective of the PERT research team was to design a planning and control system for developing the Polaris missile system, a project that was subject to a great degree of uncertainty in the performance times of its activities. PERT dealt particularly with this uncertainty. The PERT system is based on three estimates of the performance time for each activity. It distinguishes itself from other planning techniques by the use of a network monitored by statistics and computers to dovetail complex parallel and sequential job combinations.

Managers involved in the planning function warmly accepted PERT because it enabled them to cope better with the increasingly rapid pace at which technological changes were being introduced. Previously, management could afford pauses between various stages of research, design, and engineering; today, technology and the rapid introduction of new methods and processes make it necessary for these different stages to overlap. PERT has given management the tool with which to coordinate and control this. It enables management to plan complex programs and to evaluate their progress continuously. Management groups who use PERT quickly see potential and actual problems, because the system constantly gives status reports and determines the shortest time in which a project can be completed.

At about the same time PERT came into existence, another planning technique known as *CPM* (Critical Path Method) was developed by the duPont Corporation in connection with a construction program. The approaches of PERT and CPM are similar, although one originated in the military and the other in private industry. In contrast to PERT, CPM was developed for programs consisting largely of deterministic activities, such as construction and maintenance projects. CPM omits statistical considerations and is based on a single estimate of the average time required to perform the activities in question. Although these distinctions between CPM and PERT are historically correct, with the passing of time the two techniques have merged, and the result is usually referred to as a *PERT-type system*.

Development of the PERT network

The basis of both CPM and PERT is the project network diagram. A simple example is shown in Figure 7-2. The two major components of this type of diagram are events and activities. The diagram is, therefore, a pictorial representation of the interrelationships among all required events and activities in a particular project. An *event,* usually depicted by a circle, is the instant of time marking either the start or the accomplishment of a plan. An event can be the product of one or several activities. It must, however, occur at a specific instant of time. An event cannot be considered accomplished until all activities leading to it have been completed.

An *activity,* usually depicted by an arrow, is the time-consuming element of a network. An activity is the work required to accomplish an event, and it cannot start until all preceding activities have been completed. A network begins with a single event and finishes with a single event and is made up of many intermediate events related to one another by activities. Events must take place in the proper sequence—for instance, the frame of a house cannot be constructed before the foundation is laid, and none of the other work can be started before the frame is finished.

The network is essentially an outgrowth of the Gantt, or bar, chart developed by Henry L. Gantt in the beginning of this century. Gantt designed this chart primarily so that he could visualize the time element of a program in relation to the progress of the work. The bar chart graphically depicts the activities of the project and the sequences of occurrence of the various activities. Figure 7-3 is a bar chart for the construction of a house. The plain bars are the plan; the shaded bars show the progress in relationship to the plan at the end of the eighth week. The most serious shortcoming of bar charts is that they do not indicate the interdependence of various activities. The mere fact that activities are scheduled for simultaneous or overlapping time periods does not necessarily make them related or interdependent.

This same shortcoming was found in the milestone chart, the next step in the evolution of PERT. The milestone chart breaks up the long bars into shorter periods of time, each of which represents the accomplishment of an event within the long-term job (see Figure 7-4). Although the milestone

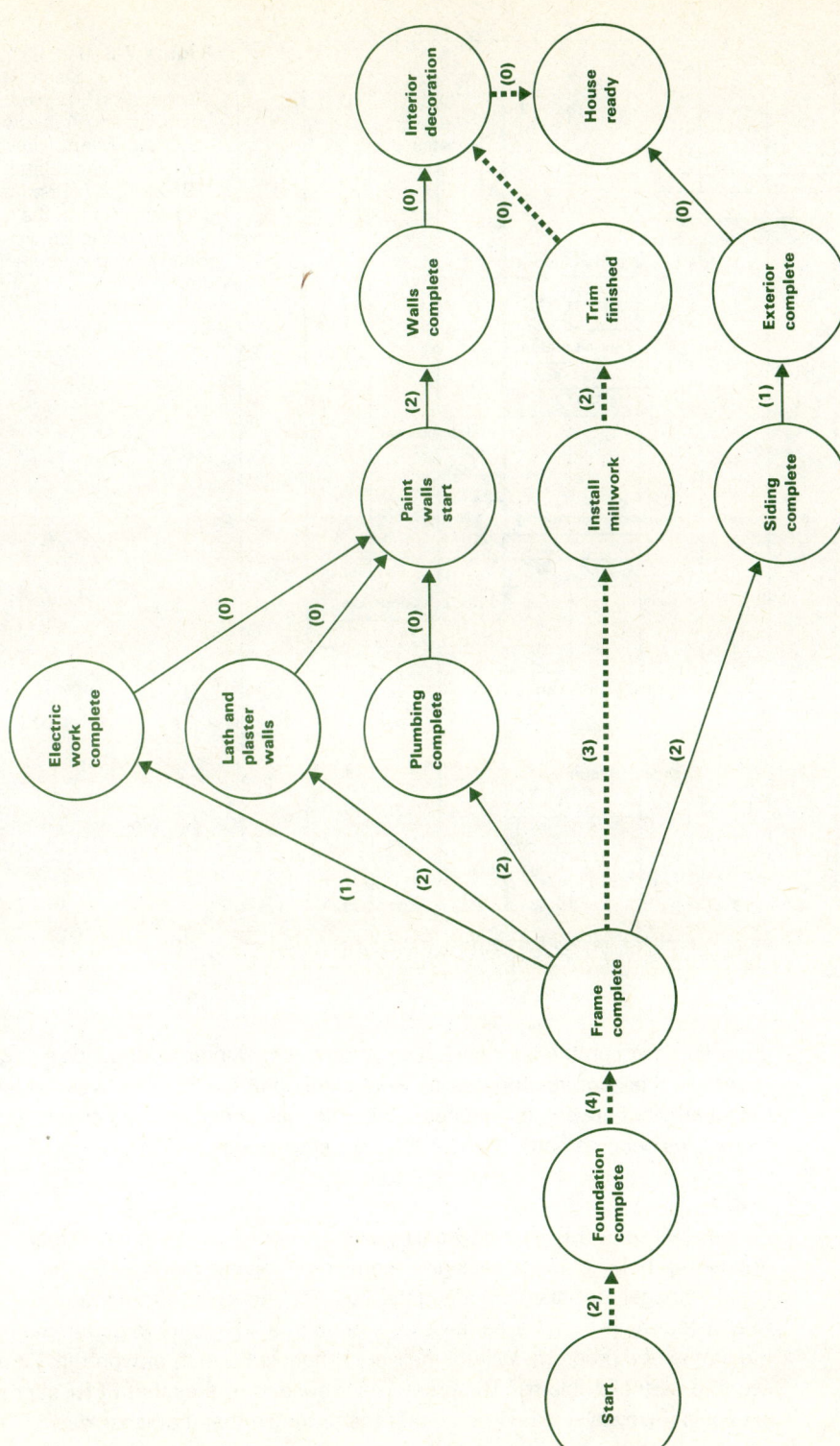

Figure 7-2 Project network diagram
Source: K. L. Dean, *Fundamentals of Network Planning and Analysis* (St. Paul, Minn.: Univac Division, Sperry Rand, 1962), p. 68. Reprinted by permission of the Sperry Univac Division of the Sperry Rand Corporation.

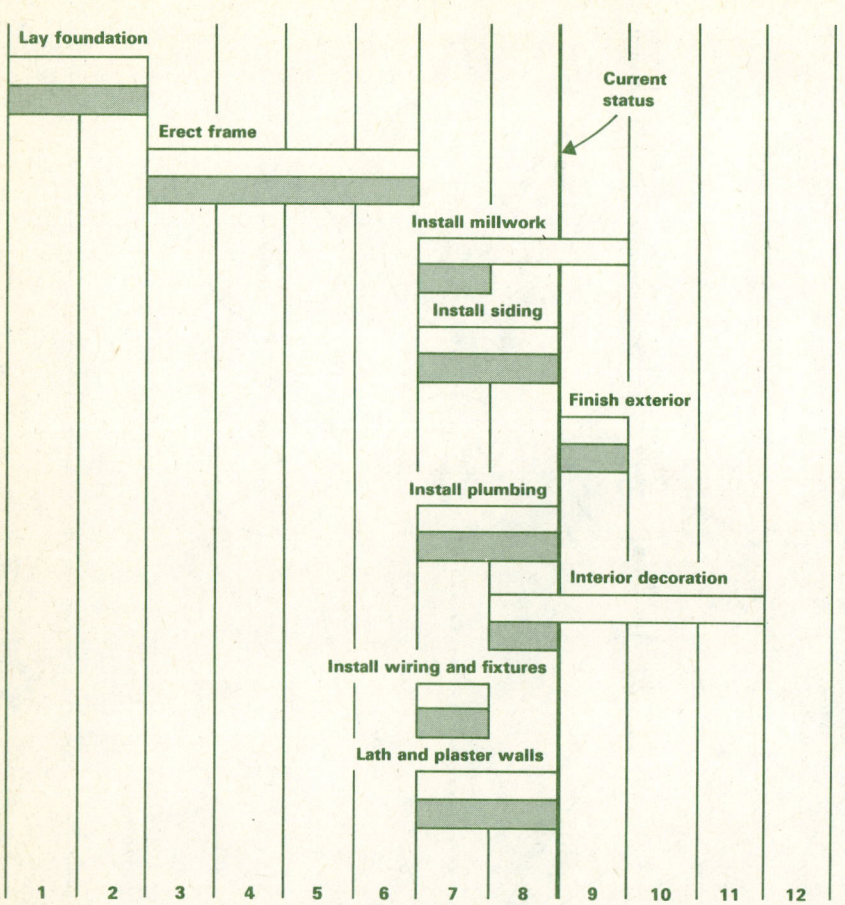

Figure 7-3 Bar chart
Source: K. L. Dean, *Fundamentals of Network Planning and Analysis* (St. Paul, Minn.: Univac Division, Sperry Rand, 1962), p. 67. Reprinted by permission of the Sperry Univac Division of Sperry Rand Corporation.

chart improved on the bar chart, it still did not show interdependencies. However, these interdependencies were clarified in the PERT network by the use of arrows between milestones. Thus, the milestones became events and the arrows became activities (see the third step in Figure 7-4).

Value

As we shall see, PERT has its weaknesses. It is not a panacea for all management problems, but it does give them some relative magnitude. The usual management planning meetings illustrate this point. From four to twenty-four high-priced executives sit around a table and try to determine the status of a program: Will the delivery schedule be met, or won't it? What seem to be the problems? The group is surrounded by fires that PERT cannot extinguish. However, PERT can direct the group so that it at least knows which fires to quench first. In addition, the PERT technique assists in pre-

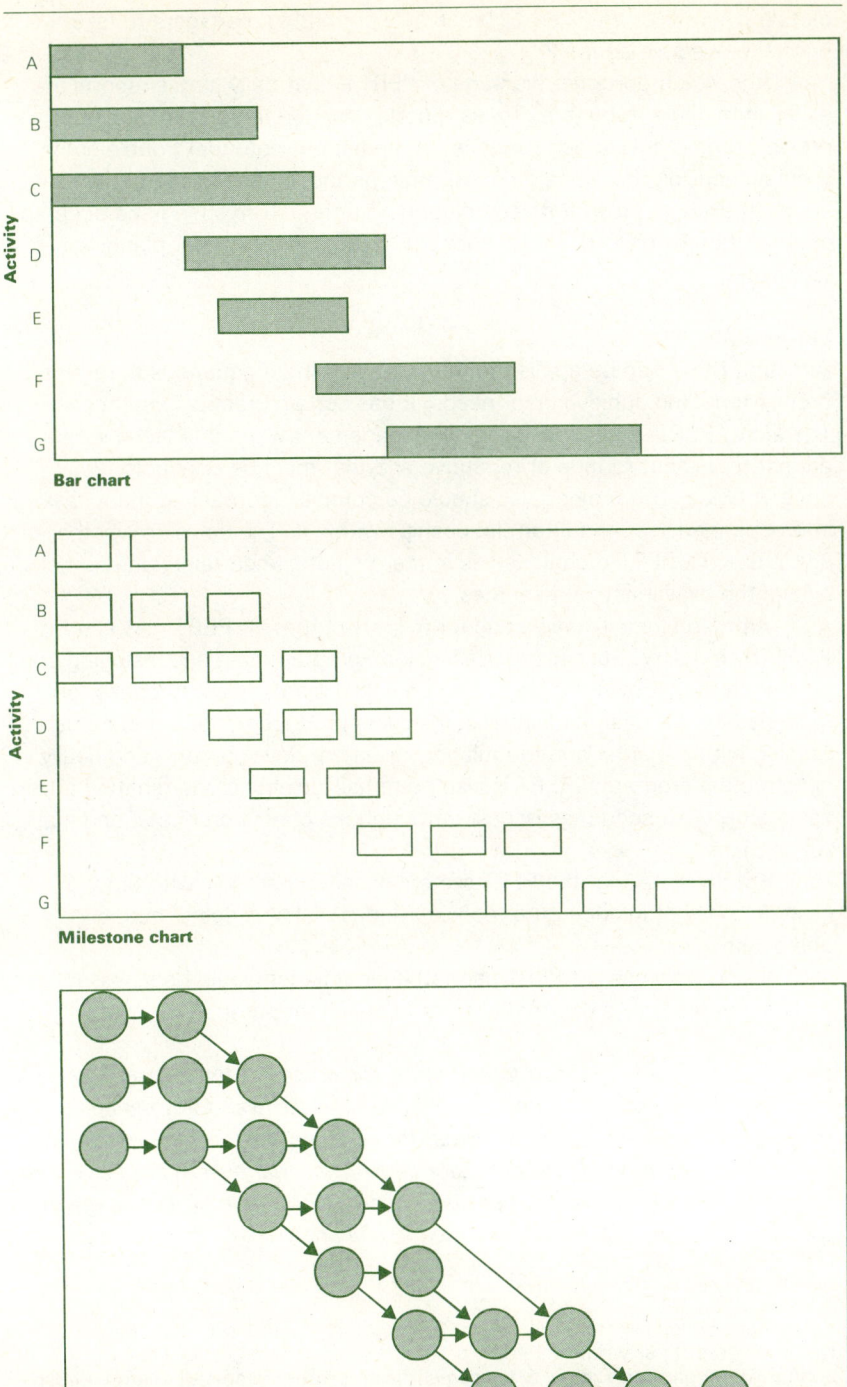

Figure 7-4 The evolution of PERT
Source: Harry F. Evarts, *Introduction to PERT* (Boston: Allyn and Bacon, 1964), pp. 16–17. Copyright © 1964 by Allyn and Bacon, Inc.; reprinted by permission of the publisher.

dicting where fires are likely to break out, permitting managers to take normal preventive action.[10]

Another important advantage of PERT is that daily status reports are easily obtainable through it. These reports describe the current status of a project, predict future performance, and point out potential trouble spots, thereby focusing the manager's attention on those parts of the project that are most likely to prevent its completion on time.[11] The speed and accuracy of simulation with PERT are far superior to those of any other planning technique.

Limitations

Although PERT can be applied in many management situations to reduce project time and achieve labor needs, it has certain practical limitations. Therefore, PERT is primarily used by management when it is faced with a project that is not routine or repetitive and that must be conducted only once or twice. The project also should be complex, containing many tasks, interdependencies, and interrelationships within it. The decision whether or not to use the PERT technique lies in the project's uncertainty and complexity and the availability of resources.

Although initially developed for military purposes, PERT now is used widely by industry. Successful uses include programming and installing computers; shutting down and restarting chemical plants, blast furnaces, oil refineries, and similar installations; installing production control systems; running pilot projects; and formulating research, development, and heavy construction programs. PERT is also potentially useful in coordinating advertising programs, securities issues, introductions of new products, and marketing plans.

Strictly speaking, the PERT system is concerned only with time; of itself, it does not include other considerations, such as costs, quantity, and quality.

If one weakness of PERT had to be identified it would be its essentially passive character. As one management consultant put it:

the input information is rearranged, but it still comes to the manager as a mass of information which he must analyze himself. Even for [managers] who might become skilled in such analysis, the time required would undoubtedly reduce their action effectiveness accordingly. [The manager's] prime responsibility is still to take action, rather than absorb information. The manager has plenty of data; what he needs is a meaningful analysis.[12]

---

[10] K. L. Dean, *Fundamentals of Network Planning and Analysis* (St. Paul, Minn.: Univac Division of Sperry Rand, 1962), p. 12.

[11] John S. Baumgartner, *Project Management* (Homewood, Illinois: Richard D. Irwin, 1963).

[12] Ibid., p. 48.

Designing the network

PERT methodology requires complete project planning: full consideration and detailed specification of all activities and their interrelationships. Failure to plan completely would lead to an incorrect solution.

In order to design a PERT network, one must first prepare a list of all activities necessary to complete the project. After the network has been designed, the next step is to make estimates of the time required to complete each activity. In order to achieve accuracy, those persons who are most familiar with the activity are generally requested to make three estimates: (1) an optimistic time (t_o), the length of time required if no complications or unforeseen difficulties arise in performing the activity; (2) a pessimistic time (t_p), the length of time required if unusual and unforeseen complications arise in carrying out the activity; and (3) a most likely time (t_m), the length of time in which the activity is most likely to be completed. These three time estimates are used to arrive at a statistically weighted average time, the expected time or elapsed time, (t_e), for the activity.

The expected time is calculated by the formula $t_e = (t_o + 4t_m + t_p)/6$. Logically, the expected or elapsed times, t_e, for the various activities can be used to calculate the earliest expected time (T_E) that an event can be expected to occur. T_E is equal to the summation of activity times from the beginning to a given event.

A simple PERT network is shown in Figure 7-5. Working backward from the final event through the network, we can determine the latest allowable time (T_L) for the events by deducting t_e. The latest allowable time is the latest time an event can occur without affecting completion of the final event. Whenever for an event T_L is greater than T_E, that event can be delayed for the amount of the difference without affecting the outcome of the project. This difference is called slack (S), and the ability to determine it is one of the outstanding characteristics of PERT. The path with the least slack is the longest one between the beginning event and the final event. The *critical path* is the sequence of activities linking the starting time with the final event that requires the greatest expenditure of time to accomplish.

Other uses

The foregoing discussion should have clarified our earlier point that PERT is not only a significant planning tool but also a powerful controlling one. Having a PERT program enables managers to concentrate their attention on critical activities. With the help of the information received on slack time and the critical path, managers can direct attention to those aspects that require corrective action. A manager will know precisely which item is out of control and what to do about it and it alone. If the item is on a slack path, then possibly no action is necessary. If an item on the critical path is not on time, however, then managers may marshal resources from a slack path to aid those activities on the critical path in need of help and correction. PERT provides managers with a wealth of information that normally is not easily

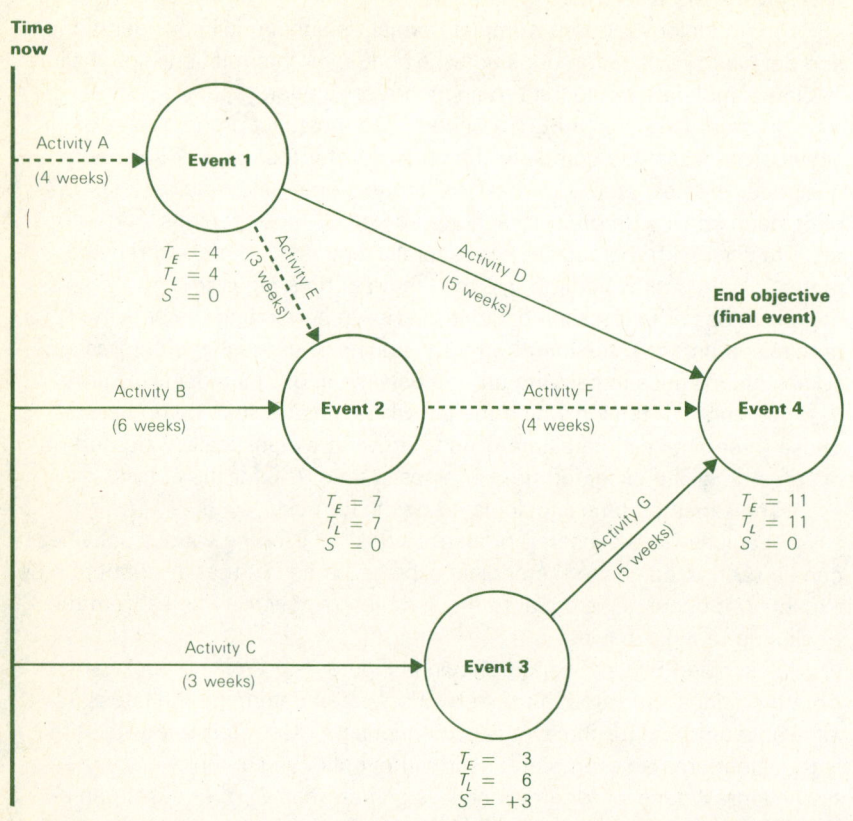

Figure 7-5 A PERT network. The critical path (dashed line) is 11 weeks in length, from "Time now" to 1 to 2 to 4.
Source: Adapted from John S. Baumgartner, *Project Management* (Homewood, Illinois: Richard D. Irwin, 1963), p. 167.

accessible. By isolating critical areas and focusing managerial attention on them, PERT in itself is an application of the principle of management by exception.

The advantage of PERT can be seen more clearly by considering that when a program that is not on PERT is behind schedule, the whole program may require overtime. PERT, however, will enable managers to decide exactly where the overtime would do the most good.

Limitations of planning

While considering the specific limitations of PERT and other short-range planning techniques, managers must also bear in mind the more general limitations on the overall planning process. These limitations exist in spite of the thoroughness with which managers may have established the process's premises, chosen its techniques, and gone about its planning. Planning is looking into the future. The accuracy of forecasts and the premises derived from them is one of planning's limitations. As long as managers recognize these limitations, they will plan flexibly, providing alternatives to enable them to switch plans if need be. Managers must also know that the further in the future their plans are, the less reliable they will be. The nature of the enterprise may also limit planning. As we have demonstrated, the dynamic rate of change in industries may play havoc with plans.

Internal limitations

Philosophy

In addition, other internal and external planning limitations exist. Often a certain philosophy of management has become so ingrained in an enterprise that it limits planning. For example, a company that has been manufacturing a high-cost, high-quality product for many years may find its quality concepts to be so deeply embedded in the minds of managers and employees that it cannot plan and carry out successfully the manufacture of a cheaper product. Or if a company has been working on the philosophy of cost-plus, it will be difficult to change this basic attitude. Again, companies that have grown very rapidly may not have made the necessary transition to large-scale thinking. In contrast, companies that have expanded greatly to meet emergency production conditions often find retrenchment and planning difficult when the emergency is over.

Previous decisions

Another serious internal limitation on planning is caused by previous decisions and actions. Once capital has been invested in equipment, future planning is limited. In some planning situations, a manager might be wise to disregard an ill-advised sunken cost; in practice this is difficult. To this extent, then, capital already invested puts limits on the flexibility of planning. Some aircraft companies, for example, are attempting to convince the commercial airlines that the new generation of aircraft should be a derivative — a modification — of present models. The resulting advantages of using present equipment are obvious.[13]

Consider another example. One of the authors has been involved in research and consultation with the nursing home industry. Nursing home administrators are faced with a difficult planning situation. First, they do not have a strong tradition of managerial planning. Second, governmental regulations are putting increasing pressure on them to upgrade the quality of their services; this pressure requires more sophisticated planning. Finally, to the administrator the regulations change so rapidly from year to year that they are most difficult to forecast. Thus, nursing home managers are caught in a Catch-22 paradox; the forces requiring planning (regulations) are highly unpredictable. It is not easy to plan for the unknown.

[13] Richard Within, "Aircraft Industry Must Make 1980's Decisions Very Soon," *Sunday Oregonian,* September 5, 1976, p. F7 (New York Times News Service).

Expenses and time

Expenses and time are also real limitations to planning. No more expense should be incurred in planning than will be recovered from ensuing benefits. For all practical purposes, a large company can afford a greater amount of planning than can a small company. However, even a small company sometimes can afford substantial plans, especially when the plans cover repetitive operations that, if properly planned and executed, can provide large savings. In such circumstances, planning involves expense but it will still pay off. The more detailed the plan, the greater the expense. Likewise, the longer the plan runs into the future, the costlier it will be. Wise managerial judgment is necessary to balance the expense of preparing plans against the benefits derived from them.

Occasionally, time itself seriously limits planning. Planning is time consuming, and when time is important, the span available will necessarily dictate the thoroughness and pervasiveness of the planning. In most organizations with a good record of planning, conditions of this sort do not occur too often; if they do, prompt action is sometimes more important than the advantages of thorough planning.

External limitations

A number of external planning limitations—conditions of the external environment over which managers have little or no control—also exist. Overall national and international climates are examples of such external conditions, as are the policies of large unions. Each of these can place serious limitations on managerial planning. Consider, for example, the long-standing tension between labor contracts and the steel industry's plan for further mechanization and automation. According to industry, further mechanization will call for changes in certain working conditions and will be outlined in future contracts. If the union is not willing to agree to them, revision—often resulting in significant planning limitations—may be necessary. Managers simply will not be able to plan on as much mechanization and automation as they would like to because of such limitations.

This completes our discussion of the planning function. By any measure, planning is in its infancy compared to the other managerial functions. The contrast is particularly striking when we compare planning with the organizing function, described in Part III. Indeed, the subject of organizing and organization is the most developed of all the managerial functions. This is reflected by the large segment of the book given over to the discussion of organizing activities.

Ten ways to keep your planning on target

Corporate planners, like other managers, can benefit from the experience of others. Here are 10 hints that may help your company's planning department stay on target.

Set goals for the planners
Guard against wasting time on nonessentials. William P. Frankenhoff, chairman of William E. Hill & Co., warns against "working things out to seven places." Says Stanford Research Institute's James E. Matheson: "People gather the information they know how to gather, rather than what is important. You need to put your effort where you are not expert."

Stay flexible
Dow Chemical Co.'s director of corporate planning, J. E. Mitchell, says too many plans "are too inflexible and involve too many numbers. We stress fast response time. We worry about getting too bureaucratic." Avoid communicating through computer printouts, says Mitchell. Use people-to-people contact instead.

Keep a balanced outlook
"The point is not to overreact, to understand that when the business cycle is at its maximum rate of change, it is probably the worst possible time to start making changes in your strategy," says General Electric Co.'s Reuben Gutoff. In a year like this, he says, the trick is to position yourself for an upturn in the economy.

Involve top management
Harvard's Professor James P. Baughman says the chief executive officer has more influence on the planning process than any other variable. "He can make or break a plan depending on the vibes he sends out in a crisis," says Baughman. Says Planmetrics, Inc.'s Gary L. Neale: "The real planner—whatever his title—should be reporting to the CEO, or be the CEO."

Beware of future spending plans
Managers always underestimate. "Operating guys never expect to be spending money two or three years from now," says Tyler Corp.'s C. A. Rundell, Jr., "If you look at a division's capital spending program, it will estimate $14-million this year, $8-million next year, but only $4-million for the three years after that."

Test the assumptions behind forecasts
"Operating people depend too much on trade association forecasts, and the economists that trade associations hire are too optimistic," warns Mead Corp.'s William W. Wommack. The problem is compounded, he says, because when "you get two sets of data you tend to believe the one you want."

Reward those who dispel illusions
"The toughest thing to get rid of is the Persian messenger syndrome, where the bearer of bad tidings is beheaded by the king," says William S. Woodside, American Can Co. executive vice-president. "You have to lean over backwards to reward the guy who is first with the bad news. Most companies have all kinds of abilities to handle problems, if they only learn about them soon enough."

Don't focus only on today's problems
"The thing that makes planning most difficult now is the recession," says Johns-Manville Corp.'s Andrew C. Boush. "Operating managers need to get away from everyday firefighting."

Establish goals before you plan
Otherwise, short-term thinking takes over. "The pressure to show short-term earnings-per-share gains," says Cresap, McCormick & Paget, Inc.'s Donald Miller, "is one of the biggest deterrents to effective long-range planning."

Let managers do their own planning
Too often operators are operators, planners are planners, and never the twain shall meet. Exxon Corp., says planner Brice A. Sachs, is moving more of the "hip shooters" (operators) into the ivory tower (planning department). This practice, he says, is one way to "inject into all those macro projections the vitality of real life."

Source: Reprinted from the April 28, 1975, issue of *Business Week* by special permission. © 1975 by McGraw-Hill, Inc.

Summary

Planning is the function by which managers commit resources to the future. Effective planning is facilitated by systems thinking, which reminds the manager that organizational units and activities are interconnected.

Strategy is the instrument of policy; it is the means for carrying out policy. Tactics, on the other hand, are specific activities designed to achieve limited, short-range objectives. Whereas strategy is primarily a top-management responsibility, tactics tend to be formulated at lower managerial levels. The basic dilemma in planning is the trade-off between committing resources and retaining flexibility.

There are several techniques by which managers plan. Chief among them are forecasts, pro forma statements, budgets, and PERT. While these techniques are not infallible, because of both internal and external constraints, they do help managers bring a reasonable measure of order to their jobs.

Discussion questions

1. Suppose you are a football coach. What parts of your job would you consider strategy? long-range planning? tactics?
2. Devise a PERT network that describes your college career. Compare the result with your intuitive feeling about your progress.

Supplementary readings

Kast, Fremont E. "A Dynamic Planning Model." *Business Horizons* 11 (June 1968):63–64.
Lorange, Peter. "Formal Planning in Multinational Corporations." *Columbia Journal of World Business,* Summer 1973, pp. 83–88.
Pollak, Jerry L., and Taft, Martin I. "Urban Planning: Ripe for Systems Analysis." *Journal of Systems Management* 22 (January 1971):12–17. Reprinted in *Dimensions in Modern Management,* 2d ed., edited by Patrick E. Connor. Boston: Houghton Mifflin, 1978.
Schoeffler, Sidney; Buzzell, Robert D.; and Heany, Donald F. "Impact of Strategic Planning on Profit Performance." *Harvard Business Review* 52 (March–April 1974):137–148.
Steiner, George A. "Comprehensive Managerial Planning." In *Contemporary Management: Issues and Viewpoints,* edited by Joseph W. McGuire, pp. 325–350. Englewood Cliffs, N.J.: Prentice-Hall, 1974.
"A Think Tank That Helps Companies Plan: Project Aware Uses Delphi Forecasting to Predict the 1980s." *Business Week,* August 25, 1973. Reprinted in *Dimensions in Modern Management,* 2d ed., edited by Patrick E. Connor. Boston: Houghton Mifflin, 1978.
Wheelwright, Steven C. "Strategic Planning in the Small Business." *Business Horizons,* August 1971, pp. 51–58.

Cases for Part II

Case II/1

The Mohawk Shoe Company

The Mohawk Shoe Company employed about 250 people to manufacture women's shoes in a small community in a largely rural area of southern Illinois. The employees were not unionized, and the company had a good relationship with its workers. Marian Jackson had just started as the supervisor of the finishing room, after working for many years in the New England shoe industry. Her line superior was Carl Sullivan, the plant superintendent.

A few days after Ms. Jackson began work, one of her employees asked for a four-week leave of absence to undergo surgery. Jackson was not familiar with the company's policy regarding leaves of absence. She told the employee that she would answer in a few days.

During the lunch period, Marian had an opportunity to ask Don Adami, the fitting room foreman, about the company's policy regarding leaves of absence. He told her that there was no policy to guide her, and that she should use her own judgment and make her decision depending on the validity of the request. Dissatisfied, Jackson made it her business to ask Jim Levis, the lasting room foreman; he gave the same answer. Obviously, there was no such company policy. Jackson, a newcomer to the organization, was eager to make the right decision.

Before Jackson could think any further about the first request, however, another employee came to her and asked for a six-week leave of absence to go on a trip to Europe with her daughter. Since her daughter was working for an airline, the trip would be at a reduced rate; the employee did not want to miss this chance of a lifetime. Both requests were made when the department was busy working on spring orders, which had to be delivered in time for Easter sales.

Questions

Ms. Jackson would like to know how to decide the two requests.

1. Where should she look for an answer?
2. How could this confusion have been avoided? Who is at fault?

Case II/2

The Central Lumber Company

Jack and Fred Billing are cousins who inherited a small, wholesale lumberyard in a rural community in Iowa. Since boyhood, they had worked part time in the family business; they began working full time after finishing high school and junior college. Their fathers, who had started the Central Lumber Company about forty years ago, have retired recently to their farms. During its forty years of business, this company has been one of the most successful of a number of wholesale lumberyards in the area that sell to retail hardware stores. In the last ten years, one wholesaler after the other went out of business due to lack of managerial talent and to intense price competition. Most of the lumber wholesalers still in business have started to sell directly to consumers; in other words, they are retailers as well as wholesalers.

The Central Lumber Company is the only lumber wholesaler that still caters to a number of hardware stores in the area. Central stocks a large inventory, and frequently it, too, sells at retail to the ultimate user, usually when the local stores do not have the particular merchandise in stock or when customers think they can purchase more cheaply at the yard. However, Central has two separate price lists: a wholesale list (for hardware stores) and a retail list (for ultimate consumers).

As things stand now, Jack and Fred realize that the retail part of their business is only a small portion of its total volume; but that portion is steadily growing. They are wondering whether now would be a good time to leave the wholesale field and enter the retail business completely, or whether they should continue with some retail business in addition to their wholesale activities.

Questions

1. If you were called in for consultation, what would you advise them to do?
2. How should they go about planning such a move?
3. What are some of the areas in which Jack and Fred could use forecasts and assumptions of the future?

Case II/3

The good citizen

The Airway Dress Company has its headquarters in St. Louis. For many years, the firm manufactured all its products in the metropolitan St. Louis area. However, during the last fifteen years it has moved its manufacturing facilities into several smaller communities in Missouri and neighboring Illinois. These small towns were eager to have plants located in them, and they offered the usual incentives—no traffic congestion, low taxes, quiet surroundings, a loyal work force, and so on. Right from the start, management made it a policy to become a good member of the community, not only by providing a substantial payroll for the town, but also by encouraging its local managers and employees to be active in civic activities, clubs, church work, local government, and charity drives.

The employees of the plant in Podank, Missouri, certainly did their share in this respect, and the company's own annual contribution to the Community Welfare Drive has increased each year—it is currently almost a third of the total pledges. It has now reached the point where the chairman of the annual drive "suggests" to the company how much is expected from it as a donation.

Although the company is earning a profit, the intense competition in the industry and the influx of imports from abroad have kept the profit a moderate one. The management of the Podank plant has submitted the question of how much this year's contribution should be to the president of the company at St. Louis headquarters.

Questions

1 If you were the president, how would you decide this matter?
2 Has the company gone too far in being a good citizen?
3 Is all of this a legitimate concern of the company?
4 If you were a substantial stockholder, how would you decide this matter?

Case II/4

The Optico Company

The Optico Company, located near Boston, Massachusetts, manufactures sophisticated optical and photographic equipment used by the U.S. Air Force and NASA. The company was founded early in 1960 by two young scientists, an engineer and a physicist. Ever since its inception, the company has sold primarily to government agencies. By 1974, 98 percent of all sales was to the U.S. government.

At that time, greatly concerned about the firm's overreliance on government business, the board of directors, a group consisting of the two scientist-founders and five persons from banking and leading industrial concerns in the Boston area, urged the executives to diversify the product line. The board suggested that 50 percent of sales should be to the private sector of the economy. Thus, early in 1975, Optico introduced its version of the instant camera, which incorporated a few of the already patented features of Optico's military and space products. The camera was a success; orders began arriving at an unexpected rate, and soon the backlog of orders amounted to millions of dollars. The managers quickly realized that within one year the company's civilian business could amount to $20 million in sales. Because their current volume of government orders was the same size, they had apparently succeeded in achieving their fifty-fifty objective.

In the middle of 1975, a large, national mail order house proposed that Optico produce a special version of the camera for it under one of its brand names. The catalog house was willing to guarantee annual orders amounting to $15 million. This, of course, would change significantly the character of Optico, from a military supplier to one concerned primarily with consumer goods. Because such a change would alter the nature and objectives of the company, as well as involve it in all the problems of producing and merchandising, the proposal was submitted to the board of directors.

Questions

1 If you were on the board, how would you decide?
2 What considerations would sway your decision?
3 If the company made the switch what new planning premises would have to be considered?

Case II/5

The closing of Middletown

The Waggoner Electronics Company, with annual sales over $30 million, has four manufacturing plants. Headquarters and one operating unit are located in Chicago; the other plants are in California, New England, and Middletown, Indiana. The last plant was bought at a low price right after the Korean War. At that time, it seemed more expedient and economical to buy rather than to build a modern plant in a more suitable location.

However, as the years went by, the rapid growth of Waggoner Electronics ended, at least temporarily, and the firm found itself with excess capacity. Therefore, at the end of 1974 the question of closing the Middletown plant arose in the meeting of the board of directors. Middletown was a small town of about twenty-five thousand people, with two large factories employing a total of about five thousand. The Waggoner plant, a smaller enterprise, was located in an older multistory building, and cost studies indicated that the plant's efficiency was significantly less than that of the other three Waggoner plants. The Middletown factory employed about two hundred and fifty people, of which thirty-five were managers and supervisors. The employees of Waggoner, Middletown, belonged to a strong union but had established no contract provisions for plant closure or separation pay.

Most members of the board could see the advisability of closing this factory, but some voiced serious concern about the impact such a closing would have on the local community. Most of the workers were middle-aged, family wage earners who had little prospect of finding employment in the two large factories still operating. Also, there seemed little likelihood that the building could be sold or leased because no new industry seemed to be moving into Middletown. Some of the directors pointed out that a firm has social responsibilities; others took the opposite view, stating that their decision would be based only on company considerations. After a lengthy discussion, the board appointed a three-member committee to work out proposals to ease the social impact of closing the plant and to submit its plans to the board of directors.

Questions
1 Which side of the board would you have supported?
2 If you were on the committee, what areas would your proposal cover? What plans and provisions would you make?

Case II/6

The Elbert Manufacturing Company

Jack Elbert is the president and majority stockholder of the Elbert Manufacturing Company, a small but rapidly expanding enterprise that produces machinery for the metal-working industry. He started the business in 1961 with only a few employees; by 1975 he had seventy-five employees on the payroll. Annual sales increased from $60,000 to nearly $3 million during the same time period.

Elbert wants to pursue his original goal of providing machinery for the metal-working industry. Although he has hardly begun to make a niche for his company in this large market, he realizes that in a few years he may branch out into manufacturing machinery for plastics and other industries as well.

Not surprisingly, the company has been a one-person organization. Elbert realizes that he is trying to do too much; because of the firm's rapid growth he cannot devote enough attention to organizational arrangements, objectives, and goals. Before he delegates authority and creates new departments, Elbert wants to establish policies that will guide the decision making of the managers he plans to appoint. He expressed his intentions to formulate policy in a meeting with his three key people—Sam Powers of the production department, John Seeger from sales, and Ann Fingert, who has been handling the accounting and financial parts of the business. It would not be correct to call these three persons managers; they had been deciding very little without first consulting Elbert.

All three were delighted that company policies were finally going to be specified. Powers urged the president to define policies prohibiting smoking and eating in the plant, because current practices were hurting production. Seeger wanted the president to set down clear-cut policies regarding salespeople's compensation, prompt deliveries, and scheduling of incoming orders, because these would help him in his sales efforts. Fingert wanted policies to cover specific problems, such as the number of voucher copies to be submitted for cash disbursements and the allocation of expenses for repairs and maintenance, that had been the source of misunderstanding.

Questions

1 Should Elbert follow the suggestions of these three people?
2 Are policies needed to solve these problems?
3 What would you suggest if you were Elbert's consultant?

Part III

Organizing

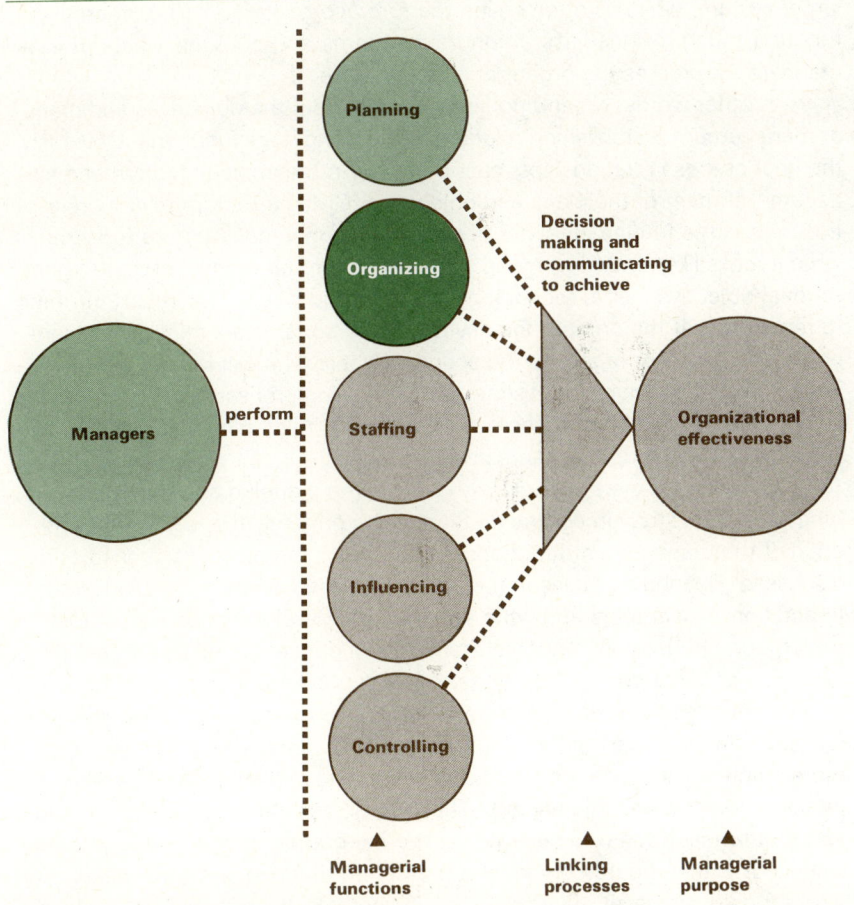

The organizing function Organizing is based on the goals and objectives of the organization, which are formulated through the planning process. Managers design their organization to best facilitate goal accomplishment. In turn, the design establishes relationships among the various parts of the organization. This is the essence of the organizing function.

Rarely are the systems and contingency concepts so well demonstrated as in the organizing function of management. Organizing, by its very nature, requires managers to think in terms of systems and to design relationships among activities in a way that assures efficient achievement of the organization's goals. The designs that evolve reflect managers' perceptions of the relationships among the parts of the organization and the kind of feedback system needed to control it.

The roots of organizing lie in planning. The designs that emerge from the planning effort reflect the social, economic, and technological experience of the organization and express its expectations in concrete form. The organizing process, then, enables an organization to accomplish its designs by helping managers to plot the activities needed to attain them. These activities form subsystems that are synchronized and harmonized into a larger system, which is often called the *formal organization*. The organizing function thus provides links among subsystems and coordinates them in a manner that creates the organizational structure.

In other words, organizing flows directly from the objectives and plans of management, establishing relationships among work functions. Obviously, the goal of these relationships must be to aid in the implementation and accomplishment of the plans and objectives. Giving structure to work relationships is the fundamental act of organizing. How the structure turns out, what it looks like, and how it works are contingent on many factors—organizational objectives, size, technology, culture, and so on. The important thing to realize is that the organizing activity is impersonal; work relationships are established without regard to the specific people who will function in them. Thus, the tone in which we discuss the organizing process must be impersonal. Later, in the Parts of the book that deal with staffing and influencing, we introduce personal elements into the design.

Although they are very closely related, the planning and organizing functions are a study in contrasts. Planning is probably the least well developed of the management functions; organizing is the most researched and discussed. Recently, studies in the latter area have accelerated still further. In addition, researchers and writers in the behavioral sciences have found the organizing function congenial to their own concepts and research skills.

The study of complex organizations has grown to include subjects traditionally treated in other functional areas: for example, decision making (usually treated as part of the planning function), small-group motivation and morale (influencing), communication (influencing and controlling), and incentives (staffing and influencing). The incorporation of more and more subject matter leads some to believe that the integration of management theory will occur within the framework of organization theory or systems theory. For our purposes, however, we retain the conventional breakdown and analytic separation of the five management functions and deal, in this Part, with classical organization concepts. Nevertheless, many new notions in modern organization theory will be introduced in this section, as well as in other Parts of the book.

Accepted organization theory rests on several major premises: *division of work* is essential for efficiency; *coordination* is managers' primary responsibility in the organization of work; the *formal structure* is the main vehicle for organizing and administering work activities; and the *span of management* sets outside limits on the number of people who are responsible to a given manager.

Organization theory continues to have great relevance to basic managerial problems of work relationships, authority, responsibility, coordination, delegation, and so on. Designing these relationships in the most effective manner possible, taking into account the conditions within which they must operate, is the essence of managers' organizing responsibility.

Chapter 8

Introduction to organizing: Two underlying concepts

Objectives of the chapter

1. To identify and describe two major concepts that underlie the function of organizing.
2. To define *span of management*.
3. To explore the meaning of organizational shape.
4. To relate span of management to organizing.
5. To consider the relative advantages and disadvantages of broad and narrow spans.
6. To define *authority*.
7. To relate authority to organizing.
8. To identify the major sources and types of authority.

Organizing tasks and resources is a dynamic process. It rests, however, on two stable concepts: span of management and authority, as shown in Figure 8-1.

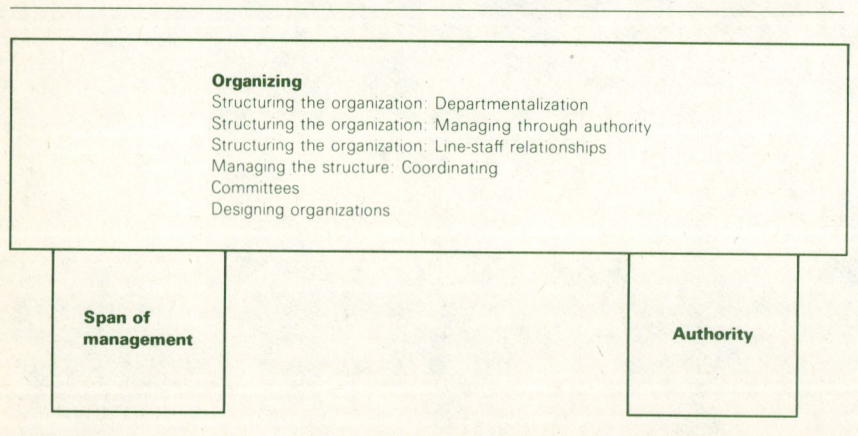

Figure 8-1 Concepts basic to organizing

The first concept is concerned with the *scope of supervision*. Establishing departments and creating levels of management are not ends in themselves. In fact, they are expensive: first, they require department managers and staff, thus raising overall administrative costs; second, as departments and levels are created, coordination and control problems increase. Why, then, should managers departmentalize their organization? The answer: one cannot manage an infinite number of subordinates. Therefore, managers establish different areas of activity—departments—and place someone in charge of each one. The way in which this departmentalizing process is carried out depends on the span-of-management concept, a concept that refers to the number of subordinates who can be effectively supervised by one individual.[1]

The second underlying concept is *authority,* the official basis through which managers command work. Where it comes from and how it is used are of fundamental importance in helping the organization perform its tasks and, thus, accomplish its goals. Goal accomplishment, as we have seen, is the reason that the organizing function is conducted. Therefore, authority is basic to organizing.

An ageless concept: Span of management

That managers cannot supervise unlimited numbers of subordinates is not a new problem. Moses ran into it, and the manner in which he handled the problem is described in Exodus 18:17–26. Moses took his father-in-law's advice:

For this thing is too heavy for thee. Thou art not able to perform it thyself alone. . . . I will give thee counsel. . . . Thou shall provide out of the people able men and place such over them, to be rulers of thousands, and rulers of fifties, and rulers of tens. And let them judge the people at all seasons; and it shall be that every great matter they shall bring unto thee, but every small matter they shall judge; so shall it be easier for thyself and they shall bear the burden with thee.

The same problem, of course, prevails today. How many subordinates can a manager effectively supervise? Despite research, it is not possible to pinpoint the exact number. Some surveys say that, at the upper level, the span of management can embrace four, five, or even eight subordinates. When he was supreme commander of the Allied forces, General Eisenhower had only three line subordinates reporting to him. General Ian Hamilton said, in the early 1920s, that from three to six people is the optimum number of upper-level subordinates:

---

[1] The term *span of management* is often called *span of control, span of responsibility,* or *span of supervision.*

132 Organizing

The average human brain finds its effective scope in handling from three to six other brains. If a man divides the whole of his work into two branches and delegates his responsibility, freely and properly, to two experienced heads of branches he will not have enough to do. The occasions when they would have to refer to him would be too few to keep him fully occupied. If he delegates to three heads he will be kept fairly busy whilst six heads of branches will give most bosses a ten hour day. Those data are the results of centuries of the experience of soldiers, which are greater, where organization is in question, than those of politicians, business men or any other class of men. [2]

What should the proper span be? As the contingency approach suggests, the answer is unclear; it depends on a variety of factors. Let us consider the mathematics first.

Span and organizational levels

Imagine a situation, illustrated in Figure 8-2(a), where there are 256 subordinates on one organizational level reporting to a single executive. Then, assume that the executive decides that 256 subordinates are too many and that only 4 should report to him or her. There are now 64 employees reporting to each of 4 subexecutives. By creating subexecutives, however, we have established two levels of organization and a total of 5 executives [8-2 (b)]. Assume that 64 subordinates are still too many, and this figure is cut to 16. Now, the organization requires three executive levels, for a total of 21 executives [8-2 (c)]. Each of the 5 executives on the upper levels will have 4 subordinates; each of the 16 executives on the lowest level will have 16 subordinates. The span of management has been reduced considerably from the original 256.

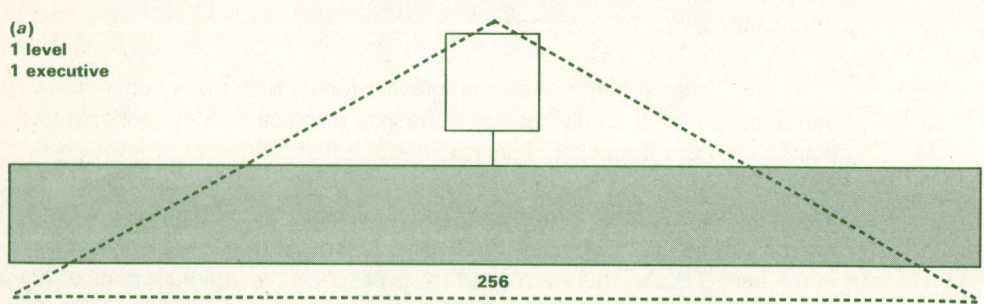

Figure 8-2 Organization levels and spans of management

[2] Sir Ian Hamilton, *The Soul and Body of an Army* (London: Arnold, 1921), p. 229.

133 Introduction to organizing: Two underlying concepts

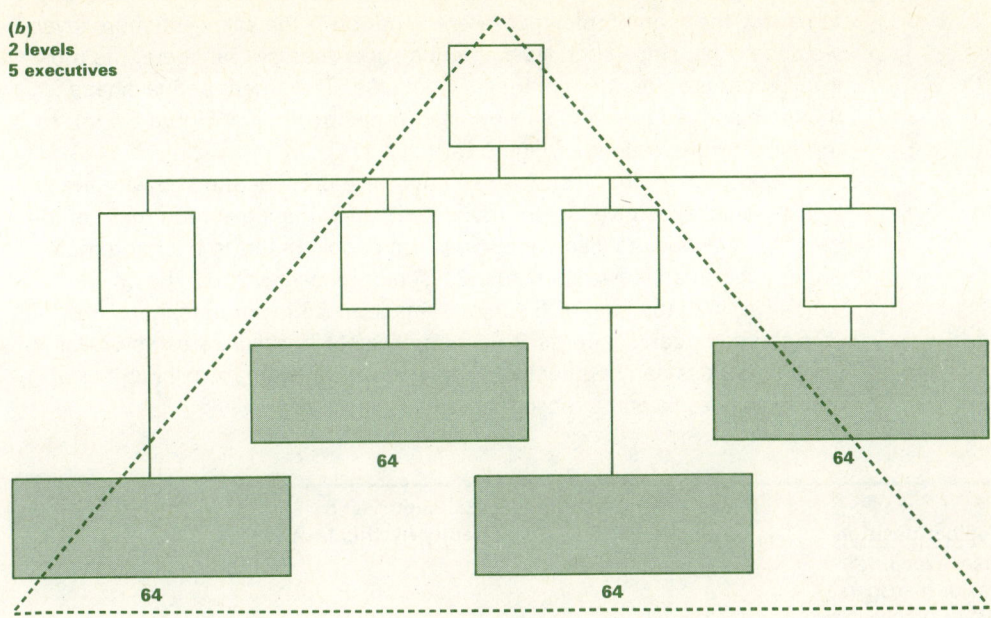

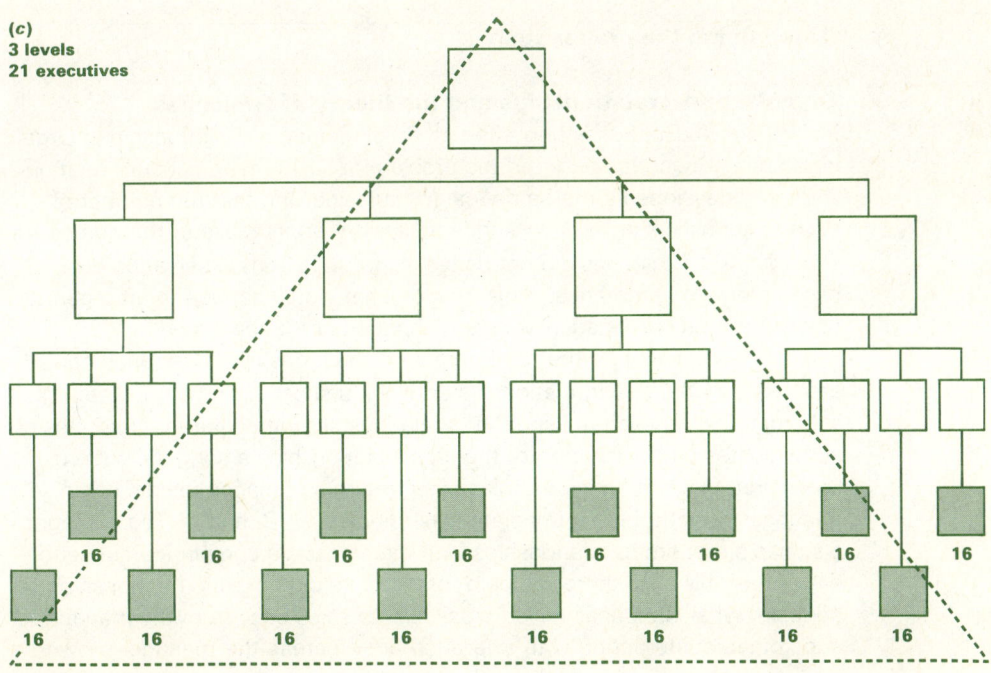

Figure 8-2 (cont.)

This obviously extreme example illustrates what occurs when we begin to narrow the span of management: the narrower the span, the more levels we need. And, since each level must be supervised by managers, the more levels there are, the more managers we need. The organizational shape is thus transformed from the shallow, flat, broad pyramid of Figure 8-2(a), to the tall, narrow pyramid of Figure 8-2(c).

Consider another example: an enterprise of moderate size with five levels—chief executive, senior managers, junior managers, foremen, and clerks or line workers (see Table 8-1). Ten people report to each foreman, and 6 junior managers report to each senior manager. Thus, the chief executive, with the help of 6 senior managers, 36 junior managers, and 216 foremen, can supervise 2,418 employees. This illustrates how a fairly large enterprise can be effectively managed, even with a small number of supervisory levels and a reasonably small span.

Table 8-1 Levels of supervision

Level	Typical position	Number of persons on this level	Total supervised directly by this level
1	Chief executive	1	6
2	Senior managers	6	36
3	Junior managers	36	216
4	Foremen	216	2,160
5	Clerks and line workers	2,160	—

Determining the proper span

Organizational relationships and the theory of Graicunas

In 1933 V. A. Graicunas published an article entitled "Relationship in Organization."[3] Graicunas analyzed the problem of subordinate-superior relationships and developed a mathematical formula showing that the number of such relationships increases exponentially with an increase in the number of subordinates. Graicunas did not derive his formula from observation but based it on a mathematical projection of what would happen to an organization if the span of management were changed at the top.

When calculating the total number of relationships, Graicunas considered not only the direct relationship between a superior and immediate subordinates, but also the superior's relationships with different groupings of subordinates and, furthermore, the cross-relationships among the subordinates. For example, in a particular organization a manager has direct single relationships with three immediate subordinates, B, C, and D. The manager also has direct group relationships with each possible combination of subordinates. In this case there will be a total of nine direct group relationships. In addition, what Graicunas called *cross-relationships* arise from the manager's subordinates interacting with one another. Whereas the manager's own

---

[3] Reprinted in Luther Gulick and Lyndall F. Urwick, eds., *Papers on the Science of Administration* (New York: Institute of Public Administration, 1937), pp. 183–187.

direct relationships with individuals increase in proportion to the addition of subordinates, the group relationships and cross-relationships increase much more than proportionately.

Graicunas' formula is expressed by this equation:

$$R = n\left(\frac{2^n}{2} + n - 1\right)$$

where R equals all types of relationships that might concern management and n is the number of subordinates. By substituting various values for n, we can determine their effect on R. The results of substituting values of 1 to 10 are shown in Table 8-2.

Table 8-2 Total possible relationships with variable number of subordinates

Number of subordinates	Total number of possible relationships
1	1
2	6
3	18
4	44
5	100
6	222
7	490
8	1,080
9	2,376
10	5,210

From this table, we can see that 4 subordinates and their superior can engage in 44 relationships. If, however, 1 more subordinate is added, 100 relationships result. This illustrates the exponential increase that results from adding even 1 subordinate. A 25 percent increase in the number of subordinates will result in 127 percent increase in possible relationships.

Contingency factors in determining the span

The key word in the last sentence above is *possible*. There actually will be far fewer relationships, since employees do not engage in every working relationship possible. There are several organizational and managerial factors that influence the determination of the proper span.

First, clear and complete organizational *policies* can markedly reduce the amount of time a manager must devote to making a particular decision—especially if the decision concerns a recurring problem. The more comprehensive the policies, the larger the span of management can be.

Second, the availability of *staff experts* to provide timely and informal advice to line managers allows them to increase their span. That is, if specialized staff makes a full range of expert advice and service available, managers' time will be freer, and their span can be wider.

Third, high *subordinate competence* increases the number of people that a manager can supervise effectively, because the manager can allow these subordinates to exercise their discretion. As a result, close—and therefore time-consuming—supervision is not necessary.

Fourth, the application of *objective standards* influences relationships and thereby affects the proper span of management. Objective standards—for example, a weekly schedule with clearly identified milestones—enable people to check whether or not they are on the right track. They therefore do not need to report to their supervising manager very frequently. Also, objective standards make it possible for a manager to concentrate on exceptions—areas where performance is deviating from expected results.

Finally, the *nature of work* performed under the manager's supervision is significant. If the work is uncomplicated, a larger number of subordinates can be supervised effectively. Part of the reason for this is that supervision is often built into work processes. For example, the pace of work on an assembly line is controlled by the speed of the conveyors. Generally, the simpler and more uniform the work, the greater the number of persons who can be supervised by one superior.

This point is emphasized time and again by Lyndall Urwick. In particular, he states that if the work of subordinates does not interlock, there is less need for extensive subdivision, or levels of control; therefore, a broader span is possible. He cites Sears, Roebuck to illustrate that there is no reason why twenty stores situated in different towns and operating on a more or less standardized pattern should not be controlled effectively by a single executive.[4]

If on the other hand, the manager supervises activities that are highly important and complicated, the span of management must be small or a great deal of authority must be delegated. Thus, the district manager of a company that runs a chain of small discount or outlet stores in several cities will probably be fully taxed by supervising just five or six store managers. Competitive factors are more intense:

The stores are harried by the unfriendly attitude of local merchants and the outright opposition of some manufacturers. There is little policy or procedure to guide him, so the store manager is forced constantly to refer to headquarters or to try to gather facts and decide himself on most operating and management problems.[5]

Span: How large?

As we have seen, the span of management is affected by many factors. We have established that the narrower the span, the more managerial

---

[4] Lyndall F. Urwick, "The Manager's Span of Control," *Harvard Business Review* 34 (May–June 1956):45.
[5] Louis A. Allen, *Management and Organization* (New York: McGraw-Hill, 1958), p. 76.

levels that will be needed. This poses a problem: should an organization have a broader span or more levels? There are advantages and disadvantages to each. Let us first consider the disadvantages of additional levels.

Disadvantages of many levels

Operating a large number of organizational levels requires a larger number of executives. They, in turn, incur a larger expense in executive salaries. In addition to extra salaries, the firm will have to pay the costs connected with extra staff and clerical personnel. In short, levels cost money.

Increasing the number of executives also makes communication more cumbersome. Communications often are distorted as they go up and down the channels of command. The more layers through which they must pass, the greater the danger of omission and misinterpretation. To avoid these difficulties, some executives have decided that contacts between units should be carried out in the most direct way—laterally. However, at the same time, each member of the organization is to keep his or her superior fully informed, thereby ensuring one level of vertical communication. If this practice is advocated by management, many matters can be solved quickly and satisfactorily at lower levels. Fayol suggested this as a solution and proposed a "gangplank" or a bridge to overcome these effects.[6]

There is another disadvantage to an excessive number of levels: loss of morale. Subordinates on the lowest levels of the executive hierarchy could feel discouraged because they never hear directly from the boss. This particular situation is hard to remedy; in large organizations, communicating throughout all levels is virtually impossible. Consequently, efforts to improve human relations have been aimed mainly at the point of direct contact between an immediate superior and a subordinate.

Disadvantages of wide span

Interestingly enough, the problem of morale has been the basis for criticism not only of the excessive use of levels but also of the excessive widening of the management span. Some people have objected to the idea of a limited span on the grounds that it prohibits democratic participation. Those advocating a flat organization pyramid with a wide span of control and few levels of management maintain that this allows a minimum of social and administrative distance. In reply, Urwick and other writers point out that nothing hurts morale more quickly and more completely than poor communication and indecisiveness—the feeling that those in authority do not know their own minds: "And there is no condition which more quickly produces a sense of indecision among subordinates or more effectively hampers communication than being responsible to a superior who has too wide a span of control."[7]

There is no doubt that a careful balancing of the inefficiencies of levels against those of span is necessary. Nevertheless, extending executives'

---

[6] Henri Fayol, *General and Industrial Management,* trans. Constance Storrs (London: Pitman, 1949), pp. 34–36.
[7] Urwick, "The Manager's Span of Control," p. 43.

spans of management, beyond what they can reasonably handle, in order to reduce the number of levels is not necessarily the cure for administrative distance. Of course, it is desirable to restrict the number of levels as much as possible and to eliminate any level that is not vital.[8]

The trade-off problem

Despite the recommendations of Urwick and others, the concept of a narrow span of management is often disregarded. In many instances, span has been increased in an attempt to encourage democratic participation and to discourage feelings of distance. In other cases, managers' desire to keep the chain of command as short as possible has resulted in the same response. They may believe that overly close supervision discourages initiative and self-reliance among subordinates, and they realize that such supervision would be physically impossible if the span of management were large.

In the last analysis, resolving the problem of span versus levels requires a trade-off. Basically, if an organization wishes to avoid the disadvantages of an excessively large number of levels, it must increase the span of management. This inevitably will require granting greater discretion to subordinates so that they may work effectively without continual direct supervisors. In short, to avoid the problem of too many levels, managers must give up some control. This is an organizing decision that managers must be willing to face.

Wide span: Some examples

How do companies respond to the arguments for and against a large span of management? Consider three of the largest.

- *International Business Machines* Between 1940 and 1947, IBM eliminated one of its levels of management entirely. By doing this, it enlarged the job content of foremen and plant managers and reduced that of middle management.
- *Sears, Roebuck* This company studied the problem carefully. It organized one group of stores with a steep organizational pyramid and another group with a wide span of management. In this second group, approximately thirty merchandise managers reported to one superior. Sears then studied sales volume, profit, and morale, and found that the stores with the flat type of organization were superior in all respects to those organized along more conventional lines. The flat organization had been successful because managers who had a large number of subordinates reporting to them had no choice but to delegate authority. This improved not only the subordinates'

[8] Urwick, "The Manager's Span of Control," p. 45. See also Lyndall F. Urwick, "The Span of Control—Some Facts About the Fables," *Advanced Management* 21, no. 11 (November 1956):5—15; and Herbert A. Simon, "The Span of Control: A Reply," *Advanced Management* 22, no. 4 (April 1957):14.

morale but the quality of their performance as well. Also, managers, knowing that they must delegate a considerable amount of authority, took greater care in choosing, guiding, and training their subordinates.

- *Bank of America* This giant financial concern also has a flat organizational structure. It has nine hundred branches in the state of California and in various foreign countries, offering more than sixty banking services. *They all report directly to corporate headquarters.* Top management believes that this enables branch managers to be self-reliant local businesspeople with a maximum opportunity to make judgments and decisions on their own, in many highly specialized and divergent areas. At headquarters, specialists are available, if needed, to provide guidance in each of the many activities. But this does not alter the fact that the nine hundred branch managers are directly accountable to the president.

IBM, Sears, and Bank of America are just a few examples of the recent trend toward a broader management span. Clearly, less weight is being given today to the prescriptions of the early writers, who stated that a manager was able to oversee directly the work of five or, at the most, six subordinates.

A second concept: Authority

We indicated at the beginning of this chapter that the delegation of authority is a managerial process that supports the organizing function. Before we can examine either the process or the function, however, we must familiarize ourselves with a concept that underlies them both—authority. This discussion could be titled "Authority: What It Is"; the discussion in Chapter 10, "Authority: What Managers Do with It."

The source and nature of authority

We generally credit Max Weber, a German sociologist, with providing the classic definition of authority. He defined authority as "legitimate power," which involves the willing and unconditional compliance of subordinates; this compliance rests on their belief that it is legitimate for the manager to give commands and illegitimate for the subordinates to refuse to obey.[9]

Early students of management borrowed from social scientists, including Weber, to buttress their experience-based beliefs about the nature, purpose, and origin of authority. To them it was a necessary building block in the formation of an organization. Henri Fayol spoke of authority as "the right to give orders and the power to exact obedience."[10] He went on to say that

---

[9] See Max Weber, *The Theory of Social and Economic Organizations,* ed. Talcott Parsons, trans. A. M. Henderson and Talcott Parsons (New York: Free Press, 1947).
[10] Fayol, *General and Industrial Management,* p. 21.

authority was not to be conceived of apart from the sanctions, rewards, or penalties that go with the exercise of power.

Since Fayol's time, other views of the nature and source of authority have arisen. Two of those views essentially contradict one another. They are called the *formal-authority*, or "top-down," theory and the *acceptance*, or "bottom-up," theory.

Formal-authority theory

The formal-authority theory is a top-down theory because it traces the flow of authority downward from basic social institutions to top management to subordinates (see Figure 8-3). Even the president of a company receives authority from the board of directors who, in turn, receive their authority from the owners. In formal theory, the ultimate source of managerial authority in America is the constitutional guarantee of the institution of private property:

Under our democratic form of government the right upon which managerial authority is based has its source in the Constitution of the United States through the guaranty of private property. Since the Constitution is the creature of the people, subject to amendment and modification by the will of the people, it follows that society, through government, is the source from which authority flows to ownership and then to management.[11]

This view of authority is consistent with that of Weber, cited earlier. A manager receives the right to issue commands from top management; the command is legitimate because it comes from a legitimate source; therefore, subordinates are obliged to comply. The problem with this view, of course, is that it does not adequately solve some important philosophical questions. Specifically: Does a manager, in fact, have the unquestionable right to command compliance if the order seems immoral or unethical to the subordinate? Even more to the point: Who does confer (or deny) that right? Only top management? Or, do the subordinates have some say in the matter?

Recently one of the authors was told a story. The owner of a small firm had dictated a letter in which he apologized to a client for failing to deliver on a promise. The letter noted that his secretary, whom he named, had misplaced the order. In point of fact, the owner himself had not wanted to deliver and had deliberately let the matter slide until it was too late. The secretary would not type the letter; the owner claimed it was "illegitimate" for her to refuse. Who decides whether a "right to command" exists?

[11] Elmore Peterson and E. Grosvenor Plowman, *Business Organization and Management*, 4th ed. (Homewood, Illinois: Richard D. Irwin, 1958). pp. 84—85.

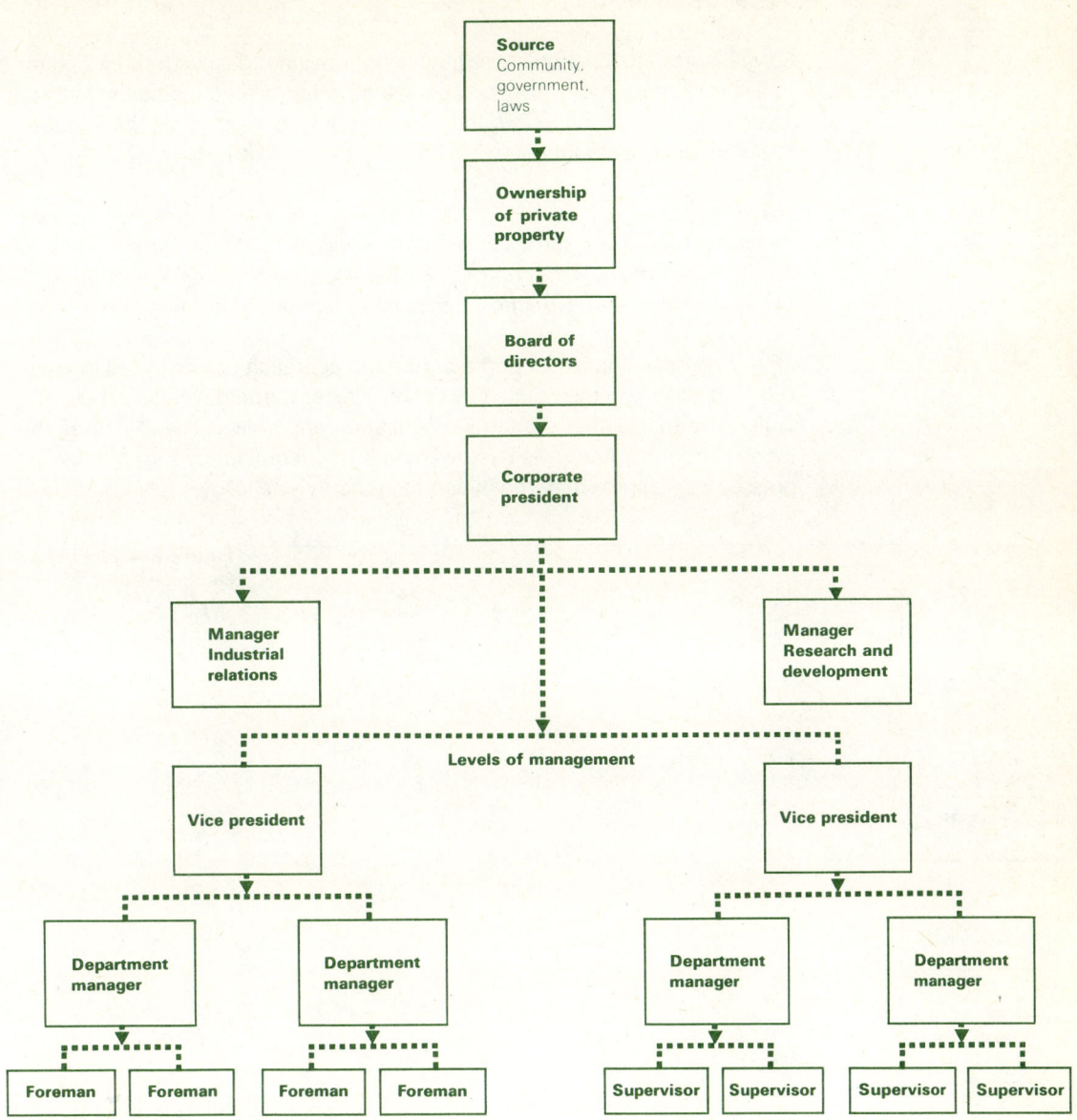

Figure 8-3 Flow of formal authority

Acceptance theory

Formal-authority theory, as we mentioned, does not deal with the problem above very satisfactorily. Several people have formulated a different view. Their position, summarized in the following definition, stresses the acceptance theory of authority:

In joining the organization [the employee] accepts an authority relation; i.e., he agrees that within some limits (defined both explicitly and implicitly by the terms of the employment contract) he will accept as the premises of his behavior orders and instructions supplied to him by the organization.[12]

This definition, reflecting a bottom-up approach, is illustrated in Figure 8-4. It is based on the points of view of Chester Barnard, Mary Parker Follett, Herbert Simon, Robert Tannenbaum, and others. They all agree that management's authority is bestowed on it by subordinates. Barnard expresses his "approximate definition of authority" as follows:

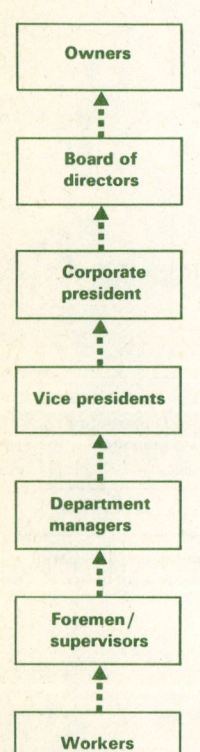

Figure 8-4 Flow of acceptance authority

---

[12] James G. March and Herbert A. Simon, *Organizations* (New York: Wiley, 1958), p. 90.

Authority is the character of a communication (order) in a formal organization by virtue of which it is accepted by a contributor to or "member" of the organization as governing the action he contributes; that is, as governing or determining what he does or is not to do so far as the organization is concerned. According to this definition, authority involves two aspects: first, the subjective, the personal, the accepting of the communication as authoritative . . . ; and, second, the objective aspect—the character in the communication by virtue of which it is accepted. . . .

If a directive communication is accepted by one to whom it is addressed, its authority for him is confirmed or established. It is admitted as the basis of action. Disobedience of such a communication is a denial of its authority for him. Therefore, under this definition the decision as to whether an order has authority or not lies with the persons to whom it is addressed, and does not reside in "persons of authority" or those who issue these orders.[13]

The key aspect of acceptance theory is that a manager has no effective authority unless and until subordinates confer it; that is, although managers may have formal authority, this authority is effective only if subordinates accept it. Essentially, Barnard equates the acceptance of a communication (order) with the acceptance of authority. Barnard also states that a subordinate accepts a communication as authoritative and, therefore, complies only when the following four conditions are met simultaneously:

1 When the subordinate can and does understand the communication.
2 When the subordinate believes that the communication is not inconsistent with the purpose of the organization.
3 When the subordinate believes the communication to be compatible with his or her personal interests as a whole.
4 When the subordinate is able mentally and physically to comply with the communication.

The accept-comply process is this: each individual possesses a "zone of acceptance."[14] An order in this zone will be accepted without conscious question. These orders generally fall within the range of requests and duties that were anticipated when the subordinate accepted employment. As long as this is the case, the subordinate will accept the orders and will comply with the authority that initiated them. If a communication (command) falls outside the zone, the subordinate considers it and then decides whether or not to accept it. The range of compliance alternatives is portrayed in Figure 8-5.

To illustrate the acceptance theory, consider a familiar situation: students sign up for a course, Management 302. On the first day of classes,

---

[13] Chester I. Barnard, *The Functions of the Executive* (Cambridge, Mass.: Harvard University Press, 1938), p. 163.
[14] Herbert A. Simon, *Administrative Behavior* (New York: Macmillan, 1945).

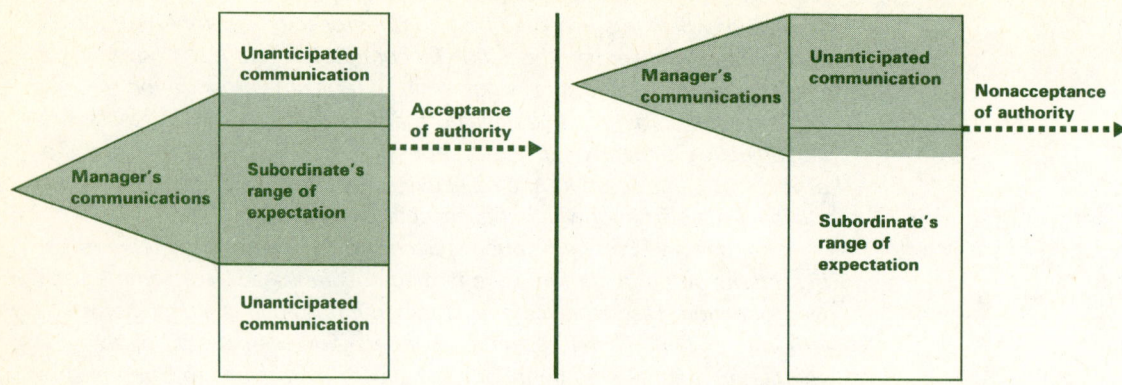

Figure 8-5 Expectations, communications, and acceptance of authority

the professor distributes a syllabus. Pared to its essentials, the syllabus requires the students to perform the following tasks: read a textbook, participate in some classroom activities (cases and exercises, for example), and write two midterm examinations and a final. So far, no problems. The students sigh and go about the term's business.

However, if the professor's syllabus contained an additional requirement—that 20 percent of the course grade would be based on the quality with which the students mow the professor's lawn—what would happen? The answer is obvious. The students would say to themselves, "Wait a minute, are we really going to do this?" They then would decide to mow the lawn or to complain to the professor or to complain to a college administrator or to drop the course. The point is, though, they would *decide*—consciously and explicitly. The command, "Mow the lawn," falls outside their zone of acceptance and the students must decide whether or not to accept it—whether or not the command is legitimate.

The organizational character of authority

Authority comes from everywhere. As Robert Bierstedt says, "Authority is always a property of social organization. Where there is no organization there is no authority."[15] Authority, in other words, is vested in organizational roles. In no way does it belong to the individual who occupies a particular role. Although individuals have the privilege of exercising the authority inherent in their positions in an organization, they do not retain this privilege when they leave. Since organizational roles consist of behaviors

---

[15] Robert Bierstedt, "The Problem of Authority," in *Freedom and Control in Modern Society*, ed. M. Berger, T. Abel, and C. Page (New York: Van Nostrand, 1954), p. 72.

that are consistent with the expectations and requirements of the bulk of an organization's members, authority that is inherent to a role is based on a legitimacy conferred by everyone. The manager of the firm's engineering design department has the right to assign duties to the draftsman in the department because there is an organizational consensus that this function is a legitimate part of the manager's organizational role. The professor has the right to assign readings, cases, term papers, and examinations—but not lawn mowing—to students for the same reason.

Bases of authority

If organizational authority—the right to command others—typically is conferred by consensus of the organization's members, on what basis does this conferral take place? What makes it seem right for one person to obey another? Several people have attempted to answer this question; Weber was among the first. He identified three bases of authority, which he called *traditional, legal-rational,* and *charismatic*.[16]

Traditional authority is, as we might suspect, rooted in tradition, or custom. As Weber wrote, it "rests on the belief in the sacredness of the social order."[17] The lord of the manor, the father in a patriarchal society, the mother in a matriarchal society, all represent rulers whose commands are recognized as legitimate because they have been hallowed by custom.

Legal-rational authority is rooted in the official and rationally enacted rules of the organization. People obey a command because it is consistent with organizational regulations specifying authority relationships. The bureaucratic organization is the clearest example of this basis for authority. Managers give orders and subordinates obey them because this is the way the organization is set up. In Weber's words, "Obedience is not owed to anybody personally but to enacted roles and regulations which specify to whom and to what people owe obedience."[18]

Charismatic authority rests on the personal devotion of the follower to the ruler. The ruler has such compelling personal qualities that the follower accepts commands as inherently right and legitimate. The warrior hero, the prophet, and the great demagogue are all examples of people who rule on the basis of charismatic authority.

Interestingly, in Weber's classification scheme, technical or managerial competence plays a part only in legal-rational authority. Neither custom nor personal devotion depend on the ruler's administrative skill. In Weber's organizational system, however, a manager is selected for a position (office) and allowed to continue in that position—therefore, to issue commands—

---

[16] Weber, *Theory of Social and Economic Organizations.* See also Max Weber, "The Three Types of Legitimate Rule," trans. Hans Gerth, *Berkeley Journal of Sociology* 4 (1958): 1–11.
[17] Max Weber, "Three Types of Legitimate Rule," p. 3.
[18] Ibid., p. 2.

only if the manager's administrative skills are adequate. For Weber, *organizational* authority is based on organizational laws (legal) and the pursuit of organizational goals (rational).

Building on Weber's idea and those of other writers, Peabody examined bases of authority in three organizations: a police department, a welfare agency, and an elementary school.[19] In his study, he asked members of these organizations to describe the kinds of authority they tended to encounter in their work. Peabody concluded that there are four principal bases on which authority rests: external authority, authority of position, authority of competence, and authority of person.

External authority is authority derived from sources outside the organization: "a police officer acts legitimately because the agency he is in is a part of the local government, operating in accordance with laws passed by a city council. The city council, in turn, is elected by the people, who are defined as the ultimate source for all authority."[20]

Authority of position derives from a position or office; it does not derive from the person who happens to occupy that office. Of course, as Peabody points out, a manager who wants to exercise positional authority in an effective manner almost invariably needs some measure of authority based on professional competence and human relations skills.

Authority of competence is based on technical knowledge and experience, not on the person's title. Thus, a command from a member of a bomb squad, an aircraft mechanic, an anesthesiologist, or a gardener may be obeyed, not because of who the "commander" is or what the "commander's" organizational title is, but because of what he or she knows.

Authority of person depends on the unique personal qualities of the ruler. Followers obey because they want to please or help the person giving the command.

Exercising formal authority: there are good days, and there are bad days

During World War II, so the story goes, an army general especially well known for his abrupt and uncompromising command style was on an inspection tour. One day he was visiting an army post that was located in the States and used as a training center, or boot camp. While walking down a street he was thoroughly ignored by a man in fatigues who was working on top of a utility pole. The general told a colonel to have the man report to him; his lack of respect for the general's rank could not go unremarked. The man replied that he was busy and continued working. The general was furious and demanded to know the man's name and company.

The name has long been lost. The company was American Tel and Tel.

[19] Robert L. Peabody, *Organizational Authority* (New York: Atherton Press, 1964).
[20] Joseph A. Litterer, *The Analysis of Organizations*, 2d. ed. (New York: Wiley, 1973), p. 439.

Types of authority

Based on Weber's and Peabody's analyses, we can identify three major types of organizational authority: positional authority, functional authority, and personal authority. A manager might possess all three, but need not. We shall discuss them separately and then see how they interact.

Positional authority

Positional authority is based on acceptance of a manager's position in an organization. Although we have discussed this source of authority extensively, there are several more ideas connected with it.

Positional authority is, in a sense, institutional. Subordinates accept the legitimacy of a manager because they recognize the manager to be an agent of an organization that they believe has social validity. This authority is impersonal; it resides in the position and in the organization in which it is found.

Ultimately, positional authority is bestowed by society. We have seen that the right to manage is inherent in the institution of property which, in turn, is supported by law that flows from the people. This concept applies not only to private property but also to property that is state owned, such as that in socialist countries. In the first case, the delegated right to manage comes from individuals who personally own property; in the second instance, it comes from the state, which administers property in the collective interest of the masses.

We find positional authority in all organizations: religious, military, educational, fraternal, and service, as well as business. The nonbusiness organizational structures likewise rest on social acceptance of those who occupy their positions of authority. Employees, church members, or soldiers may not like a particular executive, minister, or officer, but they comply because of the legitimacy of that individual's position. Soldiers often are reminded that they are not saluting the person but the uniform.

Conventional organization theory has concentrated almost exclusively on this type of authority. As a consequence, vertical superior-subordinate relationships have been the focal point for discussions of authority as a form of influence. There are, however, other dimensions to authority that are not based on the legitimacy of the position.

Functional authority

People will accept, follow, or be influenced by an expert; authority based on expertise is called *functional authority*. The influence that an expert exercises is quite different from positional authority. We accept experts' advice because we recognize that they know more about a subject than we do. However, we must need an expert's knowledge in order for us to be influenced. The needs of students of management, for example, draw them to professors of management and to executives, not to engineers and technicians.

Functional authority exists in all the traditional branches of learning and crafts as well as in business and arises from the division of labor and specialization of work. In business, functional experts emerge in organizational planning, sales, finance, accounting, production, research and development, personnel, and so on. The expertise enjoyed by people in a particular functional area often creates a firm bond of allegiance between superior and subordinates.

Whereas positional authority is impersonal, functional authority is mixed. In one sense, it is highly personal; an *individual* possesses knowledge, skill, and information. On the other hand, society in general and organizations in particular require that specialized roles be filled. Rewards are offered to encourage people to learn the skills needed to perform the functions of these roles. If the functions become obsolete, those having skills in them are displaced. We frequently label this *technological displacement,* but it may reflect changing values. For example, there is less demand today for scholars of classical Greek than there is for accountants.

In conclusion, functional authority, like positional authority, rests on acceptance. However, functional authority stems from a legitimate base of knowledge rather than from a legitimate social institution.

Personal authority

We will not devote much space to personal authority here, since we analyze a parallel subject in Chapter 24. However, we should reemphasize several points at this time. First, personal authority is closely associated with an individual. Unlike positional or functional authority, it is not based in social institutions. As its name suggests, its rests on an individual's personal attributes—a kind of personal magnetism by which a ruler is able to command followers. People accept personal authority because they see that the stated aims of the leader are consistent with their own needs. The appeals of the great national and religious leaders of the past have attracted those who felt similarly and therefore were quite willing to accept the legitimacy of the spokesperson.

However, personal authority is not restricted to well-known historical figures. It is found among managers in business organizations, soldiers of all ranks in the military, administrators in education, and so on. Although the scope of a leader's appeal is restricted in these cases to people in immediate contact, nevertheless the influence of such personal authority on behavior is real. It is capable of motivating people to spontaneous cooperation in pursuit of individual as well as collective goals.

Interaction of the sources of authority

We have now seen in broad outline the three types of authority found in organizations. Managers must rely on at least one type of authority to secure willing collaboration from others, or their effectiveness will be reduced considerably or blocked completely.

In most modern organizations, in fact, managers cannot rely exclusively on a single source of authority to ensure acceptance. In the past, most people believed that it was sufficient to base one's right to manage on the legitimacy of the social institution. This attitude was related to the idea that managers would automatically receive compliance from and be accepted by subordinates, because they represented the property rights of owners.

Such views have changed tremendously. Now, authority must be earned by demonstrating expertise in a given area, by exhibiting personal leadership ability, or both. Business itself is experiencing major technological changes that have forced modifications in the occupational character of employees. More and more experts are being employed. They, in turn, place greater weight on the role of functional authority.

Much the same can be said regarding personal authority. People entering the work force today expect more than simple economic satisfaction from their jobs. Therefore, management must develop a climate of satisfaction designed to fulfill a wide range of human needs.

However, these newer developments do not entirely undermine the practical significance of positional authority as a form of influence. Positional authority is still important in modern organizations, but contemporary managers view it as only one of the several bases on which they can gain acceptance.

Summary

We have introduced this Part by describing two fundamental concepts that underlie the process of organizing. The first concept is known as span of management; it refers to the number of subordinates a manager can supervise effectively. Authority, the second underlying concept, has to do with the right to give commands and expect that they will be complied with.

For a given number of people in an organization, managers find that if they reduce the span they will have to increase the number of levels in the hierarchy. Organizational managers must deal with this trade-off. Too many organizational levels may produce distorted communications; a narrow span, on the other hand, allows the manager to supervise closely and helps reduce employees' feelings of distance from their supervisor. There also can be problems with too few organizational levels. Although messages do not have very far to travel vertically, a large number of subordinates may make it extremely difficult for the manager to communicate with them.

There has been some debate over the years as to the source of authority. The formal-authority theory, the top-down view, holds that the right to command others comes from the top—higher management, shareholders, the general public. The acceptance theory, or bottom-up view, holds that authority comes to the ruler from those who are ruled. Subordinates' zone of acceptance determines the range of commands that are perceived by them to be a legitimate part of the manager's job.

Finally, various management writers have suggested several bases of authority: traditional, legal-rational, charismatic, external, positional, competence, and personal. Based on these suggestions, we can identify three major types of organizational authority: positional authority, functional authority, and personal authority. In modern organizations, effective managers tend to exercise command using a blend of these types appropriate to their individual managerial situations. We will explore this situational aspect of organizing in successive chapters.

Discussion questions

1 A foreman in a manufacturing company was heard to say: "These folks from the production control department come down here, restudy jobs, and change job standards. Then they walk away and leave us to sell our people on the idea that they should work harder to make the same money." What problem in organizational authority is bothering this foreman?
2 Apply the ideas of span of management to family life. Consider, for example, differences that probably exist between a family of one child and a family of four children.
3 We discussed the trade-offs between levels of span. Thinking ahead, what other variables enter into this exchange?
4 Thinking of your own career prospects, would you be happier as a subordinate in an organization with a narrow span of management or in one that has a broad span? In which organization would you prefer to be a manager?
5 What are the bases of your professors' authority over students? What does your answer suggest about the interaction of authority types?
6 What are some assumptions—about work, managing, and human nature, for example—that underlie any discussion of span of management?

Supplementary readings

Barnard, Chester I. *The Functions of the Executive.* Cambridge, Mass.: Harvard University Press, 1938.

Carzo, Rocco, Jr., and Yanouzas, John N. "Effects of Flat and Tall Organization Structure." *Administrative Science Quarterly* 14 (June 1969): 178–191.

Koontz, Harold. "Making Theory Operational: The Span of Management." *The Journal of Management Studies,* October 1966, pp. 229–242. Reprinted in *Dimensions in Modern Management,* 2d ed., edited by Patrick E. Connor. Boston: Houghton Mifflin, 1978.

Peabody, Robert L. *Organizational Authority.* New York: Atherton Press, 1964.

Simon, Herbert A. *Administrative Behavior,* 3d ed. New York: Free Press, 1976.
Urwick, Lyndall F. "The Manager's Span of Control." *Harvard Business Review* 34 (May–June 1956): 42–50.
Weber, Max. "The Three Types of Legitimate Rule." *Berkeley Journal of Sociology* 4 (1953): 1–11. Reprinted in *Dimensions in Modern Management,* 2d ed., edited by Patrick E. Connor. Boston: Houghton Mifflin, 1978.

Chapter 9

Structuring the organization: Departmentalization

Objectives of the chapter

1 To describe the fundamental characteristic of all societies: the division of labor.
2 To discuss one particular form of organizational division of labor: departmentalization.
3 To describe various forms of departmentalization—by function, by product, by territory, by customer, by process and equipment, and by time.
4 To evaluate the relative advantages and disadvantages of the different forms of departmentalization.
5 To describe the ways in which managers combine the various forms of departmentalization.

Organizations exist because one or two individuals cannot do a job by themselves. In other words, people establish an organization as a vehicle to perform tasks. This is what organizations are all about. Creation of this vehicle involves the process known as *division of labor*.

Dividing work into specialized units permits a group of people, performing together, to accomplish more than can one individual attempting a whole task alone. The result of dividing work is a pattern of task and authority relationships. Expanded to the enterprise as a whole, we call this pattern the *organization's structure*. In this chapter, we consider the development of organizational structure by means of a managerial process known as *departmentalization*. In successive chapters, we examine other means that are used by managers to develop their organization's structure.

Evolution of the division of labor

The practice of dividing labor is as old as history, but in no area of human endeavor is it more evident than in warfare. From earliest times, armies have been divided into service units—archers, infantry, cavalry, and supply—whose effectiveness resulted from their coordinated use in a commander's strategy and tactics. These military divisions remained unchanged for centuries. An appreciation of the benefits of the division of labor also appears in the classics. Cicero, for example, called it the basis for civilization.

Specialization and efficiency

Centuries later, economists viewed the division of labor as the most important factor in commerce. Adam Smith, in his famous book *The Wealth of Nations*, published in 1776, discussed the division of labor at length, using as his example the manufacture of a pin. The production of this seemingly insignificant item required several operations. Smith observed that several persons, each making an entire pin, produced far fewer pins in a day than did several specialists working together. Production increased when each activity in pin making became the responsibility of a person specialized in that task. The drawing of the wire, the cutting and sharpening of the point, the fitting of the head to the shaft, and the placing of the completed pin in a card were separated; the coordinated use of workers doing each of these tasks created high pin productivity.

The clear connection between specialization and efficiency has led manufacturers to attempt to increase the division of labor. In addition to greater efficiency, division of labor permits the use of relatively unskilled people in simple routine tasks. This, of course, reduces labor and training costs. Division of labor was made possible, in part, by the availability of massive numbers of unskilled workers. These workers, many of them immigrants, have provided the backbone of industrial development in the United States since the late eighteenth century. This situation is changing, however.

Perhaps the greatest monument to specialization and the division of labor is this country's automobile industry, pioneered by Henry Ford in the 1920s. Today, the mass production of cars using semiskilled workers in large numbers is commonplace. The same is true of the radio and television, home appliance, and garment industries. There is little doubt that the division of labor and specialization gave impetus to mass production, which in turn provided the basis of industrialization and the increasing levels of affluence in our society.

The division of labor also resulted in social evils with which we have contended for nearly a century. In the early stages of American industrialization, vast numbers of immigrant workers were concentrated in large urban areas. The human misery associated with slums in New York, Pittsburgh, and Chicago is well known. The attendant evils of crime, suicide, and exploitation are also recorded. We need not review all this, but our discussion would not be complete without the recognition that industrialization in the United States has not been an unmitigated good.

Steps in the division of labor

Through the division of labor, tasks are broken down, as naturally as possible, to allow both mental and physical specialization. Probably the most primitive basis for dividing labor in most societies has been sex. The various activities associated with having and caring for a family, for example, are usually divided among the males and females of a species. But organizations grow beyond the size of the family unit; tasks multiply as technology and products become more sophisticated. In this complex industrial and technological age, people constantly seek to increase their effectiveness. Managers' quest in this regard is reflected in their organization's structure. Let us see how this process works.

One of the first things that happens when people create an organization is that they divide up their work. As the organization grows and tasks become more numerous and varied, this division of labor usually is formalized. Thus, in a new, small manufacturing firm, Michael, Kristen, and Frank might share in performing required tasks. Eventually, however, they will find it necessary for each of them to take on principal responsibility for one set of tasks. The process is diagrammed in Figure 9-1.

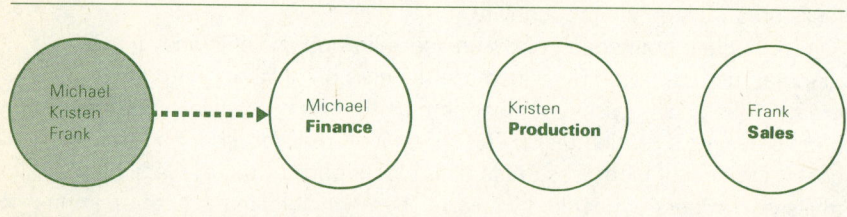

Figure 9-1 Dividing labor horizontally

As the firm grows, experiencing more and more demand for its product, Michael, Kristen, and Frank are likely to hire additional personnel to help them. As the number of employees (and tasks) increases, their organization might take on the relationships depicted in Figure 9-2.

What has happened in Figure 9-2 is similar to what has happened in Figure 9-1. In both cases, labor has been divided into distinct tasks. In Figure 9-1, technical labor was divided (into finance, production, and sales). In Figure 9-2, managerial labor has also been divided, to produce the several vertical levels shown (vice president, plant manager, department manager, foreman). To make the division of managerial labor effective, authority must be delegated; this process is discussed in the following chapter.

Departmentalization

Within each of the managerial levels shown in Figure 9-2, technical labor has been divided: vice president, production; treasurer; vice president, sales;

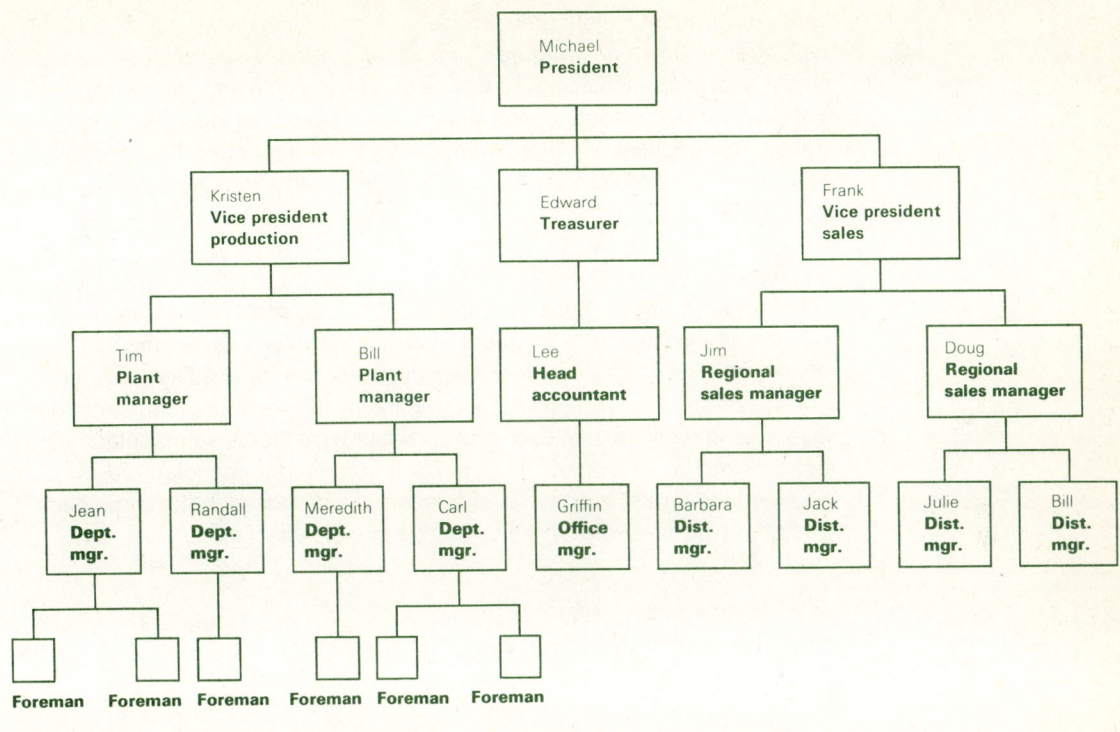

Figure 9-2 Dividing labor horizontally and vertically

two plant managers; two regional managers; several department and district managers; and so on. Dividing technical labor into several departments, plants, functions, and other organizational units is a process known as *departmentalization*. Departments are commonly organized by function, product, territory, customer, process and equipment, or time.

Departmentalizing by function

Grouping activities by the functions of an enterprise is one of the most widely used patterns of departmentalization. All organizations create some product or service. In addition, they often must market their product or service and finance their ventures. Thus, firms frequently have production, sales, and finance departments because these three major functions are found in nearly every business and nonbusiness organization.

The terminology describing basic functions varies considerably. In a distributorship, the production function will be called *buying*. In an airline or railroad, production is called *operations* and sales, *traffic*. One hardly finds a distinct selling function in a hospital, but the "delivery" of health services is common.

That nearly every enterprise has some functional departmentalization is especially evident in young enterprises, which almost always begin with this type of organizational structure. A functional structure seems to be well suited to organizations created by one or a few people and closely supervised by the proprietor(s). Here, the immediate problem is to get things done—the emphasis is on operations. At a later time, after the enterprise has grown, the problem of changing to a different type of departmentalization may arise.

Example

Departmentalizing by function organizes tasks into major functional areas. All work of the same or a related kind is placed under a single chain of command. The manager of manufacturing is in charge of all manufacturing activities throughout the enterprise, regardless of where the plants might be located and regardless of how many product lines are being manufactured. For example, in a company that has been organized to manufacture wooden and metal furniture, both types of furniture are produced in the same plant and both types are sold by the same salespeople (see Figure 9-3).

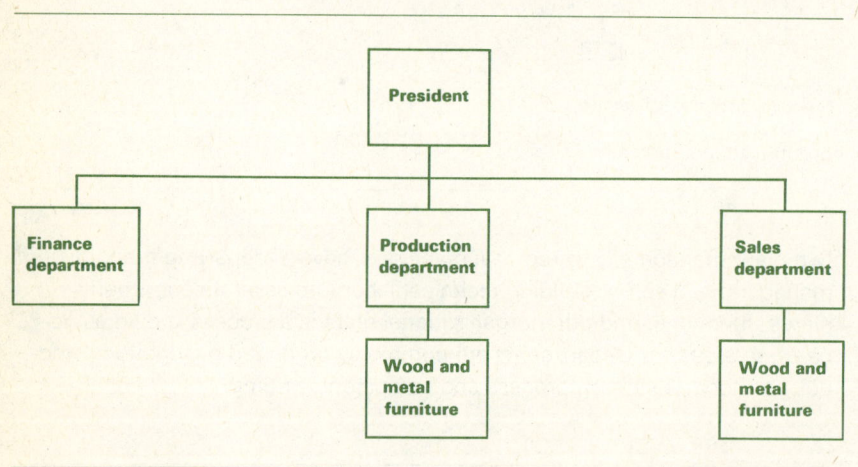

Figure 9-3 Functional departmentalization in a small company

As the enterprise grows, additions are made to existing functions. Such growth, however, necessitates separating the production and sales of wood furniture from those of metal furniture. Separate departments now handle these functions (see Figure 9-4). As we saw earlier, this departmental increase also adds levels to the areas that the managers of functional departments must supervise.

In most companies, managers of the production, sales, and accounting departments report directly to the chief executive, usually the president. These departments have large budgets and employ many people. However, a major department may occasionally become a minor one. For

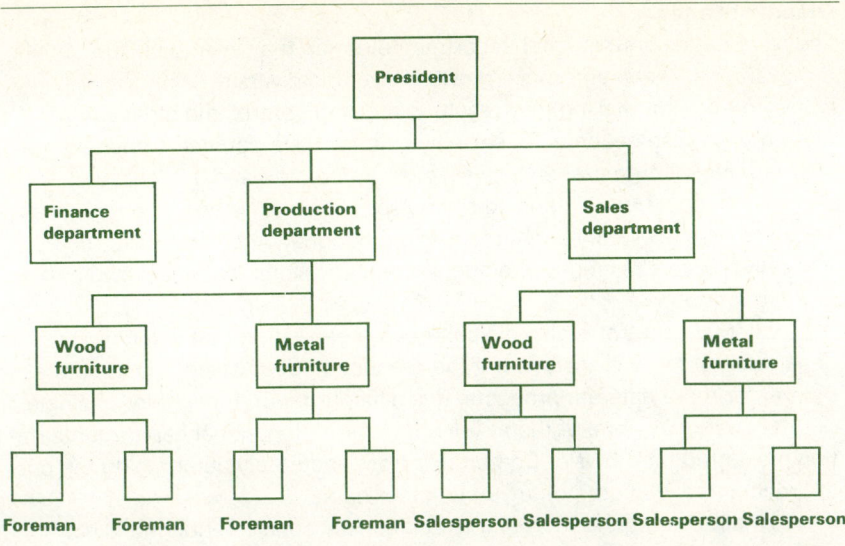

Figure 9-4 Functional departmentalization in a larger company

instance, wartime shortages may transform the duties of a sales force into the mere allocation of the available finished products to customers. This situation changes when the war is over and, with the return of a buyer's market, selling again becomes a major function. Such a change could also work in reverse. Many firms have found that, owing to the acceleration of technological competition in the industry, the once minor function of research and development (R&D) has become their lifeblood. Changes like these remind us that situational factors have a significant impact on the way managers operate or, in this case, organize.

Advantages

Functional departmentalization has many advantages. It provides a logical way of arranging activities. Also, by facilitating specialization, it leads to economical operations. It groups functions that naturally seem to belong together and are performed by the same specialists with the same equipment and facilities. With functional departmentalization, each department and its manager are concerned with one type of work. If production is concentrated in a single department, for example, peaks and valleys in the demand for one product can very likely be minimized by the peaks and valleys of a second product. Thus, both equipment and facilities are used optimally. Additional economies result from pooling and combining a number of administrative activities, such as receiving, shipping, maintenance, and the like. Finally, functional departmentalization also can improve coordination within a single function, because one executive will take the responsibility for all related activity. Coordination is more easily achieved if a single function is not diffused into several different divisions.

Disadvantages

The advantages of functional departmentalization may eventually turn into disadvantages as an enterprise grows in size and diversity. With growth, delays in decision making may result. Exercising control and measuring performance also become increasingly difficult. As a company grows, moreover, additional organizational levels must be created and a larger total number of people must report to supervisors. This slows down communications because, as we already noted, in a functional organizational structure only the chief executive can coordinate decisions that affect two or more functions.

Effective control is also difficult in an organization that is functionally departmentalized. For instance, if the production department manufactures a dozen or more different products, it is difficult, if not impossible, to single out the cost of any one of them. For a long time, functional departmentalization prevented the Chrysler Corporation from accurately determining the cost of producing a Plymouth or any of its other cars.

Finally, an organization that is functionally departmentalized is not a good training ground for all-around managers. Its managers have little opportunity to learn to manage the entire range of the different functions. Instead, they become expert only in their particular function and tend to deemphasize the importance of other functions. Once transferred from a functional position to an executive job, a manager may emphasize that original function. A former sales executive who becomes the president of a company often remains concerned with sales and neglects overall management functions. This, of course, is not really a shortcoming of departmentalization; it is, rather, a shortcoming of the executive. Functional departmentalization, however, can easily lead to this particular kind of managerial preoccupation.

Departmentalizing by product

If an organization continues to grow, sooner or later it must modify its functional departmentalization and adopt another system. When should this change occur? A thorough analysis of the organization is necessary before such a decision can be made. The amount of sales in itself is an insufficient basis for the decision. A firm doing less than $10 million business a year, for example, might efficiently departmentalize by products or territories rather than by functions. On the other hand, it is interesting to note that in 1920, when General Motors switched from a functional structure to product divisions, its annual sales were in excess of $500 million.

Under product departmentalization, an executive is in charge of and responsible for all activities—engineering, manufacturing, selling, and servicing—that relate to a particular product. It is of no importance where the division is located, whether it is close to the home office or geographically removed; the division is organized around a product, not a territory.

Product departmentalization divides a large company into smaller and more flexible administrative units. These units recapture some of the advantages of a smaller functional organization that disappear when the functional organization grows larger. Emphasis on products encourages expansion, improvement, and diversification. There is no doubt that in a functional organization certain products receive more emphasis than others. Although such emphasis is perfectly normal and understandable, it may harm some products, particularly those that require more promotion and more sales effort in order to achieve their place in the market. Problems of this sort are more easily resolved in a product division.

Example

Let us assume that our hypothetical firm now manufactures plastic as well as metal and wood furniture. Having decided to departmentalize on a product basis, the organization takes the form indicated by Figure 9-5, with each product grouping now coordinated at the divisional level. The president retains centralized advisory groups, which help in the overall management of the enterprise. Product departmentalization has proved successful in all functional areas except labor relations, finance, and the like. Since the labor relations department may deal with large national unions, it is essential that it remain centralized. For obvious reasons, it is also desirable that the president and top management should control financial management for the firm. Similarly, market research and R&D should be located on the corporate level. Operating as staff groups, people involved in these activities can lend valuable assistance to all divisions as well as perform needed research functions for the corporation as a whole.

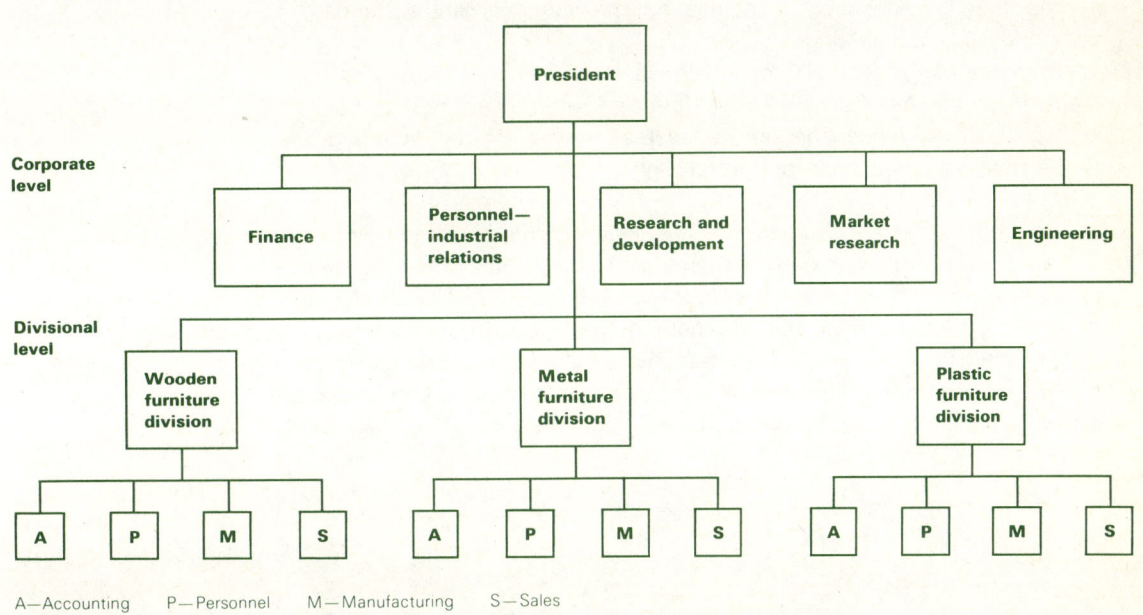

Figure 9-5 Product departmentalization

An organization should consider departmentalizing by products if the characteristics of the manufacturing, engineering, and selling of the particular products lend themselves to it. Each product should be suitable for separation from other products and should be optimized by its own production facilities and sales organization. The various divisions of General Motors—Buick, Cadillac, Chevrolet, and the others—remain among the best-known examples of product departmentalization. The duPont Corporation is another excellent example of an enterprise that, around 1921, decided that product expansion and diversification could best be facilitated by grouping its departments or divisions along principal product lines. Within each division, production, sales, and research were established as line functions. The managers of these three functions remain on the same level as and report directly to the general manager of the individual product division.

Departmentalizing: Not a new problem

In building the organization from the bottom up we are confronted by the task of analyzing everything that has to be done and determining in what grouping it can be placed without violating the principle of homogeneity. This is not a simple matter, either practically or theoretically. It will be found that each worker in each position must be characterized by:

1 The major *purpose* he is serving, such as furnishing water, controlling crime, or conducting education;
2 The *process* he is using, such as engineering, medicine, carpentry, stenography, statistics, accounting;
3 The *persons or things* dealt with or served, such as immigrants, veterans, Indians, forests, mines, parks, orphans, farmers, automobiles, or the poor;
4 The *place* where he renders his service, such as Hawaii, Boston, Washington, the Dust Bowl, Alabama, or Central High School.

Where two men are doing exactly the same work in the same way for the same people at the same place, then the specifications of their jobs will be the same under 1, 2, 3, and 4. All such workers may be easily combined in a single aggregate and supervised together. Their work is homogeneous. But when any of the four items differ, then there must be a selection among the items to determine which shall be given precedence in determining what is and what is not homogeneous and therefore combinable.

Source: Luther Gulick, "Notes on the Theory of Organization," in Luther Gulick and Lyndall F. Urwick, eds., *Papers on the Science of Administration* (New York: Institute of Public Administration, 1937), p. 15.

Other companies also are organized by product division. Department stores, for example, organize each department along merchandise lines. One finds the same product departmentalization, so to speak, in commercial banks. Their loan activities, for instance, are broken down into separate departments for commercial, personal, and industrial uses.

This departmental grouping can at times lead to coordination difficulties within the organizational structure. Also, successful managers of a product division may try to enlarge their empire by acquiring more and more power. Dangers of this sort can be prevented by the existence of a general staff, centralization of finances, and major policy determination by the top management of the enterprise. This, broadly speaking, is the arrangement at General Motors, duPont, and other large enterprises: decentralized product divisions with centralized control—particularly of financial matters—at headquarters.

Departmentalizing by territory

Another way to departmentalize is geographically. This type of organization is frequently used by physically dispersed enterprises, where the various branches produce the same goods or perform similar services at each location. For example, the United States Postal Service and the Federal Reserve System are departmentalized by territories. In all twelve Federal Reserve districts and in all post offices, basically the same functions are performed.

Advantages

Private businesses use geographic departmentalization for several reasons. Often, the needs of the customers or the characteristics of the product demand it. There is little doubt that territorial departmentalization serves the local markets with greatest efficiency. It permits managers to consider particular local circumstances that might be overlooked if activities were functionally departmentalized at headquarters. It also permits managers to utilize local salespeople who are familiar with local conditions. Furthermore, territorial departmentalization produces certain economies. It reduces the cost of transporting raw materials to the plant and finished products to the customer. It cuts delivery time. In addition, geographical groups supply a good training ground for versatile managerial talent. Because territorially departmentalized enterprises perform almost all functions in all territories, a manager's experience will be well rounded. Figure 9-6 shows an organization that is departmentalized on a geographical basis.

Managers must balance the advantages derived from geographic departmentalization against the additional expenses involved. This kind of departmentalization has obvious advantages for companies engaged in the insurance, telephone, railroad, and oil industries. Geographic departmentalization is also important where perishability is a problem, as in the processed-food industry. The advantages of geographic departmentalization are particularly important in production and sales, and therefore they are often handled in this manner. In contrast, there seems to be little reason to departmentalize finances on a territorial basis. As a matter of fact, financial management succeeds best if it remains centralized at headquarters. The

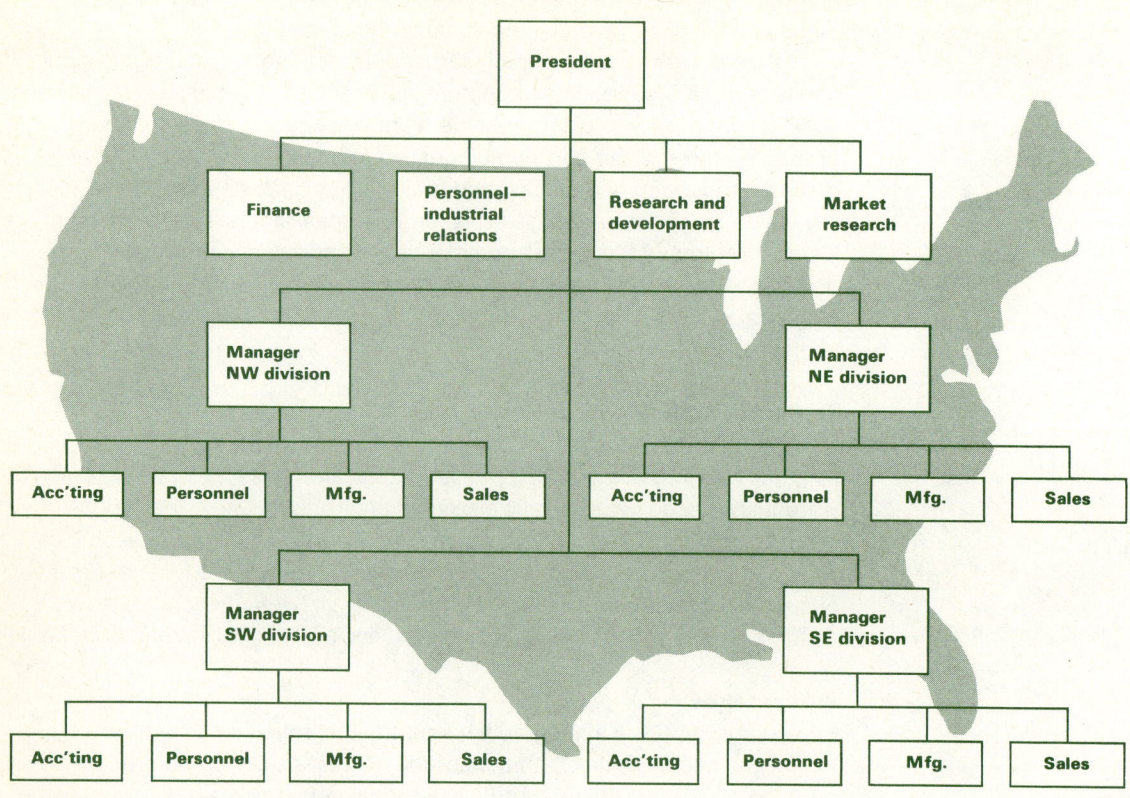

Figure 9-6 Geographic departmentalization

same reasoning holds for the overall personnel function and, generally, for industrial relations. Of course, each region has its own local personnel and finance staff in addition to the centralized staff at headquarters.

Sometimes managers may decide to departmentalize only one of the functions on a territorial basis. Sales, for instance, is almost universally organized along geographical lines. Most firms divide the country into sales territories, and all selling activities are regulated accordingly. In such cases, other functions, such as production, personnel, and finance, remain centralized.

Departmentalizing by customer

Managers also departmentalize based on customer consideration, thereby showing their paramount interest in the welfare of their customers and in the attention given to them. There are many examples of organizations departmentalized along customer lines: a university whose night programs and day programs comply with the requests and special needs of its various "customers"; department stores, which often partially departmentalize by customer as well as by product. Many stores maintain budget departments that carry a full line of merchandise, but of a different quality and at a lower price. Then, again, customers may be classified by age, as are the clientele of the teen shop in a department store. Manufacturers of motors, likewise, may distinguish among industrial users, distributors, and institutional customers.

Sales activity is often the function best suited to departmentalization on a customer basis. Salespeople who call on industrial users are better qualified to deal with these customers than if they were to call also on distributors and institutional customers. The various groups of customers have different needs to which the enterprise must cater. However, the production function of an enterprise need not be departmentalized in a similar manner. It is unlikely that a manufacturer of electric motors would differentiate in its line among motors bought by industrial users, distributors, or other customers, although it might manufacture different types of motors to suit each set of customers. There is also little likelihood that the overall finance function would be broken down along customer lines. However, a derivative finance function, such as consumer credit, can be separated as a distinct activity. The General Electric Credit Corporation is an example.

The advantages of customer departmentalization also bring with them disadvantages. Frequently, there will be pressure for special treatment and special consideration for certain customers. And, customer departmentalization may result in the underutilization of some company facilities. In some instances, the disadvantages of customer departmentalization are overshadowed by the advantages; an enterprise has much to gain by catering to the special and individual needs of its customers.

Departmentalizing by process and equipment

Activities can also be grouped according to the process involved or the equipment used. This form of departmentalization, which is employed in many manufacturing enterprises, often brings great economic advantage. For instance, in order to achieve maximum economy, it might be necessary to run a particular piece of equipment around the clock. Blast furnaces in steel mills must be kept in constant operation. The decision to departmentalize by process or equipment is usually made on the basis of cost, that is, on the basis of economic considerations.

Departmentalizing by time

Another common practice is to departmentalize according to time. Enterprises, such as hospitals and public utilities, that function around the clock often organize activities on this basis. Usually activities grouped this way are first departmentalized on some other basis, say product or function. Then, within that category, they are organized into shifts. Thus, the production department will contain a machine shop and an electrical shop (functions); each shop will have a day shift and a night shift (time).

Undoubtedly, functions performed during night hours are similar to, or the same as, those performed during the regular day shift. Nevertheless, such groupings create serious organizational questions. How self-contained should each shift be? What relationships should exist between regular- and special-shift executives?

A composite organizational structure

Departmentalization is not an end in itself; it must lead to the realization of the enterprise's objectives and permit coordination. To achieve this, managers often use more than one method of departmentalization, thereby ending up with a mixed structure. Because each method of departmentalization has its advantages and disadvantages, managers must balance the gains derived from one kind against the disadvantages of another.

It is possible, for instance, that an enterprise may organize its selling function first by territories and then, farther down the line, by customers. A large enterprise producing office machinery could conceivably break up its Manhattan sales activities in the following manner: the downtown office calls on banks and brokers; another office handles insurance companies; a midtown office deals with the textile and retail trade; and an uptown office serves the petroleum, manufacturing, and transportation industries. Or, a divisional sales department may be organized along customer lines and, at lower levels, along territorial lines. Any mixture is perfectly acceptable as long as it fulfills the purpose of the enterprise.

Figure 9-7 shows a company that has been departmentalized by functions at the primary level. On the intermediate level, production has been departmentalized by products, and sales, by territory. On the next level, the production function has been departmentalized by the process and equipment used. The territorially grouped sales districts have been further regrouped along narrower territorial lines and, at the lowest level, have been departmentalized by customer—industrial users, retailers and distributors, and institutional users. Figure 9-7, then, shows a *hybrid structure,* an organization that has departmentalized along function, product, process and equipment, territorial, and customer lines.

Summary

Division of labor is basic to all forms of organized activity. For centuries, managers have known that dividing tasks into specialized components is important to increase efficiency. Assembly line operations in automobile,

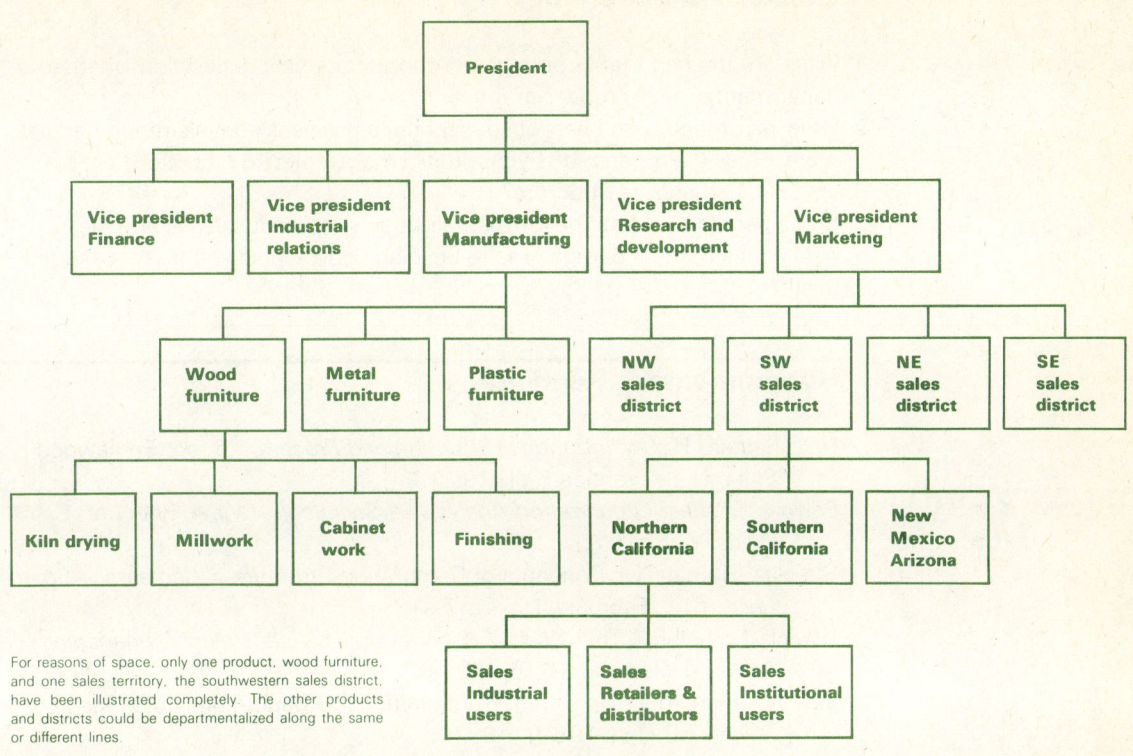

For reasons of space, only one product, wood furniture, and one sales territory, the southwestern sales district, have been illustrated completely. The other products and districts could be departmentalized along the same or different lines.

Figure 9-7 Organization structure with composite departmentalization

electronics, home appliance, garment, and other industries exemplify this belief.

As an organization grows or as tasks become more complex, managers divide labor. Horizontal division of labor is the division of technical labor into departments, plants, functions, and other organizational units. It is conducted by the process known as *departmentalization*. Departmentalizing commonly occurs on the basis of function, product, territory, customer, process and equipment, or time. Each basis has its strengths and weaknesses. Managers choose one or another form of departmentalization, depending on the contingencies faced by their organization.

In actuality, managers usually combine two or more kinds of departmentalization. Frequently, organizations will be divided into individual product groups (product) operating in a region (territory), with such functions as finance and industrial relations retained at corporate headquarters (function). These hybrid structures are well suited to the complexities of managing a variety of human and nonhuman resources in a frequently unpredictable environment.

Discussion questions

1. What are the important contingency considerations in a decision whether to departmentalize by product or function?
2. Draw an organization chart of your school's business administration department. How is it organized? By product? By customer? By function? Isn't it actually a composite structure?
3. Some people think that departmentalization simply establishes artificial boundaries that encourage empire building. How would you try to avoid this result?

Supplementary Readings

Hall, Richard H. *Organizations: Structure and Process,* 2d. ed. Englewood Cliffs, N.J.: Prentice-Hall, 1977.

Perrow, Charles. *Organization Analysis: A Sociological View.* Belmont, Calif.: Wadsworth, 1970.

Stieglitz, Harold "On Concepts of Corporation Structure." *Conference Board Record* 11 (February 1974): 7—13.

Urwick, Lyndall F. "That Word 'Organization.'" *Academy of Management Review* 1 (January 1976): 89—92.

Whiting, Richard J. "In Defense of Functional Organization." *Management Review* 58 (July 1969): 49—52.

Chapter 10

Structuring the organization: Managing through authority

Objectives of the chapter

1. To describe the vertical division of labor—that is, the division of managerial labor.
2. To define *delegation of authority*.
3. To identify the organizational and managerial principles underlying delegation of authority.
4. To trace the three major steps that occur in the process of authority delegation.
5. To examine the factors that affect managers' decisions of how much authority to delegate and when to do so.
6. To define *decentralization of authority*.
7. To describe factors that bear on effective decentralization.
8. To examine the relative advantages and disadvantages of extensive decentralization of authority.
9. To examine decentralization as it affects various organizational functions.
10. To consider recent trends that affect decentralization.

We have seen that managers help to accomplish their organizations' work by dividing labor. Specifically, they departmentalize, grouping task activities on one or more bases: function, product, territory, customer, process and equipment, and time.

As we noted in the last chapter, however, organizing involves more than grouping similar tasks together. Managers also must be able to give commands regarding the performance of work. In short, managers need authority. Thus, in addition to dividing up tasks—departmentalizing—managers must make certain that people possess the authority necessary to carry out their managerial responsibilities.

Referring to Figure 10-1 (a reproduction of Figure 9-2), we see that Michael, Kristen, Tim, and Jean all have administrative responsibilities. However, these responsibilities differ in important ways. At the lowest level, Jean

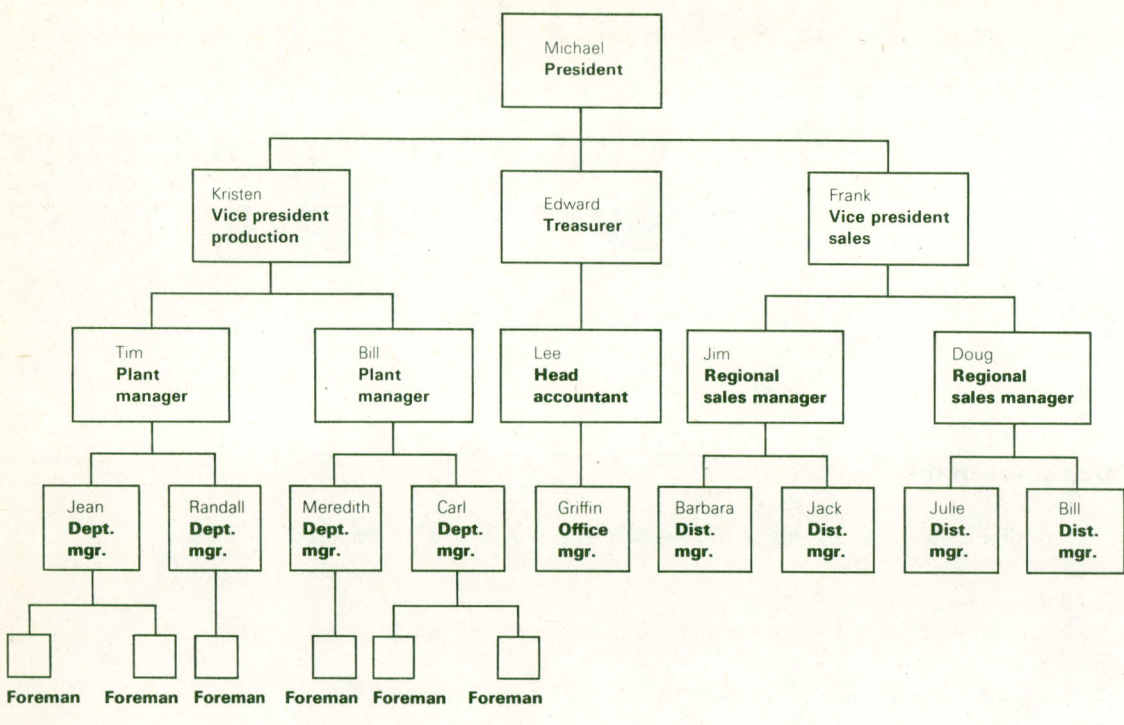

Figure 10-1 Horizontal and vertical division of labor

is responsible for supervising day-to-day production operations in her department; Tim manages overall production performance of one of the company's two plants; Kristen is concerned with the company's total production activities in both plants; and Michael must make certain that all organizational resources are coordinated so as to facilitate effective performance of all three major tasks (finance, production, and sales) and to ensure that organizational goals are satisfactorily met. Jean and her foremen must deal with the nuts and bolts of day-to-day activities; Michael's managerial responsibilities encompass broad and long-range matters of policy. *Delegation* is the process by which these people acquire the authority to carry out their various sets of responsibilities. *Decentralization* refers to the degree to which authority is delegated, or dispersed, throughout the organization.

Delegating authority

As we mentioned in the last chapter, one of the kinds of work that is divided in organizations is managerial labor. As managerial tasks are divided into increasingly specialized components, the organization takes on more and more administrative levels, thus adding to the hierarchy.

The scalar chain

The line of vertical authority relationships from superior to subordinate throughout the organization is commonly called the *scalar chain*. Scalar relationships are important to the overall functioning of the organization. In particular, they are found in what Mooney and Reiley[1] termed the critical administrative elements of principle, process, and effect.

The purpose of organization is to unify effort, which finds its principle in authority. Authority enters into the process with the scalar chain, that is the hierarchy or "line," as it is sometimes called. Its effect is the assignment and integration of functions. The scalar process has its own principle in leadership. But leadership can only enter into process with delegation and its final effect is . . . responsibility for the performance of a particular task.[2]

As can be inferred from the quotation, scalar relationships are based on the positional type of authority, which we discussed in Chapter 8. The scalar chain provides the structure for one of the most important managerial principles—unity of command.

Classicists on the scalar chain

Classical writers on management were convinced of the importance of scalar relationships: Lyndall Urwick, coeditor of the highly influential *Papers on the Science of Administration,* stated unequivocally that

adjustment of [managers'] authorities and responsibilities to each other and their continuous correlation constitute one of the main tasks of leadership in any enterprise.

The evolution of ideas on this question has been comparatively simple. Originally almost all undertakings were organized on what has been called the "line" or, incorrectly, the "military," principle. Emphasis was placed on the importance of the "scalar process."

The considerations which appeared of greatest importance were that there should be clear lines of authority running from the top into every corner of the undertaking and that the responsibility of subordinates exercising delegated authority should be precisely defined. Since, in all cases, concrete objects, physical boundaries or the limits of some well known technical process, offer the simplest and readiest means of definition, the unitary or serial methods were almost universally adopted in subdividing and grouping activi-

---

[1] James D. Mooney and Alan C. Reiley, *Onward Industry!* (New York: Harper & Row, 1931).
[2] Lyndall F. Urwick, "The Functions of Administration," in Luther Gulick and Lyndall F. Urwick, eds., *Papers on the Science of Administration* (New York: Institute of Public Administration, 1937), p. 123.

ties into tasks. [The] supervisor at each level [is] totally responsible for every aspect of his subordinates' work.*

In their 1931 volume, *Onward Industry!,* Mooney and Reiley argued that the fundamental principle of effective management was that of coordination—resources and tasks must be coordinated if unity of purpose is to be served. Such relationships played an important role in this science:

The supreme co-ordinating authority must rest somewhere and in some form in every organization . . . It is equally essential to the very idea and concept of organization that there must be a process, formal in character, through which the coordinating authority operates from the top throughout the entire structure of the organized body. †

---

* Lyndall F. Urwick, "Organization as a Technical Problem," in Luther Gulick and Lyndall F. Urwick, eds., *Papers on the Science of Administration* (New York: Institute of Public Administration, 1937), p. 51.
† James D. Mooney and Alan C. Reiley, *Onward Industry!* (New York: Harper & Row, 1931).

Unity of command

Although there are complications brought on by various contingencies that managers face, in general, the delegation of authority flows on a one-to-one basis. That is, a subordinate is accountable only to the superior from whom he or she receives his or her authority and to no one else. This is known as *unity of command.*[3]

The unity of command principle is highly regarded by classical theorists because it provides one of the principal means for coordinating resources, tasks, and other activities. Through unity of command, responsibility for coordination can be pinpointed; people are not confused by having two bosses; lines of accountability are clear. Figure 10-2 contrasts two situations, one with unity of command and the other without it.

Since biblical times, people have observed that it is difficult to serve two masters. Such a situation often creates confusion and results in unsatisfactory performance by the subordinate. Which of the two superiors has the authority to delegate duties? Which duties take precedence?

The process of delegation

There are three chief and interrelated aspects of the delegation of authority: (1) the assignment of duties by an executive to immediate subordinates; (2) the granting of permission (authority) to make commitments, use resources,

---

[3] We discuss the unity of command principle in connection with line authority relationships in several other contexts in this book. The frequent mention of this principle emphasizes its importance to management.

171 Structuring the organization: Managing through authority

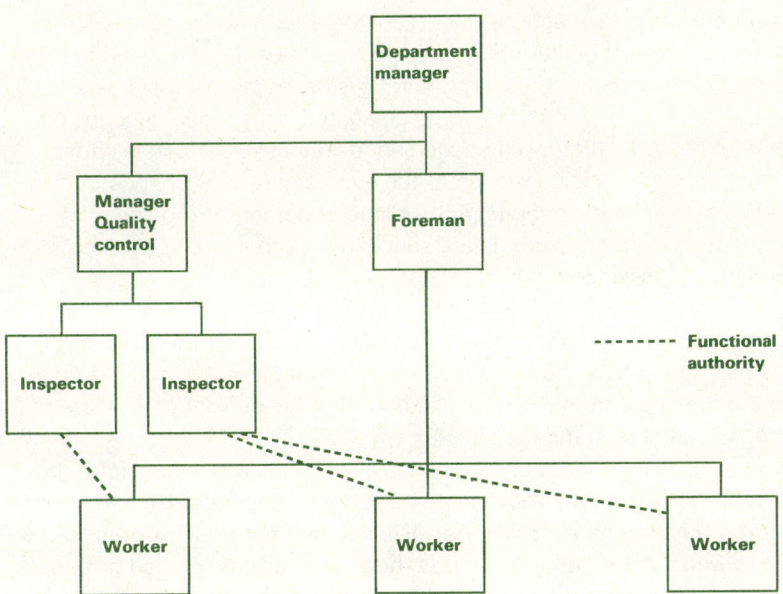

Figure 10-2 The unity of command principle

Unity of command: Each subordinate has only one superior, the foreman.

Without unity of command: Each worker is responsible for an aspect of work to the quality control department, provided this department has functional authority over the line. Workers are also responsible to their foreman.

and take all actions that are necessary to perform the duties; and (3) the creation of an obligation (responsibility) on the part of each subordinate to the delegating executive to perform the duties satisfactorily.[4]

Assigning duties

When assigning duties, managers must decide how to allocate work among subordinates in order to achieve a balance between an effective span of management and a reasonable number of managerial levels. In reviewing

---

[4] William H. Newman, *Administrative Action*, 2d ed. (Englewood Cliffs, N.J.: Prentice-Hall, 1963), pp. 185–186.

their own functions and duties, managers will see which ones they can delegate to others and which they cannot. Some duties are so routine that they could be done best by another. Other functions can be delegated only to subordinates who possess the skill to perform them effectively. Still other functions cannot be delegated at all and must be done by the managers themselves. Some decisions will not be so clear cut; a number of management duties could fall into any of the three groups. In these cases, the decision to allocate a specific duty to a subordinate will often depend on the number and quality of the subordinates available.

Granting authority

The second aspect of delegating is to grant authority to make commitments, use resources, and take actions necessary to perform allocated duties. In this stage, managers confer on the subordinate the right to act and to make decisions within a limited area. Naturally, it is necessary for managers to determine the scope of authority to be delegated. This scope depends on the area of authority that top management itself possesses and is intrinsically related to the duties assigned to the subordinate. Any change in those duties will necessitate a change in the scope of authority. The scope of authority delegated to a subordinate should be appropriate for successfully performing the assigned duties.

Contingency considerations How much authority and what kind of authority should be granted to a subordinate are contingent on several major factors. These factors range from the essential nature of the delegation process to the pragmatics of operating a complex endeavor.

A reminder: We mentioned that scalar relationships, which form the structure for delegation, are based on positional authorities. Thus, remember that duties are assigned and authority is delegated not to people but to positions within the enterprise. Unless these positions are staffed by people, however, the assignments and the delegation of authority are meaningless. That is why one commonly speaks of the delegation of authority to *subordinates* instead of the delegation of authority to *subordinate positions*. The following points are important if managers are to conduct successfully the vertical dimension of their organizing function—delegation of authority.

Clarity of understanding Effective delegation of authority requires a clear understanding of the nature and extent of the authority being delegated. The understanding must be clear to both subordinate and superior. Moreover, the authority must be clear to other people involved, managers and nonmanagers alike. Ambiguous authority often leads to reduced performance. Charts, manuals, and job descriptions aid considerably in managers' clarifying efforts.

Authority germane to duties Managers must remember that delegated authority should be directly related to the duties assigned to the subordinate and to the results expected. In particular, managers must make sure that they have delegated enough authority so that the subordinate is able to obtain the expected results. The subordinate, on the other hand, should accept responsibility only for the functions encompassed by his or her authority. If the subordinate is given more authority than is needed, loose management results.

Specific or general delegation   Managers must recognize the nature of a particular organizational situation before determining whether to delegate authority specifically or generally. Very often the nature of the task to be performed is a decisive factor in the decision. For example, authority can be delegated *specifically* if a task is routine and requires little skill, like digging in a gravel pit or working on an automotive assembly line. However, if the task is that of a research physicist, management may wish to delegate authority *generally,* thereby giving scope to the full range of that physicist's talents. To generalize from this example: the higher a task's formalization, the more specifically authority can be delegated. *Formalization* is a term that refers to the extent that formal roles and regulations govern the work behavior of the person to whom authority is being delegated.[5]

There are times when the scope of authority cannot be made very specific, even though specificity may be desirable. This is particularly true in a new enterprise or in a new venture within an existing organization. In such cases, managers themselves might not fully realize the scope of a new activity and, therefore, would not know how much authority to delegate. However, once the task has begun to take shape, conferences clarifying the nature of authority should be encouraged.

The exception principle   The scope of delegated authority defines the area within which a manager has decision-making responsibility. If situations arise outside this scope, the manager must refer these exceptional problems upward, thereby conforming to what is commonly known as the *exception principle.*

This principle is often overused. Incompetent and insecure managers frequently refer too many exceptions upward. By doing so, they weaken the delegation of authority. Sometimes, high-level managers are tempted to make a decision in an area where they have delegated the decision-making authority. Even though they may have formerly made decisions in this area, these managers must now refrain from interfering unless they are dealing with a truly exceptional problem.

Shared and splintered authority   Managers may, at times, delegate joint authority to two or three subordinates, because they may want the decisions in a given situation to be shared by them. For example, the president of a corporation might want the vice president in charge of production, the sales

---

[5] For a comprehensive discussion of formalization and its impact on delegation and other organizing matters see Richard H. Hall, *Organizations: Structure and Process,* 2d ed. (Englewood Cliffs, N.J.: Prentice-Hall, 1977).

manager, and the chief engineer to decide jointly which products will be carried in the product line for the coming year. In many respects, shared authority is the wave of the future, particularly in space-age industries.

In addition to shared authority, the concept of splintered authority is frequently found in organizations. This concept reflects a situation in which an individual manager possesses all the authority needed to make decisions within his or her own department but faces a problem that bridges more than one department. In order to solve this particular problem, several managers pool their decision-making authority.

Revoking delegated authority Managers sometimes must revoke a delegated authority. As activities change, authority relationships often need realignment and reorganization. This may mean that the managers will now exercise the authority themselves or will delegate it to someone else. Managers may even delegate more authority if circumstances demand it. Naturally, such realigning and reshuffling of authority should not take place too often. Most people in an organization can understand the necessity for reassigning authority from time to time, but, if this happens too frequently, they will become demoralized, apprehensive of the uncertain climate. The phrase "Who's in charge here?" is not always amusing to people in this type of situation.

Delegation by results expected When managers state exactly what they expect, when they expect it done, and by whom, they delegate authority by the results expected. Naturally, it is managers' responsibility to make certain that subordinates know the results expected. Edward Schleh points out the significant advantages that delegation by results will produce:[6]

1. It produces real accomplishment by a subordinate instead of "spinning wheels."
2. Through it, managers can set up job standards to provide a basis for judging performance and can establish a system of controls.
3. It helps to minimize politics in an enterprise. If expected results have been clearly laid out and standards to measure them defined, some tangible record of performance is available to judge an individual's contribution to the organization.

Management by objectives (MBO) is clearly based on these principles.[7]

---

[6] Edward C. Schleh, *Successful Executive Action* (Englewood Cliffs, N.J.: Prentice-Hall, 1956), pp. 19–23; and *Management by Results* (New York: McGraw-Hill, 1961).

[7] MBO is an important managerial approach that is gaining in popularity. See the discussion in Chapter 17. For a thorough review of MBO see Stephen J. Carroll, Jr., and Henry L. Tosi, Jr., *Management by Objectives: Applications and Research* (New York: Macmillan, 1973).

Creating responsibility

The third major aspect of delegating authority is the creation of an obligation to perform assigned duties satisfactorily. The acceptance of such an obligation by an individual creates responsibility. Without responsibility, the process of delegating authority is not complete.

Responsibility is the obligation to perform a duty or carry out granted authority. The essence of responsibility is *obligation*. By accepting employment, by accepting the obligation to perform assigned duties, an individual implies the acceptance of responsibility. In other words, responsibility results from a contractual agreement in which a person agrees to perform certain duties in return for certain rewards.

Responsibility may be a continuing process, or it may be terminated by the accomplishment of a single action. The relation between the president of a corporation and the plant manager is an example of continuing responsibility. On the other hand, the responsibilities existing between the president and someone from outside the firm, who has been hired to spend some time evaluating the salary structure of the company, will be terminated when the study is finished and the recommendations are made.

Accountability   In addition to the concept of responsibility is that of accountability. This term has long been used by the military, where to be accountable means to keep accurate and adequate records and to safeguard public property. The term has become increasingly important to writers in the area of management in discussing managerial control. Thus, we speak of people having the authority to carry out an assigned task and being accountable to their superiors for the success of that task.

Authority and responsibility   As we have already noted, authority and responsibility should be commensurate. Inequality between delegated authority and responsibility produces undesirable results. If authority exceeds responsibility, a misuse of authority can easily occur. On the other hand, embarrassment and frustration can be the only result if one accepts responsibility without adequate authority to take the necessary actions to perform required duties and fulfill obligations.

In some situations, however, authority and responsibility cannot be equalized. In emergencies, executives often are forced to exceed the bounds of their authority. Sometimes, managers are delegated authority for a task for which they cannot be entirely responsible. Sales managers, for example, are often given the authority to sell the entire output of a factory and are required to accept the responsibility for obtaining the planned sales volume. In other words, they have to accept responsibility for something they cannot control. The sales manager can neither compel customers to buy nor foresee changes in economic conditions or unexpected maneuvers by competitors that may greatly affect sales. Sales managers accept responsibility to use all material and human resources available to obtain the best results possible. They can be held accountable for making the best effort possible and for no more.

The need for balance between authority and responsibility is widely recognized. However, balance must be applied with discretion, and, from time to time, it has been questioned. Urwick, although generally advocating the principle of parity between authority and responsibility, agrees with Barnard that, at times, individuals are placed in a position where they have responsibility but cannot have authority.[8] Often, executives wish for subordinates who are more willing to assume responsibility. These executives seem to be inviting their subordinates to bid for authority that they have not yet seen fit to grant them and to accept responsibility that they have not yet been asked to assume.[9]

Decentralizing authority

One of the major considerations affecting the delegation of authority is decentralization. As we have seen, when managers delegate authority they must determine the answer to the complicated question: How much of what authority should we grant to whom for what purpose? Before they can give a comprehensive answer, however, the managers have to ask another question: To what degree do we want our organization decentralized?

Before proceeding, we should state that the concepts of decentralization and centralization are not absolutes. One can speak accurately of them only in terms of degrees; they are concepts at opposite ends of a continuum. An organization is relatively centralized (or decentralized); that is, authority is dispersed, or delegated, to a relatively small (or large) degree in the organization.

Centralization represents upper management's systematic and consistent reservation of major policy-making authority. The extent of centralization depends on the amount of independent judgment and discretion executives can exercise, the degree of authority delegated, and the qualitative nature of the decisions made on each level of the organization. Ernest Dale[10] illustrates this point well in his statement that the decentralization of authority in an organization increases with four factors:

1. The number of decisions made lower down in the management hierarchy.
2. The importance of decisions made lower down in the management hierarchy (the greater the sum of capital expenditure that can be approved by the plant manager without consulting anyone else, the greater will be the decentralization in this area).
3. The increase in functions affected by decisions made at lower levels (companies permitting only operational decisions to be made at separate branch

---

[8] Lyndall F. Urwick, *Notes on the Theory of Organization* (New York: American Management Association, 1952), pp. 51–52.
[9] Dalton E. McFarland, *Management Principles and Practices* (New York: Macmillan, 1958), p. 217.
[10] Ernest Dale, *Planning and Developing the Company Organization Structure*, Research Report No. 20 (New York: American Management Association, 1952), pp. 149–150.

plants are less decentralized than those also permitting financial and personnel decisions at branch plants).
4 The less checking required on the decision (decentralization is greatest when no check must be made; less when superiors have to be informed of the decision after it has been made; least if superiors have to be consulted before the decision is made. The fewer people to be consulted, and the lower they are in the management hierarchy, the greater will be the decentralization).

Centralization

Highly centralized authority is common in small enterprises and is often necessary if the enterprise is to survive in a competitive environment. In a highly centralized organization the chief executive is in close touch with all operations, makes all decisions, and gives all instructions. In certain organizations small enough to have this type of centralized administration, the chief executive does not care to or is in no position to delegate much authority.

On the other hand, many small firms in the electronics and space industries are loosely organized. In them, managers have delegated a great deal of authority to highly trained and educated scientists and engineers. In these organizations, such decentralization provides the best way to make effective use of valuable human resources.

Decentralization

Limited decentralization

Variations on the degree of decentralization of authority are innumerable. In some situations, authority is decentralized to a limited degree. Top management initiates policies and programs but delegates their applications in day-to-day operations and planning. In many medium-sized manufacturing firms, for example, such authority is delegated to the production manager, but this delegation has its limitations. The production manager is responsible for getting the work out: scheduling the production, requisitioning the various materials and supplies, hiring employees, and handling personnel matters within the union agreement. There may be, however, a number of matters that require final approval by top management: matters regarding inventory policy, purchasing machinery, hiring supervisors, and changing pay rates. Authority to decide these questions is not delegated to the production manager.

This kind of arrangement is advantageous because it limits the number of executives that a firm needs to employ. In addition, it relieves top management of numerous details, leaving them free for matters of greater importance. There are probably thousands of enterprises in the United States that are organized on the basis of limited decentralization of authority.

Bottom-up management: Extreme decentralization

Extreme decentralization can be seen in what William B. Given, Jr., has called "bottom-up" management.[11] At the time his book was written, Given was the president of the American Brake Shoe Company, an enterprise made up of ten divisions operating sixty widely scattered plants. Utilizing bottom-up management, he tried to encourage the initiative of all subordinates down the line so that the impetus and the ideas would flow from the bottom up.

Given was not merely dealing with the usual concept of decentralization; instead, he was dealing with decentralization carried a step further, with a radically different effect. Call it *progressive decentralization,* if you wish, assuming *progressive* to mean spreading from one part to others. Such decentralization not only takes the strings off subsidiary presidents and department heads, but also gives superintendents, foremen, chief clerks—people all along the management line—a stimulating sense of personal freedom, freedom to think and plan boldly.[12] Each manager, each division, each unit, feels a proprietary responsibility for its own activities. The manager must plan how to do the job best; and must also do the job. Under this arrangement, top executives cannot exercise detailed controls; their principal duties are to help subordinates to do a better job.

When to decentralize

Relatively high centralization or, at most, limited decentralization of authority is most logical in the early stages of organizational development. However, most managers must eventually face the problem of when to make a systematic effort to decentralize authority to the lowest possible level. Such a decision will involve major changes in the organizational structure and in the general managerial philosophy. It also will necessitate changes in the habits and attitudes of individual managers. Accordingly, it is not a step to be taken casually.

Some contingency considerations

Fortunately, managers have guidelines available to help them. Effective increase of decentralization is contingent on a number of situational conditions.

Product departmentalization   In Chapter 9 we examined that period in the growth and development of the enterprise when it becomes necessary for management to switch from a functional departmentalization to a product division. The same factors that indicate a need for establishing product divisions also indicate that it is time to decentralize authority. As a matter of fact, product division only becomes effective when accompanied by such decentralization. As soon as the enterprise diversifies into product lines,

---

[11] William B. Given, Jr., *Bottom-Up Management* (New York: Harper & Row, 1949).
[12] Ibid., pp. 5—6.

authority must be delegated to the various divisions for maximum results and accountability.

Scope of managerial activity Departmentalization by product is not the only factor that determines the proper time to decentralize. For example, decentralization becomes necessary when top managers find themselves so burdened with daily matters that they do not have time to perform their planning adequately or to maintain a long-range point of view. In this situation, they will probably want to make a concerted effort to delegate authority to lower echelons.

Task environment Occasionally, an enterprise delegates authority in order to keep its position in the market. Decision making may have become so cumbersome that other companies can adjust to prevailing market conditions more readily and quickly, gaining a major advantage. Difficulty in coping with rapid and unpredictable changes in the labor and financial markets also will indicate the need for decentralization of authority.

Pros and cons

The advantages of decentralization are obvious: it relieves executives of time-consuming detail work and frees them for more important problems. Subordinates can make decisions without waiting for approval from a superior, thus increasing their flexibility and permitting prompter action when speed is essential. In addition, decentralization of decision-making authority may produce better decisions, since the manager on the spot usually knows more about pertinent factors than the manager at headquarters. Likewise, decentralization tends to increase the morale of lower-level executives, their interests, and their enthusiasm for their work. It also provides a good training ground for junior executives.

    The disadvantages of decentralization are equally clear. As authority is decentralized, executives increasingly resemble operators of small independent businesses. As a consequence, duplications of service might develop. Also, executives in the field may come to feel that they no longer need the advice of specialists assembled at headquarters. Under these conditions, the specialists would not be utilized fully and the division or department managers would not receive technical advice or services that they really could use.

    Another disadvantage of increased decentralization is loss of control and the related problem of suboptimization. In this situation, the relatively autonomous units of a company optimize their own profitability, but in so doing decrease the net effectiveness of the organization. Many large companies devise controls to minimize this possibility.

How much to decentralize

Managers are faced, time and again, with the problem of how much decentralization to permit. Naturally they must choose a pattern of delegation that is sound for the organization. Although much executive-subordinate delegation follows a traditional pattern, new problems do arise. Thus, decentralization and delegation of authority are continuous functions requiring constant checks to ensure that they are still appropriate and adequate for the particular organization.

Some contingencies

No simple formulas exist for determining the appropriate amount of decentralization. There are, however, several situational factors that managers must take into account. That is, the amount of decentralization is ordinarily contingent on a number of factors.

History of the organization   Historical growth of an organization is frequently a factor in gauging the decentralization of authority. Organizations that expand from within and show little delegation of authority, often, have grown under the vigorous centralized direction of the founder-owner.

Companies that have been formed through business combinations, amalgamations, and mergers usually function with a great amount of decentralization. In these instances, recentralization of authority would be foolish. In time, the acquiring company must provide for proper coordination and controls, but it still may maintain the decentralized structure. The reverse can also be true. Sometimes the existing management of a firm being merged cannot be entrusted with the future of the enterprise; sometimes the controlling group had prior plans to install its own management as soon as the acquisition is completed. In these cases, the acquiring company revokes much of the authority previously possessed by the managers of the merged company.

Availability of managers to implement decentralization   Decentralization and delegation of authority cannot occur unless enough managers of sufficient ability are available to discharge the responsibilities involved. If managers do not have the necessary ability, authority cannot be granted. Managers may find themselves complaining about a lack of trained people but, at the same time, using this lack as an excuse for not decentralizing. To avoid this impasse, many firms develop and train managerial labor by pushing decision making down into the lower ranks of the organization. In the early stages of managers' careers their scope of authority will be small, but as they acquire experience, they will be given more authority.

Dispersion of operations   Geographic dispersion of operations also has some bearing on decentralization. Such dispersion increases the problems of communication and coordination. Therefore, one is likely to find more delegation of authority in dispersed operations. Usually, a local manager can manage better than can an absentee manager. Yet, geographic dispersion does not necessarily result in decentralization. For example, the local managers of chain stores usually have no authority over pricing, advertising, inventory, and purchasing; instead, all these decisions are controlled from a central office. An important series of research studies, conducted in England, showed that geographic dispersion in manufacturing firms gave line workers a high degree of control over their daily operations, while major decision making was retained by corporate headquarters.[13] In this situation, performance is decentralized, but authority is centralized.

Costliness and significance of decisions The costliness and significance of typical management decisions will greatly affect the degree of delegation and, thus, the amount of decentralization that is feasible in an organization. Generally speaking, the more costly and significant the decisions, the higher the level of the managerial hierarchy in which they should be made. Costliness can be expressed in dollars and cents, in worker hours, or in units of output. Costliness can also be intangible, such as the effect of a certain decision on an organization's reputation.

Control over capital funds In most enterprises, decisions regarding the expenditure of capital funds are not broadly delegated; they often are considered so vital to the life of the enterprise that top management reserves authority for them. Some enterprises, however, have given their managers considerable authority over capital expenditures. At General Electric, the operating department general managers may make commitments up to $500,000. Ralph J. Cordiner, former president of General Electric, has said, "I believe that too much of a fetish has been made in the past of capital expenditures. A manager can lose a lot more money on inventory, foolish pricing policy, careless personnel staffing, or poor production scheduling."[14]

Size of enterprise The larger the firm, the greater the difficulties in achieving efficient and effective teamwork. Realization of the diseconomies of size often leads to decentralization, or the division of the enterprise into a number of autonomous or nearly autonomous units. In these units, decisions can be made with more speed and at a point closer to the place of action. Time can be saved, paperwork reduced, misunderstandings in communication diminished, and friction held to a minimum.

Dynamics and type of enterprise The decentralization of authority also will be greatly influenced by the dynamics of the particular enterprise. If the organization is part of an industry that is expanding much more rapidly than expected—for instance, electronics—top management will be overburdened with numerous decisions that it probably would not have had to make in the normal course of events. This dynamic condition will force top management to decentralize as quickly as possible, even though some managers to whom

---

[13] D. S. Pugh, D. J. Hickson, C. R. Hinings, and C. Turner, "The Context of Organization Structures," *Administrative Science Quarterly* 14, no. 1 (March 1969):91–114.

[14] Ralph J. Cordiner, *New Frontiers for Professional Managers* (New York: McGraw-Hill, 1956), p. 61.

authority is delegated might make mistakes. In other words, the dynamic growth and rate of change in the industry might make it impossible to completely train enough capable managers in the lower echelons. Delegating authority will give these managers the opportunity to become more experienced.

Firms with highly diversified activities—especially those that cut across several industries—also require a large degree of decentralization. To a conglomerate corporation with divisions in divergent fields, such as electronics, lumber, shipping, steel, plastics, and chemicals, considerable delegation of authority is natural and economical. The diversification, however, could easily lead to devastating results if top management has not devised effective centralized controls to go along with the delegation.

Control mechanisms The presence of some effective control system, such as a profit center, is essential to ensure that the decentralized units of a firm function consistently with the general objectives of the enterprise. For example, General Motors has two criteria for appraising and controlling the performance of its decentralized divisions: market penetration and unit costs. The first criterion gives corporate management a reading on the effectiveness of the marketing program; the second gives data on the level of manufacturing efficiency. These criteria are broad and cover a relatively long time span—usually a year.

Other large corporations tackle the control problem by using a special corporate-level audit group. This group monitors activities in the decentralized units and sends performance reports to top management. By acquiring data on a wide variety of activities, the group gives top management a basis for carrying out its control function, and by going directly to the unit itself, the monitoring group bypasses the lengthy chain of command.

Level of morale The morale in an organization is also important to effective decentralization. If morale is low, managers may decide to increase decentralization. Generally speaking, the more authority lower- or middle-echelon managers have, and the higher their status, the higher their morale.

Concomitant with the trend toward upgrading the education and skills of the work force is the trend toward higher expectations among new, young employees. They want and expect more authority and more responsibility; they want opportunities to use their independent judgment. Managers should be prepared to decentralize, to a certain degree, in order to fulfill these expectations.

Environmental factors In our discussion of factors that influence decentralization and the delegation of authority, we have concentrated mainly on those internal to the enterprise. Since the organization is an open system, the business has little or no control over a number of external factors—labor unions, government agencies, and tax policies, to name a few. All these factors have a centralizing effect on business. For example, many firms deal with large unions and negotiate labor contracts on a companywide basis at corporate headquarters. Therefore, within the area of labor relations, authority of decision making cannot be greatly decentralized. The same effect is produced by such government control on business as price regulation. There are environmental factors, however, such as technology and competitive pressure, that lead managers to decentralize.[15]

Economic factors are also important. In periods of business decline, top executives might feel that their personal influence and experience are needed to obtain cost reductions, improved operations, uniform standards, checks on expenditures, and so forth. In general, many companies tend to centralize authority during a market decline and decentralize authority during the upward movement of the business cycle.

Decentralization in the various functions

Another way to look at decentralization is through the various functions an enterprise performs. The nature of a function will, to an extent, dictate the degree of delegation of authority and the amount of decentralization that is feasible. As we mentioned previously, the main functions in an enterprise are production, distribution (marketing), and finance; the usual auxiliary activities are personnel, accounting, and purchasing. The importance of these functions and of their relationships to one another varies from enterprise to enterprise. Also, unique circumstances sometimes necessitate centralization or decentralization in a particular case. However, some broad conclusions on the way in which these functions lend themselves to decentralization can be drawn.

In the major functions

Production Managers first tend to delegate authority over the creation of goods and services. This is especially true of the production function in manufacturing firms. Moreover, managers are likely to delegate the greatest amount of authority in this area, for as the size and complexity of production activities increase, the need for delegation increases.

This generalization seems to hold true whether production facilities are located close to the home office or not. If such facilities are physically dispersed, however, the need for delegation and decentralization becomes even more urgent. Nevertheless, overall controls must remain with top administration—through planning and examining production and operating budgets, through quality inspections, and, possibly, through a vice president in charge of all manufacturing.

Finance As we have noted, the finance function tends to be relatively centralized even in enterprises where authority is broadly delegated. The

---

[15] See Paul R. Lawrence and Jay W. Lorsch, *Organization and Environment* (Cambridge, Mass.: Harvard Graduate School of Business Administration, 1967).

reason for this is obvious: only through centralized authority can the proper application of scarce capital resources be guaranteed. In most companies, a particular manager is given a relatively small fund that can be spent without special permission from headquarters.

Operating expenditures are not as strictly controlled. Managers of manufacturing divisions are usually granted wide authority over those expenditures. However, they are subject to the usual budgetary controls. Budgets are made up at regular intervals by the operating division and are submitted to top management for review and approval. Once divisional managers receive budget approval, they have full authority in this area. However, managers are becoming increasingly aware that centralized authority over operating expenses might be advisable too. Uncontrolled expenditure in this area could also dissipate corporate capital.

Marketing At first glance, much decentralization and delegation of authority appears to exist within the marketing function. In a growing enterprise, authority over sales activities will be delegated soon after authority over the production function has been delegated. This occurs because sales activities must usually be brought to customers scattered across the country. A sales executive must have authority to adjust to these customers and to rapidly changing circumstances and conditions. Branch managers also need a wide area of discretion, so that they can give the customers the individual attention that many of them require. Therefore, the nature of distribution seems to make decentralization necessary.

A closer examination, however, shows that much of this decentralization exists in name only. In most instances, no variations in prices and discounts are permitted without the express permission of the home office; clear limits to the extension of credit usually exist; and travel and entertainment expense ceilings are often specified in detail. George Smith cites the case of a large manufacturing company where, he was told by the general sales managers, the marketing function had been completely decentralized. Certainly, all selling was done by people in the regional divisions. However, executives at headquarters decided on the product line, set up the prices, conducted sales training programs, hired the salespeople, kept track of sales, carried on the company's advertising campaign, and gave advice to regional sales managers. When the regional managers were asked whether they considered the marketing function to be centralized or decentralized, they described it as exceedingly centralized.[16]

In the auxiliary functions

Accounting Very little delegation of authority is usually associated with the accounting function, because accounting is most economically performed by

[16] George Albert Smith, Jr., *Managing Geographically Decentralized Companies* (Boston: Division of Research, Graduate School of Business Administration, Harvard University, 1958), p. 16.

a central department and the information obtained by that department is necessary for effective overall organizational control. However, if too much centralization occurs, a manager may be unable to obtain fast and accurate answers to accounting questions. Therefore, some accounting activities are often performed in the lower echelons.

The profit center: A way to decentralize

In 1921, under the leadership of Alfred P. Sloan, Jr., General Motors (GM) centralized policy making and administration, yet at the same time made provisions for highly decentralized responsibility for operations. Sloan's concept of the management of a great industrial organization was

to divide it into as many parts as consistently as can be done, place in charge of each part the most capable executive that can be found, develop a system of coordination so that each part may strengthen and support each other part; thus not only welding all parts together in the common interests of a joint enterprise, but importantly developing ability and initiative through the instrumentalities of responsibility and ambition—developing men and giving them an opportunity to exercise their talents, both in their own interests as well as in that of the business.*

In particular, GM has decentralized on a profit-center basis. This method of organization enables the firm to benefit from large-scale production while retaining the advantages of a well-managed small business. Decentralization provides GM with the flexibility to change operations and improve its products. It enables GM's managers to make effective use of their talents by giving them maximum scope to exercise their freedom of action. It also gives many individuals additional opportunity to develop executive ability and initiative.

More specifically, profit-center decentralization permits the general manager of each division to manage and operate his or her domain. Each manager is responsible for planning, for building and staffing the organization, and for controlling results. Each manager designs, develops, produces, and sells his or her own products. Each purchases materials and parts, either from outside suppliers or from other divisions of the company, the choice depending solely on where he or she can obtain the best product at the lowest price. Each manager competes with every other division of GM *and* with every other company that makes a similar product. The division manager is fully responsible for the success or failure of the division and is rewarded accordingly.

---

* "The Development and Growth of General Motors," statement before the Subcommittee on Anti-Trust and Monopoly of the United States Senate Committee on the Judiciary, by Harlow Curtice, former president of the General Motors Corporation (December 2, 1955), p. 8.

The division manager, however, is not completely autonomous. The General Motors philosophy envisions decentralized operations and responsibilities with coordinated control. Thus, the manager's efforts are guided by a comprehensive framework of centralized planning, coordination, and control.

Personnel Since managing means getting people to do things, and since people vary widely in their capabilities, attitudes, and responses, managers must have the authority to deal with them as individuals and to modify broad personnel policies to accommodate particular cases. Therefore, within the area of personnel activities there should be as much delegation of authority as possible.

In some personnel areas, however, a high degree of centralization is desirable and, in practice, exists. Union dealings require centralization of authority. Wage and salary administration, appraisal procedure, job evaluation, bonus and fringe benefit arrangements, and executive development programs also tend to be highly centralized because of the need for consistency across the organization in these areas.

Purchasing The amount of decentralization and delegation of authority in the purchasing function depends largely on the purchases involved. Capital goods are usually purchased centrally because they represent a substantial capital investment. In enterprises where the divisions produce different product lines, the tendency toward decentralized purchasing is greater. An enterprise that uses products of a perishable nature probably also delegates purchasing authority. Furthermore, semi-independent and competing divisions usually practice decentralized purchasing. If a division's performance is judged by its income statement, it is only fair to give it a free hand in its purchasing. Even if purchases are widely decentralized, however, there are usually general purchasing policies and procedures. In some enterprises—those involved in merchandising, for example—almost all purchasing activities are highly centralized. Store managers, however, might have the authority to cater to special local needs and to purchase appropriate items as they need them.

Recent trends

The tendency toward decentralization

In recent years, decentralization has been a growing trend. In fact, having a decentralization program has become one of the most discussed issues in the world of management. The cost of such a program should be considered as a long-term investment in managerial training and in improved morale among all ranks of the managerial hierarchy. However, each organization must devise its own structure. No two organizations are alike; each has its own history, problems, opportunities, and personnel.

Any organizational structure will change from time to time. Therefore, a program of decentralization cannot be devised, put into force, and then forgotten. Periodic adjustments must be made in the delegation and flow of authority among various units and levels in the company. Smith suggests that managers approach this problem with the following thoughts:

Let us look, perhaps more intently than usual for a while, at the way we have allocated authorities and powers between the headquarters organization on the one hand and the local divisions on the other hand. Let us see if we are having decisions made and actions taken at the levels where they can best be made. Let us ask the divisions what things they would like to decide which they now can't decide. What do they have to decide which they wish the headquarters would decide for them? Let us ask similar questions of the headquarters people. [17]

Smith's approach permits a continuous scrutiny of the decentralization process as well as some give and take on the part of local executives and the executives at headquarters.

The effects of computer systems

What effect does computer technology have on the centralization-decentralization issue? Increased reliance on computerized decision making and information systems has tended to slow down or even reverse the trend toward decentralization. Both of these technological innovations encourage recentralization. They do so by eliminating one of the compelling reasons for decentralization—managers' inability to keep up with the increasing size and complexity of the enterprise. Aided by computers, management can relocate most decision making at a central point. There the computers will efficiently process information and rapidly make it available. Computers will enable top management to extend its thinking and decision-making range, thus making delegation of authority less necessary.[18]

It is, of course, impossible to gauge precisely the computer's impact on important variables, such as morale, organizational structure, and the independent judgment of individuals. Although the computer seems to be a force toward centralization, the degree to which managers decide to exploit it is another matter. In fact, the growing popularity of minicomputers[19] is producing an interesting problem for managers: top management can use the computers for more and better information by which to make decisions themselves; on the other hand, the small size and cost of these devices allows them to be distributed throughout the organization, thereby increasing decentralization.[20] Since, as the philosopher once said, it is easy to predict almost anything except the future, we will have to await further developments before knowing the resolution of this problem.

---

[17] Ibid., p. 20.
[18] Harold J. Leavitt and Thomas Whisler, "Management in the 1980's," *Harvard Business Review* 36 (1958): 41—48.
[19] See Michael Cashman, "Small Business Computers," *Datamation,* June 1972; and "Minicomputer for Business Use," *Journal of Accountancy,* August 1973.
[20] George Glaser, "The Centralization Versus Decentralization Issue: Arguments, Alternatives, and Guidelines," *Data Base* 2, no. 3 (Fall—Winter 1970): 1—7.

Summary

A major way in which managers divide their labor is vertically, through the process of delegation. This process involves three chief aspects: assigning duties, granting authority, and creating responsibilities. It enables managers to confer the necessary authority to enable people to carry out their duties. The line of vertical authority relationships from superior to subordinate throughout the organization is commonly called the *scalar chain*. There are several factors on which effective delegation is contingent.

The degree to which authority is delegated, or dispersed, throughout the organization is termed the organization's degree of decentralization. There are no hard-and-fast rules that dictate whether an organization should be decentralized to a high or low degree. Managers must consider such factors as organizational history, form of decentralization, scope of managerial responsibility, environmental conditions, and so forth.

Finally, managers are not required to decentralize to the same degree in all areas of the organization. Some functions may be relatively decentralized, while others are controlled from a central headquarters. The trade-off is essentially that between flexibility and control.

Discussion questions

1. To decentralize is to lose control. What does this statement mean? If you were generally an advocate of decentralization, how would you respond to it?
2. What is the nature and extent of decentralization in this course?
3. If your professor put you in charge of a group of six students assigned to write a term paper, to what degree would you delegate authority?
4. Would such factors as length of assignment, availability of library materials, and time left before the paper is due affect your last answer? How? What does this tell you about resources and delegation?

Supplementary readings

Glaser, George. "The Centralization Versus Decentralization Issue: Arguments, Alternatives, and Guidelines." *Data Base* 2, no. 3 (Fall–Winter 1970): 1–7. Reprinted in *Dimensions in Modern Management*, 2d ed., edited by Patrick E. Connor. Boston: Houghton Mifflin, 1978.

Maier, N. R. F., and Thurber, J. A. "Problems in Delegation." *Personnel Psychology* 22 (1969): 131–139.

Staiger, John G. "What Cannot Be Decentralized." *Management Record* 25 (January 1963): 19–21.

Starkweather, David B. "The Rationale for Decentralization in Large Hospitals." *Hospital Administration* 15 (Spring 1970): 27–45.

Worthy, James C. "Organizational Structure and Employee Morale." *American Sociological Review,* April 1950, pp. 169–179.

Chapter 11

Structuring the organization: Line-staff relationships

Objectives of the chapter

1 To describe the division of managerial labor into staff activities.
2 To specify what is meant by organizational staff.
3 To define and describe staff—that is, functional—authority.
4 To examine common relationships between line and staff personnel.
5 To identify some frequent sources of conflict between line and staff.

We have been discussing the managerial function of organizing. We have suggested that the division of labor is at the heart of this function. We examined horizontal division of labor—departmentalization—in Chapter 9 and vertical division of labor—delegation—in Chapter 10. We now come to the third major way in which labor is divided.

Line and staff

When the importance, scope, or sheer volume of a managerial task becomes so great that it threatens to overwhelm an individual manager, a logical step is to divide that task. One of the ways to divide the work is into specialized components. Thus, the manager can bring in someone to handle narrowly specialized aspects of the overall administrative task. Such a person, termed *staff,* assists the manager (called *line*) in the performance of the managerial work.

Ultimately, every organization reaches a point where specialized staff contributions are required. Because the typical executive—even a chief executive—cannot be a master of all the information necessary for successful decision making, he or she hires staff groups to supply technical data and advice. Staff work revolves around the performance of specialized activities, the utilization of technical knowledge, and the creation and distribution of technical information concerning the functions that are important to line managers.

Historical evolution of staff

Staffs can be found in the history of many organizations. Most followed a similar pattern of development: as the organizations became larger and larger, top management could not possibly fulfill all the demands of its position. It needed the help of others in carrying out its job. A convenient way for management to enlarge its scope was to make use of various kinds of aides. One finds applications of the staff concept in ancient Athens and Rome, in the College of Cardinals, and in the different divisions of the Curia, which serve as advisers to the pope. Today, the president of the United States can call on many staffs. For instance, the Council of Economic Advisers gives staff advice on economic conditions. In fact, staffs are important even before the presidency is achieved; they are critical in presidential campaigns. That staff people are essential to their organized efforts is patently apparent; hardly a week goes by without some segment of the news media presenting an analysis of key staff people "surrounding the candidate."

The staff concept also has been developed for centuries within European armies. Traces of staff are found as far back as the days of Julius Caesar. The Prussian general staff, conceived in the early nineteenth century by General von Scharnhorst, was created to help commanders in the field handle the many auxiliary functions related to running an army. Many of the ideas developed for this staff are still in use. One of them, the concept of rotating officers between staff and line duties, can be seen in business today. This practice enables staff personnel to have firsthand experience with operating problems and line personnel to learn the advantages of staff assistance. International Business Machines (IBM) is one example of the many companies that follow this idea in training their executives.

Evolution of staff in organizations

Staff work plays a major role in contemporary organizations. Both the number of people involved in staff activities and the number of different types of staff work are increasing. As Figure 11-1 indicates, this increase has accelerated over the years, moving from about a dozen or so in 1915–1920 to about two dozen in the 1930s, and increasing rapidly in the period from World War II to 1960.

The process by which staff activities develop is a fairly straightforward one. As organizations grow, chief executives expand their responsibilities. Because they are the only officials who can handle certain duties properly and because there is probably no one with whom they can share some responsibilities, they must do more and more themselves. At some point, they will attempt to remedy the situation by introducing subordinate managers into the organization—that is, by departmentalizing and delegating authority. As time goes on, however, they find that their span of management is so large they cannot add any more managers and still give them all adequate attention. Chief executives also discover that they are not able to coordinate available information or plan properly.

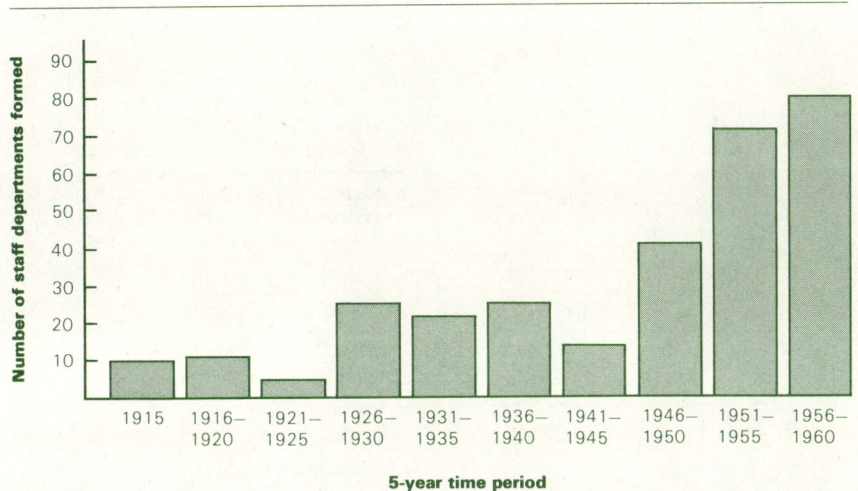

Figure 11-1 Number of staff departments created in 30 companies *Source:* Joseph A. Litterer, *The Analysis of Organizations,* 2d ed. (New York: Wiley, 1973), pp. 584–585.

Under these conditions, the executive may appoint one or more assistants, creating a personal staff that will help to perform duties that cannot be delegated. Although these assistants can provide general aid, in all likelihood none of them is well enough qualified to advise and guide the executive in the more difficult aspects of such areas as labor relations and law.

Eventually, the personal staff becomes inadequate. Not only the chief executive but also other managers now seem to need expert advice and guidance on problems of scheduling, operations research, input-output theory, taxes, new concepts of engineering, marketing, and so forth. First-line supervisors need help in recruiting workers, assistance in training them, and advice in handling their complaints and grievances. They need the expertise of skilled technicians to set up quality standards, to schedule production, and to perform many other associated activities.

At this point, specialized staffs are developed within the organization. Staff positions are created, each in a special field, to provide advice and counsel to any division or member of the organization in need of a particular type of aid. This development is traced in Figure 11-2.

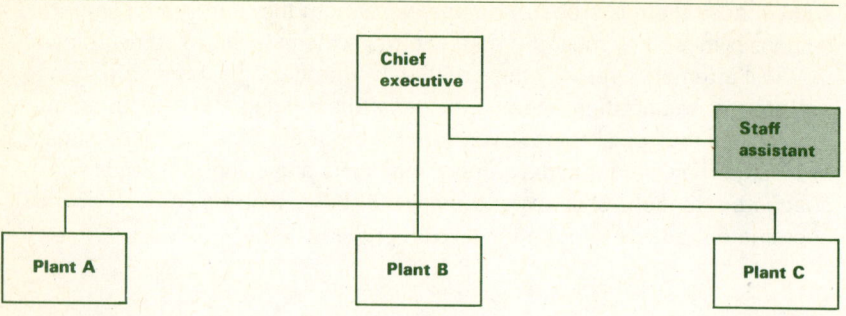

Figure 11-2 The evolution of staff

First stage: Personal staff created

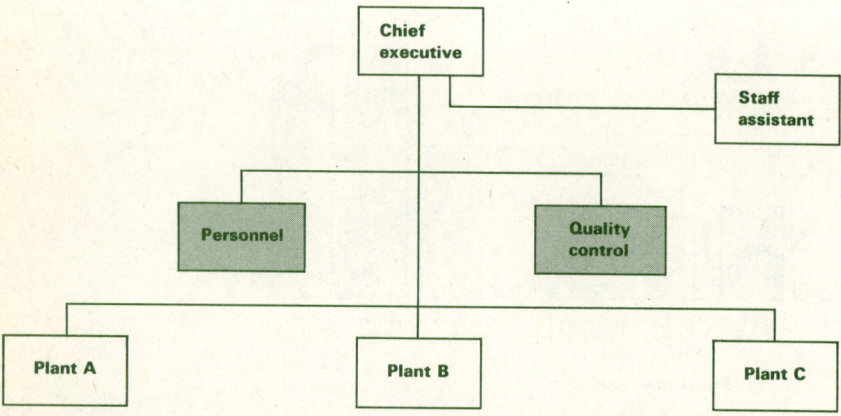

Second stage: Specialized staff added

Role and authority of staff

As we have stated, the staff guides, advises, counsels, and serves the line personnel. In reality, the staff does what chief executives might do themselves if they possessed all the necessary special knowledge.

Much of the information and advice that the staff provides flows to the line personnel, and it is their privilege to accept, alter, or reject this advice. Since, in most instances, staff has been established to provide good information, counsel, and advice, it is usually in the interest of line managers to follow staff suggestions. However, they are under no obligation to do so. When they do follow staff suggestions, they transform the suggestions into line commands, which are then issued as line orders.

Basically, we can see that line and staff possess different authority. Staff authority is not inherently inferior to line authority. Line authority is derived from the chain of command or the organizational hierarchy based on superior-subordinate relationships; it is positional authority. Staff authority is based on expertise in specialized activities.

It is conventional, and correct in most instances, to say that staff authority provides expert advice and counsel to the managers who have line authority but lacks the right to command them. There are two exceptions to this concept of staff authority. First, a manager of a staff department exercises line authority over the subordinates in that department. This relationship provides no real organizational problem, since a line within a staff is merely a secondary chain of command attached to a primary line organization. Second, a staff may have functional authority. If this is the case, staff may exercise special, but restricted, command over the line. Let us consider this type of authority.

Functional authority

Although functional authority is a classical idea, it is often misunderstood and misapplied. It is one of the more difficult ideas to group in the analysis of authority relationships. Functional authority is delegated to an activity and gives members of the activity the right to command. This right is based on the members' expertise in a narrow area of specialization, such as quality control. The delegation of functional authority enables managers to exercise control over those who are not their direct line subordinates. However, authority granted in this manner is confined to the specialized area for which it was delegated.

A simple chart, Figure 11-3, reflects the relationships brought about by the delegation of functional authority in a production department. The chart shows that the quality control manager through the inspectors has functional authority over the work of foremen in other departments. This means that if the quality inspectors find an operation "out of control" they can require that operation's foreman to suspend production until the problem is corrected.

Functional authority versus unity of command

There is no doubt that functional authority violates the principle of unity of command by introducing a second superior for one particular element of work (see Figure 11-3). Functional authority is often called *limited authority*, but this is a misnomer; a person either has authority or does not. Functional authority gives its holder full right and power to command—but in a restricted and specialized area.

Either line or staff personnel can assume functional authority. However, such authority is usually conferred on staff people because of their knowledge of specialized subjects, such as engineering, law, accounting, packaging, and design. Functional authority given to a line officer is known as *functional line authority;* that given to a staff person is known as *functional staff authority.*

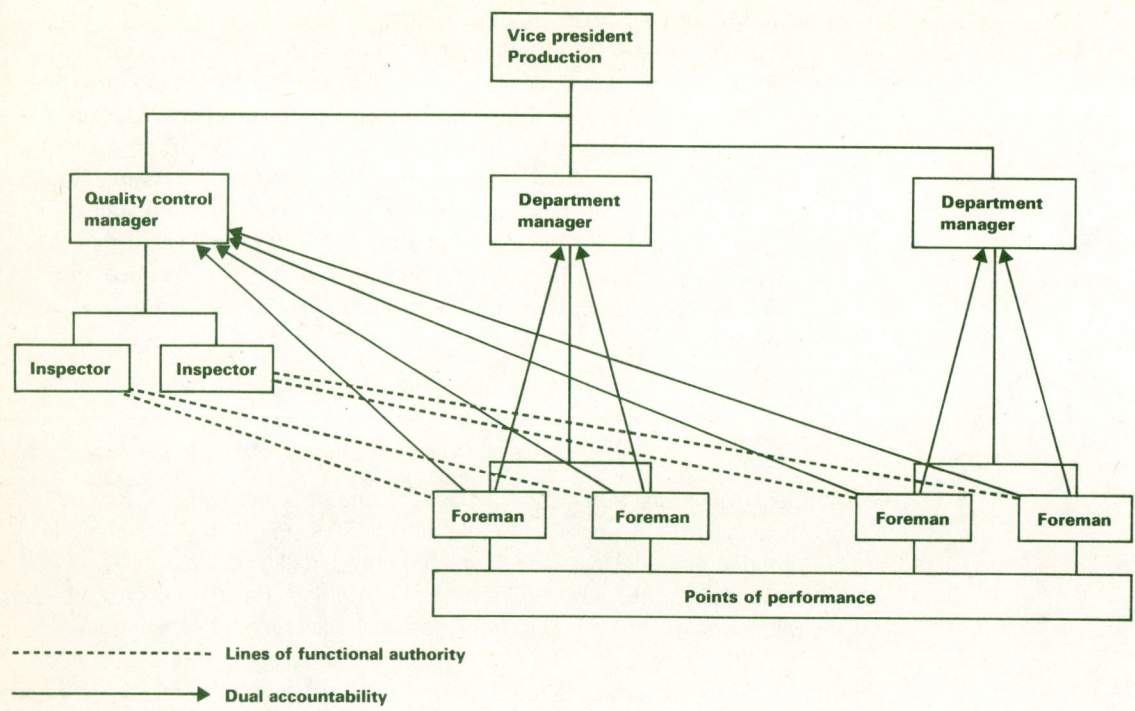

Figure 11-3 Functional authority

Functional staff authority

If an organization is large enough, staff work itself becomes differentiated into five functions: service, advice, control, initiation, and innovation.[1]

Service staff groups usually render some specialized function, such as maintenance. Their activities are indispensable to the organization, yet they are passive because they must be called into action by others.

A staff group, like market research, may supply information and suggest strategies. The group is responsible for generating appropriate data on request and on its own. Again, the line has the option to use the data and recommendations or to reject them.

Staff also helps to implement the control function. For example, the quality control staff group checks to ensure that actual performance meets standards. However, staff performing in this capacity must act after the fact—after action has been initiated by the line.

Some staff groups, like production control and scheduling, set actions into motion rather than monitor results. These staffs aid in synchronizing many of the activities that contribute to the output of a complex operation.

---

[1] These categories were suggested in Leonard Sayles, *Managerial Behavior* (New York: McGraw-Hill, 1964), chap. 6.

Finally, some staffs create new ideas. While all staffs may innovate to some extent, certain staffs, like those in research and development, have innovation as their primary responsibility.

Since staff work is dynamic, the responsibilities of a particular staff may not always remain the same. Indeed, several of the staff groups extend their influence so that they are not merely passive reactors to the line, but active agents of organizational change. Let us consider two examples.

Personnel One of the duties of an organization's personnel staff is to oversee union contracts, interpreting clauses and implementing grievance procedures. This staff guides, counsels, and advises line managers on the handling of grievances brought before it. However, staff people generally do not have the authority to decide and settle grievances. Their recommendations usually are incorporated into managerial decisions issued under the authority of the appropriate line personnel.

However, line managers may decide that, since a particular staff person is an expert in handling grievances, he or she should decide and settle those grievances and thus ensure uniform interpretation throughout the company. In this case, functional staff authority has been conferred on the staff personnel expert; that individual has full authority to determine whatever settlement he or she considers appropriate. The staff expert is now able to issue a settlement order and to sign it. Within the limits of the specialized functional area for which authority has been delegated, the staff person's role has been changed completely. The expert has now been clothed with functional authority—authority originally assigned to line, and line alone.

Accounting As another example of functional staff authority, consider a manufacturing enterprise with headquarters in New York and manufacturing plants in St. Louis and Los Angeles. Each of these plants is run by a manager who has been given sufficient authority to take full charge of local operations. The plant manager has full authority over all employees in the plant, regardless of the functions they perform. Each plant maintains some separate accounting records and, naturally, the local manager is given full line authority over the accounts in the plant. However, it is the task of the chief accountant at the central office in New York to maintain accounting records for the entire enterprise. In order for the accountant to be able to fulfill this responsibility, the necessary authority is needed. Therefore, the enterprise has conferred on the chief accountant the functional staff authority to determine the methods and manner in which the individual plant accountants are to perform their work. Without this authority, the chief accountant would be unable to ensure consistency in the records of the entire company and might become involved in serious conflicts with local plant managers. For instance, it is conceivable that the accountant in the St. Louis branch might charge depreciation on machinery at a much higher rate than that applied at the Los Angeles plant but at a much lower rate than the one used at headquarters.

In other words, the chief accountant has functional staff authority over the accounting activities in the St. Louis and Los Angeles plants, and the

196 Organizing

local plant manager has the authority and responsibility to see that the local plant accountants perform their work exactly as prescribed by the chief accountant. This, of course, violates the unity of command principle, because the local plant accountants now have two superiors, the chief accountant and the plant manager. However, this disadvantage is offset by the advantages of companywide standard accounting procedures.

Exercising functional authority

Generally speaking, functional authority is most effective when exercised over the operating line manager most directly concerned, bypassing several intermediate operating layers (see Figure 11-4). However, the senior line executives in these intermediate positions should be kept informed of the delegation decision.

Although this type of delegation is expedient, it can create problems. For instance, a person in a functional unit might need to issue directives to a manager who is actually a superior; thus, recalling our previous example, a vice president could receive instructions from someone below him or her in rank, who is in charge of accounting procedures. In this situation, the subordinate exercising functional authority is actually using the superior's authority. If the individual exercising functional authority is technically competent and if the use of authority is clearly understood and accepted, the arrangement will succeed. Functional authority can provide an effective short cut in accomplishing objectives.

In summary, although the orders issued by staff managers with functional authority are not really orders but merely representations of management's final decisions, the effect of these orders is the same as if they had come down through the direct channels of command. The line supervisor is responsible for seeing that they are carried out. If that individual believes that a particular order is wrong or unwise, he or she may appeal to a higher line executive for a change. Following a more expedient route, the individual

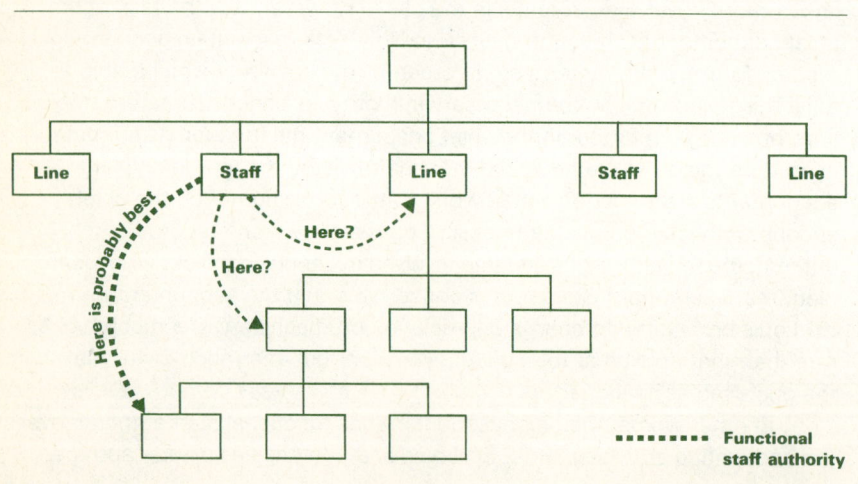

Figure 11-4 Flow of functional authority

might first see the staff members who issued the order. However, until and unless the order is changed, the line manager is expected to see that it is carried out.

Advantages and drawbacks

The main advantage of the delegation of functional authority is that it permits maximum effective use of staff specialization. A staff member given functional authority can intervene in line operations at any point that management designates. The price of this advantage is, of course, violation of unity of command. This drawback may indeed cause real frictions in some organizations. However, many feel that giving staff direct authority in restricted areas of line performance contributes more to efficiency and coordination than it detracts.

The problem that functional authority poses—conflict between the principles of unity of command and of specialization—has no general solution. It is an integral part of the overall set of relationships between staff and line.

The relation of staff to line

Staff-line relationships involve both structural and human aspects. They are reflected in the three basic problems discussed here: the levels of staff participation in organization, the relationship between line growth and staff growth, and the human relations problem of line and staff.

Levels of staff participation in the organization

Companywide service

In general, staff groups either perform companywide service or are in one of the three specialized basic business functions. The personnel department is companywide in scope. Figure 11-5 shows the personnel staff attached to the line organization between the president and the vice presidents.

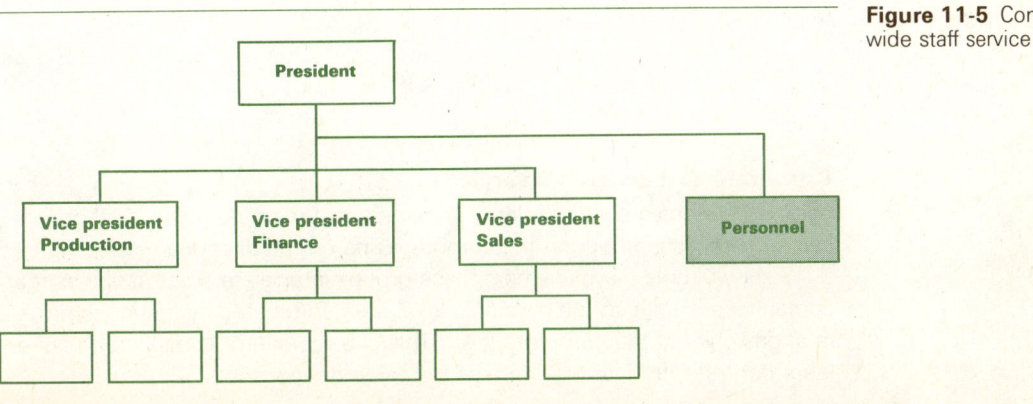

Figure 11-5 Companywide staff service

This does not mean that the personnel manager is higher in company rank than are the vice presidents. All it tells us is that the personnel department is available to give service and advice to the manager of each of the line departments. Each such department has problems with which personnel can help. These problems range from the recruitment, selection, and placement of personnel to training, employee service, and wage administration.

Service within a function

The other common form of staff participation, service within one of the basic functions of the company, is shown in Figure 11-6. Notice the positions of the staff departments under consideration. The quality control staff is concerned with the maintenance of standards at the point of production. The market research staff gathers data to assist in the development of marketing strategies and programs. The authority of these staff groups does not cut across the entire organization; rather, their work is limited to the functional area where their specialized knowledge is best utilized.

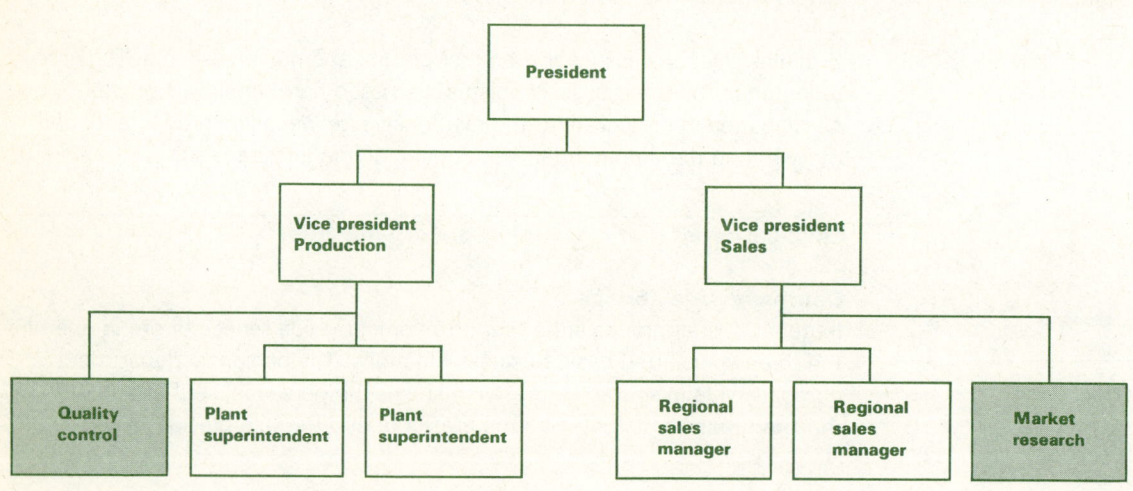

Figure 11-6 Staff service to the basic business functions

Corporate and divisional service

As organizations grow and relationships become more complex, staff groups can be established both on the corporate and on the divisional levels. Figure 11-7 shows three ways in which these groups interrelate. First, it shows that personnel activities at the divisional level are coordinated by the industrial relations chief at the corporate level. This allows uniform administration of a labor contract, for instance, across the three divisions.

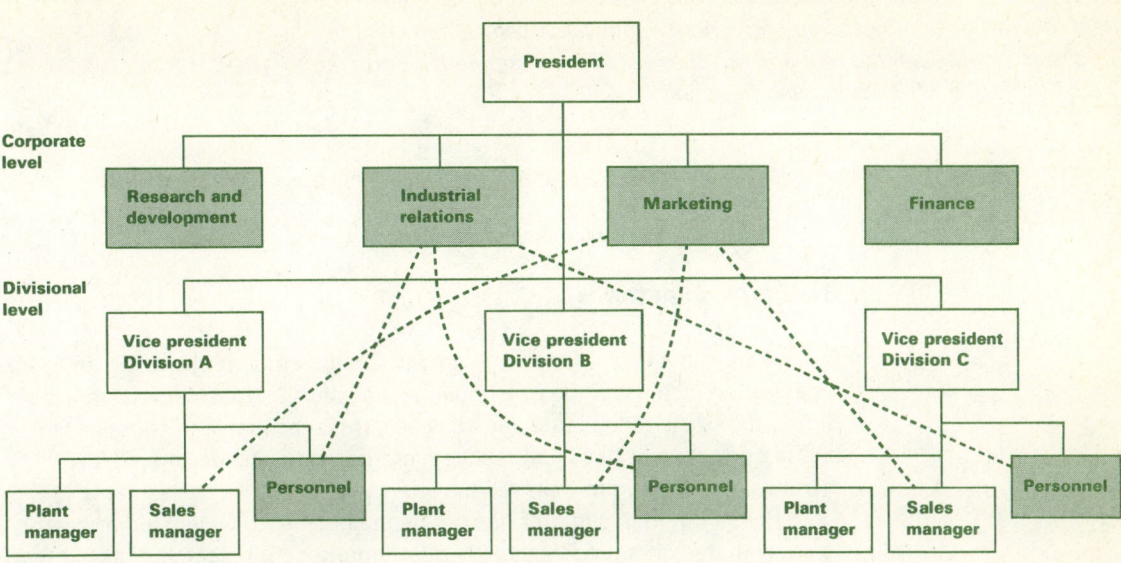

Figure 11-7 Corporate and divisional staff organizations

Second, the marketing department on the corporate level can supply consumer research data or coordinate sales efforts in the three divisions, or both. This department may assume the pure staff function of supplying information and advice to the divisions' sales managers. Or, in another organization, it might have both line and staff roles, coordinating and supervising activities as well as giving information.

Third, although the research and development group does not have continuous direct relationships with the divisions, its work in such areas as new product development and the improvement of internal operating methods and techniques eventually affects all of them.

Line and staff: Helping relationship?

There is a famous story that illustrates one of the problems frequently experienced by line managers and their staff personnel:

A plant manager and a staff engineer were on a hunting trip. One morning the engineer woke up early and went into the brush to get a lead on a tiger, which was reported to be in the vicinity of their camp. The manager was about to join his companion when he heard two shots and a blood-chilling roar, and heard his friend run toward the tent yelling, ''Open the flap! Open the flap!" Just as the manager ripped open the flap the engineer ran into the tent, chased by a huge snarling tiger not twenty yards behind him. As the engineer ran through the tent and out the rear flap, he shouted, "You take care of this one while I bring another one!"

Source: Adapted from John Stanley Baumgartner, *Project Management* (Homewood, Illinois: Richard D. Irwin, 1963), p. v.

Staff growth patterns

According to the law of functional growth, as the amount of work in an organization increases, the functional relationships increase at a faster rate. Since staff exists to facilitate line activities, it is reasonable to suppose that after a certain point has been reached in organizational size, the staff will increase at a faster rate than will the line.

Research on this matter has not been conclusive. Older studies seem to show that such a tendency holds true; more recent research does not support this conclusion. For example, Alan Filley[2] found no simple relationship between the growth of line and the natural increase of staff. Instead, he saw staff emerging at any point in a company's life span as a result of executive decision making.

Human problems of line-staff relations

Although relationships between line and staff may be clearly specified, conflict often arises. In many enterprises, in fact, there is continuous warfare—sometimes open, sometimes concealed—between line managers and staff. At times, this antagonism exists in both the higher and the lower echelons of the organization. In all fairness, we should state that there are also many cases where line and staff work together as a team, solving problems with cooperation and coordination.

Line complaints

Where staff-line conflict does exist, it may diminish the functioning and productivity of the enterprise. How does such conflict arise? One of line managers' most common complaints is that staff wants to usurp line authority. Another common complaint is that the advice of staff is academic, theoretical, and unrealistic. Line managers contend, moreover, that since staff personnel are not responsible for ultimate results, they tend to propose untried and untested ideas. However, line would sometimes willingly put these ideas into effect if the staff would discuss and explain them properly.

[2] Alan C. Filley, "Decisions and Research in Staff Utilization," *Academy of Management Journal* 6 (September 1963):220–231.

But such explanations are often expressed so technically that they are difficult for line to understand.

Another complaint is that staff thinks in a vacuum. Line managers believe that staff specialists are so involved with their own specialties that they do not think in terms of the objectives of the enterprise as a whole. This complaint is common and at times quite valid. Equally justified are those who point out that line managers will be blamed for failures, but staff will try to take the credit for successes.

Staff complaints

Staff people have their case, too. One of the most frequently heard staff complaints is that line managers resist new ideas and are not willing to accept the rapid progress of a particular specialty. Another common complaint is that line does not make the proper use of available staff; often, those line managers who need specialized advice the most hesitate to ask for it. Such line people seem to think that asking for staff advice is admitting ignorance or defeat. Then, again, staff often complains that some line managers, after going through the motions of asking for advice, reject the suggestions either because they really did not want them in the first place or because they distrust the staff adviser. Another complaint frequently made by staff is that it does not have enough authority. Staff people often believe that if they have arrived at the best solution, they should be able to put it into action.

As we have seen, these line-staff problems result in large part from the confrontation of two kinds of authority—the authority based on position and the authority based on expertise. Since each requires special personal qualifications, it is no wonder that line managers, who possess different training, aspirations, expectations, and responsibilities, disagree with staff over organizational and operational problems.

Other specialized organizational functions

Several other organizational positions cannot strictly be called either line or staff. The preponderance of these are held by assistant-to and liaison personnel.

"Assistant-to"

The assistant-to belongs to a single executive's personal staff. Usually, assistant-to functions are performed by one person who does a wide variety of jobs for the executive. This person does not have line authority. Rather, the assistant-to acts as an "extension of the arms and the mind" of the executive, gathering information, doing special research projects, and generally acting to relieve the executive of details that cannot be delegated to a staff group or left to a secretary. From time to time, the role of assistant-to is used in management training to show young executives how high-level officers function.

The assistant-to also helps by serving as a bridge between the executive and other parts of the organization. Such a person often can circulate more comfortably than can the executive. Other organization members therefore may be able to sound out the assistant-to to learn the executive's position on an organizational issue.[3] Executives, of course, understand this function very well. They often use their assistants in a reverse fashion, to disseminate information in an informal way. Politicians in particular have raised this process to a fine art.

Liaison

The liaison function is quite a different kind of activity. Liaison people act as representatives for their firm in dealings with other firms. For example, a large aircraft manufacturer often has liaison representatives in the plants of some of its suppliers to ensure that components are produced according to standards and to help the supplier overcome whatever technical problems might be encountered. Very often, liaison people are used to coordinate public utility firms operating in the same power network system (see Chapter 12). Liaison work is used also between government agencies and private contractors.

The traditional organizational structure

We have been discussing the traditional structure of formal organizations. The label *traditional* is used for several reasons. First, the structures that it represents are those most often encountered in the real world. Second, its forms are those that have received the most attention in the past from scholars of management and sociology. Indeed, as we have discussed, the German sociologist Max Weber's work on the nature of bureaucracy established the foundations of formal organization theory. And, third, such systems are those found in historical studies of the military, government, or church. In other words, the traditional model of organization is not restricted historically to business.

Specifically, traditional theory is still most appropriate for organizations that

1 exist in a relatively stable environment.
2 employ a high proportion of semiskilled and unskilled workers.

[3] Thomas Whisler, "The Assistant-to in Four Administrative Settings," *Administrative Science Quarterly* 5 (1960):181–216.

3 use a fairly unadvanced technology in achieving a relatively uncomplicated product.
4 are not gigantic in size, judged by the number of people employed.

These four points more or less define the limits of the traditional model. Most business firms fit within these limits and, therefore, find this form of organization quite useful. Appendix A demonstrates some of the ways in which traditional principles are translated into organization charts and manuals.

Line and staff: Helping relationship?

Time: Mid-1965.   Subject: The war in Vietnam.
As far as Washington was concerned, [the war] was something they slipped into more than they chose; they thought they were going to have time to make clear, well-planned choices, to decide how many men and what type of strategy they would follow, but events got ahead of them. The pressures from Saigon for more and more men would exceed Washington's capacity to slow it down and think coolly, and so the decisions evolved rather than were made, and Washington slipped into a ground combat war.

But it was not something that the military in Saigon slipped into; the planning of troops, the need for them and how to use them was something that had long been in the contingency planning stage, and now, slowly, MACV was moving toward it, careful not to ask for too much too soon lest it scare the White House; in fact, CINCPAC was far more aggressive than Westmoreland in the early days; Westy was asking for small units and the Joint Chiefs of Staff was asking for three divisions, a figure far larger than the commander dared ask for, fearing that it might blow the whole thing.

In April the military arm of MACV was asked to do an estimate for Westmoreland on the enemy capacity for reinforcement; when the assignment was given, no one knew what the answer would be. But when Colonel William Crossen, one of the top intelligence officers, put it together he was appalled: the number of men that Hanoi could send down the trails without seriously damaging its defenses at home was quite astonishing. The North was very small but turned out to have a very large army. When Crossen came up with his final figure he could not believe it, so he checked it again, being more conservative in the use of enemy figures, and still he was staggered by what he found; the other side had an amazing capacity and capability of reinforcing. When he brought the study to Westmoreland's staff and showed the figure to a general there, he looked at it and said that it was impossible. Not impossible at all, answered Crossen, checked and double-checked. "Jesus," said the general, "if we tell this to the people in Washington we'll be out of the war tomorrow. We'll have to revise it downward."

So Crossen's figures were duly scaled down considerably, which was a good example of how the Army system worked, the staff intuitively protecting the commander from things he didn't want to see and didn't want to hear, never coming up with information which might challenge what a commander wanted to do at a given moment. Because the Westmoreland staff in February, March and April of 1965 knew that he wanted to get in the ball game with combat troops, it did everything carefully, never getting ahead of itself. The design was in private, if the truth were to be known, rather grand, but Lyndon Johnson was a great salami slicer, and no one was smarter than Westmoreland at knowing how much salami to order at a given time, how much he would be allowed to carry home.

Source: David Halberstam, *The Best and the Brightest* (New York: Random House, 1972), pp. 544—545.

The traditional model has been much criticized, however. A number of scholars say that it has internal inconsistencies and, therefore, does not work well; that it is not responsive to the needs of the people in the organization; and that it does not adapt easily to change. Some of these criticisms are treated in Appendix B, following Chapter 12.

Summary

Staff activities are the result of the third way in which managers divide organizational labor. In addition to dividing labor horizontally through departmentalization and vertically through delegation, managers often develop positions that are assigned highly specialized tasks to perform. These positions are called *staff*.

The authority of staff personnel derives from their expertise. This authority occurs either in the form of advice and counsel or in actual commands to other organizational personnel. The latter case reflects functional authority, in which the staff person is operating within the guidelines sanctioned by the organization—especially top management.

Functional authority is a useful managerial device that attempts to avoid the problem of managers' issuing commands in areas in which they are unskilled. On the other hand, functional authority violates the principle of unity of command, producing predictable problems. Functional authority frequently takes one of two forms: the staff person issuing commands to line personnel, like the personnel officer who determines who is and who is not eligible for a particular training program, or the staff person working for line management but following instructions of a senior staff person, say, at corporate headquarters.

Typically, staff people perform advising duties; frequently, however, they operate as assistants-to and as liaisons with other organizational members. Staff-line relationships are fraught with conflict. This conflict stems primarily from the differences in education, orientation, and responsibilities of the two types of work.

Discussion questions

1. What dangers do you see in managers' placing too much reliance on staff? too little?
2. If you were in charge of a staff department, which function (service, advice, control, initiation, innovation) would you like your department to perform for the rest of the organization?
3. Is line-staff conflict inherently harmful?
4. What organizational mechanisms (procedures, official authority relationships, and so on) should be used to minimize the harmful effects of line-staff conflict?

Supplementary readings

Belasco, James A., and Alutto, Joseph A. "Line and Staff Conflicts: Some Empirical Insights." *Academy of Management Journal* 12 (December 1969):469–477.

Browne, Phillip J., and Golembiewski, Robert T. "The Line-Staff Concept Revisited: An Empirical Study of Organizational Images." *Academy of Management Journal,* September 1974, pp. 406–417.

Dalton, Melville E. "Changing Line-Staff Conflict: Its Causes and Cure." *Personnel* 39 (1962):11–15.

———. "Conflicts Between Staff and Line Managerial Officers." *American Sociological Review,* June 1950, pp. 342–351.

Gulick, Luther. "The Theory of Organization." In *Papers on the Science of Administration,* edited by Luther Gulick and Lyndall F. Urwick. New York: Institute of Public Administration, 1937.

Logan, Hall H. "Line and Staff: An Obsolete Concept?" *Personnel,* January–February 1966, pp. 26–33. Reprinted in *Dimensions in Modern Management* 2d ed., edited by Patrick E. Connor. Boston: Houghton Mifflin, 1978.

Sampson, Robert C. *The Staff Role in Management.* New York: Harper & Row, 1955.

Toussaint, Maynard N. "Line-Staff Conflict: Its Causes and Cure." *Personnel* 39 (1962):11–15.

Appendix A

Preparing formal organization charts and manuals

This discussion concerns the details of formally depicting and explaining organizational division of labor. The method: organization charts and manuals. Many firms utilize these tools; managers find them helpful in conducting their organizing function.

Organization charts

Organization charts graphically portray an organization's structure. They show the skeleton of the organization's structure and depict basic relationships and groupings of positions and functions. The charts are relatively easy to construct. Usually, they begin with the function under consideration usually shown as a box. Each box represents one function. The various boxes are then interconnected to show the groupings of activities that make up departments, divisions, or other parts of the organization. By studying the position of the boxes in their scalar relationships, we can readily determine who reports to whom.

    Organization charts can be of considerable assistance to managers. Charts not only portray the existing organization, but they also can be used to improve communications and personnel relations and to analyze the organization for future planning purposes. Some organizations, in fact, have two charts: one depicting the existing organization and another—a so-called master plan that the company has designed as a long-term objective—showing the ideal organization.

    Sometimes, managers do not recognize the numerous uses and purposes of charts. Managers who do not chart their organization give several reasons for neglecting this valuable tool. Some are concerned that the chart is likely to emphasize an individual's superiority or inferiority, or to give people who occupy rectangular boxes an exaggerated feeling of security and a lifetime claim to their positions. Other managers believe that it is easier for them to change the organization if there is no chart, or they believe that if one has been drawn up it should be kept secret. These objections indicate that management does not fully understand a chart's purpose, advantages, and limitations.

Advantages

As people draw its structure, they cannot help but analyze the organization. Through this analysis, structural faults, duplications of effort, and other inconsistencies that lead to lowered performance are revealed. Situations of this nature occur most frequently in enterprises where rapid expansion has occurred and where management, because of the speed of expansion, did not pay much attention to the organization per se.

Organizational charting also can be a great help in personnel administration. An organization chart will often indicate possible progression lines for managers in firms concerned with management development programs.

Charts provide a simple guide to organizational make-up. Most people within an organization have a keen interest in knowing where they stand, where their superior stands in relation to the higher echelons, and so forth. When organizational adjustments are made, publication of before and after versions of the organization chart can provide one of the most effective means of informing the members of the enterprise of the various changes.

Limitations

At best, an organization chart is merely a snapshot of the existing structure. Furthermore, it holds true only as long as the organization's status quo is maintained. As soon as changes occur, the chart is as outdated as yesterday's newspaper. It is, therefore, imperative to chart changes within the organization at once.

As we have implied, the information transmitted by a chart is limited. It shows only what is on the surface. It does not show informal relationships, which may be numerous and important. The chart also fails to show precise functions, amounts of authority, and responsibility. Although these shortcomings are substantial, they do not negate the value of the chart.

Responsibility for charting

When securing data for organizational charts, some companies are concerned only with current structure; they do not attempt to inject organizational analysis. Other companies, however, combine data procurement with a systematic approach to organizing.

Responsibility and authority for the preparation, review, and final approval of the organization chart lies with line management, generally with the chief executive. In individual departments this responsibility would probably rest with the head of the department. However, especially in large corporations, a specialized staff department at the corporate level often is charged with the duty of advising line management on the preparation of its organization charts. In some companies, this is done by the organization planning department or the department on organization. In either case, the individuals who are charged with preparing the organization chart usually obtain most of their data from the incumbents in various positions. In addition, they speak to the heads of units to get an overall idea of how each unit is organized. After all the data are collected, a temporary draft is prepared and reviewed. Once the draft has been verified, the final organization chart is drawn up and distributed as a portrayal of the organizational structure. Regardless of the amount of help and advice such a department will give in preparing, reviewing, and drawing the organization chart, approval and endorsement of the final document are the responsibility of line management. Final approval for its publication and distribution usually comes from the chief executive.

Types of charts

Vertical

Although different types of organization charts are available, an organization should plan to use consistently whatever type it has selected. About 95 percent of all business firms choose the vertical organization chart, which presents the different levels of organization in a step arrangement, with the senior executive placed at the top of the chart and the successive levels of management depicted vertically in pyramid form. This type of chart shows functional relationships, chains of command, and interconnecting lines of subordinates, and gives enough captions to clarify the structure.

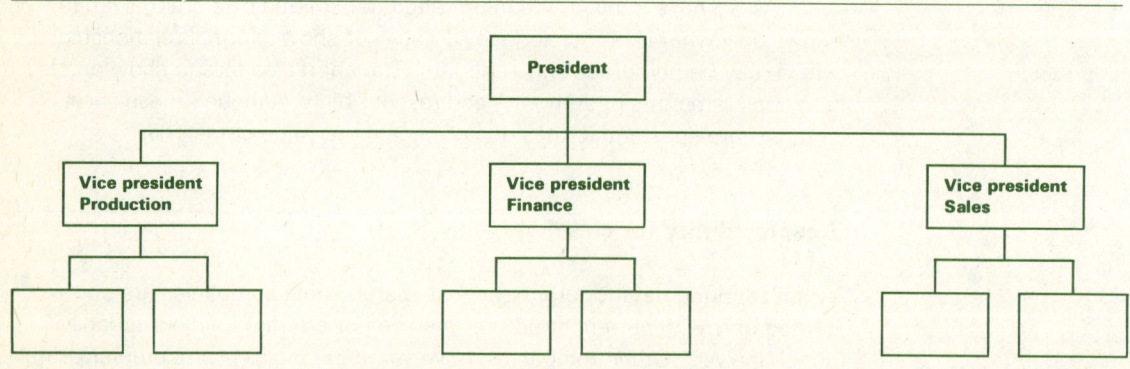

(a) Top-line management

Figure A-1 Conventional forms of organizational charting

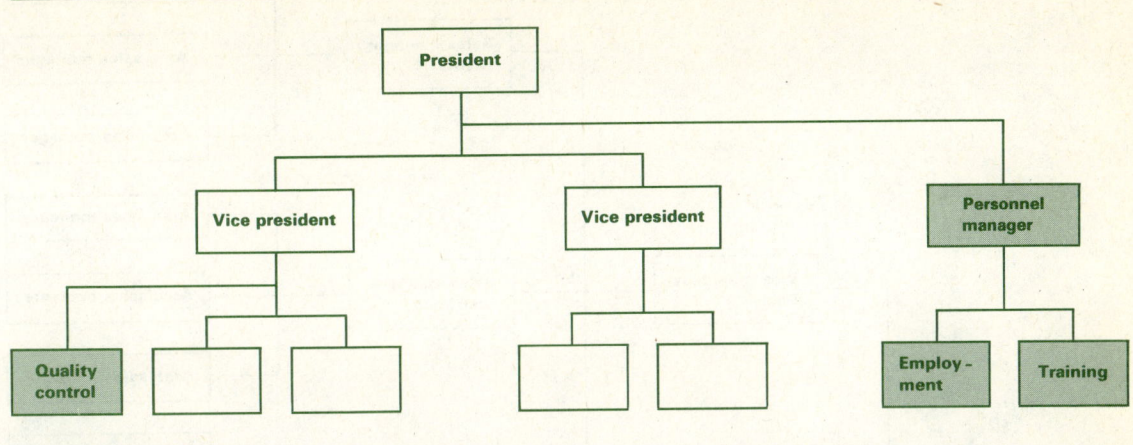

(b) Staff included

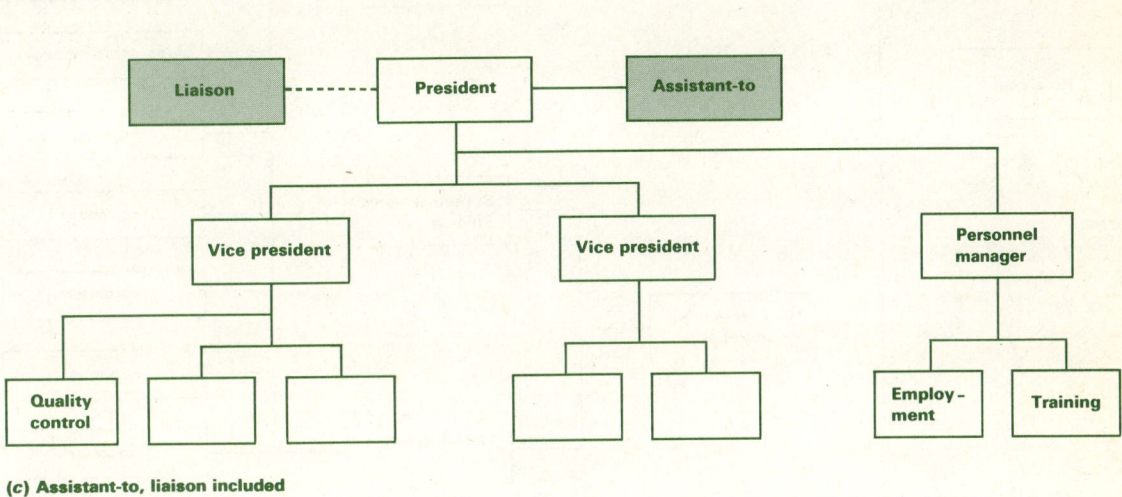

(c) Assistant-to, liaison included

Figure A-1 (cont.)

Special relationships can be indicated, as they are in Figure A-1, by the positioning of functions and lines on the chart. The straight-line organization chart should show the lines of authority clearly, the functional relationship of activities (that is, sales, production, and so on), and, to the greatest extent possible, the activities that are on the same level (that is, vice president, production; treasurer; and vice president, sales).

Often it is impossible to tell from the organization chart whom managers consider to be staff. This situation can be corrected easily by drawing a

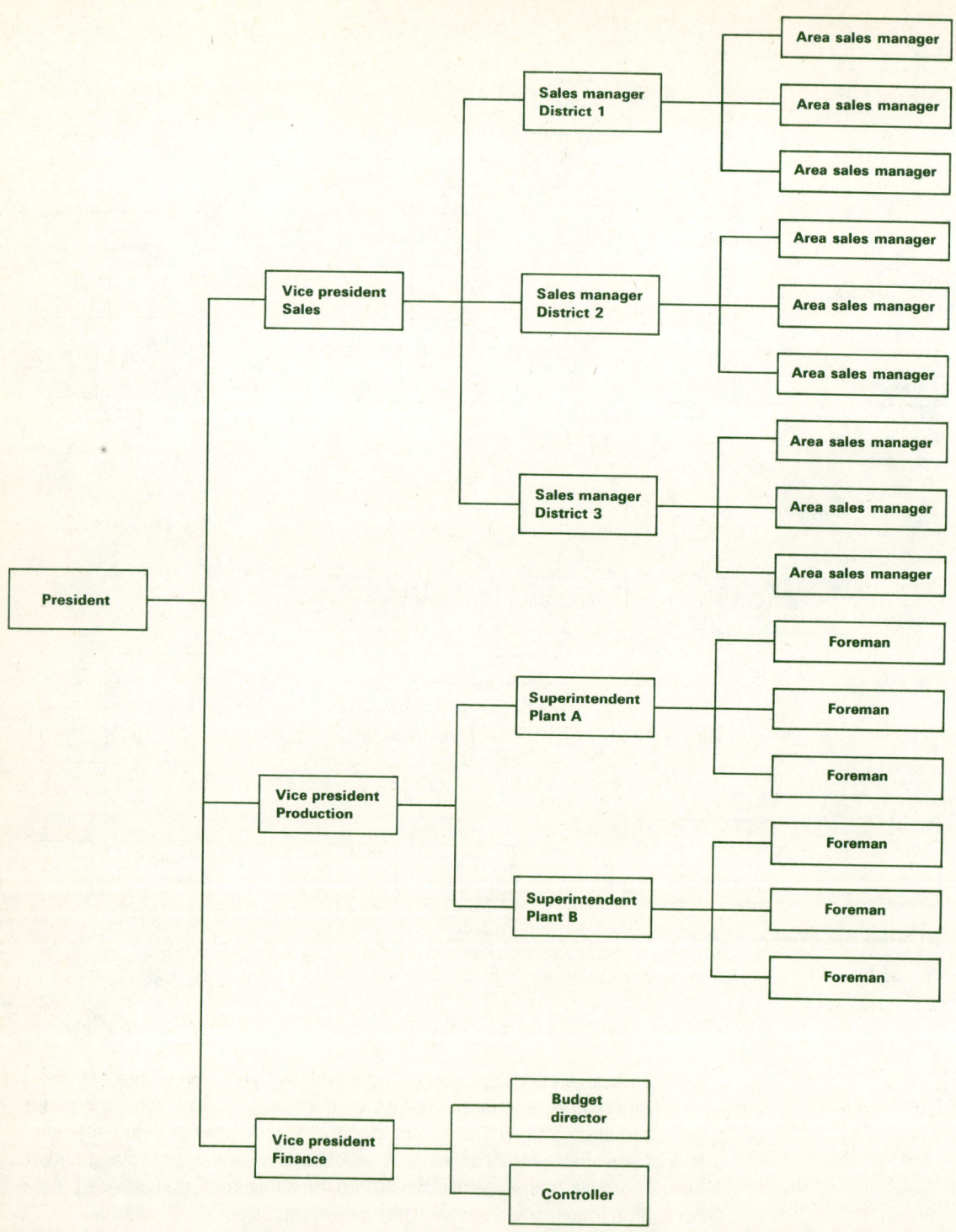

Figure A-2 Horizontal organization chart

horizontal line from one of the vertical trunk lines of the primary organization to the staff function (quality control, personnel, and so on) and its secondary chain of command, as in Figure A-1(b). Other special organizational personnel also can be designated on the vertical chart and related to the basic organization. In part (c) of Figure A-1 we see how this is done in the cases of a liaison person and an assistant-to.

One of the chief advantages of vertical organization charts is that they can be easily read and understood; the downward flow of delegation, for instance, is clearly shown by connecting lines. One of their limitations is that, like all organization charts, the information they convey is only partial. Another limitation is that unless a special device is adopted, either line or staff, even if on the same level, will appear subordinate to the other, depending on which appears higher on the chart. The same impression results if one division of an organization has more levels than another. For instance, a three-level organizational unit may show the foremen on the lowest level, whereas they may be on the third level in a five-level organizational unit.

Horizontal

Although vertical organization charts are the most conventional type, horizontal charts, which read from left to right, are occasionally used (Figure A-2). One of the advantages of this type of chart is that it minimizes the importance of hierarchical levels. It emphasizes functional relationships.

Circular

A third type of organization chart, commonly known as the circular chart, is illustrated in Figure A-3. In this chart, the position of the chief executive is located in the center of concentric circles. Positions of equal importance lie on the same concentric circle. This arrangement eliminates any position at the bottom of the chart and shows the flow of formal authority from the chief executive in many directions. Unfortunately, at first glance a circular organization chart may seem somewhat confusing.

Additional charting considerations

Many other considerations should be kept in mind when charting an organization. Charts may have differing purposes: organizations can be charted according to functions, products, or geographical locations. Chartmakers may choose to ignore certain factors: in some charts no attempt is made to distinguish between line and staff functions, and they are shown on the same reporting level. Other charts differentiate line and staff by means of light and heavy lines or by the position of the lines, as we have done.

Managers must also remember charting difficulties. They must consider the problem of drawing a chart so that it reveals the true relative status of the positions and the various departments shown. In addition, mechanical considerations may appear important. Executives may be concerned by the

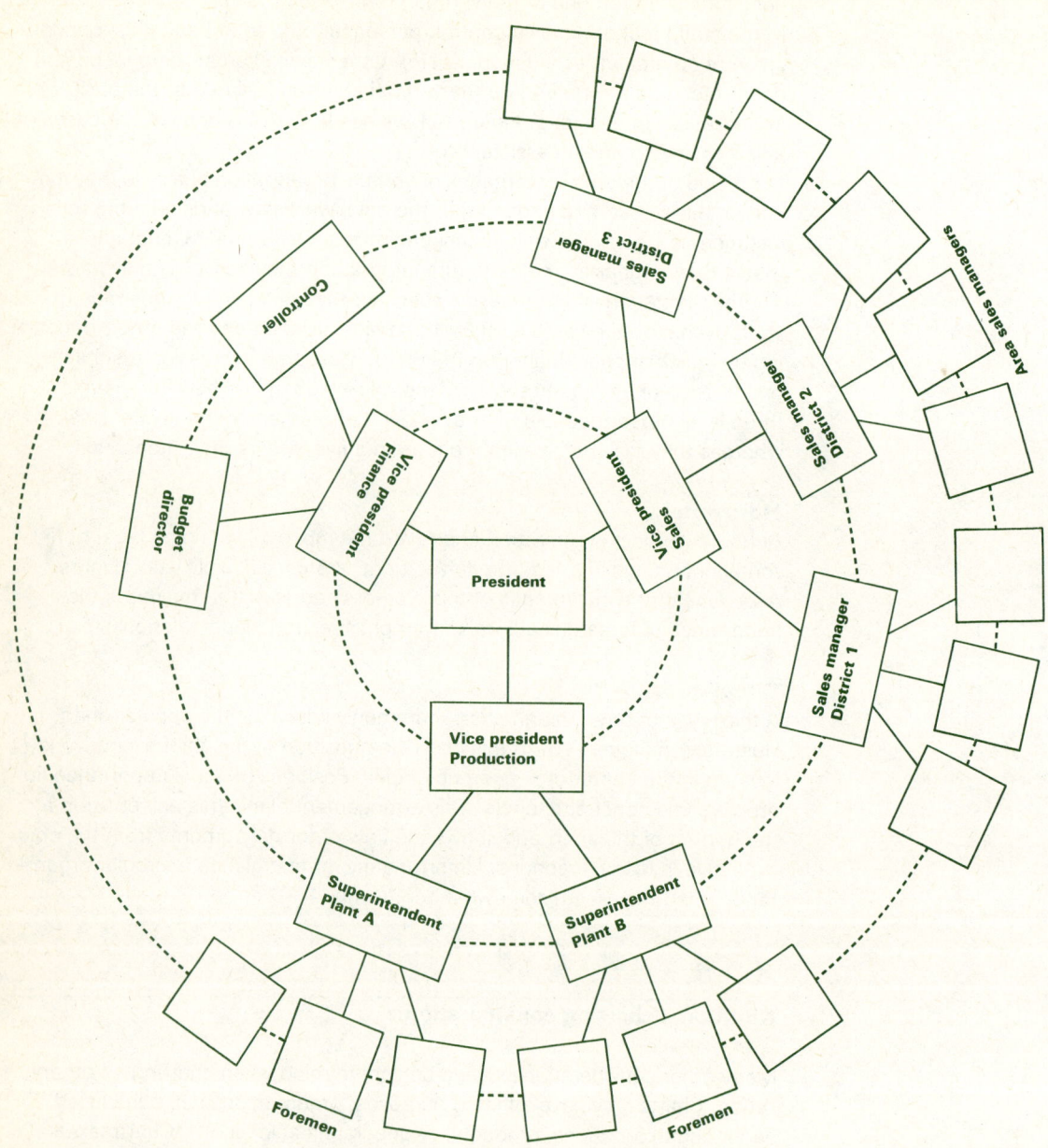

Figure A-3 Circular organization chart

placement and orientation of a chart on the page, the balance of the chart, the simplicity, the amount of white space, the identification of contents, the date of the chart, the conservation of space, and so forth.

Organization manuals

The organization manual is another helpful tool for effective organizing. Although compiling a manual involves a considerable amount of work and expense, larger enterprises have found the effort worthwhile. A manual provides, in comprehensive written form, decisions regarding the company's organizational structure; it defines the scope of authorities and responsibilities of management positions and the channels to be used in obtaining decisions or approvals of proposals; it is also helpful in the selection, orientation, development, and appraisal of management personnel. A manual specifies the scope of each manager's job and its relationship to the other positions within the organization. A manual also serves to reiterate for the individual executive the long-term objectives of the enterprise.

Naturally, some drawbacks to organization manuals exist. As we have indicated, compiling them and keeping them up to date are time consuming. Also, manuals sometimes have a confining effect. Likewise, they may reveal sensitive relationships.

Content

An organization manual normally pictures an entire organization with its various departments and functions. In it can be found a statement of the objectives of the company, its policies, a definition of terms, a definition of organizational principles, a discussion of organizational problems, job descriptions, a guide to the use of names and titles, organization charts, and so on. An organization manual often contains a brief statement of the firm's underlying philosophy. Such a statement might cover the quality of company products, pricing, teamwork, service, good citizenship, and the like.

Job descriptions

All manuals contain job descriptions, although some contain more than others, depending on the size of the group for which the manual is intended. Job descriptions generally indicate the principal duties and functions of the position, the scope of authority, and its channels. Two job descriptions are shown in Figures A-4 and A-5.

In compiling job descriptions, as in drawing organization charts, information is usually obtained from the incumbent. Again, such work can expose organizational discrepancies—dual responsibilities, fuzziness of assignments, overlapping of efforts. Checking and verifying position descriptions with the incumbent often can lead to clarifications and to necessary reorganization. Other advantages, revealed in the discussion of charting, also apply here.

Before we leave this topic, we should note that there is some confusion in the use of the terms *job description* and *job specification*. Generally speaking, the former objectively describes the elements of a position, whereas the latter specifies the qualities a person must possess in order to perform the job adequately. In certain companies, job descriptions are extended to include some personal qualities. Where this is not done, such specifications must be drawn up separately.

REPORTS TO: Division Director

SUPERVISES: Assigned Staff

BASIC FUNCTION:
   Under the direction of the Director, performs related clerical and administrative duties and relieves departmental supervisors of as much office detail as practical.

MAJOR DUTIES:
1. Prepares and edits memos, routine letters, and other materials for typing by the word-processing center.

2. Acts as liaison and maintains flow of communication between supervisors and other departmental personnel.

3. Relieves supervisors of clerical and administrative duties such as filing correspondence and memos, replying to standard requests for information, and completing routine administrative reports.

4. Prepares routine notices and bulletins, arranges for meetings, makes appointments and reservations, and maintains a calendar of important items in supervisor work schedules.

5. Acts as liaison between a supervisor and the public when supervisor is out of the office, keeping him informed of items, and routing or answering routine items.

6. Maintains an updated list of division staff work load, assignments, and/or availability for use in assigning project responsibility, promotional activity, or staffing.

7. Assists in assembly, draft copy, and editing response to invitations for firm qualifications and proposals.

8. Performs other duties as required.

Figure A-4 Job description: Assistant to division director

Titles

There is little agreement on the use and meaning of titles. For instance, the chief executive officer of one of the divisions of the duPont Corporation is called the general manager. In this capacity, the chief executive officer presides over a division empire whose capital investments and sales probably each run into the hundreds of millions of dollars. On the other hand, the chief executive officer in another enterprise with the same or, more likely, a

Figure A-5 Job description: Executive vice president, finance and administration

```
REPORTS TO: President

SUPERVISES: Assistant Secretary
            Chief Accountant
            Controller
            Manager of Management Information Systems
            Manager of Office Administration
            Staff Attorney

BASIC FUNCTION:
    Plans and directs treasury, administrative, accounting,
    purchasing, legal, secretarial, real estate, and insurance
    activities for the firm and its subsidiaries. Provides the
    President with general and administrative assistance.

MAJOR DUTIES:
 1. Appraises the corporation's financial position and issues
    periodic financial reports. Determines and arranges for
    required capital.

 2. Directs the Manager of Office Administration in the
    improvement and standardization of administrative systems
    and procedures.

 3. Directs the Controller and others in the maintenance of
    reports and analysis for management control and the profit
    improvement program.

 4. Directs the Chief Accountant in providing procedures and
    systems necessary to maintain proper records and to afford
    adequate accounting controls and services.

 5. Directs the Manager of Management Information Systems in
    satisfying the firm's information needs.

 6. Directs the Staff Attorney in providing legal counsel and
    guidance. Responsible for federal agency contracting
    procedures.

 7. Supervises the overall evaluation of the utilization of
    corporate physical properties.

 8. Assists the President in preparing short- and long-range
    plans.

 9. Formulates and recommends operating policies and objectives,
    or changes in existing policies and objectives.

10. Directs the preparation of and issues the corporation's
    Annual Report and other reports to stockholders.

11. Discharges duties of the President in his absence or
    disability.
```

considerably lower volume of investment and sales would probably be called the president.

Although the use of titles may vary considerably among different organizations, within a single organization titles must have a definite meaning and must be used consistently. Therefore, the organization manual should clearly specify the allocation of titles to executives in both staff and line operations.

Doing so permits prompt identification of comparable status within organizational levels. Such comparability often is facilitated by using a basic title, such as manager, to which an adjective is added connoting the rank, for example, assistant manager. Possibly another or several more adjectives will be included to describe the activities of the particular executive, for instance, assistant sales manager, fuel oil, West Coast.

Preparation and revision

Although ultimate responsibility for the organization manual rests with the chief executive, an assistant or the staff department primarily concerned with organizational planning usually aid in its compilation. Because making an organization manual is costly, its scope should be confined to the important targets of top management activities. Also, unless a manual is revised regularly, it can quickly become outdated. Therefore, annual, semiannual, or even quarterly revisions are necessary.

Chapter 12

Managing the structure: Coordinating

Objectives of the chapter

1 To trace the relationship between division of labor and coordination.
2 To define *coordination*.
3 To describe the coordination process in modern organizations.
4 To describe the various methods and types of coordination that exist in modern organizations.
5 To relate coordination to the basic managerial functions.

The division of labor creates a need for coordination. That is, performing tasks requires labor to be divided among various organizational units. As a result, managers must coordinate the activities of these units to assure that common objectives are pursued effectively. Why? Principally, because the division of labor inevitably leads to specialization. Specialists, with their narrow range of training and activities, often develop relatively narrow perspectives. Over time, production people tend to view organizational problems as production problems, engineers view them as engineering problems, sales managers view them as sales problems, and so on. Thus, coordination is required. The process is described in Figure 12-1.

As we have discussed, the use of division of labor (decentralization) has increased in modern organizations and, consequently, so has the need for coordination. We can only marvel at the coordination required for a modern automobile assembly line. Thousands of parts must be fed from subsidiary lines into the main line, at precisely the right moment, to make a car according to specifications. No less complex is the coordination required for a contemporary Health Maintenance Organization (HMO). A clinic, hospital, pharmacy, preventive-medicine center, geriatric unit, and a dozen other organizations rolled into one, the HMO requires that a myriad of tasks, resources, people, and activities be coordinated.

Coordination is necessary not only to the organization's production processes—but to management as well. Managers provide the systems that divide all labor into specialized tasks. They then coordinate these tasks so that the objectives of the organization may be achieved. Division of labor and coordination are the natural imperatives of organizational management; they exist in the smallest informal groups and in the largest corporations. Both are central to the understanding of the organizing process, for the division of labor is the reason for organization.

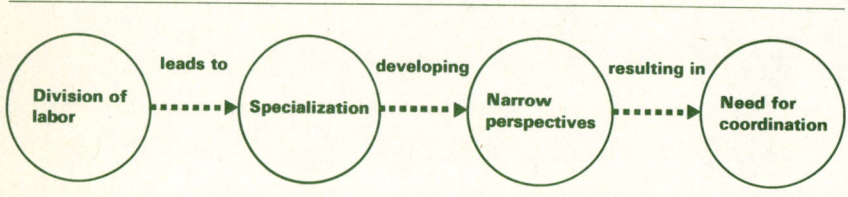

Figure 12-1 The need for coordination

The meaning of coordination

Definitions and interpretations

Regardless of where and on what level in the organization the division of labor takes place, the need for management coordination arises simultaneously. Because the division of labor is universal in organizations, coordination is a universal process too. *Coordination is the conscious process of assembling and synchronizing differentiated activities so that they function harmoniously in the attainment of organizational objectives.*

As Fayol saw it, coordination pulls together all the activities of an enterprise to make possible both its working and its success. The well-coordinated enterprise, he believed, bears the following marks: each department works in harmony with the other departments; each department, division, and subdivision knows the share of the common task it must assume; and each department and subdivision adjusts its working schedule to circumstances. Fayol found that these requirements are not always fulfilled and postulated three reasons for this. First, each department knows and wants to know little of the others; second, watertight compartments exist between divisions and offices of the same department exactly comparable to those between different departments; and third, no one thinks of the general interest. He wrote: "This attitude on the part of the personnel, so disastrous for a concern, is not the result of preconcerted intention but the culmination of non-existent or inadequate coordination."[1] To remedy this situation, Fayol suggested a weekly conference of department heads to facilitate a coordinated and current plan of action. If such weekly meetings could not be held

---

[1] Henri Fayol, *General and Industrial Management*, trans. Constance Storrs (London: Pitman, 1949), p. 104.

at all or if they could be held only at longer intervals, Fayol urged the use of liaison officers to link departments.

Other writers view coordination differently. For example, Ralph C. Davis looks at coordination primarily as a vital phase of control.[2] Louis A. Allen cites coordinating as a managerial function alongside planning, organizing, motivating, and controlling.[3] However, he goes on to say that most coordination will be accomplished automatically if sound objectives, policies, procedures, and organization are established.[4] James D. Mooney defines coordination as "the orderly arrangement of group effort, to provide unity of action in the pursuit of a common purpose."[5] He calls coordination the first principle of organization. By this he means that coordination embraces all the principles of organization in toto—nothing less. Mooney's statement best expresses the universality of the coordination process; coordination means unity of action in the accomplishment of objectives.

Ordway Tead provides another definition of coordination: "Coordination is the effort to assure a smooth interplay of the functions and forces of all the different component parts of an organization to the end that its purposes will be realized with a minimum of friction and a maximum of collaborative effectiveness."[6] Coordination, in effect, synchronizes the actions of people within an organization, and one of the important goals of every management is to achieve this synchronization. Chester I. Barnard even goes so far as to say that under most circumstances "the quality of coordination is the crucial factor in the survival of organization."[7] Coordination is not a separate nor distinct activity of management; it is a part of all the managerial functions, transversing the entire management process.

Coordination and cooperation

The term *coordination* should not be confused with *cooperation;* there is considerable difference between them. Cooperation indicates an attitude of a group of people: their willingness to help each other. Coordination is more inclusive, requiring more than desire and willingness. For instance, consider a group of people attempting to move a heavy object. Even if they are sufficient in number, are willing and eager to cooperate, are trying to do their best to move the object, and are also fully aware of their common purpose, in all likelihood they will fail. Only when one of them takes charge

---

[2] Ralph C. Davis, *The Fundamentals of Top Management* (New York: Harper & Row, 1951), p. 19.
[3] Louis A. Allen, *Management and Organization* (New York: McGraw-Hill, 1958), p. 24.
[4] Ibid., p. 43.
[5] James D. Mooney, *The Principles of Organization*, rev. ed. (New York: Harper & Row, 1947), p. 5.
[6] Ordway Tead, *Administration: Its Purpose and Performance* (New York: Harper & Row, 1959), p. 36.
[7] Chester I. Barnard, *The Functions of the Executive* (Cambridge, Mass.: Harvard University Press, 1938), p. 256.

and gives the proper orders, to apply the right amount of effort at the right place and the right time, will their efforts succeed. It is conceivable that, by coincidence, cooperation alone could have brought about the desired result. But managers cannot rely on coincidence. Although cooperation is always helpful, and its absence could prevent all possibility of coordination, its presence will not assure coordination. Coordination must be a conscious managerial effort exercised through the functions of planning, organizing, staffing, influencing, and controlling.

Self-coordination

Although coordination is management's job, subordinates are not exempt from doing all they can to help the effort. Alvin Brown calls the subordinates' efforts "self-coordination," which he defines as "the effort of independent responsibilities to achieve the harmonious or reciprocal performance of their own responsibilities."[8] In other words, each person in a group must recognize the effects of his or her own performance on others and coordinate his or her activities with those of others.[9] Herbert Simon speaks of self-coordination in a similar way.[10] However, neither self-coordination nor self-adjustment is a substitute for the overall coordination introduced by management that is necessary to the success of the enterprise.

Achieving coordination

The difficulties of coordinating

In spite of cooperative attitudes and self-coordination by each member of a group, duplication of action and conflict of effort will occur unless managerial synchronization exists. Through coordination, managers can bring about a level of accomplishment far greater than the sum of the individual parts.

We must caution, however: coordination is not easily attained. Each interest group stresses its own view of how organizational purposes should be accomplished and tends to favor the policy that will further its interests. These differences in viewpoint are a problem to all levels in a managerial hierarchy. It takes thoughtfulness, listening power, and good will to see and understand the relationships involved in working with higher and lower groups.

Difficulties in achieving coordination arise for various reasons, one of which is the growth of the enterprise. With growth, the task of synchronizing an increasing number of jobs and multiplying daily activities becomes more complicated and more important. A complex organizational structure involv-

---

[8] Alvin Brown, *Organization of Industry* (Englewood Cliffs, N.J.: Prentice-Hall, 1947), p. 354.
[9] *Ibid.*, pp. 108–128.
[10] Herbert A. Simon, *Administrative Behavior*, 3d ed. (New York: Free Press, 1976), p. 104.

ing more subordinates also adds problems of communication. Moreover, advanced products and methods bring about new worker-machine relationships, which create coordination needs unheard of before. Now person, machine, and function all must be coordinated within the framework of sophisticated, space-age technology. Management theory has just begun to feel the effects of these developments.

Human nature also can lead to coordination problems. Often managers, preoccupied with the work in their own units, hesitate to become involved in other areas even though their activities might have significant bearing on them. They, likewise, tend to think primarily of the welfare of their own departments and do not consider the overall welfare of the enterprise. Such tendencies may lead to suboptimization—the maximizing of the returns of one division or department at the expense of the firm as a whole. This is particularly likely to happen if managers are rewarded on the basis of their departments' financial performances.

Contingencies in coordinating

In its essence, division of labor involves breaking a large task into several smaller ones. The resulting smaller tasks are, therefore, linked; coordination is the process by which these linkages are maintained and exploited.[11] Managers employ several means to effect coordination. The methods they use are contingent on the nature of the situation within which the coordination has to occur. There are three principal methods commonly employed.[12]

Coordinating by standardization

When conditions are relatively stable, managers frequently use standardization as their chief coordinating device. Events that are few in number, highly predictable, and repetitive can be "programmed." Managers establish standard rules, regulations, and routines, making each action consistent with the other actions that are linked. The way to coordinate the registration of eight thousand college students each semester is to establish a standard set of procedures that everyone follows.

Coordinating by plan

When conditions are somewhat unstable, involving a relatively large number of events some of which are not highly predictable, managers establish schedules, or plans, to coordinate actions. Thus, while each activity may not be programmed down to the last detail, a schedule of planned events can be followed. Probably no two students go through a four-year degree program taking exactly the same courses at precisely the same time. Yet, the college

---

[11] Joseph A. Litterer, *The Analysis of Organizations,* 2d ed. (New York: Wiley, 1973), p. 448.
[12] This discussion borrows from James D. Thompson, *Organizations in Action* (New York: McGraw-Hill, 1967), pp. 55–56; and James G. March and Herbert A. Simon, *Organizations* (New York: Wiley, 1958), pp. 158–164.

is able to coordinate movements of the students through its various curriculum programs by using schedules as guides.

Coordinating by mutual adjustment

When conditions are highly dynamic, managers must rely on mutual adjustment to effect coordination. Events are often unpredictable in terms of the time they will occur and the form they will take; these events must be coordinated by people using their judgment. Notice of and information about unexpected events have to be communicated among the people involved in coordinating those events. As March and Simon point out:

To the extent that contingencies arise, not anticipated in the schedule, coordination requires communication to give notice of deviations from planned or predicted conditions, or to give instructions for changes in activity to adjust to these deviations. . . . The more . . . variable and unpredictable the situation, the greater the reliance on coordination by [mutual adjustment].[13]

Reliance on standardized rules and regulations in unstable situations could prove disastrous. Indeed, one of the major difficulties with the classical management approach has been its insistence on managing "by the book." Appendix B discusses this and similar problems more fully.

Types of coordinating

Managers employ the various coordinating methods in three different organizational dimensions: vertical, horizontal, and diagonal. Each dimension has its own characteristics and problems.

Vertical

Vertical coordination exists among different levels of an organization—for example, between the vice president in charge of manufacturing and the manager in charge of wood furniture, and between that manager and the millwork foreman (see Figure 12-2). Vertical coordination is secured by delegating authority together with the means and manner of supervising and controlling. As we know, delegated authority carries great weight. However, vertical coordination cannot be achieved by threat alone. Instead, it must be the result of a superior's efficient and expert performance of his or her managerial functions.

Horizontal

Horizontal coordination refers to coordination among people and departments on the same organizational level. For example, planning and implementing a new promotional program might involve working arrangements among the vice president in charge of manufacturing, the vice president in charge of marketing, and the vice president in charge of finance (Figure 12-2). Horizontal coordination is needed so that when the marketing depart-

---

[13] March and Simon, *Organizations*, p. 160.

ment is ready to market the new item, the manufacturing department will be able to fill the orders. Financial arrangements already will have been made to establish the required amount of outstanding credit and to ensure that the necessary funds are available for raw materials, parts, and so on. Each of the executives involved in this coordination manages his or her own department and has no authority over either of the other executives. Horizontal coordination cannot be commanded; it must result from superior managerial skills. If horizontal coordination is insufficient or inconclusive, however, a matter can be carried to a level of the managerial hierarchy high enough to be responsible for all the activities in question.

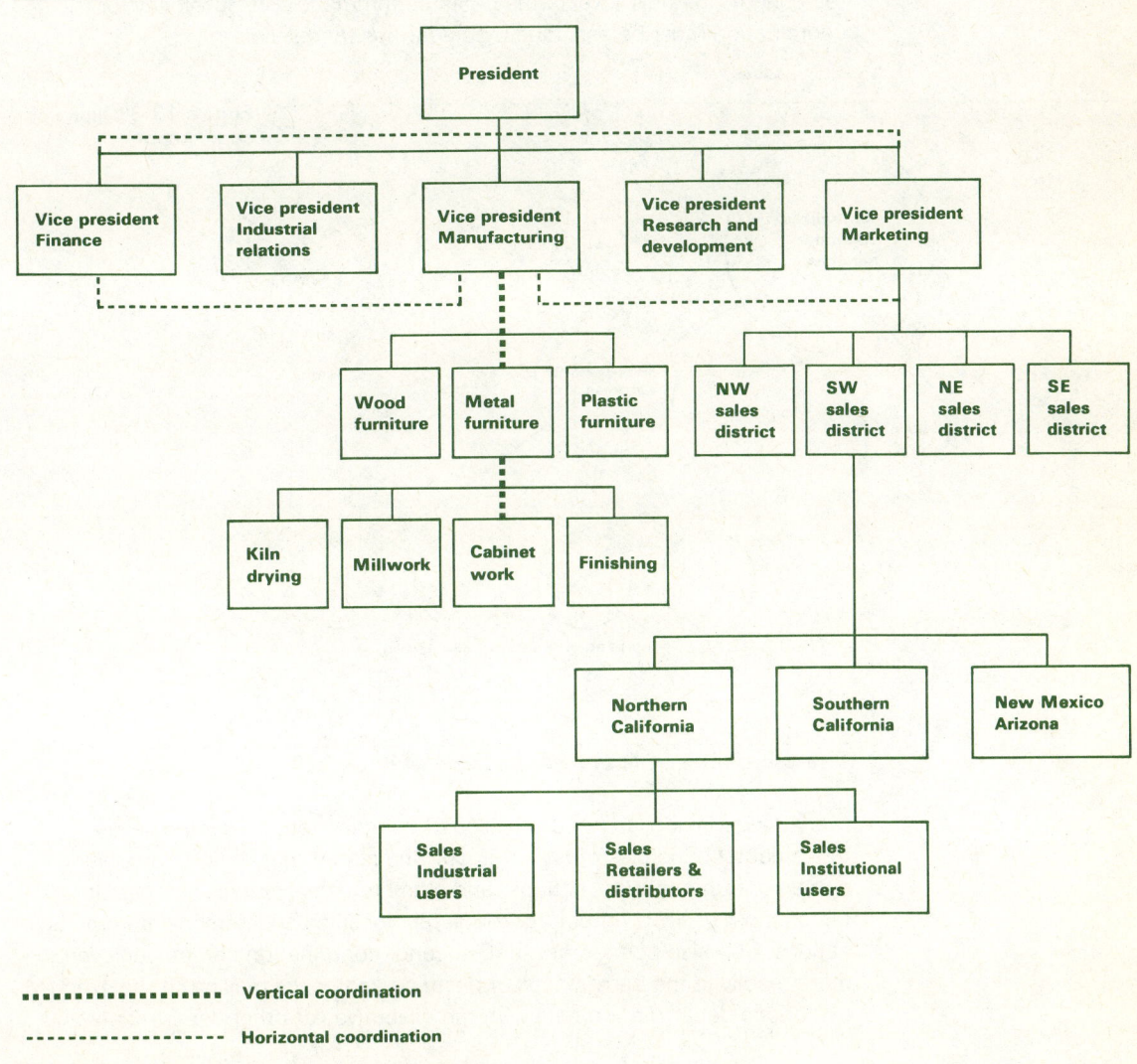

Figure 12-2 Vertical and horizontal coordination

Diagonal

In a small enterprise, coordination among the various functions and managers of different departments is facilitated by the proximity of working arrangements, close contacts, and short lines of communication. However, in a large organization the problems become more complicated, requiring diagonal coordination.[14] In this situation, both levels and positions on a chain of command are superseded so that all can take advantage of a special service. For example, operating departments and individual projects may all have access to a centralized computer service (see Figure 12-3). Allocation of the computer service resources, in this case, often has to be coordinated by negotiation between the users and the computer personnel. This process involves complex interrelationships that cannot be coordinated simply by resorting to the next level in the chain of command. Responsibility for the coordination must be assumed by the parties themselves.

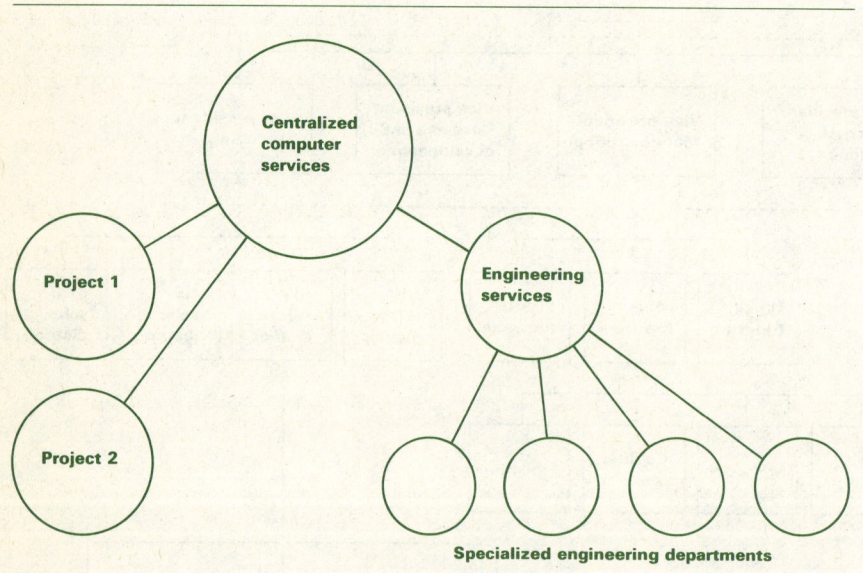

Figure 12-3 Diagonal coordination

The principles of Mary Parker Follett

Mary Parker Follett, in her discussion of coordination, presented several fundamental principles of organization. She stated that, first, coordination—agreement on methods, actions, and ultimate achievement—can be attained most easily by direct horizontal relationships and personal communications. She also pointed out that, second, coordination can be achieved more readily in the early stages of planning and policy making. If the executive of one department meets with the executives of other departments and

---

[14] Leonard Sayles, *Managerial Behavior* (New York: McGraw-Hill, 1964), pp. 58–82.

confronts them with a finished policy, coordination naturally becomes difficult. But "if the head of the production department, *while* he is forming his policy, meets and discusses with the other heads the question involved, a successful coordination is far more likely to be reached. That is, you cannot, with the greatest degree of success for your undertaking, make policy-forming and policy-adjusting two separate processes."[15]

In a third principle of coordination, Follett illuminated the process of communication. She stated that all factors in a situation are reciprocally related. That is, when A works with B, who in turn works with C and D, each of the four is influenced by all the persons in the total situation. "This sort of reciprocal relating, this interpenetration of every part by every other part, and again by every other part as it has been permeated by all, should be the goal of all attempts at coordination."[16] As a fourth principle, Follett pointed out that coordination is a continuing process that cannot be left to chance. Managers must continually work at it so that they will not be suddenly confronted by unforeseen developments.

Coordination and the five managerial functions

When management plans, it must immediately coordinate. Top executives should discuss various plans and alternatives, while they are still flexible, with the managers of all departments so that everyone will have the opportunity to express doubts and objections at once. If these managers are involved in planning at the initial stages, the chances for coordination are good. For instance, the thoughtful manager will plan an advertising campaign in conjunction with the production manager, the sales manager, the vice president in charge of finance, the publicity manager, and so on, thereby synchronizing the efforts of all individuals involved.

Concern for coordination also should permeate organizing activities. It should be foremost in managers' minds as they group and assign various activities to subordinates and create departments. In the process of organizing, managers should establish departments and define their relationships in such a way that coordination will result. For instance, placing related activities that must be closely synchronized in the same administrative unit will facilitate coordination.

Often, poor coordination is caused by a lack of understanding (Who is to perform what?) or by the failure of management to delegate authority and responsibility clearly. Fuzziness easily can cause duplication of effort instead of synchronization. This is most likely to happen when two executives both feel responsible for the same activity. The heads of the purchasing department and the maintenance division, for example, might both consider it their function to buy repair and spare parts. Committees are often formed to

---

[15] Henry C. Metcalf and Lyndall F. Urwick, eds., *Dynamic Administration: The Collected Papers of Mary Parker Follett* (New York: Harper & Row, 1942), p. 298.
[16] Ibid., p. 299.

facilitate coordination among individuals and departments. Some writers strongly recommend this practice, because it gives unit heads a reason to hold formal and informal meetings.[17] Often managers set up committees expressly to bring together the people whose activities must be coordinated and, by doing so, provide a setting that will foster horizontal coordination.

Managers also should bear in mind coordination when considering staffing decisions. They should make certain that there are the right number of executives in the various positions to ensure the proper performance of company objectives.

Coordinating in effective organizations

One of the most informative research studies conducted in the last several years is that of Professors Paul R. Lawrence and Jay W. Lorsch.* Among the questions they examined was: How do managers of effective organizations coordinate activities and resources? The researchers examined organizations in three industries: plastics, food, and container. These industries operated in environments that ranged from relatively stable and predictable to relatively dynamic and uncertain. This is what they found:

- *Dynamic environment (plastics industry)* Managers employed special departments, permanent teams of personnel from several organizational functions, direct managerial contact, and various formal procedures.
- *Moderate environment (food industry)* Managers employed special individuals (not departments), temporary teams, direct managerial contact, and formal procedures.
- *Stable environment (container industry)* Managers employed only direct managerial contact and formal procedures.

The lesson from this? The organization *is* an open system; the external environment *is* important in determining which internal coordinating devices need to be employed.

* Paul R. Lawrence and Jay W. Lorsch, *Organization and Environment* (Homewood, Illinois: Richard D. Irwin, 1969).

In influencing, managers are again involved with coordination. The purpose of giving orders, instructing, coaching, teaching, and generally supervising subordinates is to coordinate their various activities in such a manner that overall company objectives will be reached in the most efficient way. In assessing the relationship of good supervision to coordination, Alvin Brown defines coordination as "that phase of supervision which is devoted to obtaining the harmonious and reciprocal performance of responsibilities of

[17] For example, see Ernest Dale, *Planning and Developing the Company Organization Structure,* Research Report No. 20 (New York: American Management Association, 1952), p. 116.

two or more deputies."[18] Supervisors can never completely relieve themselves of the duty of watching the progress of the various activities under their direction.

Finally, coordination is related directly to controlling; the very nature of the controlling process brings about coordination. Frequent evaluation of operations helps to synchronize the efforts of subordinates. If managers find that performance is not proceeding as planned or directed, they should immediately take remedial action to correct whatever deviations have occurred. This action should at least improve future coordination.

Good communications are immeasurably helpful in all coordination efforts. Personal contact is probably the most effective means of communication. However, written communications, reports, procedures, bulletins, and the numerous modern mechanical devices that ensure speedy dissemination of necessary information to various subordinates are also helpful. Recent developments in electronic data processing can aid considerably in communication efforts, as can devices like PERT.

Liaison people

Although coordination will always remain the line manager's responsibility, special employees have sometimes been charged with coordinating tasks. In situations where executives cannot maintain sufficient personal contact to provide all the informal information desired, a liaison person may be utilized. Such a person must be thoroughly familiar with operating conditions in the division so that they can be explained to the other divisions with which the liaison is in close contact. Then, conditions in other divisions must be reported back to the liaison's own unit. In large business concerns with widely scattered headquarters, offices, plants, and branches, a liaison person is frequently useful and appropriate.

Liaison people, however, do not have the authority to commit their operating divisions, and their use should never be considered a substitute for more direct means of securing coordination. The practice of relying on liaison people became widespread during World War II, when the position of coordinator (or expediter or liaison officer) was created to assure coordination among departments, suppliers, resources, and subcontractors. As modern organizations face increasingly unstable conditions, the use of liaison personnel becomes correspondingly important. In an especially important research study, Lawrence and Lorsch found that high-performance firms in relatively unstable plastics and food industries relied on special units and personnel for coordination.[19] These means of coordination were made part of the organization's structure, with official duties and responsibilities. These findings are probably portents of things to come.[20]

---

[18] Brown, *Organization of Industry*, p. 354.
[19] Paul R. Lawrence and Jay W. Lorsch, *Organization and Environment* (Homewood, Illinois: Richard D. Irwin, 1969).
[20] See Paul R. Lawrence and Jay W. Lorsch, "New Management Job: The Integrator," *Harvard Business Review* 45 (November–December 1967):142–151.

How managers coordinate external interdependence

There are two chief problems managers have in coordinating interdependence in external relationships: (1) managing uncertainties caused by the unpredictable actions of competitors; and (2) managing uncertainties resulting from noncompetitive relationships with suppliers, creditors, government agencies, and customers. How do they deal with these problems?

Six major strategies are commonly employed. Their relative advantages and disadvantages are reflected in the table.

Strategy	Advantages	Disadvantages
Merger	Completely absorbs interdependence	Requires resources sufficient to acquire another organization; may be prohibited by antitrust laws, or infeasible for other reasons (for example, a governmental unit cannot be absorbed by a firm).
Joint ventures	Can be used for sharing risks and costs associated with large, or technologically advanced activities; can be used to partially pool resources and coordinate activities.	Is available only for certain types of organizations, though less restricted than merger (COMSAT, for instance, brings together government and business).
Interlocking directorates	Relatively inexpensive.	May not provide enough coordination or linkage between organizations to ensure performance; coopted person may loose credibility in original organization.
Personnel movement	Relatively inexpensive; almost universally possible.	Person loses identification with original organization, lessening influence there; linkage is based on knowledge and familiarity, and on a few persons at most, not on basic structural relationships.
Regulation	Enables organization to benefit from the coercive power of the government.	Regulation may be used to harm the organization's interests.
Political activity	Enables organization to use government to modify and enhance environment.	Government intervention, once legitimated, may be used against the organization as well as for its benefit.

Regardless of the strategy employed, managing external relationships involves exchange: the organization acquires the resources it needs but at the same time its managers must promise to do certain things in return. Thus, while establishing and managing interorganizational linkages are important, there is a cost: the loss of the organization's autonomy.

Source: Based on Jeffrey Pfeffer, "Beyond Management and the Worker: The Institutional Function of Management," *Academy of Management Review* 1, no. 2 (April 1976):36–46.

External coordination

In addition to the need for internal coordination, there is a need for coordination with factors external to the enterprise—changes in the competitive situation, government activities, technological advances, and the interests of the general public, the owners, and the employees. Coordination also must exist between an organization and related enterprises, such as shippers, suppliers, and carriers, as well as between the organization and the economy at large. All these external factors add to the already difficult task of internal coordination.

Much is being written about relationships among independent but integrated firms, such as power companies in an electrical distribution network. Obviously, coordination among these firms must be highly sophisticated and is of crucial importance. That organizations operate in a complex set of subsystems is obvious when issues of coordination are considered. In fact, this is one of the most important current managerial problems.[21] It should be pointed out that, through new tools and devices and a more thorough understanding of managerial functions, knowledge of how to obtain coordination is becoming broader. Managers' ever-increasing problems of coordination can thereby be offset by ever-increasing knowledge of how to perform their managerial skills.

Summary

Coordination is one natural imperative of organization; the need for it is inevitable, produced by its companion imperative, division of labor. Although several definitions of coordination can be formulated, it is essentially the conscious process of assembling and synchronizing differentiated activities so that they function harmoniously in the pursuit of organizational objectives.

There are several methods that managers commonly employ to effect coordination. They coordinate by standardization, by plan, and by mutual adjustment. Coordinating by standardization is appropriate under highly

---

[21] An extensive treatment of interorganizational relationships is contained in a special issue of *Organization and Administrative Science* 5, no. 1 (Spring 1974).

stable conditions. As conditions become more dynamic and uncertain, managers increasingly rely on coordination by plan and mutual adjustment.

Coordinating methods are employed in three organizational dimensions—vertical, horizontal, and diagonal—and in each of the managerial functions. Each dimension and function has its own characteristics and problems.

Managers are relying increasingly on liaison personnel to facilitate their coordinating responsibilities. Although such people usually do not have authority to commit resources, they are helpful in situations that require frequent exchange of ideas and information.

Finally, managers must deal with more than the coordinating of activities and resources internal to the organization. Coordinating interorganizational relationships is becoming more and more important as organizational systems become more complex and interdependent.

Discussion questions

1 How are the characteristics of coordination reflected in group assignments in your college courses?
2 Why does self-coordination take on added significance when we consider organizational situations in which diagonal relationships are crucial?
3 What coordinating problems are faced by your college bookstore? What coordinating mechanisms are used to deal with those problems? Do they work? If you were the bookstore manager, which mechanisms would you employ?

Supplementary readings

Hall, James L., and Leidecker, Joel K. "A Review of Vertical and Lateral Relations: A New Perspective for Managers." In *Dimensions in Modern Management,* 2d ed., edited by Patrick E. Connor. Boston: Houghton Mifflin, 1978.

Lawrence, Paul R., and Lorsch, Jay W. "New Management Job: The Integrator." *Harvard Business Review* 45 (November—December 1967): 69—83.

Litterer, Joseph A. *Analysis of Organizations,* 2d ed. New York: Wiley, 1973.

Pfeffer, Jeffrey. "Beyond Management and the Worker: The Institutional Function of Management." *Academy of Management Review* 1, no. 2 (April 1976):36—46.

Sayles, Leonard. *Managerial Behavior.* New York: McGraw-Hill, 1964.

Thompson, James D. *Organizations in Action.* New York: McGraw-Hill, 1967.

Wren, Daniel A. "Interface and Interorganizational Coordination." *Academy of Management Journal* 10 (March 1967):69—83.

Appendix B

Problems with traditional structures

This appendix discusses some difficulties with traditional organizational structures. In particular, traditional, or bureaucratic, methods of organizing generate two sets of problems: those for members—the people who work, are patients, are incarcerated, or who otherwise participate in the organization; and those for the organization itself.

Problems for people

Traditional forms of organizing have an undesirable impact on organizational participants in two areas: attitudes and behavior. Let us consider them in order.

Attitudes

People's attitudes are affected by what they experience over their life. It is not accidental that children develop attitudes similar to those of their parents, that people from different parts of the country develop different attitudes, that people in penitentiaries develop attitudes different from those of people in convents. Of course, this is an oversimplification, since people with similar experiences do not develop identical attitudes regarding all subjects. Still, the point is valid enough: people with similar experiences tend to develop similar attitudes, especially toward subjects relevant to those experiences.

There is mounting evidence that people's experiences are occurring more and more within organizational structures. The bureaucracy is everywhere: individuals spend the better part of their lives in one or more work-related, educational, governmental, religious, or recreational organization; more—so do their parents, their friends and their parents and friends, their next-door neighbors, their children, and so forth. Despite differences in occupation, social class, and geography, people have at least one universal experience: the bureaucracy.

We know, further, that the bureaucratic experience is focused: one emphasis is on differences between individuals, often in a superior-inferior sense; another emphasis is on efficiency. Of course, there is nothing necessarily wrong with efficiency; we might reflect, however, that there are other human values—values made subordinate by the bureaucracy to efficiency. As people's experiences increasingly take place in bureaucratic settings, the value of efficiency becomes increasingly reflected in their attitudes. "For the good of the organization" becomes a major consideration in managerial decisions and assessments of employees, who then are rewarded for their loyalty, seniority, personality, and so forth. It is hardly surprising that organizational participants develop, over time, attitudes largely congruent with the demands of the bureaucracy.

Behavior

Despite the insistent pressure by the bureaucracy, organizational participants typically have certain individual needs they wish to express. Independence, self-development, some measure of control over their lives—these are a few of them. The bureaucracy, however, tries to suppress this expression, telling the individuals simply to obey their bosses and follow the rules.

What do the individuals do? They learn to cope. Specifically, they attempt to follow the rules in their own way, accommodating themselves to bureaucratic pressures. Different people develop different ways of accommodating, of course. Some exploit the rules as much as possible, maximizing their climb up the organizational ladder. Others simply withdraw, declining to play at all; they do their job, collect their pay, and obtain their satisfaction elsewhere. These people, of course, are barely even there; they leave their minds and spirits at home. Still others suffer from an inconsistency: they want to follow the rules, obey the boss, and achieve organizational success, but they cannot bring themselves to do so. The rules appear inane or the boss ignorant or the reward system biased—whatever the reason, these people spend their careers being torn by their desire to succeed in the organization and their psychological inability to pursue that success. In all three cases, the bureaucracy has pressured the people into behaving in ways they might not have behaved had it not been for those pressures.

Problems for the organization

The prescriptions of the bureaucratic form of organization have some undesirable effects on the organization itself. In particular, bureaucratic managers' desire to control organizational activities, resources, and people leads to several problems. Specific problems that have been identified stem from two sources: the bureaucratic emphasis on rules and the use of delegation.

Rules

Bureaucratic managers tend to employ a substantial number of rules and procedures. The purpose of doing so is to ensure that workers operate (behave) in a predictable manner. That is, one way to control workers' behavior is to require them to follow highly specific rules. The purpose of ensuring predictable worker behavior is to enable managers to feel confident that they will obtain reliable performance from their employees. The problem with this, however, is that some unintended results occur. Specifically, the rules take on meaning beyond what was intended—they become ends in themselves. That is, the rules become more important than the purposes for which they were originally created. Thus, people tend to follow the rules blindly—even when they do not apply to the specific problem at hand. If you have had any dealings with the registrar's office, you know how this happens.

But, then again . . .
(or, Cheer up—Things could be worse)

French bureaucracy's control of and interference in all aspects of society can be compared with those in no other country outside the Soviet bloc. There is virtually no sphere, save the religious (and even here not entirely, because in Alsace the government still pays the salaries of clergymen), which escapes its embrace. In education, the arts, radio and television, public works, taxation, scientific and scholarly research, diplomacy, transportation, the military, technology, development, finance, social welfare, the judiciary, energy, and of course the entire police force from traffic cops to riot troops, the French civil service holds partial or complete monopolies. A French citizen deals with his national government through an administrative machinery that affects his life, from cradle to tomb, in everything from his gas, electricity, and (unitemized) telephone bills to parimutuel off-track betting and state lotteries.

By comparison, the United States, with its networks of state and local governments and its extensive private sector, all of which compete and tangle with the federal bureaucracy, appears to be a veritable anarchy of decentralized authority. Indeed the case of the French Minister of Public Instruction who could boast to a visitor, "At any given moment of the academic day, I know precisely what page of the civics textbook the eighth-graders of France are studying," is without precedent, if not inconceivable, in the U.S., where a Secretary of HEW doesn't know what's going on down the hall, let alone in a public high school in San Francisco.

The major differences between the American and the French bureaucracy, however, are not so much uniformity and centralization as political influence and control. The extent of the French civil service's political power is enormous and subtle in ways which few Americans would countenance. In France locally elected mayors of towns and cities may be suspended, as may municipal councils, through administrative decree. The city of Paris has no mayor at all, and even the decision of whether to build a Left Bank expressway lies in the hands of the central government. The decision to construct a public swimming pool in Antibes and half of the money to pay for it come from Paris. Newspapers and magazines may be seized at the printing presses by administrative decree, as indeed they often were during the Algerian crisis. And the popularly elected National Assembly may occasionally be by-passed altogether while the government rules through its bureaucracy by administrative ordinance, as happened for a time in 1967.

Source: From a review by Steven Englund of Ezra N. Suleiman, *Politics, Power, and Bureaucracy in France: The Administrative Elite* (Princeton, N.J.: Princeton University Press, 1975), in *New York Review of Books* 22, no. 8 (May 15, 1975):33. Reprinted with permission from *The New York Review of Books,* Copyright © 1975 Nyrev, Inc.

Second, bureaucratic managers tend to use rules as a decision-making crutch. Categories of decisions are created; when a problem arises, the manager says, "Oh yes, this is a type B—4 problem, requiring a type B—4 solution." Actually it may be a type B—$4\frac{1}{2}$ problem, but since there are no predetermined type B—$4\frac{1}{2}$ solutions, the nearest solution is used. Thus, a third type of problem, stemming from heavy emphasis on rules, is that managers tend not to search extensively for alternate solutions to problems.

There is a fourth difficulty generated by managers' reliance on rules and procedures to control worker behavior. In effect, rules tell people the type of behavior that is minimally acceptable. Workers respond by behaving in that minimally acceptable fashion; and managers then respond by enacting more rules, and the cycle continues.

In short, when managers rely too heavily on rules and procedures to control workers, they often get more than they bargain for. These intended and unintended results are illustrated in Figure B-1.

Delegation

The second set of organizational problems generated by a bureaucratic style of managing stems from the use of delegation. As we have seen, delegating authority helps managers develop workers with relatively specialized skills. Their specialized competence enables these people to carry out their delegated tasks and, thus, contribute to organizational goals.

235 Problems with traditional structures

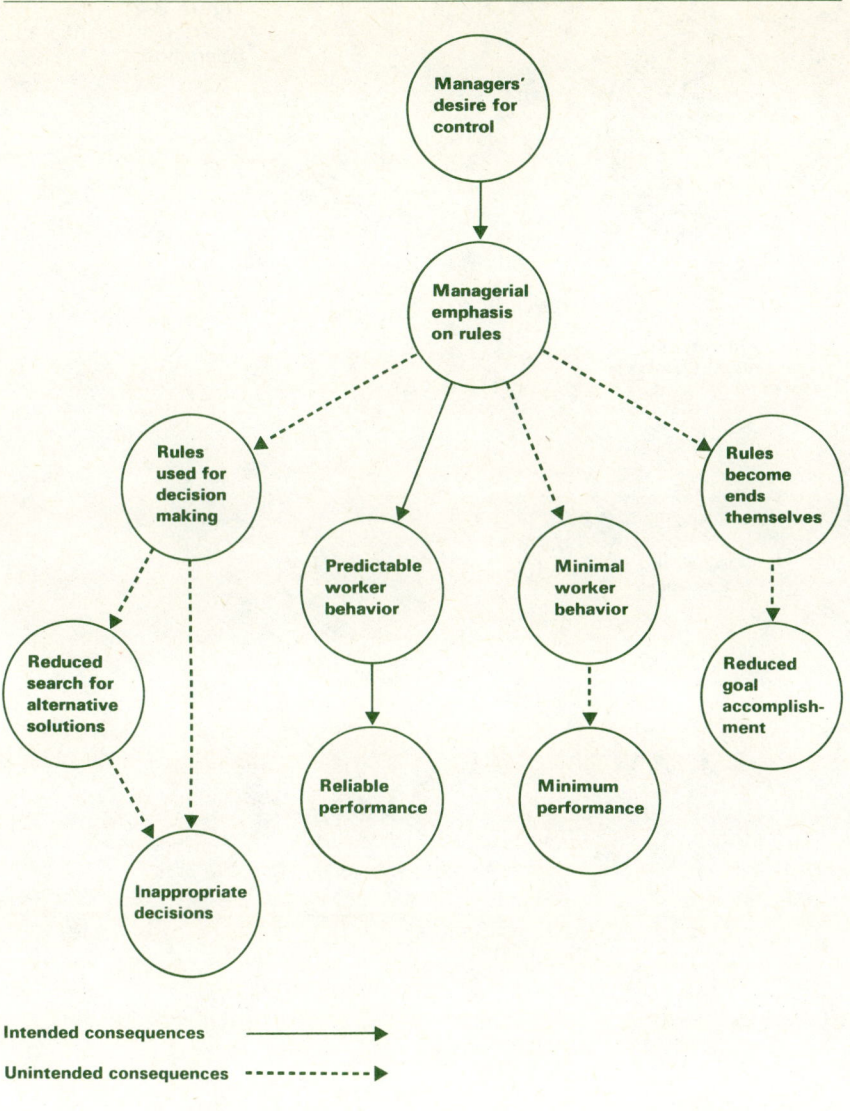

Figure B-1 Consequences of reliance on rules

Unfortunately, other things happen, too. Specifically, the specialists increasingly pay attention to their subunit goals, often at the expense of overall organizational goals. We have, in fact, seen in Chapter 12 that it is this sort of phenomenon that necessitates systematic and continual coordination. These intended and unintended consequences are illustrated in Figure B-2.

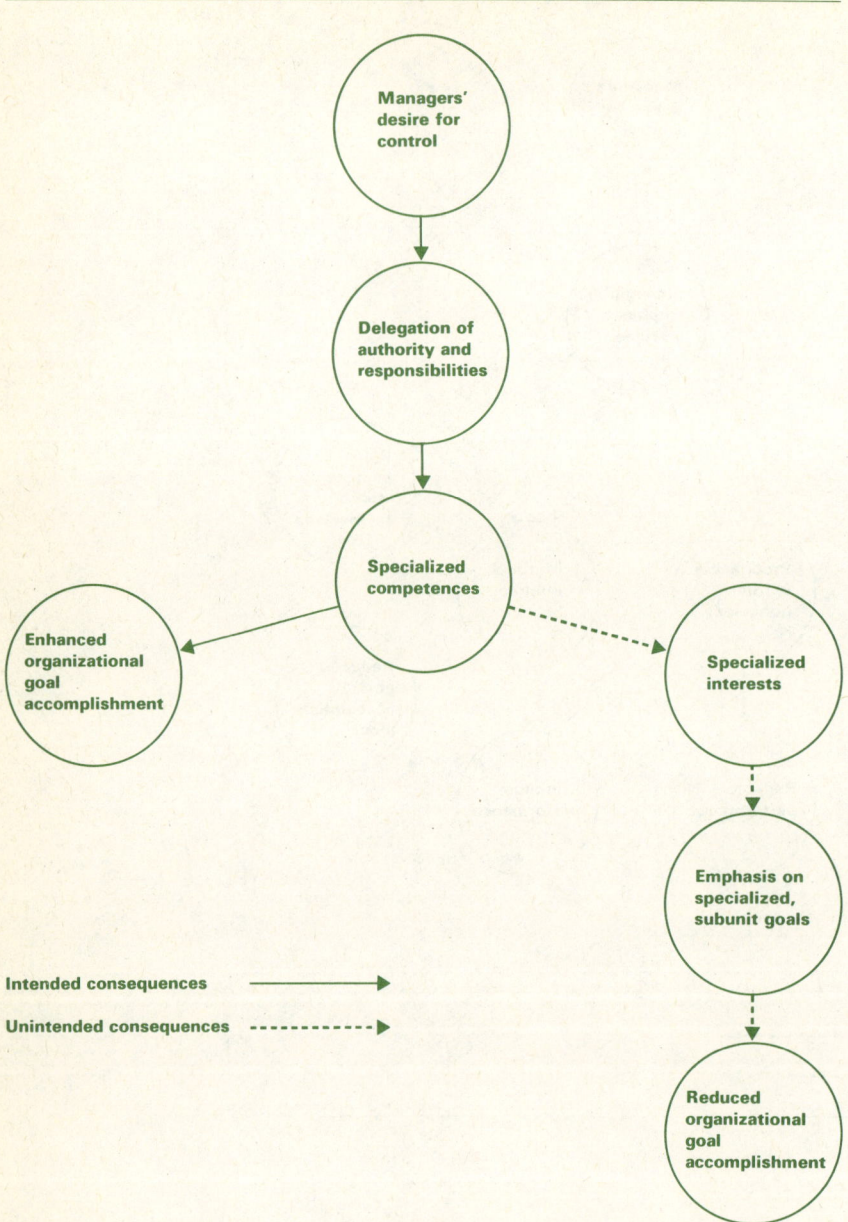

Figure B-2 Consequences of reliance on delegation

Conclusion

Although traditional forms of organizing have proved popular and durable, they are not without their difficulties. In particular, they develop problems for the people participating in the organization and for the organization itself.

In essence, it is its rigidity that is at the root of the bureaucracy's difficulties. To be effective, managers must organize with more flexibility than the traditional forms allow. We consider some alternative forms of organization in the next two chapters.

References

The student who is interested in considering further the various problems and difficulties engendered by traditional forms of organization will want to examine the following materials:

Argyris, Chris. *Integrating the Individual and the Organization.* New York: Wiley, 1964.
———. *Personality and Organization.* New York: Harper & Row, 1957.
Gibson, James L.; Ivancevich, John M.; and Donnelly, James H., Jr. *Organizations*, pp. 273–275. Dallas: Business Publications, 1976.
Gouldner, Alvin W. *Patterns of Industrial Bureaucracy.* New York: Free Press, 1954.
March, James G., and Simon, Herbert A. *Organizations,* pp. 36–47. New York: Wiley, 1958.
Merton, Robert K. "Bureaucratic Structure and Personality." *Social Forces* 18 (1940):560–568.
Presthus, Robert. *The Organizational Society.* New York: Knopf, 1962.
Selznick, Philip. *TVA and the Grass Roots.* Berkeley, Calif.: University of California Press, 1948.

Chapter 13

Committees

Objectives of the chapter

1 To define committees as organizing devices.
2 To examine the role of committees in modern management.
3 To describe the types of committees found in contemporary organizations.
4 To review the relative benefits and costs of managing by committee.
5 To identify factors that contribute to effective committee operation.

Problems with traditional structures, such as those described in Appendix B, have prompted managers to devise improved methods for organizing. The committee is one such device. For one thing, as we have seen, the larger an organization grows, the more difficulty an executive has administering its affairs and handling its problems. One way that managers cope with this difficulty is by establishing committees and turning over specific problems and issues to them. A committee is a group of people who function collectively. It differs from other units of management in that its members normally have additional duties and devote only part of their time to committee activities.

The word *committee* evokes various reactions. When properly used and wisely selected, committees can be a great asset to any organization. However, the committee device has been abused. Badly organized committees often delay action, and many perceive them as useless debating societies—"a collection of the unfit appointed by the unwilling to perform the unnecessary."

In spite of their bureaucratic image, committees—sometimes known as boards, commissions, or task forces—are widely used. Government activities generally involve a great deal of committee work. In some instances, government committees are created to investigate a certain problem; in others, they are created to manage a government agency, such as the Atomic Energy Commission. Educational institutions make extensive use of committees and boards. Religious organizations often depend on them to achieve greater lay participation in church affairs.

Committees are also widespread in business. In a survey of twelve hundred respondent firms, 94 percent of the firms with more than 10,000 employees and 64 percent of the firms with fewer than 250 employees said they had formal committees.[1] A board of directors is a committee established by law for all corporations.

Types of committees

Function and level

Committees can be classified by function and by level of organizational hierarchy to which they are attached. In the upper echelons, we commonly find policy, executive; finance, audit, bonus and salary, product, and nominating committees, and many others named after the functions they perform. Corporate committees, divisional committees, and departmental committees also exist. At the lower levels, we find grievance committees, suggestion committees, safety committees, and others. Clearly, the committee device has been used for almost every task. However, managers should use the committee form only when group action will be advantageous, as discussed in Chapter 23.

Line and staff committees

A committee investigates, debates, and discusses a problem and concludes its deliberations with a recommendation. If this procedure results merely in guidance, counsel, and advice, the committee is acting in a *staff* capacity. However, in many instances a subject is presented to a committee for decision. In this case, the committee is acting in a *line* capacity; it is called a *plural executive* and is managerial in nature. The duPont Corporation has used this type of line committee management for top policy decisions since 1921.

Although most committees are either line or staff, at times they are neither. This is the case when a committee is appointed merely to receive and pass information. Whatever its type, the committee is one of several devices that facilitate lateral relationships in organizations.

Temporary or standing committees

Committees can also be classified by longevity. A *temporary committee* is appointed for a particular purpose and will be disbanded as soon as it has

[1] A. C. Filley, "Committee Management: Guidelines from Social Science Research," *California Management Review* 13 (Fall 1970): 13.

accomplished its task. A *standing committee* has a permanent place in the organization and deals with recurring problems. Finance and budget functions are handled by standing committees.

Often, meetings and conferences are called on the spur of the moment, when an executive feels the need to discuss certain matters with several department managers. The executive, in this instance, is not creating a committee. Large lectures and meetings, likewise, are not committees, even though the speaker may have to field questions. In both instances, group action—the typical characteristic of committees—is lacking.

Committees: Some assets

Combined opinion

If a committee is properly selected and motivated, its deliberation and judgment can be an outstanding asset to an organization. Committee members can bring to their meetings a range of experience, background, and ability that one manager could not possess. This is especially important when decisions must be made on questions to which there is no clear answer. Then, expert advice in different fields must often be obtained. A committee member from one department or field may be able to direct the attention of other committee members to aspects of the problem that they might not have seen. Because the free exchange of ideas stimulates and clarifies thinking, committee members must be able to present their ideas clearly and must be willing to submit them to the critical appraisal of the other members of the committee. In this way, problems can be analyzed collectively. Frequently, staff uses committees to solicit a wide range of opinion and, thereby, improves the quality of advice it gives to management.

Coordination and cooperation

The committee device can also promote coordination. Each committee member, by listening to other members' suggestions and thinking, becomes aware of the purposes and problems of other departments. He or she will understand how his or her activities affect their functions and should become more considerate of the other departments and more aware of the necessity for synchronizing individual efforts with theirs. Managers who have participated in committee problem solving are likely to cooperate more fully in the execution of the solution. Thus, committees promote planning coordination.

Development of executives

Committee meetings provide an excellent proving ground for executives. Committees afford such people an opportunity to observe other departmental situations and to think about problems from an overall organizational point of view. Top management also can observe executives in action in such meetings. These people must be able to present thoughts clearly, defend them, and think through their implications. Committee debates and discussions can certainly broaden these qualities.

The committee is also an excellent training ground for junior executives. The appointment of such people to committees will enable them to become acquainted with the attitudes of other executives and with the way in which decisions are made. Because junior executives are not always required to participate actively in committee deliberations, they benefit principally from listening and observing.

Associated with training benefits is the continuity of thinking fostered by committee membership. Few committees replace all members simultaneously; instead, they make full members out of junior executives who have previously sat in on committee meetings, or they provide continuity by retaining several older members who know the reasons for previous decisions and actions. A desire for continuity also provides a rationale for the election of only one third of the members of the United States Senate at any one time.

An outgrowth of using committees as a special training device for young executives is the multiple management plan originated in 1932 by McCormick and Company and adopted, with modifications, by several hundred other companies. McCormick has established four junior boards for younger executives: the factory board, the sales board, the institutional sales board, and the board of directors. Although none of these junior boards is an official part of the corporate structure, they all examine company policies and operations and can make recommendations to the senior board of directors whenever they unanimously decide to do so. According to Charles P. McCormick, the purpose of the junior board is not to bypass the judgment of the more mature people, "but to supplement that judgment with new ideas."[2]

Representation of interest groups

Committees also give representatives of different interest groups a chance to discuss a subject that affects them all. Thus, executives and specialists of various departments and activities can work as a team. Each interested party is assured proper representation, morale is improved, and participation and involvement are fostered. As we mentioned earlier, committees also help to produce balanced group integration and judgment.

At times, however, concern with proper representation can be carried too far. It is essential to appoint capable, rather than just representative, members to the committee.[3] "Representative" members may not be able to

---

[2] Charles P. McCormick, *The Power of People: Multiple Management up to Date* (New York: Harper & Row, 1952), p. 12.
[3] Andre L. Delbecq, "Citizen Inputs for Decision Making: The Advisory Group," paper presented to annual meeting of the Academy of Management (Kansas City, August 1976).

contribute to the committee or to integrate their ideas with those of the rest of its members.

Committees: Some liabilities

Committees have several disadvantages that executives should consider before committing a problem to group action. Only after weighing the disadvantages with the advantages can managers determine if a particular question should be referred to a committee.

High costs

Committees consume time. Their pace is slow because each member is entitled to speak and to try to convince other members of his or her point of view. This process, of course, leads to even further discussion. Meetings can be further slowed by a committee member's unnecessary verbiage.

Meetings cost money as well as time. Time spent in committee meetings is not spent elsewhere; every hour consumed by a committee meeting costs the organization in dollars and cents. In addition, committees often require travel and its associated expense. Moreover, preparing for meetings and providing a committee staff, and often a secretary, costs money. Obviously, a single executive could reach a decision in a much shorter time and at less expense. The problem, however, is whether or not that decision would be as good as the one reached by committee deliberation.
If it were not, then the benefits of committee action would probably be substantial enough to make up for the additional cost involved.

Effectiveness limited to certain situations

When will a group make a better decision than will an individual? This question has received considerable attention, and answers to it vary. Generally speaking, a group makes routine decisions effectively but does not perform as well as the individual in creative problem solving. This conclusion has profound implications today, when committees are used to make company policy, perform research on new products, build morale, increase worker participation, and train junior executives.

A survey by the American Management Association has indicated other problems that executives feel are suitable for committee decisions. Table 13-1 presents the survey's analysis of the relative merits of individual versus group action in various management activities. We can see that most managers prefer to settle jurisdictional disputes within the company by committee. Many managers prefer that committees formulate company objectives. Although not shown specifically in the survey, the distribution of bonuses and the establishment of salaries for executives often are determined by committee. In most other functional areas, however, the survey shows that individual action is considered essential. In at least 50 percent of the cases involving organization, leadership, execution, or decision making, managers believe that the use of a committee would be undesirable and, in fact, ineffective.

Table 13-1 Percentage of cases in which managerial functions can be effectively exercised by a committee

Management function	A. Can be exercised by committee effectively	B. Same as A, but can be exercised more effectively by individual	C. Individual initiative essential; may be supplemented by committee action	D. Individual action essential; committee ineffective
Planning	20	20	25	35
Control	25	20	25	30
Formulating objectives	35	35	10	20
Organization	5	25	20	50
Jurisdictional questions	90	10	—	—
Leadership	—	—	10	90
Administration	20	25	25	30
Execution	10	15	10	65
Innovation	30	20	20	30
Communication	20	15	35	30
Advice	15	25	35	25
Decision making	10	30	10	50

Source: Adapted by permission of the publisher from *Planning and Developing the Company Organization Structure,* Ernest Dale, Research Report No. 20, © 1952 by American Management Association, Inc.

Divided responsibility

In addition to the limitations on the situations in which committee action is effective, there are limitations on the sense of responsibility it evokes. When a problem is submitted to a committee, it is submitted to a group. Therefore, it becomes everybody's—and nobody's—responsibility. Theoretically, each member of the committee should shoulder the responsibility, but in reality this does not occur.

Many people who gladly accept individual responsibility do not seem to feel the same sense of responsibility when serving on a committee. Therefore, committees often are willing to settle for reasonably satisfactory solutions. If such solutions are wrong, the committee, not the individuals comprising it, is blamed. There is no way to overcome the thinning out of responsibility; this is one of the serious disadvantages of the committee.

Danger of weak compromise decisions

Committee decisions are often unanimous, even if only majority agreement is required. This tradition is based on politeness, mutual respect, cooperative spirit, and other considerations of this sort. However, a unanimous agreement often signals watered-down action and weak compromise. Very often, in fact, the compromise decision will reflect the lowest common denominator of agreement. Therefore, this type of decision probably will not be as strong, as positive, or as good as it would be if an individual had considered the various aspects and made the decision.

A committee, however, often reports not only the majority recommendation but also the minority one. Having both opinions will probably be helpful to the executive making the final decision. Also, the danger of a weak compromise is lessened when both majority and minority opinions are submitted.

Groupthink

Committee members must be careful that they do not fall victims to a phenomenon known as *groupthink*. Basically, groupthink occurs when committee members' deliberations are dominated by their desire to agree, even at the expense of a realistic appraisal of the problem facing them. Professor Irving L. Janis* has described such fiascoes as the failure to prepare for the attack on Pearl Harbor, the Korean War stalemate, the Bay of Pigs invasion, and the escalation of the Vietnam war as resulting from groupthink at the highest policy levels.

There appear to be eight principal symptoms of groupthink:

1 *An illusion of invulnerability*   Members become overoptimistic and ignore danger signals.
2 *Rationalizing*   Members rationalize away those warning signals that they are unable to ignore completely.
3 *High moral purpose*   Members believe unquestioningly in their uncommonly high morality, which enables them to ignore the ethical or moral consequences of their decisions.
4 *Stereotyping*   Members hold and adhere to clearly drawn stereotypes of the enemy, causing them to assess incorrectly the risks in dealing with that enemy.
5 *Pressure applied to deviants*   Members who show signs of deviating from the committee's position are pressured back into the fold.
6 *Self-pressure applied*   Members agree in public, keeping silent (even to themselves) about misgivings.
7 *An illusion of unanimity*   Members develop the belief that the committee decision is unanimous, thus reducing their critical thinking as individuals.
8 *Mindguarding*   After the decision is revealed, members guard their minds from information contrary to the decision. The adage is revised: "My mind is made up; I don't want any more facts."

---

* Irving L. Janis, "Groupthink," *Psychology Today,* 5 (November 1971):43–46, 74–76; *Victims of Groupthink* (Boston: Houghton Mifflin, 1972).

Strain on interpersonal relations

One last limitation of committees is that they tend to place considerable strain on interpersonal relationships. Some organizations, therefore, establish programs to develop interpersonal competence. Some firms, TRW Systems is one example, have used sensitivity training to help employees settle problems among themselves. We will have more to say about this training technique in Part V.

Effective operation of the committee

After management has weighed all advantages and disadvantages and has decided to establish a committee, it must make plans that will ensure effective committee operation.

Clear definitions of function, scope, and degree of authority

Managers must clearly define the function and scope of committees. The basic functions of a marketing committee, for example, could be described in this way:

To review and coordinate marketing activities of the various operating and selling units of the company and coordinate them with other management functions, especially manufacturing. To develop plans for more effective analysis and control of distribution costs, pricing, inventory control, market analysis and forecasts, product service, basic advertising, trade mark policies, and market forecasting in so far as they affect the company as a whole.[4]

The scope of the marketing committee could also be delineated:

The duties and responsibilities of this Committee cover all matters concerned with the sale of products by any operating division. The committee shall not concern itself with the normal marketing activities of any individual operating or selling unit of the company unless such activities appear to require consideration from an overall company policy viewpoint.[5]

If a committee has a stated scope and duties, it is not likely to flounder. This statement will also provide committee members and higher executives with a scale on which to judge the committee's performance. Furthermore, it helps to clarify the committee's relationship to other organizational units and its connections—if any—with a particular executive's job.

---

[4] Ernest Dale, *Planning and Developing the Company Organization Structure*, Research Report No. 20 (New York: American Management Association, 1952), p. 259.

[5] Ibid.

Managers also must specify the degree of authority to confer on a committee. They must state clearly whether the committee is to serve in an advisory, informational, or decision-making capacity. And, they must specify whether the committee is to function as staff or to perform the job of a plural executive.

Selection of appropriate members

The quality of a committee's work is only as good as its members. Members should be capable of working together. They should be willing to see one another's viewpoint, be able to integrate their thinking with that of other members, and be careful to avoid compromise at the least common denominator. They also must respect each other, even if they disagree.

Members of a committee are usually of the same organizational rank and independent of each other. This ensures that their deliberations will not have any superior-subordinate connotations. It is difficult and uncomfortable, for instance, for a vice president to oppose the chairperson of the board. If committee members are chosen from different departments, these difficulties of rank are more easily overcome. Selecting members from different departments also helps to assure proper representation of the various interests that will be affected by the committee's actions. The importance of wide representation cannot be minimized; however, as we pointed out, representativeness is not as important as ability.

When selecting able committee members, a manager should choose individuals who are familiar with the objectives of the enterprise, who know how the organization operates, and who have the imagination and the ability to present their ideas effectively. They also should have the courage of their convictions and the strength to maintain their point of view until it has been proved wrong. Although each member will not possess all these attributes, each should at least be capable of expressing and defending personal opinions in the presence of a group.

Management analysts have found that committee members work together more productively and gain satisfaction from their committee experience if they share goals. However, not all committees should be homogeneous in composition. Some tasks are accomplished more effectively than are others in a competitive group atmosphere.[6]

Reasonable number of members

A committee should be large enough to provide thorough group deliberation, a wide range of opinion, and broad sources of information. However, it

---

[6] Filley, "Committee Management," pp. 18–19.

should not be unwieldy. Many believe that a committee should be limited to three or four members, whereas others feel that from six to ten is a reasonable number. Sometimes, the purpose for which a committee is established will, by necessity, dictate its size. If a committee has been appointed to coordinate activities, for example, it must include representatives of all the divisions to be coordinated. If a large committee must be formed to consider a particular subject, the group can sometimes be broken into various subcommittees that will consider smaller aspects of the general problem. In order to reduce size, managers also might designate certain individuals to be part-time committee members. Such members would attend meetings whenever their special knowledge was pertinent or whenever they could benefit from the day's discussions. Generally, smaller committees, of approximately five members, will perform tasks most effectively and will supply maximum satisfaction to participating members.

Thorough preparation for meetings

In order to make committee meetings more effective, an agenda should be prepared and circulated in advance. Too often, members go into a meeting inadequately prepared because they do not know the committee's agenda. Under these conditions, their contributions cannot be as effective as they otherwise would be.

Staff support also is necessary to effective committee work. Often, a committee is provided with its own staff, which prepares information, gathers data, and so forth. If it does not have its own staff, the committee must be able to call on advisory staffs available throughout the organization to supply background information and other detailed material. Such factual material provides a basis for committee evaluation of questions under consideration and gives a broader perspective to committee matters.

Committee procedures

Committee meetings are more effective if certain procedures are followed. Minutes should be composed and distributed to committee members before subsequent meetings; and, subsequent meetings should be planned well in advance so that members have adequate notice. Often, executives who are active on a number of committees find that meeting dates conflict. Although an executive can send an administrative assistant to a meeting as a representative, that assistant usually cannot speak for the executive and can fulfill only a reporter's role. These schedule conflicts often can be avoided by proper planning. Some companies have resorted to a scheduling board to keep track of executives' commitments and, actually, pin them down for executive meetings.

The right chairperson

A most important individual in every committee operation is the chairperson. The chairperson's skills will often determine the success or failure of committee activities. Chairpeople plan meetings, prepare agenda, and see to it that the proper background information is available before the meetings. During meetings, they provide leadership, guide the proceedings, call on speakers, and generally set the tone of the discussion. Good chairpeople can minimize many committee shortcomings. They can conduct sessions in a formal or relaxed manner, depending on the circumstances. They also can integrate committee deliberations. Naturally, chairpeople should not dominate discussion—this would annihilate the value of group deliberations. However, they can summarize discussions and try to integrate them into an effective solution or recommendation.

When, as sometimes happens, a person without much leadership ability is selected as chairperson, one of the other members of the committee will very likely become a de facto chairperson. In such a case, managers would do well to remove the originally appointed chairperson from the committee.

Group interaction

Even without the guidance of a chairperson, most committees would eventually arrive at some conclusions through the dynamics of group interaction. However, experience has shown that when several committees deliberate concurrently, some arrive at conclusions—and better conclusions—before others do. This occurs because some chairpeople can structure group interaction more successfully than can others. Structuring involves such things as keeping the discussion on the relevant subject, assessing the quality and ability of committee members, and choosing appropriate procedures and methods for the types of individual and subject involved. The various members of a committee all have individual patterns of behavior and points of view. The chairperson must know how to handle the membership so that its viewpoints and attitudes fuse, and an effective team results.

Naturally, each committee member thinks first of how a new proposition will affect him or her and the working environment. This tendency can easily lead to unnecessary friction. Therefore, the chairperson must develop some common basis for evaluating propositions. First the chairperson must establish agreement on the nature of the problem under discussion. Then, he or she must see that everybody understands the issues. Only after these steps have been achieved can the members of the group effectively interact and achieve a successful solution.

Although the chairperson plays a pivotal role in all committee interactions, he or she may appear successively as an autocrat and as a democrat. At times, even the most permissive, democratic chairperson must exercise tight control over a meeting. The decision to do so will, of course, reflect the chairperson's ability to understand and to structure group interaction.

In summary, an effective chairperson must master two leadership roles: a role that emphasizes leader control over task activities and a role that emphasizes group building and the maintenance of committee social relations. Although it is desirable that the chairperson play both roles, they are frequently shared by at least two people.[7]

Follow-up of committee action

If a committee has been acting in a staff capacity, its findings need relatively little follow-up. The chairperson will report the committee's recommendations to the initiating line executive. Of course, since committee members will be interested in the executive's reaction to their recommendations, the executive should provide appropriate feedback. If recommendations are not accepted, a mutual discussion would be beneficial.

If a committee has been acting in a managerial capacity and has been charged with authority to make decisions, a different situation arises. In this case, a member of the committee usually executes its decisions, and that member must be chosen. Usually, the chairperson or secretary of the committee will be asked to act in an executive capacity for the committee as a whole. However, sometimes a divisional representative is more appropriate. If the committee has been dealing with matters that normally belong within the realm of one operating division, it is better to have that particular operating executive execute the decision. In such an instance, functional authority is conferred on the committee, but executive authority is left to the regular operating executive.

Evaluation of committee work

Committees, like other parts of an organization, need periodic evaluation. A line executive must check to see whether or not the purpose for which the committee was established is still valid and whether or not the committee is operating efficiently within the terms of its purpose and scope. Without such review, committees may remain unnecessarily self-perpetuating.

Summary

Committees play increasingly frequent and important roles in the managing of modern organizations. There are many types of committees, depending on their purpose. Committees are formed at virtually every organizational level

[7] Ibid., p. 17.

and within every functional area. In addition, there are line and staff committees, which may be temporary.

Committees are definitely with us

College students should have little doubt that the committee is a popular organizational form. Colleges and universities tend to have a great number of faculty-student committees involved in every part of school life. Recently, the student newspaper of a large state university published a list of committees of which students are members. Here is the list:

1. Academic advising
2. Academic deficiencies
3. Academic regulations
4. Academic requirements
5. Advancement of teaching
6. Alumni association board of directors
7. Board of physical recreation
8. Broadcast media
9. Campus plan
10. Classroom television
11. Commission on the status of women
12. Computer
13. Concert
14. Convocations and lectures
15. Curriculum
16. Educational activities
17. Educational media and services
18. Equal employment opportunity
19. Examinations
20. Facilities planning and use
21. Fiscal priorities and long-range planning
22. Financial aid
23. Financial aid (scholarships subcommittee)
24. Human rights commission
25. International education
26. Library
27. Men's intercollegiate athletics
28. New student programs
29. Rally
30. Recreational sports
31. Registration and scheduling
32. Residency
33. Student activities
34. Student conduct
35. Student discipline and appeal board
36. Student fees
37. Student health
38. Student publications
39. Student recognition and awards
40. Student services advisory council
41. Student traffic court
42. Undergraduate admissions
43. University discipline
44. University housing
45. Women's intercollegiate athletics

You might find it amusing to compare this list with one from your school. Oh—there is one more committee, not shown. What else? The Committee on Committees.

As with most organizing devices, committees have their assets and their liabilities. On the positive side, the committee form enables a variety of information and views to be brought to bear on problems; it also provides an opportunity for managers to develop their administrative skills. On the negative side, committee deliberations take up a lot of time and run the danger of producing narrow, weak decisions, owing to the members' tendency to compromise.

Managers can improve a committee's efforts by providing its members with a clear charge, selecting appropriate members, and keeping the committee well informed and on the right track during its deliberations. Finally, managers must assess the performance of the committee on a regular and comprehensive basis.

Discussion questions

1. Under what circumstances (organizational, task) should members of a committee compete with one another? cooperate with one another?
2. In your experience of working with other people in groups, what group size seemed the most effective? the most satisfying?
3. There are probably a great many faculty-student-administration committees working in your school or department. Ask the people involved in these committees to describe the advantages and disadvantages that they see in committee work. Next, ask them if they can suggest alternatives to the committee form. What conclusions can you draw from your poll?
4. Has any committee of which you have been a member suffered from groupthink?

Supplementary readings

Filley, A. C. "Committee Management: Guidelines from Social Science Research." *California Management Review* 13 (Fall 1970):13–22. Reprinted in *Dimensions in Modern Management,* 2d ed., edited by Patrick E. Connor. Boston: Houghton Mifflin, 1978.

Janis, Irving L. "Groupthink." *Psychology Today* 5 (November 1971):43–46, 74–76.

───. *Victims of Groupthink*. Boston: Houghton Mifflin, 1972.

O'Donnell, Cyril. "Ground Rules for Using Committees." *Management Review* 15 (October 1961):63–67.

Chapter 14

Designing organizations

Objectives of the chapter

1 To identify important organizational characteristics that managers can vary.
2 To identify factors that constrain this ability to vary organizational characteristics.
3 To examine a modern organizational design: the matrix structure.

The purpose of this chapter is to introduce the subject of organizational design. Organizational design is the logical conclusion to our previous discussions. The organizing question that continually faces the manager is: What is the best way to organize my unit? As we have been emphasizing, the answer is: It depends. The manager's immediate response: On what? In this chapter we answer this last question. Before we can deal with the question, however, a brief review is in order. First, we must make clear what element is being designed. Second, we must remember the situational nature of management.

Design characteristics

When we say "organizational design," to what are we referring? For purposes of this discussion, let us think about three major organizational characteristics that managers can vary, depending on their situation. These characteristics are *differentiation* (departments), *formalization* (rules), and *centralization* (authority).

Differentiation

Differentiation refers to the division of organizational labor. Labor is divided three ways: horizontally, into departments; vertically, into managerial levels;

and into specialized tasks that are performed by staff personnel. The way in which these divisions occur is important. Span-of-control considerations, for example, make it clear that managers' ability to supervise varies as the degree and nature of vertical and horizontal differentiation vary. Because of the systems nature of organizations, the impact that each kind of differentiation has on managerial action is conditioned by other aspects of organizational structure. Specifically, the degree to which organizational rules and regulations are formalized and the extent to which authority is centralized also affect the ability of managers to meet their responsibilities.

Formalization

Formalization is the organizational technique of prescribing how, when, and by whom tasks are to be performed. In particular, formalization refers to the degree to which explicit rules and regulations govern the behavior (task and otherwise) of organizational participants. Like differentiation, formalization can vary in degree. The time of day that work begins serves as a simple example. An organization that is highly formalized might require workers to be at their desks by 8:00 A.M. or be docked a half-hour's pay; an organization with a relatively low level of formalization may have no rules (and few expectations) about the time work begins, just as long as the work is done.

From an operational standpoint, formalization is reflected by two things: the degree to which rules and regulations exist and the degree to which they are enforced. The more that managers use specific job descriptions and rules manuals and the less variation they allow, the more formalized is the organization.

As with differentiation, formalization may vary even within an organization. Departments that have relatively simple and repetitive tasks to perform and that require a fairly low level of technical skill on the part of the employees usually find that a relatively high level of formalization is useful. This, for example, might be the case for clerks who record and file client applications for welfare services. On the other hand, departments that are responsible for the performance of complex tasks at a high skill level usually require a low level of formalization. This is often the case for such personnel as computer programmers, system analysts, and career counselors.

In the former case, high formalization is helpful in assuring that tasks are performed in as uniform and least wasteful a manner as possible. The latter situation, however, is incompatible with a lot of rules and regulations; in this case, low formalization allows the skilled employees the latitude, or discretion, necessary to perform their complex tasks. High formalization would likely do more harm than good.

Note: Formalization is related to a worker's latitude, or areas of discretion. This concept is integral to the third critical feature of organizational design: centralization.

254 Organizing

Centralization

Centralization concerns the degree to which authority is distributed throughout the organization. Authority is the organizational right to see that organizational tasks are performed. The process by which authority is distributed—by which a level of decentralization is established—is known as *delegation*.

Situational management

Recall from Chapter 1 our discussion of the open-systems and contingency approaches. There we noted that the organization operates in an environment that consists of a number of components—other organizations, sociopolitical-economic forces, market demands, and so forth (refer back to Figures 1-1 and 1-2). Managers must take these factors into account in guiding the fortunes of their organizations. Further, the way they deal with the factors depends on their organization's goals.

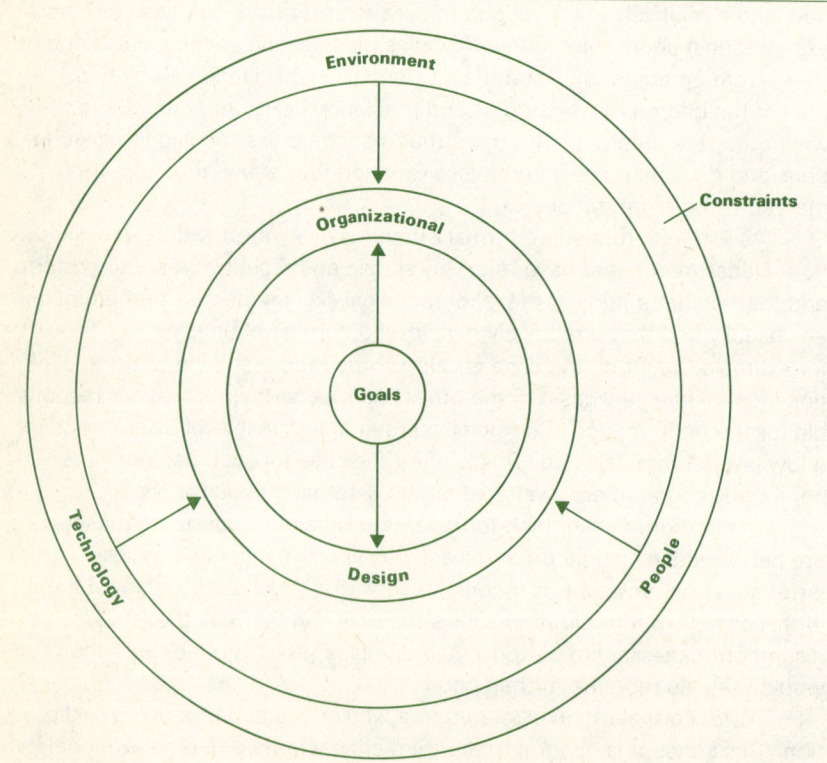

Figure 14-1 Designing the organization

Thus, the answer to the question: What is the best way to organize my unit? is: Managers should organize so as to achieve their organization's goals, given the various constraints under which the organization labors. This situation is illustrated in Figure 14-1. As Figure 14-1 indicates, the major factors constraining organizational design are the external environment, the organization's technology, and the type of people who populate the organization. Let us consider these various organizational design factors.

Organizational goals

We noted in Chapter 1 that organizations are established and perpetuated for the purpose of performing a task—cure the ill, manufacture and sell shoes, educate the young, and so forth. As a way of performing the organizational task in an orderly (rational) fashion, managers pursue a set of goals and objectives. Some typical objectives were discussed in Chapter 4 (refer back to Figure 4-1 for a brief review).

That managers know their organization's goals is vital. Managers must structure their organization so as to facilitate the effective pursuit of its primary objectives. For example, if an organization is concerned primarily with economic objectives, its managers will try to establish procedures that maximize efficiency. If an organization is concerned primarily with a service or political goal, such as a national presidential campaign organization, its managers will try to decentralize authority and to make greater use of participative structures (committees, for example).

Further, different units within the same organization may pursue different goals and, consequently, have different designs. Thus, we can observe an aerospace firm's manufacturing division to be structured like a classic bureaucracy, with large spans of control, high formalization, and high centralization and the firm's research laboratories, on the other hand, to be loosely structured, with relatively narrow spans (owing to the nature of research supervision),[1] low formalization, and low centralization.

Design constraints

Differences between the manufacturing division and the research laboratory can be attributed, initially, to differences in their primary objectives. However, the differences would not remain if constraints on the two units were not also different. Again, the principal constraints with which managers must deal are the external environment, the organization's dominant technology, and the organizational members.

---

[1] Peter M. Blau and W. Richard Scott, *Formal Organizations* (San Francisco: Chandler, 1962).

External environment

There have been several attempts by organization theorists to examine the effects of environment on the way managers design their organizations. The two most significant studies have been those by Burns and Stalker and by Lawrence and Lorsch.

The Burns and Stalker study

In 1964 Burns and Stalker published an important book about managing.[2] Based on a comprehensive study of twenty industrial firms in the United Kingdom, the researchers concluded that environmental forces are felt directly by the organization. Specifically, they reported two major types of environment: dynamic and static. *Dynamic environments* are those characterized by rapid changes in markets, technology, economic conditions, and so forth. *Static environments* are characterized by relative stability in those same conditions.

The importance of the Burns and Stalker study is: the discovery that the organizational designs effective under dynamic environmental conditions differed from those that were effective under static environments. Managers designed "organic" organizations to operate under dynamic conditions. In addition to low levels of formalization and centralization overall, organic-organization managers emphasized collaboration and authority based on knowledge rather than position.[3]

In contrast, managers designed "mechanistic" organizations to operate under static conditions. Mechanistic-organization managers relied on high formalization, high centralization, directives, and position-based authority.[4]

The Lawrence and Lorsch study

Another famous research project on the subject of organizational environment was conducted by Lawrence and Lorsch. In examining organizations in the plastics, food, and container industries,[5] the authors set out to answer the following questions:[6]

1. How do the environmental demands facing various organizations differ? How

---

[2] Tom Burns and G. W. Stalker, *The Management of Innovation* (London: Tavistock, 1964).

[3] See the analysis by Ralph M. Hower and Jay Lorsch, "Organizational Inputs," in John Seiler, *Systems Analysis in Organizational Behavior* (Homewood, Illinois: Dorsey Press, 1967).

[4] Ibid., p. 168.

[5] Jay W. Lorsch, *Product Innovation and Organization* (New York: Macmillan, 1965); Paul R. Lawrence and Jay W. Lorsch, "Differentiation and Integration in Complex Organizations," *Administrative Science Quarterly*, June 1967, pp. 1–47; Paul R. Lawrence and Jay W. Lorsch, *Organization and Environment* (Homewood, Illinois: Richard D. Irwin, 1969); and Jay W. Lorsch and Paul R. Lawrence, eds., *Studies in Organization Design* (Homewood, Illinois: Richard D. Irwin and Dorsey Press, 1970).

[6] Lawrence and Lorsch, *Organization and Environment*, p. 16.

do environmental demands relate to the internal functioning of effective organizations?
2. Is it true that organizations in stable environments make more exclusive use of the formal hierarchy to achieve integration? If so, why? Because less integration is required? Or, because in a certain environment these decisions can be made more effectively at higher organizational levels or by fewer people?
3. Is the same degree of differentiation in orientation and in departmental structure found in organizations in different industrial environments?
4. If greater differentiation among functional departments is required in different industries, does this influence the problems of integrating the organizations' parts? Does it influence the organizations' means of achieving integration?

In essence, the Lawrence and Lorsch research supported and extended that of Burns and Stalker. Put briefly, managers of effective organizations in different environments employed different means of coordination. Traditional techniques of coordination—rules, procedures, plans, and the chain of command—were effective when the organization operated under static environmental conditions. Systems techniques—teams, specifically designated coordinators, and task forces—were effective when the organization operated under dynamic environmental conditions.

Organizational technology

Without going into an extensive discussion, we must note a second critical factor on which organizational design is contingent: task technology.[7] Basically, *technology* is a term used to denote the way in which work is performed. Every task has a dominant technology, whether it is putting pockets on a piece of clothing, teaching a class of fifty management students, or putting a job hunter in touch with a company that is hiring.

Managers must design their organizations in a way that is compatible with the organizations' technology. More specifically, managers must take into account the *complexity* of the organizational technology. Technological complexity is concerned with such characteristics as the task's routineness, the number of separate variables involved, predictability of results, and so forth. The fundamental rule is: the more complex the technology, the more organic the organizational design must be.

People

The third critical design factor is the people who comprise the organization's membership. Particularly significant is the degree of cosmopolitanism

---

[7] For a comprehensive and original treatment of technology and organizational design see James D. Thompson, *Organizations in Action* (New York: McGraw-Hill, 1967).

characterizing the organization's population. Basically, *cosmopolitans* are people who are oriented to their profession, its other members, and its work standards. In contrast, *locals* are people who relate—are oriented—much more directly to their local situation; usually, locals rate high in organizational loyalty.[8]

Generally, the higher people's cosmopolitan orientation, the more they value such things as decentralization, autonomy, knowledge-based authority, and so forth. The manager of basic research scientists would be ill advised to design the organization in a highly mechanistic fashion.

A design example

As we have indicated, three major design characteristics that managers vary are differentiation (departments), formalization (rules), and centralization (authority). Each of these components varies within and among organizations; that is, each component varies on a continuum from high to low. Therefore, the manager must see to it that these components are compatible with each other and with the overall organizational mission.

Two situations

Effective relationships among the design components may best be described by illustrating two extreme situations.[9] In the first, the organization (enterprise A) is operating under environmental conditions that are relatively stable. That is, social, political, and economic pressures have changed little in recent years and show no sign of changing greatly in the foreseeable future. Furthermore, the work that enterprise A performs is relatively straightforward, involving, on the part of the employees, a great deal of work that is repetitive, predictable, small in its scope and altogether routine.

In such an organization, a relatively high level of *formalization* (many rules) would be appropriate, because rules and regulations would serve to facilitate the performance of tasks with a minimum of wasted energy. Specifically, demands of both outside conditions and task requirements are stable, predictable, and routine; responses to these demands can—and should—be

---

[8] The original description of these orientations is contained in Robert K. Merton, "Patterns of Influence, Local and Cosmopolitan Influentials," in *Social Theory and Social Structure*, rev. ed. (New York: Free Press, 1968), pp. 441–474. The concept was focused in the organizational setting by Alvin W. Gouldner, "Cosmopolitans and Locals: Toward an Analysis of Latent Social Roles," *Administrative Science Quarterly* 2 (1957):281–306 and 2 (1958):444–480.

[9] This section is based on Patrick E. Connor, "Organizational Structure: An Administrative Tool," Institute for Manpower Studies Paper No. 5 (Corvallis: Oregon State University, 1976).

equally stable, predictable, and routine. Rules and regulations help to create these responses.

Second, the nature of the demands, together with the low skill requirements of the employees, makes decentralization (the use of judgment and discretion by subordinates) unattractive. So, enterprise A's level of *centralization* should be relatively high.

Finally, enterprise A is able—at least, as far as our example goes—to have relatively few administrative levels (low *vertical differentiation*) and many subordinates reporting to an administrator (high *horizontal differentiation*). This recommendation is consistent with those preceding: the routineness of the tasks, the lack of discretionary behavior, the extensive rules governing task performance, all mean that one manager can supervise a relatively large number of people.

In brief, then, the conditions in which enterprise A operates suggest that the organization should, for maximum effectiveness, have a relatively short and fat shape, a high degree of formalization governing task behavior, and a high level of centralized decision making.

If, for a second organization, enterprise B, conditions are sketched that are relatively opposite to those facing enterprise A, it can be seen that different design conclusions are called for. B operates under socio-political-economic conditions that are fairly dynamic—continually changing, frequently in unpredictable ways. Furthermore, the work that enterprise B performs is complex, involving a large number and variety of organizational resources that must be assigned, scheduled, and coordinated. These tasks are nonroutine, requiring B's employees to exercise the sophisticated skills they have acquired in their extensive professional training.

For enterprise B, high *formalization* could prove disastrous. Probably B's managers should see to it that necessary guidelines are established; within these guidelines, however, employees will, owing to task and environmental requirements, exercise their professional judgments. Thus, the level of *decentralized* decision making should be considerably higher than that in enterprise A. Finally, regarding *differentiation*, it turns out that many organizations in circumstances similar to B's find it most effective to assign a relatively few number of individuals to a supervising manager. This arrangement is helpful for two reasons. First, the typical manager is unable to supervise effectively a large number of people performing a variety of complex tasks. Second, the relationship between a supervisor and a subordinate, if both are skilled professionals, is likely (or at least ought) to be one of colleagues, rather than strictly superior-subordinate. Having only a few subordinates allows a manager to enjoy the benefits of such a relationship.[10]

In brief, then, the conditions in which enterprise B operates suggest that the organization should have a relatively tall and thin shape, a low degree of formalization governing task behavior, and a low level of centralized decision making.

---

[10] Blau and Scott, *Formal Organizations*.

Two designs

The differences between enterprises A and B lie principally with the external conditions facing them and their internal task characteristics—over neither of which do their managers have significant control. Socio-political-economic demands are relatively stable, or static, in A's case, while they are rather turbulent, or dynamic, in B's. These conditions have important implications for the manner in which managers should design their organizations.

The differences between A and B can be illustrated by their design profiles, as shown in Figure 14-2.

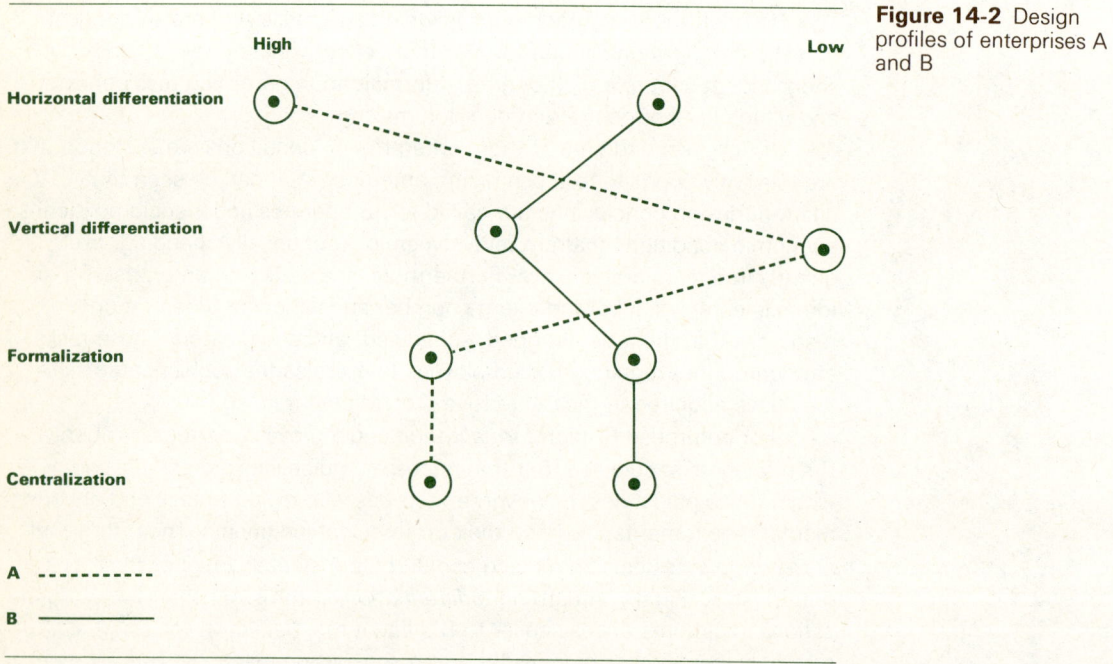

Figure 14-2 Design profiles of enterprises A and B

Remembering that A and B are extreme organizational examples, the design profile of a more typical organization will be (is) rather less composed of extremely high or low coordinates. Nevertheless, given the kind of conditions sketched for enterprises A and B, the profiles illustrated in Figure 14-2 represent ideal combinations of design properties.

Perhaps it is this concept of design profile that best enables us to understand that critical managerial question: What is the most effective structural arrangement—profile—that I can design, given the environmental conditions and task requirements of my organization?

Design issues for the manager

1 The design of an organization structure is the important outcome of the organizing function.
2 The three principal characteristics (design) that managers can vary are forming departments, establishing rules and regulations, and decentralizing authority.
3 The way in which managers choose to design their organization depends on (1) their goals, (2) environmental conditions, (3) the unit's technology, and (4) the nature of their employees.

A contemporary design: The matrix organization

As our society moves into the 1980s it is more and more likely that managers will have to design their organizations to cope with dynamic conditions.[11] The design that currently is seen as the most compatible with these conditions is that known as the *matrix* configuration. The matrix organization is the direct outcome of the vastly complex demands that advanced military and space technology has placed on American industry and is one of the most important developments in contemporary management theory and practice. Although matrix organization can be applied effectively to nonmilitary work, it was originally devised to handle contracts for weapon systems.

The matrix idea

Basically, a matrix design attacks an increasingly familiar problem: jobs (projects) come and go, depending on various customers' needs, but basic functions (such as engineering, economics, manufacturing, and marketing) continue to be required. If an organization grows geographically, it cannot develop a stable of experts in every technical area in each geographic office.

So, how can an enterprise compete for a technical contract in both Seattle and St. Louis? How can an engineering firm put highly qualified people into the field in both San Francisco and Washington, D.C.? A matrix organizational design helps solve this very real managerial problem.

The idea is this: corporate managers employ technical personnel—engineers and scientists, for example—in a functional area; as specific projects come along, the people are assigned on either a full- or part-time basis to those projects. The organization is able, then, to field groups of highly expert personnel to tackle a variety of problems without having to have a huge number of such people on its payroll.

[11] See Warren G. Bennis, *Changing Organizations* (New York: McGraw-Hill, 1966); Warren G. Bennis and Paul E. Slater, *The Temporary Society* (New York: Harper & Row, 1968); and Alvin Toffler, *Future Shock* (New York: Bantam Books, 1970).

Purpose

The essential purpose of the matrix organization is to secure a higher degree of coordination than could be obtained in a conventional line structure. Work is organized around projects; it is not limited to specialized departments, as in the typical line organization. The matrix organization is, in a sense, an overlay on conventional organizational structure. Although it draws on traditional structure for various skills, as we see in Figure 14-3, projects themselves are clearly identified and directed independently, from their inception to the manufacturing stages. The need for this type of structure is evident, especially when a firm has several projects underway.

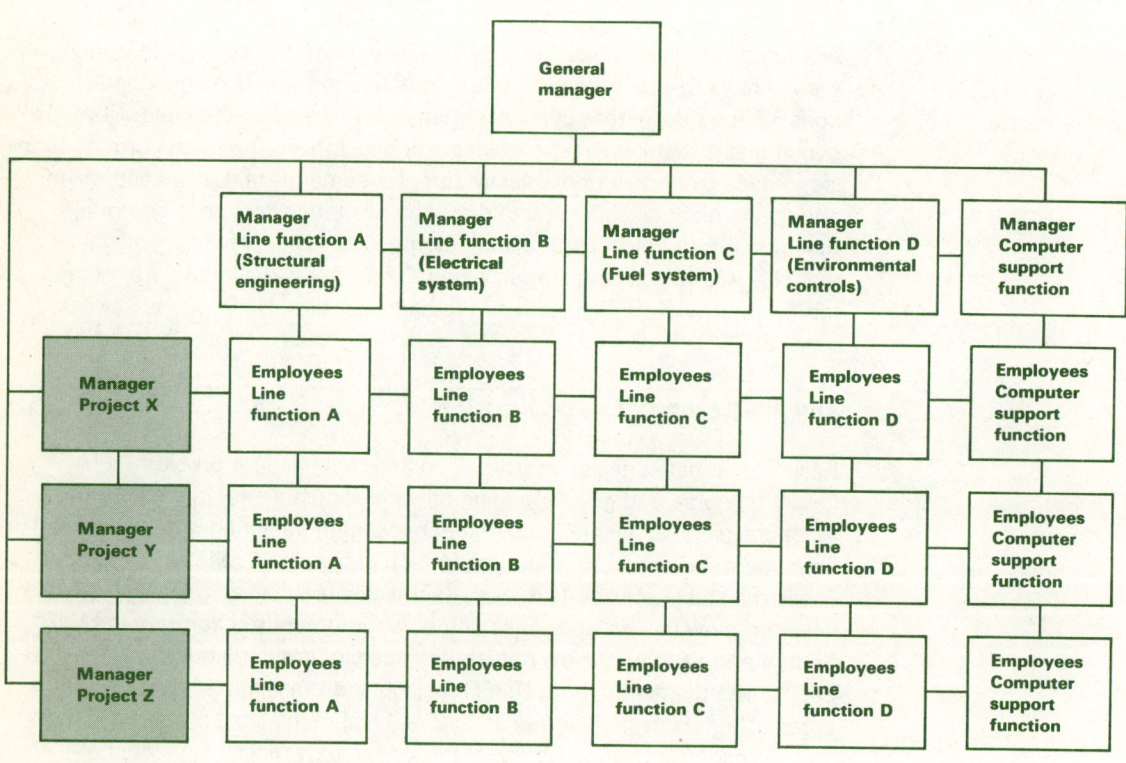

Figure 14-3 Matrix organization design

Two basic organizational segments can be seen in Figure 14-3: the conventionally organized engineering departments and the three project activities. Projects have their own managers, who see the projects through to completion. They draw the people they need from the functional (engineering) departments and coordinate their work from the design phase to testing and manufacturing. When a project is ended, personnel return to their functional departments to be reassigned to new projects.

An example

CH2M-Hill is an engineering consulting firm with approximately twelve hundred employees. The company is headquartered in Corvallis, Oregon, and has several branch offices throughout the United States. About five years ago, top management decided that a matrix organization would be the most appropriate design for the firm's needs.

Management's reasoning went like this: the company had grown dramatically in the preceding several years, becoming involved with highly technical engineering problems in many parts of the country. Such growth presented an important managerial problem. The company could not have top experts everywhere, so how could it take maximum advantage of the expertise it did have? The answer, basically, was to have its top experts on call. That is, corporate management encouraged the development of a group of experts in one location—Denver, for instance. Then, when an engineering job developed in Salt Lake City, a task force would be formed to work on that problem as a specific project. When the project was completed, the Denver-based people would either return home or move on to another project. Figure 14-4 portrays the design that has been developed for the firm.

The design enables the company's managers to coordinate the problems (projects) encountered in various geographic regions with the skills contained in several functional areas, or *disciplines,* as they are called. The ongoing character of this relationship is suggested by the design's slightly different representation in Figure 14-5.

Conclusion

The matrix organization has a number of advantages. It eases coordination and allows for rapid assessment of the status of any given project. It makes the job of maintaining effective contact between the contractor and the contractee simpler. In addition, it provides an orderly way of phasing projects in and out of an organization.

The matrix organization introduces whole new sets of relationships.[12] Whereas conventional structure and classical management theory stress vertical chain of command relationships, the matrix structure emphasizes horizontal and diagonal relationships. Clearly, such lateral relationships are necessary if the required exchanges among project managers and conventional department managers are to occur.

[12] See David I. Clelland, "Understanding Project Authority," *Business Horizons,* Spring 1967, pp. 63–70; and Jay R. Galbraith, "Matrix Organizational Designs: How to Combine Functional and Project Forms," *Business Horizons,* February 1971, pp. 29–40.

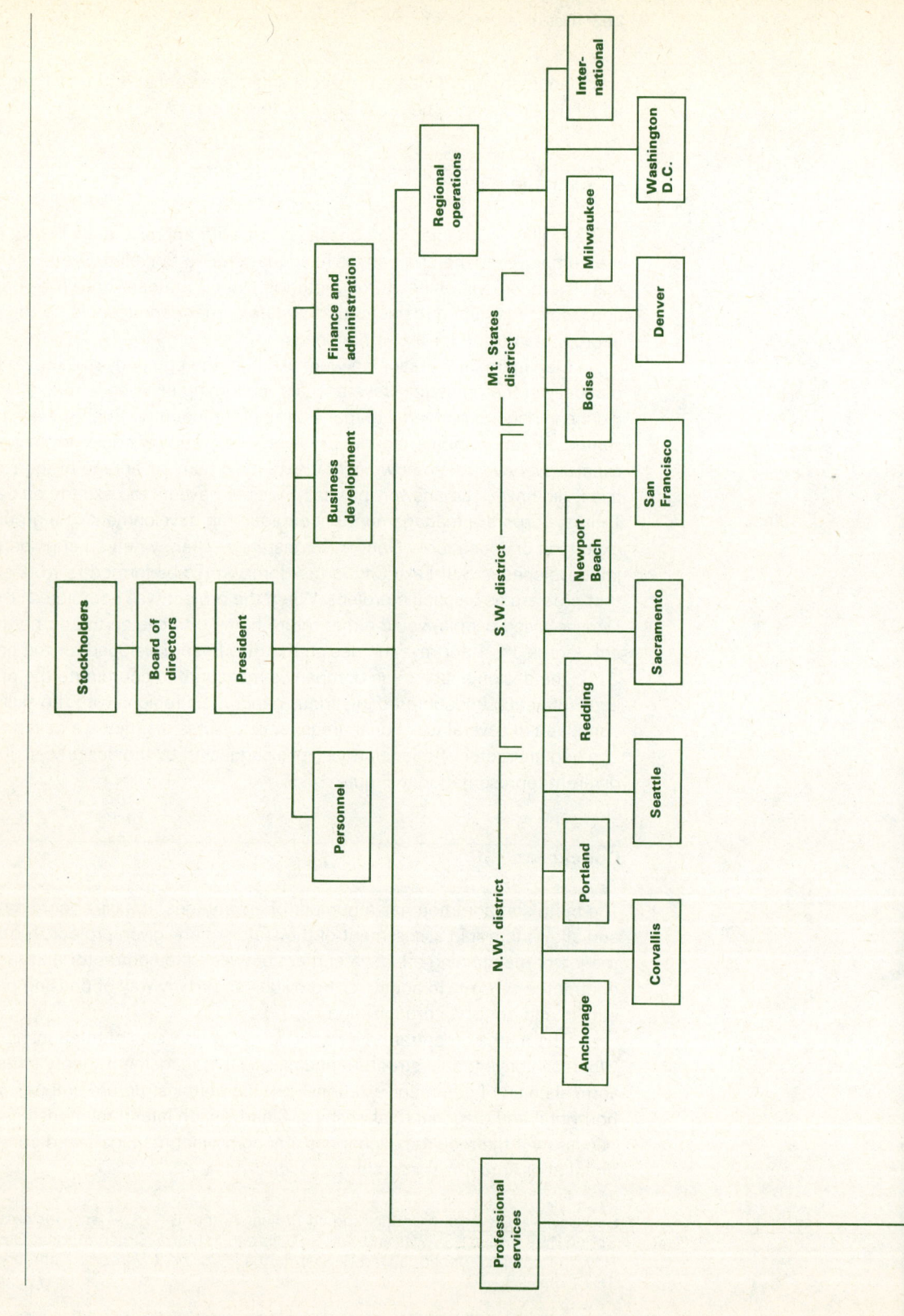

264

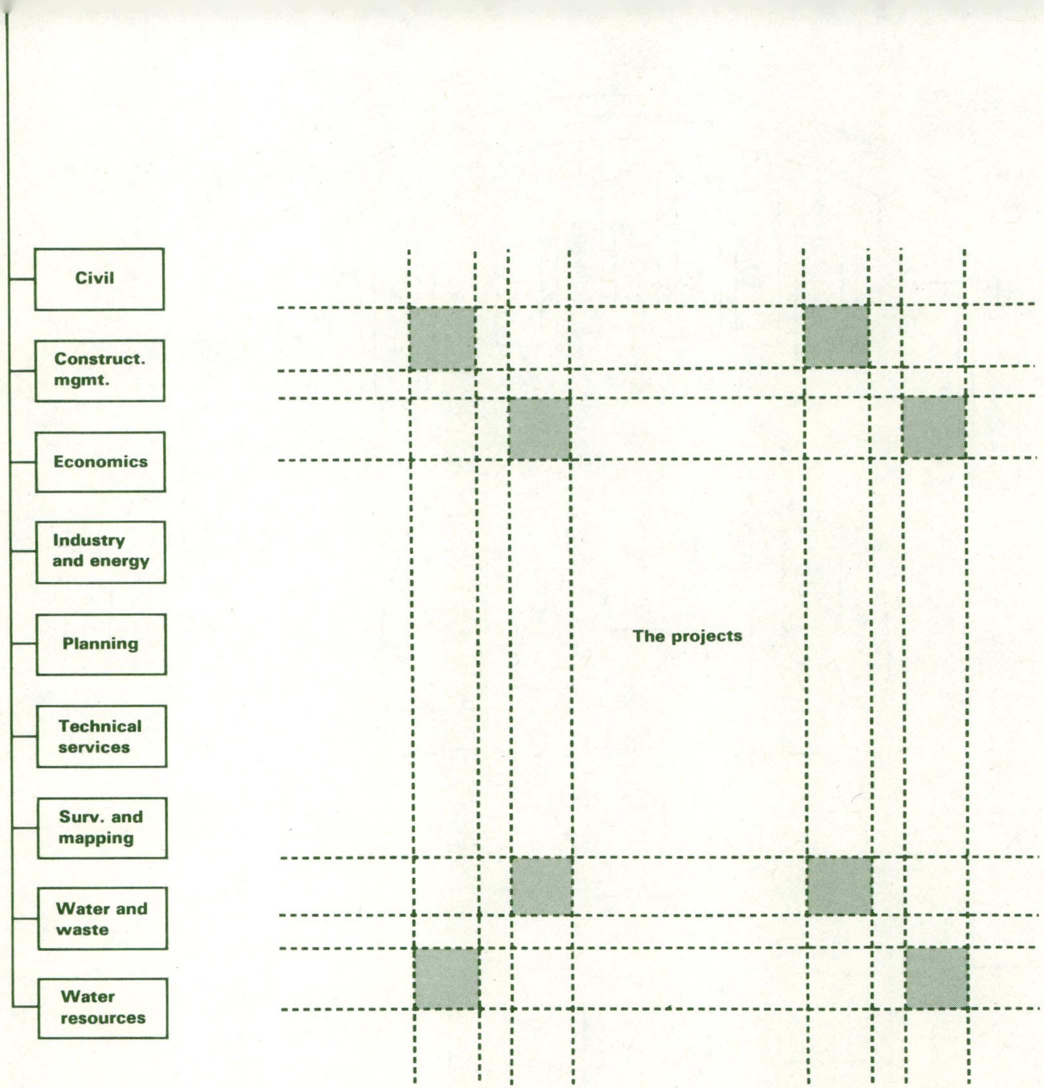

Figure 14-4 CH2M-Hill matrix (a) Reprinted by permission.

The projects

Civil
Construct. mgmt.
Economics
Industry and energy
Planning
Technical services
Surv. and mapping
Water and waste
Water resources

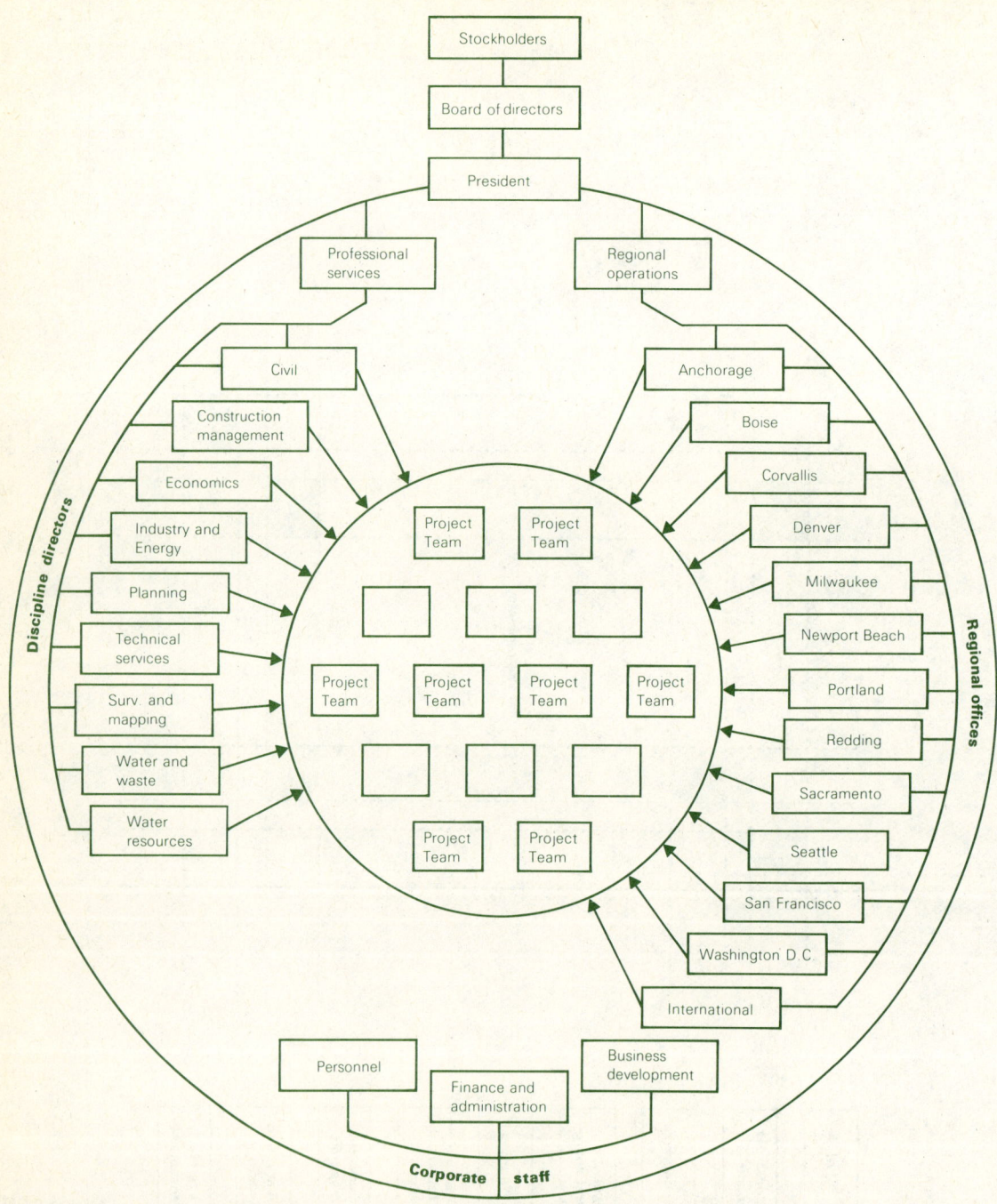

Figure 14-5 CH2M-Hill matrix (*b*) Reprinted by permission.

Organizing a professional school or an R&D department is very much like mixing oil with water: It is easy to describe the intended product, less easy to produce it. And the task is not finished when the goal has been achieved. Left to themselves, the oil and water will separate again. So also with the disciplines and the professions. Organizing, in these situations, is not a once-and-for-all activity. It is a continuing administrative responsibility, vital for the sustained success of the enterprise.

Herbert A. Simon

Summary

In deciding the best way in which to design an organizational unit, managers must consider several factors: the unit's goals, the environmental conditions in which it functions, the dominant technology by which the goals are accomplished, and the type of people who populate the organization.

What elements do managers design? We have focused on three design characteristics: differentiation (departments), formalization (rules and regulations), and centralization (authority). Basically, the rule is: a dynamic environment, complex goals and technology, and professional employees encourage an organic design; a mechanistic design is more appropriate where conditions are static.

The dynamic/organic situation has become increasingly prevalent. The matrix organization, a major design used in this situation, employs people in basic, functional departments and then assigns them to various projects as needed.

Discussion questions

1. Why would a high-technology engineering firm be designed differently than a pulp mill?
2. Content aside, would you design a senior management course differently than a freshman introduction to business course? How?
3. The matrix organization and the process of project authority violate the unity of command principle. What are the theoretical reasons for this violation? the practical reasons?

Supplementary readings

Carzo, Rocco, Jr. "Organizational Realities." *Business Horizons,* Spring 1961, pp. 95–104. Reprinted in *Dimensions in Modern Management,* 2d ed., edited by Patrick E. Connor. Boston: Houghton Mifflin, 1978.

Connor, Patrick E., and Bloomfield, Stefan D. "A Goal Approach to Organizational Design." In *Prescriptive Models of Organizations,* edited by Paul C. Nystrom and William H. Starbuck. Vol. 5. North-Holland/TIMS Studies in the Management Sciences. Amsterdam: North-Holland Publishing, 1977. Reprinted in *Dimensions in Modern Management,* 2d ed., edited by Patrick E. Connor. Boston: Houghton Mifflin, 1978.

Horton, Forest W., Jr. "Organization and Management Techniques in the Federal Government." *S.A.M. Advanced Management Journal* 35, no. 1 (January 1970):66—77. Reprinted in *Dimensions in Modern Management,* 2d ed., edited by Patrick E. Connor. Boston: Houghton Mifflin, 1978.

Raube, S. Avery. "Principles of Organization." In *Company Organization Charts,* pp. 7—13. New York: National Industrial Conference Board, 1954. Reprinted in *Dimensions in Modern Management,* 2d ed., edited by Patrick E. Connor. Boston: Houghton Mifflin, 1978.

Ross, Joel E., and Murdick, Robert G. "People, Productivity, and Organizational Structure." *Personnel,* September—October 1973, pp. 9—18. Reprinted in *Dimensions in Modern Management* 2d ed., edited by Patrick E. Connor. Boston: Houghton Mifflin, 1978.

Shetty, Y. K. "Is There a Best Way to Organize a Business Enterprise?" *S.A.M. Advanced Management Journal,* April 1973, pp. 47—52. Reprinted in *Dimensions in Modern Management,* 2d ed., edited by Patrick E. Connor. Boston: Houghton Mifflin, 1978.

Cases for Part III

Case III/1

The A. B. Electronics Company

The A. B. Electronics Company manufactures a variety of electronic components, some of which are used for consumer items and others of which are sold to producers of military equipment. Its sales for 1976 amounted to $10 million. When the company started in 1965, it was departmentalized along functional lines; as its activities increased, they were assigned to the appropriate functional departments. All parts, regardless of final use, were produced in the production department; all sales were handled by the sales department, and so on. As time went on, a large monolithic organization was created; and, it often was difficult to find out exactly who was responsible for delays and errors. It also was difficult to give one or the other item sufficient emphasis when needed.

All of this came to a head when the president, Sam Marshall, received a telephone call from one of the company's customers. The customer complained that a delay in shipping some electronic components was holding up the assembly of military aircraft and that these government orders had to be shipped on time. On checking, Marshall found that this particular company had been buying a great number of components and deserved more attention and service than it had been getting.

He decided to assign one person to this project and chose Larry Brandt, who had worked as an engineer for the company for many years and knew most of the people in the plant. Marshall felt that Brandt was a good choice, because he would understand the problems better than someone would who had no engineering background; also he was well liked and seemed to get along well with people. The president, in assigning the job to Brandt, simply stated that it was Brandt's duty to see to it that the orders for the aircraft company come through production on time and that they be delivered as promised. He was to report directly to Marshall.

In order to acquaint himself with the problems, Brandt traced the steps involved in the orders—from the point of sale through engineering, scheduling, production, inspection, and shipping. Of course, there were many other areas as well, but these departments were the most important ones. The head of the engineering department, his former boss, was eager for Brandt to succeed in his new assignment and gave him all the assistance he needed. There were no delays in engineering, and, on checking further, Brandt found that the major problems and bottlenecks were occurring in the production and inspection departments. Brandt spent a lot of time and effort in these departments and ran into some serious problems. In the beginning, he tried mild persuasion with the various supervisors and foremen. The superintendents of production and inspection resented his interference. They told him that there were other jobs on the floor, too, and that these had to be finished as well; and they told their foremen not to let Brandt bother them. Although Brandt initially did show some results, the usual delays began to recur.

Brandt reported his activities and frustrations in his second report to Marshall and urged the president to arrange his job so that it would be possible for him to obtain results. He said that under those conditions he would gladly assume responsibility for the job; but if that was not possible, he would prefer his old job back.

Questions

1. What were some of Brandt's problems?
2. Did Marshall give Brandt an assignment that could be fulfilled? If you were the president, what would you do now? Be sure to consider the organizational implications of your answer.

Case III/2

The concerned boss

Nellie Hillcrest is the director of nursing services at Jackson County Hospital; she has overall authority and responsibility for all patient care. Several years ago, she appointed Fred Palmer to be the operating room supervisor in charge of all surgical procedures. A short while ago, a new air flow system, essential to certain surgical procedures, was installed in four of the operating rooms. Jean Kelly, working under Palmer, is the head nurse in charge of these four rooms. Hillcrest has shown considerable interest in the results of this new installation and has spoken with Kelly, on many occasions, to learn the progress. She has expressed to Kelly her general disappointment with the results and functioning of these four rooms.

Palmer has also been very interested in the results of the new installation, and he, too, has been in close touch with Kelly and the chief of that surgical specialty. While reviewing and discussing the activities in her section, Kelly informed Palmer of Hillcrest's frequent inquiries and her expressed disappointment, saying that Hillcrest's attitude and behavior were disturbing her very much. Palmer, who has been generally satisfied with the results so far, is reluctant to discuss this whole situation with Hillcrest, since she has not said anything directly to him about the matter.

Questions

1 Has Hillcrest been seeking information and expressing her reaction in a correct manner?
2 Should Palmer do anything about the situation? If so, what?

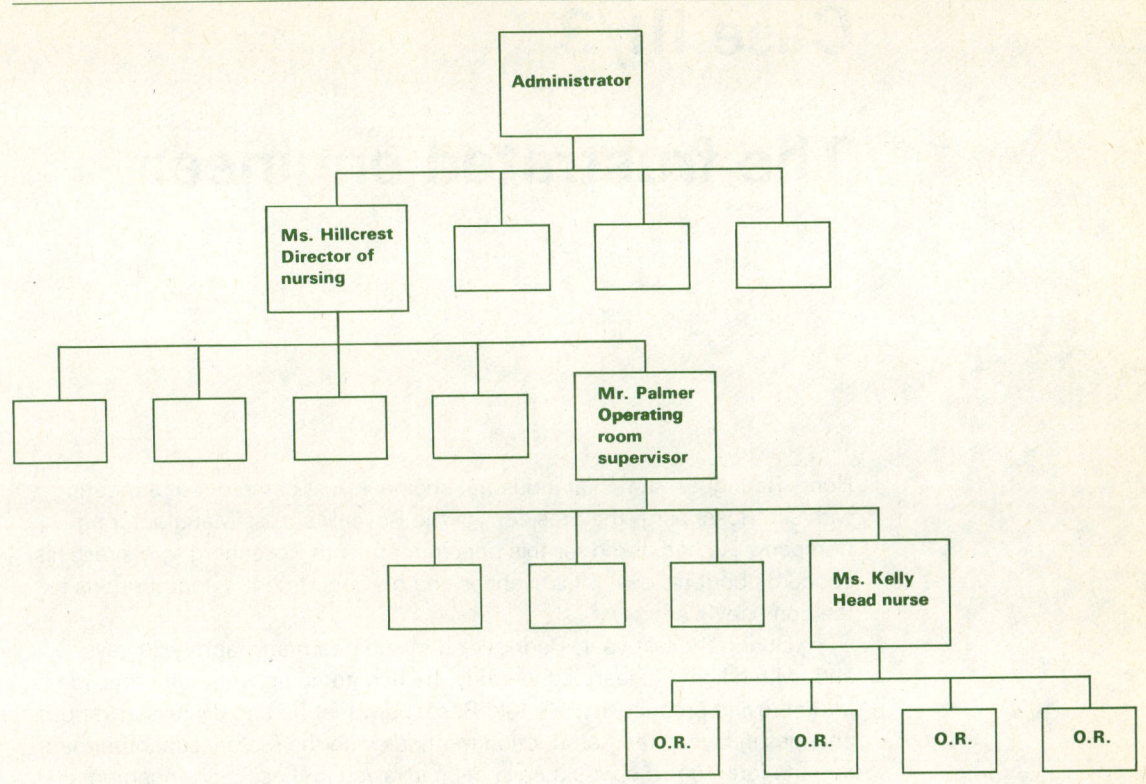

Figure III/2-1

Case III/3

The frustrated engineer

Henry Rodriguez, the chief industrial engineer, just came out of a meeting with Jim Rosenberg, the president of the Royal Mattress Manufacturing Company. He had asked for this appointment with Rosenberg to express his concern about his own effectiveness and his department's contributions to the company's efforts.

During the last year, Rodriguez had initiated many factory surveys, and, with diligent research and study, he had come up with numerous ideas for improving productivity. He told Rosenberg that he had discussed various changes in layouts and production methods with the factory superintendent and the foremen who would have been involved in these rearrangements. He had tried to show the superintendent that carrying out certain steps would simplify production, increase effectiveness, and, ultimately, result in better performance.

Rodriguez understands that industrial engineer is a staff position in the Royal Mattress Company. Therefore, he had tried everything he could think of in order to "sell" his ideas to the line managers in the production department. All to no avail. He had decided to speak to the president and to ask for the authority to make these changes and improvements. Rosenberg turned down the engineer's request.

Questions

1. What should Rodriguez do now?
2. Did Rosenberg make the right decision?
3. How can the president make certain that the industrial engineering department will make a real contribution to the firm and justify the expenses involved in the department's operation?

Case III/4

The Fabric Outlet Stores

Fabric Outlet Incorporated owns and operates a large number of retail stores that specialize in fabrics at discount prices. Primarily in midwestern states, the stores usually are located in suburban shopping districts. Each store is known by a different name, although "Fabric Outlet Incorporated" and the Chicago headquarters' address appear in small letters on each store's door. A central warehouse in Chicago supplies each store with new merchandise.

The local managers can return fabrics to Chicago whenever they feel that they have received too much of a certain type or that they will not have the customers for it. The local managers have a good deal of authority in managing the local store: they hire and fire employees, establish store hours, design the layout, reduce prices if necessary, and so on. A few functions—accounting, reporting, finances, and advertising—are centralized at headquarters; the directives in these areas are issued from Chicago. The effectiveness of a local manager is measured by the volume of sales and the overall profit of the individual store before taxes.

In the last few months, companywide sales have decreased. Other discount fabric stores have been opened and local department stores have run a greater number of sales in their fabric department. Fabric Outlet's president believed that an increase in advertising would counteract this trend and directed all store managers to double their advertising space and outlays. The advertisements were prepared in Chicago and featured the corporation's name prominently—the local store's name was mentioned in small print. Several store managers contacted Chicago and pointed out that they should have the authority to do their own advertising, featuring their individual store's name. In the final analysis, each store paid for the advertisements as a part of expenses.

Questions

1. Has Chicago headquarters practiced broad delegation of authority?
2. How would you allocate authority within the corporation's network?
3. Which functions should remain centralized at headquarters?

Case III/5

The manager's dilemma

The manager of the transportation department, Helen Wagner, recently received a directive stating that the plant manager must give permission for all overtime and Saturday work before such work is scheduled. Previously, each department manager had authorized overtime whenever the need for it arose. However, the company had been experiencing a severe profit squeeze and was looking for ways to reduce costs and other expenditures. In the past, Wagner had little occasion to schedule overtime and did not think that the directive would hamper the performance of her duties.

However, a new situation arose. Because of unforeseen delays in production, orders began to pile up. This bottleneck, which was soon alleviated in the factory, shifted to the transportation department. Here, the increased workload and unexpected absences combined to slow the shipment of orders. Wagner feared that some orders would be canceled if they were not shipped before the week was over but felt her employees could not complete their task during normal work hours. She was convinced that overtime would help the situation. She tried to contact the plant manager, John Mainelli, who was out of town and could not be reached. Wagner had heard that, some time ago, the plant maintenance manager had faced a similar problem and, realizing that delay in making the needed repair would have made the job more difficult and costly, had authorized overtime without the necessary permission. When Mainelli had returned, he had seriously criticized his subordinate and instituted disciplinary action.

The transportation manager did not know what to do. If she authorized overtime, she would exceed her authority; if she did not, shipping would be delayed and orders canceled. She tried contacting the president of the company, Mainelli's line superior, who was also out of town and unreachable. Finally, Wagner decided on the safe course: she did not authorize overtime. Some of the shipments did not go out on time, and some orders were canceled.

Questions

1 If you had been in charge of the transportation department, what would you have done?
2 What would you do if you were the president of the company?
3 How might a similar situation be prevented?

Case III/6

The Good Samaritan Hospital

Sister Estelle Marie is the administrator of the Good Samaritan Hospital in Bedlam, Ohio. She was elected to this position in 1970, after obtaining a masters degree in hospital administration, by the governing board of her religious community. Good Samaritan is a general short-term community hospital with beds for two hundred patients. Because it is the only hospital within a hundred miles, its occupancy rate has been hovering between 90 and 95 percent, far above the average rate for hospitals of its type. At this time, a new wing containing a hundred additional beds is being constructed.

The administrator heads up to the governing board, which is made up primarily of members of her religious order. When Sister Estelle took office in 1970, she decided to appoint a lay advisory board to bring the hospital into closer contact with the needs of the business community and the area in general, to interest the area in the workings of the hospital, and to serve as a source of sound advice. The board, composed of local lawyers and executives in manufacturing, construction, banking, and retailing, has been meeting monthly for over three years.

The discussion in last month's meeting was prompted by the construction and expansion program underway, and it centered around the hospital's organization. When the administrator distributed a chart showing the current organization (see Figure III/6-1), two or three board members noticed the large number of department heads who reported directly to the administrator. They wondered if the wide span of management were straining the smooth functioning of the hospital. They suggested narrowing the span, because they expected a 50 percent increase in facilities and activities in the near future.

The administrator assured them that she had been able to handle the department heads because of their competence. She did not think that the increase in beds would change the picture; the various functions would remain the same, although their magnitude would increase. Therefore, she intended to carry on with the same organizational structure. As further justification, she remarked that twenty-three people report directly to the manager of the local Sears, Roebuck store, who apparently is able to function efficiently.

Questions

1. Do you agree with the administrator?
2. What changes would you suggest? Why?
3. Design a revised organization chart.
4. What are the advantages of the lay advisory board? the shortcomings?

Figure III/6-1 The Good Samaritan Hospital

```
                         Governing
                           board
                             |
                        Administrator
                             |
   ┌─────────────┬───────────┴───────────┬─────────────┐
 Nursing       Dietary              Laboratories      X ray
 services      services
   |             |                       |              |
 Personnel    Central                  Medical        Therapy
              supplies                 records
   |             |                       |              |
 In-service   Pharmacy                Admissions     Controller
 education
   |             |                       |              |
 Maintenance  Housekeeping             Laundry       Purchasing
```

Part IV

Staffing

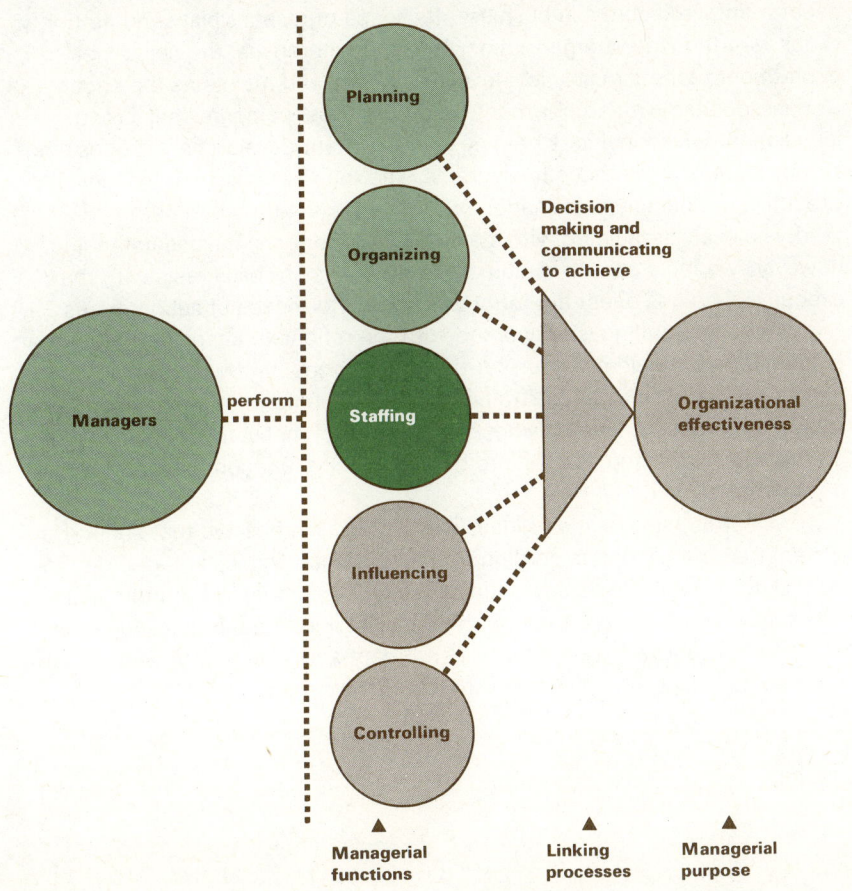

The staffing function Staffing is the managerial activity that maintains, develops, and regulates the human resource system of an organization.

Staffing supplies and maintains the people who run a planned and organized system. It is a human resource function indispensable to the management process. Staffing takes place after tasks and task relationships have been established. Work is first defined, then divided, and finally people are found to do it. Staffing includes recruitment, selection, placement, training, appraisal, and compensation of personnel.

Managers are responsible for staffing their own departments in such a way that the capability of the workers matches their authority. To achieve effective use of human resources, an organization needs a rational staffing program—one that balances job requirements with employees' capabilities. However, such balance is not easily achieved; most managers do not have direct access to the labor market for recruitment, nor do they have the specialized skills needed for the selection of employees. This situation has prompted the development of a specialized staff function—personnel—to aid and advise managers in meeting their staffing needs.

Personnel was the first specialized staff function to achieve widespread departmentalized status in business. Its scope of responsibility and authority varies with the type of organization. In some enterprises, the personnel department recruits mainly low-level employees and maintains the paperwork associated with employment. In other cases, personnel has broad jurisdiction, which includes training, management development, counseling, compensation, fringe-benefit programs, and the recruitment of high-level executives. A personnel management department with broad authority, then, is closely associated with staffing. To prevent any misunderstanding, however, we must note that ultimate staffing responsibility rests with the executive who has direct authority over the performance of subordinates.

Although staffing is concerned with the rational management of human resources, we should not interpret this function too narrowly. Staffing also has its motivational aspects. Training and development, as well as compensation and other staffing activities, are sources of motivation and influence. To this extent, staffing shades into the influencing function, which we will discuss in Part V.

We stress several major ideas in this Part. We observe that staffing is a system that is designed according to the contingency needs of an organization. Determination of these contingencies is a segment of both forecasting and appraisal activities. Based on the data obtained from forecasting and appraisal, executive development, recruitment and selection of new managers, and compensation programs can be administered.

Chapter 15

The staffing process

Objectives of the chapter

1 To give an overview of the staffing function.
2 To describe the scope of the human resource system.
3 To emphasize that staffing is a line management responsibility.
4 To examine some staffing policies.
5 To identify special staffing problems.

Staffing is a human resource function. Like other functions, it is a task that managers perform continuously, sometimes in a highly independent way, but most often in collaboration with the personnel department. The purpose of staffing is to achieve optimal use of managerial resources through rational human resource systems and programs. An enterprise needs a constant supply of capable executives moving through the system from recruitment to retirement. These people are the vital force of the organization, more valuable to it, in many ways, than efficient operational methods or money in the bank. Management is an organizational asset of primary importance; therefore, it is necessary that incumbent executives ensure the protection and expansion of this asset.

The scope of the human resource system

The staffing function is composed of a number of programs that include management recruitment, selection, placement, training, development, welfare, appraisal, and compensation. In a systems sense, these programs are related to one another, although not necessarily in the order given. The programs are not isolated. They depend for direction on organizational objectives and policies, forecasts of executive requirements in the future, and control over program results. Further, the organization is subject to environmental contingencies that have direct bearing on human resource policies.

Figure 15-1 illustrates the relationships among various elements in a human resource system.

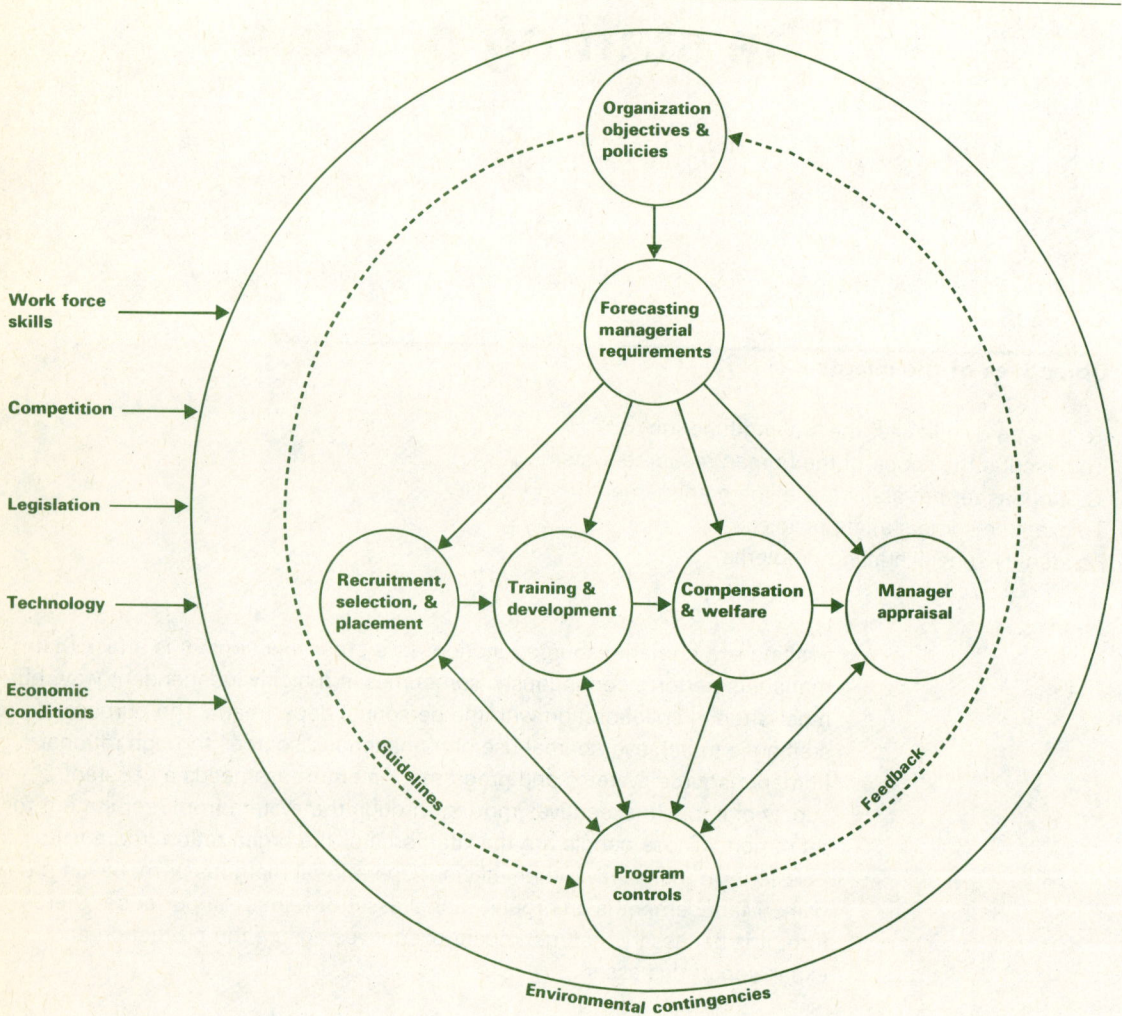

Figure 15-1 A human resource system

Figure 15-1 refers to many situations. For example, suppose a bank goes into the consumer small-loan business, using the credit card as the chief means for the expansion. This goal sets certain forecasting premises about the expected size and extent of the new service. Assumptions have to be made about the number of managers to recruit and the skills they will need. Channels for recruiting them have to be examined. Standards for selecting managers must be established. Placing those hired in new jobs must be considered. In addition, some managers might have to be trained in the computer technologies associated with the credit card business. Of course, decisions about compensation have to be made, and the performance of the people in the new activities, judged.

Throughout this process, other factors are operating as well. For instance, the law requires that equal opportunity for employment be available to women and members of minorities. This is an external contingency that regulates the personnel practices of the organization. Also, the new division is subject to a variety of internal program controls, such as compensation guidelines, that apply throughout the organization. Finally, each program has its own control measures, feedback to higher levels of management, that describe its effectiveness in achieving results.

In general, the human resource system is composed of interacting programs, environmental contingencies, objectives, forecasts, control standards, and feedback. Managers are responsible for the operation and maintenance of this system so that human resources are effectively used. The problem is complicated by two elements: the specialized skills needed in many instances and the division of responsibility for staffing between line and staff managers.

Human resources objective

In 1968, PPG adopted a formal set of corporate objectives. The prime objective is the Financial Objective, but the first objective in support of the Financial Objective is our Human Resources Objective. We think its position as number two is very significant. I'd like to read part of our objective to you because it provides the basis for the rest of the talk: "The company's continued financial success depends upon its ability to attract, develop and retain in its service dynamic and enthusiastic people whose personal goals include the achievement of excellence in their work. A continuing program of periodic assessments of current performance and potential for advancement is the keystone to our management development program."

Source: John N. McLaughlin, "The Management Development Side of Manpower Planning," a speech to the Second Annual Conference of Human Resource Systems Users, *A Record of the Proceedings* (1972) p. 53. Used with permission.

The general nature of staffing

A line function

The responsibility for an executive personnel program starts with top-line management and permeates the entire organization. Each line manager, although possibly not active in original recruitment and selection, must make certain that subordinates are properly developed, trained, and, in due time, promoted. This line function is as important as planning, organizing, influencing, and controlling. Needless to say, subordinates cannot be passive in the staffing process; they must promote their own career progress.

Chief executive's ultimate responsibility

Naturally, the ultimate responsibility for an executive personnel program lies with the chief executive. Specifically, the chief executive must monitor and support the staffing program and make certain that all executives meet their staffing obligations. For instance, an executive may be unwilling to part with a junior executive, even though a promotion would benefit the enterprise as a whole; this executive does not understand the nature of the staffing function.

Of course, the chief executive's staffing responsibility is delegated by the board of directors. The board, in turn, bears a responsibility to the stockholders to perpetuate the corporation. The directors' duty can be interpreted to mean that they should know what is being done to prepare candidates to replace the top executive and fill other top management positions. It is a duty of the board to formulate a company policy of managerial development throughout the organization. Only by so doing can the board ensure an orderly succession in the company.

Sometimes the authority and responsibility for staffing are delegated to a committee composed of high-level executive officers who represent the entire range of company operations. This committee is likely to include the chairperson of the board, the president, and the vice presidents in charge of the chief operating units. A staff member from the personnel department may serve as the executive secretary of the committee and may even hold the title of director or coordinator of executive development.

Staff assistance

Although line management cannot dispose of its staffing responsibility by assigning it to a staff unit, line officers often call on staff members for help with this program. Staff specialists, usually in the personnel department, can be useful in almost every phase of executive development. For instance, they can assist department heads in appraising their subordinates; they can aid them in determining their training needs; and they can help in devising suitable programs for individual cases. They also might guide executives in the coaching and counseling of their subordinates and may keep records of the various training activities.

Staffing policies

Promotion from within

One of the most frequently encountered staffing policies is filling responsible positions by internal promotion rather than by importing executives from outside the company. Generally, this policy leads to improved morale and a favorable corporate reputation. In addition, it is often less costly for the enterprise to promote from within. For these reasons, many firms publicly announce, in their recruitment programs, that they adhere strictly to this promotion policy, and they ensure it by specific administrative measures. The success of such a policy, of course, depends on whether or not the incumbents are qualified for their new responsibilities and whether or not they are at least as good as executives in comparable positions in competitors' enterprises.

A policy of promoting from within has limitations. At times, employees will question a promotion, feeling that the right person has not been selected. Although an outsider can engender similar complaints, company morale does not seem as greatly impaired as when the policy of promotion from within seems inequitable. Therefore, if one of three inside executives of equal status must be chosen to fill a position, management might be wise to bring in a new executive from the outside and keep all three where they were. This situation is often encountered in nonbusiness settings, for example, in universities. Instead of selecting a dean from a group of qualified professors, it is sometimes more expedient to bring in someone new from the outside.

A strict policy of inside promotion depends on the constant availability of a sufficient number of qualified executives for its success. Sometimes the most promotable junior executives are in training when an opening develops, and none is far enough advanced to take over. Promoting only from within also can easily lead to inbreeding. From time to time, most organizations can profit from the injection of new blood. This is particularly necessary in an enterprise that depends on fresh approaches for its existence, such as advertising and public relations firms.

If a company pursues a policy of promotion from within in the strictest sense, current employees are in a more or less monopolistic position. They compete only with each other, not with anyone from the outside. Management, however, should be free to select the best possible candidate, regardless of the candidate's origin. Therefore, a promotion from within policy should be modified by the words "whenever feasible."

Top management may also specify the opposite policy, stating that certain key positions—a minority—should be filled by outsiders. Such a policy is often pursued by companies that depend on a rapidly growing and changing technology. Because inside talent cannot be developed fast enough, these firms must hire outside specialists and experts.

Other staffing policies

In addition to formulating hiring and promotion policies, management must also issue staffing rules, procedures, methods, and directives. For example, it may rule that when a vacancy occurs in an important position it must be filled promptly. Procedures and methods for announcing noteworthy promotions must also be detailed. Perhaps such promotions will appear in a special column of an organization's official house publication.

Sequence of steps in staffing

The first step in the staffing process is to determine the type of managerial skills needed by an organization. A current organization chart will indicate existing managerial positions; it will not forecast future needs. Staffing requires projections of organizational changes. In addition, management also needs written job descriptions enumerating the various duties and responsibilities connected with each of the present managerial positions. These will enable staffers to draw up a list of specifications setting forth the education, experience, ability, and minimum personal qualities required of the people who are to fill each job. With the help of this information, management will know what to look for in a potential candidate.

The second step in staffing is to determine the number of executives management will need and the time at which they will be needed. In order to do this an inventory of available executives must be taken. By looking at those who are currently employed, management can ascertain, to some degree, who will be available three or five years hence and how many vacancies will occur. By comparing the current picture with the ideal organizational structure, management might also find that it wants to create certain new positions. Both the new positions and the vacancies in the old ones will have to be filled. Thus, management's next step is to determine which of the available incumbent managers will be capable of filling them. This necessitates an appraisal of the effectiveness of personnel in their present jobs and an analysis of their development and potential for promotion. Management should provide opportunities for personnel growth. In fact, the fourth step in the staffing process is to set up development programs for just this purpose. Development programs, in time, enable executives to move into positions of higher responsibility.

Naturally, the positions at the bottom of the executive ladder must be filled by outside people. Therefore, as a fifth step in the staffing process, the enterprise must initiate a basic executive training program. As a last consideration within the staffing function—though not the least important—management should devise an executive compensation plan.

Of course, there is no special magic in this sequence of steps. Staffing activities should be designed to accommodate organizational needs and circumstances. Most staffing programs usually parallel one another. In large organizations, where personnel is a well-developed staff department, any number of such programs will be going on at the same time. However, the specialized work of a personnel staff, for example, in executive development, is under the authority of line executives. New programs or revisions of old programs cannot be undertaken without line management approval.

The chief source of control over personnel activities is the budget. Managers can accomplish very little if funds are not available. Therefore, personnel officers have to *sell* their programs and plans to the line. They must convince the line that what they propose—for instance, a management by objectives program—will result in greater managerial effectiveness and an increase in value of the human assets of the organization. Personnel managers must struggle for dollars in their budgets in the same way as do managers of other functions and departments.

Special problems of staffing

Certain staffing problems do not occur in other managerial functions; they result only from the personal nature of staffing.

The problem of measurement

The rewards of adequate staffing are often intangible. What is the value of a large number of junior executives who have received many years of expensive training and who have acquired sufficient capabilities to undertake middle- and high-level positions? The high quality of executive talent will eventually influence the financial performance of the enterprise. But, in the short run, good business conditions may obscure the low quality of executive talent. The reverse, of course, is also possible.

Although no item on the balance sheet reveals the cost of neglecting executive development, poor spirit and low morale are sure indicators of such neglect. In the long run, management's concern with a systematic executive personnel program will pay off. The effort to create a human-assets accounting system, a more precise method of measuring the resource value of people in an organization, indicates the importance of this area.

The small number of staffers

The staffing process does not involve a large number of people; usually, ten to fifty people carry on its activities. Even in companies with hundreds or possibly thousands of executives in various ranks, only a small number of people decide whom to hire, whom to fire, and whom to promote. However, although the number of staffers is small in relation to the total number of employees, the magnitude of the consequences of their activities can be formidable; the quality of the executives they select will greatly influence the ultimate success of the enterprise.

Nonstandardized positions

Another challenge to staffers is the lack of standardization in managerial positions. Even similar positions in different organizations may require different technical knowledge and skills. Again, people who hold the same title in different enterprises do not always hold the same job. Although a sales manager will perform some functions common to sales managers in any enterprise, it is probable that the position in one will include functions not included in another. The way to understand a job is to study it. Only through study can people become familiar with the duties that have been assigned to a position in a particular organization.

Generally speaking, the problem of nonstandardized positions is most apparent in highly technological organizations, which rely heavily on project management. The purpose of project-designed organizations is to assemble people with special technical skills for a prescribed time period to execute a particular undertaking—for example, the Viking Project, whose mission was to place a landing vehicle on Mars. Such projects are staffed with the understanding that after they have been completed, the people in them will be reassigned to other projects within the organization or let go.

Summary

Staffing is a management activity devoted to acquiring, maintaining, and improving an organization's human resource assets. The staffing process is an integrated system composed internally of objectives, policies, programs, and controls. This system interacts with numerous external contingencies that directly influence the nature and direction of personnel policies and programs. Line managers have the primary responsibility for staffing, and they exercise final authority over staffing programs. Specialized personnel people assist and advise the line by recommending and implementing programs.

Promotion policies, managerial succession, hiring procedures, executive development, performance evaluation, and compensation are critical ongoing staffing tasks. There is no particular sequence in which these tasks are conducted. In complex organizations, specialized programs are designed to fit these and other staffing activities. The personnel department in such organizations has a strong involvement in these programs, but ultimate authority over them vests in the line. Staffing in large, complex, highly technological organizations is complicated by difficulties in measurement, the small number of specialized personnel managers, and the existence of nonstandardized positions.

Discussion questions

1 Discuss the ways in which the concepts of systems and contingency can be applied to the staffing process.
2 It is said that at General Motors, there are four people qualified to assume any given managerial position in the company. Why would this be the case?

Supplementary readings

Gooding, Judson. *The Job Revolution.* New York: Walker, 1972.
Wortman, Max S. "Manpower: The Management of Human Resources." *Academy of Management Journal,* June 1970, pp. 198–206.

Chapter 16

Forecasting executive needs

Objectives of the chapter

1 To examine the process by which an organization's future requirements for executives are determined.
2 To analyze the external and internal factors that underlie the demand for executives.
3 To review the uses of various forecasting techniques.
4 To relate the forecasting activity to other processes in the staffing function.

Every organization has a constant flow of managers through its structure. A variety of factors determine the rate of flow. The purpose of forecasting is to anticipate, in quantitative and qualitative terms, the number of executives with specific skills that will be needed in the future. Forecasts are the first step in the staffing process. They consist of calculating the internal executive requirements of an organization and the external contingencies that will affect how the requirements are satisfied.

Management uses numerous techniques to make these calculations. Position descriptions and skill evaluations are very valuable in determining the types of executive needed. Inventories of current executives and replacement tables are useful in determining the number of existing executives and the time at which they will be needed. These methods help management to visualize the total needs of the organization and the broad executive skills and talents required. They also make it easier for management to understand the groupings and relationships of positions.

External factors in the demand for executives

Contingencies in an organization's environment must be considered in forecasting, although managers seldom have direct control over them. These factors include work force issues, employment opportunity issues, legislative issues, and economic issues.

Work force issues

The demand for capable managers always exists. The growing size of business, the complexity of administration, the intensity of competition, all contribute to this demand. The impact of government and unions also intensifies the need for more and better managers. Well-trained, capable, professional executives must make decisions in many areas that vitally affect the owners, the employees, and the public in general.

The situation during World War II revealed the importance of the staffing function's role in the development of managers. At that time, large numbers of capable middle management personnel went into the armed forces, reducing the flow of competent young people who normally would have moved up to higher positions and creating substantial gaps in managerial successions and promotions. Because of this, key executives remained in their positions long beyond retirement dates, until competent successors were found. As a result, many companies in the postwar period discovered that they had competent high-level management, but only a few people in the junior- and middle-executive ranks. This condition stimulated strong interest in executive development programs; in fact, many such programs were first introduced in the postwar period.

The low birthrate in the 1930s limited the number of executives now in their forties. The need for managers in the thirty-five- to fifty-five-year-old age group will probably extend into the 1980s. However, the "baby boom" from 1946 to 1948 means that more people in their early thirties are presently coming into the labor market. Some of them will be candidates for managerial positions, and, consequently, the average age of executives overall probably will decline. A forecast must take into account the number of people available and their average age in determining staffing contingencies.

Industry issues

Employment opportunities in management vary according to industry. In 1975, using the decade of 1960 to 1970 as a base period, the number of managers rose 9 percent. This is half the rate of expansion for all employees over the same time period. Self-employed managers continued to decline, while salaried managers grew slowly. From this perspective, managing does not seem to be the rapid growth occupation that it was considered previously. This general picture, however, is deceptive. For example:

- While managers in manufacturing rose by only 9 percent, managers in retail trade grew 27 percent.

- Managers in food services are up 12 percent.
- Managers in public employment (government) rose 27 percent.
- The managerial occupation in banks and financial management rose 1000 percent.[1]

The intensity of forecasting depends, to a large extent, on the industry. In an industry that is rapidly expanding, a great deal of forecasting effort must be made to ensure accurate anticipation of future executive needs; forecasting probably is less demanding in industries that are relatively stable.

Legislative issues

Social legislation is a third important contingency in forecasting future executive needs. Antidiscrimination and affirmative-action laws at the federal, state, and local levels of government impose forecasting premises on management. Such laws, backed with stiff penalties for noncompliance, force those who forecast executive staffing needs to take women and minorities into consideration. However, government selection guidelines, affirmative-action plans, fair-employment legislation, civil-service regulations, and labor contracts, coupled with company policies on hiring and promotion, present forecasters with contingencies that may not always be consistent, and these inconsistencies often complicate the forecasting process.

Economic issues

Naturally, general economic conditions will influence staffing forecasts. A strong economy usually means that an organization will increase its number of executives. The reverse is also true. But, since no one is able to forecast these economic trends with great accuracy, the question becomes: How much executive slack should an organization support?

Executive slack is both an insurance policy and a source of flexibility. As an insurance policy, a management cadre is maintained even though it is not fully utilized, something particularly evident during periods of economic downturn. Companies that have established an effective management team tend not to break it up immediately when there is a slowing of economic activity, ensuring that people will be available when economic conditions change for the better.

Executive slack permits flexibility. For firms dependent on project contracts, this is a critical consideration. Usually projects contracted for by government agencies or private companies require that the managers are specified. It is desirable, therefore, that people to name be available in the organization when project proposals are submitted. As a practice, managers

---

[1] Adapted from Constance B. Dicesare, "Changes in the Occupational Structure of U.S. Jobs," *Monthly Labor Review,* March 1975, pp. 31–32.

cannot be hired simply on the basis of a proposal, and, then, let go if the proposal is rejected.

Like any insurance policy, executive slack is something that is bought. The amount of money top management wants to spend on it depends on two elements: management's view of the risks in the economic environment and the value management places on organizational flexibility. In whatever way these matters are resolved, economic forecasting premises for staffing are based on them.

Internal factors in the demand for executives

A very large number of internal factors underlie the demand for executives, and it would be impossible to account for all of them in forecasting executive needs. However, the factors combine into two main categories: forecasting factors that arise from strategic organizational decisions and forecasting factors that arise from personal employee variables. Table 16-1 lists some of the chief factors in each category.

Organizational decisions	Personal variables
1 Growth — contraction	1 Internal transfers of executives
2 Diversification — centralization	2 Turnover
3 Technological change in products or processes	3 Retirement
4 Goal reorientation	4 Death

Table 16-1 Internal forecasting factors

Organizational decisions are critical determinants of the need for executives. Plans for increasing the size of an organization usually increase the need for more executives. However, this increase in demand generally is not linear. Beyond a certain point in size, additional growth of the organization may not require proportionately more executives; rather, more intense use may be made of executives already on the payroll. Conversely, organizational plans may call for contraction; in such instances, forecasts must be made of the net decrease anticipated in the number of executive personnel.

Often, as an organization's size increases, more specialized tasks appear. The forecasting problem in this situation is to determine the number of executives required and the skills that they will need to perform these tasks. This aspect of organizational change is sometimes accompanied by changes in technology, where new products, processes, and systems are developed. Diversification of activities has a counterpart usually discussed in terms of centralization. Centralization supplies a coordinating service in organizations. These activities are frequently accomplished by staff control groups, such as cost control and production control. The executive composition of staff groups is initially a forecasting problem.

Equal opportunity

American employers find themselves caught in a classic squeeze play as they try to obey the law and meet the demands of the marketplace. On one flank, they are besieged by the complex and often conflicting directives emanating from the Equal Employment Opportunity Commission, the Office of Federal Contract Compliance, at least 15 separate Federal compliance agencies, and innumerable state and local commissions. On the other, they are attacked by a swarm of special interest groups, representing every cause from women's liberation to veteran's rights, who demand special hiring and promotion privileges for their members. The Federal courts' propensities to hand down adverse decisions accompanied by stiff penalties in fair employment litigation, and the recession-induced need to reduce newly integrated labor forces, may become the proverbial straws breaking employers' backs. It is easy to understand employers' bewilderment and resentment as they look vainly for a way out of what appears to them to be a hopeless mess.

Source: Felix M. Lopez, "Employment Opportunity—How Equal Can It Be?" *Conference Board Record.* September 1975, p. 41. Used with permission.

Finally, organization growth (or contraction), diversification, and new technologies may require a change in organizational goals. New objectives have implications for forecasting executive needs. If an organization moves from a single-purpose operation, like milling wheat into flour, to a multipurpose activity, like running retail chains of donut stands and marketing frozen processed bakery goods, then executive requirements will change drastically.

Another major task in forecasting is to anticipate executive mobility and the vacancies created by it. In some instances, such as retirement, promotions, and transfers, planning for managerial change can be done easily right down to identifying specific individuals. All that is necessary is an adequate personnel data system that keeps track of where people are and where they are going.[2] In other cases, involving management turnover or death, forecasting cannot be precise. Overall, however, it is possible to estimate managerial attrition and to plan for the orderly induction and movement of people through the managerial ranks. Some amount of executive slack is useful for adjusting to unforeseeable events.

These eight elements are basic factors in planning staff requirements. When executive appraisals are added to them, management can accurately forecast its executive needs. Thus, staffing rests on forecasting, and fore-

[2] Robert B. Maxwell, "The Succession Planning Side of Manpower Planning," *Proceedings.* The Second Annual Conference of Human Resource Systems Users, 1972, pp. 79–97.

casting rests on planning and executive appraisal. Line executives must assume forecasting and planning functions, although they may call on staff to work out technical details.

Determining the types of executives needed

Position descriptions

Many techniques are available to help management determine executive needs; position descriptions provide one. However, there is no single list of specifications for the executive position because each position is unique. Still, the duties, objectives, and results expected of each job in each organization should be described in as much detail as possible. Likewise, the experience and specific knowledge required for successful performance of each job should be defined. This is a time-consuming, but valuable, process. An enforced analysis of the content and requirements of positions provides an objective guide to selecting candidates for promotion. It enables management to choose the candidate who best fulfills the specifications of a particular position and, hence, is likely to succeed in it. A clear catalog of position descriptions is necessary to plans for the growth and development of members of the organization.

Position descriptions also play an important role in the selection of new personnel. A statement of the position's requirements will minimize biases and prejudices among those in charge of the selection process and will provide a definite standard to guide executives in interviewing prospective employees.

The need for continuous review

Any program runs the danger of becoming calcified, and this is clearly the case with a program of position description. Positions must be audited frequently by the personnel staff to determine the extent to which the job content has changed. Any organization will be changed considerably by new technology and the creative efforts of executives who occupy top positions. The extent and character of such change ought to be determined so that accurate information can be provided for forecasting executive needs. This feedback will, in turn, lead to the creation of better plans for executive recruitment and development programs. Figure 16-1 describes this process.

Human specifications

Because position descriptions merely state the duties, objectives, relationships, and results expected and do not tell specifically what to look for in appraising a candidate, it is necessary to translate duties into human specifications. These specifications outline the experience, age, and personal characteristics thought necessary for each position. It is relatively simple to determine experience specifications by analyzing the duties involved in the present job and the type of previous knowledge and practice required for its successful performance. It is more difficult, however, to quantify personal characteristics. Most of the following discussion, therefore, deals with this problem.

Check lists would simplify the job of specifying desirable personal characteristics, and much effort has been spent in trying to devise such lists. Although the efforts generally result in descriptions that could serve as broad executive standards, they are useless "for the practical purposes of development of particular persons for particular positions in particular companies in particular situations."[3]

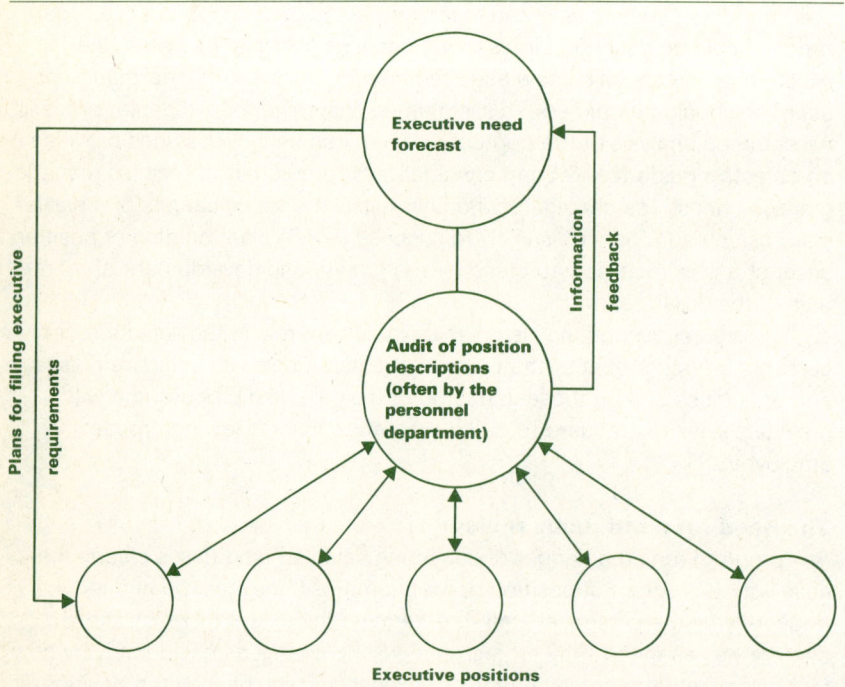

Figure 16-1 Position description program

Two primary factors invalidate any standard list of executive personal traits. First, there is no generally accepted set of objective criteria for judging a good executive. The success of a worker can be determined by measuring output, but the success of a supervisor must be measured by subjective factors that are not easily quantified. As one goes higher in the

---

[3] Myles L. Mace, *The Growth and Development of Executives* (Boston: Division of Research, Graduate School of Business Administration, Harvard University, 1950), p. 20; and C. Wilson Randle, "How to Identify Promotable Executives," *Harvard Business Review* 34 (May–June 1956):123.

managerial hierarchy, it becomes increasingly difficult to measure performance objectively. Also, no standardized executive position descriptions exist. As we mentioned earlier, technical and job knowledge requirements vary even if job titles are the same.

Since lists of characteristics for the ideal executive cannot be formulated, managerial abilities and capacities must be viewed in their relationship to a specific organizational environment. Management determines desired personal traits by the content of each job. Among the personal characteristics often mentioned in drawing up job specifications, in appraising candidates, and in planning further executive development are intelligence, analytical ability, initiative, skill in communication, willingness to accept responsibility and the leadership position, a sense of moral values, and sound judgment.

The measurement of these executive traits is also extraordinarily difficult. Some organizations, including International Business Machines, have developed elaborate psychological techniques to identify executive talent. However, the evaluation of the character attributes of people in relation to organizational needs remains an intuitive process.

Skills

Robert L. Katz has suggested what he considers a more useful approach to identifying qualified executives. His approach is based not on "what good executives *are* (their innate traits and characteristics), but rather on what they *do* (the kinds of skills which they exhibit in carrying out their jobs effectively)."[4] He suggests that effective management rests on three basic skills: technical, human, and conceptual. *Technical skill* includes the performance and understanding of technical activities. *Human skill* encompasses understanding and motivating individuals and groups. *Conceptual skill* implies the ability to coordinate and integrate the activities and interests of the organization and channel them toward a common objective. Katz suggests that this three-skill approach can provide guidelines for the promotion of executives, the development of members of the organization, and the testing and selecting of prospective personnel.

For example, the principal need at lower levels of the organizational structure is for technical and human skills; at the higher levels technical skill becomes less important, and the need for conceptual skill increases. At the highest level of the hierarchy, conceptual skill is of paramount importance.[5] It would be helpful to know how much of each skill people must possess on each step of their career development, but this would not be a substitute for job analysis and position description.

---

[4] Robert L. Katz, "Skills of an Effective Administrator," *Harvard Business Review* 33 (January–February 1955):33.

[5] David W. Ewing, "The Knowledge of an Executive," *Harvard Business Review* 42 (March–April 1964):91–100.

Determining the number of managers needed

Top managers often say that their organization always has room for good people. Frequently, managers bring competent executives into an organization without a clear-cut idea of what they are to do. In most cases, the results are devastating. These people either create disturbances and frictions by interfering with the functions of other executives, or they become tired of waiting for an appropriate assignment and leave the organization, disillusioned.

Executive inventories

To avoid situations of this sort, management must carefully determine the kinds of executive that will be needed, the number that will be needed, and the time at which they will be needed. To accomplish this, a complete review of current executive inventory is necessary. Even in companies where no fixed retirement age exists, this inventory should include the ages of present executives. Although mortality tables can be of some help, it is impossible to forecast the life span of individual incumbents. Past experience, however, can be a good guide in estimating the number of vacancies likely to be caused by serious illness, resignation, or other separations.[6] Many companies find that reviewing the total number of separations over several years yields a more reliable estimate than would a monthly or quarterly review. In this connection, the level of management where losses occurred should be considered.

An overall forecast of executive needs must be modified if the enterprise anticipates expansion or contraction in the foreseeable future. Obviously, such a forecast is highly speculative since numerous changes can take place before it is fulfilled: expansion plans can accelerate or collapse; personal situations can make projected transfers or promotions impossible; and a variety of external factors can intervene. Yet, in spite of such uncertainties, yearly, three-year, five-year, or even ten-year forecasts of vacancies in the executive ranks should be made and reviewed annually.

Replacement tables

Top management also must know the timing of executive vacancies. To obtain this knowledge, replacement tables spanning one, three, five, or ten

---

[6] A survey by Arch Patton on the "Trends in Executive Compensation," *Harvard Business Review* 38 (September–October 1960):147–148, reveals that within a six-year period major shifts have occurred in the top management of 55 percent of a very large sample of major companies listed on the New York Stock Exchange. That this trend has continued is shown in the 1969 survey by the same author, "Executive Compensation in 1969," *Harvard Business Review* 39 (September–October 1969):152–157.

years are frequently compiled by the chief executive or by the managers of each division. Such tables list each key position, the person in it, and the approximate date when this position may be vacated (see Table 16-2). Of course, these tables are subject to change and should not be regarded as rigid or automatic schedules.

Table 16-2 Executive need summary (department heads and above)

Position	Present incumbent	Placement required					Reason
		1978	1979	1980	1981	1982	
President	J. Brown				X		Retirement
Vice-president finance	S. Green			X			Possible promotion
Controller	B. Black			X			Possible promotion
Director management planning	—	X					New position
Vice-president and general manager, "X" division	—		X				New product division to be formed
General sales manager, "X" division	—		X				New division
Manufacturing manager, "X" division	—		X				New division
General sales manager, paint division	S. William	X					Inadequate performance
Manufacturing manager, paint division	G. Gray					X	Retirement
Division controller, paint division	L. Blue		X				Possible early retirement—health

Source: Willys H. Monroe, "Strategy in the Management of Executives," *Business Horizons* 6 (Spring 1963): 38. Copyright, 1963. Foundation for the School of Business at Indiana University. Reprinted by permission.

Should first-line supervisory positions be included in replacement tables? First-line supervisors are managers; they do direct the work of their people. However, this particular position requires a considerable amount of technical skill, including familiarity with the operation of the machinery and equipment, the ability to make minor adjustments, and the capacity to show workers how the work is done. Normally, people with high managerial potential are not assigned to these partially nonmanagerial supervisory jobs. Instead, most managements hope that enough first-line supervisors can be found in the ranks of the workers and do not include these positions in their replacement tables.

As a general rule, replacement tables list not only the dates when managerial positions may be vacated but also the reason for the vacancies. Some reasons, such as those involving retirement age and ill health, can be deduced from the inventory of current executives. Others, however, may depend on prior performance appraisals. Such appraisals will indicate those who are doing a good job in their present position, those who are promotable, those who need additional development before promotion, and those who, specifically, might be capable of filling each position at the time it becomes vacant. An analysis of performance appraisals combined with replacement tables also focuses attention, at an early date, on those positions for which no replacements or only weak ones are available. This gives managers a good idea of the number of positions that can be filled by promotions from within and the number for which outside executives or management trainees will have to be recruited.

Moreover, since premature death, unexpected health problems, and voluntary separations can interfere with the best-planned replacement tables, some executive slack should provide managers with runners-up, people who are able to step into a key post in the event of an unexpected vacancy. Large organizations are in a better position than small ones to have more of such talent available.

For an organization to manage its executive personnel rationally in the way we have suggested, it needs to have prior performance appraisals on all individuals in managerial roles. Appraisal programs are crucial to executive forecasting and, also, to executive development and training programs.

Summary

Forecasting executive needs is an aspect of the planning process. Its purpose is to anticipate how many executives with what skills will be required by the organization. Both external and internal factors determine the need for executives. Among the external factors are the composition of the work force, the nature of the industry, governmental legislation, and economic changes. The internal factors that influence an organization's executive forecasts fall into two categories: organizational decisions and personal variables. Organizational factors involve strategic decisions about the objectives and growth of an enterprise; personal variables focus on the career aspects of individual employees and include the critical element of executive mobility. A rational approach to forecasting internal organizational management changes requires managers to have position descriptions, human specifications, skill inventories, and replacement tables at their disposal.

Discussion questions

1. Discuss the internal and external factors that underlie an organization's demand for executives. How precisely can such a demand be calculated?
2. You have been asked to discuss with a group of high school students what it is like to be a college student. Write a description of a college student.
3. For the same discussion, prepare a skill inventory.

Supplementary readings

Dicesare, Constance B. "Changes in the Occupational Structure of U.S. Jobs." *Monthly Labor Review,* March 1975, pp. 31–32.

Lopez, Felix M. "Employment Opportunity—How Equal Can It Be?" *Conference Board Record,* September 1975.

Monroe, Willys H. "Strategy in the Management of Executives." *Business Horizons,* Spring 1963.

Pati, Gopal C., and Fahey, Patrick E. "Affirmative Action Program: Its Realities and Challenges." *Labor Law Journal,* June 1973, pp. 351–361. Reprinted in *Dimensions in Modern Management,* 2d ed., edited by Patrick E. Connor. Boston: Houghton Mifflin, 1978.

Chapter 17

Performance appraisal of managers

Objectives of the chapter

1. To analyze the process by which managerial performance of job-related activities is reviewed and evaluated.
2. To explore the nature of a performance appraisal system.
3. To review the techniques of performance appraisal.
4. To discuss the implementation of a performance appraisal program.
5. To consider management by objectives as an approach to performance appraisal.
6. To evaluate management by objectives as a system of management.

Performance appraisal is a formal evaluation of an employee's job-related activities that is conducted by a superior and that covers a specified period of time, usually not more than one year. Performance appraisals are essential to planning of staff requirements and to trainee selection and development. They also help management to identify individuals with potential for promotion. Additionally, they provide a source of information about the training and development needs of older managers. However, the primary use of performance appraisals is to judge the effectiveness of managers. Are they and the amalgam of units and departments they run contributing to the achievement of the organization's goals?[1]

Traditionally, the evaluation of managers, by one technique or another, is an integral part of most personnel management programs. A Conference Board survey, Table 17-1, shows that over 70 percent of 293 companies reporting have formal appraisal of managers. Such appraisals are, as the table indicates, concentrated at the lower- and middle-management levels. There does not appear to be any startling differences in practices among the industries surveyed.

---

[1] See Stanley Sloan and Alton C. Johnson, "New Context of Personnel Appraisal," *Harvard Business Review* 46 (November–December 1968):14–30.

Industry (number of companies)	Management level*		
	Lower	Middle	Top
Manufacturing/processing (148)	73	73	57.4
Insurance (39)	66.6	64.1	46.2
Banks/financial service (65)	78.5	70.7	56.9
Wholesale/retail trade (41)	78.0	73.3	48.8
Total (293)	74.1	71.3	54.8

Table 17-1 Prevalence of management performance appraisal systems (percent of companies)

*For the purposes of this study lower management is defined as supervisors, foremen, crew chiefs, and so on. Top management is defined as the CEO and/or president and the immediate reporting personnel.
Source: Adapted from Robert I. Lazer, "The 'Discrimination' Danger in Performance Appraisal," Conference Board Record, March 1976, p. 62. Used with permission.

Even though appraisal programs are widespread and well established in organizations, they have been surrounded by controversy. This chapter reviews performance appraisal activities in a systems framework, discusses some of the issues they raise, and concludes with a discussion of two techniques that have been developed to overcome some of the problems.

An appraisal system

The appraisal process is related to a larger human resource management system.[2] This system is composed of three main elements, as illustrated in Figure 17-1. The first element is *work analysis* and review based on job descriptions, job specifications, and broad organizational objectives. These subsystems provide the standards against which individual performance is measured. The second element is the *formal appraisal process,* wherein the actual performance—the quality of skill and motivation a person applies to the job—is evaluated. The third element is the *use of the formal appraisal.* Although there are more, the figure illustrates four uses of appraisal in the human resource system: planning executive requirements, transfer and promotion (and termination), merit salary rating, and executive development. For purpose of example, we apply the formal appraisal to merit salary ratings.

A basic principle of performance appraisal is that every employee should receive *feedback*. If workers have been rated in the top 10 percent of those appraised, they should be told why, to reinforce their already high level of performance and to indicate what implications this rating has for future promotions, transfers, and development plans. The workers in the lowest 5 percent should also be given the reasons for their unsatisfactory performance, what it might mean in terms of their career, and the remedial steps necessary to improve it.

[2] Nathan B. Winstanley, "Performance Appraisals and Management Development: A Systems Approach," *Conference Board Record*, March 1976, pp. 55–59.

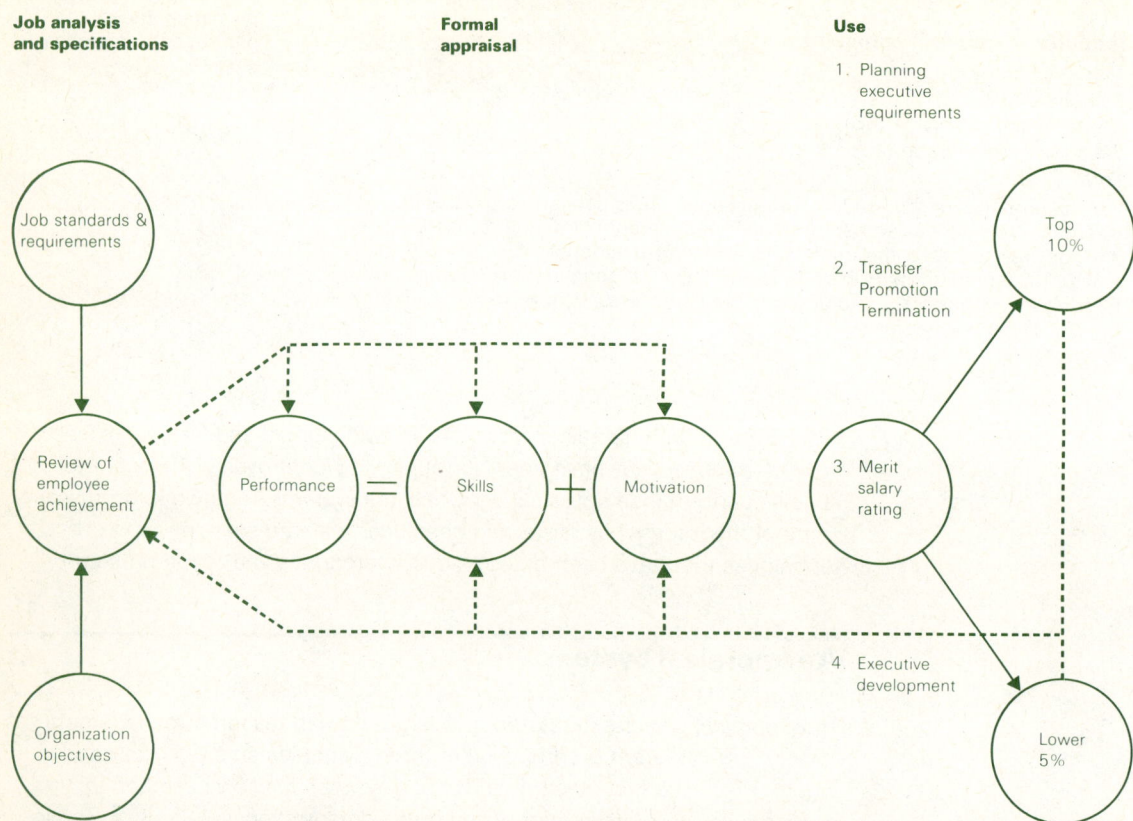

Figure 17-1 An appraisal system
Source: Adapted from Nathan B. Winstanley, "Performance Appraisals and Management Development," *Conference Board Record,* March 1976, p. 57. Used with permission.

The appraisal system is both a guide for merit rating and a basis for promotions and executive development. When a manager appraises a subordinate to decide if a salary increase is warranted, the appraisal is concerned exclusively with the subordinate's performance in a current job. When a manager appraises for purposes of possible promotion, however, the employee's potential for growth and further advancement is evaluated.

By specifically defining an individual's strengths and weaknesses, an appraisal becomes a basis for improving the quality of current job performance. Only by appraisal is it possible to isolate weaknesses and formulate a development program to overcome them. The early discovery of such weaknesses often prevents them from becoming more serious, damaging to the individual and to the enterprise.

The appraisal is also a source of information—letting managers know where they stand with their bosses. Employees have the right to know how well they are doing or what they can do to improve their present performance and advance in the company.

In some instances, managers need reassurance about their future in the organization. To carry this idea a bit further, appraisals can be an important incentive to the members of an organization. Often managers in a large organization have the feeling that their individual contributions, which necessarily appear small, are lost and forgotten. Appraisals can assure managers that their work is appreciated and that they have development opportunity.

The uses of appraisals that we have been discussing are emphasized by Douglas McGregor's summary of their three major purposes:[3]

1. *Administrative* Appraisals permit an orderly and rational way of determining promotions, salary increases, transfers, terminations, and development potential.
2. *Informative* Appraisals supply data to management on performance of subordinates and to the individuals on their strengths and weaknesses.
3. *Motivational* Appraisals create a learning experience for subordinates that motivates them to improve.

The appraisal process

Most organizations use appraisal forms to evaluate employees' performances. Patz, reporting on his research into appraisal practices, writes:

Some appraisal forms consist of a long list of elaborate rating scales; others contain only a few simple scales; still others require the boss to write a paragraph or two concerning his subordinate's performance. Some companies maintain a central file for all appraisal forms; others do not. In the absence of a central file, the appraisal form usually remains with an employee's immediate superior or with his division or department head.[4]

These forms reduce the elements to be measured to the most objective terms possible. Although there are innumerable types, most of the forms include a number of different criteria for measuring job performance, intelligence, and personality. In deciding which criteria are appropriate to its forms, management should study the specific requirements of its different jobs. These requirements differ, of course, according to the function and the level of position. The number of criteria should be kept to a minimum in order to make the form reasonably manageable. Likewise, the number of categories of evaluation—does this well, needs more instruction, does poorly—should be kept to a minimum, yet should give the appraiser sufficient choice.

[3] Douglas McGregor, *The Human Side of Enterprise* (New York: McGraw-Hill, 1960), pp. 82–88.
[4] Alan L. Patz, "Performance Appraisal: Useful but Still Resisted," *Harvard Business Review* 53 (May–June 1975):75.

Among the specific criteria most frequently mentioned in appraisal forms are quality of work, character, knowledge, ambition, leadership, communication facility, and promotion potential. Since these words often mean different things to different people, further definition is usually included. Explanatory words and phrases also are added to the rating categories in order to assist the appraiser.

Since an evaluation is based on a subordinate's performance in the job, it is essential that appraisers keep job content in mind. Also, forms often require that appraisers support their conclusions with evidence. This assures that the appraisal is made with thoughtfulness and diligence and helps to avoid superficial approval or disapproval. A request for evidence can, for example, discourage what has been termed the *halo effect*, in which a high rating on one factor leads to unmerited high ratings on other factors.

Who should appraise?

In most firms, the immediate superior fills out the appraisal forms; but in some enterprises, the appraisal is made by the immediate superior together with two others from the superior's level who know the person being appraised. Some companies prefer to have the appraisal made by a group consisting of the immediate superior and two members at the superior's level, one of whom does not know the employee to be appraised. Of course, the immediate superior can generally make the most effective appraisal of how an individual has actually performed on the job. The superior is in the best position to observe and judge an individual's initiative, interpersonal skills, quality of performance, and delegation abilities. Although there is no substitute for the firsthand knowledge and experience of the immediate superior, it is possible that the appraisal may have certain shortcomings. It is understandable, although unpardonable, for executives to underrate good subordinates for fear of losing them. This is one reason many companies have instituted group appraisals. Sometimes one rater can add to the knowledge of another. Also, these committee deliberations help to assure the use of uniform standards in judging an individual's performance. Of course, it is advisable that an individual's job description and any standards of performance be clearly understood before the members begin their appraisal.

Some companies believe that appraisals are more accurate if made independently by the appropriate executives rather than in conference. Such companies attach considerable significance to the contrasts between these ratings. They feel that they have removed the danger of single-member dominance of rating committees. No matter how rating groups are organized, however, they should include the immediate superior of the appraisee and that person's superior. In addition, they should include two or more managers who have had some contact, though not necessarily a close working relationship, with the appraisee.

During the evaluation, the appraisers should not see copies of prior appraisals. This restriction ensures that the employee is judged on the basis of present performance alone. If independent appraisals are made by several different appraisers, a staff person might be called on to summarize the various conclusions, or the appraisers might meet in subsequent discussion to transcribe the results.

Regularity of appraisal

Appraisals of management personnel should be made routinely once a year. This period is normally considered long enough for growth and change to manifest themselves. People should be appraised after six months in new and responsible positions. Periodic appraisal reminds individuals that they are not forgotten; they know that whatever improvement they make will be noted and will, very likely, carry them to higher positions.

How far down?

Most companies appraise all managers from first-line supervisor to top executive. They do not, however, appraise hourly workers and try to locate, develop, and utilize potential managers from their ranks. The reason often given for this is that union rules and the slowness of promotions make it impractical to conduct such appraisals.

However, some organizations, particularly in government, periodically appraise all employees and conduct individual superior-subordinate appraisal discussions. Managements that do not follow this practice might reexamine their policy; some members in the hourly wage earners group undoubtedly have administrative potential.

Review of the appraisal

By a higher executive
If an appraisal is made by an individual, rather than a committee, the appraiser's superior should review the appraisal. This ensures that the appraiser will make the evaluation as thoroughly and objectively as possible, because it may have to be justified to a manager on a higher level in the organization. In addition, this keeps the manager well informed about the promotability, potential, and need for improvement of all executives in the department, at the same time indicating the effectiveness of the rater's own appraising, coaching, teaching, and directing ability.

With a subordinate
The appraisal conference between superior and subordinate is very important. Some managers feel that a conference is unnecessary, because they are in daily contact with their subordinates. This, however, is not enough. Subordinates know that they have been appraised formally, and they are understandably eager to have a firsthand report. They also may want to discuss private matters with their boss. An appraisal conference is not

always easy. Although positive judgments can usually be communicated effectively, it is difficult to communicate criticism without generating resentment and defensiveness. Day-to-day criticism is much easier to accept than the formal criticism of an appraisal; it is not threatening, whereas formal criticism is. However, the effective manager can channel criticism into positive suggestions for self-development and growth. Counseling an executive about preparation for new responsibilities and ways to improve performance is an art, and each interview must be adapted to the individual case.

Conducting the interview Although an appraisal interview should be held shortly after the appraisal has been performed, the appraiser should still review the reasons for the opinions expressed. At the outset, the appraiser should emphasize that the appraisal is a training device designed to benefit the individual and the enterprise. If the subordinate, though not an outstanding person, performs satisfactorily, the superior should minimize criticism and suggest one or two moderate improvements. If the appraisal indicates that the subordinate is highly proficient, much of the interview should center around the types of experience that can further this employee's growth and development. An interview succeeds best when a manager plays the role of a coach, helping an individual to determine targets and the steps necessary to reach them.

Negative judgments In the discussion thus far, we have not mentioned the possibility that an executive might have to be removed. Top management must be sure that all managerial positions are properly filled. Changes may be necessary if an employee has not lived up to the potential expected. Conceivably, periodic appraisals will reveal that a promotion has been a mistake or that a manager's performance has fallen below expectations. When this becomes evident, performance appraisals form the basis for possible demotion or discharge. The supervising executive is often reluctant to face this situation. However, the superior must correct the situation. In most instances, the correction will amount to no more than reassignment to a position of lesser importance. But, if an individual has had several opportunities to show ability and has been unable to perform the functions assigned, discharge is the only solution.

Implementing the appraisal program

There are four basic guidelines in implementing the appraisal process: keep it simple, keep it separate, keep it contained, and keep it participative.[5] Simplicity is important since the chief goal of appraisal is to divide the above-average from the below-average employees. Elaborate techniques confuse people more than they lend precision to a process where the vari-

[5] Ibid., pp. 79—80.

ables involved defy precise measurement. Performance appraisal often is kept separate from other techniques, which include management by objectives, that are used to evaluate performance. This is a limited view of performance appraisal; since it is a part of the overall appraisal system it can, and should, be used to achieve other objectives as well, for example, employee development. The information collected in the appraisal process should pertain only to the individual's performance for a current time period and whether or not the individual is promotable. All out-of-date appraisals should be destroyed. Finally, the process must involve a give and take between the manager and the person appraised; in other words, it should be participative.

Difficulties in appraising

Although managerial appraisal has become routine in most large firms and even in many medium-sized firms, there are still numerous executives who do not believe in it. This may be partly because of the difficulties involved in effective appraisal. For one thing, it is very hard to measure the quality of performance of various employees because each of them is an individual with different capacities. In addition, measurement is complicated by the dynamic changes that take place as an individual grows in years and experience. Although great efforts have been made to learn more about people, there is still no exact way of measuring human qualities.

A further difficulty in effective appraisal is that standards for executive performance often do not exist. There is no question that formulating such standards is a line manager's job, but there are many questions as to how precisely these standards can be established. Obviously, a position description alone is not enough; it lists only what a person does. What is needed is a statement of the conditions that exist when a job is done well. Although some larger enterprises have made progress in setting standards of this type, much remains to be accomplished.

Another appraisal problem stems from the fact that appraisals of effectiveness are often based on recent incidents that are not representative of the subordinate's performance. To counteract this, a superior must draw conclusions as objectively as possible from overall performance. However, the appraiser probably cannot help but inject some conscious or subconscious bias and prejudice into the appraisal.

Additionally, some say that performance appraisal allows the superior to "play God" with the subordinate. The appraisal is an extremely powerful instrument in the superior's hand: the subordinate's career progress often depends on it. Bad appraisals, which are, of course, recorded and made a part of employees' permanent personnel files, stay with them throughout their employment at the company. As a consequence, some employees feel that they must conform to the wishes of their superiors even though they might believe that their bosses' decisions are not in the best interests of the company. It may even develop, as Harold Leavitt explains, that "the young executive finds it hard to separate good from his boss's approval of it."[6] Thus, performance appraisal of the conventional type places employees in a highly dependent position, which could stifle initiative and creativity.

To overcome this problem, William Evan suggests a system of appeal.[7] This would give an individual the right to take a case to a higher management board, if the individual feels he or she has been unjustly appraised. This right would free the individual from the pressing need to conform. However, programs of this type are by no means prevalent in industry, partly because the feeling against bypassing one's immediate superior is deeply ingrained.

Other critics have pointed out that a performance appraisal is misleading since it does not really measure performance. This is a valid criticism because the conventional paper and pencil evaluation cannot measure results in any significant way. It simply reflects a manager's subjective judgment of a subordinate, which is based on rather vague personal qualities.[8] It does not give a meaningful indication of how the subordinate is really doing.

Thus, problems with performance appraisal arise from three sources: interpersonal relations, measuring techniques, and the intangible aspects of most managers' jobs. These issues seem so formidable to the effectiveness of conventional appraisal systems that other approaches have been developed to overcome them.

The assessment center approach

The managerial assessment center is a rather widely used appraisal approach. Following its development in 1956, by the American Telephone and Telegraph Company (AT&T), some one thousand organizations have applied this technique, or a variation of it, to executive evaluation. Finkle writes that the phrase *assessment center* "refers to a group-oriented, standardized series of activities which provide a basis for judgments or predictions of human behaviors believed or known to be relevant to work performed in an organizational setting."[9]

A combination of techniques is used to assess employee performance. Usually, groups of managers are given a series of situational exercises or tasks, designed and standardized for rating purposes, to perform. Their performance is evaluated by groups of assessors. Coupled with the situational exercises are other methods of assessment, involving testing, interviewing, and peer rating.

[6] Harold J. Leavitt, *Management* (Chicago: University of Chicago Press, 1964), p. 127.
[7] William M. Evan, "The Organization Man and Due Process of Law," *American Sociological Review* 26 (August 1961): 540–547.
[8] See Patrick E. Connor, "A Critical Inquiry into Some Assumptions and Values Characterizing OD," *Academy of Management Review*, October 1977.
[9] Robert B. Finkle, "Management Assessment Centers," in Marvin D. Dunnette, ed., *Handbook of Industrial and Organizational Psychology* (Chicago: Rand McNally, 1976), p. 861.

Is performance appraisal discriminatory?

The future emphasis placed on performance appraisal systems, and the direction this emphasis will take, appears to be in the hands of the courts. The definition of appraisal as an employment test has already begun (as evidenced by *Brito*). It may only be a matter of time before the use of appraisal data in making employment decisions is unequivocally defined as the use of a "test" and brought under the constraints of the EEOC and OFCC selection Guidelines.

The feeling of many of the personnel executives interviewed is that appraisals relying on ratings of personal characteristics present a serious disadvantage, especially when compared with appraisal systems revolving around preset performance objectives. In the latter approach, validation criteria are an integral part of the process. The objectives to be accomplished are inherently important to the job and, as a result, job relatedness is automatic.

On the other hand, rating scales designed to measure subjective personal characteristics are seen as not being inherently job related. Moreover, as one personnel vice president points out, each trait or scale might have to be validated for its individual relationship to particular jobs. This type of appraisal system is also seen as violating many of the standards established by the selection guidelines.

Obviously, the impact on business and industry of a court ruling equating performance appraisals with employment selection tests could be tremendous. If companies find any adverse effect on protected groups, then many may be expected to drop their formal appraisal programs; others may attempt validation studies; or temporarily equalize the impact of the appraisal score on each group of employees (by converting these scores to percentiles for each group) until a definitive study can be conducted. And the remainder will undoubtedly continue present practices until forced into action by a complaint or finding of discrimination (and thereby risk any number of judgments against them, including class action back-pay awards).

Source: Robert I. Lazer, "The 'Discrimination' Danger in Performance Appraisal," *Conference Board Record,* March 1976, p. 64. Used with permission.

Table 17-2 shows the variables measured in programs of five organizations. The information about individual performance on these variables is used to make staffing decisions, such as placement, promotion, transfer, and the like. This approach differs from conventional performance appraisal techniques in that it attempts to predict a manager's potential for success in future assignments. Obviously, assessment center data should be used with regular appraisal information on actual work performance so that a comprehensive profile of the individual manager is available for staffing decisions.

Table 17-2 Comparison of variables from selected programs

AT&T	IBM	Sohio	IRS	Wolverine Tube Division of Universal Oil Products
(Bray & Grant, 1969)	(Hinrichs, 1969)	(Thompson, 1970)	(DiCostanzo & Andretta, 1970)	(McConnell, 1969)
Organization and planning	Self-confidence	Amount of participation	Decision making	Intellectual ability
Decision making	Written communications	Oral communication	Decisiveness	Oral communication
Creativity	Administrative ability	Personal acceptability	Flexibility	Oral communication skills
Human relations skills	Interpersonal contact	Impact	Leadership	Written communication skills
Behavior flexibility	Energy level	Quality of participation	Oral communications	Leadership
Personal impact	Decision making	Personal breadth	Organization and planning	Creativeness
Tolerance of uncertainty	Resistance to stress	Orientation to detail	Perception and analytic ability	Self-objectivity
Resistance to stress	Planning and organizing	Self-direction	Persuasiveness	Behavior flexibility
Scholastic aptitude	Persuasiveness	Relationship with authority	Sensitivity to people	Primacy of work
Range of interests	Aggressiveness	Originality	Stress tolerance	Realism of expectations
Inner work standards	Risk taking	Understanding of people		Range of interests
Primacy of work	Oral communications	Drive		Energy and drive
Oral communications skills		Potential		Acceptance
Perception of social cues				Organization and planning
Self-objectivity				Initiative
Energy				Decision making
Realism of expectations				Motivation
Bell System value orientation				
Social objectivity				
Need advancement				
Ability to delay gratification				
Need for superior approval				
Need for peer approval				
Goal flexibility				
Need for security				
Staff prediction				

Source: Robert B. Finkle, "Managerial Assessment Centers," in Marvin D. Dunnette, ed., *Handbook of Industrial and Organizational Psychology.* © 1976 by Rand McNally College Publishing Company, Chicago. Page 872, Table 1.

The management by objectives approach

Management by objectives (MBO) is a highly popular managerial appraisal technique. It is applied in varying degrees of elaborateness, in thousands of organizations. Peter Drucker is usually credited with being the first person to describe the MBO process;[10] however, George S. Odiorne has been the most active in promoting its cause.[11]

While procedures for implementing MBO programs differ, there are four points that all programs have in common:

1. Specification of organizational goals with objective measures of organizational performance.
2. Conferences between a superior and a subordinate about that subordinate's goals.
3. Agreement between the superior and subordinate on the subordinate's goals that are consistent with organizational goals.
4. Review of progress by superior and subordinate toward achievement of jointly determined goals.

The dynamics of this process involve close consultation between superior and subordinate. For instance, in steps 2 and 3 both the manager and the subordinate jointly agree on those areas of performance that will be subject to appraisal and what the appraisal criteria will be. Suppose a regional sales manager and a district manager are concerned about setting sales quotas for the next six months. The regional manager feels that a 5 percent increase over last year is a reasonable expectation; the district manager believes that only 2 percent is possible. The regional manager and district manager meet and discuss the reasons for their figures. As a consequence, a 4 percent increase is agreed on and becomes one of the standards on which the performance of the district manager is judged. The same sort of process can be pursued to define and measure other results and standards of performance.

The most significant feature of MBO is that it is motivational, in the sense of receiving a "commitment by individual managers to achieve measurable objectives."[12] The technique involves a high degree of appraisee participation in all aspects of the appraisal process. The appraisee participates in the review and analysis of results at the end of the appraisal period; the appraisee helps to decide the kind of management development or training program necessary to improve his or her effectiveness; and the appraisee helps set the standards for the next appraisal period.

---

[10] Peter F. Drucker, *The Practice of Management* (New York: Harper & Row, 1954).
[11] George S. Odiorne, *Management by Objectives* (London: Pitman, 1965).
[12] E. Allen Slusher and Henry P. Sims, Jr., "Commitment Through MBO Interviews," *Business Horizons*, April 1975, p. 5.

MBO as a system

Management by objectives is a good deal more complex than what we have suggested above. It involves a general philosophy of management that stresses the necessity for an integrated organizational system, as well as a number of highly specific techniques for implementing this system. A comprehensive MBO program encompasses many aspects of the staffing function, such as planning and control of staffing needs, executive development and career planning, compensation, and overall evaluation of organizational goals. Figure 17-2 illustrates a model of an MBO system.

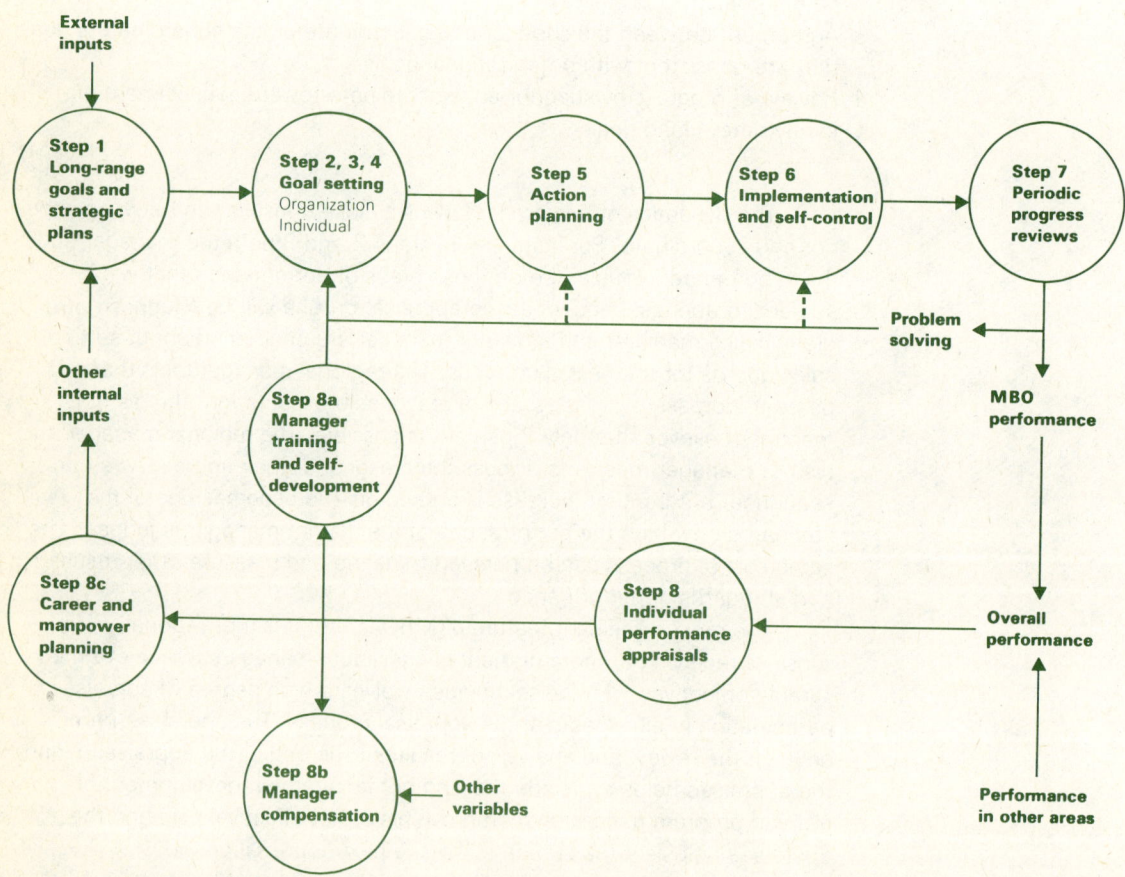

Figure 17-2 MBO as a system
Source: Anthony P. Raia, *Managing by Objectives* (Glenview, Illinois: Scott, Foresman, 1974), p. 20. Used with permission.

MBO and organizational objectives

Relating MBO to other staffing activities requires that those involved, particularly in higher levels of management, think in terms of measurable objectives and priorities of goals. While this is difficult to do in many instances, statements of resources and time commitments in various areas can be made. These statements serve as guidelines at lower levels of management where specific objectives are easier to set.

Given the nature of MBO as an appraisal system, the existence of tangible objectives gives managers, at every level of the organization, a powerful source of feedback on performance. Such feedback is not only useful to the person being appraised, but it also provides information necessary for the adjustment of organizational goals and strategies.

MBO and compensation

While there is debate on this issue, there are strong arguments in favor of linking MBO to merit compensation. MBO usually has more objective standards for rewarding (or not rewarding) people for performance. Therefore, it is motivationally reinforcing because individuals can see a direct relationship between their accomplishment of objectives and financial rewards associated with it. However, as Table 17-3 indicates, people tend to see the relationships between MBO and compensation differently, depending on whether they are being appraised or are doing the appraising.

Table 17-3 Managerial perceptions of the relationship between MBO and merit compensation

		Response percentage					
Question	N	Don't know	Very little bearing	Little bearing	Some bearing	Considerable bearing	Almost sole determinant
1 To what extent is goal attainment used to merit compensation consideration for you?	625	41		2	17	36	3
2 To what extent should goal attainment be used in merit compensation considerations for you?	625		1	3	37	54	4
3 To what extent do you use goal attainment in merit compensation considerations for your subordinates?	462		9	5	33	50	3

Source: William H. Nobley, "The Link Between MBO and Merit Compensation," *Personnel Journal,* June 1974, p. 426. Reprinted with permission, *Personnel Journal* copyright June 1974.

The results on question 1 show that a significant number of people failed to see the link between MBO and merit compensation when they were being appraised by their superiors. At the same time, an overwhelming majority in question 3 felt that they used MBO criteria in relating compensation to the performance of their subordinates. This data suggests the need for good communication and the consistent use of MBO appraisal information if effective links are to be made between it and merit compensation.

MBO and career planning

MBO appraisal conferences provide managers with useful information for personal career planning and the planning of organizational programs for the development of executives. All executive development efforts must be undertaken with specific needs in mind. MBO can create a framework of information around which such programs can be built.

Most obvious, however, is the application of MBO results to individual career planning. They can indicate deficiencies in performance and show the manager specific steps to take to overcome them. Certain training programs might be called for, reallocation of time could be required, and a rethinking of career alternatives may be suggested. Of course, MBO feedback is not all negative from an individual's standpoint. It can reinforce a manager's behavior in areas of high performance. As such, MBO gives a person a realistic evaluation of his or her potential and expectation for career progress.

MBO as an integrative process

MBO focuses managers' attention on the interdependent nature of the human resource system of the organization. In the process of doing so, MBO puts at management's disposal techniques for integrating this system. For example, MBO opens a two-way channel of communication between superiors and subordinates. However, more is required than formalizing the subordinate's role in the appraisal process. A favorable environment is produced by MBO in which people can legitimately express their feelings without fear of reprisal from their superiors. Finally, MBO has significant implications for the controlling function. Its emphasis on feedback allows managers to check and, if necessary, to alter plans, given the level of human performance experienced in operations.

An appraisal of MBO

In spite of its popularity among practitioners in organizations and researchers in universities, MBO has not lived up to its promise of more effective human resource management. Perhaps its popularity raised people's hopes too high. MBO is not a program that can simply be turned on and left to run by itself; nor is it alone capable of achieving organizational effectiveness. MBO is not a panacea for organizational ailments; it will not make a sick organization healthy. Gielgold writes:

A more useful way to look at MBO is as a diagnostic tool, or a ''discloser''— an agent which in the process of application reveals the status of structure and climate, and, ultimately, how badly or how well management is really doing its job.[13]

Summary

Performance appraisal is a formal evaluation of an employee's job-related activities conducted by a superior. The appraisal system—which includes work analysis, performance appraisal, use of results in other parts of the system (for example, compensation and training), and feedback of findings to the employee and higher levels of management—is an essential part of human resource management.

Conventional appraisal processes use various rating scales and written statements of evaluation of employee performance. Most often, appraisal is done by the immediate superior of a manager, but sometimes group appraisals of an individual are conducted. Usually the appraisal period should be no longer than one year. Traditional appraisal methods have numerous shortcomings. Among the most serious are lack of objective standards and the problem of appraisers' bias. In an attempt to overcome these difficulties, the assessment center and MBO approaches to appraisal have been recommended and applied by many organizations.

Discussion questions

1. Discuss the nature of the appraisal system used by the professor in this course to evaluate your performance. How is it similar to the performance appraisal system discussed in this chapter? How is it dissimilar?
2. How can grading become a more effective developmental process for students?
3. Some states require MBO programs to be used in their agencies; for example, school systems. Discuss the pros and cons of legislating managerial techniques.

Supplementary readings

Hyatt, James C. "More Concerns Use 'Assessment Centers' to Gauge Employees' Managerial Abilities." *Wall Street Journal,* January 3, 1974, p. 15. Reprinted in *Dimensions in Modern Management,* 2d ed., edited by Patrick E. Connor. Boston: Houghton Mifflin, 1978.

McConkey, Dale D. "Measuring Managers by Results." *Personnel Journal,* December 1962, pp. 540–546. Reprinted in *Dimensions in Modern*

---

[13] William C. Gielgold, "MBO After All These Years," *Conference Board Record,* July 1975, p. 52.

Management, 2d ed., edited by Patrick E. Connor. Boston: Houghton Mifflin, 1978.

McGregor, Douglas. *The Human Side of Enterprise,* chap. 6. New York: McGraw-Hill, 1960.

Oberg, Winston. "Making Performance Appraisal Relevant." *Harvard Business Review* 50 (January–February 1972):61–67. Reprinted in *Dimensions in Modern Management,* 2d ed., edited by Patrick E. Connor. Boston: Houghton Mifflin, 1978.

Patz, Alan L. "Performance Appraisal: Useful but Still Resisted." *Harvard Business Review,* May–June 1975.

Chapter 18

Executive change and development

Objectives of the chapter

1 To identify some common purposes underlying management development programs.
2 To emphasize the importance of enhancing the quality of the managerial group through a variety of off-the-job experiences.
3 To tie in executive development programs with the appraisal system.
4 To review techniques and methods used in executive development programs.
5 To examine trends in executive development.

There is no consensus on the nature of executive development and the best means for implementing programs. In fact, there is little general agreement in theory or in practice about much of anything in this aspect of staffing. Executive development turns out to be what the management of an organization says it is: perhaps, spending the summer in a Harvard Graduate School of Business program; perhaps broad exposure to a variety of jobs within the organization. If any principle of executive development exists, it is that such programs should be tailored to suit the needs of each manager involved through a variety of off-the-job experiences.

The key word here is *tailor*. How do we know where to cut the development cloth for managers? Executives change during their organizational careers, and their development needs change with them. An enormous amount of study and research has been given to the educational and development requirements of children, adolescents, and young adults. These studies pertain to the age group from birth to twenty years of age. However, little attention has been given, until recently, to what Harry Levinson calls "the adult life cycle." He writes:

Middle age is the vast gulf between 35 and the time when every man comes to terms with his own fate. It's the time of the greatest expansion of the human personality, when the mature adult is in the widest possible contact with his environment.

But it is also a time when several things happen. He's psychologically aging and realizes he's no longer as competent and powerful physically as he used to be. . . .

As this stage of life comes along, they [executives] increasingly must give up on the individual competition. They invest themselves in the development of other people and . . . with evolving a new sense of purpose about living.[1]

Yet, it is within this period of the life cycle that executives go through profound physical, psychological, and career changes; and they also are in critical organizational positions in middle and upper levels of management. It is probably not too farfetched to say that until we know more about human development and change between the ages of thirty-five and fifty-five, executive development activities are likely to remain hit-or-miss propositions.

However, it is not management's job to do the necessary research in this field; such research is in the domain of medicine, psychology, and other behavioral sciences. Until better information is available, executive development is likely to be guided by rule-of-thumb propositions such as: executives can become obsolete and need programs to maintain their skills; executives need broadening experiences to enhance their managerial capacities; and executive development, regardless of form, should be related to organizational needs as determined in the appraisal system.

Executive obsolescence

Although executive obsolescence is hard to define for research purposes,[2] it is a fact of business life brought on not only by changing technology but also by an organizational environment that does not help its executives cope with change. In today's atmosphere of rapid change, such obsolescence has become a key issue. Unless executives keep themselves up to date and are encouraged to do so by their firms, they may quickly find their skills outmoded and may feel apathetic about learning anything new.

The problem of obsolescence is particularly evident among engineers in the aerospace industry. Assume, for example, that an optical engineer is assigned to work for two years on an exotic project, such as a missile guidance system whose design specifications are frozen. At the end of two years, when the project is completed, the engineer may know more about optical guidance systems for missile X than anyone in the world. But, who will need these skills? More than likely, new families of missiles have been developed and missile technology has advanced.

---

[1] Harry Levinson, "Executives Confront Middle Age Problems," *Boston University Alumni News*, July 8, 1969.
[2] Frederick C. Haas, *Executive Obsolescence*, Research Study No. 90 (New York: American Management Association, 1968), pp. 11–12.

Admittedly, the problem of obsolescence is more dramatic among engineers than among managers in less technical work. Nevertheless, the difficulties it poses are similar. Organizations invest large sums of money to augment managerial performance with a variety of support systems. This is particularly true in the case of computer-based management information systems. Managers must develop skills in this area, as well as other areas, to be able to apply these technologies effectively in their jobs. New technology creates a gap between existing managerial skills and the requirements of changing managerial support systems. Organizations should take the initiative through training and development to ensure that this gap is as narrow as possible.

But executive obsolescence involves more than keeping up with technologically induced organizational change. Obsolescence is a state of mind. People must want to change as social and organizational transitions strike them. Maintaining an organization's valuable managerial resources in the face of change along these dimensions is a difficult task. However, executive obsolescence will probably become a more important issue, for the factors causing it are not likely to abate. Consequently, those concerned with future executive development should address themselves to the conservation of managerial talent.

Expanding managerial horizons

The issue in executive development is not just one of conservation. It also involves the enhancement of managerial potentials. As we have said, executive development focuses frequently on providing managers with off-the-job experiences. The purpose of these experiences is to enlarge managers' horizons. This is not done solely for the sake of the individuals' general education; it serves four important organizational purposes as well. First, executive development is essential to managerial succession. Competent, qualified, and mobile people must be available for promotion or transfer when the need arises. Second, continuous improvement in managerial performance on existing assignments is desirable, and believed to be achievable, through executive development. Third, better-qualified managers are usually able to guide or coach their subordinates more effectively. In this sense, executive development is seen as a top-to-bottom, organizationwide undertaking. Fourth, executive development should provide managers with a more cosmopolitan perspective. This is particularly critical today when managers, more than ever, have to interact with managers in other organizations.

Executive development in the appraisal system

Douglas W. Bray defines management development in a way that ties it directly into the appraisal system. He states that executive development "encompasses all those actions and circumstances leading to having the needed number, and no more than the needed number, of fully effective managers at all levels of the organization."[3]

To know the number of managers and their necessary skills at every level of an organization clearly requires a great deal of planning information. Much of this information is obtained from the appraisal process, which, as we have seen in the last chapter, is designed to feed back to management data concerning the quality and location of executives presently employed.

Thus, management should know how many lower-level executives are ready to move into higher positions of responsibility. This requires determination of managerial ability and performance, with further estimation of the extent to which these two factors will respond to management development. The types of development activity chosen for management also depend on the readings received from the appraisal system.

In-organization executive development programs

The most effective means of development is by performing a job in which a positive relationship exists between boss and subordinates. Under the guidance of their superior, managers learn skills and develop the potential for advancement. No substitute has been found for this on-the-job managerial development. In fact, some companies consider it so important that they provide opportunities for managers to gain experience in a number of appropriately chosen positions of differing nature and increasing degrees of responsibility. These positions, however, are not created for this express purpose. Each time management moves an individual into such a position, it does so because it wants the job filled by a capable person and, at the same time, wants to give that person an opportunity for development. Each new assignment carries the full responsibility for satisfactory performance.

Planned progression systems

Many organizations have formalized rotation practices, so that they constitute a planned progression system. This plan provides executives with the knowledge necessary to fullfill higher-level responsibilities. There are differing opinions, of course, on whether or not executives should be well versed in the technical aspects of their positions. There is little doubt, however, that the manager of the production department, besides being thoroughly familiar with managerial functions, ought to know production processes, techniques, and methods in order to do an effective job of managing the plant. Equally, there is little doubt that the sales manager ought to know what is involved in performing various sales functions, and it is preferable that this knowledge be gained through experience.

---

[3] Douglas W. Bray, "Management Development Without Frills," *Conference Board Record*, September 1975, p. 47.

The path of progression from the lower levels of the organization often can be traced by studying the company's organization chart and job requirements. Planned progression is not a rigid path, however; it can be changed or modified to meet prevailing conditions or to allow capable individuals to be promoted into certain jobs more quickly. Most companies, in fact, have several progression paths rather than a single one, since substantially similar experience can be secured from several different positions.

Even those organizations that consider planned progression to be the main avenue to further executive growth and development should realize that deviations are sometimes necessary. It is unwise to plan an executive's path of progression in detail. One of the difficulties is that individuals do not progress at the same rate. Some perform very well up to a certain level, but do not seem capable of going further. Innumerable causes, both personal and business related, can upset even the best planned schedule.

Lateral transfers

Planned progression can limit an entire progression path to a specific function, so that a person who starts in production, for example, is expected to progress only through production department positions. Such a pattern can lead to complaints by the sales department that production people do not recognize their problems and complaints by the production department that the sales people have no understanding of the production and procurement processes. In order to resolve these misunderstandings, some companies have found it advisable to transfer people across functional lines. Such lateral shifts are often used for lower- and middle-level management but less frequently for top management.

The values derived from lateral transfers are numerous. They broaden the manager's technical knowledge and understanding of many of the functions of the enterprise; they enable the manager to coordinate and supervise an increasing number of units concerned with different functions; and they afford the manager an opportunity to acquire new managerial skills. Also, they give the manager an opportunity to work under several different executives whose coaching can be of great benefit. If an enterprise has a program of lateral transfers, it will have an increased number of channels for advancement to higher positions. Such a program will also increase the number of competitors for promotions.

There are some drawbacks to lateral transfers. Naturally, a manager dislikes seeing a subordinate leave the department after that person has developed into a capable understudy. It is also conceivable that the ambitious members of a department will be disturbed whenever a young executive moves in from another department. This drawback can be overcome, however, if management shows that there are just as many promotions out of as well as into a division.

Lateral transfers can, of course, be effectively incorporated into a planned progression program. As an example, consider a company whose chief of engineering seems to be the best candidate for the president's job—a position that, because of retirement, will be open in a few years. The chief engineer has demonstrated outstanding managerial capabilities in the designing and engineering sections of the enterprise. However, the board of directors, responsible for grooming a presidential replacement, is not certain how effective this person would be as head of the production department. They also wonder whether or not the engineer would treat the various functions of the enterprise in the proper balance. As a test, they place the chief engineer in charge of production for several years and then in charge of an entire product division encompassing activities ranging from production to sales and finance. If the engineer's performance remains good in both instances, when the president retires the directors will elect this candidate to that high position with full confidence.

Special projects

If exposure to a series of jobs cannot be arranged, there are other means for giving managers opportunities to acquire experience. They can, for example, be assigned to a special project or to some new activity in which the enterprise plans to engage. They may be put in charge of an electronics committee created to assess the feasibility and advisability of automation for the enterprise. They may be asked to introduce a new product. On such a special project, managers usually have a great amount of freedom because the newness of the project makes it difficult for top management to confine and prescribe their area of authority precisely. This gives developing executives a chance to show their initiative, perspicacity, and the many other qualities that top management is trying to appraise.

Temporary assignments

Temporary assignments also are used to provide on-the-job development. When a manager is away because of illness, vacation, or an extended leave of absence, another executive may take over temporarily. This gives the executive a fine opportunity to gain experience in the higher-level job. The immediate superior of the absentee manager is available to counsel and instruct the substitute, hence minimizing the risk that such substitution might otherwise entail.

Although the knowledge gained through this experience is of great value to the substitute, his or her performance in a temporary assignment cannot be gauged effectively for selection and promotion purposes. First, the department or activity will probably carry through on its own momentum, and no one will expect the temporary manager to undertake radical changes. Furthermore, no responsible acting manager would deviate greatly from the established pattern, knowing that he or she will not be around when the successes—or the failures—of such changes appear.

Assistant-to positions

We noted earlier that shifting across functional lines at the upper levels of management is not usually feasible. Often, however, an executive who is destined for a top-level positon lacks knowledge in some particular function. Occasionally, firms have tried to overcome this gap by creating upper-level assistant-to positions.

The assistant-to position is frequently successful as a developmental tool for junior and lower-level executives; it is not as successful when used for upper-level managers. First, upper-level managers are high salaried; whatever contribution they can make as assistants-to would not be commensurate with the expenses that the host department would have to pay. Also, assistants-to seldom can demonstrate skills because of lack of responsibility. And, the amount of knowledge gained largely depends on the instructional efforts that the department's specialists expend. All of these limitations are serious, and they have curtailed the use of the assistant-to position as an upper-level developmental device.

Coaching and counseling

Whether a company has a planned progression system and a program of lateral transfers or has more informal executive practices, it will need to stress the diligent coaching of executives by their immediate superiors, because the benefits the subordinate derives from any type of on-the-job development effort depend largely on this practice. Day-to-day relationships provide a superior with innumerable opportunities to strengthen and develop employees' capabilities.

Coaching is clearly a line duty. Although the staff of the personnel department or of the executive development group within that department can help, it is in no position to perform the coaching job for the line manager. Executives resent being trained by personnel staff, most of whom have had no managerial experience. Likewise, the coaching duty cannot be shifted to outside consultants, although they too can supply help and assistance, especially at the beginning of a development program.

Since the theory supporting any on-the-job development program is to learn by doing, the superior must provide ample opportunity for the subordinate to perform on the job. There can be no development without delegation. Only by having real authority and responsibility can a person's managerial qualities be tested and strengthened; only by giving such authority and following through on it can superiors fulfill their coaching function.

One of the most important aspects of coaching is *counseling*—teaching the subordinate the art of management. In counseling, the counselor discusses with the subordinate the performance of specific activities. These discussions usually include critical analysis of administrative skills, personal adjustments, problems of personalities, job knowledge, leadership, and so on. There is no single method of counseling. Specific techniques and styles used by one executive might be of little value to another. The important thing is to make the counseling procedure fit the specific case; each working situation might require a different method of counseling.

Critical counseling factors

A climate of confidence

A climate of confidence between superior and subordinate must exist if coaching and counseling are to be effective. Confidence cannot be achieved merely by using a gimmick or a technique, like the well-known open door policy. The manager must be available not only physically but also psychologically. To tell people to come in at any time will not create confidence if the ensuing discussions are handled in a discouraging, curt, or discourteous manner. The reduction of threat in the counseling atmosphere is essential to establishing confidence. An inappropriate remark or a thoughtless comment may shatter the rapport that has taken so long to establish. However, the climate should be such that both the strengths and shortcomings of employees may be discussed frankly.

Getting superiors to coach

Since the extent and rate of managerial development depends greatly on coaching, it is important to impress on executives the magnitude and significance of this duty. The degree of coaching practiced within a company is usually determined by the chief executive. If the chief executive practices coaching and believes firmly in it, this attitude will probably permeate the organization. In many cases, management should continuously stress coaching responsibility, pointing out that one of the factors on which each executive is appraised is his or her ability to develop subordinates.

In order to impress managers with their responsibility, some companies state that no one will be promoted unless a successor has been prepared. Although this rule can be helpful, it is not applicable in all instances. Some individuals cannot be promoted no matter how many subordinates they may coach; others have no further administrative ambitions.

Out-organization executive development programs

Modern organizations have undertaken many development activities that are conducted off premises. These activities offer broadening experiences to executives, but are less directly tied to specific job functions. One is immediately impressed by the variety of activities available. They range from studies of classic literature to transcendental meditation.

Most of these activities are conducted by universities and colleges, consulting firms, trade associations, management associations, and specialized organizations like the NTL Institute. Many organizations recommend graduate programs to their executives. Sometimes they urge pursuit of a definite goal—an advanced degree. At other times, they merely suggest that an executive take a particular course or two. Occasionally, formal educational activities take place at schools and staff colleges sponsored and maintained by the enterprise itself. Of course, only the very large enterprises can afford such an arrangement. General Electric, for instance, has established a Management Research and Development Institute at Crotonville, New York. If an enterprise does not have its own school, it might call in instructors from nearby universities. All in all, diversity characterizes out-organization executive development programs.

College and university programs

Generally, major college and university training programs are based on one of two models. In the first, executives leave the organizational scene for a specified period of time, from three weeks to six months. They meet with other executives from around the country. They live together, usually in a campus environment, and study different subjects, including policy formulation, business conditions, economics, and finance. These have been the most popular programs by far. They allow executives to get away from daily pressures and to interact with other people from different organizational backgrounds. In the process, these executives are exposed to the many points of view of their fellow students and of the faculty responsible for running the courses.

The second college model is built around a more formal academic curriculum and often leads to a master's degree in business administration. Executives who participate in this type of program pursue a course of study similar to that offered to regular students.

Special institutes

The popularity of special institutes that train executives in a more restricted subject area is growing. A good example is the NTL Institute. Executives who attend NTL programs receive training to improve their interpersonal skills so that they can become more effective leaders. In addition to NTL, there is a huge number of special institutes run by professional groups. The American Management Association is particularly active in this area.

Use of consultants

Frequently, firms use a consultant in conjunction with their own training director to create and present a development program that will satisfy the organization's special needs. This approach has been quite popular in developing programs for first-line supervision and has been used extensively for higher levels of management as well.

The subject matter in these specially designed programs is diversified, but it focuses mainly on leadership skills and management processes. Usually, the programs are condensed versions of introductory management courses and cover planning, organizing, staffing, influencing, and controlling. The degree of emphasis on each of these topics will vary from program to program. More often than not, consultants conduct these programs in a live-in environment away from the organization. A hotel, a resort, or a college campus frequently provides the facilities.

Trends in executive development

We will not attempt to list all the various training techniques in this chapter—they come and go like the Marx Brothers in a revolving-door routine—but two particular trends in executive development that seem to be emerging in practice should be noted. The first trend is toward better integration of development programs into the staffing system, in an effort to make executive development a less haphazard undertaking. It requires that management has improved decision information for forecasting, assessing executive performance and potential, and career planning. The move to acquire this type of information seems to be under way, particularly in large organizations and in their attempts to satisfy in a *rational* way the needs of the organization and the individual manager through development.

The second trend is a corollary of the first. Executive development programs have been notorious for their lack of follow-up. Seldom were serious questions asked. Were the programs achieving their stated objectives? Was behavior being changed by them in the directions anticipated? Were the right people in the programs? In short, controlling program effectiveness was, and still is, a shortcoming of most development activities. Emphasis on the systems approach to development seems to be changing this situation, because it places high priority on feedback and control of these programs in relation to other system elements. For example, one critical feedback question asks: Does the executive development program actually create a fund of promotable executives to fill positions in the process of management succession? While management practice has a long way to go in developing reliable feedback on its development efforts, attempts are under way in the form of the assessment center and MBO approaches.

Summary

Executive development practices vary widely, but they are usually designed to provide managers with a broad exposure to off-the-job experiences. The justifications for such programs are that managers grow obsolete, that managers need to be enhanced for better job performance, and that organizations need a reserve of qualified people to meet their succession needs.

Executive development programs fall into two broad categories: those that are conducted on organizational premises and those that are conducted off organizational premises. Of the programs in the first category, the ones using job rotation, planned progression, and lateral transfers are the most important. Since these methods of development require close linkages between a boss and a subordinate, effective implementation necessitates expert counseling and coaching skills.

Programs in the second category use numerous facilities and techniques. University programs and programs conducted by special institutes, professional management associations, or company schools are prevalent.

Two general trends in the practice of executive development show movement toward greater integration of programs within the staffing system and toward the creation of reliable feedback on program effectiveness.

Discussion questions

1 You work for a management consulting firm and have just been given the assignment of designing a management development program for a local company. What questions will you ask before you actually design the program?
2 What criteria will you use in determining the effectiveness of your program?

Supplementary readings

Argyris, Chris. *Interpersonal Competence and Organizational Effectiveness,* chap. 6–8. Homewood, Illinois: Richard D. Irwin, 1962.

Bray, Douglas W. "Management Development Without Frills." *Conference Board Record,* September 1975.

Schein, Edgar H. "Management Development as a Process of Influence." *Industrial Management Review,* May 1961, pp. 59–77. Reprinted in *Dimensions in Modern Management,* 2d ed., edited by Patrick E. Connor. Boston: Houghton Mifflin, 1978.

Chapter 19

Selecting and training new managers

Objectives of the chapter

1 To stress the role of the staffing system in providing a continuous flow of qualified people into the organization.
2 To indicate some public policy measures that regulate the selection of management employees.
3 To review the steps in management selection.
4 To review the principal elements in training new managers.
5 To summarize learning principles and to relate them to training programs.
6 To note some important training methods.

A crucial part of the staffing system is ensuring the continuity of management by providing an adequate flow of potential young managers into the organization. The quality and quantity of this flow are determined by the forecast of executive requirements and by the evaluation of managerial talent, which is part of the appraisal process.

In earlier decades, the natural flow of young people into the business sector seemed to be sufficient to supply almost all corporate needs. As enterprises began to grow in size, however, and as other appealing avenues of employment opened up in society, business firms began to find their existing sources of potential executives inadequate, and it was necessary to undertake an active search for new sources of talent. Across the country, their recruiters combed the campuses of colleges and universities for suitable personnel. The now annual parade of "body snatchers" on the campus each spring is a sure sign that the academic year is nearing its close. Some companies prefer graduates from the liberal arts colleges, whereas others lean toward the graduates of schools of business administration. Although campus recruitment has become common in recent years, a number of companies followed this practice as long ago as World War I.[1]

---

[1] Henning W. Prentis, Jr., "The Task of Managing," in H. B. Maynard, ed., *Top Management Handbook* (New York: McGraw-Hill, 1960), p. 119. Mr. Prentis, the former chairman of the board of Armstrong Cork Company, describes his firm's experience with campus recruiting.

For all practical purposes, then, junior executive training means the preparation of college graduates for managerial jobs. No doubt some schools provide their graduates with a better background on which to base such training than do others. Each organization will sooner or later find its best source. A college education, however, is not an absolute prerequisite for entry to a management training program. Every employee of an organization, regardless of formal education, should have the opportunity for promotion. Foremen should be asked to nominate candidates from the worker ranks for preparatory training, and those who pass the usual tests and executive interviews should be selected as management trainees. In most instances, though, this practice provides only a fraction of the total number of executive trainees needed. Hence, colleges have increasingly become *the* source of candidates for management training programs. Higher education has eliminated the need for corporate executive farm clubs, much as it has eliminated this need for professional football and basketball teams.

Recruitment and selection

It is interesting to observe the recruitment activity on university campuses from year to year. Larger firms recruit consistently, regardless of business conditions. They realize that the aging process of executives continues through good years and bad ones. Other companies, those that have not yet solidified their junior executive training program, may allow hiring to fluctuate with general business conditions. This is a shortsighted view, and one that indicates that some managements are not yet fully convinced of the benefits of a regular recruiting effort. Sporadic hiring of outstanding young people will sooner or later be reflected in a poorly balanced age distribution among upper-level executives.

Public policy issues in recruitment

Legal requirements for nondiscriminatory hiring practices imposed by federal, state, and local governments are among the most important external contingencies management must consider in its recruitment and selection policies. At the federal level, numerous laws and agencies prohibit discrimination, among them Title VII of the Civil Rights Act of 1964, the Age Discrimination in Employment Act of 1967, the Equal Pay Act of 1963, and the Equal Employment Opportunity Commission. All forbid discrimination based on race, color, religion, sex, and national origin. Additionally, Executive Order 11246 requires affirmative-action plans for certain employers.

Thus, as James Hollander writes, "equal employment opportunity has evolved from a 'do good' program into a legal obligation that can have severe consequences for any employer that falls short of its requirements."[2]

[2] James Hollander, "A Step-by-Step Guide to Corporate Affirmative Action," *Business and Society Review*, Fall 1975, p. 67.

Probably, the most cited example is the AT&T case, which cost the company $15 million in back pay and $23 million in promotion and wage adjustments.

Given these developments in public policy, an organization must extend recruitment to women and minorities when seeking applicants who are qualified to enter management training programs. That such efforts are under way is evident; but equal-employment opportunities in executive positions are still a distant goal. What appears to be happening at this time is a federal crackdown on large organizations, like AT&T and some universities, in the hope that others will fall in line. These efforts have not seemed, as yet, to have brought about the massive voluntary compliance sought for affirmative-action programs.[3]

Nevertheless, affirmative action is in the air, and rightly so, since it requires the equitable use of human resources that have been previously underemployed. To begin, management should issue a policy statement in support of affirmative action, and this statement should be distributed to managers throughout the organization with orders for implementation. Based on work force analysis, managers can pinpoint various executive areas in the organization where women and minorities are underrepresented. Recruitment efforts now should focus on overcoming these deficiencies through outreach programs and advertising. When these channels are opened for all, initial screening can begin.

Initial screening

The first step in the recruiting process is *screening.* This takes place when the firm's recruitment officer—a member of the personnel staff or a line executive—visits university campuses and speaks to potential candidates. It is especially important that a corporation send as recruiters individuals who are well informed about their company and who know what kind of trainees to seek. A large corporation like General Motors hires as many as a thousand graduates each year and, in order to do so, may have to interview twenty-five thousand. A well-qualified recruiter can develop valuable relationships between the company and the college placement counselors, thus facilitating the process of putting the right students into the right spots.

Each firm has certain minimum hiring requirements, and in the first interview a good recruitment officer should be able to eliminate candidates who do not fulfill them. Although there is a great diversity in these requirements, almost all firms stipulate that applicants be young, for it will be years before they are ready for senior executive jobs. If applicants are approximately twenty-five to twenty-eight years old (the upper age limits set for most management trainees), at the age of forty-five to forty-eight they could, theoretically, step into high-level executive positions and still serve the firm for approximately twenty years before retirement at age sixty-five.

[3] Patrick E. Fahey and Gopal C. Pati, "Trying to Be Equable About Equal Opportunity," *Conference Board Record,* September 1975, p. 37.

Why the Cubs don't win pennants

Then, Wrigley recalls, when Jackie Robinson broke into the major leagues with the Dodgers in 1947, there was a rush to sign up Negro ballplayers. Wrigley cautioned against haste. He told his associates: "We aren't going out and hire a Negro ball player just because it is popular to have a Negro ball player. When we have a Negro ball player, he will be an outstanding ball player. He has to be outstanding, or it is going to reflect on his race. He has to be better than any white boy because he will be under the microscope and in the limelight."

In the early 1950s, the Cubs had a young Negro second baseman at Los Angeles who showed great promise. For two successive years, the Cubs brought him to the spring training camp, where he sparkled. But in the exhibition games, he could do nothing. In a major league uniform, playing against mostly white major leaguers, he was terrified.

Late in 1953, Wid Matthews came up with a Negro second baseman named Gene Baker, who met Wrigley's requirements. A few days later Matthews informed Wrigley that he had bought another Negro player from the Kansas City Monarchs.

"Who?" Wrigley asked.

"Fellow named Ernie Banks."

"Gee whiz!" Wrigley answered. "We are bringing up one Negro player this year. Why did you go out and get another one?"

"Well," Matthews replied, "we had to have a roommate for the one we've got."

Source: From *Philip K. Wrigley* by Paul M. Angle. Copyright 1975 Rand McNally & Company.

The recruiter also must try to learn many other things about the candidates in this preliminary interview. Although it is difficult to judge maturity, the recruiter will form an impression of some of its facets—the candidates' interests, views, common sense, drive, and initiative. It is always easier to eliminate candidates who are obviously unfit in these respects than to determine degrees of fitness for those who do seem to qualify.

The recruiter's next task is to encourage applicants who have not been eliminated to become active candidates for the training program. The recruiter will, of course, discuss compensation with potential trainees. Starting salaries have become a problem; they must be comparable to what other firms offer, but they must be consistent with the company's overall compensation system, thereby assuring that reasonable increases can be given to trainees once on the job.

At one time recruiters rolled out the red carpet to woo candidates; those days have passed. Competition for jobs has grown keener due to the large number of college graduates in the labor market, restrained hiring because of economic conditions, and preferential hiring resulting from affirmative-action programs.

Interviewing, testing, and final selection

The next step in the recruitment process is the initiation of a series of thorough interviews, which are normally conducted at the headquarters of the firm. Although the interviews are usually supervised by the officer in charge of the training program, a number of other corporate executives also participate. It is necessary that line officers interview the candidates so that the final selection decision reflects a consensus of several different types of experienced executives.

In assessing a candidate, the interviewer will look for intelligence, analytical capabilities, facility in communicating, personality, interests, and motivation. The intelligence of the candidate can be determined by checking scholastic records and various aptitude tests that have been taken before and during a college career. In order to assess analytical ability, the interviewer may present the candidate with a certain problem and observe how it is solved. Because the same problem is given to all candidates, the interviewer can rate the quality of particular solutions. The candidate's interests and ability to communicate are easily appraised during an interview.

Usually, selection tests supplement the interviewing procedures. These tests are designed to add data from a source other than the people who have talked with the candidate. Testing can be done on many facets of an individual's abilities, often on the same characteristics that an interviewer tries to assess. Interviewing combined with testing is aimed at predicting a candidate's potential for success in the organization.

In final selection, management must beware of the tendency to pick candidates who are too much alike. Since great stress often is placed on the need to secure adaptable young people schooled in managerial skills, greatly concerned with human relations, and displaying characteristics that will make them good members of a smooth working team, organizations often neglect individuals with new and even unorthodox views who will question existing practices and generate ideas for constructive change. To do so disregards the dynamics of business and neglects the need for innovators.

Training

After selection, the new employee enters a program designed by the organization for new managers. Before we discuss this type of program, however, some preliminary remarks about training are necessary. Training involves "any organizationally initiated procedures which are intended to foster learning among organizational members . . . the desired learning is in a direction which is intended to contribute to overall organizational objectives."[4] Management must consider training needs and objectives and principles of learning.

---

[4] John R. Hinrichs, "Personnel Training," in Marvin D. Dunnette, ed., *Handbook of Industrial and Organizational Psychology* (Chicago: Rand McNally, 1976), p. 832.

Assessing training needs

Training needs must be assessed before an organization commits itself to a program. The process of assessment includes a review of organizational goals, and job and work force analyses.

Training must be consistent with overall organizational objectives while it reinforces any new goals management may want to achieve. For example, management may intend to implement an affirmative-action program, which requires the hiring of minority management trainees. This goal will influence the type of program used.

Job analysis is critical to the assessing of needs, since it determines the content of the training program. It provides information about job requirements and the skills needed by managers for effective performance. Although there is a great deal of flexibility in management, it is necessary to have an understanding of the nature of the jobs for which people are being trained.

Finally, work force analysis reveals the level of management skill and quality, as well as its present composition and future requirements. Such work force data, available from the management appraisal system, are valuable for indicating strong and weak points in the management group.

Training objectives

Once organizational training needs have been assessed, thought should be given to the objectives of training. Training objectives fall into three broad categories: transmitting information, changing attitudes, and developing skills.[5]

A large part of an organization's training efforts involves transmitting information. This provides the trainee with a general orientation into organizational policies and procedures. A person in sales training, for example, must know the company's product line, pricing structure, division of territories, credit policy, and so on.

A second objective—indoctrination—should modify trainees' preconceived ideas about the organization and the job. Every organization has a unique culture to which trainees must be introduced if they are to work effectively with other managers.

Finally, training should impart skills on three levels: content, interpersonal, and conceptual. *Content skills* are those skills that people need in order to perform the technical aspects of their jobs. *Interpersonal skills* include the human relations skills that are essential both to leadership and to effective teamwork. *Conceptual skills* pertain to a person's ability to think in abstract terms about system relationships: How does the job performed relate to other jobs in the organization? How do the decisions made influence the decisions of others in the organization?

---

[5] William G. Scott and Terence R. Mitchell, *Organization Theory* (Homewood, Illinois: Richard D. Irwin, 1976), pp. 355–357.

Principles of learning

Learning is closely related to training objectives. It is the means by which individuals acquire the content, interpersonal, and conceptual skills necessary for effective performance. Learning, therefore, implies a *change* in individual behavior that is long term in nature and that usually results from experience or practice.[6] Researchers have observed a number of principles that underlie the learning process:

- *Motivation* The person should want to learn; thus, the learning process should be made as attractive as possible to stimulate participation by the trainee.
- *Reinforcement* The trainee should receive positive rewards for the successful accomplishment of learning tasks.
- *Practice* The trainee should be given the opportunity to repeat learning tasks; the greater the repetition, the more likely the trainee is to master the task.
- *Relevant material* The learning material should pertain to the goals the trainee is seeking through employment in the organization.
- *Transfer of learning* To have maximum effectiveness, learning material should be transferable to the job or jobs the trainee will perform.

Training programs

Shortly after people have been selected for a training program, they will need to learn the history and tradition of the enterprise, its position within the industry, its market standing, its objectives and policies, and its general structure and organization. This information is often available in books, booklets, manuals, or brochures; if not, lectures are given.

Presupervisory work

After becoming acquainted with the enterprise, trainees will enter a period of presupervisory work. The length of this period varies greatly from a brief six months to one or two years and sometimes even longer. The presupervisory period is intended to give trainees experience in all kinds of nonmanagerial jobs. For instance, in a manufacturing concern the trainees may go first into the stock room, from there into the shipping room, and then spend several months on the production floor. They may also spend some time in the production control department, scheduling department, purchasing department, accounting department, and in the general offices. Later, they may be placed for several months in the sales department at headquarters, probably selling to the customers in the field. The exact order and selection

---

[6] G. A. Kimble, *Principles of General Psychology* (New York: Ronald Press, 1956), p. 192.

of the nonmanagerial jobs will differ depending on the needs and character of the enterprise. All trainees will not do the same job at the same time. After a given amount of time is spent at a certain job, the trainees are reshuffled. Thus, by the end of several years, all will have had approximately the same amount of diversified work experience.

Advantages and shortcomings

The advantage of varied presupervisory work experience is obvious: it affords the trainee an opportunity to perform differing jobs. There are, however, certain disadvantages. Some trainees learn the details of a job in a shorter time than do others and, therefore, waste much of the time they spend on the job. Many regular employees resent trainees because they are the chosen few who will eventually be promoted into higher positions. A further disadvantage is that those in charge of the particular departments used for training will have to bear the costs of training the junior executives, knowing that they will probably not remain long enough to make a productive contribution. Nevertheless, these and numerous other disadvantages are far outweighed by the great advantage of having trainees who have done many jobs. Furthermore, if all the trainees follow an established presupervisory route, supervisors eventually will accept this procedure as a matter of course, and, with time, much of the friction will disappear.

Trainee appraisal

At the end of each presupervisory assignment, the executive responsible for supervision rates and appraises the management trainee. The appraisal is sent to a staff specialist from the personnel department, or more specifically from the executive development program, who serves as trainee administrator and counselor. From time to time, this counselor reviews the record of each trainee, deciding whether or not the trainee has the capacity for further advancement. If not, the trainee probably should be encouraged to leave. This decision should be made in the first years of employment; in the long run, frankness can only be beneficial to the young man or woman.

Additional presupervisory training

In addition to presupervisory experience in actual work situations, many firms use other devices to broaden the exposure of trainees before assigning them to supervisory levels. Two of the more commonly used are work in an assistant-to position and rotation in observation posts. Through these devices the trainee is exposed to certain aspects of company operations without actually doing the work.

Assistant-to positions

The assistant-to positions connected with an executive training program differ from those associated with line and staff. In the latter instance, assistants are assigned to overburdened executives to relieve them of some of their duties. In executive training, the position is created primarily to help the trainees by exposing them to managers' daily activities. It is more effective to put trainees into assistant-to positions after they have had some kind of work experience within the enterprise.

Trainees' assistant-to positions usually are not permanent, and only a few executives are assigned trainees. Trainees are there to learn and only add to the burdens of executives. Executives, of course, are generally responsible for the success or failure of the assistant-to position as a training device. If executives make a real effort to be good teachers and coaches, trainees will benefit. For this reason, only executives who have proved that they have these capacities should participate. In the beginning, assistants-to do very little other than some of the leg work for the executives. However, if the executives are good teachers, they will be able to make more and more use of the trainees, and the trainees will be exposed to a multitude of managerial activities. This, of course, presupposes not only the superiors' abilities to teach but also the trainees' desires to learn. Hence, the assistant-to position is often created especially for a particular trainee; after it has served its purpose, it is abolished.

Observation assignments

The observation assignment also permits trainees to gain exposure to various managerial functions. When it is used, trainees are assigned on a rotating basis to different managers whom they observe as they perform their functions. The obvious disadvantage of this training device is that trainees might not know what to look for; they might not be far enough advanced in their training to distinguish between the activities that are worthwhile observing and those that are not. In addition, some managers feel that the trainee should not be allowed to observe certain confidential activities and decisions. Also, some managers resent observation assignments because the trainees actually perform no work, although their salary is charged to the department.

Nevertheless, under proper auspices, observation assignments are beneficial. They give trainees an opportunity to examine and discuss thoroughly the work being done. However, an observation assignment may not improve managerial skills, because it does not involve any practice or impose any responsibility for action. The special value lies only in the information gained.

Assignment to managerial positions

After sufficient exposure to presupervisory experiences, the trainees are appointed to supervisory jobs. From then on, they must show what they have learned and will continue to learn by managing. They have to direct subordinates' efforts toward achieving the enterprise's goal. They change from doing things themselves to having things done by others; they plan, organize, staff, influence, and control.

For first supervisory jobs, trainees are assigned to one of several line or staff positions. Sometimes, the trainees who prefer staff positions are assigned to line jobs to qualify them for operating functions later on. At other times, trainees will be placed in fields completely different from those in which they specialized in college, thus improving their adaptability and versatility. Initial supervisory assignments are by no means permanent; generally, trainees are rotated just as they were in their nonmanagerial, presupervisory period. The type and extent of rotation depend, among other things, on the needs of the enterprise, its plans for expansion, and the dynamics of the industry. In addition, they depend on the individuals' needs.

Junior executives who have progressed to the supervisory level usually spend several years at a certain job. During this time they must prove their value before they can progress to another job. If top management has decided on a system of rotation as a training device, then certain managerial jobs must be set aside and staffed only by executive trainees. These are regular managerial positions within the organization, but positions that will offer the trainee-manager a suitable opportunity for development and experience. There will be a rather rapid turnover rate in departments staffed by trainees, so top management should minimize the loss in efficiency by making certain that the positions above and below the one being filled by a trainee-manager are held by experienced individuals.

One of the greatest advantages of this kind of rotation is that the trainee-manager gains an understanding of interdepartmental relationships and the importance of coordination and cooperation. One of the major disadvantages, in addition to the difficulty of selecting suitable positions and the initial loss of efficiency, is the lowering of morale among subordinates who work in the departments that the trainee-managers supervise. These subordinates resent the fact that, although they may be qualified, they will never achieve a managerial position within their own department because such positions always go to a trainee. Those who are ambitious and feel that they are at a dead end will probably leave the enterprise, whereas older subordinates, unable to leave, will remain and be resentful. This is a disadvantage that usually cannot be overcome, and top management must make certain that it is outweighed by the advantages derived from the rotation procedures.

Additional training devices

Some supplementary devices can be worked into the junior executive training program. These include use of committees, junior boards, conferences, courses, university programs, trade association programs, and many other arrangements that contribute to a well-rounded training experience.

Committees

There is little doubt that service on committees is of considerable educational value to executive trainees. It is useful to place young managers on committees composed mainly of experienced executives so that they will become acquainted with various company problems and points of view. They will have the opportunity to observe how department managers defend their attitudes and opinions in front of a committee and how they adjust themselves to the overall needs of the enterprise. This will broaden trainees' knowledge, for the problems under consideration usually have causes and consequences far exceeding any one member's area of competence. Committee experience will also warn young executives against believing that their point of view is always right; it will show them the importance of having an open mind on all complex issues.

Junior boards

The junior board is a committee created for training purposes and is composed only of junior executives. In this arrangement, junior executives at various levels meet as a quasi—board of directors, deliberating over problems they have encountered and suggesting changes and ideas that they consider proper and good for the enterprise. Their suggestions are passed on to regular managerial boards and, if they warrant, to the board of directors. Participation in this kind of deliberation broadens the outlook of the trainee.

The problems selected by junior boards are usually fairly general. This affords trainees an opportunity to acquire considerable knowledge in almost all aspects of the enterprise. It is a sign of recognition for a young person to be elected and reelected by fellow trainees for membership on a junior board. In fulfilling assignments as a board member, young executives have a chance to develop important skills, such as leading a discussion, leading the investigation of a problem, and preparing and presenting a report. Junior boards are a good additional training device for potential executives; and the suggestions they generate can be of substantial benefit to the enterprise.

Training outside the firm

Management often sends trainees to conferences held by trade or management associations. Much can be learned if these conferences are properly conducted, and if they come at the right time in the trainees' development. In addition to conferences, top management often decides to enroll trainees in formal university courses or university programs. These and innumerable other external training devices are desirable if they stem from well-qualified sources.

A shopping list of training methods

There are many training methods to make the learning process easier, whether training is conducted on or off the organization's premises. Combinations of these methods are used in training programs:

- *Lecture* A one-way transmission of information to the trainee.
- *Directed conference* A discussion by trainees of preselected topics by a conference leader, to emphasize certain points or conclusions.
- *Films and television* Pertinent films and video tapes shown to trainees on specialized subjects.
- *Case study* The discussion, analysis, and solution of narrative problems by trainees, which often require them to make policy and action decisions on the case material.
- *Simulation techniques* Attempts to duplicate, in the training setting, situations that trainees may actually encounter on the job. There are many methods available, including role playing, in-basket simulations, and business games using a computer.
- *Laboratory training* A technique, like sensitivity training, that involves the trainee in group processes in order to learn interpersonal skills.

Evaluation of training programs

Evaluation is a vital, though often neglected, step in training activities. Managers must decide whether or not the organization's program has produced the desired changes in trainees' behavior. It would seem easy: simply observe and measure trainees' attitudes and behavior before entering and after leaving the training program.

The problem of evaluation is complicated, however, by a number of factors. First, training goals are difficult to state in quantifiable terms, especially if they involve changes in trainees' interpersonal and cognitive skills. Second, long-term learning changes are usually sought. Consequently, follow-up on trainees must continue for several years after the program to see if what they learned has stayed with them. Third, while initial changes in behavior may be positive, trainees may go into departments in the organization that are not supportive of the skills and attitudes learned. If this is the case, the trainees are likely to lose these skills. Such a situation is not entirely the fault of the program; often the problem lies in the departmental environment. Evaluation can indicate areas where training objectives and departmental leadership and culture are not compatible.

All in all, if an organization invests its resources in management training programs, it must take the final step and evaluate results to ensure that the program is accomplishing its goals.

Summary

Recruitment and selection of new managers are the initial steps in ensuring a flow of people to provide continuity of management. Presently, organizational recruitment policies are strongly influenced by antidiscrimination laws and affirmative-action programs. Within the framework of these government-imposed contingencies, recruits are screened, interviewed, and selected to be new managers. Once hired, the new managers enter training programs.

In designing training programs, management must assess its training needs, decide training objectives, and apply principles of learning. Training programs take many forms. Usually, they include a lengthy presupervisory period, supported by various types of training experiences, such as junior boards, assistant-to positions, committee assignments, observational assignments, and so on. An essential part of all training programs is their continuous evaluation to determine if they are meeting organizational objectives.

Discussion questions

1 Prepare an inventory of laws that regulate the recruitment and hiring of new people for managerial positions.
2 Discuss the relationship between performance appraisal and the process of selecting and training new managers.

Supplementary readings

Dill, W. R.; Hilton, T. L.; and Reitman, W. R. *The New Managers.* Englewood Cliffs, N.J.: Prentice-Hall, 1962.

Hinrichs, John R. "Personnel Training." In *Handbook of Industrial and Organizational Psychology* edited by Marvin D. Dunnette. Chicago: Rand McNally, 1976.

Hollander, James. "A Step-by-Step Guide to Corporate Affirmative Action." *Business and Society Review,* Fall 1975, pp. 67—73.

Odiorne, George S. *Training by Objectives.* New York: Macmillan, 1970.

Chapter 20

Executive compensation

Objectives of the chapter

1 To point out the economic and tax factors that influence the level of executive compensation.
2 To describe the principal aspects of a compensation program.
3 To review the chief forms of direct financial compensation.
4 To review various methods of indirect financial compensation.
5 To discuss some contingencies that influence the operation of compensation programs.

Classical economic theory tells us that an individual is paid according to the contribution that person makes to the revenue of an organization. While this makes rational sense, it does not lead us very far in determining why the chief executive of corporation A earns four times more than the chief executive of corporation B earns, even though their companies are of comparable size and in the same industry.[1]

Executive compensation practices vary widely among organizations. They are influenced by external conditions, such as the economy, tax laws, the stock market, and so on. As an aspect of the staffing function, executive compensation centers mainly on direct and indirect financial incentives. These include salary, bonuses, pensions, stock options, and a number of perquisites. The purpose of compensation management is to achieve organizationwide equity and consistency in the administration of programs. Beyond this, the compensation system must provide financial incentives that reward and encourage high managerial performance, as well as provide salaries that are competitive with other organizations for comparable jobs. Added together, the direct and indirect pay schemes, the nonfinancial incentives, and the external contingencies that influence compensation form a very complex picture of which we can give only the most general view.

[1] "Who Gets the Most Pay," *Forbes*, May 15, 1976, p. 225.

Salary determinants

The level of executive pay is affected by organizational size, type of industry, and the amount of managerial responsibility. Generally, for comparable positions, a large company pays higher salaries than does a smaller company. One study indicated that average compensation ranged from $103,000, for companies with $50- to $100-million sales, to $390,000, for companies with over $5-billion sales.[2] However, there is some evidence that a company's size is not quite as important a determinant of salary as it has been in the past. According to a *Dun's Review* survey, of the executives who make $100,000, more than two thirds work for companies in the $100- to $500-million sales bracket.[3] These salary figures are for the chief executives of the corporations.

While these surveys have mixed results, an earlier study by Arch Patton showed that there is a fairly stable distribution of salary percentages among executives in the four highest levels of the six hundred organizations reporting. Table 20-1 shows, for example, that in 1961 the number 2 executive received an average of 71 percent of the salary of the chief executive, the number 3 executive received 59 percent of the number 2 executive's salary, and so on. Such percentages held firm for an eight-year period.

Table 20-1 Salary relationships among top executives (percent of chief executive's salary received)

Position	1954	1955	1956	1957	1958	1959	1960	1961
Chief executive	100	100	100	100	100	100	100	100
Number 2 executive	70	71	70	69	73	72	73	71
Number 3 executive	58	58	57	57	60	60	61	59
Number 4 executive	51	51	51	52	55	55	54	54

Source: Arch Patton, "Trends in Executive Compensation," *Harvard Business Review* 38 (September–October 1960): 144–154, and "Executive Compensation in 1960," *Harvard Business Review* 39 (September–October 1961): 152–157.

The level of salary for a company's chief executive sets the standard for the other executives. In dollar terms and among similar firms: if the chief executive receives more money, the lower levels of management will also receive more money; if the chief executive receives less money, the lower levels of management will also receive less money.

Since Patton wrote, several factors have combined that may alter his conclusions about salary percentages. They are the combination of the tax laws with inflation and recession. The net effect of these factors is a compression of earnings among people making under $52,000 a year and a widening of the gap between these people and those who earn over $52,000 a year. Inflation, of course, means that executives will press for

---

[2] "Compensation Currents," *Compensation Review,* Fourth quarter 1975, p. 3.
[3] "Compensation Currents," *Compensation Review,* First quarter 1975, p. 5.

wage adjustments upward, and this results in a larger tax bite. For most middle managers the more pay received, the less is kept in after-tax income, because progressive taxation exists up to the $52,000 cut-off point.[4] These contingencies make compensation planning difficult, especially in terms of maintaining equity and consistency in the program.

Executive salaries differ considerably from industry to industry. Manufacturing firms appear to pay the highest salaries; the largest top-executive salaries in 1973 were in the automobile industry, for example. After manufacturing came companies in the wholesale and retail trade. Service industries — which include insurance, real estate, and banking[5] — are among the lowest paying.

The magnitude of an executive's decision-making role is crucial in determining salary level. This statement, however, raises an interesting question. Is an executive really paid on the basis of the size of the reponsibility or on the profitability of the unit's operation?[6]

There is evidence to indicate that the magnitude of responsibility, not profitability of the activity, is becoming the crucial factor underlying salary. Arch Patton, for example, talks about the "disassociation of pay and profits" and states that this is a relatively recent development. To substantiate this he points out that, in 1965, "only a few industries were detected which showed a positive correlation . . . between the level of top management pay and return on sales or invested capital."[7] More recently, a study of 183 companies with declining profits showed that just 52 of them reduced the salary of the top executive.[8]

Internal consistency and external competitiveness

The three factors we have just discussed are not the only determinants of executive compensation. They are supplemented by two closely related and somewhat overlapping considerations: internal consistency and external competitiveness. *Internal consistency* requires that the salary system reward jobs according to their importance in the organization. It attempts to minimize the pay inequities that arise when one job has fewer responsibilities than another, but carries a higher salary. *External competitiveness* demands that executive compensation meet that of other firms. The reconciliation of these two factors is often difficult. Frequently, the market demand for certain specialists, like computer technologists and systems analysts, does not respect the internal salary structure of any particular firm.

[4] Otto Maurer and M. Kasey Hellerman, "Executive Compensation in the 1980s," *Conference Board Record*, April 1976, p. 27.
[5] "Compensation Currents," *Compensation Review*, First quarter 1975, p. 6.
[6] Malcom S. Salter, "What Is 'Fair Pay' for the Executive?" *Harvard Business Review* 50 (May–June 1972): 6–13, 144–146.
[7] Arch Patton, "Top Executive Pay: New Facts and Figures," *Harvard Business Review* 44 (September–October 1966): 96; and "For the Chief, Sales Set the Pay," *Business Week*, September 30, 1967, p. 174.
[8] "Compensation Currents," *Compensation Review*, Fourth quarter 1975, p. 2.

Internal evaluation of management positions

In order to achieve an equitable internal alignment of management positions, it is necessary to determine the proper relationships among the salaries of the positions; and, in order to do this, it is necessary to evaluate each position systematically. This procedure, called *job evaluation*, is a standardized method of appraising the worth and value of each job in relation to other jobs. Although job evaluation methods can be used for any position, the present discussion is concerned only with the evaluation of management positions. Such evaluations should be performed by a committee of representative top-managers to assure that all managers receive equal attention and concern. Once a number of such positions are appraised and their worth and value determined, it is a simple matter to figure out the relative compensation for each managerial job. The compensation of the chief executive and of a limited number of other very high corporate officers is determined by the board of directors.

The evaluation of executive jobs for compensation purposes has been criticized because such evaluation is concerned with the job itself, not with performance. Some say that carrying this factory-oriented concept of job evaluation to executive positions brings an unrealistic rigidity into the compensation structure, particularly at upper levels. As Patton puts it: "The closer to the top of the company pyramid an executive climbs, the more he makes his own job."[9] In other words, Patton believes that it is pointless to speak about job evaluation of top positions, in reality, because evaluation can relate only to what an individual manager has made of his or her job in comparison with what others have made of theirs. In his opinion, the critical element in evaluating the upper-level positions is the contribution managers in such positions make to the decison-making process. Although it is relatively easy to distinguish major decisions from the less important ones, it is much more difficult to determine who makes or influences which decisions and whose decision-making contributions go beyond functional responsibilities.

External compensation alignment

An executive compensation structure also must align equitably with those of other firms. Otherwise, the enterprise will not be able to retain its capable managers or, when necessary, to attract executives from the outside. Because of the differing size, nature, and specific job characteristics of enterprises, it is much more difficult to obtain proper external alignment than it is to achieve internal balance. Clearly, many executive duties performed in one enterprise may not exist in another.

---

[9] Arch Patton, "What Is an Executive Worth?" *Harvard Business Review* 39 (March–April 1961): 71.

349 Executive compensation

In addition to direct compensation, many companies provide supplementary benefits that are not readily quantifiable and comparable. The report on trends in executive compensation published by the Conference Board is a good source of information on these supplementary benefits as well as on other aspects of compensation. These reports analyze the compensation data of about twelve hundred companies listed on the major stock exchanges. Management can use such data to see whether or not its own executive compensation structure is sound internally and externally.

Other forms of direct financial compensation

Other forms of financial remuneration round out a company's executive compensation program. These range from offering managers financial incentives designed to increase their annual income to providing deferred income for retirement, a policy that provides distinct tax advantages. Table 20-2 lists both the objectives and techniques of the major compensation practices.[10]

Table 20-2 Compensation practices

Technique	Objective
Incentive compensation	1 Dollar profit improvement 2 Increased return on investment 3 Improved individual performance
Stock option	1 Proprietary attitude toward costs and profits 2 Dollar profit improvement
Qualified profit-sharing plan	1 Increased individual attention to company profits 2 Dollar profit improvement
Qualified retirement pension plan	1 Greater loyalty to the company 2 Lower turnover

Source: The Use and Effectiveness of Management Compensation Programs (New York: Cresap, McCormick and Paget, Management Consultants, 1963), pp. 1–4.

Incentive and bonus systems

Many firms have bonus systems, which supplement base salaries, to provide a financial incentive for managers. The purpose of these plans is to encourage higher managerial productivity and, thereby, to contribute to the profitability of the firm. Although the amount of a bonus will fluctuate, it generally composes a substantial portion of an executive's annual income.

[10] For a more detailed account, see George W. Hettenhouse, "Cost/Benefit Analysis of Executive Compensation," *Harvard Business Review* 48 (July–August 1970): 120–121.

In addition to their motivational function, bonus plans are useful for attracting new managers to a company. Roche found, in a study of mobile executives, that people moving to another company expected a 43 percent increase in their bonuses on the average, while those not moving expected a 31 percent average increase. He writes: "The prospect—and that is all it is in most cases—of a sizable bonus increase is undoubtedly an important lure in recruiting an executive into another organization."[11]

One of the problems with the bonus system is that it is often difficult to measure the degree to which the efforts of a particular executive have contributed to the results of a particular year. Business may have good results because economic conditions were unusually good; success may have had little to do with the efforts of the particular executives. As a matter of fact, it has been found that executives often exert more effort when economic conditions are poor; yet, company profits will necessarily remain low.

Clearly, the basis of incentive compensation presents a problem. Theoretically, it would be a good idea to relate the standard measurement to the work of the individual and pay a cash bonus. A sales manager, for example, would receive incentives based on the amount of sales; for other managers, the bases might be production output, reduction of costs, and so on. But none of these bases necessarily provides an accurate reflection of true managerial performance. Increased sales might result from business conditions or the poor performance of competitors; they might also be a by-product of inflation. Increased production could be caused by overwork, speed-up, and other devices which will look good in the short run but will eventually harm the enterprise. The same applies to incentives based on savings in costs and expenses. A manager might postpone needed replacements, repairs, and maintenance in order to earn a bonus. Adequate controls can, however, minimize these problems.

Generally, incentives are related to overall performance of the enterprise; they are, therefore, based on profits. Large companies frequently establish a bonus fund. This fund, a fixed percentage of the net profits, reflects not so much the contribution of an individual as the teamwork of all executives and is earmarked for bonuses either in cash or in company stock. In some cases, this percentage is set aside regardless of the return on invested capital; in others, it is not set aside until a certain percentage return is earned on such capital. The division of the bonus fund among participating executives is determined by the board of directors or by a special bonus committee. Naturally, the larger the enterprise, the larger the fund will be and the larger the number of executives who will participate in it.

One extreme case can be found at General Motors, where the bonus fund for 1972 operations (distributed in 1973) amounted to over $101 million, distributed among approximately 7,100 employees of the corpora-

---

[11] Gerald R. Roche, "Compensation and the Mobile Executive," *Harvard Business Review* 53 (November–December 1975): 59.

tion. The amount of money available for employee bonuses is determined by a complicated formula based on the corporation's net income. In the same year, the bonus fund for the Ford Motor Company amounted to over $64 million, disbursed among approximately 6,800 managers of the company. The amount was based on 6 percent of the profits after 10 percent of the capital used in the business had been deducted.

Incentive payments are frequently made in the form of cash. This has the advantage of satisfying the immediate financial needs of executives—needs that usually peak during the early and middle stages of their careers. However, as the executive progresses into higher income brackets (up to 50 percent), a growing portion of the cash payment will be consumed by taxes. Therefore, deferred payment plans with their tax-saving features have become increasingly popular. There is, however, the danger that preoccupation with tax saving and emphasis on retirement will cause some of the incentive value to the bonus to be lost.

Stock options

Stock option plans, during the past years, became a major device for attracting and retaining capable executives. These plans give company executives the right to purchase a certain amount of the company's stock at a stated fixed price. From 1950 until 1964, options could be granted at as much as 15 percent below the market price of the stock on the day they were granted. Under changes introduced by the Internal Revenue Service in 1964, the options cannot now be granted at less than current market price on the day they are declared. There is no obligation on the part of executives ever to exercise their options, and naturally they will not do so unless the market price of the stock advances far enough so that it pays for them to take action. In other words, if an option is declared when the market price of the stock is $50 per share, executives might want to wait until its price goes up to $55 before exercising their option to buy at $50. This waiting period, however, cannot extend beyond five years from the date the option is declared, whereas prior to 1964 the option expired in ten years. Profits derived from stock options are considered long-term capital gains and are taxable as such, provided the buyer holds the stock for at least three years. Before 1964, a six-month holding period was sufficient to qualify for the lower capital gains tax rate.

Such arrangements attract executives in the high income tax brackets. For them, stock options are preferable to substantial salary increases, which are taxed as normal income. However, the effects of the 1964 and 1969 revisions of the tax law virtually eliminate the possibility of capital gains profits from options. The law and severe slumps in the stock market have hampered the incentive value of stock option plans.

Even with these problems, many organizations still cling to the stock option. For example, a study of one hundred top industrial firms in 1974

A half-century of options

Stock options appeared in the early 1920s when capital gains were given favorable tax treatment under the Internal Revenue Code. However they were not widely used as a form of executive compensation until encouraged by the special tax advantages accorded them by the Code in 1950.[a] Thereafter the practice of granting stock options grew rapidly—too rapidly, in fact, for some government observers. Opposition on Capitol Hill mounted as a long and steep "bull" market frequently produced compensation Congress deemed disproportionate to the original objectives of the Code.

Consequently, in the Revenue Act of 1964 the legislation more strictly circumscribed the tax benefits accorded the options. And when these rules failed to stem the growth of the practice, the Tax Reform Act of 1969 was passed with provisions to limit the benefits even further. This soon prompted serious reevaluation of stock option plans by virtually all companies having them. Nevertheless, as recent surveys confirm,[b] a majority of firms decided in favor of retaining the mechanism.

Doubts have arisen once again, however, with the onset of the "bear" market of 1973. But this time the question in the minds of many corporate compensation executives is not whether the stock option plan should be continued, but what can be done about those options that are deeply under water. The frequency of such questions now being put to The Conference Board confirms the answer to that question is far from clear.

[a] Senate Report 2375, 81st Congress, Second Session.
[b] See Harland Fox, *Top Executive Compensation* (The Conference Board, 1974).
Source: Burton W. Teague, "Rescuing the Drowning Executive Stock Option," *Conference Board Record*, February 1975, p. 43. Used with permission.

showed eighty-seven companies used stock options in one form or another.[12] Why do these plans survive? Burton W. Teague writes:

One reason might be that options granted at the current market level could result in substantial gains for executives if, as some market analysts suggest, a new bull market may be in the making. Another reason could be that no one has yet devised an alternative means of granting tax-favored income to the executive at no measurable cost to the company. The cost/yield ratio is unbeatable, assuming the stock price rises.

But perhaps the prime reason can be found in the durability of the mechanism itself. The current desultory stock market is not the first crisis the stock option plan has faced. For the past two decades it has shown its ability to survive economic downturns and opposition by both government and stockholders.[13]

[12] "Current Compensations," *Compensation Review*, First quarter 1975, p. 8.
[13] Burton W. Teague, "Rescuing the Drowning Executive Stock Options," *Conference Board Record*, February 1975, pp. 40–44.

Profit sharing

Profit sharing is a popular form of executive compensation. Much like bonus-type incentive plans, profit sharing generally provides an annual distribution of funds to executives based on overall company performance. Unlike regular incentive plans, however, cash distributions are not made in the year earned. Rather, they are credited to the executive's account and allowed to accumulate over the years. Frequently, these funds are invested in the common stock of the firm with the anticipation of future appreciation. Such anticipations were certainly fulfilled in the case of the celebrated Sears, Roebuck plan, in which modest dollar investments grew to sizeable proportions for the participants.

Because of their deferred character, profit-sharing plans are being integrated with retirement programs. Typically, an executive must be with a company some years, usually five to ten, before receiving any vesting privileges in the firm's contributions. This means that the executive cannot take any of the company's contributions to the program if he or she changes jobs before the vesting period expires. Such a feature is a strong incentive for an executive to stay with the company. Indeed, in some companies, funds do not vest until retirement age is reached.

Pension plans

As we pointed out previously, high income tax rates have led top management to devise forms of deferred executive compensation. Prior to retirement, such compensation is not subject to income taxes. Executives are often much more interested in an assured income after they retire than in an increase in income at a time when they are already receiving high salaries. This is one reason why the popularity of pension plans has greatly increased. A pension plan provides executives with a reduced, though still sizable, income following retirement. And, although they will still have to pay income taxes on pension income in retirement years their tax brackets by then will be considerably lower.

Retirement benefits have become more generous since the 1950s, which marked the beginning of modern business pension systems. Benefit ranges tend to follow industrial patterns, with banks and insurance companies leading in terms of pension paid as a percentage of current salary. Figure 20-1 shows these percentages for the top three executives in one thousand companies across industry lines.

In addition to pension plans, there are other types of deferred executive compensation. For example, some enterprises enter into contractual agreements with executives stating that when they retire they will be available on a consultant basis to the enterprise for a fixed income. Other arrangements establish compensation levels for executives if they are elected to the board of directors. Still another form of deferred compensation involves a contract made between the enterprise and the retired executive, in

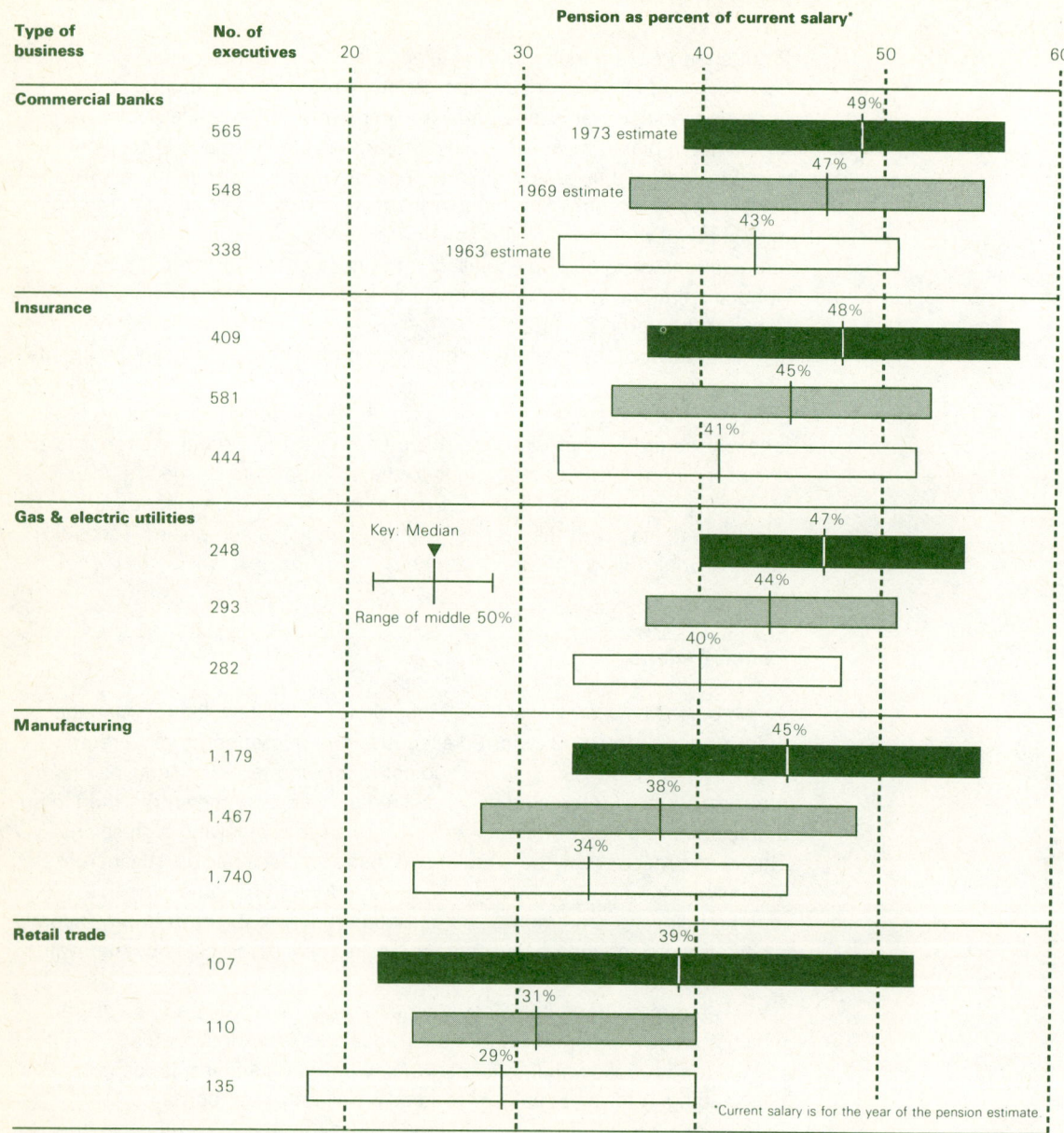

Figure 20-1 Estimated pension as percentage of current salary, 1973, 1969, and 1963, by type of business
Source: Harland Fox, "Top Executive Pensions," *Conference Board Record*, February 1975, p. 38. Used with permission.

which the executive is paid a sum of money for not working for any other firm, particularly for a competitor. In all these arrangements, care must be taken that there is no doubt about the deferred nature of the income and that the device is not merely intended to evade current taxes. Expert advice about legality and tax considerations should always be obtained.

Indirect financial compensation

Executive perquisites (perks) are an important element of compensation planning. "Perks" cover a multitude of items, from membership in luncheon clubs to tuition assistance for executives' children. Few, if any, of these perks are performance related. They are available to executives as benefits of employment with an organization. As might be expected, practices regulating the nature and amount of these benefits differ considerably from organization to organization. Generally, a package of benefits is worth between 5 and 15 percent of a manager's pretax salary. Since organizations have so many benefits to choose from (see Table 20-3), management should aim for a mix of perks that will be most attractive to its executives.

Table 20-3 Executive perquisites: A selected list

1 **Insured or Internal Revenue Service qualified benefits**
   Voluntary supplementary retirement benefits
   Voluntary supplementary life insurance and disability insurance
   Officers and directors liability insurance
   Profit sharing, thrift saving, stock purchase plans

2 **Special privileges**
   Financial counseling services
   Company loans for stock option exercise, stock purchase, home purchase, education, personal investment, and so forth
   Company cars
   Paid memberships (initiation and dues) to country clubs, athletic clubs, luncheon clubs, dinner clubs, professional associations
   Liberal expense accounts
   Extra time off from work, sabbatical leaves
   Company housing, hotel suites
   Income deferral
   Employment or termination contracts
   Combined business and vacation trips
   Second office in-home or near-home location
   Executive medical examinations
   Executive dining room privilege
   Unique investment opportunities.
   Special office decorating allowance

3 **Expense assumptions**
   Educational assistance (tuition, dependent scholarships or loans)
   Discounts on company products, services, or use of company facilities
   Uncovered family medical and dental expenses

Source: Robert A. Sbarra, "The New Language of Executive Compensation," *Personnel,* November–December 1975, p. 12. Reprinted by permission of the publisher from *Personnel,* © 1975 by AMACOM, a division of American Management Associations.

Compensation contingencies

Compensation borders closely on motivational issues, which we discuss in the next Part. However, there are three practical contingencies that often have some bearing on the success of a compensation program: communication, participation, and disclosure.

Communication

Direct and indirect compensation to managers make up a large part of the cost of doing business. Therefore, managers should know what their total compensation package is worth for informational, as well as for motivational, reasons. Managers can use many techniques to obtain this information. One, the benefit audit approach, is illustrated in Table 20-4.

Table 20-4 Summary page from a typical benefit-audit statement

	Your total pay package	
	Your yearly contributions	Estimated cost if you bought it all
Basic and major medical	$138	$1,101
Salary continuation and disability insurance	none	2,261
Life and accident insurance	none	535
Pension plan	none	3,021
Social security	632	1,264
Total	$770	$8,182
Net value of benefits		$ 7,412
Annual salary		$35,000
Total pay package value		$42,412

This report tells you what your company-provided benefits can mean to you and your family at retirement or in case of illness, disability, or death. There is no way of knowing how many dollars you will actually receive. The table above, however, shows your yearly contributions and the estimated cost in annual individual insurance and benefit policy premiums if you were to buy this protection and income yourself. The company pays the full cost of your basic and major medical insurance, salary continuation, long-term coverage, and your pension. You and the company together share the cost of social security and the medical insurance program.
Source: George W. Hettenhouse, Wilbur G. Lewellen, Howard P. Lanser, and Howard L. James, "Communicating the Compensation Package," *Personnel*, November–December 1975, p. 22. Reprinted by permission of the publisher from *Personnel*, © 1975 by AMACOM, a division of American Management Associations.

Participation

Soliciting planning information from managers on the compensation program is often worth the effort and expense entailed. This is particularly true in the case of executive perks. There is little point in preparing a package of benefits without finding out what the people who will receive them want and need. Often, a survey of executives will indicate the kinds and amounts of benefits desired, in addition to a distribution of benefits in a compensation package.[14] Such information will help establish a highly regarded compensation system, which may cost no more than if the managers' participation in designing the program had not been sought.

Disclosure

Secrecy of managerial salaries is another issue in compensation. Most managers believe that salary information should not be disclosed. However, some behavioral scientists argue for greater openness about salaries, feeling that such openness has motivational advantages; others maintain that disclosure depends on the situation. For example, Thompson and Pronsky found that disclosure works best where performance can be measured objectively, where people are not closely interdependent on the job, where job standards can be specified clearly, and where efforts and results can be related over short periods of time.[15] Since these conditions do not apply to many managerial jobs, it appears that discretion about salaries often is the best strategy.

Summary

The objectives of compensation management are equity, consistency, motivation, and competitiveness. Most modern organizations offer their executives compensation packages. These packages may include salary, bonuses, stock options, profit sharing, and pension plans. In addition to these direct forms of financial compensation, there are also a number of executive perquisites that must be considered as part of the total compensation picture. The value of the compensation package should be communicated to all managers. And, sometimes it is advisable to encourage managers' participation in the design of certain aspects of the program.

Discussion questions

1. "No one is worth $750,000 per year salary." Debate both sides of this statement.
2. We often hear about the relative merits of being "a big fish in a small pond" versus being "a small fish in a big pond." How does this cliché translate into compensation issues for the individual?
3. How would you value the perks that go with managerial positions?

[14] Lawrence M. Baytos, "Employee Participation in Compensation Planning," *Compensation Review*, Second Quarter 1976, pp. 25–38.

[15] Paul Thompson and John Pronsky, "Secrecy or Disclosure in Management Compensation," *Business Horizons*, June 1975, p. 74.

Supplementary readings

Maurer, Otto, and Hellerman, M. Kasey. "Executive Compensation in the 1980s." *Conference Board Record,* April 1976.

Ricklefs, Roger. "Executive Fringe Benefit: Cold Cash." *Wall Street Journal,* September 5, 1973. Reprinted in *Dimensions in Modern Management,* 2d ed., edited by Patrick E. Connor. Boston: Houghton Mifflin, 1978.

Roche, Gerald R. "Compensation and the Mobile Executive." *Harvard Business Review,* November–December 1975, pp. 53–62.

Cases for Part IV

Case IV/1

The likely candidate

The Allen Company is a manufacturer of electronic components, with several manufacturing and assembly plants in various locations in the United States. The position of branch manager has become vacant in a plant located in a medium-sized midwestern city. The company president, Charles Dubois, appointed an ad hoc committee, consisting of three line executives at headquarters to search for a suitable manager. The committee was charged with screening potential candidates and making a recommendation to the president from among present employees, if possible, in line with Allen's policy of promotion from within. With the help of an effective appraisal system, which keeps management informed of junior executives' progress, it was not difficult to reduce the number of suitable candidates to a few. After checking all available records, reviewing personnel history, and interviewing possible candidates, the committee informed Dubois it was ready to submit its suggestions to him.

In an executive meeting, the search committee suggested two good candidates to fill the branch manager's position. One of them is Jack Smith, thirty years old, who joined the company about eight years ago, after graduating from college. Smith has been through various phases of the executive training program and has held several positions in a number of plants, the last being that of assistant plant manager in southern California. He has a record of good performance wherever he has been. Smith is married and has two children.

The other candidate is George O'Connell. He is thirty-five years old, married, and has three children. He has worked for the Allen company for the past twelve years, joining it after graduating as a mechanical engineer. He, too, has moved through various responsible positions within the firm and has an excellent record. In his most recent position, he has served for three years as a customer's service manager in the Chicago plant. While living in Chicago, O'Connell has been studying part time toward a master's degree in business administration, which he will receive shortly.

After listening to the committee's presentation and studying the records of the two candidates, Dubois suggested that O'Connell visit headquarters for a personal interview. The president was sure that O'Connell was a better choice for the job than was Smith. Before the meeting ended, Louise Hillsdale, a member of the search committee, thought she should give Dubois some additional information. She said:

"We checked out the candidates very carefully. In so doing, we learned that Mrs. O'Connell has a dark complexion and Oriental features. She is from the Philippines. The O'Connells met while both were undergraduate students and married after graduation; they have three school-age children. We also learned that she is quite a joiner of organizations and causes, and by this I do not mean garden clubs, literary societies, or art appreciation groups."

Questions

1 Does Hillsdale's statement throw a different light on the situation?
2 Should considerations of this sort be part of managerial selection criteria?
3 If you were Dubois, what would you do now?

Case IV/2

The hatchet man

Several members of the board met for lunch and casually began to discuss the replacement of Harvey Simon, who is due to retire from the presidency in about six months, when he reaches the mandatory retirement age of sixty-five. Simon, who was not at the luncheon, has been the chief executive officer of Hargrove Press for twenty years. He has managed the company with a steady hand and has achieved moderate annual growth: the firm showed steady profits and paid its regular dividends. Some of the directors often thought that Simon was overly concerned with maintaining his management position and did not provide the necessary dynamics for all the potential growth of the company.

Also, Simon had surrounded himself with a group of executives of similar ideology and drive. Although most did a fair job in fulfilling their duties, they were imbued with the philosophy of management maintenance and a degree of apathy. None of them would make a suitable president, with the necessary drive and capacity to increase the volume of sales and to expand the activities of Hargrove Press. Therefore, the board had decided to go outside the company for a replacement, preferably to someone working for a competitor, even if the compensation arrangements would be high.

While they were discussing the problem of succession, Dick McDonough, a member of the board, suggested that it might be a good idea also to bring in a proven professional administrator for a one- to two-year period, for the express purpose of cleaning up the old organization. The arrangement would have to be clearly understood by the new chief executive and would have to remain confidential. A great deal of discussion followed McDonough's suggestion.

Questions

1 McDonough's suggestion is, basically, to appoint a "hatchet man." What do you think about this type of appointment?
2 Do you think someone would accept this type of appointment?
3 Do you think this is a good solution?

Case IV/3

The board's dilemma

The executive committee of the board of directors of Unico Company met over lunch to discuss the recent resignation of the president, Fred Rosa. Rosa had been president for a year. Before the appointment, he had held important executive positions, over many years, in other leading companies, and he had come highly recommended. He was the third president to resign within the last three years. The reason for his resignation—as confidentially told to some members of the committee—was Francis Chesterfield, the former president of the company and current chairman of the board. Chesterfield's failing health and age caused him to relinquish the presidency three years ago. At that time, he was sixty-one years old, four years younger than the mandatory retirement age of sixty-five. The directors elected him to be chairman of the board while searching for a new president to serve as chief executive officer.

Rosa's reason is the same as that of his two predecessors. Apparently, Chesterfield, after leaving the president's office, still wants to run the company. He overrules the president, does not keep him informed, and generally undermines his position. The members of the executive committee are pondering what to do. They realize that this situation must be dealt with effectively, otherwise the company will be unable to attract executives from the outside. And, since Chesterfield never believed in nor practiced broad delegation of authority, the company cannot rely on a sufficient supply of experienced executives from within. None of the parties involved holds any large portion of the company's stock.

Questions

1. What steps should be taken now?
2. How can such a dilemma be avoided in the future?

Case IV/4

The informal promotion

Betty Nichols, R.N., graduated from the local university with a bachelor's degree in nursing and, after a few years as a regular staff nurse, was persuaded to take a head nurse's position in the medical-surgical division of St. John's Hospital. This job involves the supervision of many beds and a good number of R.N.'s, L.P.N.'s, nurses aides, and orderlies.

Time was always a problem to Nichols. Although she believed in and practiced delegation, she could not resist remaining involved in direct patient care more than she should. This demanded time that she needed to oversee the daily round of administrative problems that came to her.

When Nichols found that one of her employees, an experienced L.P.N. named Rose Simpson, was eager to take on additional responsibilities, she began to assign some administrative work to her. Simpson did an excellent job and began to handle more and more administrative details for Nichols. After some time, she, in effect, filled the job of assistant head nurse, although such a position did not exist on the hospital's organizational chart.

After many months had passed, during which this informal arrangement worked smoothly, Nichols requested a promotion for Simpson to the position of assistant head nurse. The director of nursing services was willing and able to create such a position; however, it was felt that Simpson lacked adequate formal education for the job and that the hospital accrediting agency would insist that an R.N. hold such a position.

This situation left Nichols with a difficult problem. She could not obtain a change in status or even a salary increase for Simpson because she was already receiving top wages as an L.P.N.

Questions

1. What should Nichols do?
2. Should Nichols have allowed Simpson to perform the administrative work?
3. What should Simpson do?

Case IV/5

The appraisal interview

Janet Baker, the director of marketing for the Ace Distributing Company, has just finished the annual evaluations of her immediate line subordinates. Among them was an evaluation of Henry Lorenz, the sales manager. Lorenz has been with the company several years. Although he is doing a good job in the field, he has serious shortcomings in a number of other areas. Baker often has tried to discuss these areas with him, but to no avail; Lorenz simply will not accept criticism and has done nothing to correct his shortcomings.

Thinking of the forthcoming evaluation interview, Baker decided to contact her former professor at the university to see whether or not he could suggest a method of approaching Lorenz. The professor suggested that she ask Lorenz to evaluate himself, so she sent Lorenz an evaluation form and requested that he return it within a week. Lorenz returned it promptly, and Baker found that he not only had given himself a superior rating on each point but had concluded that he was ready for a more challenging position in the company.

Baker was studying the evaluation again as the door opened and Lorenz came into her office for his evaluation interview.

Questions

1. How desirable are self-evaluations?
2. Did Baker's former professor give her poor advice?
3. Should Lorenz accept and correct his shortcomings?
4. How would you handle the evaluation interview with Lorenz? Role-play the interview.

Case IV/6

Simmons Retail Chain Store: Selection of an auditor

Harry Jamison, the employment manager of the Simmons Retail Chain Store Company, returned to his office from a luncheon engagement with two assistant controllers where several important matters had been discussed. Among them was the company's expansion program, which included the establishment and acquisition of new stores throughout the southwestern part of the country. These changes, plus the normal amount of turnover, had greatly increased the need for additions to the company's accounting and internal auditing staffs.

Several of the traveling auditors had been promoted to more responsible positions, some were made regional controllers, and others were brought into the Chicago office as department heads. Two experienced employees had retired during the past year, and four had left the company to take positions with other companies. As a result of these changes and difficulties in hiring new auditors as replacements, eight requisitions for either experienced accountants or auditors were in the employment office. It was desirable but not necessary that the auditors be certified public accountants.

The assistant controllers were convinced that ten years of accounting or auditing experience was necessary for an individual to qualify as a retail chain store auditor. Harry Jamison believed that it might be possible to employ college graduates with specialized training in accounting, place them on a planned job rotation program, and develop them into auditors in five or six years. Simmons' policy, however, was to hire only experienced personnel, so Mr. Jamison usually sought auditors through newspaper advertisements and private employment agencies.

The pressing problem of the moment was to fill the immediate vacancies with qualified people. In recent years, Jamison had experienced extreme difficulty in hiring new auditors. Part of the problem was that the starting salary paid to a new auditor was somewhat lower than the prevailing rate in the Chicago area (about $500 a year lower). Jamison believed,

Source: Reprinted from *Problems and Policies in Personnel Management,* 2nd edition by Joseph W. Towle, Sterling H. Schoen, and Raymond L. Hilgert. Copyright © 1972 by Houghton Mifflin Company. Used by permission.

however, that most of the problem lay in the nature of the job itself. Simmons' auditors were required to travel extensively and to be away from their homes for long periods of time, sometimes several months. Qualified accountants with family responsibilities objected to the long absences from home, and often turned down positions at Simmons because of this problem. Several auditors had resigned in the past specifically because they disliked being away from their homes on extended assignments.

Harry reached into his pocket and pulled out a newspaper clipping which the chief controller, Mr. Griffin, had given to him. It was a section from the want ads and was heavily marked with pencil. It read:

Wanted

Position in accounting or auditing work by well qualified man with 25 years of financial experience with two corporations and one bank. Long service in responsible positions marred by one human error, an embezzlement. Interested in discussing employment with corporations executive needing the services of good accountant, controller or auditor. Single. Will travel. Box M-103.

The penciled notation indicated that Mr. Griffin was willing to talk to this man. However, Harry knew that Mr. Griffin was aware of the company's unwritten policy against hiring people with prison records. In addition, this applicant was probably in his late forties or early fifties, and the company seldom hired men over forty years of age.

Just then the telephone rang. It was Mr. Griffin.

"Harry," said Mr. Griffin, "how about my requisitions for accountants and auditors? Look, boy, this thing is getting serious. We need men and fast."

Jamison answered, "Griff, I've been saying for years that we need to establish some type of policies or training program in regards to where, when, and how we're to get and keep qualified auditors. It's going to be a tough proposition to find eight experienced men right away."

"Maybe so," replied Mr. Griffin, "but the problem is that we need auditors today. I say, let's get whatever men we can get today and worry about the policies some other day when we can afford to think about them. Do you think we should talk to the guy in the want ad who has the prison record?"

For a moment, Jamison pondered what his reply should be.

Questions

1. Should Jamison reply to the ad and set up an interview?
2. What do you think of the company's unwritten policy against hiring people with prison records?
3. What should the Simmons Company do to avoid such a dilemma? Would hiring accounting majors after graduation be the answer?

Part V

Influencing

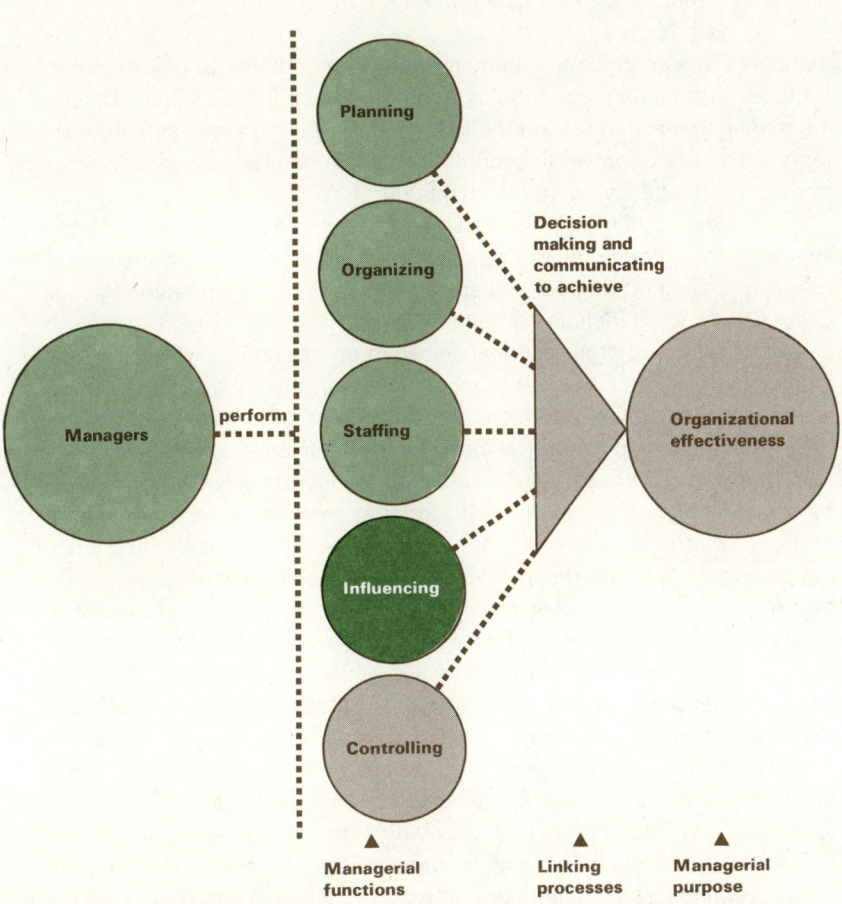

The influencing function Influencing enables managers to evoke goal-directed action from others in the organizational system. It is a human resource function, one particularly concerned with behavior—individual, group, and organizational.

To perform effectively, managers must be aware of the human activities in which they take part and must understand how they affect, and are affected by, other people. Managers must be sensitive to interpersonal relationships if they expect to influence any of the people who surround them. And, clearly, managers must influence if they are to fulfill their role of getting things done through others.

Influencing others, in a planned, purposeful way, is a skill. In the past, however, influencing was done on a hit-or-miss basis. Little purposeful or scientific planning was involved, except that provided by the early management pioneers in the form of work incentive programs. Moreover, negative persuasion or coercion through disciplinary action seemed to be more common than were positive incentives. This was largely a result of the domination of traditional organization theory by the notion of hierarchy. Generally speaking, the vertical chain of *command* was considered to be the only relevant system for evoking action in an organization.

As we have seen, the behavioral sciences, offering new dimensions to managers' understanding of human motivation and behavior, were not introduced into management theory and practice until the 1930s. No longer did managers have to rely on the limited ability of economic incentive systems or the use of power to secure action. The behavioral sciences pointed to new, more effective methods of influence.

Today, the influencing process is concerned mainly with the interpersonal and intergroup relationships that each executive must manage in order to obtain collaboration and cooperation in achieving organizational goals. Older fields, which include human relations, and newer ones, like organizational behavior and organizational development, contribute directly to the influencing process. Their contributions are felt in two ways: through research and conceptual development and through the training methods they have devised to help executives become more effective influencers.

In management circles the influencing function is known by many names. Sometimes it is called *motivating;* at other times, *actuating;* and often, *directing.* Regardless of the name, the behavioral view of the influencing process focuses on the question: How do managers obtain the most and best from subordinates while creating a climate for personal fulfillment? Or, what constitutes effective superior-subordinate relationships?

Recently, behavioral analysis of the influencing process has been applied to other organizational relationships, notably to the interaction among managers of roughly the same rank. Today's complex organizations contain numerous managerial specialists, whose presence compounds the number of existing lateral or horizontal relationships. New technologies, complicated structures, well-educated employees with high levels of expectations, all make management's influencing function more challenging. The modern organization is clearly an intricate network of influence patterns. It cannot be easily categorized into a series of superior-subordinate relations.

Thus, the theoretical climate has changed, and with it our thinking. We now speak of interdependencies among elements and functions of organizations; we discuss horizontal, vertical, and diagonal flows of information and resources. The behavioral sciences help us to find meaning in these new concepts; they provide the knowledge that enables managers to perform their influencing functions more effectively.

Chapter 21

The influencing process

Objectives of the chapter

1 To review the meaning, bases, and types of authority in the organization.
2 To consider the meaning and uses of power in the organization.
3 To examine influence—a process based on the combined exercise of authority and power.
4 To introduce the principal factors found in the influencing process.

Influencing is the process by which people are induced to act in ways they otherwise might not. The basis of influence is usually some sort of power or authority.

This Part is devoted to the complexities in the influencing process. In this chapter, we introduce the subject by discussing power and authority as bases of influence and presenting the major ideas encompassed in the process.

Authority

Authority has already been treated at some length in Chapter 8, so we need not dwell on its characteristics. A brief review, however, is probably in order.

Bases of authority

In one of the earliest examinations of authority, Max Weber identified three bases of authority:[1]

---

[1] Max Weber, *The Theory of Social and Economic Organizations*. See also Max Weber, "The Three Types of Legitimate Rule," trans. Hans Gerth, *Berkeley Journal of Sociology* 4 (1958): 1–11.

- *Traditional authority*   Rooted in tradition, or custom.
- *Legal-rational authority*   Rooted in the official and rationally enacted rules of the organization.
- *Charismatic authority*   Rooted in the personal devotion of the follower to the ruler.

Building on Weber's ideas and those of some other writers, Peabody concluded that there are four principal bases on which authority rests: external factors, position, competence, and personal qualities.[2]

Types of authority

We can identify three primary types of organizational authority:

- *Positional authority*   Based on acceptance of the position that a manager holds in an organization.
- *Functional authority*   Based on expertise.
- *Personal authority*   Based on personal magnetism, through which a ruler is able to command followers.

A manager might possess all three, but need not.

Compliance

People comply with authority that they perceive to be legitimate. They accept it because they believe that the goals and communications established by such authority are consistent with their personal needs and values. This is the only way that spontaneous and willing collaboration can be produced. Much of authority's legitimacy used to be based on an employee's automatic acceptance of vertical chain of command—type relationships. However, with the growing complexity of firms and the increasing need for technical experts in business, other kinds of organizational relationship are becoming important. These include the lateral (horizontal) relations among managers, which we have discussed.

Such relations, rather than being based on the chain of command, are founded in the interdependency of functions. These relationships foster an entirely different form of managerial behavior, one in which compliance, cooperation, and coordination of tasks are achieved through such activities as:

1. *Creative problem solving*   In which effective managerial teams produce inventive decisions that are satisfying to the organization and to the individuals on the team.

[2] Robert L. Peabody, *Organizational Authority* (New York: Atherton, 1964).

2. *Bargaining and negotiation* Through which managers mutually exchange resources in order to improve the performance of their departments.
3. *Win-lose conflict* In which two managers or groups of managers compete, the outcome resulting in a defeat for one and a victory for the other.

Thus, compliance and coordination are much more challenging to achieve when functional and personal authority supplement conventional reliance on traditional authority. Employees cannot be ordered to act on the assumption that they accept the chain of command.

Power

Superficially, power is a straightforward concept. It is a form of domination giving its possessor the ability to direct the actions of others toward predetermined goals. As applied to organizations, this definition of power is based on two important ideas.

First, managers are able to influence the behavior of others because they control some of the organization's resources. These resources, which managers can either distribute to subordinates or withhold from them, consist of the values that people seek from employment. They include money, opportunity for advancement, security, and satisfying work assignments. Although these values are stated in positive terms, they also have a negative side if any or all are withheld.

Second, that power is necessary is implicit in our definition. People do not always willingly and spontaneously accept authority. Power is latent in every organization; it is an ever-present potential available to secure action when authority fails. It is natural that people bring to organizations diverse motives and needs. Frequently, these motives and needs will correspond to organizational objectives, but occasionally they will not. When this incongruence between organizational goals and individual goals occurs, power must be used to influence.

Sources

Power rests on managers' ability to administer incentive and sanction systems. These systems are, in turn, based on the resources controlled by management. Therefore, power, like traditional authority, is institutional and impersonal.

However, we have also said that power is latent. It appears only when legitimate authority is not perceived by subordinates. Thus, whether power is needed or not, the extent of its application is highly personal and depends greatly on the kind of interpersonal relationship that exists between superiors and subordinates. If subordinates willingly accept their superiors, the superiors will seldom need power to achieve their goals. Of course, the reverse is also true. Clearly, the application of power relates directly to an individual's leadership ability and situation within a particular department or other organizational unit.

Moreover, it is a matter of personal administrative skill to know when to use power and what kind of power to use. Management has at its disposal several positive incentives and negative sanctions. Their appropriate use and timing is crucial for the effective operation of an organization.

Outcomes

It is interesting to examine the views of Herbert Simon on the use of power because they are shared by many contemporary management scholars. Simon believes that dominating employees by power is not an effective way to manage an enterprise; he therefore speaks of the "poverty of power."[3] He sets forth several reasons for his belief.

First, power is not a one-way street. Although managers can derive seemingly overwhelming power from the resources at their disposal, employees can retaliate in a number of ways—through absenteeism, waste, minimum compliance, slowdown, and malicious obedience.[4] Overreliance on power to secure objectives is dysfunctional from an influencing standpoint. In other words, power meets resistance, which tends to require more power to overcome, generating more resistance, and so on.

Second, although managers' control of positive motivators, such as financial rewards, may seem to provide them with a strong source of influence, this source is not as strong as it appears to be. Behavioral scientists have shown that employees work for more than money. Therefore, influence based solely on financial incentive is likely to produce insufficient results.

Third, in a very practical sense, using power costs more than securing compliance through acceptance.

Authority, power, and influence

A mixture of authority and power exists in any concrete administrative situation. Of course, it is desirable that managerial authority be accepted in any such situation; to the extent that it is not, power fills the *influence gap*. Figure 21-1 visually portrays the nature of this idea.

This figure shows a situation in which the manager has much, but not total, subordinate acceptance. To compensate for the deficiency, the manager uses some latent power to move the group toward departmental objectives. This influence gap may merely represent one employee who has not wholly accepted the manager's authority, or it may be that the whole work

---

[3] Herbert A. Simon, "Authority," in *Research in Industrial Human Relations*, ed. Conrad M. Arensberg et al. (New York: Harper & Row, 1957), pp. 108–110.
[4] A maliciously obedient employee actually complies to the letter of a command and eliminates all flexibility from the execution of the task. Often this results in the failure of a project and the embarrassment of the superior, without blame to the subordinate, "who was only following orders." See Peter C. Reid, "A Case of Malicious Obedience," *Supervisory Management* 8, no. 7 (July 1963): 4–8.

group has backed off slightly from full acceptance. Whatever the case, power is necessary for the achievement of the aims of the department.

The sociologist Robert Nisbet presents a somewhat different conception of the relationship between authority and power.[5] He believes that these two concepts are different sides of a single coin—and that the coin itself is influence.

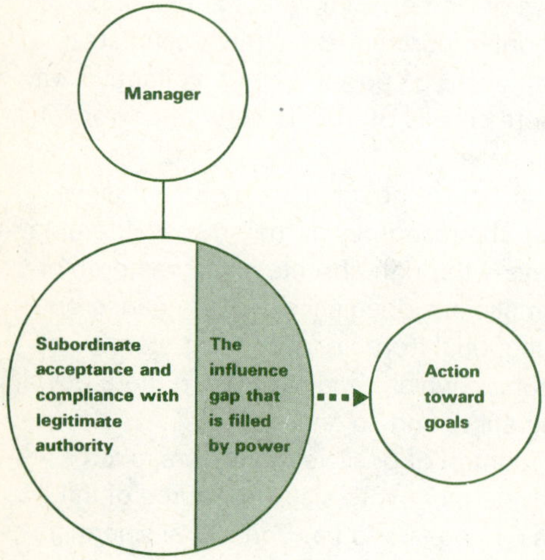

Figure 21-1 Power, authority, and the influence gap

Still another view of the authority-power relationship is provided by the influence continuum shown in Figure 21-2. It is hard to conceive of any management situation where both elements are not present to some extent. However, one element tends to predominate. Nevertheless, because there is an infinite number of points on any continuum, there can be an infinite number of power-authority mixes. The crucial factor from a managerial standpoint is to pick the optimal mix for the situation. At point 1 in Figure 21-2, the use of power predominates. This might occur when a manager supervises a number of low-skilled manual workers who have little, if any, identification with the values of the organization.

At point 2, we might assume that the manager is supervising a number of highly trained CPAs who possess considerable professional commitment and a greater identification with the goals of their department, if not the whole firm. To influence their subordinates successfully in this type of situation, managers must build on the acceptance of legitimate authority rather than power. For a variety of reasons, most of which we have already discussed, today's managers submerge power as far as possible beneath the surface of superior-subordinate relations.

---

[5] Robert A. Nisbet, *The Sociological Tradition* (New York: Basic Books, 1967), pp. 3—7.

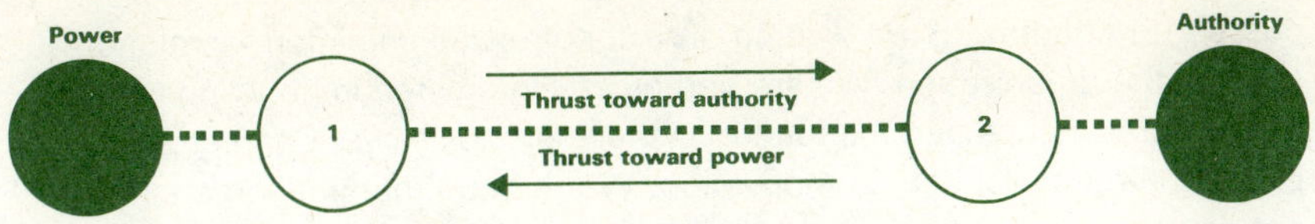

Figure 21-2 The influence continuum

In summary, managers must mix authority and power in a manner suitable to the human and organizational variables that they confront. Part of the art of management lies in selecting the mode of influence that will lead most effectively to the accomplishment of organizational objectives and, concurrently, provide satisfaction for the people in the firm. Another part lies in creating a mix of power and authority that will optimize flexibility and adaptation to change. Critics say that reliance on power to obtain compliance unduly rigidifies the organization. Acceptance of authority, on the other hand, facilitates change.

Contingency factors in influencing

As we shall see, effective influencing is contingent on a number of factors, the most important being: characteristics that individuals bring with them to the organizational situation, certain properties of that situation, and situational conditions that develop with time.[6] Figure 21-3 illustrates these factors and their effect on developmental relationships.

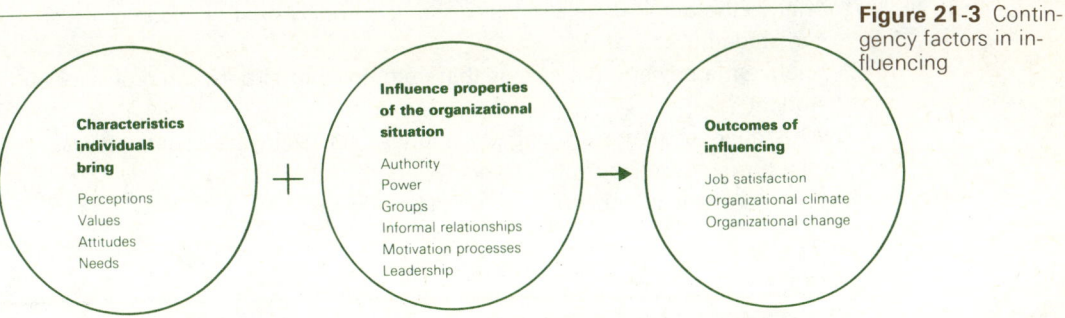

Figure 21-3 Contingency factors in influencing

This Part is divided into chapters that deal with the various factors depicted in Figure 21-3. Chapter 22 is concerned with the basic unit of organizations—the individual. Specifically, the chapter describes basic individual characteristics, focusing on perceptions, values, attitudes, and needs.

[6] For a thorough treatment of this idea, the student is referred to George C. Homans, *The Human Group* (New York: Harcourt Brace Jovanovich, 1950).

The importance of these characteristics to people's behavior also is discussed. In Chapter 23 we expand our scope, examining informal relationships in the organization. We are particularly interested in how and why people form groups and the functions these groups serve. Chapter 24 explores the nature of human motivation. We then tie that phenomenon to a critical managerial task—leadership. We conclude our discussion of influencing with an examination of its important outcomes: organizational climate, job satisfaction, and organizational change.

Summary

The influencing process primarily rests on the exercise of authority and power. Managers' authority is usually of one or more types: Positional, functional, and/or personal.

Power differs from authority. Authority is rooted in legitimacy; power is based on ability—the ability to control resources, thereby evoking compliance from subordinates. If managers rely on power to be their chief means of influencing, they are likely to experience some undesirable outcomes. Typical of these are employee retaliation, insufficient results, and high cost. Successful managers use authority as much as possible in exercising influence, tempered with power when necessary.

Discussion questions

1 Analyze the authority relationships that commonly exist between professor and student.
2 Analyze the power relationships that commonly exist between professor and student.
3 What changes that are taking place in your university are affecting these relationships? outside your university?
4 What forms of influence are used in this course?

Supplementary readings

Bierstedt, Robert. "An Analysis of Social Power." *American Sociological Review* 15 (1950): 730–738.
French, John R. P., and Raven, Bertram. "The Bases of Social Power." In *Studies in Social Power,* edited by D. Cartwright, pp. 118–149. Ann Arbor: University of Michigan Press, 1959. Reprinted in *Dimensions in Modern Management,* 2d ed., edited by Patrick E. Connor. Boston: Houghton Mifflin, 1978.

Hickson, D. J.; Hinings, C. R.; Lee, C. A.; Schnech, R. E.; and Pennings, J. M. "A Strategic Contingencies' Theory of Intraorganizational Power." *Administrative Science Quarterly* 16 (June 1971): 216–229.

Presthus, Robert V. "Authority in Organizations." *Public Administration Review* 20 (1960): 86–91.

Rogers, Mary F. "Instrumental and Infra-resources: The Bases of Power." *American Journal of Sociology* 79 (1974): 1418–1433.

Chapter 22

The individual in the organization

Objectives of the chapter

1. To identify specific human aspects of managing: perceptions, values, attitudes, and needs.
2. To describe the ways in which perceptions are formed and their importance.
3. To define and describe values and attitudes.
4. To examine the ways in which values and attitudes underlie people's behavior.
5. To identify the variety of needs that people attempt to satisfy.
6. To describe the importance of needs in affecting people's behavior in the organization.

People bring to their organizations a number of characteristics: opinions, attitudes, values, perceptions, and needs. These characteristics are, of course, integral to people's behavior, and managers must recognize and deal with these factors if they want to be effective motivators and leaders. In this chapter, we consider four of the most important factors: perceptions, values, attitudes, and needs.

Perception

Individuals experience an incredible number and variety of sights, sounds, smells, tastes, and tactile sensations. *Perception* is the process by which they take in all these stimuli and make sense of them. Social scientists define it this way:

When . . . one understands the relationships of objects which were previously merely raw, undifferentiated sensory experiences, he is said to perceive these objects.[1]

[1] Julius Gould and William L. Kolb, eds., *A Dictionary of the Social Sciences* (New York: Free Press, 1964), p. 491.

Basically, the process of perceiving works in this way: individuals experience a set of stimuli (sights, sounds, smells, and so forth) and mentally arrange them in some way that makes sense for them, thus developing an organized perception. For example, we observe a witness at a congressional committee hearing begin a statement, stop, talk to someone sitting nearby, and then finish the statement on a somewhat different note. We take in all the various sight and sound stimuli and form our perception: the witness was advised, probably by a lawyer, that the statement needed to be altered.

Reality: Interpreted or created?

Three baseball umpires were discussing their approaches to their job.
"I calls 'em as I sees 'em," said the first.
"I calls 'em as they is," remarked the second.
The third, and probably wisest, observed, "They ain't nothin' till I calls 'em."

Our knowledge of the witness, the lawyer, the committee's purpose, and the circumstances may add further to our perception. That is, perceptions are formed when stimuli are organized by means of some existing *frame of reference*.

Frame of reference

As children gain experience and maturity they begin to learn that certain patterns of stimuli have meaning. Thus, children learn not to touch a glowing burner on the top of a stove and not to put a hairpin in an electrical socket. They quickly learn to organize other stimuli. For example, on a warm summer day, there are children playing outside and the sound of a bell tinkles a few blocks away—an ice-cream truck is approaching. A child who has never experienced—never seen, heard, or even read about—an ice-cream truck would not form that perception. The child would not have the proper organizing device—a frame of reference.

Where do people acquire their frames of reference? Basically, through experience. Parents and teachers help children to develop accurate and useful frames. The army adds its contribution, as does the university. Often, managers attempt to suggest frames of reference to new employees ("Well, that's fine in school, but the way we do things *here* is . . ."). Frames of reference are important because they are the lens through which we experience and interpret reality.[2]

[2] E. Brunswick, *Perception and the Representative Design of Psychological Experiments,* 2d ed. (Berkeley: University of California Press, 1956).

Selective perception

Frames of reference allow stimuli to be organized into a sensible pattern. One of the ways in which this happens is for some stimuli to be selected and others to be rejected, or screened out. As an experiment, attend a nature movie with two friends, one of whom has strong antigun views and the other, an ardent hunter. After the film, listen to each of them describe the movie; their respective descriptions should indicate clearly the way in which people perceive selectively.

On a more mundane level, it is evident that people screen out many stimuli, while accepting and processing others. Traffic noise, background music, ringing telephones in a large office—all are stimuli that are screened out. The sound of an automobile collision, our name being paged over an intercom system—both are stimuli that are processed. Often we are unaware of the selecting process; the roar of silence that follows an air conditioner's sudden halt is a case in point.

Finally, selective perception operates in task behavior. The most obvious situation is one we have discussed before: specialists viewing and acting on problems based on their specialized perspectives. A few years ago, researchers had twenty-three managers read and evaluate a long, factual case about a steel company. There were six sales, five production, four accounting, and eight miscellaneous managers. All were asked to identify the major problems facing the company. The result: virtually all managers identified as most critical a problem closely related to their specialty.[3] In short, we tend to hear what we want to hear, see what we want to see, and screen out contradictory information.

Frame of reference (writer unknown)

Dear Mom and Dad:

Since I left for college I have been remiss in writing and I am sorry for my thoughtlessness in not having written before. I will bring you up to date now, but before you read on, please sit down. You are not to read any further unless you are sitting down. Okay?

Well, then, I am getting along pretty well now. The skull fracture and the concussion I got when I jumped out of the window of my dormitory when it caught on fire shortly after my arrival here is pretty well healed now. I only spent two weeks in the hospital and now I can see almost normally and only get those sick headaches once a day. Fortunately, the fire in the dormitory, and my jump, was witnessed by an attendant at the gas station near the dorm, and he was the one who called the Fire Department and the ambulance. He also visited me in the hospital and since I had nowhere to live because of the burnt-out dormitory, he was kind enough to invite me to

---

[3] Dewitt C. Dearborn and Herbert A. Simon, "Selective Perception," *Sociometry* 21 (1958): 140–143.

share his apartment with him. It's really a basement room, but it's kind of cute. He is a very fine boy and we have fallen deeply in love and are planning to get married. We haven't got the exact date yet, but it will be before my pregnancy begins to show.

Yes, Mother and Dad, I am pregnant. I know how much you are looking forward to being grandparents and I know you will welcome the baby and give it the same love and devotion and tender care you gave me when I was a child. The reason for the delay in our marriage is that my boy friend has a minor infection which prevents us from passing our premarital blood tests and I carelessly caught it from him.

I know that you will welcome him into our family with open arms. He is kind and, although not well educated, he is ambitious. Although he is of a different race and religion than ours, I know your often-expressed tolerence will not permit you to be bothered by that.

Now that I have brought you up to date, I want to tell you that there was no dormitory fire, I did not have a concussion or skull fracture, I was not in the hospital, I am not pregnant, I am not engaged, I am not infected, and there is no boy friend in my life. However, I am getting a D in History and F in Science and I want you to see those marks in their proper perspective.

Your loving daughter,
Susie

Source: W. E. Scott, Jr., and L. L. Cummings, eds., *Readings in Organizational Behavior and Human Performance*, rev. ed. (Homewood, Illinois: Richard D. Irwin, 1973), p. 72.

Managerial implications

Experiencing, selecting, organizing, and interpreting stimuli occur as we drive down the street, listen to a rock concert, or perform tasks at work. We primarily are concerned, of course, with this last context. The way in which people perceive stimuli — that is, accurately or inaccurately — is very important to managers. Specifically, effective managers must be able to understand and handle distortions in the perception process. There are three particularly important ways that this process generates inaccurate information: stereotyping, halo effects, and perceptual defense.[4]

Stereotyping

One of the ways people deal with complicated sets of stimuli is to use stereotypes. A *stereotype* is a convenient category into which people are put on the basis of some characteristic. Two of the most important classes of stereotypes are based on ethnic and occupational characteristics. So-called

[4] Sheldon S. Zalkind and Timothy W. Costello, "Perception: Implications for Administration," *Administrative Science Quarterly* 7 (September 1962): 218–235.

ethnic jokes are based on generally agreed-on (although not necessarily accurate) stereotypes. Priest, professional wrestler, accountant, labor-union official, politician, psychiatrist—all these occupational titles suggest different sets of images, and these image sets constitute stereotypes.

Stereotypes can be harmful. When people are stereotyped, they are perceived as members of a category, rather than in terms of their own unique qualities or deficiencies. Many ethnic group members have suffered from just such a process. Allport[5] has provided an excellent example of the power of a stereotype:

Mr. X   *The trouble with Jews is that they only take care of their own group.*
Mr. Y   *But the record of the Community Chest shows that they give more generously than non-Jews.*
Mr. X   *That shows that they are always trying to buy favor and intrude in Christian affairs. They think of nothing but money; that is why there are so many Jewish bankers.*
Mr. Y   *But a recent study shows that the percent of Jews in banking is proportionally much smaller than the percent of non-Jews.*
Mr. X   *That's just it. They don't go in for respectable business. They would rather run night clubs.*

Managers must be especially careful not to evaluate or otherwise deal with people on the basis of stereotypes.

Halo effect

Another way in which people perceive incompletely is to allow an impression of a person in one area to dominate their impressions of that person in another area. Students who are always present in class, turn in work on time, and show enthusiasm often are evaluated more highly in the course than their technical performance merits. The halo surrounding them leads to the instructor's misperception of their competence. "We are known by the company we keep" is an adage that acknowledges the power of the halo effect. It need hardly be said that managers must be careful not to succumb to this distortion process.

Perceptual defense

Finally, people often screen out perceptual stimuli that make them uncomfortable. Social psychologists have found, for example, that subjects do not recognize obscene or taboo words flashed rapidly on a screen as well as they do neutral words.[6] People in organizations often tend to reject original ideas suggested by new employees. "Not invented here" reflects the perceptual

---

[5] Reprinted by special permission from Gordon W. Allport, *The Nature of Prejudice* (Reading, Mass.: Addison-Wesley, 1974), pp. 13–14.
[6] L. Postman, J. S. Bruner, and E. McGinnies, "Personal Values as Selective Factors in Perception," *Journal of Abnormal Social Psychology* 43 (1948): pp. 142–154; and E. McGinnies, "Emotionality and Perceptual Defense," *Psychological Review* 56 (1949): 244–252.

defensiveness that many old-timers exhibit. Otherwise, they are confronted with a fact (new employees can have good ideas) inconsistent with a stereotype already held (people must be around long enough to earn the right to participate in an important way).[7] The danger that perceptual defenses hold for distorting information is obvious. Managers must guard continually against allowing such processes to obscure their accurate perceptions.

Perceiving

(a) (b) (c)

A famous experiment was performed by Robert W. Leeper* in 1935. He showed one half of his subjects the *a,* and the other half the *b* version of the above figure. He then showed everyone the *c* version. All the subjects that had first seen the old hag picture (*a*) saw only the hag when first viewing the ambiguous drawing (*c*). Ninety-five percent of those who had first seen the young woman (*b*) saw only the young woman when first viewing the same ambiguous drawing. The subjects had formed an initial frame of reference and then locked in on that view. Are employees equally affected by managers' actions?

* Robert W. Leeper, "The Role of Motivation in Learning: A Study of the Phenomenon of Differential Motivation Control of the Utilization of Habits," *Journal of Genetic Psychology* 30 (1962): 1–15.

Values and attitudes

People bring more than perceptions and perceptual processes to their jobs. They also bring—and form—values and attitudes. Most behavioral scientists

[7] Don Hellriegel and John W. Slocum, Jr., *Organizational Behavior* (Saint Paul, Minn.: West, 1976), pp. 86–87.

recognize that values and attitudes are important factors underlying behavior. Let us consider some of the reasons managers must be aware of employees' values and attitudes.[8]

Values and attitudes and behavior

Basically, a *value* is a person's idea of something desirable: "A value is a conception, explicit or implicit . . . of the desirable which influences the selection from available modes, means, and ends of action."[9] More concretely, values can be thought of as "abstract ideals, positive or negative, not tied to any specific object or situation, representing a person's beliefs about (ideal) conduct . . ."[10] Values are essentially global beliefs that guide people's behavior regarding several specific objects and situations.

Attitudes, on the other hand, are narrower than values, and more focused. An *attitude* is a person's feelings, thoughts, and behavioral tendencies regarding a specific object or situation. Engaging in interpersonal relationships may be a strongly held value for many middle managers; they may translate that global value into an attitude favoring active participation in decisions by their subordinates. Thus, one of the functions of attitudes is to enable the individual to express more general—and underlying—values.[11]

Behavior tends to reflect values and attitudes. People's perceptions and responses to stimuli are determined, in large part, by the values and attitudes they bring to a situation. In fact, the best we can do is *infer* values and attitudes from behavior. After all, behavior is the only thing we can observe directly; we can only guess at what is going on in a person's mind or psyche.

Despite their impreciseness, values and attitudes are accepted generally as factors that underlie behavior. Behavior in organizations is no exception. Therefore, managers must recognize the part that values and attitudes play in relation to the managerial functions as well as the organization itself.

Values, attitudes, and managing

Effective managers must consider the values and attitudes that people bring to their jobs, together with those they form at work. For example, there is evidence that when people make a decision together, as a joint action, their

---

[8] This section borrows from Patrick E. Connor and Boris W. Becker, "Values and the Organization: Suggestions for Research," *Academy of Management Journal* 18 (1975): 550–561.
[9] Clyde Kluckhohn, "Values and Value Orientations in the Theory of Action," in Talcott Parsons and Edward A. Shils, eds., *Toward a General Theory of Action* (New York: Harper & Row, 1962), p. 389.
[10] Milton Rokeach, *Beliefs, Attitudes, and Values* (San Francisco: Jossey-Bass, 1968), p. 160.
[11] Daniel Katz and Ezra Stotland, "A Preliminary Statement to a Theory of Attitude Structure and Change," in S. Koch, ed., *Psychology: A Study of a Science* (New York: McGraw-Hill, 1957), pp. 423–475.

perception of the decision's worth varies according to their values. Specifically, the more similar their values, the more useful they perceive the decision.[12] Obviously, managers should be careful that such similarities do not improperly affect their decision-making processes.

Reflections on Indian children

People said, "Indian children are hard to teach. Don't expect them to talk."
One day stubby little Roy said, "Last night the moon went all the way with me, when I went out for a walk."
People said, "Indian children are very silent. Their only words are no and yes."
But small, ragged Pansy confided softly, "My dress is old but at night the moon is kind. Then I wear a beautiful moon-colored dress."
People said, "Indian children are dumb. They seldom make a reply."
Clearly, I hear wee Delores answer, "Yes, the sunset is good, I think God is throwing a bright shawl around the shoulders of the sky."
People said, "Indian children have no affection. They just don't care for anyone."
Then I feel Ramon's tiny hand and hear him whisper, "A wild animal races in me since my mother sleeps under the ground."
People said, "Indian children are rude. They do not seem very bright."
Then I remember Joe Henry's remark, "The tree is hanging down her head because the sun is staring at her. White people always stare. They do not know it is not polite."
People said, "Indian children never take you in. Outside their thoughts you'll always stand."
I have forgotten the idle words that people said.

Source: Juanita Bell, *Squol Quol* (newspaper of the Lummi Indian tribe).

Values and attitudes affect managers' behavior in other ways. In particular, the way managers choose to exercise control over subordinates appears to be related to the managers' values.[13] Even more interesting is the mounting evidence that managerial values and attitudes interact with those of subordinates and affect the subordinates' promotional opportunities.[14]

---

[12] John W. Drake, "The Backgrounds and Value Systems of Transportation Modeling Project Participants and Their Effects on Project Success," *Transportation Research Forum Proceedings* (1973), pp. 659–672.
[13] Ray Hesel, "Value Orientation and Pupil Control Ideology of Public School Educators," *Educational Administration Quarterly* 7 (1971): 24–33.
[14] Johann M. Pennings, "Work Value Systems of White Collar Workers," *Administration Science Quarterly* 15 (1970): 397–405; and John Senger, "Managers' Perceptions of Subordinates' Competence as a Function of Personal Value Orientation," *Academy of Management Journal* 14 (1971): 415–423.

Needs

In addition to perceptions, values, and attitudes, there is something else that people bring to, and develop within, the organization: *needs*. Put simply, we say that people have needs when they lack, or are deficient in, something they want. In general, this lack generates within them a drive to overcome the deficiency. There are, of course, many needs that people bring to their jobs. Depending on how specific one wishes to be, a list of needs can be drawn that covers from one to over fourteen thousand separate needs.[15]

A hierarchy of needs

It is most useful to consider needs in a few major categories. This view was expressed by the well-known psychologist Abraham Maslow. He postulated a hierarchy containing five levels of needs. We may visualize it as a pyramid (see Figure 22-1).

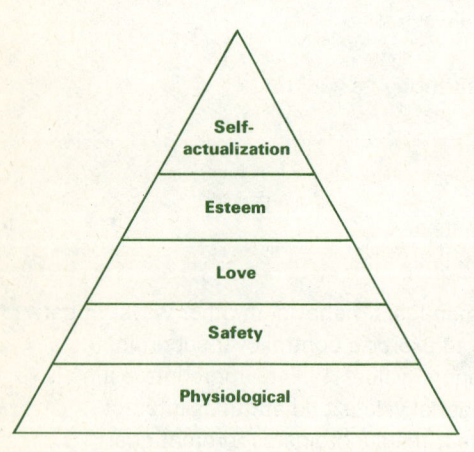

Figure 22-1 Hierarchy of needs
Source: Abraham H. Maslow, *Motivation and Personality,* 2d ed. (New York: Harper & Row, 1970).

The lowest order of needs are *physiological*. These needs encompass people's biological demands—hunger, thirst, sex, elimination, and so on. *Safety* needs follow. These involve relief from certain physical threats in the environment—for example, safety from attack. The need for *love* appears on the next higher level. It is usually expressed as a person's need for warm

---

[15] Lyman W. Porter, Edward E. Lawler, III, and J. Richard Hackman, *Behavior in Organizations* (New York: McGraw-Hill, 1975), p. 40.

supportive relations with others, such as family and friends. The need for *esteem* is dual in nature and quite complex. People need self-esteem, which often comes from mastery over part of their environment—for example, being the best hunter in the tribe or being an outstanding accountant. People also need *others* to esteem and recognize their accomplishments. The linkage between these two aspects is evident: it seems likely that self-esteem derives from the esteem received from others.

Self-actualization, the highest level of need, is the most difficult to describe. It has been said that this is the need "to become what one is capable of becoming." It is here that we find the key to the meaning of fulfillment. Unlike the other four needs, which may be satisfied, self-actualization never is fully realized. This failure may result from the potential of the human spirit; once activated, it seems capable of limitless expansion and variation.

The hierarchy of needs seems to relate to age. That is, each level appears to be associated with certain periods in an individual's life span. Physiological and safety needs are paramount in infants' lives. As children grow older, love needs become important. When they reach young adulthood, esteem needs dominate their energies. If people are successful in satisfying these needs, they may move on to self-actualization later in life. This last step does not necessarily follow, however, since social or organizational demands may arrest progress at the esteem level or lower. This problem is the basis of the conflict between organizational and individual goals.

Final comment

Ours is a collective society. More specifically, organizations are systems of social relations. What this means, of course, is that people who are members of organizations participate in social relationships. Inevitably, these social relationships occur in the context of small groups. Thus, in order to complete our discussion of needs, wants, and drives, we must consider the principal setting for behavior in the organization: the small group. This subject is taken up in the next chapter.

Further, people possess a variety of needs and drives. These needs and drives combine in individuals to form their *motivational structures*. How and why people are motivated is the subject of Chapter 24.

Summary

There are several human aspects of which managers must be aware. First, people bring a variety of perceptual processes to their jobs. Perceptions are developed by means of basic frames of reference, through which individuals experience and organize—make sense of—the multitude of stimuli with which they are bombarded. Frames of reference may distort perceived information by selective perception, stereotyping, halo effects, and perceptual defense mechanisms.

Second, people bring many values and attitudes to their jobs. They also develop values and attitudes as a result of their jobs. Managers must be aware of these human characteristics, since they underlie and guide workers' behavior.

Finally, people are driven to satisfy a complex set of needs and wants. Most important are those ranging from physiological to self-actualizing, including aspiration, achievement, and group needs. Needs form the basis of human motivation, a subject of principal importance to effective managers.

Discussion questions

1 How quickly do you form a perception of an instructor at the beginning of a term? What sorts of stimuli do you primarily use in forming these perceptions?
2 Would you want to be a manager that is quick to form perceptions of subordinates? slow to form perceptions of subordinates? For which type of manager would you prefer to work?
3 How would you go about inferring your subordinates' sets of needs?
4 Which of your behaviors can you tie in with your values?

Supplementary readings

Herzberg, Frederick. "The Motivation-Hygiene Concept and Problems of Manpower." *Personnel Administration* January—February, 1964, pp. 3—7. Reprinted in *Dimensions in Modern Management,* 2d ed., edited by Patrick E. Connor. Boston: Houghton Mifflin, 1978.

Institute for Social Research. "Facts and Fictions About Working Women Explored: Several Stereotypes Prove False in National Study." *ISR Newsletter,* Autumn 1972, pp. 4—5. Reprinted in *Dimensions in Modern Management,* 2d ed., edited by Patrick E. Connor. Boston: Houghton Mifflin, 1978.

McClelland, David C. "That Urge to Achieve." In *Think,* pp. 19—23. New York: International Business Machines, 1966. Reprinted in *Dimensions in Modern Management,* 2d ed., edited by Patrick E. Connor. Boston: Houghton Mifflin, 1978.

Morse, John J., and Lorsch, Jay W. "Beyond Theory Y." *Harvard Business Review* 48 (May—June 1970): 61—68. Reprinted in *Dimensions in Modern Management,* 2d ed., edited by Patrick E. Connor. Boston: Houghton Mifflin, 1978.

Chapter 23

Informal relationships

Objectives of the chapter

1 To examine informal aspects of the organization.
2 To define and describe small groups.
3 To define the ways in which groups affect people's behavior.
4 To examine the ways in which managers can use small groups to solve problems.
5 To describe relationships between formal and informal aspects of the organization.

The individual and the formal task structure constitute two main elements of a complex organization. A third, and equally significant, element is the social subsystem, traditionally known as *informal organization*. Informal relationships—powerful as a source of influence—interact with and modify the other two elements. Most of what is known about informal relationships comes from sociology and social psychology. Studies conducted within these two disciplines center on small-group behavior and provide what is, perhaps, the most convenient approach to the subject. Adopting this approach, we will begin by asking why people join small groups. This will involve us in a more specific inquiry: What benefits are derived from small-group participation? Next, we will broaden our discussion and delve into the nature of the informal organization and its relationship to formal organization. Finally, we shall briefly observe informal working relationships that seem to incorporate other patterns.

Before beginning, however, we must recognize that there is a basic difference between the small group and the informal organization. The small group is a component of the informal organization and constitutes its nucleus. In the first sections of this chapter we will discuss the small group; then, we shall expand our discussion to the informal organization.

Why people form groups

Why do people form groups?[1] What advantages do they gain from these associations? Why do smaller subgroups emerge within large aggregations of people? The answers to these questions are straightforward: people have a basic need to associate with their fellow humans in groups; and these groups should be small enough to permit intimate, direct, and personal contact among individuals. The satisfactions that are derived from these associations cannot be obtained from working in a big organization, living in a large city, or learning in a sizable high school or college. The group provides individuals with satisfactions different from those that they can get from any other source.

Attraction to specific groups

Individuals, however, do not gravitate randomly to just any small group. They follow a pattern that has certain general characteristics. First, the group must arise spontaneously within larger aggregations of people. It usually has no more than ten members; though, it may be as small as two members.

Second, small groups attract individuals who share similar values. These people interact, mainly by communicating, to produce a consensus on values and standards of behavior (called *norms*) that is essential to the group's effective accomplishment of its objectives.

Third, all groups have certain goals that they seek to fulfill. The goals are important to the group and to each individual member. These goals usually involve task achievement and emotive satisfactions. The *task* often involves some specific outcome that can be achieved only by a group collaboration, such as family members sharing chores for a picnic. *Emotive satisfactions* are the rewards that each individual experiences from participating in the group endeavor. Task and emotive satisfactions are often closely related. We discuss important exceptions later in the chapter.

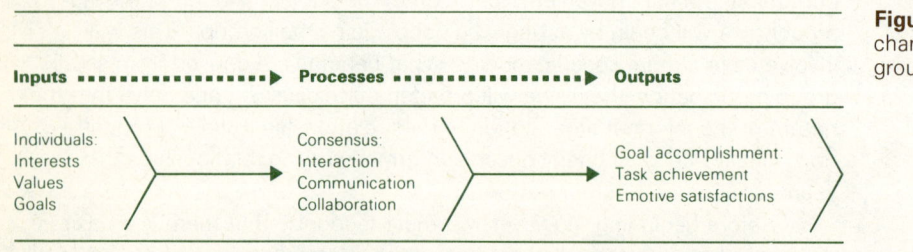

Figure 23-1 General characteristics of small groups

[1] The basic reference in group behavior is George C. Homans, *The Human Group* (New York: Harcourt Brace Jovanovich, 1950).

Figure 23-1 sums up these three characteristics. Small groups process inputs to create outputs. The inputs are individuals with various interests, values, and goals. The group processes of interaction, communication, and collaboration allow the members to reach a consensus, without which the outputs of goal accomplishment would be difficult to achieve.

Benefits from group participation

Satisfaction

Because an individual in a group is surrounded by others who share similar values, the group reinforces the individual's own value system. This is a formal way of saying that it is usually more comfortable to be around people who think the same way we do. Such an explanation illuminates the basic satisfaction a person gains from group participation. Forming groups to supply this satisfaction is as natural as eating or sleeping.

However, additional factors are present. Groups help people to accomplish tasks that they cannot accomplish alone. As we have already noted, task facilitation provides personal satisfaction through cooperative effort. A task may be essentially economic, like work, or it may be social and recreational. Barn raising, common among pioneer farmers, was both a work and a social event.

Group output includes both task and emotive content. On the emotive side, the group is a source of psychological satisfactions. For example, the group provides a person with status by enabling that person to belong to a distinct and, more or less, exclusive organization. It also allows an individual an opportunity for self-expression—it provides a forum and, generally, sympathetic listeners. Individuals that participate in a group receive satisfaction for their recognition, participation, and communication needs. In some instances, people can even find an outlet for their leadership drives in the group.

A good deal of evidence shows that in an organizational setting such satisfactions are often not available from work itself. However, jobs that are boring, fatiguing, and monotonous are offset to some extent by social relationships among workers. Managers, too, derive emotive satisfaction from their colleagues as well as mutual support—another of the major benefits of group participation.

Support

Group reinforcement of individual values is, of course, a form of support. However, the concept of support goes beyond this; the group, in a very real way, insulates the individuals from the complexity and hostility of a vast, impersonal society. Often, when people enter an organization for the first time they feel considerable anxiety. Their surroundings are unfamiliar, their future uncertain. Their first inclination is to seek out others in a similar situation and to form a friendship with them. Where several people are in the same circumstances, a small group may arise on this basis alone. However, usually it does not last very long after the initial fear of the new environment wears off.

More lasting are groups that arise from the members' perception that collective action is necessary to prevent the encroachment of outsiders. People who perceive that they will be involved in an organization for a long time may form such groups in an attempt to maintain the status quo. We find examples of this in prisoner of war camps, in teen-age gangs, and, to a degree, in business organizations.

In business, groups may restrict workers' output. Such restrictions have been interpreted as a protest or a protective form of behavior. Protests usually occur against high standards of output or other aspects of working conditions. Protective behavior may attempt to ensure that output standards will not be increased even though higher productivity may be possible.

To generalize, whenever people mutually perceive that their environment creates a need for protection or protest, they may form small groups. They do so because they realize that action is most effective when engaged in collectively. Often, such groups form the embryo of a larger, more formalized organization. Certainly, the labor movement had its beginnings in a few informal groups of workers.

Groups and perceiving

The work group is a major factor in influencing people's attitudes and setting standards for their behavior. Further, because persons tend to adopt group standards unconsciously, groups profoundly affect perception. That is, the very way people see or understand events is greatly determined by their group experiences.

A classic experiment illustrated the effect of a group on individuals' perceptions.* The researchers used a dark room with no visual standards by which people could orient themselves. It turns out that in such a setting, people invariably perceive a fixed point of light as moving back and forth slightly. Test participants looked into a box in which they could not see anything except the apparently wavering point of light. After looking for a while, each subject reported how much the light seemed to move. The report was not made known to others making similar observations. Each person reported a certain distance—for example, 2 inches for one subject and 3 inches for another. Then the subjects were grouped in twos and threes and asked to give their estimates of movement, this time in the presence of fellow subjects. Group members did not consult one another; they simply continued to give their own estimates and to hear the estimates of others. The previously wider individual estimates converged toward a new group estimate, or norm.

* See Muzafer Sherif and Carolyn W. Sherif, *Social Psychology* (New York: Harper & Row, 1969), pp. 201–220.

After the oral reporting was completed, the groups were broken up and each person was asked to record his or her own judgement privately. Significantly, the individuals retained the *group* norm, carrying with them the estimate that had been established when they all were together.

There are two lessons to be learned from this and similar experiments. First, people often derive their opinions from groups, and second, they often are unaware of that fact. The individual's values and perceptions usually become tangled and modified by the norms of the group.

Information

A third reason why people form groups is to secure information. The so-called grapevine is an important means of satisfying the communication needs of individuals. Of course, a person does not have to be in a small group to receive information from the grapevine, but it helps.

In fact, research into communication patterns shows that people tend to form groups in an effort to cluster around the individual who is the focal point in a communication network (see Figure 23-2). Thus, possession of information may be considered to be an important prerequisite of group leadership. This is true whether we are talking about formal or informal organization. An individual who has information is able to satisfy the communication needs of others and can reduce a great deal of uncertainty in others' minds. The small group facilitates this process, even though the information transmitted may be false or misleading.

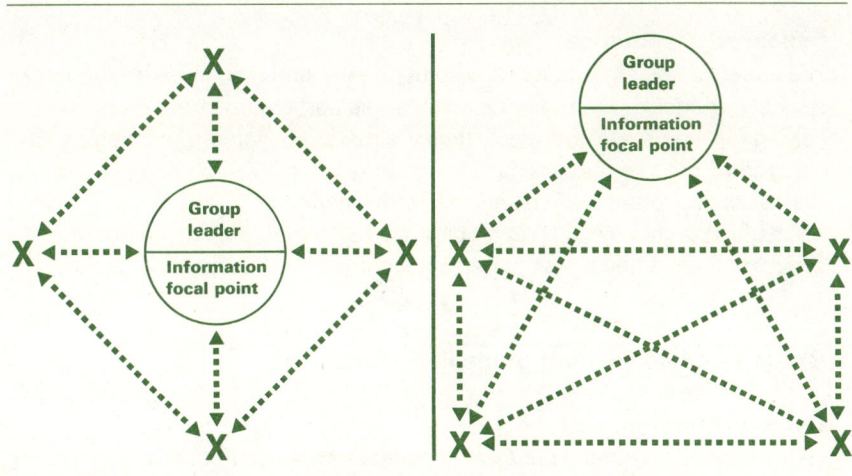

Figure 23-2 Communication patterns of small groups

Work group effectiveness

We do not exaggerate when we say that a substantial proportion of the work that is performed in organizations is done within the group context. How well work groups perform their functions—solve problems, as it were—is, therefore, of no small importance to effective management. What are the relative merits of the group (as opposed to the individual) problem solving?[2]

Group problem solving: Some assets

Greater knowledge
Committees, boards of directors, and the like typically are designed to include members who represent a variety of occupations, values, objectives, and interests. This variety gives the group more information and knowledge than has any one of its members; and each member, with a somewhat different source of expertise relating to the group's problem, can fill in the knowledge gaps of other members.

More approaches
Individuals tend to develop tunnel vision in their thinking and their approaches to problems. The interaction of group members can stimulate the search for more approaches by challenging one another's thinking. For example, consider the problem of providing adequate job training for the unskilled. Solutions vary: increase the number of jobs available, emphasize development of short-range skills rather than long-range career orientations, delegate more discretion to paraprofessionals, increase support to programs for the disadvantaged, and so on. Each is only a partial solution; the total solution to the problem involves a combination of these elements.

Increased acceptance
The effective implementation of a solution frequently requires the support of several individuals. If a project's staff people participate in the problem solving for their specific project, they are more motivated to accept a solution and to assume responsibility for making it work. A high-quality solution that lacks acceptance will be less effective than a lower-quality solution that has high acceptance. Solving problems is more than a technical matter; it includes the additional task of persuading others to accept the solution.

Group problem solving: Some liabilities

Overconformity
When social pressures emphasize consensus and camaraderie and frown on disagreement, a work group can become an instrument for maintaining conformity. Agreeing with and accepting a decision by group members, therefore, is not necessarily related to the quality of the decision reached. Of course, if a group's duties are primarily advisory in nature, the manager can serve as a check on the group's decisions.

---

[2] This section is based on the discussion of Don Hellriegel and John W. Slocum, Jr., *Management* (Reading, Mass.: Addison-Wesley, 1974), chap. 13.

Domination by an individual

A work group's effectiveness can be reduced if one individual, who is neither forceful nor dynamic, dominates its activities. The best problem solver may not have the opportunity to influence and, therefore, upgrade the group's decisions. This problem is accentuated when a group has an appointed leader. Managers must be aware that, when they use and participate in a group setting to work on problems, they may well be the dominating element.

Goal displacement

The job of a problem-solving group is to create a viable solution. To accomplish this, the members must consider alternatives. Some people come into the group vigorously supporting their preferred alternatives. Such people often become too concerned with bringing neutral members to their side and refuting those with other suggestions. The resulting—and operating—goal becomes one of winning the argument rather than finding the best solution to the original problem. This process, called *goal displacement*, can obviously lower the quality of the decision. In this situation, it is usually desirable to start over again, generating alternatives and delaying the evaluation of alternatives.

Conclusion

In general, managers can use groups for effective decision making in the following circumstances:

1 The task requires generating, integrating, and evaluating information and alternatives.
2 There is a high need for acceptance of and commitment to the decision on the part of people affected by the outcome.
3 A variety of people possess the knowledge or expertise required to solve the problem.
4 The climate is conducive to group discussion; helping and sharing are encouraged and rewarded.
5 There is sufficient time to allow the group to explore and consider alternatives.

Nature of informal relationships

We turn now to a larger entity, the informal organization, of which small groups are a part. Before analyzing its structure and behavior, we must reaffirm one important point: both the informal organization and its main component, small groups, exist in a still larger social system. The nature of social systems varies: it may be a neighborhood in a city, a unit in the military service, or the formal structure of a business firm. Often, a system is so large that individuals feel lost in it; therefore, they form small groups.

Now that we are aware of this pattern, we can turn to the characteristics of the middle-level organizational structure—the informal organization.

Structure

The structure of the informal organization is determined by the different status positions people hold in relationship to the organization. There are four status positions: group leader, member of the primary group, fringe status, and out status. By using sociometric techniques to measure the type, duration, and frequency of contact among people located in a close geographic area, we are able to determine who holds which status position and, thus, draw a picture of the informal organizational structure. Suppose, for example, that we wanted to determine the structure of a group of nine people working in an office. These people are located in a close general area, and there are no artificial barriers, like walls, to prevent them from associating with one another frequently if they wish. Common sense tells us, however, that each person will not associate with each of the others with equal frequency. Rather, they will be selective in their associations, regularly including some and excluding others.

This is the phenomenon that we want to measure, and *sociometry* is the device that measures it. Through a simple questionnaire and some rough observations, an outsider can obtain, in a rather short time, an accurate picture of the informal organization of the workers. On paper, the picture looks something like the model of the atom often described in elementary science books (see Figure 23-3).

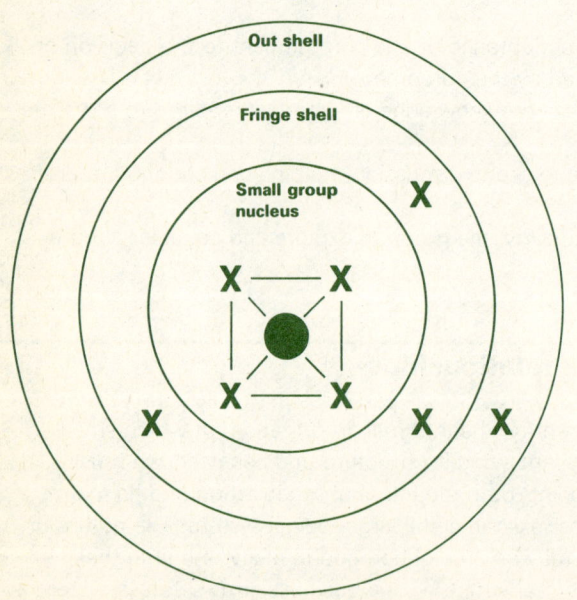

Figure 23-3 A model of informal relationships

The solid square in the nucleus represents the leader of the small group. Clustered around are four other members. Their association is close, and their interaction and communication is intense. In a practical sense, these five people enjoy one another's company, go for coffee and lunch together frequently, and often meet for dinner and a show after work. The person who is the leader is the dynamic force in the group, crystallizing opinions, setting objectives, and the like.

The three people in the fringe shell of the informal organization are newcomers. They are being evaluated by the smaller group for acceptance or rejection. Eventually they will move either into the nucleus or into the out shell.

The person in the out shell has been rejected. Although part of the office force, this person has not been accepted by the members in the core group. Such rejection can affect the person's behavior profoundly, especially if the person wants badly to belong to the nucleus group. Of course, if the rejection is mutual, the person in the out shell can survive easily.

We must stress that the entire informal organization is a system of interaction. The structural diagram that depicts it cannot capture all of its behavioral complexities. Most certainly, the interactions of the nuclear group members modify each member's individual behavior. This group's behavior also has a marked impact on the individuals in the two surrounding status shells. Conversely, the people outside the nuclear group could have a marked impact on those inside. They could, for example, be perceived as threats. If so, the nuclear group will modify its behavior toward them. Finally, the informal organization as a whole interacts with other subsystems, particularly with the formal organization.

Behavior

We have just indicated that the informal organization influences its members' behavior. This is an obvious but exceedingly important observation. A manager cannot hope to understand individual behavior without knowing the forces that shape it, and the informal organization is a significant force.

In order to understand why the informal organization has influence over individual behavior, we can refer to our earlier discussion of the reasons for joining groups. There we stated that groups are capable of granting or withholding the advantages of group membership. Thus, if individuals want acceptance by a nuclear group in an informal organization, they must modify their behavior so that it corresponds to the standards and values of the group. However, indifference to group acceptance does not eliminate them from the informal organization. They are still in the system, and their behavior will be influenced to a greater or lesser degree by the values and behaviors that predominate there.

Another characteristic of behavior in the informal organization is that it resists change. It does not resist all changes, however; only those that are interpreted as a threat. Let us assume, for example, that a group of staff engineers has been working together for some time in a close area of a department and has evolved a satisfying social relationship. Management may decide, however, that it would be more efficient to reorganize the office. This decision could involve shifting the engineers to several different locations in the department. The move would break up the pattern of social relations among the engineers, possibly destroying the group.[3] Often, threats of this type of change are countered by resistance—complaining, slowing work, reducing quality, being absent, and so on. Without understanding the dynamics of group behavior, management could not possibly hope to influence the group's acceptance of change.

Leadership

Although we will discuss organizational leadership more fully in the next chapter, we can make several points here about informal leadership. First, leadership in the informal organization tends to be situational, with the selected leader having the optimum combination of intelligence, sensitivity, and communication skills appropriate to the situation.

Second, the group leader is chosen democratically. He or she acquires the leadership role by a consensus of the group members.

Third, the leader is the dominant personality in the group. He or she functions to help satisfy members' task and emotive needs. However, from time to time, we observe groups where these aspects of the leadership role may be shared. The sharing may be brief, depending on the needs of the group. For example, one person may assume leadership of the group because he or she has some skill the group requires to accomplish a particular task. The regular leader, sensitive to the group's need, temporarily will take a back seat.

Finally, we often observe a division of labor in a group. In addition to bringing specific task skills to the group, we find members playing out their roles both in the task and the emotive categories. The leader integrates these diverse activities so that the processes of the group work well.

Relationships between formal and informal organizations

The informal organization is clearly a product of natural human social processes. This kind of organization will appear wherever people gather together to gain benefits that the larger organization cannot provide. Thus, the informal organization can aid the formal organization: it supplies satisfaction for individuals and high morale for work teams.

Some early theorists tended to picture the informal organization as antagonistic to the formal organization's goals. They viewed management's role as one of trying to manipulate the group into accepting formal goals.

---

[3] For a fascinating example of this process, see E. L. Trist and K. W. Bamforth, "Some Social and Psychological Consequences of the Longwall Method of Coal-Getting," *Human Relations* 4 (1951): 1—38.

However, managers should be aware of the positive nature of the informal organization and cease to dwell on it as a source of conflict.

Currently, we realize that a clear distinction between formal and informal organizations does not exist. Instead, both formal and informal organizations are parts of a complex system. These parts interact within the system, each modifying the other in the process of achieving goals. This does not mean that the goals of these subsystems are necessarily the same; they may be mutually reinforcing, conflicting, or may bear little relationship to one another. Regardless of the nature of the goals, however, there is no question that they interact. Thus, the expectations and satisfactions of the people in both formal groups and informal subsystems will be influenced in several directions.

Of course, managers must constantly strive to create an organizational climate in which the legitimate satisfaction and expectations of individuals and their informal groups can be fulfilled. It is foolish for managers to suppose that the functioning of the formal system alone can provide the entire range of satisfaction necessary for high morale among employees. The informal organization has a positive contribution to make in this respect. As such, it should be nurtured by management.

Informal working relationships

Just as the informal organization is a departure from the specific structure that exists in formal charts and manuals, so are informal working relationships. They are less dramatic but nonetheless profoundly influential on organizational behavior. Informal working relationships encompass all the job-related activities that are carried out in ways not specified in formal organizational documents or in ways different from those that are specified. Behavior pertains to work, but it deviates from formally prescribed patterns. The most obvious example of this is the informal bypass of the chain of command that many use to communicate on some aspect of work.

In Figure 23-4, electrical engineers who work on circuit design cut directly across the chain of command to consult with and take work to the supervisor of draftsmen, the dashed line shows the informal relationships between them. This bypass speeds up requisitioning drawings and working out technical details. Following the prescribed channels of communication would be burdensome and time consuming.

It is impossible to describe all the informal working relationships that can exist within formal organizations.[4] The point to remember was made by a management scholar who observed that if everyone adhered to the formal organization in the day-to-day operation of a company, nothing would get done. Informal working relationships introduce a considerable degree of flexibility into any organization.

---

[4] For an illuminating discussion of various patterns of informal relations see John Pfiffner and Frank P. Sherwood, *Administrative Organization* (Englewood Cliffs, N.J.: Prentice-Hall, 1960), pp. 18–27.

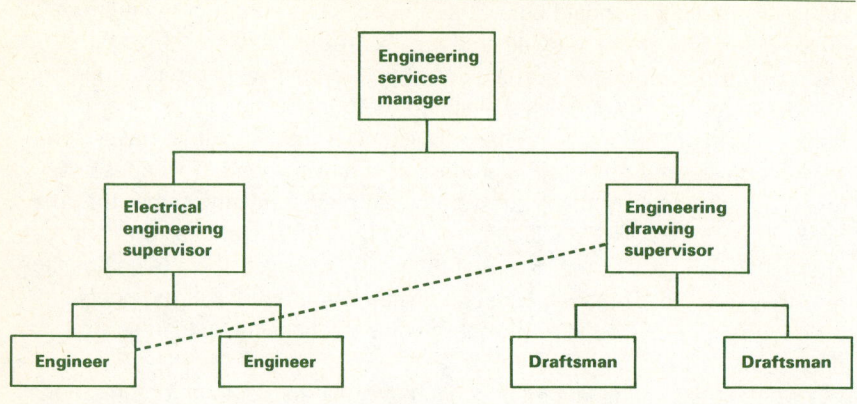

Figure 23-4 Bypassing the chain of command

Summary

Small groups are a basic element in organizations. Managers must recognize that small groups will form, and that they are important in affecting people's behavior.

People form or join groups because they derive some benefits from doing so. In essence, groups satisfy various needs for liking, approval, information, and affiliation. They also help to reinforce individuals' perceptions, values, and attitudes and to reaffirm their identity.

Groups not only provide support to individuals, they also provide a vehicle for effective task performance. Specifically, under certain conditions, groups can be used as effective problem-solving devices. In general, compared to an individual, groups bring to problems greater knowledge and more approaches, and generate greater acceptance of the solutions by the members. On the debit side of the ledger, groups can suffer from too much conformity, domination by a single member, and goal displacement.

In addition to the small group, there is a whole network of nonofficial relationships among organizational participants. This network is generally referred to as the informal organization. Informal relations have an indentifiable structure and strongly influence people's behavior. In fact, many organizational tasks are performed by means of informal relations.

Discussion questions

1. When you first arrived at college, what group associations did you make? What goals did you have in making these group connections?
2. "There is nothing so tyrannical as a small group." What does this statement mean? *Hint:* Consider the tolerance of a high school clique for deviant behavior.

Supplementary readings

Greene, Charles N. "The Satisfaction-Performance Controversy: New Developments and Their Implications." *Business Horizons,* October 1972, pp. 31–41. Reprinted in *Dimensions in Modern Management,* 2d ed., edited by Patrick E. Connor. Boston: Houghton Mifflin, 1978.

Homans, George C. *The Human Group.* New York: Harcourt Brace Jovanovich, 1950.

———. *Social Behavior: Its Elementary Forms.* New York: Harcourt Brace Jovanovich, 1961.

Pfiffner, John M., and Sherwood, Frank P. "Non-Formal Aspects of the Organization." In *Administrative Organization,* pp. 18–27. Englewood Cliffs, N.J.: Prentice-Hall, 1960. Reprinted in *Dimensions in Modern Management,* 2d ed., edited by Patrick E. Connor. Boston: Houghton Mifflin, 1978.

Chapter 24

Motivation and leadership

Objectives of the chapter

1 To explore the nature of human motivation.
2 To discuss various theories of motivation.
3 To relate motivation to personal satisfaction and job performance.
4 To discuss managers' leadership responsibilities.
5 To consider various leadership theories.
6 To show the relationship between leadership style and motivation.

Satisfaction, productivity, turnover, waste, cooperation, and a host of other important variables depend on the manner in which workers are induced to behave. Behavioral scientists have shown that motivation and leadership are central factors in the effective influencing of people at work.

The nature of human motivation

Human behavior is goal directed. Peoples' unsatisfied needs motivate their actions. A person needing food searches for something to satisfy hunger; a sense of achievement motivates an individual to advance in an organization; a person writes poetry to fulfill a creative urge. Underlying motives are individual attitudes, which are feelings or predispositions about something. Attitudes are formed by an individual's upbringing, education, environment, and many other circumstances that combine to form personality.

The enormous variety of experiences to which any particular person is exposed accounts for varied attitudes and, consequently, varied behaviors. This idea is expressed in the notion of *individual differences*. Several people may, for example, have strong achievement needs. However, one might seek fulfillment of these needs in business, another in education, and still another in the arts. Thus, individual attitudes, feelings, or predispositions determine the route taken to achieve a goal.

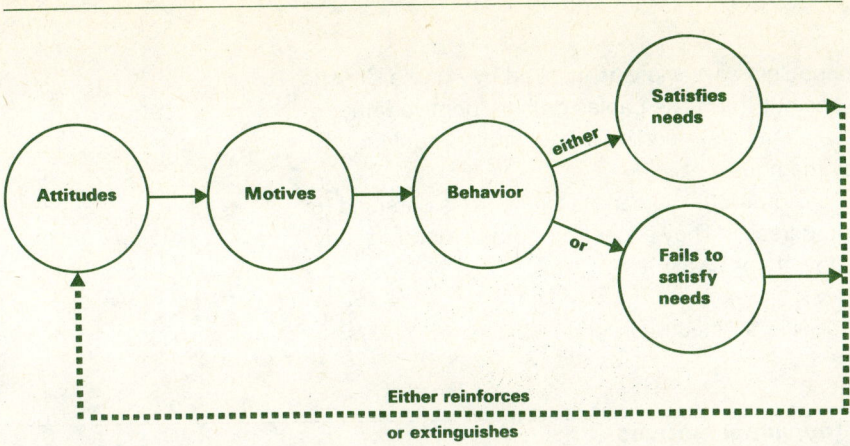

Figure 24-1 Attitudes, motives, and behavior

Figure 24-1 shows the relationships among several elements in human motivation. Attitudes shape motives, and motives lead to behavior that is aimed at the goal of satisfying a need. If the behavior is successful, and the need is satisfied, a reinforcement of the attitude occurs. If the behavior fails to satisfy a need, then the attitude tends to be extinguished, replaced by another attitude leading to different goal-directed behavior.

A person's level of aspiration is closely related to motivation. Aspirations are dynamic: they represent the ever-changing shift of goals that occurs as need satisfaction is achieved. That is, when needs are satisfied at one level, the individual usually readjusts aspirations to higher levels. An individual who is highly motivated by a need to achieve in business will not be satisfied by a low-level executive position. Once such a position is obtained, the person will strive for the next higher position and so on. After achieving a top position in a firm, objectives may shift to, say, social or governmental activities, where other possibilities exist that will satisfy achievement needs.

This endless personal search for alternatives to satisfy increasing aspirations is an important source of individual motivation. It is also a powerful factor in the concept of influence, because the wider the range of need satisfaction that an organization is able to supply, the greater will be the individual's commitment to that organization.

Motivation models

Psychologists have developed many models of human motivation. Generally, we break the models down into three categories: models of individual motives, models of motive classification, and models of the choice process.[1]

---

[1] William G. Scott and Terence R. Mitchell, *Organizational Theory*, 3d ed. (Homewood, Illinois: Richard D. Irwin, 1976).

Goal-directed behavior

London—This ingenious schoolgirl says she was inspired by Agatha Christie and Alfred Hitchcock. So she cut the brake cables on her adoptive father's car. And later set fire to the car as it sat parked in the garage, hoping it would explode and destroy the house.

A British court yesterday ordered 15-year-old Diane Irons detained for life. Said the attempted murderess, "They expect me to be a goody-goody all the time. I wanted to show them I wasn't."

Source: "Too much Agatha Christie & Alfred Hitchcock," Whitehorse, YT, *Star,* September 24, 1976.

Individual motives

One of the more interesting behavioral studies is David McClelland's research in patterns of achievement motivation—*n*(achievement) as he calls it.[2] McClelland relates levels of aspiration directly to achievement motivation and says that such motivation is learned. In some societies, the culture, the upbringing of children, and various traditions produce a low level of achievement motivation among the people. In the United States, there is a high level of achievement motivation. However, *n*(achievement) is not equally distributed throughout the population. Business leaders tend to score highly on *n*(achievement) tests. Since achievement motivation is learned, McClelland reasons, it may be possible to teach young people and lower levels of management to raise their motivation. If such is the case, then executive development programs may affect these groups.[3]

Another approach that also considers individual motives is the *competency theory,* which explains motivation in terms of people's need to master their environment. *Affiliation,* or the need to have contact with others, also is a model of individual motive.

Motive classification

Among the best known motive classification systems is Maslow's hierarchy of needs (see Chapter 22). Maslow attempted to classify needs according to *prepotency*—the lowest needs on his scale have the greatest urgency of satisfaction.

Frederick Herzberg, a psychologist who has done a great deal of research on job motivation and satisfaction, has defined a number of conditions on which satisfaction is based.[4] By analyzing the responses employees

---

[2] David C. McClelland, *The Achieving Society* (Princeton, N.J.: Van Nostrand, 1961).
[3] David C. McClelland and David G. Winter, *Motivating Economic Achievement* (New York: Free Press, 1969).
[4] Our discussion is based on Frederick Herzberg, "New Approaches in Management Organization and Job Design," *Industrial Medicine and Surgery* 31 (November 1962): 477–481.

have made to a survey, he has measured how often satisfiers and dissatisfiers appeared in work-related events described by his survey respondents and how long they produced either a marked improvement or a marked reduction in job satisfaction. Herzberg found that the most frequently mentioned determinants of improved job satisfaction (*satisfiers*) are achievement, recognition, work itself, responsibility, and advancement. The factors most frequently involved in events causing job dissatisfaction (*dissatisfiers*) are company policy and administration, supervision, interpersonal relations, and working conditions. Figure 24-2 summarizes Herzberg's findings about satisfiers and dissatisfiers along both the frequency and duration dimensions. The length of each box in the figure indicates frequency, the width indicates duration.

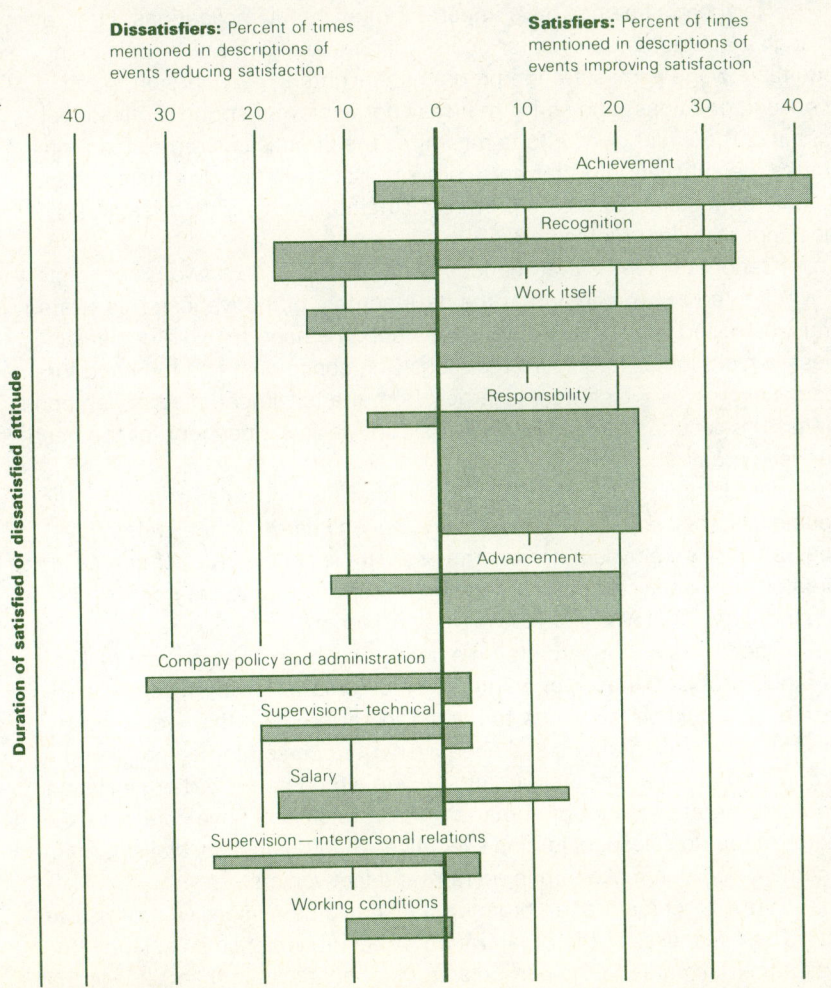

Figure 24-2 Factors affecting job satisfaction *Source:* Adapted from Frederick Herzberg, "New Approaches in Management Organization and Job Design," *Industrial Medicine and Surgery* 31, no. 11 (November 1962):480.

In Figure 24-2, the first five factors are satisfiers. If these factors are unfulfilled, they can produce dissatisfaction, as shown by the extensions of the bars to the left of point 0. If they are fulfilled, they can be strong motivators. Achievement, for example, is mentioned most frequently as a source of satisfaction, but the length of time a person derives satisfaction from any particular achievement is short. Conversely, responsibility is a long-term satisfier. Dissatisfiers tend to be relatively short term. It is interesting to note that the factors that bring about job satisfaction are not the same as those that cause job dissatisfaction. The satisfiers pertain to the content of the job, whereas the dissatisfiers reflect the job environment. Both are one dimensional in their effects. That is, the factors that appeared frequently on the right side of the scale showed up infrequently on the left side and vice versa. To emphasize these differences, Herzberg calls the dissatisfiers "hygiene factors" because they are environmental and prevent improved job satisfaction. He calls the satisfiers "motivators" because his study seems to indicate that they promote higher performance and achievement levels.

Herzberg's findings have important managerial implications. First, even though management strives for good organizational hygiene by promoting equitable wage-administration programs, enlightened supervision, good working conditions, and so forth, it may not achieve a strong motivational climate. The effect of its efforts minimizes the dissatisfiers rather than maximizes the satisfiers. Furthermore, because satisfiers and dissatisfiers relate to different aspects of the employment situation, minimizing dissatisfiers does not stimulate motivation.

Second, it seems that management must develop a two-pronged strategy, directed at hygiene and at the development of motivation. This strategy must be based on two sets of human needs: the need to avoid unpleasantness, which comes largely from dissatisfying conditions; and the need for personal growth, which comes largely from the fulfillment of satisfying conditions. The second need is closely related to Maslow's concept for the need for self-actualization.

In addition to Herzberg's findings, other evidence also shows a direct relationship between satisfaction and a work climate that facilitates the realization of employees' needs. The opposite is equally true, of course. The greater the inconsistency between employees' goals and the goals of the organization, the lower is the level of satisfaction.

These straightforward statements may obscure what is essentially a complex problem. If everyone entered an organization with the same expectations, it would be fairly easy to create an environment that would satisfy all. However, expectations and needs vary from person to person, group to group, and occupation to occupation. Even a moderate-sized organization contains a great amount of human diversity. Engineers have different expectations than do salespeople, line executives than do staff specialists, management decision makers than do rank-and-file workers.

The environment of an organization should be responsive to this diversity. To be responsive, the organization's subunits must be sufficiently free to adapt their climates to the particular people found within them. It is virtually impossible to impose a uniform style of management on an entire organization. This becomes especially apparent as the size and complexity of an organization increase.

Thus, from a motivational standpoint:

1. Managers should foster decentralization to allow lower managerial levels the freedom to work out the climate best adapted to the satisfactions sought by the people supervised.
2. Managers should increase their awareness of the needs of their subordinates and the satisfactions that they require.
3. Managers should not consider responsiveness to human satisfactions as being "soft." Instead, it reflects a philosophy that facilitates organizational adaptability and accommodates a wide variety of human differences.

Choice-process models

The third category of motivation models emphasizes what psychologists call the *choice process*. Chief among these models is *expectancy theory*,[5] which indicates that people are motivated to act along lines that lead to the highest anticipated payoffs. The model explains motivation in two ways. First, it indicates that people order the outcomes of their behavior according to their perception of the *value* of these outcomes; that is, people have priorities in the goals they seek. Second, the model indicates that people place different emphasis on the *satisfactions* that they anticipate receiving from an outcome. Thus, the value of an outcome is distinguished from the satisfaction expected. For example, money might be a highly valued outcome from work, but an individual may not receive much satisfaction acquiring it by doing a job.

Motivation to act is based on an individual's perception of the probability of achieving a goal coupled with the probability of receiving the rewards associated with the achievement. The expectancy model has been applied to predict employees' job satisfaction and job performance.

A second choice-process model deals with *exchange theory,* which pertains to how people perceive their rewards on a job relative to the rewards others receive doing the same job. Differences in rewards between what people do on a job in comparison to what they expect to obtain motivate them to reduce the differences that they believe exist. For example, if people feel that they are not rewarded adequately for work done, they will be motivated to reduce effort, to quit, or to absent themselves more frequently than management thinks is appropriate. Exchange models are associated with concepts of equity and distributive justice, which go beyond psychological theories of behavior and enter the realm of philosophy.

[5] Victor H. Vroom, *Work and Motivation* (New York: Wiley, 1964).

Motivation by managers: The leadership process

A manager is concerned with motivation because it is closely associated with *performance*. People are motivated to behave in a variety of ways. And, from a manager's point of view, it is critical for people to behave in ways that are organizationally useful. In organizations, people work for money and possibly although not necessarily, for enjoyment. Further, a structure of authority exists in an organization that imposes limitations on behavior. The freedom of action in an organization is limited, in many instances extremely so. Finally, jobs are assigned, which means that an individual often does not have a great deal of choice in what he or she wants to do.[6] Given an environment of constraints, managers try to motivate people to the highest level of job performance possible. This responsiblity is often called *leadership*.

Leadership is a process by which people are directed, guided, and influenced in choosing and achieving goals. In any undertaking, a leader mediates between the organization and the individual so that the degree of satisfaction to both is maximized. Viewing leadership as a process directs our attention to the function performed. What does a leader do? The first step in answering this question lies in understanding something about leadership roles.

The diversity of leadership roles

Most of us have seen the various individual roles usually enacted in a group situation. One person organizes the group to achieve a goal, another raises a stream of objections, another provides comic relief, still another synthesizes the ideas of all, and a final historian evaluates present action in the light of what was done in the past. These roles and many others are essential for group life. They fulfill needs of individual members of the group and are vital to group accomplishment.

Some of these roles involve leadership, others do not. Researchers in the behavioral sciences have devoted considerable attention to this distinction. They have found that, generally, leadership roles fall into two broad classifications: task and emotive.

Task roles
When leaders organize and influence groups to achieve some specified set of objectives, they are playing task roles. Whether such objectives are imposed on groups from above, whether they are imposed laterally, as in a work flow, or whether they arise spontaneously from within the groups themselves, leaders must still play their task roles in order to remain leaders and to facilitate the accomplishment of the groups' goals.

---

[6] E. E. Lawler, III, *Motivation in Work Organizations* (Monterey, Calif.: Brooks/Cole, 1973), pp. 5–6.

Emotive roles

Emotive roles are equally important, for they allow the individual needs of groups' members to be satisfied. Sometimes, these needs are related to goal accomplishment; at other times, they are unrelated to goals. In either case, the emotional needs of people are social and psychological in nature. Leaders who play the emotive role play a dual part: they help the members of the groups to experience need satisfaction, and, at the same time, they smooth the way for task performance.

Frequently, we say that the ideal leader is one who plays both task and emotive roles effectively. However, the leadership of a group can be shared without diminishing group performance or morale. In such a situation, one person takes the task role and another, the emotive role. This is not unusual. The nature of the formal organization often forces managers to be most concerned with getting a job done. If they can be accepted by their subordinates on this basis, they have gone a long way toward being true leaders and not merely the heads of their groups. However, they must anticipate that normal group processes might also select other informal leaders, who will function in the emotive role.

Leadership theories

In our concern for the functional aspects of the leadership process, we must not overlook research done on the characteristics and behavior of the leader. This subject has long received considerable attention from observers of society.

Early genetic theory

For hundreds of years, a continuous stream of observers recognized leadership as the ability to influence people in such a manner that they willingly strove toward an objective. It was believed that this ability was not a part of official position. Certain people were born to be leaders, it was said, having inherited a set of unique traits or characteristics that could not be acquired in any other way. Leadership was thought to be inherited, simply because it emerged frequently within the same prominent families. In reality, however, strong class barriers made it impossible for most people outside these families to acquire the skill and knowledge needed to become leaders.

Trait theory

As the social and economic barriers were broken down and as leaders began to emerge from the so-called lower classes of society, the early genetic theory underwent some modifications. Some of the change resulted from contributions by behavioral scientists to the literature in the middle 1930s. The first work was by writers who maintained that leadership traits could be acquired through experience, education, and training. These writers tried to focus on all the traits, whether inherited or acquired, that were found in people regarded as leaders.[7] The traits frequently included physical and nervous energy, a sense of purpose and direction, enthusiasm, friendliness and affection, integrity, technical mastery, decisiveness, intelligence, teaching skill, and faith.

The inadequacy of the trait approach soon became apparent. Seldom, if ever, did any two lists enumerate the same essential leadership characteristics. Moreover, the lists were confusing; they used different terminologies and contained different numbers of characteristics. Nonetheless, the trait approach was widely accepted for a long time. Its hypotheses seemed plausible because studies of various successful leaders almost always indicated numerous similar personality and character traits. However, the intensity and degree of the traits often varied. Likewise, theorists could reach no satisfactory consensus about the number of traits necessary for leadership, or whether or not a person could be a leader lacking some but not all of the traits. Neither could theorists determine how to isolate and identify all the specific traits common to leaders. Moreover, writers used different terminology and did not indicate which traits were the most important and which were the least important. A further weakness of the trait approach was that it did not distinguish between the characteristics needed for acquiring leadership and those necessary for maintaining it.

Although the trait approach is partially discredited today, research does show that leaders do have in common certain very general characteristics—intelligence, communication ability, and sensitivity to group needs. Such traits found interwoven in the personality of the leader must always be viewed in the context of the group. In other words, the most intelligent person in a group will not necessarily emerge as the leader. Instead, the person with the combination of traits best suited to the situation in which the group finds itself will assume leadership.

The follower theory

A more subtle theory of leadership acknowledges the follower's personality and needs. Those holding this approach maintain that the follower must also be studied, because the type of individual who will carry out leadership functions depends on the characteristics of the followers as well as the specific needs of the group at a given period of time. "It is the follower as an individual who perceives the leader, who perceives the situation and who, in the last analysis, accepts or rejects leadership. The follower's persistent motives, points of view, frames of reference or attitudes will have a hand in determining what he perceives and how he reacts to it."[8]

The follower approach does not fail to consider that certain characteristics will help one person to emerge as a leader and others to emerge as

---

[7] A prominent exponent of the trait theory was Ordway Tead in *The Art of Leadership* (New York: McGraw-Hill, 1935).
[8] Fillmore H. Sanford, "Leadership Identification and Acceptance," in *Groups, Leadership and Men,* ed. Harold Guetzkow (Pittsburgh: Carnegie Press, 1951), p. 159.

followers. It stresses the idea that the leadership function must be analyzed and understood in terms of the dynamic relationship that exists between the leader and the followers. Group members will follow a leader because they see in that person the means for need fulfillment. Yet, they see that leadership is essential if the group is to act as a unit. Therefore, group members choose a leader not only because of such characteristics as intelligence, skill, drive, and ambition but also because of functional relationships.

Although a leader may emerge as a result of agreement among group members, the reverse also may be true. A person might seek out group leadership; an individual may want to accomplish an objective that can only be attained by directing the activities of other people. A manager who has been formally appointed to a leadership position within an organization is usually in this situation.

The contingency model

In their search for leadership theory, behavioral scientists discovered the importance of situational factors that predispose certain persons to leadership. The proponents of the situational approach do not deny that the characteristics of individuals also play an important part in leadership. However, they point out that leadership is also the product of situations in particular groups. They argue that leadership will differ in each group situation. The person who becomes a leader of a group engaging in a particular activity and the leadership characteristics that are needed depend on the specific situation in which the group finds itself.

Fiedler's research has shown that the style of an effective leader must be matched to the demands of a situation.[9] For example, in job situations that are extremely easy or extremely difficult, a strong task-oriented leader is most effective. In job situations that are moderately difficult, a human relations—oriented leader is most effective, because interpersonal relationships appear to be the critical problem with which a leader has to deal in groups that are doing jobs of intermediate difficulty.

The contingency model of leadership, Fiedler argues, is useful in planning management training activities. Human relations training may be maximally beneficial for managers who supervise employees with moderately demanding jobs, like laboratory technicians and computer programmers, whereas foremen who supervise workers on routine assembly jobs may not benefit as much from such training.

Leadership style

A leader is an individual who is perceived by other group members to be in harmony with the needs of their group and responsive to the group situation.

---

[9] Fred E. Fiedler, *A Theory of Leadership Effectiveness* (New York: McGraw-Hill, 1967).

Leaders must always be recognized as such by group consensus. Appointed managers, who do not necessarily reflect subordinate group choice, are not usually regarded as leaders at the outset, though they may become leaders. If the influencing function is to be effective, it is desirable that subordinates accept their manager as a leader, and not merely as the head of their department. This is where leadership style enters, in three categories: autocratic, democratic, and free rein.

Autocratic

Autocratic leadership reflects a narrow span of management, tight supervision, and a high degree of centralization. Those who utilize the autocratic style tend to be repressive and to withhold communication other than that which is absolutely necessary for doing the job. Autocratic managers unilaterally make decisions, vesting little if any participative rights in the group. This style tends to minimize the degree of involvement of groups and individuals in the job decision-making process.

Democratic

Democratic leadership emphasizes a nonpressure orientation that maximizes group and individual participation in the decision-making process. A free flow of communication is encouraged among all members of a department so that a climate of understanding can be built on a foundation of honesty and trust. The democratic style is fully consistent with a decentralized organization and a wide span of management.

Free rein

Under the free rein, or laissez-faire, style of leadership, the organizational climate is such that people, assumed to be self-motivated, do their jobs virtually without supervision. The individual with authority leaves the group to its devices and provides little specific direction. However, the leader is available in a consultative capacity to help if requested.

Leadership style and effective influence

Obviously, each of these styles has its place in management practice; a good leader knows when and when not to use them. As a rule, free rein is most useful for establishing a leadership environment for professional people—university professors, research scientists, and others—who desire independent work and have shown the capacity for it. Free rein situations are relatively rare in industry.

A democratic style is appropriate to an organization in which rapid change is evident. Because this style creates a fairly free environment, skilled and educated people—engineers, technicians, and craftspeople—seem to thrive under it. Some writers believe that a democratic leadership style is beneficial to all organizations. This position is not widely accepted, mainly because the autocratic style is necessary to produce results among unskilled workers who are poorly prepared to participate in decision making and might be uncomfortable if urged to do so.

The preceding discussion reinforces our statement that leadership style must be contingent on the situation. However, in general, a more democratic, more open, and less pressure-laden style leads to greater leader acceptance than does an autocratic one. This factor is important in certain cases because the democratic climate is capable of greater flexibility in the face of change.

Effective influence means better motivation of employees, which requires matching leadership style to the situation. Figure 24-3 illustrates this point.

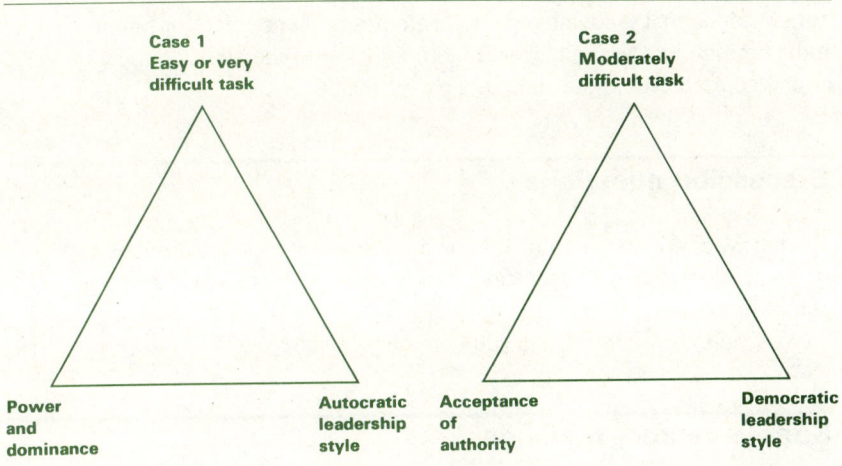

Figure 24-3 Influence triangles

In Case 1 we show an easy or very difficult task situation based on power and dominance. Its prevailing leadership style is autocratic. Case 2 exhibits a moderately difficult task situation where acceptance of authority is high and the need to rely on power and dominance is low. We have seen that the democratic style is appropriate for this situation.

We have stressed throughout this chapter the situational character of management practice. Frequently, cases occur where the Case 1 triangle applies and should be used by management. However, change is carrying managers and organizations further and further within the boundaries of the Case 2 triangle. Its methods are viewed by management scholars and practitioners as the approved and most effective way to run an organization.

In a sense, we have now made a complete circle. We started this chapter by saying that people are motivated to action by unsatisfied needs. Then, we went on to show how leadership style must be designed to fulfill employees' and organizations' needs. The next chapter takes this discussion a step further, by considering organizational climate and change.

Summary

Human behavior is goal directed, which means that it is motivated toward the satisfaction of unmet needs. Models of motivation are explanations of need-satisfying behaviors. These models fall into three categories: individual motives, motive classification, and choice processes.

Managers are interested in motivation because it is related to performance on the job. Since it is essential that people be motivated to behave in organizationally useful ways, managers must influence employees' actions through leadership. There are many leadership roles, but they have been classified into two general categories: task roles and emotive roles.

Underlying explanations of leaders' behavior are several theories of which, at present, the contingency model is the most influential. Its basic conclusion is that leadership style—autocratic, democratic, or free rein—must be matched to the task situation. Effective leadership is critical to improved employee motivation and performance.

Discussion questions

1 In what ways are Herzberg's findings confirmed by your experiences as a student? Identify specific satisfiers and dissatisfiers with which you are confronted.
2 What style(s) of leadership do you generally exhibit? Why?

Supplementary readings

Fiedler, Fred E. *A Theory of Leadership Effectiveness*. New York: McGraw-Hill, 1967.

Herzberg, Frederick. "The Motivation-Hygiene Concept and Problems of Manpower." *Personnel Administration,* January–February 1964, pp. 3–7. Reprinted in *Dimensions in Modern Management,* 2d ed., edited by Patrick E. Connor. Boston: Houghton Mifflin, 1978.

McClelland, David C. "That Urge to Achieve." In *Think,* pp. 19–23. New York: International Business Machines, 1966. Reprinted in *Dimensions in Modern Management,* 2d ed., edited by Patrick E. Connor. Boston: Houghton Mifflin, 1978.

Tannenbaum, Robert, and Schmidt, Warren H. "How to Choose a Leadership Pattern." *Harvard Business Review,* 36 (March–April 1958): 166–168. Reprinted in *Dimensions in Modern Management,* 2d ed., edited by Patrick E. Connor. Boston: Houghton Mifflin, 1978.

Vroom, Victor H. *Work and Motivation* (New York: Wiley, 1964).

Chapter 25

Organizational climate and change

Objectives of the chapter

1. To emphasize that organizational climate is a consequence of managerial decisions about design.
2. To describe some design strategies or alternative models of organizational design.
3. To relate organizational design to morale, satisfaction, and productivity.
4. To discuss the outcome of morale and job satisfaction.
5. To consider the relationship between organizational design and adaptation to change.
6. To discuss various dimensions through which organizations can be changed.

Managers must regulate organizational structure and processes so that performance is raised and human satisfaction is increased. The atmosphere in which the influencing activity is conducted is called the *organizational climate*. This climate is designed by managers, and it is composed of contingencies that help the organization adapt to changes, satisfy employee needs, and raise the effectiveness of operations. Thus, organizational climate is closely associated with employees' attitudes, needs, and expectations. It is also related to leadership and motivation. But the climate of an organization is more than the total of its component parts; it is a complex meshing of a variety of contingencies into a behavioral system that has strong implications for managerial practices and results.

A major cause of personal dissatisfaction arises from the conflict between organizational and individual goals. The first systematic analysis of this problem was made by Chris Argyris.[1] Argyris saw a conflict between the individual who seeks activity and independence through psychological development and the bureaucratic, formalized organization that keeps the individual in an infantile state of passive dependence. The organization's work climate, as Argyris described it, stifles an individual's natural desire for freedom and self-determination. Because of this, many symptoms of conflict

---

[1] Chris Argyris, *Personality and Organization* (New York: Harper & Row, 1957), chap. 2.

manifest themselves in turnover losses, waste, slowdowns, lower productivity, lack of innovative and creative behavior, nonacceptance of leadership and authority, and so forth. However, probably the most serious consequence of bureaucratic organization is that it blocks the individual's psychological maturation. This represents a lamentable squandering of human resources.

Generally, the blame for this situation must be placed on the organization itself. It is often so inflexible, so dedicated to rigid bureaucratic norms, so divided into specializations of labor, that it is incapable of providing the opportunity for individuals to achieve a wider range of work satisfactions. These conditions, combined with centralization of authority and autocratic managerial behavior, submerge the individual in the system and reduce the opportunity for self-realization.

Although we have stated these outcomes in an extreme manner, they do reflect a major thrust in current management theory. Organizations must create an improved climate if they are to fill the legitimate needs of the people in them. In fact, numerous forces are present in modern society that make this improvement imperative.

Among these forces are advancing technology, highly skilled labor, professionalization of management, and the rising expectations of employees that they will have a more satisfying work experience than that of their parents. But of all the new and dynamic forces that have confronted the modern organization since the close of World War II, perhaps the most important of all is the phenomenon of change itself.

That we live in a rapidly changing world is a commonplace observation. This change has forced on organizations a need for flexibility and adaptability never before experienced. Many writers, notably Warren G. Bennis,[2] have stated that the key criterion for judging organizational health is the organization's ability to cope with change. Moreover, they go on to say that the typical bureaucratic, highly formalized organization is poorly suited to the demands for change.

A crucial factor affecting an organization's ability to cope with change is its climate. Research in the behavioral sciences has shown that certain leadership styles, decision-making structures, communication patterns, and the participation levels are more apt to gain acceptance of change than are others. Let us look at two pioneering approaches to how managers can develop an organizational climate that is flexible for both change and effective motivation.

Organizational climate theories

Theory X and Theory Y

Douglas McGregor observed that people placed in an organizational climate will behave in a particular manner, based either on the assumptions of

[2] Warren G. Bennis, *Changing Organizations* (New York: McGraw-Hill, 1966).

Theory X or those of Theory Y. A manager who fits into the Theory X group leans toward an organizational climate of close control, centralized authority, autocratic leadership, and minimum participation in decision making. This manager accepts this combination of characteristics because of certain assumptions about behavior. Theory X assumptions, according to McGregor, are:[3]

1. The average person dislikes work and will avoid it as much as possible.
2. Most people must be threatened or forced to make the effort necessary to accomplish organizational goals.
3. The average individual is basically passive and prefers to be directed rather than to assume any risk or responsibility. Above all else, people prefer security.

A Theory Y manager operates on the basis of vastly different assumptions, believing that an effective organizational climate has looser, more general supervision, greater decentralization of authority, less reliance on coercion and control, a democratic style of leadership, and greater participation in decision making. The assumptions on which this type of organizational climate is based are:[4]

1. Work is as natural as play or rest and, therefore, is not avoided.
2. Self-motivation and inherent satisfaction in work will be forthcoming in situations where the individual is committed to organizational goals. Hence, coercion is not the only form of influence that can be used to motivate.
3. Commitment is a crucial factor in motivation and is a function of the rewards coming from it.
4. The average individual learns to accept and, even, to seek responsibility, given the proper environment.
5. Contrary to popular stereotypes, the ability to be creative and innovative in the solution of an organization's problems is widely, not narrowly, distributed in the population.
6. In modern organizations, human intellectual potentialities are just partially realized.

In a later book, McGregor observes that these assumptions are not simply ends of a continuum.[5] He believes that they represent distinctly different views of human nature. Theory X views people mechanistically; they are simply a depersonalized factor of production. Theory Y views people as affecting and being affected by others; and, as such, people simply cannot be taken for granted. McGregor underscores the notion that Theories X and Y represent beliefs held by managers. They constitute the foundations on which organizational climate can be built.

Which organizational climate will produce the best results? One is inclined to say that climate fostered by Theory Y because, on the surface, it

---

[3] Douglas McGregor, *The Human Side of Enterprise* (New York: McGraw-Hill, 1960), pp. 33–34.
[4] Ibid., pp. 47–48.
[5] Douglas McGregor, *The Professional Manager* (New York: McGraw-Hill, 1967), pp. 79–80.

is humanistic and less harsh than that of Theory X. It is also more optimistic about human motives at work. However, sentiment alone is not sufficient for judging the effectiveness of an organizational climate or leadership style; we must evaluate organizational climate separately in each situation. For now, let us say that under some conditions Theory X works best, and under other conditions Theory Y works best. Although this is not a complete answer, we shall discuss the matter further after we look at another theory of organizational climate.

Likert's theory

Rensis Likert's concept of organizational climate in many ways resembles McGregor's, yet contains several differences. Likert proposes four systems of organizational climate: System 1, exploitive; System 2, benevolent authoritative; System 3, consultative; and System 4, participative group. Each of these systems is composed of six elements, which Likert feels are key ingredients of organizational climate. The six are leadership, motivation, communication, decision, goals, and control. Their dimensions can be measured on a continuous scale so that managers may rate their organization's climate.[6]

Obviously, Systems 1 and 4 define organizational extremes. They embody autocratic and democratic leadership climates, respectively (in McGregor's terms, a Theory X climate and a Theory Y climate). Likert observes that the climate found in most American industry lies in the center—somewhere between System 2 and System 3. Interestingly, however, when asked, "What is the most effective climate?" the majority of managers tend to select the democratic end of the scale. This leads Likert to conclude that managers do not execute what they, in essence, believe to be successful leadership styles and organizational practices.

The chief difference between McGregor's and Likert's theories is that McGregor's does not view organizational climates as a product of managerial design, whereas Likert's does. Superficially, this may appear to be a small distinction, but in reality it has wide implications. Likert feels that an effective management is one that operates in a climate on the participative (democratic) end of the scale. He thinks that managers should consciously strive to mold their organizational climate in this manner because people working within it will experience higher levels of need satisfaction and, hence, will become better employees.

McGregor, while endorsing the positive human values flowing from democratic management, says implicitly that Theory X, or an autocratic climate, may be more effective in certain situations. Management should not be locked into a strategy that may prove inappropriate to its particular situation.

---

[6] For a full discussion see Rensis Likert, *The Human Organization* (New York: McGraw-Hill, 1967), pp. 14–24, 120–121.

The current consensus

An article in *Fortune* magazine gives us some insight into the consensus on the question: What is the best organizational climate?[7] Most writers appear to underscore organizational contingencies as the leading determinants of climate. Thus, in organizations having a stable environment and using employees of low-level skill, a more nonparticipative, autocratic kind of climate appears to be effective. And, in rapidly changing firms with highly educated and skilled employees, more democratic forms of management obtain the best results.

However, writers who admit the value of autocracy in some cases will say that organizations that find this type of climate conducive to effective influence are dying out. In twenty to thirty years, autocratic bureaucracy will be nothing more than a curiosity. The forces bringing about this change and requiring a more democratic climate are technology, education, and professionalization of management.

Organizational design

As we saw in Chapter 14 the changes produced by new technology, new consumer and employee demands, and new ecological awareness are placing extraordinary demands on management.[8] Study after study has indicated that the type of organizational design best suited to cope with such change is the organic system[9] — a type of design that emphasizes openness, flexibility, and maximum employee participation in the formation and fulfillment of organizational goals.

Closely related to organizational change are the processes of integration and differentiation.[10] As organizational change occurs, the degree of *differentiation,* or specialization, in organizations increases. Likewise, as specialization increases, *integration* must increase. In other words, greater specialization requires greater coordination. Management must increase the degree of collaboration that exists among various segments of the organizational structure. Various techniques help in this process. They include analyzing the design of structural relationships, training and developing managers' interpersonal skills, and improving the climate of the job to increase employees' satisfaction.[11]

---

[7] Robert C. Albrook, "Participative Management: Time for a Second Look," *Fortune* May 1967, pp. 166–170, 198–200.

[8] For a discussion of present-day environmental turbulence see Alvin Toffler, *Future Shock* (New York: Random House, 1970).

[9] Tom Burns and G. M. Stalker, *The Management of Innovation* (London: Tavistock, 1961).

[10] Gene W. Dalton, Paul R. Lawrence, and Jay W. Lorsch, *Organizational Structure and Design* (Homewood, Illinois: Richard D. Irwin, 1970).

[11] Wendell L. French and Cecil H. Bell, Jr., *Organization Development* (Englewood Cliffs, N.J.: Prentice-Hall, 1973).

Certain outcomes are expected from an improved organizational climate. Among the more critical are employees' morale, satisfaction, and productivity.

Morale and satisfaction

Many writers distinguish morale from satisfaction. They say that *satisfaction* is associated with an individual's experience, whereas *morale* pertains to the spirit of a group. It is correct for a manager to say, "The morale of the people in my department is high," when referring to subordinates as a group. When speaking of individuals, the manager might say, "Smith is satisfied with the job." This seems to be a natural usage, so we will preserve it. However, a difficulty exists: in behavioral research the factors used to measure group morale often are used to measure individual satisfaction. Terminology can become confusing. However, this is partly a methodological problem, and we will try not to let it distract us as we discuss morale.

The components of morale

Morale is widely studied, and, as one might expect, it is defined in many ways. Yet, most scholars agree about some aspects of it. The consensus is that morale is a group feeling that results in intense goal-directed effort. This feeling is caused by group members' perception that they share similar values about the accomplishment of a worthwhile objective. When working together is essential for achieving a goal, morale often makes the difference between success and failure. This is true in any collective undertaking—business, educational, military. We may expand our definition of morale by looking at its four components more closely:

1. *Group feeling*   This may be thought of as a type of togetherness, a belonging with others who are dedicated to accomplishing similar ends. The stronger this feeling is, the more intense will be the effort expended in goal-directed behavior.
2. *Goal-directed behavior*   Since group action is not directionless, the component is indispensable to morale. Goal-directed behavior must always aim at something; it may be task oriented, recreational, social, protective to the group, and so on.
3. *Shared values*   A group's behavior becomes welded around a perception of shared values, acknowledged by group consensus. If the group shares values, by implication it shares mutual and compatible expectations. This allows the group to act as one in achieving its objective.
4. *Worthwhile objective*   The last factor actually expresses the norms that determine acceptable group behavior and the rewards that come from group effort. In general, the higher the rewards, the greater will be the group effort.

Morale contingencies

Many determinants affect the way these four factors will function in a specific group situation. That is, the level of morale in any group results from conditions both inside and outside the group. Separating the internal from the external determinants is not easy, because they interact closely. However, for purposes of simplification, we will try to make such a separation.

Internal contingencies

Values and objectives   The higher the rate of agreement among members of the group on values and objectives, the higher will be the morale. It is only natural that such agreement will reduce potential conflict and allow group members to concentrate their energies on goal accomplishment.

Probability of success   The higher the probability that joint action will accomplish goals, the higher will be the morale, because group members perceive a strong likelihood of success from their collaboration. If the reverse is true, morale tends to be lower.

Actual success   This is also an important determinant of morale, because if the group achieves its goals, morale tends to be high; if the group constantly fails, morale tends to be low.

Individual satisfaction   The higher the degree of individual satisfaction of group members, the higher the morale of the group as a whole. However, morale is not merely a sum of individual satisfactions; a circular relationship exists between these two factors. High personal satisfaction leads to high morale, which in turn tends to raise the level of satisfaction even higher, and so on. In other words, individuals obtain personal satisfaction from being in a high-morale group.

External contingencies

Job or task   Work itself is intrinsically satisfying if it is geared to the needs, skills, experience, and education of group members. Because managers, to a large extent, determine the content of jobs, they must have a good program of personnel administration to assure satisfactory selection, placement, appraisal, promotion, and transfer of people according to their interests and desires. The personnel program must also meet the staffing needs of the firm. At one time, it was felt that the nature of a job was fixed by technology and nothing could be done to alter it; we now know that work can be changed within a given technological framework to make it more stimulating.

Type of supervision   A good deal of research supports a policy of looser, more general supervision that allows a higher degree of individual and group determination of work activities. A direct relationship seems to exist between the amount of workers' participation and the level of morale. The interpersonal skills of a manager also have much to do with morale levels.

Nature of the control systems and amounts of pressure at work   These related factors also have considerable influence on morale levels. Morale tends to be lower when control systems are tight and output pressure is high. In the process of automobile assembly, workers are paced (controlled) by an assembly line and experience great pressure to get work done.

Group identification with the goals and values of the organization   When people feel that they work for an organization that has worthwhile objectives, their morale is favorably affected. Of course, the organization's objectives and the way they are implemented are a function of management's philosophy and the administrative skill of the executives.

The outcomes of morale and job satisfaction

Even though high morale and job satisfaction are values that managers endorse and attempt to achieve, they do not exist apart from other important variables. We must ask, therefore: What relationship do these values have to turnover, absenteeism, accident rates, and productivity? This question is of considerable importance to managers because it relates directly to costs and to the efficient use of human resources.

A tremendous amount of research in the behavioral sciences has been formulated to shed light on these relationships. Victor Vroom, who has reviewed this literature extensively, has pointed out some emerging patterns:[12]

1. Higher morale and job satisfaction result in lower turnover. This pattern is consistent throughout the research.
2. Although high morale and job satisfaction also result in lower absenteeism, this pattern does not appear quite as strongly.
3. The same kind of statement seems to apply to the relationship of morale and satisfaction to accidents. However, because of the small number of research studies in this area, the evidence is inconclusive.
4. Finally, and most interestingly, research findings do not give a clear picture of the relationship between morale and productivity.

For years it was assumed that a positive relationship existed between morale and productivity, that high productivity would result from good morale. Indeed, many respectable, early research findings did show that this relationship prevailed in some enterprises. The human relations movement was inspired by such findings. One of the chief aims of this movement was

---

[12] Victor H. Vroom, *Work and Motivation* (New York: Wiley, 1964), chap. 6.

to devise means to improve morale so that management would experience lower unit labor costs from satisfied, highly productive employees.

Researchers in the early 1950s, however, created doubts that the results of earlier studies could be generalized. One study, conducted in an insurance company, showed no convincing evidence of a connection between employee attitudes and productivity. As more findings were published, it became clear that the morale-productivity relationship could appear in many forms—low morale and high productivity, high morale and low productivity, high morale and high productivity, low morale and low productivity. Such findings suggest that morale and productivity may be independent variables. In arguing for this interpretation, Vroom holds that the conditions providing job satisfaction are not necessarily identical to those that lead to higher employee performance.

The present state of affairs does not satisfy people who are looking for straight answers. Management could easily justify the cost of installing morale-building human relations devices in firms if it could be proved that they work better than traditional incentive systems do. However, management must now think twice about morale-productivity contingencies. Since climate is a major factor in organizations, managers need alternative strategies for changing climate to improve morale, productivity, job satisfaction, and all the other human variables that are essential for effective performance.

Changing organizations

Job change

Mass-production, assembly-line technology designed work so that tasks were reduced to their simplest elements. Employees could learn jobs quickly, since they only needed the minimum skills necessary to perform tasks efficiently. Workers were thought of as parts in a machine, easily replaceable and interchangeable with other parts.

This approach to job design began to change in the 1950s. Research studies pointed out that all was not well on the assembly line; it created many human problems that equally productive alternative job designs could avoid while increasing human satisfaction.

One alternative design is called *job enlargement*. This is an effort to widen the scope of a job by incorporating a number of minor tasks into a single larger task. For example, a worker, instead of putting one gear into a transmission box, would assemble the entire transmisison. Job enlargement challenges workers by providing less boring repetitive tasks. Frequently, job enlargement also includes opportunities for job rotation and, when possible, flexible work hours.

Job enlargement is a horizontal change in job design; *job enrichment* is more inclusive. In these programs, workers not only have greater responsibility but also more discretion, with significant opportunities for decision making. Job enrichment, consequently, has a vertical as well as a horizontal dimension. It gives workers a chance to contribute to the job design process, which previously was considered to be exclusively management's domain.

Apprenticeship training

Under the old form of apprenticeship a boy was taken into a shop and turned over to a foreman, who was expected to teach him the trade. The foreman, himself very busy in his regular duties and usually more adapted by experience and inclination to the production of manufactured materials than to the training of boys, would turn the boy over to an assistant foreman, who in turn would pass him down the line until he landed under the supervision of a mechanic, skilled or partly skilled as the case might be, but not often able to impart his skill to the boy. Frequently, also, the run of work in a shop was not sufficiently varied to give the boy broad experience of instructive character. Even though the boy's superior might possess the ability to impart to him his knowledge, and might also be able to give him such a varied assortment of work as to afford a broad opportunity to learn the trade, the apprentice was himself seriously handicapped by his own limited education. Employed at work that required the use of drawings, he could usually neither understand them nor could he make a simple mechanical sketch. If a mechanical operation required the use of mathematical formulae that were not included in his limited school experience, the apprentice would have to forego doing the higher grade of work that such knowledge would have brought within his range. The apprentice became, therefore, the victim of the daily or weekly requirement of the shop.

Source: John R. Commons, *Trade Unionism and Labor Problems* (Boston: Ginn, 1921), pp. 235–236.

Changing decision roles

If employees have a say in affairs and are able to influence those decisions that directly affect them on the job, their satisfaction is higher and, sometimes, so is their productivity. A number of years ago, Lester Coch and John French, in a study of a garment manufacturing firm, showed that through employees' participation, turnover was reduced, learning new jobs was accelerated, and changes were accepted, not resisted.[13]

Increased employees' participation and an expanded definition of such participation have increasingly become the theme of management philosophy. Whereas earlier studies stressed the need for factory workers to have greater say in their jobs, today the meaning of participation has broadened to become almost synonymous with democratic management. However, the

[13] Lester Coch and John R. P. French, Jr., "Overcoming Resistance to Change," *Human Relations* 29 (1948): 512–532.

basic idea remains: when people—and this includes rank-and-file workers, technical specialists, and managers—receive the opportunity to exercise more responsibility, judgment, and discretion in their jobs, they derive more satisfaction from work.

All this makes good sense if we relate it to technology and the changing character of the work force. People are entering the labor market today with more education and greater skills than ever before. Furthermore, they are conditioned to expect more from work than economic satisfactions. Because of these widening expectations, a repressive work climate will stifle employees' innovative capacities.

Participation is a tangible way of decentralizing authority in an organization, by allowing employees a greater degree of self-determination. The idea alters organizational decision roles considerably—classical organization theory has managers making decisions unilaterally. In participative systems, employees can contribute to decisions about both job goals and methods by which these goals will be met. Usually, participation in the latter is more common than in the former. In either case, however, participation requires a major change in organizational design.

Changing organizational processes

Human relations feel the emphasis of this aspect of organizational change. Obviously, one purpose of behavioral science is to provide managers with more effective techniques for using human resources. The search for such techniques has been going on for years, and in the 1970s organizational development (OD) emerged as a popular approach for changing the organizational climate. French and Bell write:

> *Organizational development is a long-range effort to improve an organization's problem-solving and renewal processes, particularly through a more effective and collaborative management of organization culture—with special emphasis on the culture of formal work teams—with the assistance of a change agent, or catalyst, and the use of the theory and technology of applied behavioral science, including action research.*[14]

OD is a long-term program. Its main direction is toward improving interaction processes among groups and individuals, by using a resource person, called a *consultant* or a *change agent*, to facilitate change.

It is important that we understand the background of OD. It joined two basic movements: research and theory in the behavioral sciences and laboratory training (sensitivity training). The result of this merger was an action-oriented effort that is humanistically inclined toward bettering the organizational climate. Employees expect more from an organization's climate today than they did a generation ago, and there is little doubt that the next

---

[14] French and Bell, *Organization Development*, p. 15.

generation will make even greater demands than does the present one. Organizations must respond to these demands not only for the good of the employees, but also for their own sake. The viability of an organization depends on how well its managers cope with change. The repressiveness of traditional organization is no longer justifiable. The truly responsive organization maximizes individual freedom and responsibility, thus fulfilling rising employee expectations.

Summary

One reason that managers design organizations is to have positive effects on employee behavior. The way in which contingencies are structured influence the organizational climate, which, in turn, has consequences for morale, productivity, and satisfaction. Morale is composed of contingencies that are both internal and external to a group. Favorable contingencies are likely to increase employees' satisfaction, reduce turnover, and reduce absenteeism; their impact on productivity still is not clear. High morale does not *necessarily* result in high productivity.

The organizational climate also has consequences for adaptation to change. Since many organizations exist in a turbulent environment, managers must cultivate flexibility. Organizational change strategies may be designed along three dimensions: job change (job enlargement or job enrichment), changing decision roles (participation), and changing organizational processes (OD).

Discussion questions

1. Do you find that your various professors exhibit either Theory X or Theory Y views? What outcomes (class atmosphere, student productivity) result from these different views?
2. Assume that the grade you receive in a course is the only measure of your productivity as a student. To what extent is this grade a function of your satisfaction with the course?

Supplementary readings

Bennis, Warren G. *Changing Organizations*. New York: McGraw-Hill, 1966.
French, Wendell L., and Bell, Cecil H., Jr. *Organizational Development*. Englewood Cliffs, N.J.: Prentice-Hall, 1973.
Greene, Charles N. "The Satisfaction-Performance Controversy: New Developments and Their Implications." *Business Horizons*, October 1972, pp. 31–41. Reprinted in *Dimensions in Modern Management*, 2d ed., edited by Patrick E. Connor. Boston: Houghton Mifflin, 1978.

Lawler, Edward E. "Workers Can Set Their Own Wages—Responsibly." *Psychology Today,* February 1977, pp. 109–110, 112. Reprinted in *Dimensions in Modern Management,* 2d ed., edited by Patrick E. Connor. Boston: Houghton Mifflin, 1978.

Morse, John J., and Lorsch, Jay W. "Beyond Theory Y." *Harvard Business Review* 48 (May–June 1970): 61–68. Reprinted in *Dimensions in Modern Management,* 2d ed., edited by Patrick E. Connor. Boston: Houghton Mifflin, 1978.

Cases for Part V

Case V/1

The punctual president

Ben Cohen, the president of the Coday Manufacturing Company, is preparing for a meeting. He called the meeting to clear up what he considers a bad situation in the company.

During the past year, Cohen has had numerous complaints from both the union and the factory superintendent regarding employee punctuality. In the production department, it has been a shop rule that every worker must be at his or her station at 8:00 in the morning and remain working there until 4:30 P.M., with the exception of clearly stated rest and lunch breaks. Salespeople and engineers have not followed any similar rule, and production workers have been complaining about the comings and goings at all hours of the day.

Cohen has asked the superintendent of the plant, the sales manager, and the director of engineering to come to the meeting. He has been mulling over the way in which to approach the subject—how firmly he should lay down the law—when Beverly Gallo, the personnel manager, happens to phone. Cohen tells her that he is busy preparing for a meeting and, as an afterthought, he invites her to also be present.

Questions

1. Did Cohen take the appropriate step by calling a meeting?
2. How should he approach the subject? Should he lay down firm rules and regulations regarding starting and quitting times for the entire company?
3. What position should the sales manager and the director of engineering take?
4. What should the personnel director's role be?

Case V/2

The zealous graduate student

Jane Smith was an administrative resident at St. Margaret's Hospital. She was spending a year there as a requirement to receive her degree in hospital administration from a local university.

Like most hospitals, St. Margaret's had a number of building and renovation projects underway, and Smith noticed that expensive and sophisticated equipment and machinery often lay around for weeks before it was installed, because the rest of the work had not progressed to the stage of installation. As her term project, Smith devised a system that involved careful planning among the hospital administrator, the associate administrator in charge of the particular project, the chief of the medical specialty involved, the purchasing department, and the firm doing the construction work. She even designed a simple-to-use network analysis with the help of the members of the computer department. Her report concluded that thousands of dollars could be saved if these department heads would adopt a formal planning procedure.

Jane's proctor, Tom O'Malley, who was an associate administrator at the hospital, was delighted with her report and discussed it at the next executive committee meeting, which many of the people involved attended.

The reaction was not good. The department heads resented that a graduate student, who was doing her assigned residency at the hospital in order to learn, had the audacity to involve herself in such a problem; and they disliked the suggestion that their actions were costing the hospital thousands of dollars. They stated that Smith was no longer welcome.

O'Malley told Smith about the outcome. Both wondered why they had received such a reaction.

Questions

1 Where did O'Malley and/or Smith make their mistake?
2 How can the committee's reaction be explained?
3 Assuming that the facts, the reasoning, and the conclusions of the report were right, what should have been done to avoid the final outcome?

Case V/3

The new directive

For the past fifteen years, the Claymont Manufacturing Company has produced valves and other small parts to be used in aerosol spray cans. Most of its employees have worked for the company for a long time and are not unionized. For many years, Len Williams, the president of the company, has wanted to change work hours during the summer months, to help his employees avoid some of the rush-hour traffic and to enable them to enjoy more daylight hours after work. The regular work hours for all factory and office personnel are from 8:00 A.M. to 5:00 P.M., with an hour off for lunch. Williams intends to change these hours to from 7:30 A.M. until 4:00 P.M., with only half an hour off for lunch.

He knows that many of his employees will prefer the new hours. However, he also knows that this new arrangement will cause hardships for a number of employees: those that drive to work with their spouses; those that are in car pools; those that depend on babysitters; and those that enjoy sleeping late in the morning. Williams also expects some objections from those whose work depends on the work of outsiders whose day begins later and ends later.

Williams had entertained the idea of *flexi-time,* a plan that allows employees to set their own time schedules, as long as eight hours a day are spent on the job and as long as those eight hours fall between 7:00 A.M. and 5:00 P.M. However, he decided that flexi-time would create too many new problems on the production line and in the administrative office.

Therefore, Williams has decided to go ahead with the earlier work hours. He fully realizes that he could submit this change to his employees for group deliberations and group decision making and that this group participation could facilitate the change. Nevertheless, Williams intends to simply announce the new work hours four weeks before they will take effect, so that his employees can make all the arrangements that will be necessary.

Questions

1 Is Williams doing the right thing?

2 What would you prefer if you were the president of the company? one of the employees?
3 What are the advantages of group decision making? the disadvantages?
4 What problems are usually encountered when changes are introduced?

Case V/4

Juanita and her department

Juanita Mendez, age thirty, is the supervisor of the Dunhill Manufacturing Company's storeroom. She has worked for the company for five years, having spent the first three of those years as an assistant to one of the buyers in the purchasing department. That assignment familiarized her with many of the materials, parts, and supplies needed by the company. When the job of supervisor of the storeroom became vacant, two years ago, she asked for the position and was given the job. Because it was a promotion, Mendez was eager to succeed in her new position. However, the job was a challenge; the operation of the storeroom had always been a source of complaints in the company.

Mendez installed new procedures for record keeping, issuance of materials, and controls, and the department seemed to be functioning smoothly. She had six employees working for her when she started. Within two years, four of the six had left the company and were replaced. All four had been with the company for a number of years; the two who remained were older employees, who would be unable to find comparable jobs in other companies.

When the personnel director called this situation to the attention of the plant superintendent, Bob Low, under whose authority the storeroom operates, Low suggested that someone determine the reasons for the turnover. He asked his assistant, Philip Noonan, to do this, and, after speaking with the former employees and with other employees of the company, Noonan submitted a report. He had found that Mendez was a hard worker, who was eager to succeed in her job and was very knowledgeable. Many of the new methods and procedures she had originated were very good, and the department generally functioned well. However, her major weakness seemed to occur in the areas of directing, motivating, communicating, and leading. She seemed to be a rigid and formal young woman who, in her desire to succeed, ran the department with a firm hand, thereby creating considerable resentment among the employees. At times, she had embarrassed her subordinates by taking disciplinary action in public.

Low would like to know what to do. Mendez certainly is doing a good job with the material aspects of the job, but she seems deficient in the personnel area.

Questions

1 What are the major problems in this situation?
2 Should Mendez be replaced? If not, what action would you recommend?

Case V/5

The chemical laboratory

The Alpha Laboratories develops chemicals, oils, coloring, and other ingredients for use in the cosmetic industry. The firm employs a number of chemists, engineers, technologists, and clerical workers. All the chemists and engineers hold at least a bachelor's degree; the technologists have one or two years of junior college or a high-school education and a great deal of on-the-job training.

The president of the firm, Sheila Green, assigned each project to a chemist, who then carried it through to its completion. During this period the chemist could request the help of other chemists, engineers, or technologists. No particular technologist or number of technologists was assigned to a chemist. This informal arrangement always worked well; there were always technologists available to tackle new tests; and no significant delays were caused by the overuse of equipment or apparatus.

As time went on, however, the number of projects increased. Green enlarged the laboratory by adding chemists and technologists. At the same time, she rearranged the organizational setup, creating a pool of technologists with a chief technologist in charge. By creating a pool, Green hoped to conserve resources, avoid waste, and make technologists' support available to all on an equal basis. Under the new scheme, whenever a chemist needed certain tests, that person was to channel a request through the chief technologist, who would then assign someone from the pool to do the job.

After some time, delays and dissatisfaction indicated that the new system was not working. Chemists complained that they could not obtain their test results quickly. The technologists were dissatisfied and complained that the chief technologist placed too much pressure on them. Often, they said, the unavailability of testing equipment caused the delays. More technologists were put to work and more equipment was bought. Still, the complaints persisted to such a degree that, after one year, Green was tempted to go back to the informal working arrangement that she had previously used.

Questions

1 Could these problems have been avoided?
2 Why didn't the pool produce the desired results, even though its organization was rationally based?
3 The number of projects is continuously increasing. What should Green do?

Case V/6

The administrative assistant

Dr. John Wesselman is the chief of medicine at the Methodist Hospital in St. Louis. As such, he is a full-time employee of the hospital in charge of all aspects of the department of medicine. He is paid a substantial annual salary; whenever he sees private patients, his fees are paid to the hospital. He has a staff of about seventy-five people, comprised of physicians, scientists, technologists, and clerical employees. In order to ease his many administrative duties, he has hired Charles Gorham as his administrative assistant. Gorham, who holds a B.S. in business administration, has helped Dr. Wesselman greatly by ensuring that the department functions smoothly, thereby enabling the chief to concentrate on the medical and scientific aspects of his job.

The department contains specialized groups, one of which is composed of endocrinologists headed by Dr. Sarah Miller. A number of physicians, scientists, and technologists work in this speciality; all of them are full-time employees of the hospital. One of the bright young people in this area is Dr. Nat Conway, a resident, who came to the hospital with an outstanding record of achievements in other hospitals. He had come to Methodist Hospital with high expectations and great hopes for pursuing his research.

Gorham, who is well liked by most people in the department, has learned that Dr. Conway is dissatisfied and on the verge of turning in his resignation. His chief complaint is that Dr. Miller burdens him with routine work and does not allow him any time to pursue his own area of research. He was hired with the understanding that he could, and should, pursue the promising work he had started in other hospitals.

Gorham does not know what to do. He definitely considers it his duty to do all in his power to keep Dr. Conway on the staff of the hospital. He does not know if Dr. Miller is aware of Dr. Conway's intentions. However, he does know that Dr. Miller would resent it if Gorham were to discuss the matter with her. On the other hand, Gorham is reluctant to discuss Dr. Conway's case with Dr. Wesselman because it is not an administrative matter. Also, if he approached Dr. Wesselman and Dr. Wesselman, in turn, discussed the case with Dr. Miller, Dr. Miller would either resent Gorham's interference or would think that Dr. Conway had gone directly to Dr. Wesselman to express his dissatisfaction.

Question

1 If you were in Gorham's position, what would you do?

Part VI

Controlling

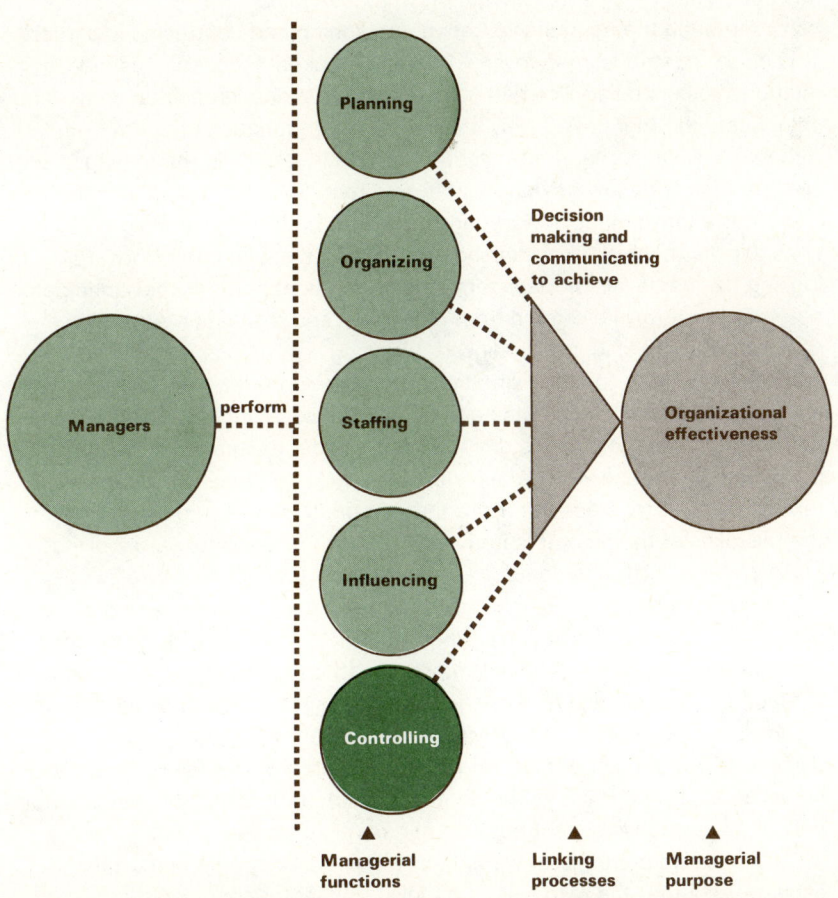

The controlling function Controlling is the management activity that ensures that organizational goals are being met, by comparing performance to the guidelines established in the planning function.

There are many misconceptions about the controlling function. One of the most serious is that controlling is concerned only with events after their occurrence. This misconception probably stems from two causes. First, most management textbooks (including this one) discuss the controlling function last, giving the impression that it occurs after the other functions have been performed. Second, in certain practical applications of control, such as quality control, deviations from standards are not picked up until after a mistake has been made or faulty workmanship has been discovered.

This after-the-fact interpretation of control only gives half the picture. We must remember that control goes on simultaneously with the other functions in a system. Control decisions affect plans, for example, just as planning decisions affect controls. In the process of planning, managers set goals, objectives, and policies, and these become the standards against which performance is checked and appraised. If any deviations occur between achievements and goals, managers must take corrective action, and this action itself may entail new plans and new goals.

Although the relationship between planning and controlling is particularly close, control is interwoven with all managerial functions; indeed, their relationship is circular. The better management plans, organizes, staffs, and influences, the more effectively it can perform its function of control, and vice versa. Clearly, the interrelatedness of the functions in the management system does not allow any one function to remain first or last in a sequence.

The after-the-fact view of controlling can be further modified when we consider that control, like planning, should be at least partially forward looking. Higher levels of management should adopt controls that anticipate potential sources of deviation from objectives and standards. As we have said, control and planning are linked: planning sets objectives, and high-level control seeks ways to offset situations that may interfere with their accomplishment. Past experience can be of considerable help in anticipatory controlling. Managers may study the past in order to learn what has taken place and where and why certain standards were not met. They can then take the necessary steps to ensure that action in the future does not follow the mistakes of the past. It is in this sense that control is forward looking, utilizing the past to anticipate the proper measures for the future.

In practice, however, the anticipatory aspect of control is seldom emphasized or realized. Deviations are corrected *after* the fact; they are not anticipated. The part of the control process that receives the most attention is reaction. The reactive aspect enables a manager to detect deviations from standards or objectives, to receive feedback information, and to correct deviations at the point of performance. We must always keep in mind, however, that proper use of the control function requires understanding not only of its corrective aspect but also of its anticipatory potential.

We would be remiss if we did not take note of another important aspect of control: the response of people. This factor pervaded our discussions of the organizing, staffing, and influencing functions. For this reason, we do not have a chapter specifically devoted to it in Part VI. However, we would like to make several points concerning it here. Control means nothing more or less than placing constraints on behavior so that what people do in organizations will be predictable. Important techniques of control that facilitate this purpose arise from specialization and specification of function, from organizational structure, and from the reward and punishment systems through which managers exercise power. Group norms—nonplanned or consciously introduced into the system by management—also exert powerful controls over behavior.

The amount of control or restraint exercised in a particular situation obviously is subject to management's discretion. Management literature mentions two extremes—tight control and loose control or close supervision and general supervision. These extremes define the degree of freedom an individual has and how much discretion that individual is permitted in performing a job. This is an important matter because the nature and degree of control over people's discretion relates directly to the climate of motivation we discussed at length in Part V.

We saw that managers are increasingly widening this area of discretion in an effort to obtain greater organizational flexibility. They realize that if control is loosened and human satisfactions on the job are enhanced, the facility of the organization to adapt to change will be increased. Looser control is, of course, accomplished by less functional specification, greater decentralization, and more participation in the decision-making process, among other things.

The degree of control can also be related to the organic or mechanistic character of an organization. An *organic* organization has free-flowing communication and an open structure that depends less on lines of authority. A *mechanistic* organization, on the other hand, has a rigid chain of command that forms a path for the movement of information along official channels of communication. Obviously, the mechanistic organization has a more closely controlled and formal, bureaucratic system. As we have said, management is tending to move away from this type of organization toward more open, organic systems.

This movement, however, should in no way suggest the complete disappearance of control in organizations. Such a situation is an impossibility. What we see is, in part, a reaction to the tight, often inhuman character of traditional control systems. However, we must keep in mind, as we have observed previously, that organizations are not universally susceptible to the reduction of human controls. Technology and the educational levels of the work force are the contingencies that make the difference. Those organizations most open to loose control structure are the ones that utilize advanced technologies, are subject to rapid change, and employ large numbers of professionally educated people.

Chapter 26

The control process

Objectives of the chapter

1 To examine the organizational control process and its relationships to the other managerial functions.
2 To present a general model of control.
3 To discuss the human aspects of control systems.
4 To consider the design of an effective control system.
5 To describe the principal steps in the control process.

Control is the management function that ensures that organizational performance is as close as possible to the objectives, policies, and standards established in the planning process. Henri Fayol writes: "Control consists in verifying whether everything occurs in conformity with the plan adopted, the instructions issued and principles established. Its purpose is to point out weaknesses and errors in order to rectify them and prevent recurrence. Control operates on everything, things, people, action."[1] However, a control system does not control performance *directly*. The techniques of control are tools that managers use in a variety of ways, depending on the strategies demanded by a situation's contingencies.[2]

Without control, management could not do a complete job of managing. Indeed, control is necessary whenever management assigns duties and delegates authority to subordinates. Managers cannot simply delegate and sit back; they must exercise control over the actions taken under the delegated authority. They must set standards, check results against them, and take corrective measures when necessary.

---

[1] Henri Fayol, *General and Industrial Management,* trans. Constance Storrs (London: Pitman, 1949), p. 107.
[2] Cortlandt Cammann and David A. Nadler, "Fit Control Systems to Your Management Style," *Harvard Business Review* 54 (January—February 1976): 66.

Although planning and setting objectives, goals, policies, and procedures are indispensable to the efficient management of an enterprise, they are not means of control. Objectives, goals, and policies generate the need for control, but they do not fulfill that need; neither does organization. Management must develop separate and distinct techniques for control purposes.

A general model of control

Organizations must have systems for information processing. These systems provide managers with information that helps them make decisions about their external environment and internal organizational processes. Such information is vital not only for control purposes but also for planning. Feedback is a particular type of information that is central to information and control systems. For any system to operate properly it must have readings on how well it is doing in relation to its environment and its internal activities. Feedback supplies this kind of information. The most commonly cited example of a feedback system is the thermostat. This instrument controls the air temperature in a room by turning on and shutting off a furnace. It constantly compares the actual room temperature with the desired temperature and takes regulating action when the actual temperature rises or drops sufficiently to trip an actuating device.

Control systems in organizations work on the same principle. They compare actual performance with desired performance. When and if the actual level deviates unacceptably from the desired level, corrective action is instituted. These similarities allow us to speak of a feedback principle in organizational control systems. More specifically, we can develop a general model of control that applies to a wide variety of systems (see Figure 26-1).

The model represents a closed-loop system composed of six elements: the inputs, the converter, the output, the sensor, the regulator, and the information that flows through the system. The controlling data — standards, objectives, policies, and the like — are inputs to the system. They originate in a larger system of which the model is a part. Similarly, if an individual sets a thermostat at 72 degrees, that individual represents a larger system providing controlling objectives for the subsystem.

Given the objectives, the close-loop system works in the following manner: the converter processes inputs to produce an output. The output is sampled by the sensor to discover if it conforms to the standards set by a higher system. If it does, the sensor takes no action. If it does not, the sensor activates a regulator, which adjusts a controlling input. *Note:* The regulator functions on only one input, not on all. This one input is crucial; by varying it, the control desired of the converter can be achieved. In other words, the converter will resume producing outputs in line with the standards.

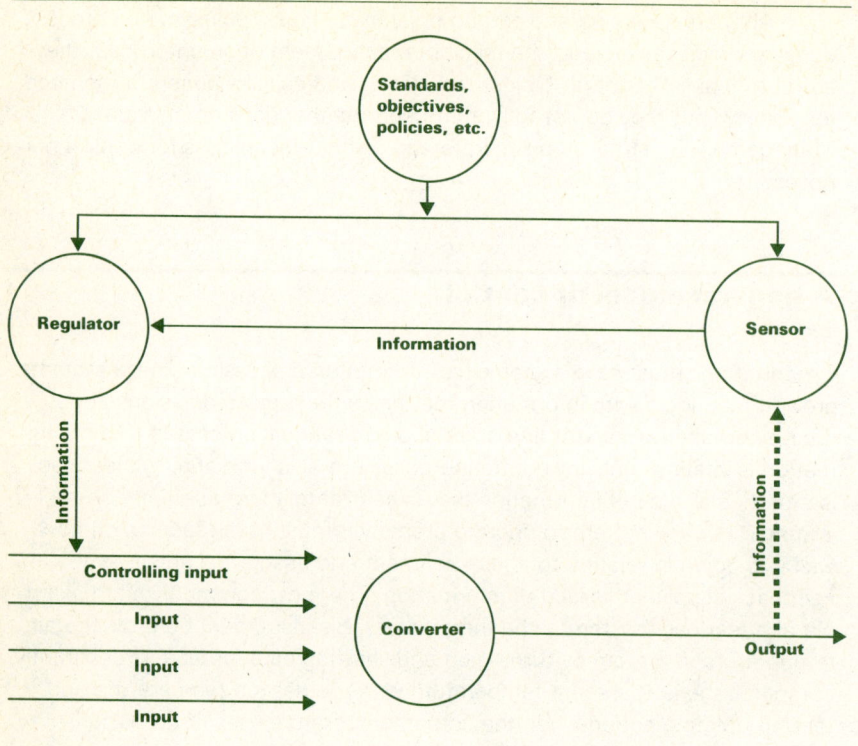

Figure 26-1 Control model

This model can easily be applied to many organizational situations. The most obvious example is the quality control in a manufacturing operation shown in Figure 26-2. The closed-loop system in this illustration applies to nail manufacturing. The inspector samples the nails being produced. If the rejection rate exceeds the allowance, the foreman is notified. The foreman acts on one of the inputs, in this case labor (a poorly trained employee), to reduce the number of faulty nails. After the input is corrected, the convertor or production line should then be able to produce more nails that meet quality standards.

Feedback is a powerful source of information for managerial control. It can be used to correct errors, to identify and solve problems, and to clarify goals for more effective employee motivation.[3] There is the danger, however, that feedback control systems are viewed in a mechanical sense. For example, Miles and Vergin write:

In the traditional control model, its critics argue, the organization is pictured as essentially machine-like. Control procedures are designed to monitor the machine's performance along a number of dimensions and to dispatch vari-

---

[3] David Nadler, Philip Mirvis, and Cortlandt Cammann, "The Ongoing Feedback System," *Organizational Dynamics,* Spring 1975, pp. 63–80.

ous reports to upper level officials. Management, in this model stands at the "control panel" alert to evidence of negative deviation from preestablished standards and procedures and ready to pull switches and twist dials to enforce compliance at any point at which such deviation may occur.[4]

While this may overstate the traditional case somewhat, the warning is well taken—managers implement control to change behavior, and, therefore, it is a mistake to disregard the mutual influence that exists between people and control systems.

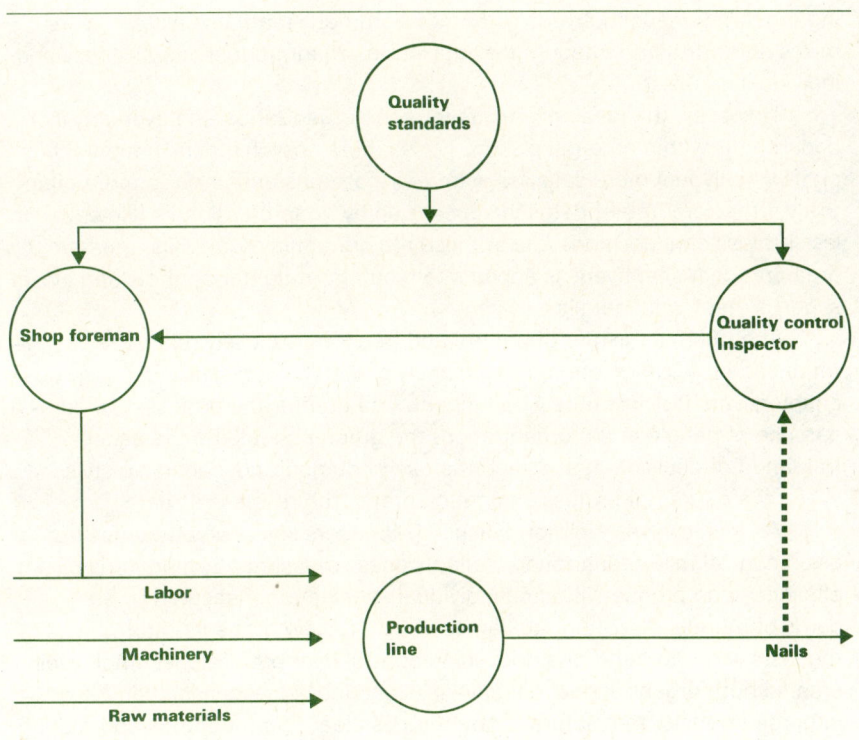

Figure 26-2 Control model applied to a quality control system

The human aspects of control systems

The amount of control that exists in an organization determines how much freedom of action individuals have when performing their jobs. However, individuals' perception of freedom is not necessarily maximized by an absence of control; some control is conducive to maximizing human perception of freedom. Control restricts not only one's own behavior, but also the

[4] R. E. Miles and R. C. Vergin, "Behavioral Properties of Variance Controls," *California Management Review,* Spring 1966.

behavior of others. The existence of control assures individuals that they will be able to predict, within limits, the behavior of others toward them. If, for example, individuals could not predict the reaction of their bosses they might feel constrained in their behavior.

A certain amount of formalization and control appears essential to regulate behavior in all situations. Because controls limit arbitrary, capricious, and erratic behavior, they make a positive contribution to individuals' perception of freedom. Theorists now think that perception of freedom is optimized when a balance is achieved between the degree of discretion and the degree of formalization in an organization. In other words, neither the extreme of tight control nor that of complete freedom is optimal for achieving organizational effectiveness. Somewhere between these extremes are mixes of control and freedom that maximize organizational effectiveness and individual satisfaction.

However, the ideal mix differs for each organization and even for each department within an organization. For example, psychiatrists in mental hospitals usually feel more satisfied with their positions and perform more effectively if they are free of detailed supervision by nonprofessionals. However, in less professional positions and in those requiring minimum skills, greater organizational effectiveness appears to result from tighter controls and closer supervision of work details.

The optimal mixture of control and freedom is closely related to organizational centralization and managerial style, which we discussed in previous chapters. Its basis is entirely contingent. The greater the professional competence of people in the organization, the greater should be the decentralization of decision making and the use of democratic leadership style. When the degree of professionalization drops, the reverse is true.

All this involves a major difficulty. Managers seek two outcomes from a given control mix: organizational effectiveness measured by standards of efficiency and productivity, and individual satisfaction measured by standards of morale. According to James Price's review of the literature, theorists seem to agree that loosening control over professional employees creates both organizational effectiveness and individual satisfaction.[5] For nonprofessionals, the picture is not quite as clear. Tight controls do produce organizational effectiveness, but they may reduce individual satisfaction and group morale.

Behavior and control

Control affects behavior in three separate situations: when a control system is installed, when actual comparison is made between standards and performance, and when the job is being performed under specific control techniques.[6] In the first instance, people may resist a new control system if they

---

[5] James L. Price, *Organizational Effectiveness* (Homewood, Illinois: Richard D. Irwin, 1968), chap. 3.
[6] Ralph Louis Benke, Jr., "Human Behavior and Control," *Managerial Planning*, July–August 1975, p. 19.

feel it is a threat to them. In the second case, which involves actual evaluation of performance, disagreements may arise over the standards of control as they relate to how an employee has done a job. In the last situation, people may try to beat the control system, if they feel it is exploiting them or not measuring the relevant aspects of job performance.[7]

These negative consequences of the control process are discussed at length in management. Control, when properly implemented, can be a powerful tool for influencing behavior. However, if control is mishandled, and if it is treated without regard to its impact on people, unwanted behavioral results are bound to occur. Therefore, serious attention must be given to the design of the control system.

Design of an effective control system

Controls must always be appropriate to the activity they monitor. The tools of control that are suitable to a sales department are different from those used in manufacturing. Even within manufacturing, the control tools used by the vice president in charge of production are different from those used by the supervisor on the floor. Likewise, the controls found in a small organization are not as elaborate as those employed by a large enterprise.

Some control techniques, however, are used in one form or another by almost all enterprises. These include standard hours, standard costs, budgets, break-even points, and financial ratios. Management adapts these and other techniques in order to devise a control system that adequately reflects the activities and needs of the particular enterprise. The size and type of enterprise will, of course, help to determine the criterion of adequacy. Any system of control should require no more reports, data, figures, and statistics than are absolutely necessary.

Consequently, controls must be designed to suit the contingencies of each situation, depending on both the *level* and the *means* for achieving objectives.[8] In project-type organizations, each project has different goals that require separate and distinct levels of performance and techniques of accomplishment. A low-technology project that requires considerable amounts of semiskilled labor should have a control system that differs greatly from a high-technology project that demands highly skilled labor. For example, the control system used in making the Mars landing vehicle for the Viking II project differs from the system used in the mass production of automobiles.

Understandability

Managers throughout the system must understand how the controls work and must recognize the standards that are to be achieved. People seem to

---

[7] Cammann and Nadler, "Fit Control Systems," p. 67.
[8] Henry L. Tosi and Stephen J. Carroll, *Management: Contingencies, Structure, and Process* (Chicago: St. Clair, 1976), p. 433.

find it easier to live with a problem they cannot solve than with a solution they cannot understand. In practical terms, this means that the system of control should be designed so that it will become less complicated as it extends farther down into the managerial hierarchy. Certainly, it must be understood by the level of management that is to apply it. This factor frequently leads to conflict between the specialists who devise systems of controls and the managers who must apply them. The incomprehensible technical language of specialists often is a barrier to understanding by lower levels of management.

Rapid reporting of deviations

An effective control system requires the immediate reporting of deviations. The sooner management is aware of such deviations, the sooner it can take corrective action. Indeed, it is more desirable to have deviations reported quickly, even if they are substantiated only by approximate figures, than it is to wait two or three weeks for exact figures. Management cannot afford the time lag; it must find means to learn of deviations expeditiously. The organizations that use electronic data-processing equipment have the great advantage of receiving data almost immediately.

Another reason for rapid reporting is that managers are prone to exert less and less pressure as time passes. They tend to concentrate on events that took place during the last few days and report them to their superiors, ignoring those that are past history. Often, the reviewing manager ends up focusing on this last bit of information instead of on the more enduring problems that should be under review. The timeliness of control information is, therefore, essential.

Inevitably, in higher levels of the organization, the control period lengthens. A parallel to this exists in the planning function. We noted that the typical planning period of the first-line supervision is much shorter than that of the middle managers, and the middle-managerial period is shorter than that of top management. Similarly, in the control process, the first-level supervisors may receive rapid feedback on performance, but top management may have to wait a longer period of time to receive meaningful control data. However, top management generally receives integrated feedback on broad segments of the system, whereas supervisors receive data pertaining only to their small slice of the organization.

Flexibility

Since the environment of every organization constantly changes, controls must be flexible. Unforeseen circumstances play havoc with the best plans. Even if management prepares planning premises thoroughly, these premises are still estimates and are uncertain. A good control system, in other words, must be designed to keep pace with the continuously changing pattern of the organization's environment. Unless control devices are flexible enough to permit change as soon as it is required, the control system is bound to deteriorate.

The practical importance of this can be illustrated by considering the budgetary control device. Typically, the amount of expense allowed in a department is based on expected sales for the coming period. If, however, the sales during that period double, managers cannot be expected to stay within their allotted budget. There must be enough flexibility built into the system so that they can cover the added expenses resulting from this substantially increased amount of business. Similarly, in their desire to stay within budgets, executives themselves should not refuse to recognize early indications of change in the internal or external environment. If they overlook such indications, they will not be able to keep pace with altered conditions as rapidly as they should.

Economic criteria

In a workable control system, the controls must be economical and must be worth the expenses involved. At times it is difficult—although always worthwhile—for management to estimate how much a particular control system is worth and how much it really costs. They must bear in mind certain economic criteria: the relative contribution the control system makes in relation to the size of the enterprise, the expenses involved, and the consequences that might follow if the controls did not exist.

Indication of corrective action

It is not enough for a control system to reveal deviations; an effectively designed control system should show the way to corrective action. At times, however, this information is not readily available. Often, a report submitted to top management has been oversimplified, and too many items have been consolidated under a single heading. A summary report does not clearly indicate below-the-surface facts. Perhaps a favorable showing in one area prevents a poor showing in another from appearing. Management can discover such occurrences by insight, accident, or by a thorough study of the detailed financial control information on which their incomplete summary is based.

Basic steps in the control process

To set up an effective control process, managers should plan four basic activities. First, in order to ascertain whether or not performance is in accordance with plans, they must set standards. Next, managers must establish strategic control points. Then, they must ensure that performance is checked and appraised. Finally, if a deviation occurs, they must have set up an apparatus for corrective action. To control effectively, these activities should be followed in the sequence indicated.

Setting standards

Standards are criteria against which we judge results. In planning, management sets the objectives and goals that the enterprise hopes to achieve. It then divides these overall objectives into narrower objectives for individual departments. From these narrower objectives, specific goals are established. Specific goals may relate to quality, production cost, time standards, sales quotas, schedules, budgets, and many other areas of detailed operations. These goals become the standards for exercising control.

Types of standards

Because the variety of specific goals is so large, the average enterprise will have a multitude of standards. Most of these will be of a tangible nature, although some will be intangible and therefore much more difficult to work with.

Tangible standards

The most common tangible standards are physical, cost, revenue, and capital. Normally, *physical standards* form the basis of all planning. They encompass the actual operation of the enterprise: where goods are produced, services rendered, and workers employed. These standards are both quantitative and qualitative. Quantitatively, they define the number of units to be produced per hour, the number to be obtained out of a cerain quantity of raw material, and so forth. Qualitatively, they refer to the durability of the product, the content of the mixture, the dimensions, closeness, and precision of machining operations, the finish, smoothness, hardness, toughness, strength, and the like. These are the physical criteria of control.

Cost standards are established by attaching monetary value to the expenses that are necessary to reach planned goals. Cost standards include direct and indirect labor costs per unit, standards per hour, standard cost for the material per unit, selling costs, overhead costs, and other direct and indirect costs.

Revenue standards are obtained by attaching monetary value to sales. Management can easily set these standards by multiplying the number of units that are forecast to be sold by the price of each unit. The revenue standard thus calculated is the expected sales volume of the enterprise for a particular period. In planning the annual sales of a department store, for example, the revenue standard might be set at a figure 10 percent above the previous year's sales. This, then, will be the expected volume for that year. The revenue standard for a hospital might be based on expected room occupancy and revenue per bed. Inflationary trends must be considered, of course, when setting revenue standards.

Capital standards are related to the amount of capital invested in an enterprise. The return on capital invested forms a frequently used standard. Other capital standards often used in analyzing the balance sheet of a firm include the ratio of current assets to current liabilities, of fixed investment to total investment, of equity capital expressed by capital stock to debt financing by debentures, notes, or bonds, and the ratio of debt to net worth.

Intangible standards

Although it is relatively easy to measure performance against tangible standards, intangibles, such as attitudes, beliefs, morale, public relations, and executive development, are much more difficult to assess. It is exceedingly difficult to measure whether or not the enterprise has reached standards of good community relations, high employee morale, and/or complete customer satisfaction.

Tools to aid executives in appraising intangible standards and drawing appropriate conclusions are being developed. Psychologists and other behavioral scientists constantly are evaluating new tests and attitude surveys. Although some of these tools will be helpful to management, they are far from the exact. Indeed, the farther away a characteristic is from the production line or from the accounting department, the more difficulty management has in setting up specific standards and measuring performance by them. Nevertheless, management must not overlook the importance of intangible standards in achieving a balanced systems of controls.

Strategic control points

The staggering variety of control standards available makes it necessary for managers to be selective in their use. One author suggests that managers should take at least two important steps before they attempt to compare actual operations with standards. First, "if control is to have effective influence on performance, the administrator should make sure that the goals are promptly identified with individual responsibility."[9] Second, since the administrator will find it impossible to review all aspects of performance, certain points must be selected to give him or her adequate information about what is going on.

It is impractical, in other words, to check the performance of each activity against all the standards that might be applied to it. As operations become more complex or as the area of managerial authority increases, such minute control becomes increasingly infeasible. Managers must concentrate, therefore, on certain strategic control points. In taking this

---

[9] William H. Newman, *Administrative Action,* 2d ed. (Englewood Cliffs, N.J.: Prentice-Hall, 1963), p. 421.

approach, managers select for use only the standards that best reflect the organization's goals and best show whether or not those goals are being met.

It is obvious that, out of the great number of strategic control points, executives must select those that are most effective for their particular undertaking. By such selection, managers can limit the number of standards necessary to achieve a comprehensive and balanced control system that accurately reflects the goals of their specific activities. It should always be remembered that what serves well in one enterprise will not necessarily serve in another.

Checking on performance

The next activity in the process of control is checking performance. This can only occur after standards have been set. Then, work can be observed, output measured, and figures and reports compiled. Checking against standards is a continuous process, which, depending on circumstances, must be performed daily, weekly, or monthly.

There are numerous ways for management to check performance. It may require written reports and summaries with or without oral presentation. The reports serve a good purpose and are necessary. However, they cannot substitute for direct observation and personal contact. Although executives will find that checking on performance by personal observation is time consuming, and although they will find that inspecting operations personally at all the strategic control points is almost impossible, they will find the techniques to be valuable. If the president of a company, for example, wishes information regarding the company's products, its reputation, the effectiveness of its publicity campaigns, there is no better way to obtain such information than to travel with area salespeople, even for short periods. Through this process, the president will gain a firsthand picture of whether or not the enterprise is reaching its tangible physical standards—a quality product, for instance—and its intangible standards of reputation, customer goodwill, and salespeople's effectiveness.

Checking performance is usually carried out by superiors after subordinates have perfomed their functions. When superiors delegate authority for these functions to their subordinates they should make certain that enough controls exist to enable them to take corrective action in case subordinates' performance does not meet the standard. In the final analysis, superiors never shift their responsibility for the function; they merely exercise control after the fact.

Occasionally, however, superiors insist on checking work before subordinates can proceed. Prior confirmation may be required for numerous reasons: superiors may be reluctant to delegate authority because they are unable to state control standards clearly; superiors may not, as yet, have completed all their planning functions and, thus, may not be able to set the standards that they expect subordinates to achieve. This lack of complete planning, with its consequent lack of standards, might be caused by the development of new areas or by superiors' ignorance of the functions involved in a particular area. In cases of this nature, superiors should have the subordinates check with them before they proceed—prior confirmation instead of subsequent controlling.

Corrective action

The last activity in the process of control is taking corrective action. Management does not control unless it performs this step whenever it is needed. If no deviations from established standards occur, then, of course, controlling is fulfilled by the first two control activities. However, if there is a discrepancy or a variation, the controlling function is not completed unless corrective action is taken.

Reasons for deviation
Management should check into the reasons for variations from standards before prescribing specific corrective measures. For example, a deviation could result from ill-chosen planning premises. It could result from the dependence of production quotas on some other department. For instance, the production quota of a machine shop could be based on its receiving a certain number of units from the casting department. A check on performance might point out that the deviation in production was caused by an insufficient foundry supply. The corrective action, in this instance, would be directed toward the casting department.

Deviations might also occur if a subordinate is unqualified or has not been given proper directions and instructions. If the latter is the case, additional training might solve the problem. If this is not sufficient, a replacement must be sought. Before taking such a step, however, the superior should be sure that the subordinate understands what is expected of him or her.

Taking appropriate action
After reviewing the different reasons for deviation, management must decide on and carry out necessary corrective action. This action might consist of a revision of standards or plans or the replacement of certain subordinates.

To visualize the entire control process, let us assume that an economic upswing has been forecast and that standards have been set accordingly. If the upswing does not materialize as anticipated, then the standards must be lowered. In this instance, corrective action also will include a revision of plans. At the moment management revises its plans it starts a completely new cycle of all managerial functions. The new plans might necessitate changes in organization, changes in staffing, changes in influencing, and, of necessity, creation of new standards for the control process. These will require checking and reappraisal, that is, a comparison of results with the new standards. If new deviations occur, additional correction will have to be taken. This example clearly shows the continuing circular movement of the controlling function and the management process in general.

The exception principle

Managers in checking subordinates' activities will find most performance adequate; they should pass over the satisfactory areas and concentrate their attention on exceptions—matters in which performance deviates significantly from the standard. This technique, named the *exception principle*, was expressed by Frederick Taylor. Taylor felt that managers should give detailed attention to unusual or exceptional items because only they warrant executive attention. Managers might even request that subordinates not send any reports on activities that are within preestablished standards.

In order for this checking process to be successful, a sense of mutual trust and confidence must exist between subordinates and superiors. Managers must know that subordinates will not hesitate to report functional exceptions or deviations, and subordinates must know that their superiors maintain confidence in their overall performance.

Do not confuse the exception principle with strategic control points. Strategic control points indicate only the points to be watched, whereas the exception principle refers to significant deviations that must be watched, regardless of where they occur.

Summary

The control function is a form of insurance, which provides that the organization operates according to performance criteria established in the planning function. Central to control is information through feedback. This information allows managers to detect deviations from standards, locate causes of deviations, and take corrective action.

Control involves more than technical systems of information and measurement. Such systems are used by managers to change employees' behavior. Therefore consideration of the impact of controls on people is essential in the design of a control system.

In all cases, the design of a control system must suit the activities being monitored. In addition, controls should be designed so that they are understandable, quick to report deviations, flexible, economical, and indicative of the corrective action to be taken. Further, control systems should be designed around sequential steps in the process, which include setting standards, identifying strategic control points, checking performance, and taking corrective action.

Discussion questions

1. Relate control to the other functions in the management process.
2. Explore your feelings about control systems. Use the examination process in your courses as a case in point. Would you be more satisfied if there were no examinations or grades?

Supplementary readings

Cammann, Cortlandt, and Nadler, David A. "Fit Control Systems to Your Management Style." *Harvard Business Review,* January–February 1976.

Sayles, Leonard. "The Many Dimensions of Control." *Organizational Dynamics,* Summer 1972. Reprinted in *Dimensions in Modern Management,* 2d ed., edited by Patrick E. Connor. Boston: Houghton Mifflin, 1978.

Chapter 27

The budget: Control aspects

Objectives of the chapter

1. To analyze the budget as a means of managerial control.
2. To describe the administration of a budgetary program.
3. To discuss the various kinds of budgets found in modern organizations.
4. To review the process by which budgets are prepared.
5. To consider the relationship between budgeting and the other managerial functions.

The budget is probably the most widely used of all available control devices. Indeed, when properly applied, budgetary control is one of management's most effective tools. Budgets express the plans, objectives, and programs of an organization in numerical terms. Therefore, the preparation of the budget is a planning and decision-making function. However, its administration is a controlling function: it establishes standards to which operations can be compared and adjusted. Like other control techniques, budgetary standards measure the progress of actual performance against the plan and, in doing so, provide information that enables management to take necessary action to make results conform with the plan.[1]

Budgeting and budgetary control

Budgetary plans generally regulate all phases of an organization's operations over a definite period of future time. Managers usually plan an overall budget for the organization and a number of subbudgets that detail departmental and divisional plans. For instance, the sales budget states revenue goals,

---

[1] James Don Edwards and Jack E. Kiger, "Financial Planning and Control," *Management Planning*, November–December 1975, p. 1.

and the expense budget states the expense limitations that cannot be exceeded if a business firm, for example, wants to realize planned income. Other subbudgets specify the plans for inventory levels, cash requirements, financing, production, purchasing, labor requirements, capital additions, and so forth.

The term *budgetary control* refers to the use of budgets to control day-to-day operations so that they will conform to organizational goals. Budgetary control involves not only constant evaluation of actual results in relation to the established goals but also corrective action when necessary.

Comprehensive and partial budgeting

If all phases of the operations of an organization are budgeted and if departmental budgets are consolidated into the overall budgetary program, then comprehensive budgeting is being used. Although many managers prefer comprehensive budgeting, a number prepare only partial budgets. For example, some prepare only a sales budget to serve as a basis for setting sales quotas and a production budget to cover activities in the production department. Others use budgets extensively for planning but not for control. Unquestionably, partial budgeting is of greater value than no budgeting, but the full benefits of budgeting and budgetary control can be realized only if a comprehensive program covers all organizational aspects and is utilized for both planning and control purposes.

Numerical expression

Although the numerical terms specified in budgets are frequently monetary, not all budgets are expressed in dollars and cents. Many are expressed in nonfinancial numerical terms. A raw materials budget is expressed in pounds, tons, gallons, or yards of specific materials. Personnel budgets are expressed in terms of the number of workers needed for each type of skill or the number of hours necessary to perform a certain activity. Likewise, finished-goods budgets are expressed mostly in units of products. If nonfinancial budgets were expressed in monetary terms, they might be too general. A company might appear to have an adequate total inventory if its budget showed only the dollar value of all raw materials together. However, if one or two particularly important items are not in the inventory, production will stop. Likewise, a monetary budget would not be detailed enough to show price changes in raw materials, although such changes might greatly influence the outcome of the production plan. Nevertheless, overall budgeting needs some common denominator, and generally this is dollars and cents. Ultimately, even nonfinancial budgets must be translated into this system so that they can be incorporated and condensed into companywide estimates and overall budgets.

Managerial budget preparation

Because budgets activate all plans, budget preparation engages management in one of its most basic decision-making activities. For budgetary purposes, management cannot merely say that production is likely to increase during the second half of the year or that selling expenses should be lower. These planning premises must be quantified and dated. There is considerable difference between making general forecasts and attaching numerical values to plans. The figures that are put into the budget represent actual operating plans; they are no longer merely predictions. They will generally be regarded as the basis for daily operations and as the standards for control. This kind of rigorous budgeting is bound to improve the quality of planning.

A line function

Broad participation in determination of budget estimates

Not only top management but also line managers, who will administer and function under the budgets, must have a part in their preparation in order to assure the advantage of improved planning that comes from budget making. People resent arbitrary orders; therefore, management must include all those responsible for executing budgets when it determines budget allowances and objectives. In order to bring about such participation, management must direct each manager to submit an individual budget.

Participation does not mean, however, that the entire responsibility for budgeting rests with subordinate managers. Before executives request managers to submit their budget estimates, they must ensure that the managers are supplied with all available information concerning past performance, new developments, and any other facts that would assist them in preparing an intelligent and attainable estimate. Once budget proposals are submitted, sponsoring managers must substantiate them in a free and spontaneous discussion with their superiors. Later, in cooperation with top managers, they will set and adjust final figures.

This is what is meant by *broad participation* in budget making. A successful budget program cannot be handed down by a budget director or budget administrator. Active support and cooperation on the various levels of line management is necessary to achieve a good budget.

Of course, the budget suggestions of subordinates do not always prevail. A superior may feel that they are inadequate or incorrect. Indeed, top management—the group with final budgeting authority—should accept no budget plans without carefully studying and analyzing them. Top management also should resolve any differences regarding budget estimates and should be sure that a definite decision is reached.

Often, budgets that have been formulated through the broad participation of all managerial levels tend to be loose. This occurs because some individuals deliberately set their budgetary estimates at a level that presents no challenge. Obviously their motive is self-protection. Usually, managers who exceed their sales budget or stay under their allotted expense budget are, at least temporarily, praised; managers who have set a stiff budget for themselves and do not live up to it are rarely complimented for what they tried to accomplish. Management can check the tendency toward budgetary looseness by making it clear that although it scrutinizes unfavorable variations between actual performance and the budget estimate, it will also scrutinize favorable performance.

Submitting realistic and attainable budget estimates is one of the criteria on which managers are appraised whenever their overall rating takes place. An effective budgetary program indicates the degree of efficiency of individual managers. For this reason, when managers develop a budgetary program, they may encounter many problems and may run into active or passive opposition. These problems must be solved, and full managerial support must be gained. If all levels of management are drawn into budgetary preparations, and all are encouraged to give the budget serious thought not only from a narrow departmental view but also from a companywide vantage point, support will probably be forthcoming.

Ultimate responsibility

In the final analysis, of course, the ultimate responsibility for the budget program lies with the chief executive. Although he or she may be assisted by other line officers and by staff specialists, the chief executive cannot turn over the authority for budget making to a staff unit. It is reasonable and often necessary to enlist staff help in constructing the budget, but budget making is always a line function.

Staff or committee assistance

Budget director

In many organizations, much of the work connected with the preparation of a budgetary program is performed by the budget director or the controller. Often this individual is in top management but holds a staff position and performs an essential, but supporting, function. The budget director provides technical assistance and advice to line personnel and supervises the process of bringing the budget estimates together in final form, after they have been prepared by the operating executives.

Budget committee

Many enterprises have found it expedient to establish a budget committee. This standing committee is often composed of the president, the vice presidents, and the budget director. In a manufacturing firm, it may consist of the president, the sales manager, the production manager, the controller, and the treasurer. In some organizations, the budget committee merely advises and, in this capacity, contributes greatly to top-level coordination. In other organizations, the budget committee adopts a line function and assumes responsibility for the complete budgetary program. Under these conditions, the budget committee considers all departmental estimates and makes any required revisions. No estimate becomes effective without committee approval. Moreover, the budget committee receives reports that compare performance with budgeted figures and, if necessary, makes changes in the budget.

Approval by the board

Top management, in most cases the president, gives final approval to the budgetary program. However, after this approval and before distribution, the complete budgetary program is usually placed in broad outline before the board of directors. A budget submitted to the board will be accompanied by a statement saying that this is what management intends to accomplish, this is why they wish to do so, and this is the probable outcome. The president points out that the budgetary program is based on certain forecasts regarding the foreseeable future, and that if unforeseen conditions should develop the budget would be resubmitted. The presentation of the budgetary program to the board is something of a formality, but it is desirable that board members understand its major aspects.

Administration of a budgetary program

Comprehensive budgeting requires that managers establish and administer a budgetary program that covers the entire operations of an organization. Although budgeting could begin in almost any area, the management of business firms usually starts by requesting the development of a sales forecast or sales budget by the sales division. Since advertising and the extent and expense of distribution also affect total sales potential, these budgets are prepared in conjunction with the sales budget.

Once the sales budget is prepared and tentatively approved, a large number of other subbudgets can be generated almost simultaneously. For example, when the sales budget and the policy regarding the finished-goods inventory are determined, managers can prepare a production budget enumerating the timing and materials required. Then, having established production requirements, managers can develop budgets for direct material requirements, direct labor requirements, and the various manufacturing expenses. At the same time, other departmental managers will be engaged in preparing budgets for administrative expenses, research outlays, capital expenditures, financial expenses, and cash. After all these budgets have been established, they are summarized in the income statement, sometimes called the *profit-and-loss statement* or the *balance sheet*. The flow of a budgetary program is shown in Figure 27-1.

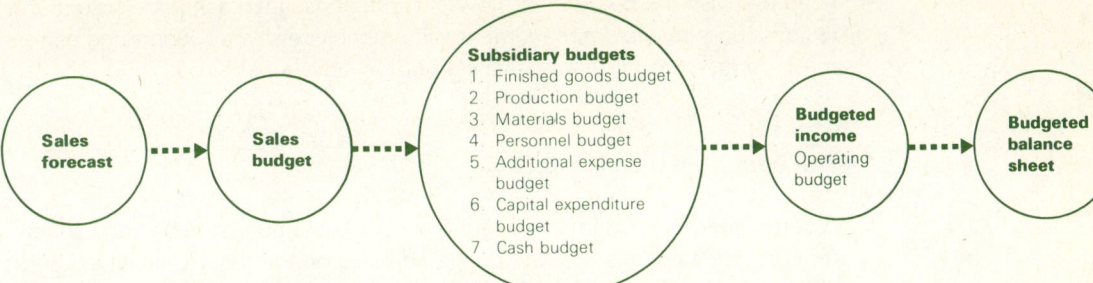

Figure 27-1 The flow of a budgetary program

Sales budget

As we noted previously, formulation of the sales budget is usually the initial step in budgeting. To do this, management must predict sales for the coming year by relying on past experience, anticipated market conditions, and all other planning considerations. Let us assume that only one product is manufactured. If no seasonal fluctuations occur, the annual sales budget can be broken down into quarters or monthly periods by simple arithmetic. If, however, a seasonal fluctuation exists and other departments, such as production, advertising, and finance, must coordinate their efforts with the sales department in order to meet the fluctuating demand, management must calculate separate sales estimates for each of the twelve monthly sales periods. The resulting budget will show the number of units to be shipped each month. If we assume that each unit is sold at a constant price, then multiplying the number of units by the price will give us the monetary value of shipments for each month.

From sales budget data, subsidiary budgets can be prepared. When all this information is assembled, the operating budget and the budgeted balance sheet may be estimated.

Budgeted income statements (operating budget)

Data from the budgets just discussed can be consolidated into what is called a *budgeted income statement*. This statement provides management with an estimate of the profit and loss from operations for the budgeted year. Many companies prepare a budgeted income statement on a monthly as well as a yearly basis. This, of course, entails additional work, but if the monthly income budget is used as a control device, it can be of great help. Like the annual budgeted income statement, it will show management approximately what can be expected under prevailing conditions during the budgeted period. If the indicated results seem to be satisfactory, management will not need to revise the budgets. If, however, the consolidated income statements indicate poor results, management will probably review all supporting estimates in an effort to change plans and to achieve a better outcome.

The budgeted balance sheet

A comprehensive budgetary program usually has a budgeted balance sheet that indicates the effect of the budgeted plans on the assets, liabilities, and net worth of the enterprise. The chief finance officer compiles this balance sheet, basing the figures on the various budgets in the program. This balance sheet indicates to managers the probable financial picture of the organization at the end of the budget period. In evaluating a budgeted balance sheet, managers should compare it with the final balance sheet that appeared at the beginning of the year. This comparison will show how the various items making up the assets and liabilities of the organization will shift by the end of the budgeted period.

Subsidiary components in a budgetary program

Finished-goods budget

Most firms will use their sales budget as a basis for a production budget. The sales budget does not necessarily reflect the production schedule, however, because in most instances an enterprise must carry at least some inventory so that it can fill orders promptly. Thus, a finished-goods budget is usually a prerequisite of a production budget. The finished-goods budget will indicate the monthly opening inventory and the monthly closing inventory. At certain times of the year, the closing inventory level will be higher than it is at other times.

Production budget

The production budget determines the number of units that must be manufactured in order to meet monthly sales requirements and maintain desired inventory levels. Suppose, for example, that a sales budget was based on anticipated shipments of fifty thousand units for the month of January. On January 1, the finished-goods budget indicated an opening inventory of ten thousand units and a desired closing inventory of twenty thousand. The production budget for the month would have to be sixty thousand units. By using the finished goods and sales budgets in this fashion, the manufacturing division is able to prepare a production budget that specifies individual monthly figures.

Materials and materials-purchases budgets

The materials budget is concerned with the number of units of raw material that a company must have in order to produce the units of goods specified in the production budget. The exact quantity of each raw material required is known to the production department, and this information provides the basis for the materials-purchases budget that is sent to the purchasing department.

Although the materials budget is stated in terms of physical units, the purchasing department will reduce it to monetary units. This materials budget can then form an element in the computations that must be made for all materials and supplies before a summary purchase budget can be formulated. When formulating its summary budget, the purchasing department must also consider the company policy on excess raw material inventories. In addition, the purchasing department should make certain that the timing of the purchases is budgeted to coincide with inventory policy and production schedules.

Personnel budget

To achieve complete budgeting, management also must estimate personnel and labor requirements. As an ingredient of this, the manufacturing division must prepare a direct labor budget based on the production budget. This labor budget, normally expressed in terms of standard labor hours, specifies the types of personnel needed—unskilled workers, skilled workers, salespeople. The seasonal fluctuations that appear in the production budget must appear in the personnel budget. If such a budget is given to the personnel department at the beginning of the year, that department will be able to prepare accordingly. Curtailment of production will necessarily be reflected in a curtailed personnel budget, and if the personnel department knows about this in advance, it can carefully prepare layoffs and discharges.

Additional expense budget

An organization incurs many expenses other than those for materials and wages. Included are advertising expenses, distribution expenses, administrative expenses, insurances, taxes, interest, depreciation, utilities, and so forth. There are also selling expenses and supervisory expenses, losses, caused by bad debts, and many other items of this nature. Because these expenses often are substantial, they too must be budgeted, at least tentatively, for the ensuing period.

Capital expenditure budget

In contrast to the additional expense budgets, the capital expenditure budget is often projected over a long range, such as five or ten years. This budget outlines in specific terms expenditures for such things as plant expansion, machinery, equipment acquisitions, and other permanent capital additions. Only the portion of the long-range capital expenditure budget that will materialize during the current year is taken into consideration in the summary budget. Since capital expenditure budgets result in monetary investments that can be recovered from operations only after a long period has elapsed, they must be planned with the greatest care. Plant and equipment expenditures have far-reaching significance not only for the future of the particular enterprise but also for the national economy. Indeed, the overall figures of capital expenditure budgets are used as one of the indicators of national economic activity.

Cash budget

Another important budget is the cash budget, usually prepared by the organization's treasurer. This budget indicates estimated cash receipts, disbursements, and resulting cash fluctuations throughout the year. In preparing the cash budget, treasurers include only those items that actually involve cash. They must bear in mind that cash disbursements do not always coincide with expense totals since such items as depreciation and bad debts are recorded as expenses but are not considered to be cash outlays. Conversely, a number of items that normally are not treated as expenses do require cash outlays. When enterprises invest cash in new machinery, for example, the machinery is not charged directly to expenses but is recorded as an asset; still, machinery requires cash outlays. Treasurers also know that the sale of merchandise on credit increases company assets but cannot increase cash receipts until the merchandise is paid for by the customer.

A properly prepared cash budget will indicate whether or not there will be enough cash available to meet the company's obligations whenever they become due. In other words, it will show management, at the beginning of the year, at what time during the year the enterprise probably will run short of cash. This knowledge enables management to choose in advance whether to secure additional capital or to change the various budgets. If the cash budget shows that the need for additional funds is only temporary, the treasurer probably will meet the current deficit by making arrangements to borrow from a bank. The cash budget will indicate how much will be needed and for how long a period. At the same time, the treasurer will make plans for repayment and will determine the size of installments. Arrangements of this nature are particularly important in industries that have strong cyclical fluctuations in sales and, consequently, in cash receipts. Many companies in such industries depend heavily on seasonal borrowing. These transactions are clearly indicated and projected in their cash budgets.

A cash budget is particularly necessary for a firm that operates on a narrow cash margin. A cash budget is also important to enterprises that have large funds available in excess of the cash needed for current operations. In such situations, the cash budget will show the amount of excess cash and the period during which it will be available. Knowing that such a situation will exist, treasurers then can invest in short-term bonds or treasury notes, instead of keeping idle cash in the bank.

Flexibility of the budgetary program

A budgetary program should be flexible and adaptable, to enable managers to cope with rapidly changing conditions. It also will permit them to revise those parts of the budget that may prove to be incorrect. There are many ways to build flexibility into a budget. Among those that we shall discuss are the length of the budget period, alternative budgets, variable expense budgets, supplemental monthly budgets, and budget reviews.

Length of the budget period

Although the length of the budget period varies among organizations, most managers choose a yearly period. Many firms break down the planned yearly budget into quarters. Some specify months only for the first quarter; others divide the entire planning period into months at the time of the original budget preparation. The selection of a definite yearly budget period and its constituent subperiods is commonly referred to as *periodic budgeting*.

If reasonably accurate budgetary estimates cannot be made for a whole year at a time, managers will use what is called *continuous budgeting*. In this case, monthly, quarterly, or semiannual budgets will be prepared. These, then, will be revised each month by dropping the month just ended and adding the following month. This technique ensures a highly accurate budgetary picture, which is capable of reflecting short-term conditions and events.

It is quite common for organizations that use either periodic or continuous budgeting also to use budgets that extend over long terms, such as three, five, ten, or even more years. Long-term budgets of this nature are formulated by top management and the board of directors. They are not operating budgets.

Alternative budgets

Another way to achieve flexibility in budgeting is to follow the system of alternative budgets, which requires that separate budgetary programs be set up for different operating conditions. At the beginning of the budget period, managers prepare three different budgets: one geared for a high level of operations, another for a medium level, and a third for a low level. All three must be approved. At the beginning of each month or each quarter, managers are told which budget will be in effect. Since such an arrangement is cumbersome and time consuming, three alternative budgets are not frequently made. Instead, managers commonly prepare two budgets: one for a high level and another for a low level of activity. From these, management can estimate mathematically or graphically what the various budget items should be under each alternative. Of course, managers must wait until operations for the particular budgeted period are completed in order to know the level of activity; only then can they see how the various items compare to the amounts budgeted. Although it is relatively easy to determine budgetary standards for different levels of activity, it is impossible to obtain an estimate of how well the organization is doing until the budget period is over. Moreover, this system of alternative budgets is suited only to an enterprise that produces a single product or performs a single service. This device also assumes that costs will vary directly with volume at a constant rate, which is not always the case.

Variable expense budgets

Similar to the system of alternative budget is that of the variable expense or flexible budget. This budget is concerned only with expenses: expenses are estimated and allowances are computed for different levels of activity. After the budget period is over, and the level of actual activity is known, managers can determine what the proper amount of expenses should have been. For example, the variable budget may indicate an allowance of $1,000 per month for supplies plus $10 per 100 direct labor hours worked. Budget allowances for supplies can easily be computed for the various volumes of activity by adding to the $1,000 base the multiple of $10 per 100 direct labor hours. This provides an expense standard adjusted to the rate of activity, a particularly useful device for the control of expenses.

Variable expense budgets, however, do not set a level of operations until after the activity has been performed. They are, therefore, of little value to the overall budgetary program. It is not possible for the purchasing agent, for instance, to wait to determine a materials-purchases budget until after the month is over. Variable expense budgets, however, do help to explain overexpenditures and unfavorable variances. Nonetheless, they are a supplement to, not a substitute for, a comprehensive budgetary program.

Supplemental monthly budget plan

Flexibility also can be achieved through the use of a supplemental monthly budget plan. Under it, a basic minimum budget for the company's operations is set up. Then, a supplementary budget is prepared each month for increasing sales volume and controlling costs and expenses. This additional budget, prepared about ten days before the beginning of the month covered, gives management funds above those already specified in the basic budget.

Budget review or budget revision

Since managers realize that flexibility in applying their budgets increases the chances of achieving or even bettering goals, they often assure flexibility by regular budget revision. At periodic intervals of one, two, or three months, they review the established budget and change it if necessary. At these times, they compare actual performance with the budget. If operating conditions have been appreciably altered, or if the comparison indicates that the budget cannot be followed in the future, they will have to revise the budgetary program.

In comparing actual results to budgeted data, however, managers must look for the cause of variation in order to be able to make the appropriate corrections and adjustments in future plans. According to J. H. Hennessy, Jr., "Variance analysis, whether it be for budgetary purposes or for day-to-day operating control, is the procedure employed in deciding when and where a predetermined level of performance is not being met and, to varying degrees, in exposing fundamental causes."[2]

An unfavorable variance by itself is not sufficient reason for changing the budget. It is a symptom and indicates the need for further investigation and explanation. A failure to reach standards, for example, could result from supervisors' inability to keep products moving through their departments. In such circumstances, budget revision would probably be unnecessary. On the other hand, a thorough analysis may indicate that sales revenue has declined because of the reduction in selling prices brought about by an industry price war. This external condition may necessitate internal budgetary changes. Similarly, managers may find that an inventory loss has resulted from a drop in raw material prices. A budget revision may also be in order to accommodate changes caused by the competitive situation. The proper action, however, cannot be taken unless an analysis is made to discover the causes for the variations from the budgeted amounts.

When this analysis indicates a definite need for revision, management must decide whether significant changes or minor changes are required for the remainder of the period. A significant revision may involve considerable work, but it is a worthwhile effort. In contrast, management may allow minor explainable variations to show up on the budget reports rather than its revising the budget.

Regular budgetary review and revision seem to be the best means for assuring flexibility within a budgetary program. They enable the budget to be a living, growing document rather than a strait jacket. At the time of revision, management can usually make quite accurate predictions of the new operating conditions. Therefore, the adjusted budget will remain a good standard of performance for management's control purposes.

The relationship of budgeting to other managerial activities

Budgets: Planning and control

Budgets are created by the planning process as an essential feature of the control system. The budget does not control; managers control using the budget as an effective device to compare and measure actual performance against plans.

[2] J. H. Hennessy, Jr., "Looking Around," *Harvard Business Review* 38 (May–June 1960):40–42.

In setting up budgets for control purposes, management should follow the existing organizational structure and accounting systems. The organizational structure will indicate budget responsibility; the accounting system will provide the categories that must be included somewhere in the overall budgetary program.

Budgets and accounting

The success of the budgetary program depends on good accounting. Because reliable historical data form the basis of many budgetary estimates, accounting records are essential. These records, however, cannot substitute for actual budgeting. Traditionally, by analyzing accounting data, executives can compare current results with those of some past period. However, such a comparison often is defective. Conditions or prices may have changed, new products may have been added, productivity may have increased or, possibly, the previous period's performance may have been unsatisfactory. Thus, a meaningful analysis of present performance can be provided only by the goals set out in the budget. However, since accountants' reports of actual operations, costs, revenues, and other financial amounts must be compared with budgeted amounts, budget and accounting categories must be identical. Comparisons would be meaningless if the classifications did not coincide.

The accounts also must accurately reflect the areas of managerial responsibility. Extreme care should be taken to make certain that supervisors have no items in their budgets over which they have no control. Moreover, close budgetary supervision requires that if several department heads are responsible for semifinished inventory, separate inventory accounts must be kept for each department.

Budgets and organization

Logically, the budget will be influenced by the organizational structure. If budgets are to be effective, they must be prepared for each unit of the organization and the managers of each unit must have clear authority to execute them. Thus, the person responsible for each department and for any performance that does not meet the budget must be clearly designated. Confusion over authority and responsibility also will make it difficult for managers to secure the data necessary for constructing the budget in the first place.

Budgets as an aid for coordination

Budgets also aid in achieving coordination. The existence and availability of the various budgets promote balanced activities among the departments.

For example, sales and production departments must coordinate closely so that the sales department does not plan to sell more than the production department can produce. Since the production budget tells precisely how much can be expected and when, the sales manager can adjust the activities in the sales department accordingly.

The use of a budgetary program is bound to improve coordination and maintain a proper balance not only between production and sales, but also among many other areas. Because work is usually interdependent, department managers, for example, will often seek information from one another while in the process of preparing the budget. This open communication and interchange of information will greatly aid in the coordination of the various plans and budgets, and will often reveal imbalances. Budgeting, therefore, can show possible inconsistencies at an early stage, while they can still be adjusted easily. Moreover, because budgetary plans must take into consideration the objectives and problems of each department and of the enterprise as a whole, they facilitate overall planning coordination as well.

The relationship of the budget to coordination and to the organizing function cannot be emphasized too strongly. This is one of the reasons why the Department of Defense undertook its celebrated Planning-Programming-Budgeting System (PPBS). PPBS was instituted in recognition of the fact that "integrated combinations of men, equipment, and installations whose effectiveness could be related to our national security objectives" must be treated as program elements and regrouped in meaningful units of activity.[3]

The problem with conventional budgeting is that it tends to segment the organization into labor budgets, material budgets, and so on. Such budgets are inappropriate to matrix-type organizations. These organizations are forcing management to think in terms of coordinated program budgets. This is an important current development that has wide impact on many functions, especially planning, organizing, and controlling.

Budgets and human problems

Budgets represent restrictions, and for that reason people often dislike them. In fact, people often approach budgets defensively, an approach they have acquired through painful experience. Many times budgets appear only as barriers to spending or as an excuse for not granting raises. In the minds of many employees, therefore, a budget often is associated with penurious behavior rather than with planning and direction.

Managers must point out that budgeting is a trained, disciplined approach to all problems and is necessary for maintaining a standard of performance. The budget should be presented as *both* a planning and a control device. A budget "may be symbolized by two wooden sticks—one neatly divided into thirty-six one-inch spaces, and the other sharply pointed at one

---

[3] Charles J. Hitch, *Decision-Making for Defense* (Berkeley and Los Angeles: University of California Press, 1965), p. 32.

end."[4] The planning concept of budgets is expressed by the yardstick; the control concept, by the pointed stick. Every manager should know that the yardstick concept often will bring forth a voluntary effort; the pointed-stick concept will bring forth reluctance and minimum performance. A study conducted by Chris Argyris concerning human relations problems and budgets led to the tentative conclusion that when budgets are used as a pressure device "they tend to generate forces which in the long run decrease efficiency." His study concluded that budget pressure seems to unite the employees against management, to place supervisors under tension and cause them to see only the needs of their own departments. Ultimately the budget, in and of itself a neutral thing, often is blamed for many problems.[5]

Most of these problems naturally arise at the point of budgetary control. It is there that deviations are discovered and that employees are criticized for exceeding budgets. Deviations from the budget necessitate explanation, instruction, and decisions. Such discussions presuppose that a satisfactory working relationship exists between subordinates and their immediate superior. Of course, executives should be certain that enough flexibility is built into the budget system to permit the common-sense deviations that serve the best interests of the enterprise.

In the final analysis, the effective utilization of budgetary procedures will depend on management's attitudes toward the budget system. On the one hand, management can consider the budget as a part of overall planning, ensuring that action will be by design rather than expediency and that a guide for spending will be available. On the other hand, management may view the budget as a control device. Management should understand its own motives and attempt to balance its position between these two factors.

Summary

Budgeting is not only an element of planning; it is a control device as well. A budget supplies tangible, numerical standards against which operations, either limited or comprehensive, can be gauged.

The preparation of the budget is a line function, which should include managers at every level of the organization. Help with budget preparation may be provided by a staff budget director or by a budget committee. However, ultimate responsibility for the budget rests with top management.

The administration of a budgetary program requires managing a flow of events, often beginning with a sales forecast, moving through the preparation of subsidiary budgets, and ending with an operating budget and a budgeted balance sheet.

---

[4] James L. Peirce, "The Budget Comes of Age," *Harvard Business Review* 32 (May–June 1954):59.
[5] Chris Argyris, "Human Problems with Budgets," *Harvard Business Review* 31 (January–February 1953):97.

Flexibility is a critical part of all budgetary programs. It permits adaptation to changing conditions that may occur during the budget period. Numerous methods exist for building flexibility into budgetary programs. Included are varying time periods, alternative expense budgets, variable expense budgets, supplemental monthly budgets, and budget review or revision. Budgeting is related to many managerial activities, including planning, controlling, organizing, accounting, coordinating, and influencing.

Discussion questions

1 Budgets are by nature short-term control techniques. If managers are performing according to short-term control measures, what are the implications for long-term performance?
2 As a manager, how would you feel if the principal times you saw your boss were when your performance deviated from the budget?

Supplementary readings

Argyris, Chris. "Human Problems with Budgets." *Harvard Business Review,* January—February 1953.

Daugherty, William, and Harvey, Donald. "Some Behavioral Implications of Budgeting Systems," *Arizona Business,* April 1973, pp. 3—7. Reprinted in *Dimensions in Modern Management,* 2d ed., edited by Patrick E. Connor. Boston: Houghton Mifflin, 1978.

Edwards, James Don, and Kiger, Jack E. "Financial Planning and Control." *Management Planning,* November—December 1975.

Chapter 28

Controlling overall performance

Objectives of the chapter

1 To discuss control techniques that are used to regulate and evaluate organizational performance.
2 To relate control techniques to the rise of information technology.
3 To consider various overall control techniques in terms of managerial use.

While the budget is a very powerful tool, it is not sufficiently comprehensive to give managers the information they need to control complex organizations. Managers have other control techniques that also are used to regulate the overall performance of an organization, such as break-even point analysis, profit-and-loss control, return on investment control, internal auditing, control units, and external auditing. Some of these techniques are used along with the budget; others are separate. In either case, these control systems require the creation and distribution to managers of information pertaining to the performance of the organization in vital areas of operations.

More and more managers are relying on computers and management information systems (MIS) to provide them with the data needed for effective control of their enterprises. It is not surprising that since 1954 the power of computer hardware to assimilate, process, and feedback data has increased greatly. However, workable systems that would permit noncomputer specialists to utilize the machines efficiently have not been perfected. Trends indicate that the software side of the computer field is developing rapidly in the improvement of person/machine relationships.[1] These MIS procedures will extend management's ability to acquire information by permitting any manager to question the computer directly in simple language and to receive control data output immediately.

[1] Kenneth W. Clowes, "Computers and Information Technology," *Management Controls*, July–August 1975.

However, technological developments in the management information field will not replace entirely the more conventional methods of overall performance control. They will improve these techniques by reinforcing them with better information for managerial planning and controlling decisions.

Break-even point analysis

Break-even point analysis is a popular conventional technique of control. The break-even chart shows the relationship of different volumes, costs, sales prices, and sales mixes, to profits. Logically, it always contains a *break-even point*, which is defined as that level of volume at which revenue equals total cost or that point at which operations shift from profit to loss or vice versa. The difficulty with this concept, however, is that the break-even point is not rigid; it changes with every management decision—with rising and falling operating efficiency; with product mix; with changes in fixed costs, variable costs, sales volume, selling price, and so on. Thus, break-even analysis is concerned with the effect of these changes on profits—or on the break-even point.

Break-even chart

Figure 28-1 illustrates a break-even chart. The vertical scale represents dollars of revenue and cost; the horizontal scale represents volume or activity in units of output. In this chart, the fixed-cost line is drawn horizontally through the fixed-cost point at $175,000; the total-cost line is drawn from the intersection of the fixed-cost line at the left vertical scale. The sales line is drawn through the zero point on the left scale. The point at which the sales and the total-cost lines intersect is the break-even point. To the right of this point the spread represents the profit potential; to the left, it represents the loss potential.

Break-even analysis using a break-even chart is made under the assumption that it is possible to identify fixed and variable components of cost with reasonable accuracy. It also assumes that at all volume levels fixed costs remain constant, and variable costs vary proportionately. This assumption, however, is only true for the volume range anticipated by management; outside this range, the pattern could change. "What the analysis purports to show is what fixed costs should be and how variable costs should act within the relevant volume range as determined by existing managerial policies."[2] As long as performance remains within this range, operations can be assumed to be relatively stable and therefore predictable on a straight-line basis.

[2] Glenn A. Welsch, *Budgeting: Profit-Planning and Control* (Englewood Cliffs, N.J.: Prentice-Hall, 1957), p. 265.

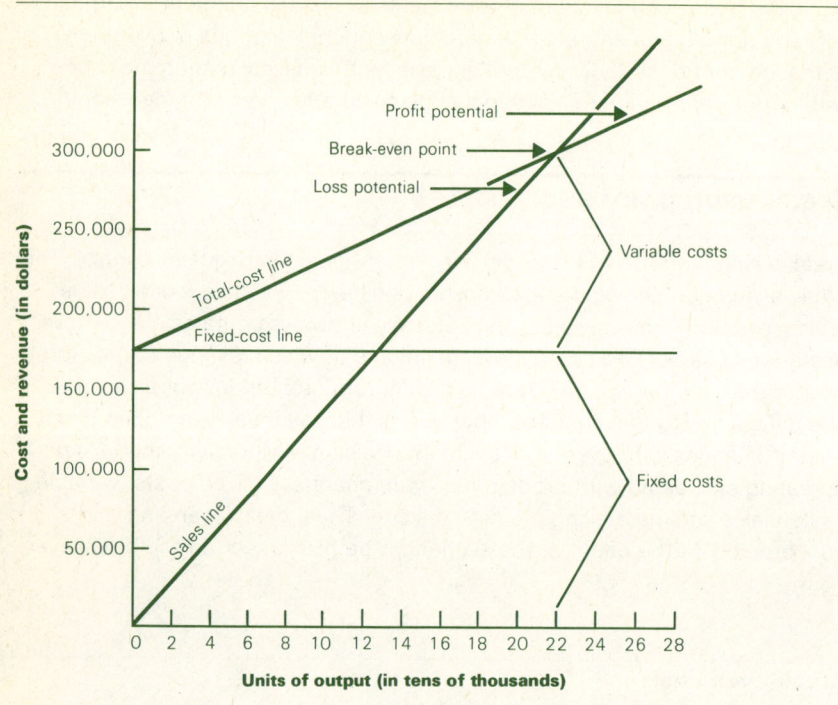

Figure 28-1 Break-even chart

As we have seen, the general terminology used in break-even analysis is that some costs are *fixed* while others are *variable.* Fixed costs or stand-by costs are so named because they do not vary as volume changes. They are those costs that "because of organization structure, style of operation, capital availability, methods of selling, size of productive capacity, and stored-up knowledge of key individuals, cannot be added or dropped at will through wide ranges of activity rate fluctuation."[3] Normally, fixed costs include depreciation, property insurance costs, property taxes, minimum-fee service contracts, costs of administrative officers, costs of keeping sales offices, and so forth.

Those costs that do vary with volume changes are, of course, the variable costs. Direct labor costs, direct material costs, and commission rates on sales are examples of variable costs. Many consider variable costs to be the costs of *doing* business; stand-by costs to be the costs of being *in* business.

These two broad groupings often shade into one another. As evidence, management often attempts to classify some costs as semivariable. In other words, within each account classification the costs are neither always completely variable nor always completely fixed. For instance, normally it could

---

[3] Fred V. Gardner, *Profit Management and Control* (New York: McGraw-Hill, 1955), pp. 28–29.

be assumed that inspection costs would vary closely with the rate of productivity. However, regardless of productivity the enterprise must maintain a reservoir of supervisory inspection ability. The reservoir is necessary, even if production should be at a complete standstill. To this extent, then, inspection costs would be a fixed cost. Similarly, because of differences in organizations, corporate structure, or industry type, certain other costs that are considered fixed in some enterprises are variable in others.

In general, the break-even chart and the break-even point reflect the efficiency and quality of the management of an enterprise. If operations are under close control, the chances are that the actual break-even point will not fall very far from the planned break-even point. If, however, no effective control exists, the break-even point could shift extensively. This may be caused by a lag in control action, the law of diminishing returns, shifts from high- to low-margin lines, growth of the company, and many other reasons.

Of course, an almost unlimited number of areas within an organization are subject to managerial controls. Each of these areas is concerned with one of the many functions or activities of the company. By and large, most general controls are of a financial nature. Unless the enterprise shows a profit or a good return on investment it cannot stay in business. For this reason, financial control of overall performance seems to be the most effective control type.

Profit-and-loss control

The profit-and-loss statement is probably the most widely used means of controlling general performance. This statement shows all the revenue, expenses, and income for a given period and, as such, is an excellent control tool for the operations of the enterprise. It serves to hold each operating department, plant, or unit rigidly accountable on a profit-and-loss basis.

In some organizations both budgetary control and profit-and-loss control are used. Using the budgeted income statement as a standard, management can make a valid comparison between it and the profit-and-loss statement. Profit-and-loss control will also become more meaningful if management has comparative income statements showing financial results for a number of consecutive years. By highlighting the increases or decreases occurring from year to year, these statements help management to do a better job of controlling.

Profit-and-loss control is effective not only in appraising the performance of the entire enterprise but also in appraising fully integrated parts of it, such as regional divisions, subsidiaries, and product divisions. This type of control, of course, calls for a profit-and-loss statement for each such division or subsidiary. Obviously, these statements necessitate considerable accounting work, which in itself is expensive and cumbersome. However, this is the only way that the contribution of each division to the income of the entire enterprise can be ascertained. Divisional profit-and-loss control requires that managers of all divisions have ample opportunity to run their division as they deem best. Naturally, they do not have authority to determine overall corporate expenses, such as those for research and administrative overhead. These will be prorated for each division.

The accuracy of a divisional profit-and-loss statement increases with the integration of the particular division. If the enterprise is departmentalized by products or if its organization follows territorial divisions, control through divisional profit and loss becomes more meaningful, because each of these organizational units is responsible for its own production and marketing operations. In such a situation, the profit-and-loss statement will truly represent management's effectiveness. Enterprises with purely functional organizational structures cannot use divisional or departmental profit-and-loss control easily, because they cannot determine the income of the various departments.

Although numerous problems occur when profit-and-loss control is applied to certain departments and divisions, it is still one of the most effective tools for controlling the general performance of an enterprise. It requires little effort to compare the profit-and-loss statements for a number of consecutive years to gauge overall past performance, and it is likewise easy to compare the current profit-and-loss statement to a tentative, budgeted statement to see how operations are progressing in comparison to the established future goal.

Calculating return on investment: The duPont example

Although a number of companies have been employing this yardstick since the end of World War II, duPont has used it since 1919. Figure 28-2 illustrates what duPont considers to be the relationships among the various factors that affect return on investment. By multiplying the turnover by the earnings as a percentage of sales, the return on investment figure is reached. Tying turnover to earnings as a percentage of sales in this way means that management clearly acknowledges that one division with a high profit rate but a low capital turnover may not be as profitable as another division that shows a high capital turnover but a low ratio of earnings to sales. Earnings as a percentage of sales reflect management's success or failure in maintaining satisfactory control of costs. Turnover shows how rapidly the capital committed to the operation is being utilized. Turnover itself is computed by dividing sales by total investment. In this case, total investment is considered to be working capital and permanent investment. Working capital, in turn, consists of inventories, accounts receivable, and cash.

In total, then, Figure 28-2 shows that executives, by properly managing an operating investment, potentially can improve the return by reducing costs or working existing investment harder. Return on investment and earnings as a percentage of sales are calculated both before and after income taxes. The purpose of this is to analyze the job being done by the industrial departments and to keep operating management aware of the impact of income taxes on profits.

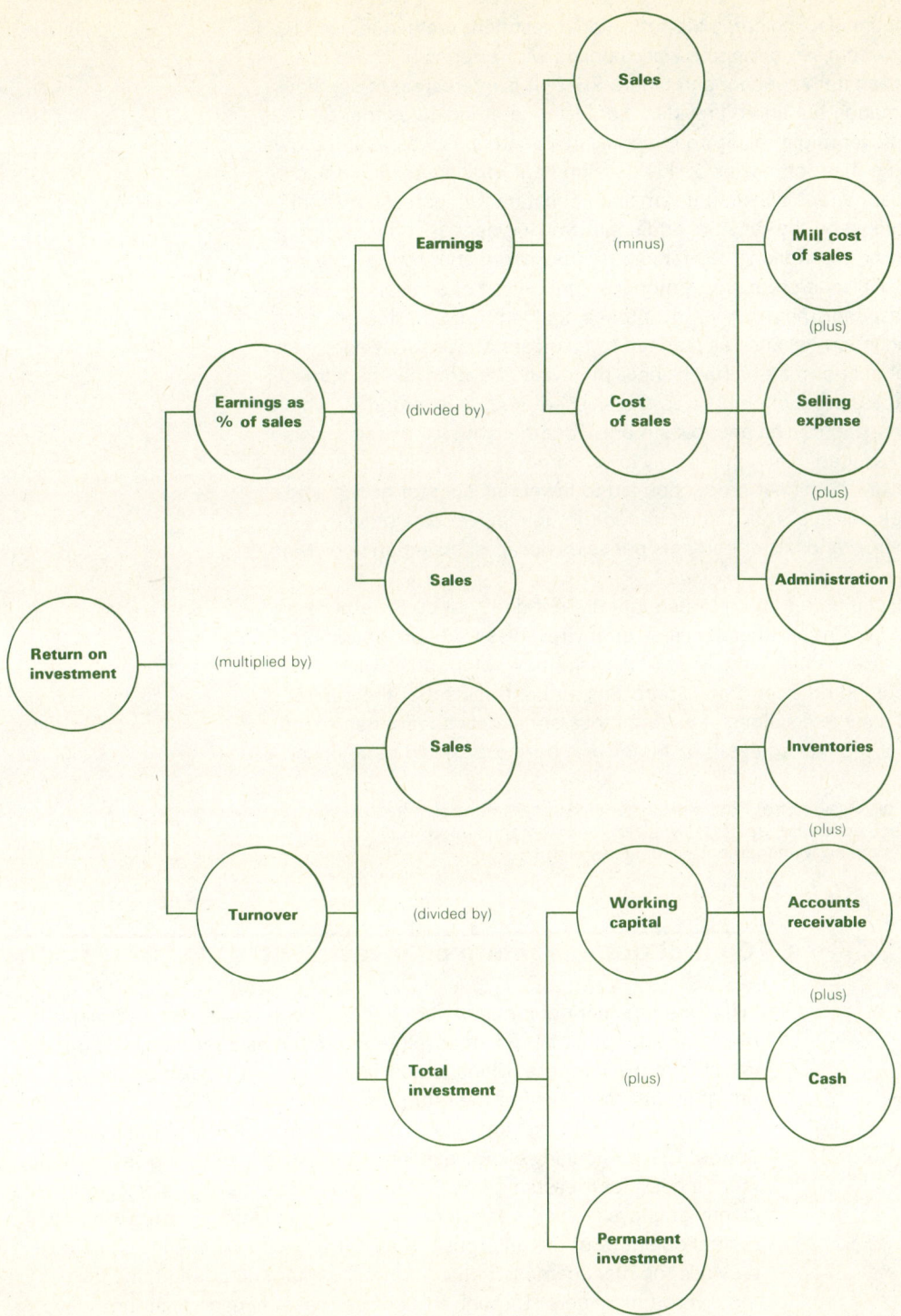

Figure 28-2 Relationship of factors affecting return on investment

The figure also indicates the return on investment technique used by duPont. Its executive committee was supplied with a series of charts that illustrated each item appearing in Figure 28-2. It is interesting to see how much information the figure provides. For instance, it indicates that decreased turnover might result from increased inventory as well as from lower sales. Tracing the root causes of this development, managers would find that if the permanent investment remained constant, an increase of total investment must be the result of additional working capital in the system. Then, checking the working capital charts, they might spot the trouble in inventories. Finished-product inventories might be out of control, for example. The reason for these higher inventories could in turn be traced to greater production, which was planned to take care of sales that had been forecast but did not materialize. Hence, the cycle of events can be summarized: excess production built up the finished-product inventories, which increased working capital and investment. Together with lower sales, rising investment resulted in an appreciably lower turnover of capital. At the same time, however, the higher production led to lower mill cost for goods sold as a percentage of sales. This can be traced through lower costs of sales, higher earnings, and better earnings per sales dollar, showing an improving net return on investment.

In calculating return on investment duPont does not consider any reductions for current or other liabilities or any reserves for depreciation. The company is aware that many different views of how return on investment should be computed exist. For its purposes, duPont holds that the capital, liability and reserve positions of an enterprise are largely a reflection of the philosophy of top management as to how the business should be financed.

Source: This discussion of duPont's return on investment control is based on information in *Executive Committee Control Charts,* AMA Management Bulletin No. 6 (New York: American Management Association, 1960).

Control through return on investment

When management controls performance through return on investment, it must consider profit not as an absolute figure but as a return on the capital invested in the business. Management's goal is still to maximize profits, but only if profits will maximize the return on investment.

There are many advantages to using return on investment as a control device. It is particularly effective in large companies, since it gives management a basis for measuring whether or not invested capital is being efficiently employed. Such a yardstick focuses management's attention on the central objective of the enterprise: the best utilization of the investment. It provides top management with a fair measure for comparing the activities of the division managers. Through this device these managers, in turn, develop a broad corporate outlook. Before requesting additional large capital investments for a division, a manager will stop to consider the impact of this on the enterprise as a whole and on the showing of his or her division. The system also permits the manager to detect speedily the source of any difficulty that is unfavorably affecting the return on investment.

Although these advantages are of great importance, particularly for larger firms, return on investment control also has certain disadvantages. How are certain general overhead expenses to be allocated? How should expenses be apportioned among divisions and departments? If some assets are used jointly, how should they be allocated to the different divisions? Also, should assets be charged at original cost, depreciated value, or replacement value? This last question is especially important in periods of inflation.

We should note also that management's emphasis on return on investment often produces too much consideration of financial factors. As a result, the divisional manager might conveniently overlook technical development, the development of junior executives, the morale of employees, public relations, and many other factors that do not contribute directly or financially (at least for the time being) to return on investment. In addition, management must determine what constitutes a reasonable return on investment. It is difficult to establish an optimum return for a particular enterprise. As a matter of fact, even comparisons within the industry might not be valid, because each firm has its own idiosyncrasies and policies. Nevertheless, many large enterprises are using return on investment to control performance and are achieving good results.

Internal auditing control

Another control tool available to management is internal auditing. Modern internal auditing, performed by a staff of specialists, began to flourish as organizations, rapidly expanding during World War II, found an increased need for close accounting supervision. Since then, modern internal auditing has become one of the most important ways to establish and maintain managerial control. However, since it was born of accounting, many executives limit internal auditing activities to verification of accounting transactions. Nevertheless, authorities in the field of accounting view internal auditing as a management control function.

Meaning and scope

The Institute of Internal Auditors defines the *internal audit* as an independent appraisal within an organization that can serve as a basis for protective and constructive help and service to management. This type of control functions by measuring and evaluating the effectiveness of other types of control. Internal auditing is concerned primarily with accounting and financial matters, but it may also deal with matters of an operating nature.

James T. Powers writes: ''The modern internal auditor does not simply analyze expense accounts; he analyzes *activities,* and groups of accounts which reflect the results of these activities, in order to evaluate the profit-improvement or cost-reduction aspects."[4] Beyond this, modern electronic data-processing technology requires that the internal auditor be versed in computer skills. This is necessary not only for monitoring these activities, but also for ensuring that proposed changes in computer programs reflect adequate internal controls. There are many examples of how susceptible computers are to manipulation for illegal purposes.

In more specific terms, internal auditing is concerned with finding out whether or not management's policies are as effective as management intends them to be and whether or not the members of the organization are carrying out such policies with thoroughness. In this way, internal auditing ascertains the adequacy of the procedures in force and, if necessary, facilitates finding improved procedures. In brief, internal auditing is constantly alert to any weakness or breakdown of controls.

Position within the organization

Obviously, it is difficult to discuss the functions of internal auditing control in specific terms since they vary considerably with the size and type of organization. However, in most established auditing systems a basic pattern of continous measuring and evaluating of all other controls exists. Most auditing systems also require an internal auditor who must be independent of all departments in which he or she performs audits. In other words, that person should not be attached to the controller's or the treasurer's office, but should report either to the chief finance officer or, even, to the head of a control unit. It is also conceivable that, in some cases, the internal auditor may report directly to the president. Internal auditing usually is considered to be a staff function. Therefore, internal auditors cannot interfere with line personnel about some of the shortcomings that they might discover. Instead, the internal auditing staff must report the situation to the responsible operating manager, who then decides whether to pursue the auditor's suggestions.

The control unit

The control unit is simply a department in which control functions are centralized. It includes internal auditing as well as other managerial control activities. This unit is a significant top-management tool and represents an important step in the evolution of managerial control. Generally, a control unit is a fact-finding and recommendations section with no administrative or operating responsibility. Normally, the overall control unit reports to the president, but such units can be utilized in lower levels of organization if the department they supervise is large enough to require internal control activity.

[4] James T. Powers, "The Meaning of the Internal Audit Function," *Management Controls,* April–May 1975.

Cracking the computer

A 15-year-old schoolboy completely cracked the security system of a major London computer time-sharing service two months ago, gaining access to the most secret files stored on the computer by other users—able to read and change them at will without anyone noticing. He used no special technical gadgets and started with no special knowledge of the computer's inner workings—instead he relied only on ingenuity and a teletype terminal in his school.

The schoolboy, Joe, is part of a new generation of "computer freaks" who explore computer systems in the same way that "phone phreaks" explored the telephone system. Joe worked on the project for only four months, until he was temporarily banned from the computer by his teacher.

Most users of the service have a terminal which is not permanently connected to the computer, and dial into it using the normal telephone system. After reaching the computer, the users must identify themselves by giving an account number and password. The trick Joe used was to listen to the sign-on procedure to learn the account name and password of highly privileged users, and then pretend to be them in order to gain access to secret files. . . .

He had the power to completely take over the system, cutting off other users, changing passwords, and even altering the bills that customers would have to pay.

In fact, he never did anything much with his privileged account numbers. He wrote to the time-sharing service and told them what he did, but he never got a reply. A new version of the operating system was introduced on the computer early this month, and Joe said he planned to check it to see if his method still worked.

Source: New Scientist, December 19, 1974, p. 81. This article first appeared in *New Scientist London,* the weekly review of Science and Technology.

Need

It is difficult to define the circumstances that make a centralized control unit worthwhile. Obviously, it is not needed in a small, compact enterprise where most of the control functions can easily be performed by the chief executive and his or her staff. The need for a centralized control unit is more apparent in a large complex organization. However, what is large? And, what is complex? Some people regard an organization with a thousand employees as large; others might not consider any firm that employs less than ten thousand to be large.

In addition to size, the dispersion of operations may indicate the need for a centralized control unit. The more dispersed the operations of the company are, the greater is the need. Complexity bears significantly on the decision to establish such a unit. The Koppers Company is an excellent example of a highly diversified company that produces a wide variety of products and services for the use of other industries. The complexity of its operations makes a centralized control unit mandatory.

Purpose

Clearly, there is no formula to determine whether or not a control unit is applicable to a particular organization. If such a unit is established, its functions and duties must be tailored to the enterprise. We can say that the purpose of a control unit, in almost all enterprises, is to facilitate orderly, efficient administration and planning by supplying a continous flow of facts to top management.

More specifically, the purpose of the control unit is to assist top executives in discharging certain phases of their duties by providing a source of centralized control information. It is conceivable that similar control units will exist in each major division to assist the divisional managers in discharging their control responsibilities. In a large organization, where top management is distant from the supervisory level, and problems of coordination are more involved and time consuming, the central control unit can help top management to be well informed about operations at all levels.

Position within the organization

The centralized control unit is a staff department, usually associated with the top echelon reporting to the president. This position conforms with sound organizational principles. Wherever a staff department must serve two or more divisions impartially and equally, it should report to a level of management above these divisions. Although management may be tempted to merge the functions of the control unit with those of the controller, to do so would be unwise. The head of the control unit should be a different executive from the controller. Even if the title *controller* is not already used in the enterprise, it is inadvisable to give this title to the head of the control unit. Traditionally, the controller is the chief accounting executive of most enterprises, and it is not generally appropriate to expand this individual's function to include the areas of planning, policy control, and so forth. The centralized control unit is concerned with much broader functions than those of the traditional accounting activities.

External auditing control

Almost all enterprises engage outside accountants to perform an audit of the financial transactions and accounts of the business, at least once a year. This audit is an examination, performed by certfied public accountants (CPAs) or chartered accountants, that serves as a basis for an expression of opinion regarding the fairness, consistency, and conformity of statements prepared by a corporation to generally accepted accounting principles.

The external audit does not establish the factual accuracy of the statements audited; it is merely an expression of opinion. Although all members of a corporation are supposed to prepare their statements in anticipation of the audit, this is generally thought of as the accountant's job and he or she does most of the work involved.

The usual form of audit used by outside accountants is a balance-sheet audit, which includes detailed verification of all important balance-sheet accounts and test checks of revenue and expense accounts, with particular emphasis on those that are closely related to balance-sheet items, such as fixed assets and depreciation. In a balance-sheet audit, all major assets, liabilities, and stockholders' equity are verified. The CPA is responsible for determining the extent of verification. No appraisal of the value of physical property contained in the balance sheet is made. That such items are valued in accordance with accepted accounting principles is certified.

Public accountants do not have primary responsibility for the accuracy and reliability of the financial data that appear on a certified statement; management alone has this responsibility. The CPAs, of course, are responsible for exercising reasonable care and diligence in conformance with established standards while performing an audit. They also have to express an opinion as to whether or not generally accepted accounting principles have been followed. However, this is usually all. Most outside accounting firms limit their audit to the verification of the accounts and do not extend it into additional functions that the internal auditing staff might perform, such as the checks on plans, policies, and procedures.

External auditing, obviously, does not directly control overall performance of the enterprise; however, by assuring that generally accepted accounting principles are met, it does exercise an indirect control, or a degree of control, over the operations of the enterprise. Although a certain amount of flexibility of viewpoint is to be expected in determining whether this is the case, no certified public accountant would certify an account where a major item had been charged off as an expense rather than being capitalized.

Summary

The control of overall performance uses a number of techniques to give management readings on the operations of an organization. These controls rely, with growing frequency, on data supplied by management information systems. These computer-based systems are used to supplement conventional control techniques, which include:

- Break-even point analysis
- Profit-and-loss control
- Control through return on investment
- Internal auditing control
- The control unit
- External auditing control

These techniques use largely financial yardsticks for controlling organizational performance, although internal auditing and the control unit are concerned with manufacturing and sales procedures as well.

Discussion questions

1 Why do modern management information systems open a whole new area of specialization in the control process?
2 Break-even point analysis is only a rough estimate and a first approximation of organizational performance. Why?

Supplementary readings

Clowes, Kenneth W. "Computers and Information Technology." *Management Controls,* July–August 1975.

Powers, James T. "The Meaning of the Internal Audit Function." *Management Controls,* April–May 1975.

Strong, Earl P., and Smith, Robert D. "Break-Even Charts." In *Management Control Models.* New York: Holt, Rinehart & Winston. Reprinted in *Dimensions in Modern Management,* 2d ed., edited by Patrick E. Connor. Boston: Houghton Mifflin, 1978.

Cases for Part VI

Case VI/1

Willard's controller

The Willard Company has six operating divisions, which range in sales volume from $25 million to $75 million. Each division is managed by a division manager, who is in full charge of the product line from design, through manufacture, to marketing. The volume of intracompany transfers is small: only a few parts and subassemblies are transferred from one division to another. At headquarters, the president, Donald Sanderson, has available a complete corporate staff to assist him in running the corporation. Edna Statler is the corporate controller. Sanderson has discussed with her his concern regarding the declining rate of profit during the past two years, and Statler has also wondered what she could do in this respect. She thinks that her office should have more influence and authority; she believes that there is "a lot of fat to be boiled out" in the divisional operations in areas with which headquarters is not familiar and to which it cannot reach.

As things are arranged, each division employs a divisional controller who reports to the division manager. Statler would like to change this and have them report directly to her office at corporate headquarters. The company follows thorough budgetary arrangements. All budgets are submitted to headquarters by the manager of each division and the divisional controller helps the manager in the design and execution of the proposed and finally approved budget. The divisional controllers report to the divisional managers, not to Statler. Statler issues instructions regarding the accounting systems to be followed and the general procedures expected in connection with budgets and performance reports from each division; she has no authority beyond this. Statler believes that this should be changed.

Question

1. Should Statler's proposal be accepted, viewing the situation from headquarters? from the divisional managers' point of view? in light of sound organizational principles and arrangements?

Case VI/2

The pricing dispute

The Zephyr Company is a widely diversified company, which manufactures and sells a multitude of products. Each product division is managed by a product manager who is in complete charge of all aspects of design, engineering, production, distribution, and servicing of that particular product. The Zephyr Company has profit center decentralization.

The radio division produces a line of high-quality portable and table-model radios. The bulk of the division's work is assembly, since most parts and subassemblies are bought elsewhere. For example, the division has been purchasing the plastic cases used in the radios from Zephyr's plastics division.

The manager of each division also has the authority to buy parts from any vendor, although, in practice, many of Zephyr's divisions provide parts for the other divisions. The prices and quality of the parts must be competitive with what is available on the outside. If a pricing dispute arises, or if a product division wishes to have a part made on the outside, the matter must be decided by the divisional purchasing agent. There always are a number of intracompany pricing disputes pending, one of which currently is affecting the radio division.

Some time ago, the president of Zephyr had instructed the engineering staff to improve the quality and appearance of the company's products. These corporate staff engineers had no line nor functional staff authority over managers of a product division or any of their employees. As one of the improvements, the corporate engineers requested the plastics division to create a shinier and smoother appearance for the radio cases. This necessitated more expensive materials and additional buffing and polishing operations. The plastics division had added the additional cost to the price charged to the radio division.

The radio division refuses to pay the increase, claiming that a change was not requested by its engineers or anyone in the radio division, and that the improvements will not make any difference in the sale of radios. The radio division maintains that it would have made other changes in its radios if it had wanted to spend additional money and that those improvements would have helped to increase sales. The plastics division states that it was ordered to make these changes by headquarters and does not see any reason why it should be saddled with these additional expenditures.

Question

1 How would you settle this intracompany pricing dispute if you were in charge of the radio division? the plastics division? if you were president of Zephyr? if you were the purchasing agent?

Case VI/3

The copying machine

The faculty office of the School of Business Administration of Martin University consists of four people who perform all the stenographic work, typing, and secretarial services needed. One important duty is the reproduction of printed material, in small or large quantities, to be used for class material, exams, or an individual faculty member's research. The school does not have a duplicating machine available on the premises. There is a print shop on the university grounds, and all papers are sent there to be reproduced. However, this takes a great deal of time. An office worker must take the papers to the print shop and pick them up. In addition, there generally is a waiting period of a few days. And, on those occasions when an announcement or a document is needed immediately, an office worker has to wait at the shop for the job to be finished.

The dean of the business school follows a detailed budget made out by the university's central administration. Whenever the faculty and the office force suggest the installation of a duplicating machine at the business school, the dean cites a lack of funds for the purchase or leasing of such a machine. Of course, the print shop charges the business school for whatever work is done, and these expenditures are covered in the school's budget.

When the faculty argues that a duplicating machine in the building would save a secretarial employee from performing a messenger's service instead of doing secretarial work, the dean states that funds are available to hire additional help, but that the budget for equipment does not permit a machine installation. Basically, although the funds for the machinery are available in the budget (now appropriated for print shop expenses and additional labor), the dean does not have the authority to transfer funds between accounts.

Questions

1. What is the purpose of detailed budgeting?
2. How can this type of situation be avoided or corrected?

Case VI/4

The administrator's problem

Max Jones is the administrator of St. Mary's Hospital, a general short-term community hospital in Cincinnati. It has five hundred beds and operates most of the time at maximum occupancy. Its total revenues amounted to $22 million for the last year. While reviewing last year's operating statement, the board of directors found that the operating surplus had dwindled to a negligible amount compared with that of other years. The board is searching for the reasons for this change and for ways to cut expenses and eliminate unnecessary expenditures.

An outlay that received much of the board's attention was $75,000 for continuing education for the employees. It covered such items as travel to meetings, membership fees for professional organizations, tuition reimbursements, educational material, books, and subscriptions to journals; it did not cover the expenses for interns and residents. The account represented all expenditures made in connection with the hospital's efforts to give its employees the chance for additional development, education, and training.

When the board asked Jones about this account, he replied that such provisions are necessary in today's labor market. Unless they are available, good employees who are eager to advance in their professions will not stay with the hospital. Also, only by exposing employees to meetings, seminars, and talks can the hospital achieve and maintain its goal of providing the best-quality patient care. After the administrator had cited these and other reasons, the board could see the need for the expenditure.

The board then asked Jones what tangible results he could show for his program and how he ascertains the effects of these developmental costs. The administrator admitted that he did not have a solid answer to that. He said he would try to set up a control system that would enable the hospital to check and appraise the validity and benefits of the expenses.

After the board meeting, Jones called Samuel Tibauld into his office. Tibauld is an administrative resident who is fulfilling the residency requirement for his master of hospital administration degree. Jones told Tibauld what the board wanted to know and asked him to devise a system to measure the effectiveness of spending $75,000 a year for continuing education.

Question

1 How should Tibauld go about this task? What approaches to the problem might Jones give him?

Case VI/5

The Elysée Manufacturing Company

Aaron Wagner is the president of the Elysée Manufacturing Company, a small, Chicago-based manufacturer of women's belts. The company's total annual sales have been approximately $1 million for the past few years. The annual after-tax profit is small. Because of the size of the company, the amount of accounting work is not enough to warrant mechanized facilities, and records are kept manually. Therefore, the accounting department requires quite some time to prepare the monthly closing figures; Wagner usually has to wait until the fifteenth of the following month to learn the past month's financial results. Since the company is small and has meager financial resources, he is monitoring operations and affairs closely. He has repeatedly told the accounting department that he would prefer to have approximate figures of each month's performance within two or three days after the end of the month than wait for exact figures until the fifteenth or later.

The chief accountant, Lena Chang, has tried to convince Wagner that all closing figures must be gathered first and that it would waste effort and incur needless double work to submit the preliminary figures to him right after the month closed. She maintains that such figures would not be correct or meaningful until all figures—returns, allowances, discounts, salespeople's commissions, inventory fluctuations— were correctly assembled. She has even said that the president would be taking real risks if he were to base plans or act on any figures other than the final ones. Because the president does not have much knowledge of accounting and the company's financial resources are small, he has submitted to the accountant's point of view. But he still wishes he could receive some relevant information sooner.

Questions

1 Do you think Wagner's point of view has any merit?
2 What are the disadvantages of acting on the basis of approximate data and information? the advantages?
3 Why should Chang's contention be supported?

Case VI/6

The fledgling company

For fifteen years, Judith Rubin had been a traveling salesperson for the Star Manufacturing Company of New York. The company sold an assortment of women's scarves, which either were produced by the firm or were imported from abroad. Rubin sold these scarves to department and specialty stores in the East. She had established a good following and a fine reputation during the many years in which she worked for this company. Her income was substantial, and she was able to save enough money to realize her ambition: to go into a similar business for herself.

About two years ago, she was able to secure sufficient bank loans and additional credit to open a manufacturing company. Ever since, her business has grown and prospered. After two years, her annual sales amount to about $250,000, and last year's operations showed an after-tax net gain of $20,000. Of course, Rubin worked day and night, personally supervising all phases of the small, growing company. She designed the scarves, watched the production, made trips abroad to select the imports, sold her products, took care of the correspondence, watched the flow of finances, and did everything else involved in building a new business. As time went on, she realized that there was a limit to how much she could do. Therefore, she placed a superintendent in charge of production and the workers, and she hired a salesperson. She already had two good office employees who had joined the company when it was founded.

Rubin knows that in order for the company to grow, she must assign activities to others and delegate to each the authority necessary to manage his or her own department. She is perfectly willing to do so, but she is greatly concerned that when she does, she will no longer be familiar with and involved in every detail. She has invested all her savings in the company and has even pledged her personal belongings to the bank as collateral for the various loans. She does not want to lose this investment. Although Rubin has a great deal of confidence in her subordinates, she knows that she still should watch all aspects of the business. She has read somewhere that "to delegate authority does not mean to lose control," and she is wondering how to set up a control system that would enable her to let others take charge of some of the aspects of the fledgling company while she remains fully aware of what is taking place.

Questions

1. How would you set up controls so that Rubin will be aware of what takes place in her small company?
2. Design a system that would provide Rubin with strategic control points to examine and, at the same time, would leave her with the time and opportunity to expand her business.

Part VII

The linking processes

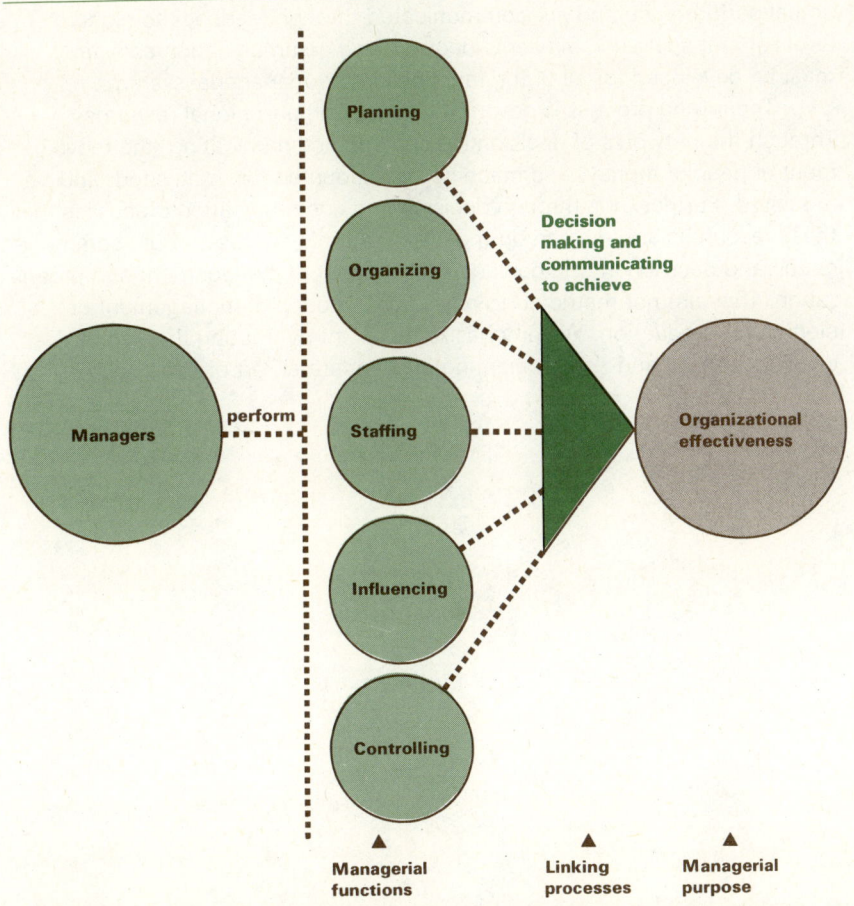

Linking the elements of the system The performance of the basic management functions is facilitated by the linking processes—decision making and communicating. In turn, these processes link the functions to organizational effectiveness.

A system, as we have seen, consists of interdependent parts, each of which affects the behavior of the others. The output of one part may supply the input for another part, and, in organizations involving people, feedback is the agent that regulates this process of interaction. The interdependent and interrelated activities of managers, described in terms of the five basic managerial functions, form a system of managerial behavior. However, the missing element must be added to the functions of planning, organizing, staffing, influencing, and controlling. This element is the linking process, a vital force in holding the managerial system together.

In this Part we consider two linking devices: decision making and communicating. The decision network and the communication network overlay and connect the managerial functions. For example, decisions about standards of control are made during planning and are communicated to control activities. Other decisions are made to implement these standards in actual performance and are communicated through feedback to higher levels of management. Similarly, decision and communication activities must be developed for all of the functions in the managerial system.

The linking processes govern the flow of organizational resources. Through the networks of decision making and communicating, the movement of people, money, and machines is accounted for, motivated, and regulated. Further, it is through decision and communication processes that these resources are focused on the organization's purpose. Thus, communication and decision efforts pervade every aspect of management and organization. They are not restricted to any single function of management or element of production. We emphasize this point by treating the two devices, decision making and communicating, in a separate Part of this book.

Chapter 29

Linking process 1: Decision making

Objectives of the chapter

1 To describe managerial decision making.
2 To identify the stages of managerial decision making.
3 To point out several of the constraints managers experience when they make decisions.
4 To describe the decision-making techniques that are available to managers.

Stewardship is a chief characteristic of professional management. Managers are responsible for the property of others, regardless of whether they are employed as hospital administrators, executives in the federal government, or business executives. The way in which that property is used or those resources are spent is managers' main responsibility.

Managerial performance is judged on the basis of how many resources are used to accomplish an organization's objectives. A wise investment broker has said that a person buys stock not in a company but in the ability of a firm's managers. The purchase or sale of shares is an expression of confidence in management. In a general way, the performance of executives is appraised by their success in managing the resources owned by other people.

Preliminary to the use or withholding of resources is the managerial act of choosing among alternative courses of action. *Decision making* is the conscious deliberation about alternative ways to use resources. Because resources are limited, the capacity of managers to exploit opportunities is limited; everything cannot be tried randomly or haphazardly. Decisions are made to discriminate rationally among available alternatives.

Managers at all levels of organization and in all functions within organizations deliberate among alternative actions. Decision making runs vertically from top management to first-line supervision, and cuts horizontally across areas of specialization, such as industrial relations, sales, budgeting, and production. Decision making is dynamically involved as a linking process, for it ties one function to another. The decisions of one manager or organizational unit are never made in isolation. Their implications and outcomes are related to other decisions throughout the organizational system.

Decision making is an indispensable part of a systems approach to management. It is basic to every function of management; the job of management cannot be understood unless the nature of decision making is appreciated.

Elements of the decision process

Decision making is in the immediate experience of all people. It begins in early childhood, when a person is first able to discriminate and select alternatives from competing stimuli. Choosing among alternatives continues until the individual dies. What piece of candy should I buy with my dime? Should I go out for soccer or basketball? What should be my college major? Whom should I marry? What job should I take? Where should I go on vacation? Common decisions, in one sense, differ little from managerial decisions. All decision makers must consider five elements (shown in Figure 29-1):

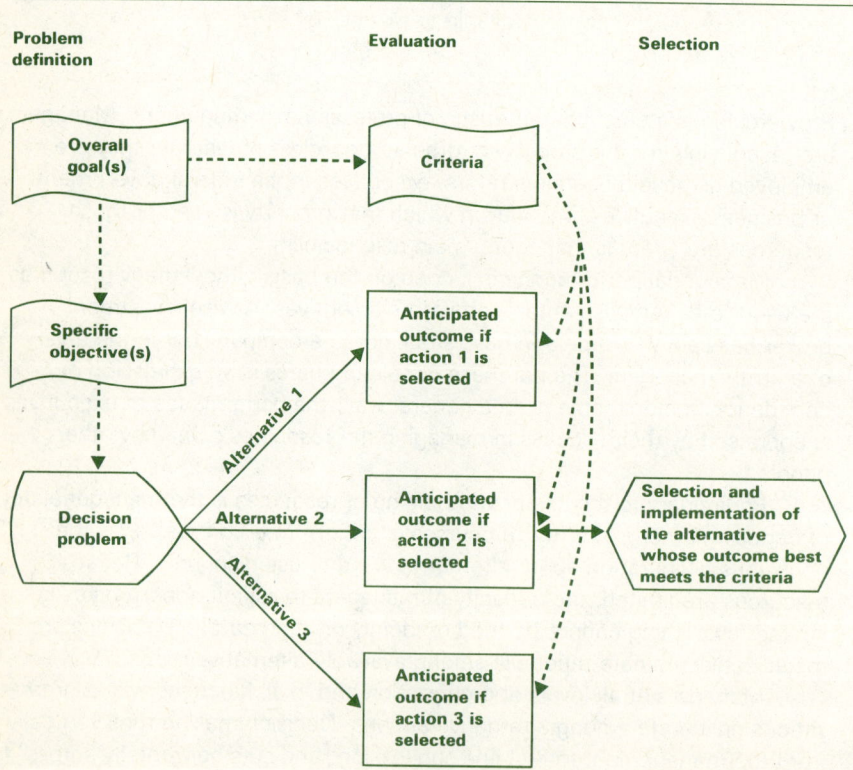

Figure 29-1 The decision process
Source: Professor Dale D. McFarlane, Oregon State University.

1 The objective sought
2 Alternative courses of action to achieve the objective
3 A prediction of the outcomes (consequences) for each alternative
4 A choice procedure (decision criteria) by which an alternative is selected
5 An evaluation of the chosen alternative

Closely related to this process are the implementation of the decision and appraisal of the effectiveness in the decision in achieving a goal. These two aspects of decision making can be intellectually separated from the choice process, but in reality they are indispensable to it. Action is the reason for making a decision. Appraisal is feedback, and it becomes *data* for further deliberations. For example, if you decide to buy one make of car and have trouble with it, this experience will color your thinking when you are ready to buy again.

Conditions for making decisions

Management writers have, by convention, identified three sets of conditions under which decisions are made. These conditions have been labeled *certainty, risk,* and *uncertainty*.

Key decision definitions

- *Objective*   A clear and concise statement of what the manager intends to accomplish with respect to a particular problem area.
- *Criteria*   A list of factors, both quantitative and qualitative, that will be examined in order to determine whether or not an objective has been achieved.
- *Action (or alternative course of action)*   A sequence of organizational activities that has been designed to achieve an objective.
- *Anticipated outcome*   A forecast or prediction of the changes in organizational performance that will result from the selection and implementation of a specific course of action.

Source: Professor Dale D. McFarlane, Oregon State University.

Making decisions under certainty

This condition corresponds to classical economic theory; it has been traditionally known as the *rational model* of decision making. According to this view, the decision maker makes optimal choices in completely specified, narrowly defined decision situations. Rational people *maximize* the values they seek by selecting alternatives that have optimal outcomes for the goals they want to achieve.

How? Rational people have set out before them a complete array of all the options open to them in a situation. Alternatives are givens and are completely known. Further, the consequences of each alternative are known. In addition, rational people have a list on which the outcomes are ordered in terms of their preferences. They select the alternative leading to the most desired outcome, which, according to the model, is the optimal solution to the problem. Figure 29-2 illustrates the situation. The decision maker simply compares each outcome against the criteria and selects the best.

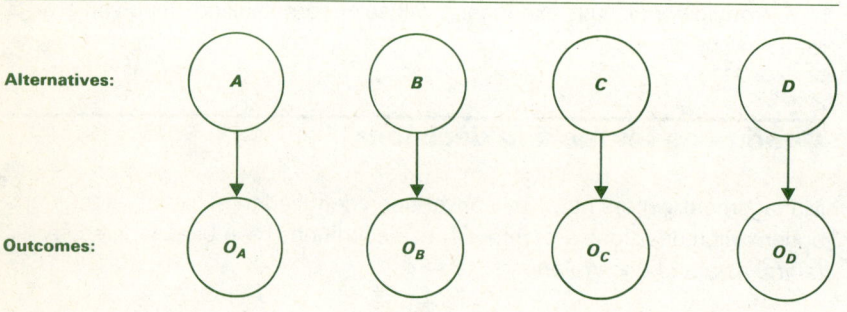

Figure 29-2 Condition of certainty (alternatives and outcomes known)

Making decisions under risk

The problem with decision making under certainty is that it never happens; decision makers never know—with certainty—all the alternatives and all the outcomes. The best they can hope for is to know the *probabilities* that various outcomes will occur (see Figure 29-3).

An interesting feature of this condition involves the nature of managerial decision making: repetition. That is, most managers, regardless of their function or hierarchical level, make roughly the same basic decision over and over. Whether it is a small ordering decision made each morning by a foreman or a substantial financial decision made every two years by a university president, managerial decisions tend to repeat themselves. Bearing this fact in mind, consider Figure 29-3. Assume you are a manager who makes some kind of decision on a periodic basis. Now, suppose that time and again alternative B appears to be the best. What will happen if you select alternative B each time you are required to make that decision? Outcome B_2, which presumably you want, occurs 90 percent of the time. That's the good news. The bad news, however, is that outcome B_1, which let us say you do not want, will occur 10 percent of the time. Thus, each time you select alternative B, you are taking a calculated *risk* that outcome B_1 will not occur.

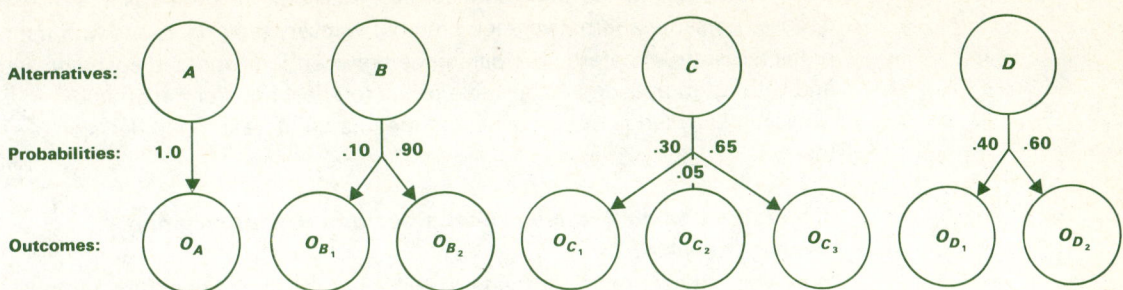

Figure 29-3 Condition of risk (alternatives known, outcome probabilities known)

States of nature

Basically, decision problems under risk (and also those under uncertainty) involve an interaction between the decision maker's choice of an alternative and the state of nature. The *state of nature* is the existence of a variable that is not under the control of the decision maker and that affects the outcome of a particular alternative. For each decision alternative there are as many outcomes as there are states of nature. Because of the multiplicity of outcomes, choice is more complex under risk and uncertainty than it is under certainty.

What is the likely choice procedure when there is risk? Let us assume that cost is the appropriate measure of the outcome. The logical choice procedure, then, seems to be to select the alternative that yields the minimum expected value of cost. If the decision is repeated many times, this procedure would minimize the sum of costs of the individual decisions.

Probability and probability distribution

Calculating costs for each alternative requires knowledge of the probabilities of the various states of nature. These probabilities can be determined, in some cases, by intuition; in other cases, they must be determined empirically. Knowledge of them makes the calculation of expected values conceptually simple, but when the number of alternatives and outcomes becomes large, the problem is difficult in practice. In these cases, by expressing the probabilities in terms of mathematical equations, the theory of probability, along with the methods of mathematical analysis, can be used to solve the decision problem.

The value of information about the state of nature

Information about the state of nature is an important element in any decision problem under risk. If decision makers can perfectly forecast the state of nature, they will be operating as if certainty existed. They will no longer choose the same alternative each time but will vary their decisions with the predicted state of nature. The difference between the expected cost with and without forecasting is the value of the forecasting information. Obviously, a knowledge of this value can mean a great deal to the decision maker.

Objective and subjective probabilities and the importance of risk analysis

In most practical problems, the probabilities of the states of nature are not known. This could mean that the decision-making problem under risk is virtually nonexistent. The fact is, however, that although accurate probabilities are usually not known, some knowledge of them is generally available through existing data and experience. Such knowledge makes an analysis under risk a convenient approximation of the intermediate case.

The importance of risk analysis is tied closely to the concept of the value of information. If estimated probabilities are used as though they were in fact true, the analysis can lead to a reasonably good decision. The reasonableness of the decision can be measured by the value of the information about the true probabilities. If we are led to virtually the same decision no matter what the probabilities, then the analysis under risk, even though not perfect, is worthwhile.

Decision making: A personal process

Social psychologists have learned a great deal about the personal process —mental and psychological—that decision makers go through.* While the specifics vary from one researcher to another, the consensus seems to be this: the decision maker goes through three stages, involving different psychological and action features. Following is a summary of the stages and their characteristics.

Information-seeking stages	*Stage 1* Decision maker becomes aware of some problem, threat, challenge, or otherwise some change in the status quo, and appraises the seriousness of that challenge.
	Stage 2 Identifies various alternative solutions.
	Stage 3 Selects most appropriate solution (satisfices).
Decision stage	*Stage 4* Commits resources to implement selected solution.
Postdecision evaluation stage	*Stage 5* Evaluates effectiveness of decision—if found wanting, go back to Stage 3 (possibly even to Stage 2 and, in extreme cases, to Stage 1).

* See, for example, Edward E. Jones and Harold B. Garard, *Foundations of Social Psychology* (New York: Wiley, 1967), pp. 186–226.

Making decisions under uncertainty

In uncertainty, the possible states of nature are known, the possible alternatives are not known completely, and the probabilities of the occurrence of both are not known at all. This situation is illustrated in Figure 29-4. This polar case is rather unlikely. But, what if it did exist? If we know nothing about the probabilities, how can a choice of alternatives be made?

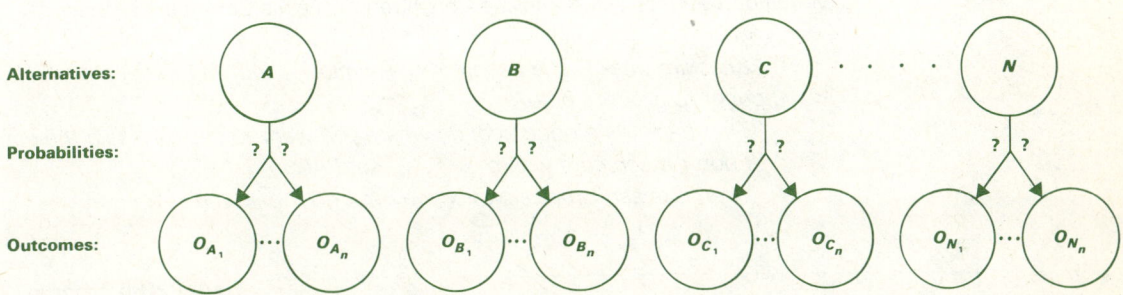

Figure 29-4 Condition of uncertainty (alternatives not known, outcomes not known, probabilities not known)

The consensus in risk analysis, at least for repetitive problems, is to choose the alternative that minimizes (or maximizes) the expected values. In uncertainty no such consensus exists. Many procedures have been proposed, among them minimax (or maximin), minimax regret, and Bayesian procedures.

The *minimax* procedure is the pessimist's approach to decisions under uncertainty. The decision maker determines for each alternative the worst outcome that could possibly occur. If outcomes are measured in cost, the maximum cost for each alternative is determined. The decision maker then selects the alternative that has the smallest value of maximum cost—the minimax. In this way, the individual is guaranteed a cost that is no higher than the minimax.

In the *minimax regret* procedure, *regret* is defined as the difference in cost between the outcome of the selected alternative and the outcome of the alternative that would have been selected had the decision maker known the state of nature. It is the opportunity cost of an incorrect decision. The minimax regret procedure states that one should choose the alternative that minimizes the maximum regret.

Bayesian procedure reverts to the expected value concept in the following way: if no knowledge of the relative probabilities of the states of nature is available, one should act under the assumption that they are equally likely. The expected value choice procedure would then follow.

Rational decision making is possible, of course, even under conditions where the lack of information or the state of nature create a situation of either risk or uncertainty. However, one problem is knowing which choice procedure is rational in a state of uncertainty. So far, the science of decision making has not provided a solution to this problem.

Rational decision making consists of sequential stages that may overlap but are, nevertheless, relatively discrete. A conventional view of the process is illustrated in Figure 29-5. The decision maker starts with the identification of the goal to be achieved. This is the obvious starting point; otherwise, pursuing a rational decision would be pointless. Reporting a conversation between Alice and the Cheshire cat, Lewis Carroll said it best:

"Cheshire-puss," she began, rather timidly, "would you tell me which way I ought to go from here?"
"That depends a good deal on where you want to get to," said the cat.
"I don't much care where . . . ," said Alice.
"Then it doesn't matter which way you go," said the cat.

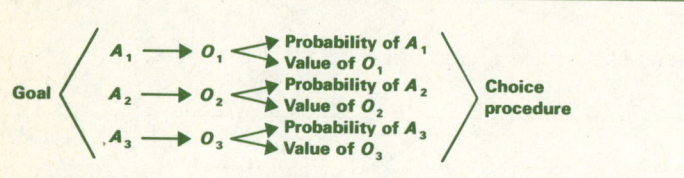

Figure 29-5 Steps in the decision process

Referring to Figure 29-5, the decision maker has three alternatives (A_1, A_2, A_3), from which to select the one that will give the best solution to the decision problem—for example, how to achieve the goal in the most effective way. Each alternative has an outcome (O_1, O_2, O_3). Outcomes are the consequences in which the decision maker's forecasts will result if a particular course of action (alternative) is followed. Associated with each outcome are two conditions that are crucial to the decision maker's selection of an alternative. The first is the estimation of each alternative's probability for accomplishing the goal. The second is the value or utility that the decision maker assigns to the outcome of each alternative. For example, if the value of O_1 is high but the probability that A_1 will accomplish the goal is low, relative to the probability of other alternatives, then the decision maker may select another alternative that has a greater probability of success even though it might have a lower payoff.

The choice procedure used to evaluate the alternatives and their outcomes depends on whether the decision situation is one of certainty, risk, or uncertainty. Any of these analyses would be appropriate in the situation just described. However, in a situation of risk or uncertainty we must add multiple outcomes to the process shown in Figure 29-5. Thus for A_1 we would have O_{1a}, O_{1b}, O_{1c}, and so on. The choice procedure will fall into risk analysis if we know the probabilities of these outcomes. The analysis will be one of uncertainty if we do not know the probabilities.

Several years ago Irwin Bross presented another way of looking at the decision maker. His approach, shown in Figure 29-6, remains a classical description of the decision process. Bross's decision maker directs attention to aspects of the decision process that are not emphasized in the conventional description. Lying beyond the decision maker, but necessary to decision making, are data, which Bross terms the "fuel of the Decision Maker."

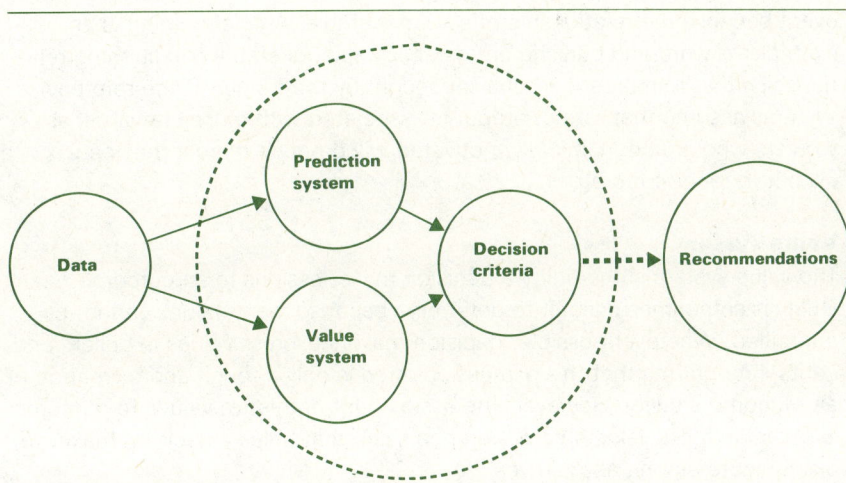

Figure 29-6 The decision makers
Source: Irwin D. J. Bross, *Design for Decision* (New York: Macmillan, 1953), p. 29. Copyright ©1953 by Macmillan Publishing Co., Inc.

Data

In some respects, goals or objectives are data, but not in the usual sense. Data are the information, in various states of refinement, available to the decision maker. Data generate alternatives, determine their outcomes, and find their probabilities and values.

Data are obtained from many sources. A sales manager who needs information to make a decision about introducing a new product has four obvious sources: (1) historical sources, which include sales records for existing and comparable products marketed by the company; (2) observations of the performance of competitors' similar products; (3) controlled tests in pilot markets; and (4) consumer attitude surveys to indicate how the new product will be accepted.

Prediction systems

A prediction system is used to help the decision maker determine the likelihood that a given alternative will produce an effect that will accomplish a goal. Systems other than probability theory can be used to make these forecasts:

1 *Persistence prediction*   Present conditions will continue. Tomorrow's weather will be like today's; a new product line will have as much success as the old line did when it was introduced.

2 *Trajectory prediction*   Change will occur at a stable rate. A hospital that experienced a 2 percent increase per year in the number of patients cared for in the past three years could expect a 2 percent increase in the next year.
3 *Cyclic prediction*   Events will recur periodically. The seasonal popularity of different types of clothing enables designers, manufacturers, and buyers to plan their activities for a year.
4 *Associative prediction*   The occurrence of one event will produce another event because the relationship of events is stable. Animal training is an example: reward and punishment establish a set of stable conditioning relationships that reinforce the behavior sought by the trainer. Piece-rate pay systems assume that rate of output is associated with money rewards; so, workers who are economically motivated will produce more if they can expect to receive more pay.

Value system

The value system is the utility a decision maker assigns to an outcome. Utility is sometimes difficult to determine because many values cannot be quantified. Wherever possible, decision makers express values in dollars and cents, recognizing that this expression often is only a rough approximation of an outcome's utility. However, the assignment of relative values to outcome is essential for developing a preference scale that helps a decision maker to discriminate among alternatives.

Decision criteria

Decision criteria have two aspects. One is the kind of analysis to use in a decision situation—certainty, risk, or uncertainty analysis. The other aspect considers whether a decision maker seeks an optimum or a satisfactory solution to a problem.

Problems with the rational model

The rational decision model is still haunted by the ghost of economic humanity, which tries to maximize its gains by seeking optimum solutions to decision problems. The model requires that all alternatives be given, their consequences known, and a complete preference scale established. The minimum requirement to enable management to make optimum choices is perfect information. This requirement, of course, cannot be met in practical circumstances, and so optimal solutions are unobtainable. Decision makers, especially those confronting complex choices, must be content with less than optimal standards. These observations prompted James March and Herbert Simon to suggest the concept of *satisfactory standards,* as opposed to optimal standards, for decision criteria. They say:

An alternative is optimal *if: (1) there exists a set of criteria that permits all alternatives to be compared, and (2) the alternative in question is preferred, by these criteria, to all other alternatives. An alternative is* satisfactory *if:*

(1) there exists a set of criteria that describes minimally satisfactory alternatives, and (2) the alternative in question meets or exceeds all these criteria.[1]

Most human decision making, whether individual or organizational, is concerned with the discovery and selection of satisfactory alternatives; only in exceptional cases is it concerned with the discovery and selection of optimal alternatives.

This approach should not be considered nonrational. Indeed, rationality enters in regardless of whether the decision maker is trying to optimize or to "satisfice."[2] A few years ago a researcher constructed a computer program to try to duplicate investment decisions of a bank trust investment officer.[3] The program used various satisficing—rather than maximizing—criteria for investing. The computer program almost exactly duplicated the officer's portfolio decisions. The notion of satisficing is much closer to the real world of decision making, where the manager cannot completely specify the decision situation or hope to gain complete information about it.

Decision making under uncertainty: It's real

A few years ago, a well-known manufacturing firm was in deep financial trouble; and so, as a direct consequence, was its host city. A critic charged the firm's management with being culpable for the community's dire straits. Local editorial writers were quick to criticize the critic, pointing out that there were some good—and unavoidable—reasons for the firm's problems:

1 The Pentagon had canceled several very large contracts.
2 Commerical customers were tightening their belts and had cut back severely on their orders.
3 Congress had scuttled a project that would have contributed greatly to the company's recovery.

In short, concluded the editorialists, the firm's problems were the direct result of events and factors in the socio-political-economic environment that were completely outside the control of company management. Therefore, company management could hardly be held accountable for failing to deal effectively with forces outside their control.

Were the editors correct? You decide. But before you decide, consider this: saying that managers make decisions in an environment that they cannot control is to state the obvious—managers make decisions under conditions of uncertainty. That's what *uncertainty* means.

---

[1] James G. March and Herbert A. Simon, *Organizations* (New York: Wiley, 1958), pp. 140–141. Emphasis in original.
[2] The term *satisfice* reflects the desire to select an alternate that is *satis*factory and that will suf*fice*.
[3] G. P. E. Clarkson, "A Model of Trust Investment Behavior," in Richard M. Cyert and James G. March, *A Behavioral Theory of the Firm* (Englewood Cliffs, N.J.: Prentice-Hall, 1963), pp. 253–267.

Boundaries of rationality

Optimization presumes unlimited flexibility on the part of managers to vary the organization to suit the actions they must take in order to maximize. *Bounded rationality* gives another picture of the limits to which maximization efforts can be carried. Managerial rationality is limited (bounded) by various elements of the decision situation that are taken as givens and do not enter the rational calculations of the decision maker. Such elements are many and are found in the goals sought by the organization or the individual. Boundaries also arise in the organizational structure, which must be maintained, and in the premises used by decision makers in planning. The research methodology used to generate data provides additional boundaries of rationality.

The use of the submarine by the Japanese navy during World War II is an interesting example of bounded rationality. The Japanese used submarines primarily as fleet-support weapons; they did not deploy them as attack weapons against shipping as did the Germans and Americans. The Japanese navy formulated its strategy on the premise that the primary goal of submarines was to defend major fleet units. This premise limited the military decision makers to alternatives within the boundaries of defensive strategy. This faulty assumption resulted in the underutilization of the Japanese submarine fleet, although the decisions made within the framework of it were rationally formulated and executed.

The submarine example shows that a decision maker can be rationally consistent but consistently wrong. Errors arise from faulty premises, irrelevant goals, and so on. The boundaries to rationality may be so blemished that effective managerial action is prevented.

On the positive side, bounded rationality maintains stability in decision situations. Everything in organizations cannot change at once. Change in some parts of an organization is predicated on stability in other parts. Decision making could not be effective if all the elements of a decision situation varied wildly. For example, a college student would find it difficult to graduate if course offerings and curriculum requirements were constantly changing. The catalog of course requirements provides boundaries that help the student to plan a program.

Boundaries of bounded rationality

The major issue that pertains to bounded rationality is the balance between stability and flexibility. From the administrative standpoint, both stability and flexibility are desirable qualities, though too much of either could stifle the organization or unhinge the decision process. But the problem, in the final analysis, seems weighted toward stability. In actual decision situations, managers must overcome considerable inertia in order to produce organizational change and to create an environment that favors adaptability.

Part of this inertia arises from the goals, objectives, policies, and premises that are taken as givens in the decision process. It is the nature of rational boundaries that they go unexamined. Adaptation to change through continuous reappraisal of the givens is essential to innovation in decision making. How can the system be opened to an examination of its basic premises? Probably, the most elementary requirement is an improvement in the flow of information to strategic decision makers. Questioning basic premises is all right, but to do so without adequate information is irresponsible. Beyond this requirement is another, somewhat more intangible because it consists of a change in management's attitude.

The examination of fundamental decision premises cannot occur without a commitment from management to an organizational design that stresses openness and freedom to explore. Conventional organizations place a premium on routine, mechanistic approaches to problem solving. Negative rewards are likely to result if an individual questions organizational givens. These constraints must be overcome in order to establish a creative atmosphere for decision making.

Decision making and organizational design

Two organizational variables affect decision making—the kind of job performed and the manager's level in the organizational structure. As a rule, the higher managers are in the organization, the greater is their authority and discretion. As the managerial hierarchy is ascended, broad, complex problems that defy routine or detailed solutions are encountered. Decision criteria are vague, and solutions to decision problems are ordinarily given in terms of policy guidelines. Under these circumstances, the boundaries of rationality are fewer and looser for upper management. Consequently, there is opportunity for creativity and innovation in the decision process. Decisions made in these situations are said to be *unprogrammed*.

Opposite conditions are found as the hierarchy of an organization is descended. Lower levels of management find greater and more precisely defined boundaries to rationality. Since their jobs are heavily involved with the implementation of basic decisions, their activities become routine. The decision process at these levels requires managers mainly to select the program out of several established programs best fitted to a given decision situation. Such decisions are called *programmed*.

This analysis of the decision process assumes a conventional organizational design. The structure of the organization is based on the specialization of work and a chain of command. For most real-world organizations, this is a fairly accurate first approximation of the decision setting. However, the fact that this analysis is a first approximation must be emphasized. Many modern organizations are far too complex to divide the decisions of managers neatly into programmed and unprogrammed categories.

For example, higher levels of management depend on managers at lower levels for information, advice, counsel, and assistance in formulating unprogrammed decisions. Therefore, lower managers can and do have a hand in shaping innovative decisions. The size of the hand depends on the expertise of lower management, the technology used by the organization to achieve its goals, and the organizational design. In turn, organizational design is a function of both technology and the level of managerial skill. The conventional model of the decision process is more closely approached by the organizational design of a firm quarrying limestone than it is by the aerospace division of an aircraft company.

The type of structure has a great deal to do with who participates in what kinds of decisions. Even such factors as management's leadership styles encourage or discourage participation in innovative decision activities. A great deal of work has been done to improve understanding of the decision process. Operations research has supplied management with certain quantitative tools to help it make better decisions.

Research report: Decision rules in group decision making

When a group of people makes a joint decision, it is necessary to have some standard or principle for recognizing when a decision has been reached. These standards are called *decision rules*. Some common rules are:

- *Consensus rule*   All group members must agree with the proposed decision.
- *Majority rule*   At least one half (sometimes two thirds) of the group members must agree with the proposed decision.
- *Plurality rule*   More group members must agree with the proposed decision than do support any of the alternative decisions.

Which decision rule is best to use? The answer seems to depend on the type of decision being made. For example, if the alternatives contain, or are believed to contain, a single correct decision, then groups using a consensus rule are more likely to be accurate (although more conservative) than majority-rule groups.

Unfortunately, most decisions made by groups do not have one clearly correct alternative; several choices are available, but it is not possible to verify the decision objectively. Policy decisions are a case in point. Which decision rule should be used in this type of situation? Consider some evidence.

In one experimental study,* 647 undergraduates served as members of mock juries, which deliberated to reach a verdict in a rape case. The students were separated into seventy-two juries: thirty-six juries used a consensus rule and thirty-six required a two-thirds majority. None of the juries convicted the defendant. When jury members later were asked for their individual opinions anonymously, it turned out that those people who were

---

* J. H. Davis, N. L. Kerr, R. S. Atkin, R. Holt, and D. Meek, "The decision processes of 6- and 12-person mock juries assigned unanimous and two-thirds majority rules," *Journal of Personality and Social Psychology* 32 (1975): 1–14.

members of consensus-rule juries continued to accept the verdicts of their group more than did members of the two-thirds majority juries.

Now, the students in this study knew they were participating as subjects in an experiment. They had little reason to believe their decisions were consequential. Consensus rule yielded more stable decisions. What about the case in which the matter being decided is important to the decision maker? Klopfer[†] used a decision topic previously rated by subjects as important. Subjects were assigned to one of sixteen consensus-rule groups, or one of the same number of majority-rule groups. Subjects in half the groups were led to believe their decision making might have real impact (high consequence), while subjects in the other groups were not (low consequence). Several days after their participation, group members were asked to make an individual decision and to rate their satisfaction with the group decision making. Subjects in consensus-rule groups making high-consequence decisions showed a tendency to reject their group's decision and revert to their own original points of view.

The conclusion to be drawn regarding decisions that have no clear best solution is: consensus rule may be a difficult criterion to achieve with important or high-consequence decisions. However, the evidence suggests that consensus rule is preferable with less important issues for producing stable decisions. Several studies also suggest that consensus rule takes more time but is more satisfying, in both cases.

[†] F. J. Klopfer, "Decision rules and decision consequence in group decision-making," unpublished doctoral dissertation, Texas Tech University, 1975.
Source: The authors wish to thank Professor Frederick J. Klopfer, Department of Psychology, Oregon State University, for preparing this report.

Operations research

Methods

Operations research involves a particular view of management's operations and a particular kind of research: "Operations are considered as an entity. The subject matter studied is not the equipment used, nor the morale of the participants, nor the physical properties of the output; it is the combination of these in total, as an economic process."[4] Operations viewed in this manner are subject to analysis by the thought processes and methods normally associated with the research work of natural scientists, physicists, and chemists. Because it makes use of general scientific methods, operations research is applicable to the study of operations in many types of organization, including business, government, and the military.

[4] Cyril C. Herrmann and John F. Magee, "Operations Research for Management," *Harvard Business Review* 31 (July–August 1953): 101.

Operations research uses a team or task force to approach a problem. This technique evolved during World War II when scholars from a variety of disciplines—natural sciences, economics, sociology, cultural anthropology, statistics, mathematics—found they could work together to solve related problems. Two early applications of operations research were the development of an antiaircraft fire-control system to defend England against German bombers and a logistical system to coordinate the movement of convoys across the North Atlantic.

Because of their varied backgrounds and training, the members of task forces do not have a common technical vocabulary and, thus, are forced to use the universal medium of mathematics, which is abstract enough to permit mutual understanding. Although no approach has been firmly established, mathematics is essential to operations research. However, businesspeople rarely are well trained in this field, and they are often at a loss when confronted with its symbols. They need not learn the language of mathematics completely in order to understand the place or use of operations research, but they must develop at least an awareness of its nature and applicability to business problems. Because the technique is still somewhat new, many managers are reluctant to incorporate it into their own managerial skills, preferring to leave their problems to operations research specialists. They may continue to avoid the technicalities of operations research while accepting its methods on faith and proven results.

Presentation of alternative solutions

Operations research has two other major characteristics that differentiate it further from customary business-related or organizational research. First, the operations research team usually attempts to investigate and study the relationship of the activity under consideration to all other pertinent elements of the business. Second, the team makes an effort to uncover, catalog, and evaluate all courses of action that might be taken. The aim is not necessarily to find one definite answer, for in many cases there is no single right answer. The final choice "is the one that will lessen or mitigate a problem or the one that will give the most beneficial results."[5] In other words, operations research presents management with an array of solutions to a given problem, the solutions being arranged in the order of their desirability and probability of success. If there is no clear evidence that one solution is more advantageous than another, the answer will most likely read: "Solution A should reduce absenteeism 20 percent but may increase personnel administration costs 6 percent. Solution B will reduce absenteeism 17 percent but will raise personnel administration costs 3 percent." This presentation of alternative solutions and costs represents the most important contribution of

[5] *Ibid.*

operations research to business management. It certainly helps executives to make decisions, but it will not make up their minds for them.

Models

A common method of applying mathematics to operations research is through the construction and study of mathematical models. The best known of these is the *accounting model:* "Assets minus liabilities equals proprietorship." This is essentially "a simplified representation on paper, in the form of accounts and ledgers, of the flow of goods and services through a business enterprise."[6] Also familiar are the various models used in physics, such as three-dimensional representations of complex molecules and the many sets of mathematical equations.

In operations research, a distinction is made between *descriptive models,* which describe the facts and relationships of various problems, and *policy models,* which are useful for planning and selecting an optimum course of action. Operations research models also can be distinguished as *exact* or *probabilistic,* depending on the degree of chance involved. A major goal of the operations research analyst is the construction of a model that constitutes the most faithful representation of the operation. The mathematical model is particularly convenient because it can be manipulated to test the probable effect of contemplated changes without disturbing the existing order of things. The ability to manipulate prevents costly failures that could result from experimenting with the actual operation of a business.

Model building can be considered a three-stage procedure. The first stage describes the situation under study in the terms of the symbolism adopted. The second stage introduces the motivational, behavioral, and technological assumptions. The third stage quantifies the process by assigning different sets of numerical values to the parameters of the model.[7] These values make it possible for the operations research team to manipulate the model so that it will yield quantitative information that shows the results the different values will produce. Much of this work has been made possible by the development of rapid computing machines.

Large segments of the business process are susceptible to such numerical treatment. Quantifiable data that can be used with considerable accuracy are readily available for most aspects of finance, shipping, production, and employment. However, when attitudes or emotional reactions are involved—particularly those relating to consumer responses, advertising, marketing, and collective bargaining—quantification is much more difficult and probably will be highly arbitrary. The calculations will not necessarily be valid because in these instances they are made on the basis of someone's

---

[6] *Ibid.,* p. 103.
[7] Robert Dorfman, "Operations Research," *American Economic Review* 50 (September 1960): 579.

own idea of the numerical value to be assigned to a feeling or attitude. In such matters, individuals' judgments vary considerably.

Techniques of operations research

In analyzing specific business problems, operations research scientists make use of techniques, such as probability theory, game theory, queuing or waiting-line theory, and linear programming. These are tools developed by mathematicians and statisticians.

Probability theory

When risk or uncertainty is present in a business decision, probability theory can be called on. According to probability theory, certain things are likely to happen in accordance with a predictable pattern. For instance, if a person tosses a coin one hundred times, the probability is that it will show heads fifty times and tails fifty times. The deviations can be set within a predictable margin.

Game theory

Game theory introduces a competitive note. It brings into a simulated decision-making situation the actions of an opponent. Both competitors are presumed to be similarly motivated: the manager is interested in maximizing gains and minimizing losses, and so is the rival. Game theory will show the highest gains with the smallest amount of losses, regardless of what the competitor does.

Queuing theory

Queuing theory develops the relationships that are involved in waiting in line. Customers awaiting service, cars at a toll gate, planes waiting to land, work in a production line awaiting inspection—each is typical of the problems that may be approached by the methods of queuing theory. The theory, in effect, balances the cost of waiting lines against the cost of preventing them by increasing facilities. The problem is figuring out the cost of total waiting—that is, the cost of tolerating the queue—and weighing it against the expense of building enough service facilities to lessen the need for the queue. Sometimes it is more costly to eliminate all delay than to keep some of it.

Linear programming

Linear programming is often applied when it is necessary to find an optimum combination or allocation of limited resources to obtain a desired objective. The resources may be the money a company has available for use, the capacity of its plant or individual machines, or its advertising budget. The objective may be the lowest cost or highest profit possible from the given resources. Linear programming must be considered in the light of the limitations on its use. A general prerequisite for utilizing it is that there must be a *linear* (straight line) relation among the factors involved. The limits of variation must be fairly well established. The volume of calculations required often is so great that a computer is essential. Linear programming has been commonly applied to transportation problems, such as those posed when standardized commodities are to be shipped from a variety of sources to many destinations.

Summary

Decision making is a process that links the basic managerial functions. Managers make decisions as a fundamental part of their organizational stewardship. In essence, all decisions involve the following elements: objective(s), alternatives, outcomes, criteria, and choice.

There are three basic sets of conditions under which decision making may occur: certainty, risk, and uncertainty. It is fair to say that managerial decision making takes place almost exclusively under uncertainty; the best managers can hope for is to improve the odds and move into a risk condition.

Rational decision makers start with data, make predictions about the future, assign utilities to various outcomes, utilize the decision criteria they believe are appropriate to their situation, and, then, form their decision recommendation. This process operates even under conditions of uncertainty, in which decision rationality is bounded, leading to satisficing rather than maximizing. Depending further on the decision situation, decisions are either programmed or unprogrammed.

Several decision-making tools have evolved out of the discipline of operations research; probability theory, game theory, queuing theory, and linear programming are a few of them.

Discussion questions

1   In general, are you a rational decision maker? Support your answer with specific examples.
2   When you decide how much time to devote to studying for each course you are taking, do you try to optimize? to satisfice? Which decision criteria do you use to allocate your study time?

3 Eventually you will have to select a major field, if you have not done so already. Can you identify the boundaries of rationality in your decision? (*Example:* My father has a CPA firm; therefore, I am majoring in accounting.)

Supplementary readings

Browne, William G. "Techniques of Operations Research." *Journal of Systems Management,* September 1972, pp. 3–13. Reprinted in *Dimensions in Modern Management,* 2d ed., edited by Patrick E. Connor. Boston: Houghton Mifflin, 1978.

Heilbroner, Robert L. "How to Make an Intelligent Decision." *Think,* pp. 2–4. New York: International Business Machines, 1960.

Kepner, Charles H., and Tregoe, Benjamin B. *The Rational Manager.* New York: McGraw-Hill, 1965.

MacCrinnon, Kenneth A. "Managerial Decision Making." In *Contemporary Management: Issues and Viewpoints,* edited by Joseph W. McGuire, pp. 445–495. Englewood Cliffs, N.J.: Prentice-Hall, 1974.

Rowe, Alan J. "Making Effective Decisions." *Chemical Engineering,* September 16, 1974, pp. 126–132. Reprinted in *Dimensions in Modern Management,* 2d ed., edited by Patrick E. Connor. Boston: Houghton Mifflin, 1978.

———. "The Myth of the Rational Decision Maker." *International Management,* August 1974, pp. 38–40.

Simon, Herbert A. "Administrative Decision Making." In *Administrative Behavior,* pp. xxv–xxvii, 67, 75–77, 80–84. New York: Macmillan, 1947. Reprinted in *Dimensions in Modern Management,* 2d ed., edited by Patrick E. Connor. Boston: Houghton Mifflin, 1978.

Chapter 30

Linking process 2: Communicating

Objectives of the chapter

1 To define and describe *communications* in formal organizations.
2 To identify various channels and means of communicating.
3 To review the ways in which communications become distorted.
4 To review the ways in which distortions may be dealt with by managers.

At its basic level, *communicating* is a process of exchanging information. It entails imparting ideas and making oneself understood by others—and understanding others, in return. As such, communicating is a process by which managers implement their basic managerial functions; without communications to link them together, the managerial functions would fail.

Rogers and Rogers cite a spectacular example of the impact that communicating can have on effective management:[1] Erwin Pawelski, a patient in the Chicago-area Veterans Administration Hospital, was misplaced for twenty-seven hours.

At 9:30 A.M. on May 1, 1975, Pawelski (who could not speak) was strapped into a wheelchair to be taken for a session of occupational therapy. There is no record of Pawelski's whereabouts for the next twenty-seven hours.

At 7:00 A.M. on May 2, someone at the hospital telephoned Pawelski's wife to ask if she had removed him from the hospital. She had not. When she rushed to the hospital, she discovered that another patient had been moved into his bed. No one knew what had happened to Pawelski.

At 1:10 P.M. the same day, Pawelski was found in a main elevator, slumped over in his wheelchair. The hospital has 3,000 employees, 1,295 patients, and 700 daily visitors. Hundreds of physicians, nurses, attendants, patients, and visitors ride the elevators every day. A hospital spokesperson

---

[1] Everett M. Rogers and Rekha Agarwala-Rogers, *Communication in Organizations* (New York: Free Press, 1976), p. 9.

made the obvious observation to reporters: "It's unbelievable that there wouldn't be one person during those twenty-seven hours offering to help this man slumped over in a wheelchair. It's a mystery what happened."

Organizing and communicating

The purpose of subdivision is to create a series of tasks within the competence of the available individuals, or tasks for which they can be trained, and to relate those tasks to each other and to the overall objectives of the corporation so that they support each other. It is, in short, to ensure coordination of effort.

The reason why people organize is always the same: to ensure that individual efforts are directed towards a common purpose and that they support each other. The latter is largely a question of timing, the timing of individual efforts. Every form of human collaboration, from two persons to 200 million, is like an orchestra. It only works really well if the individual players "keep time," so that their efforts support each other and are in accord with "the score." If a single player fails to "keep time," the whole effect may be ruined. That is why orchestras have "conductors" and business undertakings have managers.

But in an orchestra all the players can see and hear the conductor. In a business undertaking they cannot. The conductor (Chief Executive) may live in an office ten thousand miles away. Concerted action (after all a musical performance is called "a concert") then depends upon communication. That is what organization is about. A so-called "Organizational Chart" is a wiring diagram. It defines who should tell whom about what and, if anybody doesn't know, whom he/she should ask. Without orderly communication any effort at human cooperation tends to become a "disorderly house."

Source: Lyndall F. Urwick, "That Word 'Organization,'" *Academy of Management Review* 1 (January 1976): 90.

Three weeks later, Pawelski died from a cerebral hemorrhage following brain surgery. Hospital officials said that his death was not related to the unfortunate incident. Rogers and Rogers put it well:

A hospital can best be viewed . . . as an organization that devotes much of its activity to processing information. So, in fact, do most other types of organizations.[2]

[2] Ibid.

The purpose of this chapter is to examine the communicating process, pointing out its importance to managers.

The nature of communicating

Communication is successful only when mutual understanding results. Because a part of managing is getting things done through various people, managers obviously must communicate with many members of their organizations. It has been estimated that managers spend 90 percent of their time sending or receiving information. However, to assume that in all this activity communication is taking place would be erroneous. Just because managers send and receive messages does not mean that there is successful communication. The appearance of frequent misunderstandings, confusion, and disagreement is evidence that true communication often does not take place.

Communication always involves at least two parties, a sender and a receiver. A person who is stranded on a desert island, shouting for help, does not communicate. This fact is not so obvious to managers who send out a large number of memoranda. They are inclined to believe that once a memorandum has been sent, communication has occurred. This is not so until and unless information and understanding have passed between them and their intended receivers.

Understanding is a personal matter. If the idea received is the one intended, communication has taken place. However, people may interpret messages differently. If the idea received is not the one intended, communication has not taken place; the sender has not communicated but has merely spoken or written. This does not mean that the receiver must agree with the statement of the sender; he or she merely must understand it.

Each person is endowed with some capacities for communication. Of course, some persons are much more effective communicators than are others. The personal effectiveness of managers is determined, in part, by their ability to communicate. If they cannot transfer information and knowledge so that they are understood, they will not achieve the desired results. Also, managers must know how to receive knowledge and understanding from the messages sent to them by others. Only through effective interchanges can organizational policies and practices be formulated and administered, misunderstandings ironed out, long-term plans achieved, and activities coordinated and controlled.

Channels of communication

An organization's communication network has two distinct, important channels: the official, or formal, and the informal. Each carries messages from one person or group to another downward, upward, across, and diagonally.

Formal channels

Formal channels are established primarily by the organizational structure through the establishment of formal systems of authority and responsibility and by explicit delegation of duties.

Downward communication

The chain of formal command suggests that someone at the top issues an order that the next person in the hierarchy passes along to those who report to him or her, and so on down the line. Managers rely on this downward movement for the communication of directives. Through this channel, policies are transmitted to lower levels of the organization for implementation. Downward communication helps to link the levels of the hierarchy and to coordinate activities on many different levels. Generally speaking, it initiates subordinates' actions and is primarily directive.

Upward communication

Upward communication informs and reports. It carries control information about what has happened at various points of performance, as well as the opinions and attitudes of subordinates to their superiors; it must carry reports on work-related activities and actions. Managers should encourage such communication, for this is the only means by which they can determine whether or not messages have been transmitted and properly received and whether or not the enterprise is operating effectively. Upward communication shows whether the proper action has taken or is taking place to accomplish organizational objectives. The chain of command not only establishes the downward line of communication, which enables a manager to transmit directives and information to subordinates, but, working in reverse, it also creates a path for the upward line of communication, which the subordinate can use to convey information to superiors.

Lateral communication

Lateral communication also is essential for effective organizational action. Such communication occurs across departments or among people on the same level in the managerial hierarchy. For example, the manager of the production department will certainly have to communicate with the managers of the sales and accounting departments. Without such lateral communication the coordination of various functions cannot occur.

Diagonal communication

Diagonal communication occurs when messages flow between decision centers that are not on the same lateral plane of the organization's structure. Communication between line and staff groups occurs diagonally. We also frequently find this form of communication in project-type organizations. Figure 30-1 illustrates diagonal communication as well as the other formal types that we have been discussing.

Downward

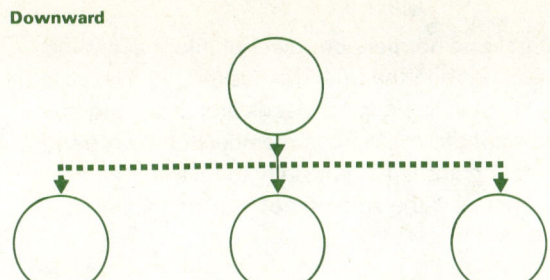

From a higher to a lower level: Carries policies, orders, directives, and performance standards. Is used to evoke action from subordinates and coordinate activities.

Upward

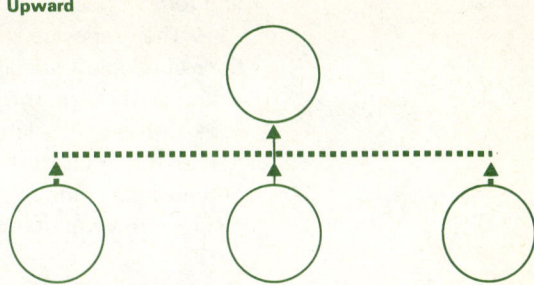

From a lower level to a higher level: Carries control information pertaining to performance. Is used as a feedback device.

Lateral

Between functions on the same organizational level: Carries information vital to the effective performance of work between functions that are interdependent. Is used to coordinate activities by the exchange of data. Also used by staff for transmitting technical information necessary to facilitate the work of other functions.

Diagonal

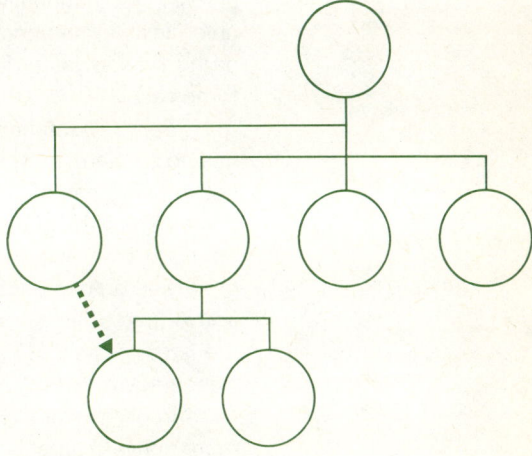

Between special staff groups and line functions: Used by staff to transmit information and advice to line. Sometimes used by staff to exercise functional staff authority.

Figure 30-1 The flow of information along formal communication channels

Informal channels: The grapevine

Although it is important to develop sound formal channels of communication, students of organization have repeatedly pointed out that groups often tend to create additional channels of communication as well. Every organization has its grapevine[3] — a network of constantly recurring, casual personal

[3] Keith Davis, *Human Behavior at Work* (New York: McGraw-Hill, 1972), pp. 261–270.

contacts that forms spontaneous channels through which facts, half-truths, and rumors pass.

The grapevine is a natural and normal outgrowth of informal organization, of people's social interaction, and their natural desire to communicate with one another. The grapevine fulfills peoples' needs and desires to be kept posted on the latest information. It gives the members of the organization an outlet for their imagination and an opportunity to relieve their apprehensions in the form of rumors. At the same time, it offers managers insight into what others think and feel.

Operation

At times, the grapevine carries factual information and news, but, as we noted above, it also carries inaccurate information, private interpretations, suspicions, and all kinds of distorted information. Like the formal communication channels, it carries such information in four directions—up, down, across, and diagonally. In addition, it carries information in an unpredictable, flexible, meandering pattern not fixed by an organization chart. The path followed yesterday is not necessarily the same as that of today or tomorrow.

Being spontaneous and having no definite pattern, the grapevine also has no stable membership. Normally, only a small number of people are active participants in it. Although the vast majority of people in an organization listen to the grapevine, few actually pass information along it. And, although any person within the organization is likely to become active in the grapevine on one occasion or another, some individuals tend to be more active than others. They believe that their prestige is enhanced by providing the latest news and, in doing so, they do not hesitate to give the news new "accuracy."

In periods of excitement and sudden change, the grapevine becomes more active than at other occasions. During these periods of insecurity and great anxiety, the grapevine gives members of the organization an outlet for their fears and apprehensions: it serves as an emotional safety valve.

Uses

The grapevine often carries important information that can help to clarify formal messages. In fact, it frequently spreads information that could not be sent through the official channels of communication. For example, occasionally an executive suddenly "resigns." Although top management cannot state publicly what actually took place, it may not want to give the impression that the executive was the victim of some unfair managerial action. In such a case, a top manager may reveal to a member of the grapevine—under the seal of secrecy—what really occurred. Leaks are not restricted to the world of politics.

Some managers believe that the grapevine should be stamped out since it often carries false, malicious, and uncontrollable rumors. Managers can no more eliminate the grapevine than they can abolish informal organization. The grapevine performs useful functions and is an important part of organizational life. It transmits information with amazing speed! "With the rapidity of a burning powder train, information flows like magic out of the woodwork past the water fountain, past the manager's door and the janitor's mop closet."[4] It is unrealistic to expect that such a spontaneous phenomenon can be stamped out.

Since the grapevine represents an enduring portion of the channels of communication, managers should learn how to live with it and how to use it. To do so, they must tune it in and learn what it is saying; they must listen and look for the meaning of its communication; they must find out who its leaders are and who is likely to spread information; and they must learn that by giving the grapevine facts, they can counter more rumors and half-truths. Managers can and should utilize the grapevine's energy. Although the best way to minimize rumors is to improve the official channels of communication, grapevine channels should not be ignored. An organization without a grapevine is unthinkable.

The communication media

Words, pictures, and actions are the media for communication. Because words are the most important symbols used, a manager must be able to employ them effectively. Words can be transmitted orally and received by listening, or they can be transmitted in written form and received by reading.

Pictures, the visual aids that a manager may resort to, from time to time, are powerful too and are particularly effective in association with well-chosen words. Managers make extensive use of pictures—blueprints, charts, drafts, models, posters, and the like. The popularity of motion pictures and comic strips also clearly proves the ability of pictures to communicate and, especially, to contribute to understanding.

Action also is an important factor in communication. Managers must not forget that their actions are interpreted as a symbol by subordinates and may be more powerful than their words.[5] Because of managers' status, all observable acts communicate something to subordinates whether they intend them to or not. A purposeful silence, a gesture, a handshake, a shrug of the shoulder, a smile—all have meaning.

By the same token, inaction communicates as well. Unexplained action, however, often communicates a meaning that is not intended. For example, if a manager orders the removal of machinery from the production floor without telling the workers why, it may upset them considerably, especially if the workers fear a shutdown or think that the plant will be moved to another city.

---

[4] Jospeh K. Shepard, "I Heard it on . . . the Grapevine," *Indianapolis Star Magazine* October 2, 1955, p. 4.

[5] Of course, this fact can backfire. Recall Attorney General Mitchell's advice at the beginning of the Nixon administration to "watch what we do, not what we say."

Written communication

Because words are the most important means of communication, we should look at their uses more carefully. Words are used in both oral and written communication. Although oral communication is more frequent, a well-balanced communication system must utilize both media. Serious inefficiency can result if, for example, managers try to communicate with their subordinates and colleagues entirely by writing. Executives who rarely call anyone for a face-to-face conference and who only rarely use the telephone must spend all their time dictating memos, leaving little time for other, more important, business. Their subordinates would have to spend an equal time reading and preparing replies to their communications as the executives did in dictating, reading, and signing them.

Written messages are indispensable at times, however. They provide a permanent record to which receivers can refer as often as necessary in order to make sure that they understand what has been said, whereas the spoken word generally exists only for an instant. Moreover, detailed instructions may be so lengthy that they must be put in writing so that they can be studied at leisure. Also, the written medium is frequently best for widepsread dissemination of information that may concern many people. Finally, written communications have a degree of formality that oral messages usually do not carry.

Oral communication

Nevertheless, in most instances, managers can achieve better understanding and can save time by communicating orally—by telephone or face-to-face conversations. Face-to-face conversations, particularly those conducted between supervisor and subordinate or line and staff managers on a frequent basis, are the heart of an effective communication system. They provide the most frequently used opportunity for the exchange of information, points of view, and instructions. No form of printed communication—nor even the telephone, the public-address system, or other artificial oral media—can equal oral contact between the various levels of management, the supervisor and the worker, and among the entire work group.

The greatest single advantage of oral communication is that it provides immediate feedback. Although the response may be only a facial expression, senders can judge how their messages have been received. Oral communication enables senders to find out immediately what receivers hear and what they do not hear. It enables the recipients to clarify meanings and resolve unexpected problems instantly. The human voice gives a message a meaning and shading that even long pages of written words simply cannot convey.[6]

---

[6] That oral communication is, in fact, more effective than written (and face-to-face communication, more effective than the telephone) has been shown by Jake Huber, "An Efficacy Comparison of Vocational Instructional/Curriculum Material Survey Techniques," (Ph.D. dissertation, Oregon State University, 1973).

Barriers to communication

The speaker and the listener are two separate individuals who live in different worlds. Many fundamental factors can interfere with and distort the message that passes between them. Every manager is familiar with the misunderstandings, frictions, and inconveniences that arise when the communication network breaks down. Most managerial problems (and human problems in general) result from poor or nonexistent communication. Breakdowns not only cost money but also injure teamwork and morale and, therefore, are significant obstacles to effective influence.

Although the variety of communication barriers is large, the most important ones can be placed into four general groupings. Some are caused by the nature of the organization's structure, some by status and position, some by language, and many by people's inclination to resist change.

Organizational structure

The intricate structure of most enterprises today involves several layers of supervision, long communication lines, complex relations among staff and line assignments, and considerable distance between workers and the top levels of management. Communication may break down because of faulty transmission at any level of supervision. To forestall potential breakdowns, managers must consider the nature and complexity of the organization's structure and determine the best channels and the most effective ways to overcome communication barriers. For instance, managers might decide to reduce the number of supervisory levels, shorten the lines of authority, provide for more participative practices, or increase delegation and decentralization.

Status and position

Obviously, the president of a company and the vice president in charge of production are on two different levels in the corporate hierarchy. Differences in status and position become apparent as one level communicates with another. In addition to the barriers to communication that usually exist between human beings on the same social level are barriers of social distance caused by the different echelons in an organization.

When subordinates listen to a message from a superior, several factors become operative. The receivers evaluate what they hear in terms of their own position, background, and experience, and they also unconsciously evaluate the sender. It is difficult for the receivers to separate what they hear from the feelings they have about the person who sends the message. Often they attribute nonexistent motives to the sender: union members often interpret management statements adversely because they are convinced that management is trying to weaken and undermine the union. Often, a company's newspaper is considered to be a propaganda organ and a mouthpiece of management, and, regardless of the truth and interest of its information, the workers read it with suspicion. Such attitudes, however justified, do not promote understanding.

Good communicators realize that negative feelings, prejudice, and barriers created by differences in status and position often result from the divergence between the listeners' and the senders' interests. Superiors can help to overcome this by putting themselves in a subordinate's position and analyzing and anticipating his or her reaction before they send the message. Often, the reactions of several subordinates must be considered. The president's announcement that the enterprise is buying a concern in a different part of the country might be interpreted by the sales manager to mean a larger sales potential, whereas the production worker in the old plant may feel the action will threaten his or her position.

The same status and position barrier also appears in the upward flow of communication because subordinates want to impress their boss. Consequently, they screen the information that is passed up the line, emphasizing what the superior likes to hear and omitting or softening what is unpleasant. At times, subordinates try to cover up their own weaknesses when talking to a person in a higher position. Often, supervisors fail to pass on important subordinate attitudes or grievances because they believe that such information would reflect unfavorably on their supervisory ability. After two or three selective screenings of this sort, a message is likely to become extensively distorted.

Language

Normally, words serve well as a basis for communication, but frequently the same word may suggest quite different meanings to different people,[7] and the particular orientation of different groups will give different meanings to the same words. In such a case, the words themselves constitute a barrier to communication. For example, when managers speak of profits, they consider them essential for an enterprise to continue as a growing business, to buy new equipment, to expand, and to provide more jobs. However, many employees may think that profits suggest unearned or unfair excess earnings derived from paying inadequate salaries. Some union members do not understand—or else understand too well—the competitive position of their employer and, therefore, cannot accept management's explanation of its position. Their orientation and interests are different, developed from another way of life.

---

[7] An entire field of study, called *semantics*, is devoted to the analysis of the meaning of words. According to one semantic principle, the structure of a person's language influences the manner in which he or she understands reality and behaves with respect to it.

Communicating: It's not the words, it's the music

The following is an excerpt from a well-known novel. To set the scene: Lewis, the narrator, is a very staid and influential English gentleman; Roger is a cabinet minister, caught in adultery and being blackmailed; Ellen is Roger's mistress; and Roger and Ellen are meeting with their friend Lewis to seek his advice.

> "What do you think, Lewis?"
> After a pause I replied, turning to Roger:
> "It's a slight risk. But I fancy it's probably time to take the offensive."
> I said it with every appearance of reason, of deliberate consideration, and perhaps as persuasively as I ever said anything.
> Roger had been talking sense. Ellen was as gifted with sense as he was: but she was made for action, her judgement was always likely to leave her if she couldn't act. I ought to have known that. Maybe, with half of my mind, I did know. But my own judgement had gone, for reasons more complex than hers, and much more culpable. As I grew older, I had learned patience. The influence I had on people like Roger was partly because they thought me a tough and enduring man; but this wasn't as natural as it seemed.
> I had been born spontaneous, excessively so, emotional, malleable. The stoical public face had become real enough, but the earlier nature went on underneath, and, when the patience and control snapped, was still, in my middle-age, capable of breaking through. This was dangerous for me, and for those around me, since fits of temper, or spontaneous affection, or sheer whims, filtered through the public screen, and sounded as disciplined, as reliable, as some part of my character had now become, and as I should have liked the rest of it to be. It didn't happen often, because I was on my guard: but occasionally it happened still, as on that evening.
> No one but my wife knew it, but for days . . . my temper had been smouldering. Like Ellen, I had gone into the pub craving for action. Unlike her, though, I didn't sound as though I needed it. The craving came out through layers of patience, mixed with all the qualifications and devices of discipline, as though it were the reasonable, considered recommendation of a wise and prudent man.*

*C. P. Snow, *Corridors of Power* (New York: Scribner's, 1964), pp. 265–266.

The problem of word meanings is aggravated by the status barrier. People on different levels often speak different languages. There are many instances in which a frustrating conversation ends with this admission. In order to avoid a breakdown in communication, communicators should attempt to use the language of the listener so they should realize that some words carry a symbolic meaning for some people and that when they use such words, they may find themselves communicating something they did not intend to say. An expression such as *management prerogatives* has acquired different symbolic meanings for management and for union representatives. The word *efficiency* has different meanings to a union leader, a worker, a manager, and an engineer. This is a lesson that many technical specialists, with their reliance on jargon, must learn.

People also speak languages that are geared to the specialized work they do. The existence of staff and technical experts in a large number of fields makes organizations sound like modern towers of Babel. Experts use their own jargon, making understanding difficult for those uninitiated in the field. Often, technical reports must undergo "translation" so that top management can use them as a basis for policy making.

Resistance to change

Resistance to change builds yet another communication barrier. All too frequently, listeners do not properly receive messages that convey new ideas. Listeners' receiving apparatus works like a filter, rejecting new ideas if they conflict with what the listeners already believe. Sometimes, this filter works so efficiently that they do not hear at all. Ultimately, listeners hear what they expect to hear. If they are insecure, worried, or fearful, this barrier becomes even more powerful. Sometimes listeners, determined to refute what they expect to hear, pay only marginal attention to a communication instead of trying to understand it.

Other barriers

Many other barriers arise from specific situations—emotional reaction; deeply rooted feelings and prejudice; physical conditions, such as heat, noise, and cold. All these obstacles can cause serious barriers to communication and, unless the senders know of their existence, they are in no position to overcome them. For this reason, managers must acquaint themselves with all potential and actual barriers to communication. They should not assume that their messages will be received as they were intended. Instead, since managerial effectiveness depends largely on the accurate transmission of information and orders, managers must do everything possible to overcome communication barriers.

Means for overcoming barriers to communication

Although perfect understanding may be impossible, there are many techniques available for improving communication. Executives ought to be familiar with several of them in order to maximize communicating success.

Feedback

Feedback is probably the most important method of improving communication. Most people are automatically aware of feedback. When sending messages, they are alert to the reactions of their receiver; they constantly seek clues from the receiver that show that they are being understood.

The following experiment, testing the importance of feedback, was conducted by Professor Alex Bavelas.[8] Two students were placed in different rooms, with identical grids in front of them and a set of dominoes. One student was asked to communicate to the other by telephone the position of an interconnected series of dominoes, explaining their relative positions in any way he felt advisable and necessary. The receiver was then to arrange his dominoes like those of the sender. The receiver could listen to the sender's instructions but could not respond or ask questions. Although the sender explained the pattern carefully and minutely, the receiver was unable to successfully complete the task. This and similar experiments indicate that some kind of feedback is essential if complex information is to be communicated successfully. Managers who think they communicate when they send so-called information memos should remember this experiment. At best a yes or no response to the sender's question of whether or not the message is understood would be helpful. However, as subsequent portions of Bavelas's experiment indicate, the speed and efficiency of communications increase as feedback increases.

The simplest way to obtain feedback is to observe receivers and analyze their nonverbal responses. Observation of expressions of comprehension or bewilderment, the raising of an eyebrow or a frown, is possible only in face-to-face communications. Therefore, one of the outstanding advantages of any oral communication is that it provides immediate feedback.

If senders wish to test comprehension verbally, they may ask receivers to repeat complex information. This is much more effective than merely asking whether or not the statement or the instruction is understood.[9] If receivers can state the gist of a message, the senders will know what has been heard, whether or not it has been understood, and what has not been understood. This process might also reveal that the receivers ascribed special meaning to a particular message that the senders did not intend. Also, during face-to-face conversation, receivers may ask additional questions and make comments, thereby making immediate feedback even more meaningful. Additional feedback can be obtained simply by observing whether or not people behave in accordance with the communication. If direct observation is not feasible, senders must watch for reports and results.

---

[8] See Elmer L. Lindseth, "Management Communication," in *The Management Team*, ed. Edward C. Bursk (Cambridge, Mass.: Harvard University Press, 1954), pp. 24–25; and George Strauss and Leonard R. Sayles, *Personnel: The Human Problems of Management* (Englewood Cliffs, N.J.: Prentice-Hall, 1960), pp. 203–204.

[9] See Huber, "An Efficacy Comparison."

Sensitivity to the receivers' world

As we have stated previously, in order to communicate successfully, senders must be sensitive to the world of the people who will receive their messages. Once managers determine the messages they want to convey, they should try to predict their impact on the feelings and attitudes of the receivers. A common ground for understanding must be established, especially if the backgrounds and experiences of receivers and senders differ considerably. If their relationship is close, managers can anticipate more easily how subordinates will interpret a message.

Managers often ignore the need for sensitivity to the employees' world. They attempt to communicate with employees in managerial terms through company newspapers filled with analyses of economic conditions, the prospects for the company, competitive problems, and so forth. However, employees often are not interested in problems of this sort. Managers are merely projecting their own interests and, in doing so, do not succeed in communicating their messages.

Effective listening

Interestingly, senders usually can overcome barriers to communication by spending more time listening. In order to have receivers hear what they want to say, speakers first should listen to the receivers. Of course, listening cannot be accomplished by a mere expression of attention. And, one who hears with the intent of finding fault and correcting, likewise, is not listening. Better communications are achieved if biases and prejudices are put aside. There is no need to agree with a speaker, but there is every necessity to try to understand him or her.

It is the listeners' job to listen to the meaning of an idea rather than to the individual words of the speaker. Listeners must be careful to discover any hidden content—the *latent content*, as distinct from the *manifest content*. Although listeners should keep their imaginations in check, they must ask themselves what is really meant. From time to time, listeners might ask, "Is this what you mean?" Managers also must listen carefully, even though they may believe that what they hear is irrelevant.

Listening greatly improves communication by reducing misunderstandings. By listening while talking, speakers can adjust their messages to fit the responses of the receivers. The adjustment opportunity provided in oral communication is one of its chief advantages.

Actions speak louder than words

As we have noted, people communicate as much by actions as by words. One of the best ways to give meaning to a message is to act in accordance with it. Managers are frequently the center of subordinates' attention, and they communicate by all observable actions regardless of intention. Naturally, barriers to communication will be overcome if verbal announcements are reinforced by action. But, if managers say one thing and do another, sooner or later their subordinates will "listen" mostly to what they do. For example, managers' statement that they are available at any time to see employees who have problems has no meaning if they keep their doors closed.

The importance of being an expert

One other aspect of effectiveness in communication should not be neglected. Because of the growing technical complexity of organizations, more and more people with professional and scientific skills are being employed. In general, such people will more readily accept their manager's communications if they perceive the manager to be technically well qualified. They tend to reject messages from those they think to be technically less competent or incapable of meeting the requirements of their specialized jobs. This tendency seems to hold true regardless of how the scientific and technically trained subordinates feel about their manager personally, as an individual, apart from his or her technical skills. In short, the authority of competence, which we discussed in Chapter 8, has its parallel in communicating.

Summary

Communicating—exchanging information among people—is a process through which the basic managerial functions are linked. As such, it is of two fundamental natures; organizational and personal.

In essence, communicating involves two parties: the sender and the receiver. Their relationship is complex. For effective communication to take place, the sender must send what he or she thinks is being said; the receiver must receive the same, and the sender must recognize that the message is being transmitted accurately. In terms of Figure 30-2, relationships A, B, and C must be identical.

There are two channels of communication: formal (vertical, lateral, and diagonal) and informal (grapevine). Likewise, there is a variety of written and oral communication techniques.

Figure 30-2 Communicating relationships

Relationship	Action
A	Sender sends message.
B	Receiver receives message.
C	Sender perceives what message receiver has received.

Managers must be aware of the many barriers to effective communication that exist in modern organizations. These develop for several basic reasons: organizational structure, status and position, language, and basic human resistance to change. Managers can overcome these barriers with such techniques as feedback, sensitivity, effective listening, actions consistent with words, and expertise.

Discussion questions

1. Consider your situation as a student. Contrast the content of messages carried through formal channels of communication with that of messages carried on the grapevine. What does this tell you about the grapevine? about so-called official channels?
2. Is it sneaky for managers to manipulate behavior by utilizing the grapevine?
3. How many forms can feedback take in organizational communication?
4. How are the principles of good communicating used in this course? abused in this course?

Supplementary readings

American Management Association. "Ten Commandments of Good Communication." New York: American Management Association, 1955. Reprinted in *Dimensions in Modern Management,* 2d ed., edited by Patrick E. Connor. Boston: Houghton Mifflin, 1978.

Case, Stewart. "Executive Communication: Breaking the Semantics Barrier." *Management Review,* April 1957, pp. 58–66.

Fisher, B. A. *Small-Group Decision-Making: Communication and the Group Process.* New York: McGraw-Hill, 1974.

March, James G., and Simon, Herbert A. *Organizations.* New York: Wiley, 1958.

Planty, Earl G., and Machaver, William. "Stimulating Upward Communication." In *Effective Communication on the Job,* pp. 123–130. New York: American Management Association, 1956. Reprinted in *Dimensions in Modern Management,* 2d ed., edited by Patrick E. Connor. Boston: Houghton Mifflin, 1978.

Roberts, Karlene H., and O'Reilly, Charles A., III. "Failures in Upward Communication in Organizations: Three Possible Culprits." *Academy of Management Journal,* June 1974, pp. 205–215.

Rogers, Carl R., and Roethlisberger, F. M. "Barriers and Gateways to Communication." *Harvard Business Review* 30 (July–August 1952): 46–52. Reprinted in *Dimensions in Modern Management,* 2d ed., edited by Patrick E. Connor. Boston: Houghton Mifflin, 1978.

Rogers, Everett M., and Agarwala-Rogers, Rekha. *Communication in Organizations.* New York: Free Press, 1976.

Scott, William G., and Mitchell, Terence R. *Organizational Theory,* 3d ed., pp. 192–209. Homewood, Illinois: Richard D. Irwin, 1976.

Conclusion

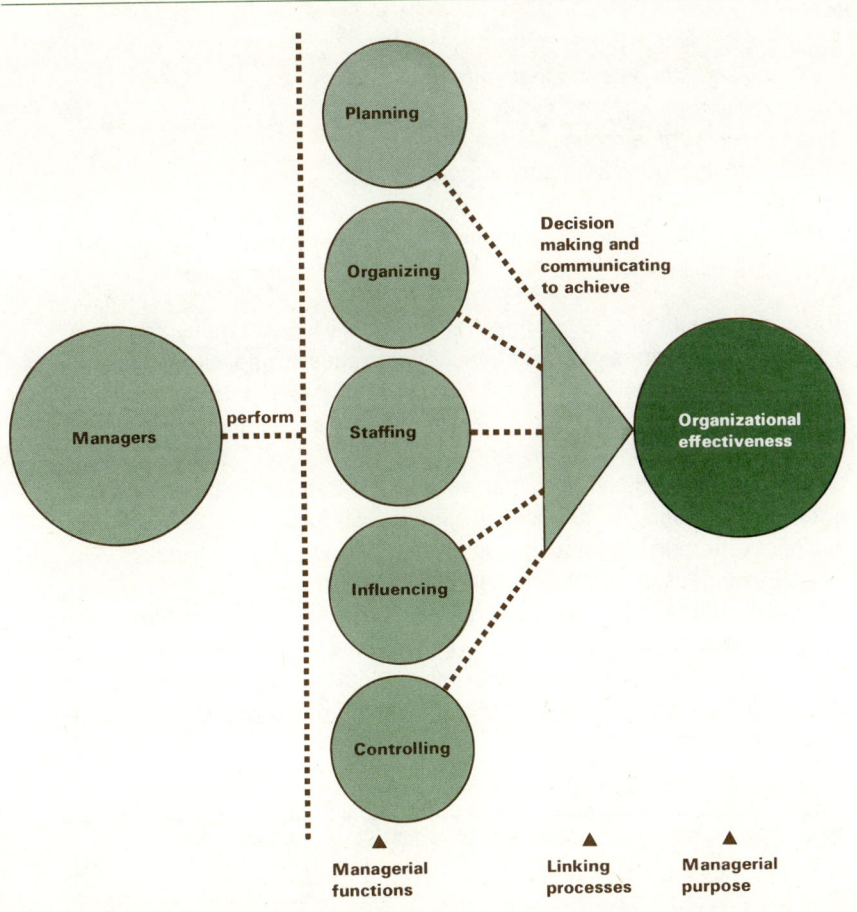

Chapter 31

Organizational effectiveness

Objectives of the chapter

1 To show that organizational effectiveness is a contingency problem.
2 To examine various methods of measuring organizational effectiveness.
3 To identify the major variables that determine organizational effectiveness.
4 To evaluate the economic and social factors that influence organizational effectiveness.
5 To consider social responsibility as an effectiveness contingency.

The improvement of organizational effectiveness is what managing is all about. In broad terms, organizational effectiveness is measured by performance in accomplishing goals, using standards based on management's past achievements and future expectations. Consequently, effectiveness is always a dependent condition, contingent on the nature of the organization's goals — and these goals can vary considerably from organization to organization. Consider, for example, the goals of a hospital versus those of a business enterprise. Obviously, the criteria for judging effectiveness will differ as much as do organizational goals themselves.

The criteria issue, therefore, makes the problem of generalizing about organizational effectiveness virtually impossible to solve. However, a great deal is being written and said about measuring organizational effectiveness and, therefore, it is necessary to examine some of the dimensions along which organizational effectiveness is considered.

Measures of organizational effectiveness: A contingency problem

Earlier, it was popular to measure organizational effectiveness by some ultimate standard, like growth, profitability, efficiency, or the like. More recently, however, the trend is toward using effectiveness models that are composed of a number of criteria that, when taken together, indicate the quality of organizational performance. Steers, in a review of seventeen models of organizational effectiveness that appear in the literature, summarizes fourteen effectiveness criteria and the frequency with which they are mentioned.[1] This list is shown in Table 31-1.

Table 31-1 Frequency of occurrence of evaluation criteria in 17 models of organization effectiveness

Evaluation criteria	No. of times mentioned ($N = 17$)
Adaptability-flexibility	10
Productivity	6
Satisfaction	5
Profitability	3
Resource acquisition	3
Absence of strain	2
Control over environment	2
Development	2
Efficiency	2
Employee retention	2
Growth	2
Integration	2
Open communications	2
Survival	2
All other criteria	1

Source: Richard M. Steers, "Problems in the Measurement of Organizational Effectiveness," *Administrative Science Quarterly,* December 1975, p. 549. Used with permission.

These many measures are, of course, very difficult to assemble into a composite effectiveness model. Mott observes that most criteria fall into three categories, which make the number of variables affecting performance more easily applicable.[2] They are:

1. *Output* The quality and quantity of a good or service created, and the efficiency with which it is produced.
2. *Adaptability* The long-term ability to cope with change in technology, culture, and behavior.
3. *Flexibility* The short-term ability to shift resources to cope with unexpected contingencies.

Regardless of the criteria selected in an abstract way, organizations will assign their own meaning and value to effectiveness measures. The weights given to the effectiveness standards depend on an organization's contingencies. A library is likely to give output, adaptability, and flexibility a far different interpretation than is a business organization. For example,

---

[1] Richard M. Steers, "Problems in the Measurement of Organizational Effectiveness," *Administrative Science Quarterly,* December 1975, pp 546—551.
[2] Paul E. Mott, *The Characteristics of Effective Organizations* (New York: Harper & Row, 1972), pp. 17—20.

libraries have a service goal; their output, in large part, is measured by circulation (quantity). However, they also must possess the kinds of books most demanded by their clientele (quality). Furthermore, they must be able to process books for loan efficiently, maintain accurate records, and minimize loss and damage (efficiency). A library system also must plan for long-range change in its clients' needs and tastes. A library district faced with the long-term aging of its borrowers will plan to order different books than one that anticipates serving a large number of young, school-aged children. It must consider adopting new technologies—duplicating techniques, microfilm, and so on. These long-range changes are related to the criterion of adaptability. Finally, a library system must have sufficient flexibility so that it can make its holdings available to subunits, for example, the mobile libraries that give rural users and shut-ins the opportunity to borrow books.

In a study of weight given to criteria of organizational effectiveness, Mahoney and Weitzel showed differences in values assigned by business organizations compared to those assigned by research and development organizations (see Table 31-2). While both rate it as the ultimate criterion of performance, their interpretations of what *overall effectiveness* means and how it is achieved differ considerably.

Thus, for any tangible measure of performance to be realistic, criteria have to be used that reflect the particular contingencies that govern the management of an organization. There is no one universal standard that is appropriate to the situational nature of organizational effectiveness. As Steers wrote: "A clear understanding of an organization's functional and environmental uniqueness is a prerequisite to assessing its effectiveness."[3]

The traditional approach to determining effectiveness

Typically, organizational performance is appraised in economic terms and is expressed as profit, efficiency, or cost. Business organizations use these measurements extensively. Indeed, the quantitative expressions of monetary gains or losses are interpreted as the final statement of management's worth. However, business is not alone in the use of quantitative standards of performance. Other organizations, which do not have dollar profit as a goal, use quantitative measures of efficiency as indicators of managerial effectiveness.

The preoccupation of modern organizations with quantitative measures of effectiveness is shown by the central role they give financial control. This is a result, of course, of the basic expectations people have of the organizations that serve them. Business owners expect profit and appreciation in value; the government expects dollar accounting for tax purposes; the customer expects a quality product at a low unit cost; and employees expect to maximize their income and fringe benefits. Thus, management's devotion to

---

[3] Steers, "Problems in measurement," p. 555.

the economic measures of effectiveness is, in large part, a response to the expectation's of the people it serves. Since our society is basically materialistic in its values, it should not be surprising that we expect the performance of organizations to be stated in quantitative terms.

Although it is an oversimplification, the criteria of economic effectiveness can be expressed by the equation: $E = O/I$. This equation is the statement of efficiency, and it implies general economic guidelines for managerial decision making and organizational behavior. The equation says that efficiency equals outputs divided by inputs. The idea behind this statement is deceptively simple, but its rules for application are profound.

Table 31-2 Ranked importance of criteria of organizational effectiveness

Research and development Dimension	General business
1 Reliability	3
2 Cooperation	12
3 Development	10
4 Turnover	22
5 Selectivity	15
6 Flexibility	14
General business	**Research and development**
1 Performance-support-utilization	14
2 Planning	10
3 Reliability	1
4 Initiation	13
5 Bargaining	20
6 Supervisory support	17

Source: Thomas A. Mahoney and William Weitzel, "Managerial Models of Organizational Effectiveness," *Administrative Science Quarterly*, September 1969, p. 361. Used with permission.

The first rule is that efficiency should be increased. By doing this, productivity is increased, costs are reduced, volume is expanded, and the organizational payoffs to owners, managers, employees, customers, and society are improved. Given these targets, the next rule is that managers should make adjustments in O or I so that the value of E is increased. For example, managers can allow output to remain constant and inputs to decrease; they can allow output to increase and inputs to remain constant; or they can allow outputs and inputs to vary so long as the value of E goes up.

Ultimately, the various engineering, economic, and accounting measures of effectiveness embody the values expressed by the efficiency equation. The life or death of business organizations depends on management's ability to work the output-input relationship. The executives' worth is decided by the way they manage the rules of efficiency. The well-being of the clients of the organization as well as the health of the organization itself depends on earnings. Earnings, in turn, depend on how well the resources of the organization are used to produce goods or services.

Application of efficiency rules

There are many examples of how the rules of efficiency are applied to organizational practice. As a first example, we should recall previous discussions of the budget and other financial controls. These provide financial examples of the workings of the efficiency principle, because they are aimed at obtaining maximum benefits for the organization at minimum costs. As we emphasized, the calculations behind budget considerations permeate the cost-benefit analysis involved in all managerial functions.

Management uses production control standards to determine various levels of resource utilization and, thereby, to reduce cost. One specific application of these controls is management's establishment of output standards for labor engaged in various jobs. Similar calculations are made for expected expenditures for capital investment in plant and equipment.

The efficiency rules are based on the assumption that the more intensive is the use of resources, the more effective is the organization. Most of the time this aspect of the calculus is reduced to quantitative terms. For example, if sales volume can be doubled without increasing the sales force, management has a positive, concrete indicator of increased marketing effectiveness. The efficiency equation is most apt to be reduced to quantitative terms in organizations with a high degree of departmentalization, specialization of labor, and mechanization of production. These conditions occur primarily in conventional manufacturing organizations, although they also could occur in organizations that process large quantities of paperwork on a routine basis.

Organizational design and effectiveness

Organizational design is at the heart of the organizing process. Managers must assign explicit responsibility to people for implementing plans. To aid this process, managers may need to establish special departments, to delegate authority, or to hire new people with required skills. Organizational design, in this respect, is crucial to control, since effectiveness is very difficult to measure unless those responsible for specific activities are clearly identified. Although organizational effectiveness is associated, in an immediate sense, with control, it also involves decision making, planning, and staffing.

Organizational effectiveness has its origins in decision making. In the decision-making process, managers set basic directions for the organization and allocate resources for programs and activities. For example, corporate management may decide to fund an employee's college tuition program, a decision that requires a diversion of stockholders' earnings. Management's decision, of necessity, involves all decision-making steps from the evaluation of alternatives to the appraisal of outcomes. In short, it encompasses those mental calculations required by the decision-making process. Thus, decision making initiates the consideration of organizational effectiveness.

Next, management must plan its program since, through planning, basic goals, objectives, and standards are formulated. If a hospital starts an educational program dealing with preventive medicine, basic objectives must be established. Is the program going to be communitywide? Is it going to involve only certain age groups? Is the program going to focus on certain subjects, like drug abuse and prenatal care? On the basis of goals formulated by answering such questions, standards of performance can be formed. How many people should become involved? By what level should drug usage be reduced? How many expectant mothers can one hospital expect to counsel? The projections derived from these further questions provide guidelines for organizational design and, ultimately, for effectiveness criteria.

Organizational complexity and effectiveness

The increasing complexity of organizations, the expanding relationships between organizations and their environment, and the growing turbulence created by technological change require that organizations introduce new methods of evaluating performance. Effectiveness criteria must be developed to cover a broader range than those covered by the economic and efficiency controls. These new organizational factors—including social and behavioral ones—need control criteria so that management can compare actual organizational performance against stated objectives. More often than not these criteria will be qualitative.

The difficulty of measuring organizational effectiveness is compounded when organizational complexity increases, when decision-making time horizons grow longer, and when a number of conflicting factors in organizational performance must be balanced.

Managers face a number of internal organizational problems when complexity grows. Top management, obviously, wants to optimize the performance of the entire organization. However, in concerns with semiautonomous subdivisions, such a goal could mean that certain segments of the organization would be forced to operate at less than the degree of efficiency that might otherwise be attained. For example, a firm could require that its manufacturing departments purchase internally the components they use, even though comparable products are available on the open market at a lower price. This policy, while increasing the unit cost of the product of a manufacturing division, contributes favorably to the overall performance of the organization.

Implicit in the simplified version of the efficiency equation is the assumption that the time span of effectiveness is measured in the short run. However, organizations that deal with advanced technologies, with research and development programs, and with extensive capital investments must take a long-range view of organizational effectiveness.[4] Immediate appraisal

---

[4] Ibid., p. 553.

of research and development activities, for example, might show their adverse effect on earnings, or the installation and use of new capital equipment could result in short-term decline in efficiency. Nevertheless, if an organization is to stay healthy in the long run, such short-term sacrifices must be made.

Finally, management's attempts to balance the interests of organizational clients are bound to affect the efficiency equation. As illustration, one executive in the electronics industry said that customers expect every television set produced to work perfectly. However, he pointed out, given the technology of mass production, there are going to be duds. In these cases, the best a company can do is to offer warranties or to replace defective sets. To make every unit perfect would involve such vast costs that the final price would be outside the reach of the mass market. Many other examples also show that effectiveness often is a compromise between what is possible in an engineering sense and what is necessary in order to make a product or service available to a wide market.

Management audits

Management audits are techniques frequently used to determine organizational effectiveness. They are substantially different from audits performed by public accountants, because they are not concerned with verification of financial data. They are performed for top management, the stockholders, or other owners, in order to survey, from the broadest possible point of view, managerial performance and, by implication, the overall position of the enterprise. Management audits start where balance-sheet audits leave off. At times, they are undertaken by management itself, but, more often, outside help is called in.

Periodic management self-audit

In the 1930s, James O. McKinsey advocated that a periodic self-audit be held in order to discover and correct management's errors. The self-audit amounts to an appraisal of all aspects of the enterprise. In order to do a self-audit, managers must determine not only the company's present position but also where it is heading and where it will be in five, ten, or fifteen years. Moreover, managers must look beyond the present and future position of the company in the industry and appraise the outlook for the entire industry. The self-appraisal covers policies, organizational structure, personnel practices, personnel inventory, physical facilities, financial resources, and all the other aspects that bear on the outcome of the organization's operations. Managers should perform a self-audit once a year or, at the very least, once very two or three years.

Audit by the American Institute of Management

The American Institute of Management, a private nonprofit organization, has conducted management audits for many years. This organization devised a list of several hundred questions to determine the quality of the management of a particular enterprise. The questions cover ten areas encompassing economic functions, corporate structure, health of earnings growth, fairness to stockholders, research and development, composition of the board of directors, fiscal policies, production efficiency, sales, and executive evaluation. A maximum number of points is assigned to each area.[5]

The individual questions, grouped by areas, are submitted to corporate officers and to outside sources. Members of the institute then analyze the answers in order to determine how many points out of the maximum attainable rating are to be given for each answer. The points are added to obtain a total for each of the ten areas. The relationship between the total number of points achieved and the maximum attainable will determine management's rating.

Management audit by outside consultants

Management audits by outside consultants are increasing. These examine a company's performance, its position within the industry, its organizational structure, and the operations of its divisions and departments. If such audits are conducted regularly—usually, on a yearly basis—management can compare current findings with prior conditions in order to discover what has been achieved and what is still required. External management audits by management consultants are similar to external financial audits by public accounting firms.

Because the quality of management is of utmost importance to the long-run performance of an organization, it may be that management audits by outside firms will become just as routine as the annual audit by independent certified accountants. This trend could even lead to the establishment of a certified management audit performed by a firm whose staff is thoroughly trained and qualified to appraise the effectiveness of an organization's management. At present, however, the prospects for such certification are remote.

Social responsibility as an effectiveness contingency

Americans today expect more from their organizations than efficient management. They feel that business and other organizations have social obligations and responsibilities. Social responsibility includes the obligations that an organization has to the general public and to specific interest groups. They arise from organizational activities that affect society to a greater degree than do the organization's ordinary affairs.

Keith Davis observed that recognition of social responsibility is growing through the acceptance by managers and the public of five basic propositions:[6]

---

[5] Jackson Martindell, *The Scientific Appraisal of Management* (New York: Harper & Row, 1950), p. 280. See also Jackson Martindell, "Management Audit Simplified," *The Corporate Director,* special issue no. 15 (December 1951), pp. 1—6; and *The Appraisal of Management* (New York: Harper & Row, 1962).

[6] Keith Davis, "Five Propositions for Social Responsibility," *Business Horizons,* June 1975, pp. 19—24.

1. With the increased social power achieved by organizations, there is a parallel necessity for increased social responsibility on the part of organizations.
2. Organizations must function as a two-way communication system—sensitive to the needs of the public and open to disclosure of their operations to the public.
3. The social cost and benefits of an organization's activities, either currently underway or contemplated for the future, should be calculated and such calculations should serve as a basis for implementing programs.
4. The social costs of an activity are supported by the consumer.
5. Organizations participate as citizens in helping to solve social problems where the need exists, provided that the organization has the skills to do so.

A study of managers' perceptions of social responsibility appears to bear out Davis's observations. Holmes found that in a five-year period, 1970 to 1975, executive attitudes changed significantly in support of policies that emphasized social responsibility and social involvement.[7] The executives who were surveyed believed that the positive outcomes outweighed the negative ones from their firm's active participation in social programs.

The arena of social responsibility

Management's decision to become engaged in areas of social responsibility can be the result of governmental legislation, of pressure from individuals or interest groups, of voluntary response to social needs,[8] or a combination of all three. For example, let us look at water quality controls. Congress has passed a law that indicates the minimum legal standards of water quality. In order to comply with this legislation, an organization would install a pollution control system sufficient to meet the minimum standards. If local fishing interests felt that these standards were not adequate to protect the fish, they could pressure management to exceed the legal standards of water purity. Finally, management voluntarily might undertake additional programs to clean up rivers and lakes in those instances where no law applies.

The arena of social responsibility has grown dramatically in the last ten years. This arena can be visualized as three expanding concentric circles (see Figure 31-1). In the center is the responsibility of management for the traditional economic operation of an organization. The next circle shows management's responsibility for the application of economic power in socially responsible ways. This obligation requires a sensitive response to a variety of public needs, such as clean air, honest advertising, equal lending opportunities in banking, fair employment practices, and so on. The last circle indicates those areas of social responsibility that include goals that society has set for itself, but that management can help society to achieve

---

[7] Sandra L. Holmes, "Executive Perceptions of Corporate Social Responsibility," *Business Horizons*, June 1976, pp. 34—40.
[8] George A. Steiner, "Institutionalizing Corporate Social Decisions," *Business Horizons*, December 1975, p. 13.

547 Organizational effectiveness

through its expertise. As Davis points out, business does not cause educational problems, but, as a citizen of a community, business has the obligation to improve the quality of education in the community.[9]

The three rings of social responsibility point managers in various directions of social action and social policy. Policies become the social criteria against which organizational performance is measured. Clearly, unless managers formulate policies based on imposed or voluntary obligations, criteria for organizational effectiveness cannot be stated.

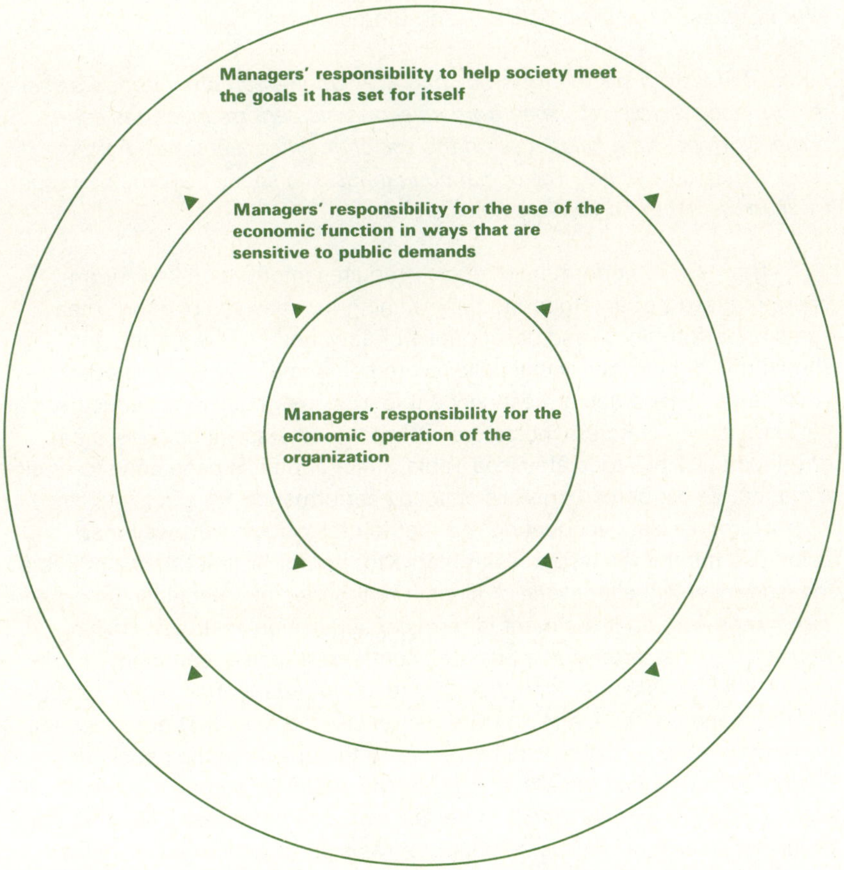

Figure 31-1 The expanding arena of social responsibility

- Managers' responsibility to help society meet the goals it has set for itself
- Managers' responsibility for the use of the economic function in ways that are sensitive to public demands
- Managers' responsibility for the economic operation of the organization

Even if managers have established social policies, the problem of judging organizational effectiveness is only partially solved. What measures of effectiveness shall managers use? Obviously, the usual economic and accounting measures of performance are hard to apply to qualitative social actions. If obligations are imposed, such as fair hiring practices and pollution controls have been, legal requirements may provide adequate control stan-

[9] Davis, "Five Propositions," p. 23.

dards. For instance, they might include a measure of the pollutants emitted in a time period or might establish the ratio of minority employees to the total number of employees in an organization. But, often such objective standards are not available. This has led managers to use such techniques as the social audit and human-assets accounting.

The social audit and human-assets accounting

The social audit is one attempt to overcome the problem of measuring social effectiveness. As defined by Davis and Blomstrom:

A social audit is a systematic study and evaluation of an organization's social performance, as distinguished from its economic performance. It is concerned with possible influences on the social quality of life instead of the economic quality of life. The social audit leads to a social performance report *for management and perhaps outsiders also.*[10]

The "social performance report" requires information flows from operating levels of an organization pertaining to measures of effort, measures of performance, and descriptions of activities.[11] This information should reflect how well social policies are being implemented. However, such data is very crude at best, since it is extremely difficult to reduce social performance to concrete indicators. Other than the social balance sheet developed by Abt Associates (see Table 31-3), little has been done to create a monetary cost-benefit analysis of social performance.

Human-assets accounting is a method for judging how well managers use the human resources available to them over time. As such, it is a measure of social effectiveness, since it recognizes that people in an organization represent an investment in terms of acquisition costs and training.[12] Rensis Likert has proposed a plan of "human resource accounting."[13] He places a dollar value on the human assets of an organization; it shows up as a bottom-line figure on annual statements. Likert argues that organizational performance, or lack of it, can be traced to the quality of the people employed. Thus, expenditures that improve the quality of human resources can be looked on as an investment rather than as a cost. For example, training programs or executive development programs are typically written off as expenses; under Likert's scheme, such expenditures could be treated as an investment that increases the assets of the concern.

[10] Keith Davis and Robert L. Blomstrom, "Implementing the Social Audit in an Organization," *Business and Society,* Fall 1975, p. 13.
[11] Raymond A. Bauer, L. Terry Cauthorn, and Ranne P. Warner, "Auditing the Management Process for Social Performance," *Business and Society Review,* Fall 1975, pp. 40–41.
[12] James A. Cannon, "Human Resource Accounting—A Critical Comment," *Personnel Review,* Summer 1974.
[13] For a description of Likert's technique see "A New Twist to People Accounting," *Business Week,* October 21, 1972, pp. 67–68.

Table 31-3 Abt Associates, Inc., social balance sheet (year ended December 31, 1971, with comparative figures for 1970)

	1971	1970
Social assets available		
Staff		
Available within one year	$ 2,594,390	$ 2,312,000
Available after one year	6,368,511	5,821,608
Training investment	507,405	305,889
	9,470,306	8,439,497
Less accumulated training obsolescence	136,995	60,523
Total staff assets	9,333,311	8,378,974
Organization		
Social capital investment	1,398,230	1,272,201
Retained earnings	219,136	—
Land	285,376	293,358
Buildings at cost	334,321	350,188
Equipment at cost	43,018	17,102
Total organization assets	2,280,081	1,932,849
Research		
Proposals	26,878	15,090
Child care research	6,629	—
Social audit	12,979	—
Total research	46,486	15,090
Public services consumed net of tax payments	152,847	243,399
Total social assets available	$11,812,725	$10,570,312
Social commitments, obligations, and equity		
Staff		
Committed to contracts within one year	$ 43,263	$ 81,296
Committed to contracts after one year	114,660	215,459
Committed to administration within one year	62,598	56,915
Committed to administration after one year	165,903	150,842
Total staff commitments	386,424	504,512
Organization		
Working capital requirements	60,000	58,500
Financial deficit	—	26,814
Facilities and equipment committed to contracts and administration	37,734	36,729
Total organization commitments	97,734	122,043
Environmental		
Government outlays for public services consumed, net of tax payment	152,847	243,399
Pollution from paper production	1,770	770
Pollution from electric power production	2,200	1,080
Pollution from automobile commuting	10,493	4,333
Total environmental obligations	167,310	249,582
Total commitments and obligations	651,468	876,137
Society's equity		
Contributed by staff	8,946,887	7,874,462
Contributed by stockholders	2,182,347	1,810,806
Generated by operations	32,023	8,907
Total equity	11,161,257	9,694,175
Total commitments, obligations, and equity	$11,812,725	$10,570,312

Source: "First Attempts at a 'Social Audit,'" *Business Week*, September 23, 1972, p. 89. Reprinted from the September 23, 1972, issue of *Business Week* by special permission. © 1972 by McGraw-Hill, Inc.

One company, the R. G. Barry Corporation, figures human resources as an investment in its annual reports. However, such figures are unaudited and are not obtained by conventional accounting practices.[14] Although its techniques are experimental, nevertheless executives in this company claim that the data obtained are useful in appraising the true cost of employee turnover and helpful in making financial decisions.

Summary

Organizational effectiveness is the bottom line of managerial practice. Figure 31-2 shows that we have come full circle in our study of managing. The feature we have added to our basic diagram to illustrate this idea is the dotted line, which indicates the connection among managers as human beings, the functions they perform, and the organizational outcomes they hope to achieve. Implied in the process of managing are two points that have been stressed in this book: first, the management process is a system in which all activities are *interrelated;* second, the management process is *situational*—all activities are influenced by contingencies.

The unsettled issues in management are the ingredients that compose organizational effectiveness. Given the enormous influence of management and organizations in America—we can truly say that we live in an organizational society—people have every right to expect a high level of economic and social performance. The difficulty is that we do not know, at present, what we should measure to determine effectiveness except in the limited area concerned with economics and efficiency.

Indeed, everyone, managers and the public alike, want improved overall performance from organizations. But this criterion is too broad. There is no single measure of effectiveness. Effectiveness is essentially a contingency problem in which multiple, midrange standards of performance must be established for each organization. This situation is even more evident as managers move into the realm of social responsibility. In the 1980s, the issue of organizational effectiveness, which in reality means *managerial effectiveness,* is most likely to be the most critical matter confronting management theory and practice.

Discussion questions

1 "Whatever it is that makes up the standards of organizational effectiveness, ultimately, it is reduced to a contingency problem." Discuss this statement.
2 If organizational goals are something other than growth (for example, stability or decline), how will the concepts of organizational effectiveness change?

[14] See "Firm's Accounting Covers 'Human Resources' Data," *Wall Street Journal,* March 21, 1972.

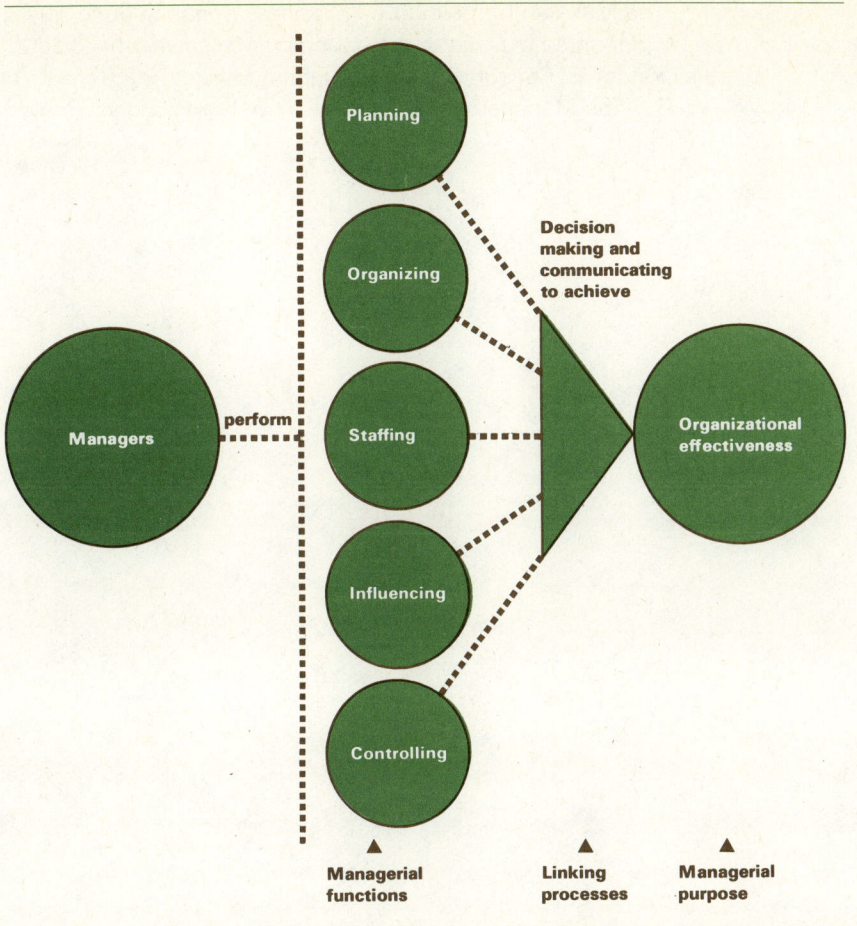

Figure 31-2 The process of management

Supplementary readings

Bennis, Warren G. "The Coming Death of Bureaucracy." In *Think,* New York: International Business Machines, 1966. pp. 19—23. Reprinted in *Dimensions in Modern Management,* 2d ed., edited by Patrick E. Connor. Boston: Houghton Mifflin, 1978.

Buchele, Robert B. "How to Evaluate a Firm." *California Management Review,* Fall 1962, pp. 5—16. Reprinted in *Dimensions in Modern Management,* 2d ed., edited by Patrick E. Connor. Boston: Houghton Mifflin, 1978.

Davis, Keith. "Can Business Afford to Ignore Social Responsibilities?" *California Management Review,* Spring 1960, pp. 70—76. Reprinted in *Dimensions in Modern Management,* 2d ed., edited by Patrick E. Connor. Boston: Houghton Mifflin, 1978.

Mee, John F. "The Manager of the Future." *Business Horizons,* June 1973, pp. 5–14. Reprinted in *Dimensions in Modern Management,* 2d ed., edited by Patrick E. Connor. Boston: Houghton Mifflin, 1978.

Scott, William G. "The Management of Decline." *Conference Board Record,* June 1976.

Comprehensive cases

Case 1

Case of the questionable communiqués

On a warm June day, Ralph Hampton, hoping to catch a breeze, stood near the window of his office at Cooper Fabrics, Inc. Gazing across the grassy fields to the neat frame houses that marked the east border of Parville, he smiled to himself. "With a little luck," he thought, "and if things keep going well, we should have the whole plant air-conditioned by this time next year."

Hampton had reason to feel satisfied. He had been with Cooper Fabrics four years as its general manager. He had seen the company pass through difficult times, but in January Cooper had finally begun to show a profit. Hampton mused, "I think we're out of the woods now, but we're certainly going to have to convince the workers to wait a little longer for that pay raise."

The Parville, New Hampshire, plant had been built in 1840 and had been operated over the years by a long succession of owners. Each, for one reason or another, had been forced out of business. Throughout this long period, the appearance of the plant had changed very little, and one generation of workers followed another with little, if any, management turnover.

In the past fourteen years, the plant had been owned by four different companies. For three years, it had been held by a manufacturer of upholstery fabrics. For the next five years, the Haber Company, a large textile combine, operated the plant to turn out a somewhat different product line. Haber had operated the plant profitably in only one year. The next owner was a company that specialized in the liquidation of plants and companies. Finally, Cooper Fabrics, an operating subsidiary of Atlas Corporation, a large conglomerate, took over the plant in order to manufacture automotive and specialty household fabrics.

It was Ralph Hampton who had seen the possibilities in the product line abandoned by former owners. A calm, slow-speaking man in his mid-forties, Hampton had previously been employed as an assistant manager of a

Source: This case was prepared by Ruth G. Newman and appeared in *Harvard Business Review* 53 (November–December 1975): 26–40, 162. Copyright © 1975 by the President and Fellows of Harvard College; all rights reserved.

Massachusetts textile concern. When Hampton took over the management of Cooper Fabrics in 1971, he selected the most suitable machinery from Cooper's two Rhode Island plants, had this equipment moved to Parville, and disposed of excess facilities and equipment. In the process of consolidating the company's operations at one location, he created a yarn and fiber processing department—an operation that the previous owners of the Parville plant had subcontracted to other manufacturers.

During Hampton's first two years, Cooper Fabrics operated at a loss. Sales were at low levels, and operations were hindered by the necessary renovations and reorganizations. The lack of income and the cost of changes and additions in the plant exerted a severe financial strain. Hampton hoped that next year's operations would be profitable enough to ease the burden.

However, sales were difficult to obtain, the textile industry was depressed, and, more significantly, potential customers were skeptical about dealing with Cooper Fabrics. It was well known in the trade that the company had recently been in the process of liquidation. Fabric buyers did not wish to deal with a company which they feared might soon be in difficulties again.

But Hampton clung to his belief that by persistently providing dependable service and high-quality products, Cooper Fabrics could dispel such doubts. Under his supervision, sales volume greatly increased during the third year and maintenance and machinery replacement costs were held to the minimum. Although the company was still operating at a loss, employment rose to more than 300 workers, and the organization began to reestablish its reputation in its trade circle. In the first month of 1974, Hampton's fourth year, the books finally recorded a small profit.

Also at the beginning of the year, William Rauls joined Cooper Fabrics as company controller. Rauls had been graduated from a leading business school five years previously and had held several positions in a large textile company before coming to Cooper. In May, his responsibility as controller was extended to include the personnel department.

Exhibit 1 Income statement—24 weeks ending June 19, 1974

Net Sales		$1,631,000
Cost of sales		1,451,000
Gross profit		$ 180,000
Selling expense	$58,000	
General & administrative expense	42,000	100,000
Operating profit		80,000
Other charges		12,000
Net profit		$ 68,000

In Hampton's view, Cooper's prospects looked bright (see Exhibit I). And he believed that more and more favorable results could be anticipated if the company continued to lower its costs and to improve the quality of its products. In June, employment had leveled off at approximately 340 workers, but actual output was still increasing. The general manager realized, however, that he could not expect to reduce actual unit costs more than just slightly below their present level. The plant was operating 24 hours a day, five days a week, with the second and third shifts somewhat smaller than the first.

Workers and working conditions

At this time 55% of Cooper's employees were men and 45% were women. Most of the jobs in the plant could be handled by members of either sex, and there were no wage differentials based on sex. Of the women, 75% were married. Whenever possible, the company tried to employ two or more workers from the same family. It was not unusual, therefore, for a husband and his wife to be working different shifts so that one of them could always be at home with the children.

The plant was surrounded by old but well-kept frame houses, once owned by the factory for rental to employees. At one time, company-owned homes were customary in the textile industry. Almost all textile mills had now divested themselves of such property, and Cooper Fabrics was no exception. Some of the workers did live in the immediate vicinity of the plant, but others commuted from surrounding towns. A substantial number traveled to Parville from neighboring areas of Vermont, over distances of 25 to 35 miles. (The textile industry was so depressed in the adjoining parts of Vermont that workers there were often forced to travel considerable distances to find work.)

The turnover of employees at the Cooper Fabrics plant was low, according to John Rider, personnel manager under William Rauls. Rider had told Hampton that the month of June was fairly typical—fourteen separations, and only five that were voluntary. Rider said that three or four of the people who had voluntarily left lived far from the plant. And, he pointed out, a large part of the remaining turnover represented relatively new employees; some of these were still in the process of finding the type of work that suited them, while others did not perform satisfactorily in their jobs. Rider emphasized that, although their employment usually was not continuous because of work stoppages, more than half the workers had been with the company for ten years or more.

Recently Rider had told Hampton, "Look Ralph, I know that it's sometimes difficult to fill in when we lose a highly skilled worker, but I still can say that the labor market around here is loose." He added, "For example, I almost never have a hard time replacing people who are absent for short periods." Rider believed that, in a large measure, the general availability of labor was due to the recession. Two of the four local textile mills had gone out of business since 1970.

Hourly wage rates at Cooper Fabrics ranged from $2.25 for battery hands (floor men) to $3.25 for weavers and $3.75 for fixers (setup and repair men). In addition to the hourly rate, weavers and fixers were paid an incentive bonus. All basic wages in the plant were subject to a cost-of-living differential which was reviewed every three months. For every eight tenths of a point change in the Consumers' Price Index, wages were raised or lowered $0.02 per hour.

Hampton believed working conditions in the factory were superior to those of many mills in the area. The one-story plant was designed so that all areas were uncluttered and easily accessible. The work areas were clean, well lighted, and reasonably well ventilated. Moreover, as noted, Hampton hoped to see air conditioning installed soon. Noise in the weave room made conversation difficult, but Hampton assumed the workers understood that this was a characteristic of textile plants.

Union and employee relations

When the plant reopened in 1970 as Cooper Fabrics, Ralph Hampton had the option of ignoring the Textile Workers Union, which formerly held jurisdiction over the plant's workers. He preferred to establish a stable union relationship from the start. Before reopening the plant, he renewed contact with the local office in Concord, New Hampshire, and secured the union's approval to rehire former workers according to management's convenience rather than according to seniority. Ultimately, 95% of the employees who had previously worked at the plant were reemployed.

Hampton could point out that union sentiment at Cooper Fabrics was rather weak—as it was throughout the southern New Hampshire area. The plant's union shop required 100% membership, but the general manager knew that only 15 to 20 members customarily showed up at the monthly union meeting.

Looking back, Hampton believed that relations with the union had always been amicable. Before the textile recession, the labor supply had been extremely tight, and the union had suceeded in winning a 5% across-the-board wage increase. When the recession became severe, a general industry movement for lower wages ensued and Cooper Fabric's wages fell back to their former level. Recently a two-year contact had been negotiated with the union.

The Haber Corporation, former owner of the Parville plant, had sponsored and emphasized athletic leagues and similar activities for the employees. Under the present management, group activities were limited to a Christmas party and an outing (see Exhibit II). One of the employees who had worked under both managements had commented on this de-emphasis to William Rauls: "Look, Mr. Rauls, there sure is a big difference in the amount of activities we've got now—you can't miss that. But I don't think there's any less loyalty to the company because of it."

Communications to the employees during the past four years had been generally routine. Notices of vacations, holidays, and union meetings were posted on bulletin boards in the shop whenever the need for them arose. Infrequently, a notice of an infraction of the rules also appeared (see Exhibit III). Management has recently subscribed to a bulletin board service which supplied the company with a monthly poster on the subject of safety or waste. John Rider reported that sometimes a particular poster created considerable interest at the plant.

Exhibit II   Announcement of "Coming Events," dated June 9, 1974

Our Annual Clambake will be held at the Central Recreation Grounds in Parville on Saturday, August 7, 1974. A fine sports program is being planned for the afternoon with prizes for all winners. There will be a charge of 50 cents for all employees of Cooper Fabrics. Guest tickets may be purchased at $2.75—children 5–12 years of age, $1.75. Detailed information will be given later, but save this date for a Grand and Glorious time.

Committee in charge

Jim Parker	Marjorie Constega	Henry Boudreau
Martha Kucak	Louis Congores	Joseph Neff
Martin Heinickie	Pauline McMahan	Bill Rider

Exhibit III   Notice dated May 10, 1974

As we find that certain of our employees are not adhering to the plant regulation applying to "starting" and "stopping" times, we are bringing the following to your attention:

   Employees are expected to be at their work or machine, ready to commence, when the starting horn blows for their shift—and to remain until the closing horn has blown at the end of their shift.

   Cooper Fabrics, Incorporated

Since Hampton had been general manager, two letters had been written to the employees. The first was a notice of production cutbacks, which was posted on the plant bulletin boards in 1971, Cooper's second year of operation (Exhibit IV). The second was a letter Hampton sent the following year, first to the union and later to the employees who received it just before their annual vacation. This letter asked the employees to accept a decrease in wages. It touched upon steps the company already had taken to curtail expenses. "You all know," Hampton stated, "that for reasons of economy we have had to cut out the cafeteria. We are giving up our company station wagon and are going to have a truck which will double for both. We are selling whatever machinery we will not use. In general, we are doing everything possible to cut our overhead and administrative expenses to the bone." Even so, the letter indicated, the company's economies amounted to only about half its losses.

Exhibit IV Announcement of production cutbacks, dated April 25, 1971

Notice to employees
Cooper Fabrics, Incorporated
Parville, New Hampshire

Unfortunately, due to present industrywide market conditions, it is necessary that for a temporary period we reduce our basic work week in some departments to a 32-hour schedule. This reduction will affect many of our employees; although in order to balance production or satisfy particular consumer demands, a portion of the mill will be operated on a full-time basis.

Please be assured that the management of your company has put off this decision to curtail operations as long as possible with the hope that business conditions would improve. We sincerely hope that this change of schedule will only be for a brief period, and want our employees to feel that we are doing everything possible to speed the return to normal operating conditions.

    Cooper Fabrics, Incorporated
    R. Hampton
    General Manager

Although Hampton presented a fairly bleak picture, the outlook described in his 1972 letter was not completely gloomy. He pointed out that the company was making great strides.

"I believe that we are now producing as good a product as was ever made in this mill. We are gaining back the good reputation that our mill used to have for quality and in the process we are getting new customers—and good ones. . . . What we offer in return for your accepting a temporary reduction in pay is that we are building job security and establishing a permanent business here in Parville."

Finally, the 1972 letter promised that any cut accepted by the union would apply in the same percentage to management and the sales force. Hampton's reasoning was that "we are all in this together and are all interested in making a go of this mill."

The 1972 letter was read to and voted on by the 25 workers who appeared at the next union meeting. (The following week, copies were distributed throughout the plant.) Unfortunately, the union president had misunderstood the letter's intent. He thought that the Cooper management was asking the employees to take a $0.60 rather than a 6% decrease in wages. This mistake generated considerable resentment among the workers at the lower end of the wage scale. Ralph Hampton did not learn about the misunderstanding until some time later. Although the company's proposal was voted down at the union meeting, an industrywide reduction was put into effect at the following contract negotiation. No letters were sent the following year. After their annual vacation, several workers stopped John Rider in the hallway to mention that they felt neglected by the omission.

"You know, they do like us to keep in touch," Rider later told Hampton.

Although the union contract called for only one week's vacation, the level of production during Cooper Fabric's first three years was such that each employee was given two weeks off. Each received a flat percentage of his yearly wages as vacation pay. No more money was allowed for two weeks off than for one, but the percentage given varied depending upon the length of service in the company.

Earlier in the current year, however, Hampton had announced that vacation time would be reduced to the one-week period stipulated in the contract. Customers had been advising him that they could no longer purchase two week's supply of fabrics in advance to keep their operation supplied while the plant was closed for vacation. Hampton felt confident that the employees would be satisfied with a one-week vacation, since the result would be more take-home pay for them. But some employees were disgruntled; they said they considered this change to be a reduction in their vacation period.

Conference in June

As he pondered both the recent success of Cooper Fabrics and his concerns about the employees' possible expectation of a raise, Ralph Hampton decided he needed to talk with William Rauls. He reached for his phone, and by three o'clock the two men were discussing the situation together in Hampton's office.

Hampton explained to the controller that, in spite of the difficult times that Cooper Fabrics had recently seen, it was almost impossible to convince employees that the company had been losing money. "Our policy has been not to make our financial statements available to the public. And the workers believe that we couldn't continue to operate if Cooper was not making a profit."

Rauls agreed that this was true.

"Another problem that seems to be related to this," Hampton continued, "is our need to persuade the workers that we're not wasting money when we replace outmoded equipment with more efficient machinery. Lots of the old-timers around here — our most experienced people, too — have worked on one machine all their lives; they've never even seen a different model. In their opinion, the machines they've been using are still perfectly good.

"Bill, you know well enough," Hampton continued, "that I believe that the way to create good employee relations is to treat my people fairly and give them cause to feel secure. I have always maintained that we need to give unswerving attention to the task of building a profitable operation. First and foremost, I'm convinced that equitable treatment and job security are what our employees value most. As a matter of fact, several of our workers recently went into civil service—and I know of a couple of men who have joined the fire and police departments here in Parville. It's a pretty good guess that these people sacrificed the higher take-home pay they get from us for jobs that give them better security. We don't want to lose any more people for such reasons in the future."

Rauls agreed wholeheartedly with Hampton's thesis that security and justice were basic in the employee's system of values. "You're absolutely right, Ralph. But building that kind of trust in the company is certainly a slow process."

"I know my way is slow," Hampton responded. "However, if I have learned anything from my previous experience with employees and customers alike, I've learned that actions speak louder than words."

"That's true, Ralph. But still, don't you think we can handle communications to our people so that they *will* listen and, what's more important, understand and want to help us achieve our goals."

"You know, Bill, your thinking interests me," the general manager replied emphatically. "I wonder whether we should experiment to see if we can find an answer to your question. Do you think we might try this: we could draft a letter explaining that we're now making a profit. That has been on my mind ever since we learned that things are going a little better this year. We would have to be sure, though, to point out that this won't allow us to raise wages. The people in the plant will know that our company situation has improved and they'll wonder why an increase isn't forthcoming."

Hampton further suggested that they might plan to send the letter so that the employees would receive it just as they began their vacation. In this way, management's best wishes for a pleasant holiday might be included. Hampton said he would draft a letter. He also asked Rauls to draft a version of the letter, and suggested further that Rauls should ask John Rider, the personnel manager, to do the same. "The three of us can get together in a week," Hampton declared with enthusiasm. "We'll compare notes and decide what sort of letter would be of most value at this time."

The three letters

One week later the three men met in Hampton's office, each with a copy of the letter he had drafted. Hampton laid them side by side on a table so that the men could read and compare them. The letters are shown in Exhibit V.

Now imagine that you are in Ralph Hampton's position. Would you select one of the letters for distribution to employees? If so, which one—and why? Or would you compose a different letter? Would you make any other changes in the plan Hampton seems to have in mind?

Exhibit V The three letters

A General manager's version
July 2, 1974

To All Employees
Cooper Fabrics, Inc.
Parville, New Hampshire

As general manager of this mill, I am happy to report that as of the 24-week period ending the nineteenth of last month, this mill has finally turned in a profit. This shows, I feel, that our constant attention to keeping overhead low and the quality of our products high is a policy which will, in the end, pay off in the form of a profitable and permanent business here in Parville. What this means to you employees is that with each passing day, your jobs become more secure, and you become safer than ever from layoffs and slowdowns.

Your cooperation in this effort has been, of course, essential to its success. By accepting wage cuts, and the necessary curtailment of activities and fringe benefits (such as a shorter vacation), you have done more than your share in making this mill a going concern. The owners of the mill must now be surer than ever that our people here are determined to keep the business in the black. Our customers are again coming to depend on our product and service, and our reputation is growing daily.

I would like to add, however, that in order to continue this favorable trend we must not allow, insofar as it is possible, any of our costs to increase. Among these expenses are employees' wages; I am sure that you can understand the necessity of holding the line on all costs, so that the present trend toward greater profitability can continue. What you are buying with a refusal to ask for more compensation is greater job security. I am sure that we can all agree that having stable employment and reasonable freedom from fears of a layoff is far better than a few cents an hour increase in remuneration.

I know that the owners of this mill are at least as pleased as the rest of us to see this business producing a return for the first time; I want you all to feel that this has been the final payoff in a long, and sometimes discouraging, team effort. Rest assured, however, that this need not be the last time we get into the black. If we can all work together, and hold the line on overhead, and keep providing the kind of dependable service and quality products which we are slowly becoming again known for, we can turn in a profit every quarter.

In closing, I want to extend to you on behalf of the whole management and administrative team here, all best wishes for a pleasant and restful vacation.

Sincerely,
R. Hampton
General Manager

B Controller's version

July 2, 1974
To All Employees
Cooper Fabrics, Inc.
Parville, New Hampshire

Dear Employees:

As you probably know, our mill here in Parville is owned by the Atlas Corporation, which also has interests in a number of other industries. We have not been one of their better investment bets, to say the least. In fact, I'm afraid that till now, we've been just about their worst—in plain language, they've had to put about $10,000 per month into our operation for the last four years, just to keep us going. They've been losing money on our mill for a number of years; but they've always felt, as we have, that we have a good crew here, and that we'd eventually start making money.

It is my pleasure to report to you that, as a result of the continued efforts of management and workers alike, we have turned in a small profit the first half of this year. We're in a difficult and very competitive business—we've had to decrease our vacation time, and modernize our equipment, just to keep our customers happy—but we've managed to show both the owners and our customers that we can turn out the best product in the business, and make a profit besides. You can be proud of this achievement, because it is due to your efforts as much as anyone else's. We on the management team can take only part of the credit: we direct and organize your work—but you are the ones who turn out our fine product.

And turn it out at a profit, as I said. But our competition from the South is tough, and the business is a very difficult one to prosper in. And the owners of the mill, though they realize they didn't have to put money into the business these past 24 weeks to keep it going, also realize that this could be just a "flash in the pan." From their point of view, they've started to make money, but they have a long way to go before they get back all the money they've put into the business over the last four years. They have to be shown that our recent profit is not just a fluke.

If we all work together as we have this first half of the year, I'm sure we can keep on turning in profits. This means, of course, that expenses have to be held where they are: management salaries and employee wages must both stay at the same level, and all frills must be kept to a minimum. Once we show the owners that we can and will turn in profits month after month, then they will be more likely to want to reward us all with increased salaries and wages, as an incentive to keep up our good work. But we all have to pitch in first and prove to them that we can do it.

We'll get much more than eventually higher wages out of continued hard work now, however: we'll be building our reputation and prestige in the business, and insuring that we'll all have jobs here for many years to come.

I want to thank you all once again for the fine work you've done; we've finally put this mill on a profitable basis, and we'll keep it there, with your help. Have a pleasant vacation, and I hope to see you all at the Clambake.
Very truly yours,
    Bill Rauls
    Controller

C Personnel manager's version
July 2, 1974

Notice to Employees
Cooper Fabrics, Inc.
Parville, New Hampshire

I would like to take this opportunity to inform all employees that there has been a change in the financial status of the Cooper Fabrics company—the company has, for the first time in four years of operations, shown a profit on its financial statements. This is a source of considerable pleasure to us in management, and so we would like to communicate it to you.

We know you will understand that, even though we are now turning out a small profit, this is no reason to expect any increases in pay for any of us. The company has lost considerable amounts in the last four years, and the parent company is in no mood to see this continue. We will all be safeguarding our jobs if we keep our noses to the grindstones and keep working at the same level of pay as previously. We are all confronted with whether we want increased salary, or no salary at all. In the sense that if we do go for greater salary now, and then begin losing money again later on as we have been, the parent firm may simply decide to liquidate this mill. The old "bird in hand" story applies here too.

We have to, in short, keep overhead low and productivity high; this is the way to keep a high profit margin. Increasing pay now might be totally premature; it would cut into a very thin profit margin that is only now showing strength. We have two parties we have to satisfy. We have the owners, who want a good profit on their investment, and we have the customers, who want good, steady service and a high quality product. We have had to update our equipment to keep turning out a good product, and we've had to cut vacations, because our customers can't stock two weeks' goods anymore. We've been satisfying the customers for some time, and now we have started with the owners, with this profit. This is only a start, however. In order to win their confidence, the profit margin must continue, and also get better. Your union has been understanding on this, and they know also that security of employment is very important in these days when layoff is constantly a possibility.

As manager of personnel, I can tell you that there are plenty of textile workers looking for work who would gladly take these jobs at present pay. Additionally, our working conditions here in Parville are the best in the area. The way to build job security now for us is to recognize the needs of the owners to have a reasonable profit on their investment.

We wish you the best of vacation holidays, and will see you when you get back.

Sincerely,
    J. Rider
    Manager of Personnel

Case 2

The case of the borderline black

David Kimball stood by the window of his Philadelphia office, looking high out over the Schuylkill River Valley. He was waiting for his Design Engineering manager, Paul Kelley, to arrive for a 10:30 conference. In his hand was a memo Kelley had sent him after the meeting of section heads the day before. It read:

"I have considered the alternatives, and clearly LSI circuits is the program to cut back. I recommend letting two of our engineers on that project go. But I thought you ought to know that one of the two is Thomas Rawlins, the only black engineer we have in Design. What do we do about that?"

Kimball, a trim and athletic 51, was manager of the Engineering Department of Industrial Computer Products, the largest division of multinational International Business Systems, Inc. He had risen far in the company and hoped to go farther.

As he gazed out the window, Kimball thought back to his student debate-team days at Cornell, when he had spoken passionately about the race question in 1940, years before the general acceptance of civil rights causes. And he remembered his satisfaction three years ago when Tom Rawlins became his first black engineer.

The sight of a jet plane arching steeply up from the Philadelphia airport brought Kimball's thoughts back to the present. He lit a cigarette to clear his mind for the conference coming up with Paul Kelley. Systematically, he assembled and sorted out his thoughts about the meeting two days ago when his boss, Harold Page, vice president in charge of the division, had announced the cutback.

Page, 60 and a product of the Depression, was a hard driver with a brilliant mind, devoted to the rapid expansion of the industrial computer

Source: This case was prepared by Theodore V. Purcell and appeared in *Harvard Business Review* 49 (November–December 1971): 128–143. Considerable credit for the preparation of the case and its interpretation goes to the author's research assistant Miss Irene E. Wylie. Copyright © 1971 by the President and Fellows of Harvard College; all rights reserved.

business. He demanded a lot from his managers. At the meeting Page had quoted part of a memo from the executive vice president, Louis Kagan, which read:

"The Automation Group of International Business Systems must take serious action. We have reviewed the rate of incoming orders and projected our expense levels from the last two quarters. I am convinced that for the balance of this year we are going to have to trim expenses throughout the Group. A 10% reduction is a reasonable target for the Industrial Computer Products Division."

The cutback was inevitable, of course, in light of the current recession, Kimball remembered thinking. IBS had grown into a successful company not only through its alertness in moving in on new technology, products, and markets, but also through its skill in controlling costs, adjusting to changing business conditions, and quickly trimming fat and eliminating unprofitable products.

But Page wanted to go further than Kagan. He had continued: "I've reviewed our incoming orders rate, our inventory, our backlog, and our cost structure, and I'm convinced that ICP can and should reduce costs 15%. I want each of our departments to take a long look at how we can cut back."

The department managers, although not surprised by Page's higher goal, had reacted negatively, for cost cutting is not easy and letting employees go is one of the hardest tasks a manager faces. Both Kimball and Toby Marotta, employee relations manager, had protested the 15% target. But Page had said, "We're determined to go beyond the demands of the New York office. I'm sorry, but you're going to have to cut your costs 15% for the next two quarters. Find ways and means to do it."

Later Kimball had called a meeting with the managers of his five sections—Software Applications, Design Engineering, Production Engineering, Drafting, and Model Shop—to inform them of Page's decision. He had talked to each about where the cost reductions should be made.

To Paul Kelley of Design Engineering he had suggested, "I think we might stretch out that LSI circuit program, Paul, don't you?" Kelley had said, "Well, I'll see what I can do about it, Dave. I think we can."

"But I didn't know," said Kimball now to himself, "that it would mean that Tom Rawlins has to go. Well, let's see what Kelley says."

"Not sure he's worth it"

"Come in, Paul." Kelley strode in and eased his big frame into a chair by Kimball's desk. Just 40, likable, craggy-faced, he looked more like a football coach than an engineer.

"Thanks for your memo," said Kimball. "I'm asking Toby Marotta from Employee Relations to sit in with us. We need advice on this." Just then Marotta came in.

At 38, Marotta was young for an industrial relations manager, but he had had broad experience in three different locations of the IBS Automation Group, and was once in operating management.

"Thanks for coming, Toby," said Kimball. "Here's the problem. In order to meet that cutback, I've asked Paul Kelley to take two engineers out of Design Engineering. Paul and I agree that the program to slow down is large-scale integration circuits. LSI circuits is a development program for our next-generation computer, so we can slow it down without hurting any systems now in production or on the market.

"But Paul tells me that one of the two people who should be cut from that project is Tom Rawlins, who, you know, is the first black engineer we hired, a few years ago. I'd like to keep Rawlins, but we're in a tight spot. Think you can help?"

Marotta smiled and shrugged. "You know me. No miracles. Just difficult questions."

Kimball turned to Kelley. "Fill us in, Paul, on your reasons for recommending that Rawlins be laid off."

"Sure, Dave," said Kelley. "I hate to do it. I've gotten to like the guy myself, but I don't see any way around it. We have three men on the LSI program. One is Jack Martin, a real hot-shot engineer. I can cut back on the program, but I can't cut back on Jack Martin. He's the center of it. The other two are Rawlins and a white fellow, Longworth Smith. Neither of them have been with us long, and neither are going to become really great engineers. And they couldn't keep LSI circuits going alone. Martin can."

"But you have about 35 engineers in Design," Marotta interjected, looking at the roster. Couldn't you let any of them go in place of Rawlins?"

"Hold on! It's 29, not 35; I've already lost 6 men and I'm pressed. But I did think of the alternatives. If I move Rawlins to another project, I'll have to take a more experienced man off it. I'm afraid Rawlins wouldn't be able to pull his own weight, and we can't afford to get behind in production now."

"Could you spell that out a bit, Paul?" asked Kimball. "What makes you think that Rawlins wouldn't cut it?"

"Let's face it," Kelley replied. "It's rough for any man to pick up a new job. It would take time before he knew it as well as someone who has been on the job nine months. I'm just not sure he would be able to catch on fast enough to maintain our schedules.

"And then there's the problem of backlash. If Rawlins bumps a white fellow, there's going to be talk of preferential treatment. As a matter of fact, there was some bad feeling several months ago among my engineers when there were rumors that some blacks over in the Manufacturing Department were favored during a layoff. If the men are resentful, they won't help Rawlins much. It would mean hours lost in poor morale."

"How do you think Rawlins would react to a situation like that?" asked Marotta.

"Well, he's a pleasant fellow—no chip on his shoulder," Kelley said. "And he's pretty well liked now. He might be able to win them around eventually, but you can't tell. It's a risk I don't feel I can take. And, frankly, I'm not sure Rawlins is really worth it. If he were white, I wouldn't even have brought it to your attention."

"He's doing much better"

Kimball frowned and made a few notations on a pad. "We'd better have a look at Rawlins' background," he said.

"Rawlins is 34 years old," said Kelley, looking at his notes. "He got a B.S. in electrical engineering from Brooklyn Poly after a stint in the Army. His grades were fair. Let's see. . . . His previous job was an electrical engineering position with a construction company, and before that he did designing of telephone equipment.

"As you know, Dave, we hired him in 1968, and I was the one who did the hiring. As I think I told you then, he did seem marginally qualified for a job in this department. After all, our men are a cut above average. I'll be honest: if he'd been white, I don't think we'd have taken him on. But he seemed to have a good attitude and real potential."

"I remember," said Kimball. "That was about the time we began to ask, 'If a person isn't perfectly qualified now, is he qualifiable?' Black engineers were hard to come by, and '68 was a good year. We could afford to take a gamble on a man who might make it. But I seem to recall that there were some problems with Rawlins at first."

"Yes, there were," Kelley said. "Rawlins had some difficulty on a design. We had a complaint from the Manufacturing Department a couple of years ago on one of his projects. He was catching his mistakes late, Toby, and he had to send through quite a few alteration notices. Then Manufacturing was sore because it slowed down their production and raised their costs."

Marotta, looking up from the notebook on which he was doodling, asked, "What's your experience with other new engineers, Paul? Have other men had this kind of problem?"

"Well, even our experienced men send through alteration notices once in a while. But this was a bad case. Sure, I've had others that bad—some that eventually turned out well—but we worry about them."

"You were able to straighten Rawlins' problem out, as I recall," said Kimball.

"Well," Kelley went on, "he is doing much better now, but the situation got worse before it got better. Part of the problem was the Drafting and Model Shop men. You know what they're like—no engineering degrees, but they know an awful lot about their particular job, and once they find an engineer like Rawlins who isn't very sure of himself, they're going to give him a hard time. Then, of course, Rawlins being black didn't help matters.

"After that problem project, some of them didn't want to work for him at all. But I had a talk with Rawlins. I told him when he is talking to these technicians, he should take a position and hold on to it. I spoke to the men too, and told them that no one is going to refuse to work for the man I assign him to."

Marotta broke in. "Let's go back to Dave's point about qualifiability, Paul. Do you think Rawlins really has the aptitude for an engineer's job in this unit? Were you able to do anything about his problem with design?"

Kimball looked up from his note pad and said, "I remember authorizing a two-week training program for Rawlins up in New York. That helped, didn't it?"

"It did," Kelley answered. "I also thought it would help to put him on this LSI project so that Jack Martin, the engineer I was telling you about, could kind of work along with Rawlins and bring him out a bit. He's been on LSI circuits ten months now and he's doing all right. He's developing, though slowly.

"But when I think how well he's responded to what we've demanded of him, it's gratifying. In the long run, Rawlins may be as good as some of the fellows I need to keep because of their experience on important jobs. But I have to remind myself that I'm not running a vocational training school; I'm managing a design unit in a highly competitive business. I really have no alternative but to recommend that he and Smith go."

"That cut will be noticed"

Kimball turned to Marotta. "Toby, your business is 'people business.' What are your reactions?"

"Just a few comments, Dave. Paul's right in hesitating to let Martin or any other really bright young guys go. You need to grow talent for Design Engineering. The service picture of these men doesn't help much, either. Rawlins has only been with IBS three years, and I doubt you have many other people with less service."

"I have a couple," said Kelley, "but they're in key positions. I can't do without them."

"Okay, let's try another tack," Marotta said. He turned to Kimball. "Could you use Rawlins in the Production Engineering Section, Dave?"

Kimball leaned back in his chair, lit a cigarette, and looked at Kelley and Marotta. "Well, fellows, of course I've thought of that, but it's impossible. I've asked the Production Engineering manager to cut back too, and I couldn't ask him to take on a new man who has no working knowledge of the products and isn't familiar with the factory end of it, not at a time like this."

Marotta nodded. "I can see that would be rough, Dave. But at the same time we've got to consider our affirmative action commitments. Let's look at the statistics. If you let Rawlins go, that means no blacks at all in the Design Engineering Section.

"But let's talk about the whole Engineering Department, which is your biggest concern, Dave. You supervise some 150 professionals and 90 non-professionals."

"That's right."

Marotta looked at his notebook. "Your nonprofessionals are 6.6% black. That's not too bad. But if you let Rawlins go, that brings your minority percentage for professionals down from 2.6% to 2%. That's low when you consider Philadelphia's large black population. That cut will certainly be noticed in our next federal contract compliance review."

"But it's not just a question of flak from the examiners, Toby," Kimball put in. "I personally feel that New York management was right in urging us to build up our black proportions in IBS, and I'd like to do what I can in our department."

"But at the same time, Dave," Kelley interrupted with some heat, "you're telling me I've got to cut two men to meet our cost reduction target. Now, the only two men I can see to let go, in all honesty, are Smith and Rawlins. We'll both be in trouble if we get our production schedules snared up."

"That's the key problem, isn't it?" said Marotta. He opened a small blue pamphlet. "Take another look at our IBS affirmative action policy: 'You should recognize that we are all expected to fulfill our Equal Employment Affirmative Action responsibilities while at the same time achieving our profitability goals. It's not an either/or situation, and one does not give relief from the other.'"

Kimball snorted. "Well, that helps a lot, doesn't it!"

"It does give you the parameters anyway, Dave," Marotta said. "Those aren't just empty words in that policy. Well, I guess the ball is in your court. It's your decision. I can't give you a pat answer."

Kimball snuffed out his cigarette and said with a sigh, "Well, thanks, fellows. I'll let you know tomorrow."

Kimball sat at his desk, solitary, concerned, puzzled. Mechanically he jotted down on a pad of paper the issues to be balanced, to be judged. The pros and the cons. The decision was his, all right.

He had to cut costs. LSI was the program to be cut in Design engineering. He respected Kelley's judgment. He wanted to retain Rawlins, but he did not want to hurt Engineering's production by preferring Rawlins over some better qualified white engineer. He considered going to Page, but promptly rejected it because he knew that Page would be unsympathetic.

He thought of the excellent reputation of the Engineering Department. He thought of his own reputation and his future. Once you got soft on one decision, you could easily get soft on any decision. But was it really getting soft?

Kimball recalled the phrases of the IBS policy guide that Marotta had read: ". . . expected to fulfill our Equal Employment Affirmative Action responsibilities while at the same time achieving our profitability goals." Big help. "It's not an either/or situation." Big help. "One does not give relief from the other." Big help.

Yet what else could those policy makers in New York say? The decision was his.

For a strange moment he saw himself at the tiller of his ketch, plunging through waves off the Maine coast. Easier to sail a boat than manage a department under pressure. You could be pretty sure of the wind and the sea and a boat you knew.

Kimball got up from his desk. He walked over and stood alone by the window of his Philadelphia office, looking over the Schuylkill River Valley.

Case 3

Crisis in conscience at Quasar

The case setting

Universal Nucleonics Company, the parent company for a number of wholly owned subsidiaries, suddenly found itself in the embarrassing position of having to report that its earnings for the year would be substantially lower than had been announced at the end of the previous quarter. Shortly thereafter, a statement appeared in the "Who's News" section of *The Wall Street Journal* reporting that Quasar Stellar Company, one of Universal's subsidiaries, had a new president and a new vice president of finance (replacing the former controller).

As time went on, the financial community learned that Universal had discovered that one of its subsidiaries had been withholding the truth, purposely distorting the facts, or otherwise misrepresenting the situation at hand in its monthly reports to corporate headquarters. By the time Universal had realized the actual condition of Quasar's financial situation, it was too late to correct it without affecting the reported year-end earnings of the parent company.

The two individuals most directly concerned at Quasar—John Kane, president, and Hugh Kay, controller—had both "resigned." It was generally agreed by the board of directors that there would be no public announcement as to the reasons for the resignations. Privately, however, one director stated flatly that out-and-out fraud was involved; another, more in tune with the times, said that the situation was directly attributable to the pressures to make good and the tendency to have a positive outlook on the outcome of all individual company problems.

Corporate headquarters was vitally interested in finding out why, given the organizational structure at Quasar, no feedback had been received independently of the president-controller monthly statement; whether any of the

Source: This case was prepared by John J. Fendrock and appeared in *Harvard Business Review* 46 (March–April 1968):112–120. Copyright © 1968 by the President and Fellows of Harvard College; all rights reserved.

other executives were involved in the reports either knowingly or unknowingly, willingly or unwillingly; and, finally, what steps could be taken to prevent a recurrence of the situation in the future.

Fact-finding team

To resolve these questions, Universal's executive committee decided that a direct approach should be taken. The executive vice president and the vice president of industrial relations for the corporation would conduct a series of interviews with the Quasar Stellar personnel who might have been involved. Both men were well qualified to appraise the situation. Jim Bowden, the executive vice president, was both an operating and a financial man, having spent a number of years in each area. Hubert Clover, vice president of industrial relations, was a former professor of industrial psychology at one of the leading business schools.

It was further agreed that each executive would interview different men, compare notes, and then speak with each other's interviewees if the situation so warranted. After studying the organization chart (see Exhibit 3-1), and the company's "Manual of Responsibilities," they decided it would be best to talk to Peter Loomis, vice president—marketing; George Kessler, vice president—manufacturing; and William Heller, vice president—engineering.

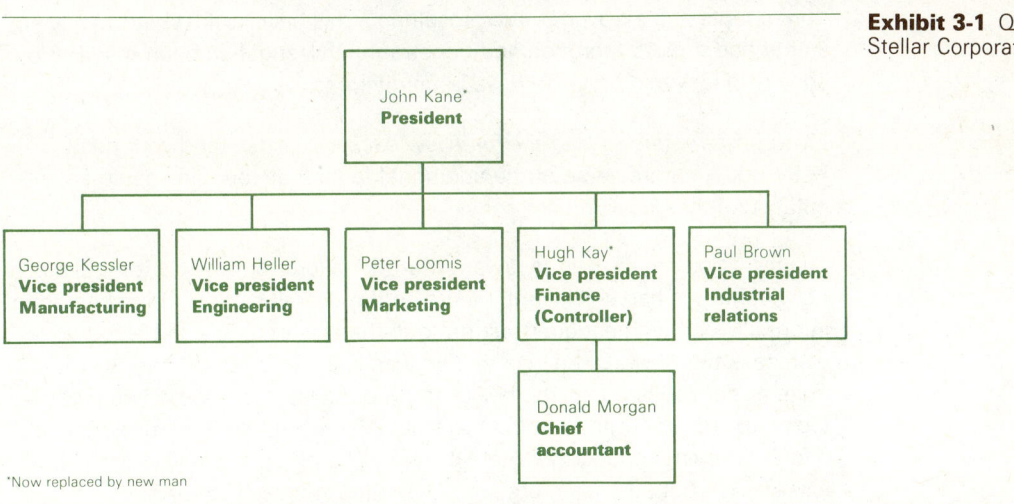

Exhibit 3-1 Quasar Stellar Corporation

Loomis' session

The scene opens in a small conference room at Quasar Stellar Company. The first man to be interviewed is Peter Loomis, vice president—marketing, who is known to be outspoken, demanding, and intensely loyal. Loomis is greeted by Hubert Clover.

Clover Pete, as you know, the purpose of our chat is to see if we can learn something from this unfortunate episode that can help to prevent such an occurrence in the future. I would like to get your version of what happened and any suggestions you may be able to offer as to what can be done to help our planning.

Loomis (defensively) Well, Hubert, you know I thought very highly of John. I'm certain you are aware that he hired me for this job. I don't mind admitting that I think the decision to fire him was unwarranted and ill advised.

Clover If there is one thing I am certain of, Pete, it is that there is no question of your loyalty to John. I hope that won't bias your outlook. As for John's resignation, perhaps the best I can say is that on the basis of all facts available, the board decided this was the only logical course of action. And if . . .

Loomis (interrupting) Let me set the record straight on two points. My loyalty to John was based on respect for his abilities — not on personal grounds. And I'm not disagreeing with you, either on the basis of the facts available at the time or on those turned up by the investigation, that the action was not warranted. But I also feel that there was too hasty a collection of facts and an overreaction resulting in his dismissal. What I'm saying is that had a more thorough and penetrating investigation been made, the conclusions would probably have been different.

Clover (attempting to lead the interview back) I understand your point, Pete, but what are some of the additional facts that you think could have influenced the decision differently?

Loomis You are most likely aware that the failure to receive the Apollo and LEM contracts had significant effects on the overall picture. But when John informally notified headquarters that our chances of receiving these two jobs were less than 50-50, he was told he was just being pessimistic. It was quite evident to him that the board of directors felt these were two prestige jobs that we simply had to get. The trouble was that while we dissipated our efforts on trying to land these low-probability programs, a half-dozen other less known, but perhaps more lucrative, opportunities slipped by.

Clover You say John told headquarters about this. Have you any idea why the so-so probabilities and the alternatives were not openly presented and discussed at the appropriate company board meeting?

Loomis To be frank, the 50-50 chance was an after-the-fact estimate. When the decision was made to pursue the two jobs, because of the pressure from headquarters and knowing what the work could mean to Quasar, I was undoubtedly too optimistic myself. A staff meeting was held in which the two marketing efforts were reviewed in detail.

Clover   Who attended that meeting?

Loomis   As I recall, there was George Kessler, Bill Heller, Hugh Kay, John, and myself.

Clover   Was it unanimously agreed that you should go after the two contracts?

Loomis (shaking his head)   Oh no! Bill felt very strongly that we should. He thought that the engineering department could gain a heck of a lot by being involved—state-of-the-art stuff. George was against the effort. He argued that production would be severely affected, because these projects would require such a long-term engineering effort before production could start. He wanted more immediate work that would occupy his work force. Hugh was with George. Not only was he worried about overhead and profits, but he had a "gut feeling" that our chances were less than what I forecast. He was right, of course. John was in favor of pursuing the contracts only if we had about a 75% chance of capturing each. John tossed the ball to me when he asked what our chances of getting the jobs were. At the time, I indicated that while I couldn't stick my neck out to 75%, I was willing to guess it would be much closer to 75% than to, say, 50% or even 60%. Considering the attitude at headquarters, the stakes, and my projection, we finally decided to go after both.

Clover   Are you saying that you didn't really feel that your chances were as close to 75% as you indicated?

Loomis   I believe they weren't. But that isn't to say that I didn't feel they could or should have been.

Clover   How long had you been with the company when this meeting took place, Pete?

Loomis   Just about nine months. I'm quite sure I know the reason for your question. Actually, I was not as familiar with the company as I should have been to express so strong an opinion on such an important matter.

Clover   Obviously, you showed a good deal of enthusiasm . . .

Loomis (interrupting again)   And, I'm afraid you'll have to agree, naiveté. Remember, however, that this is—or at least was—a gung-ho operation. I was anxious to earn my spurs. Those contracts would have put us on the map and made Quasar and Universal household words.

Clover I can certainly understand your decision to go after the big fish, but, once you found that you were out of fishing water, why was headquarters not kept informed of the deteriorating market picture? Wouldn't that have been the logical thing to do?

Loomis Logical, yes, but hardly practical. In retrospect, that is probably what we should have done, but let's go back six months. That's when our fears of a drop in production began to inject themselves. Hugh's warnings about profitability were proving to be only too accurate, and there was nothing that could be pulled in at the last minute to bridge the gap.

Clover Yes, but you must have known very early that your odds were way off.

Loomis (after a pause) Well, perhaps I did not emphasize that fact strongly enough. I assure you, however, that both George and Hugh did, since their operations were directly and indirectly involved.

Clover (bothered by Loomis' evasiveness) How, then, was the decision reached not to inform headquarters of this situation? Didn't it bother you to think that there might be adverse effects on employment?

Loomis Once the decision was made to go after the two projects, any reversal could only result in a loss of face and prestige. Like the gambler at the roulette wheel, we plunged deeper—with about the same odds—and lost. I must confess that I had my moments of doubt about our course of action. It was quite clear that people could get hurt, but that too is all part of the game. Frankly, at no time did it occur to me that I had a greater responsibility than the one I had to John. Perhaps this is wrong, but I have always felt that I owe more loyalty to my supervisor than to the company. And besides, I'm not certain to what degree personal morality should enter into business decisions.

Clover Pete, let me ask you one final question. What do you think we might do to prevent this sort of thing from happening again in the future?

Loomis Frankly, I feel that headquarters should give us more independence. For example, if headquarters had not exerted pressure on us to pursue these two contracts, we might have followed a different course. To me, what happened was that headquarters decided on a set course of action, passed the word down, and then—when it became impossible for us to follow through—they looked for scapegoats. Both John and Hugh were sacrificed because of poor headquarters policy.

Clover (rising) Thanks for a frank and open presentation of your thoughts on the situation, Pete. By the way, Jim Bowden may or may not wish to speak with you, depending on how things go in general. In any event, we'll let you know later. Once again, thanks for your ideas.

Loomis Thanks for asking. I honestly thought this might just be allowed to die on the vine without anyone looking deeper into it.

Follow-up questions

Hubert Clover brooded over his interview with Loomis, scanning his notes in a manner that suggested more sorrow and disappointment than thought. He then decided to summarize his observations and to recommend that Bowden not interview Loomis. But, after reviewing the results of Clover's conversation, Bowden concluded that there was one more thing he wanted resolved: Why had not Loomis, in routine fashion, been put in a position to send a report back to headquarters that would have been at variance with the official statement? Later that afternoon, the two men got together. After exchanging the usual pleasantries and engaging in small talk related to the previous interview, Bowden asked the specific question he had in mind.

Bowden The one thing that puzzles me, Pete, is why you were not able to transmit your misgivings about the possibility of receiving two contracts directly to the corporate vice president of marketing.

Loomis Your question, Jim, implies that I was *unable* to do this. Actually, it was always possible, but I was not *required* to do it. However, I was expected to give my observations to John and to support him in any decision he made as to how the information was to be handled.

Bowden Your answer implies to me that you were fully aware that two distorted monthly reports were sent to corporate headquarters. Am I correct in this assumption?

Loomis From what I have said to both you and John, there is no doubt that your conclusion is correct. And to be honest, I was completely aware of the distortions in the reports. I can only repeat what I said earlier this afternoon to Hubert: my loyalty is to my supervisor, and I always support him in his use of information in any way he sees fit.

Kessler's interrogation

The next man to be interviewed was George Kessler, vice president-manufacturing, who was an old-timer by Quasar standards, having been at Quasar for 15 years. He was known for his outspokenness, integrity, and forcefulness. Clover and Bowden decided that Bowden should conduct the interview with Kessler because there existed a somewhat close relationship between them. As a former operations man, Bowden had taken a direct interest in manufacturing, and he had developed a healthy respect for Kessler. Bowden greeted Kessler, and the two exchanged a few pleasantries.

Bowden   I guess we could keep up the chitchat all day, George, but I'm afraid we've got to get down to business. A fellow in your position must have seen what was coming—how in hell could you let it happen?

Kessler   I would rather continue reminiscing about old times than get into this. To answer your question, Jim, I saw what was coming; but, to turn the question back to you, how could I possibly have prevented it?

Bowden   All right, George, you couldn't have stopped it. Really, what I am asking is this: Seeing what was happening, wasn't there something you could have done to raise the storm signals?

Kessler   You know me well enough to realize that I am not one of the gung-ho types. While I had tremendous respect for John's ability to analyze a situation, I always suspected that he had a streak of the gambler in him. Let's face it; if he had pulled those two jobs out of the hat, he would have been Universal's brightest star.

Bowden   Getting back to the point, George, wasn't there some way for you to signal headquarters of what was happening?

Kessler (frowning)   You insist on pursuing this point, don't you? Jim, you know as well as I do that I answered directly to John. I'm not going to beat a dead horse; but, without going into details, I think I expressed my views strongly on the approach we were taking. Certainly, I was concerned about a number of things . . . the number of old-time employees who were going to take a beating if this thing fizzled, as it did; what might actually happen to the company overall; and what I owed to myself as well as to John. Taking all these points into consideration, I did what I thought was morally and managerially right, and I don't say that lightly. In expressing my doubts so forcefully, perhaps I did a disservice to everyone I tried to help.

Bowden   In what way do you think you performed a disservice?

Kessler   In short order, I found myself outside the actual development of the monthly reports. The result was that any influence I might have exerted in determining what information was to be generated for headquarters was cancelled out.

Bowden (nodding)   I appreciate your dilemma, George, and I also respect the position you took. But don't you feel that there might have been some way to get this back to our office?

Kessler   In weighing my responsibility to the company, corporate headquarters, employees, self, and supervisor, I may possibly have erred in following too narrow a path. It seemed to me at the time, and I feel the same way even now, that with the organizational structure we have, my only approach was to try to change things through the existing framework. My efforts failed. Perhaps I should have been more adventurous and requested—demanded, if you will—an audience with you fellows. But I am certain that if a similar situation arose again, I still would not do this.

Bowden   Then let me ask you what you think can be done to prevent this from happening in the future?

Kessler   To me, there must be an approach that will allow for greater communication between headquarters and the company office. Perhaps the answer lies in having an executive committee sign the monthly report; or possibly having each committee member prepare a short concurrence or dissent report of his own, after the pattern of the Supreme Court; or even a more direct approach of having each manager give an independent report to his respective staff contact at corporate headquarters. The fact is, so long as we have a characteristic line and staff organizational structure, we can only follow the channels of communication that the chief executive officer decides on. No self-respecting manager would consider surreptitiously reporting behind his superior's back.

Bowden (rising and extending a handshake)   George, thanks for your observations. I like your suggestion of a concurrence or disagreement by an executive committee. I hope that the next time we have a little get-together it can be under more pleasant circumstances.

Heller's interview

To some extent, the interview had merely reinforced Bowden's estimation of Kessler. However, he couldn't help but feel a sense of frustration that a man of Kessler's caliber did not find a way to communicate his misgivings to those who could have done something about the developing Quasar problem.

After reading Bowden's notes, Clover concluded there was no need for him to talk with Kessler. Instead, he decided to carry on with the next interview. The final man singled out was William Heller, vice president—engineering, an intense, serious-minded, pipe-smoking engineer whose forte was considered to be R&D, not administrative work. He too was a long-term employee, having been with Quasar over ten years. Clover met him at the door of the conference room and, with a wave of his hand, motioned Heller to a chair.

Clover   I suppose the idea of sitting down to discuss this problem is not the most appealing thing to you, Bill. I hope it won't be as painful as realizing that an R&D project is going sour.

Heller   Since your call a few minutes ago was not completely unexpected, I prepared for this by fixing myself an extra tightly packed pipe of tobacco. It will give me more time to think about your questions.

Clover What can you contribute to our understanding of the things that happened here, and do you have any suggestions as to how they might be prevented in the future?

Heller I wonder if you could narrow your question somewhat. Exactly what would you like me to address myself to?

Clover The specific problem, Bill, is this. Do you have an idea why Quasar's deteriorating condition was not reported back to headquarters? Of greatest interest, of course, is the overall condition of the plant operation, but the decline in engineering acitivty is something you can probably elaborate on in detail. Any light you can shed will be useful.

Heller While you have become more specific, I still have a wide-open field. Probably I should first outline what happened to engineering, and from this we might then be able to work into the bigger picture. How does that appeal to you?

Clover (nodding) That would be a good start.

Heller About a year ago, it became obvious that our engineering activity, including both research and development and general engineering, was going to decline. The decision was made that a joint effort with marketing would be undertaken. After a series of meetings, it was decided to pursue actively and aggressively two relatively large contracts.

Clover Those would be the Apollo and LEM contracts. *(Heller nods assent.)* When you say it was decided that those two contracts would be pursued, what did this imply?

Heller It meant that a radically new—for us—course of action was decided on. Always in the past we had operated as a subcontractor to primes on large systems. However, John and Pete took the stand that we were in a position to enter the systems area itself. Frankly, while I had initial skepticism about this approach, John portrayed the picture in optimistic terms. He was convinced that the contracts would be awarded more on the basis of marketing activity than on the engineering proposal, and he was equally confident that Pete's personal contacts would help us in capturing this work. Apparently John knew, or felt he knew, that Pete had influence with the right people where those two contracts were involved. Thus, while in the past we had been merely keeping our fingers in the pie and hoping to get a piece of the action, it was decided at that point we would go the whole hog after them.

Clover And you agreed with this approach?

Heller As I indicated, initially I was skeptical. Our organization is simply not capable of coping with proposals of this size. However, after John and Pete argued their case so persuasively, I was fully in favor of the decision. Actually, I knew it involved a lot of risk, but Quasar stood to benefit greatly if it worked out, and so I went along with them on it.

Clover   What did you think the chances were of getting those contracts, Bill?

Heller (pausing to light his pipe)   To me, our chances were less than those expressed by Pete, who, as I recall, said he figured them to be closer to 75% than to 60% or so. Frankly, I would have guessed 60% to be the upper limit on our chances for each contract. However, even at that, it seemed like a good risk because, if we had captured but one of them, engineering would have benefited greatly.

Clover   And how about the rest of the plant operations?

Heller   Here, unfortunately, I was shortsighted. While the engineering activity would benefit, in retrospect the company as a whole could conceivably lose if only one, or perhaps even if both contracts were awarded to Quasar. I might add that this point was brought out strongly by George and Hugh. To offset this argument, however, it was pointed out that while a temporary downturn might occur, in about two years Quasar would be hard pressed to satisfy the requirements for the projects. In addition, Quasar would become so well known that interim work would be easy to come by.

Clover   Might it not also have worked to Quasar's disadvantage? How can you assume that other companies would be willing to give you work, knowing that it would be short-term and that you certainly would give attention to your own contracts once it was time to begin production?

Heller   Yes, it was an optimistic outlook and probably very shortsighted from a total company point of view.

Clover   Even assuming that the decision was a good one when made, why didn't someone recognize it was the wrong course before the entire operation went sour?

Heller (puffing on his pipe for a moment)   Now you are in an area that is too deep for me. Once it was decided on to pursue those contracts, my group concentrated its efforts on the technical proposal. We are extremely thin in this area. Therefore, our R&D activity was almost totally devoted to the proposal. Let me add that for approximately a 3-month period, 10- to 12-hour days and 7-day weeks were common for my staff.

Clover   But this very activity reduced your effectiveness on current work, did it not, and resulted in costly overruns and delays on contracts already in the house?

Heller Unfortunately, yes, but that was not totally unexpected. We attempted to minimize the overruns and delays, but some were certainly inevitable. Since we were trying to maintain our staff, a lot of the added cost went into overhead and project charges as we stockpiled personnel during the initial period when the decline began to manifest itself. Of course, we had to face facts later and let some people go when it became apparent that the plans were not working out.

Clover At that point, why didn't the company reverse itself, abandon its course, and go after some short-term subcontract work? And why didn't you get back to headquarters with your problem?

Heller At that point, both John and Pete felt retreat would be impossible. Frankly I supported them against my better judgment, both because I could see no way to change their attitude, and because I had an obligation to do my utmost in attempting to rectify the situation. Now, then, your other question as to why headquarters was not informed is difficult for me to answer. What can I say?

Clover I would like a frank comment on this point, Bill.

Heller (knocking the ashes from his pipe) Both John and Pete stood high in my book. I don't pretend to be a business manager; rather, I am an engineering manager. The tangibles of engineering are something I grasp and manipulate readily, but the intangibles of business are quite another thing. In retrospect, it's easy to criticize past decisions, but I respect the decisions that were made then. I personally felt there was an obligation to the parent company, but even though I disagreed with the principle of not reporting the situation to headquarters, I accepted it as a business decision.

Clover Then you were aware, were you not, that the reports sent to headquarters distorted conditions at Quasar to such an extent that the status of projects was inaccurately reported, actual and projected earnings were blatantly inflated, and the entire status of the operation was totally misrepresented? How could you have accepted such a situation?

Heller If only I could answer you in a manner that might express my feelings at the time. Was I aware of what was going on? Yes, of course, I was. But I didn't *want* to know about it. I will go so far now as to say that I tried *not to know* what was being done. Realistically, once I accepted the basic decision to ride the thing out, I felt stuck with the consequences. There was nothing, as I saw it, that I could do to alter the course taken.

Clover Bill, did you have any opportunity to bring this to the attention of headquarters?

Heller Formally, no, of course not. No mechanism existed, or perhaps should ever exist, for circumventing top management. On a few occasions I might have had the opportunity to mention to the corporate vice president of engineering what was happening, but I certainly would not do that.

Clover (shaking his head slowly) I think you will agree such a situation should never be allowed to exist. Can you offer any suggestions as to how information of such importance to the welfare of both the company and the corporation could be made available to top management without violating any precepts—actual or imaginary?

Heller I have given considerable thought to this point. I honestly feel that what gets reported back to headquarters can only reflect what the president sees fit. I would hit the ceiling if I found out one of my project managers was reporting directly or indirectly to the president. By the same token, the president shouldn't have to guard against insurgency in his ranks. The corporation might use an internal audit team composed of knowledgeable personnel to make frequent checks on various phases of the operation. Apart from that, I've no suggestion.

Clover Bill, your pipe's been cold and empty long enough. Thanks for your comments. Hopefully, we won't need another one of these sessions with you.

Morgan's opinions

Clover discussed his report with Bowden, and they agreed that another interview with Heller was unnecessary. Then they went over the results of all three interviews in depth. When they had finished, they decided to pursue two additional questions from two other specific areas: (a) Why did the accounting people not find a way to report to headquarters? (b) What was the quality of the morale of the personnel during this period?

Accordingly, Donald Morgan, chief accountant, and Paul Brown, vice president—industrial relations, were invited to sit down with Bowden and Clover, respectively, in two simultaneous sessions. Since both corporate fact finders felt that too much briefing might tend to "lead" the interviews and stifle response, they agreed that the only statement they would make at the start would be to the effect that efforts were being made to prevent a repetition of the Quasar situation in the future.

Bowden Don, you certainly are aware of the upheaval here at Quasar, and I suspect you know pretty well the reasons for it.

Morgan Yes, I have a good idea of what's what.

Bowden I wonder if you would care to express your opinions on two specific points. First, why was it not possible to have the information fed back to corporate headquarters once the deteriorating situation began and, second, what might be done to prevent what happened from taking place again?

Morgan As standard company policy on reports, we generate our financial statements from whatever information is given to us. Our statements, in turn, are sent to the controller's office, and he does what he see fit with them. Should we receive instructions from his office to reorganize, let's say, or otherwise manipulate the reports, there is very little we can do but follow instructions. This is particularly true when matters of judgment are involved. Let me give you a for-instance: if a project is reported as being behind schedule by the program manager and, after review by the controller's office it is decided that it is not all that far behind, naturally adjustments are made. Or, say, an expected contract has not yet been received, but management decides to open up a project number anyway and begins accepting charges in anticipation of receiving the job; this too is done. So far as I can see, this is nothing more than exercising management prerogative. I will summarize my position by saying that I do pretty much what I am told. Sometimes I may not like it, but my job is not to set policy or to question decisions. Rather, it is to follow instructions.

Brown's observations

At that point, Bowden decided that he had heard enough and abruptly ended the interview. Meanwhile, Clover was undertaking his interview with Paul Brown.

Clover Paul, can you give any insight into the state of morale during the period when Quasar was apparently falsifying reports to the home office and after it became apparent that a serious problem existed?

Brown For a while, everybody acted as if they were on "pot"; everyone was filled with high expectations. To be sure, there were a couple of exceptions. But, in rapid fashion, things began to settle down and disillusionment set in. Many people sensed that there was trouble ahead and that nothing was being done. After a month or two, the exodus began, and, as you know, it still hasn't ceased. I know that some of the managers tried their best to hang onto their key people, but as usual it was just this caliber of individual who would read the writing on the wall and got out while the getting was good. I'm equally certain that a number of the other top people would have left except for loyalty to the company and their fellow employees, their years of company service, and/or other factors. My only other observation on this is that I hope our new president and controller have been selected more for solid, long-range accomplishments than for flashy, short-term results.

The interviews having been concluded, Clover and Bowden are now faced with drafting a series of recommendations on the individuals interviewed and the steps to be taken by Universal Corporation.

Case 4

Lennert Company Limited

Harry Fielding spent the evening of June 24, 1963, confiding to a close friend who he hoped would give him a different perspective on a major decision he would have to make within the next two days. At the time he was the vice-president of sales of the Lennert Company of Oshawa, Ontario, a nationally known manufacturer and merchandiser of powered lawn mowers and garden equipment. The essence of his conversation was:

"In July 1962, I left a promising job as sales manager for Kelly Foods to work with Glen Hayes when he bought Lennert. I came with him mostly because I was anxious to see how a guy who buys and sells companies works . . . The past 11 months, since we took over, have really been rough. Although I've worked like a dog, the company is not going particularly well. It will take at least four more years to turn it around, diversify the product line and get some long-run stability. I've done well with the company so far; the sale of common stock Hayes gave me when I joined him has netted me a capital gain of close to $25,000. But why should I stick with it when there are so many other opportunities that look so much better. Hayes has already checked out a couple of possibilities, and I've got a couple in mind that he doesn't know about. Also I left my old company with a standing offer, that would soon get me to the top rank of the New York head office.

"I'm sure Hayes will slowly drop out of active participation in Lennert now that the stock price has dropped. Besides he's not the kind of guy who sticks with any company for very long unless there is a capital gain potential. When he goes there is no one but myself that is presently capable of taking over. If I stayed with Lennert, the whole operation would probably be mine, with a big salary, in four or five years . . . And it could be argued that I have some responsibility to the shareholders to keep the thing going."

Source: This case was prepared by George S. Day, lecturer, under the direction of Professor Donald H. Thain, as the basis for class discussion rather than to illustrate either effective or ineffective handling of an administrative situation. Copyright 1963 by the University of Western Ontario, School of Business Administration. Reprinted by permission.

Company history

The Lennert Company was founded in 1933 by Carl Lennert of Oshawa. The original assets of the company were a new idea for producing hand lawnmowers and $4,700 that Carl Lennert raised by mortgaging his farm. Although sales were confined to the Oshawa-Toronto area, the company was able to survive and grow in the depressed market of the 1930s. However, due to material restrictions Carl Lennert suspended operations in 1940 and enlisted in the army.

In 1946 Carl Lennert was joined by two other ex-servicemen, who were able to supply some of the skills the company previously lacked. Their first major success came in 1947 when a large department store ordered 500 mowers. Money was borrowed to finance the sale and operations were expanded. For the next 10 years the three owners were fully engrossed in the company. They worked seven-day weeks, there were few vacations for anyone, salaries were limited and all expenses were carefully controlled. All problems were faced by the three men as a team. Both individually and together they had a strong determination to grow and succeed.

By 1958 the company was apparently financially sound (see Exhibit 4-1) with an established position in the field. The early diversification into power mowers and cultivators had proven very successful in capitalizing on the suburbanite's desire to work on his own lawn and garden.

Exhibit 4-1 Summary of financial results ($000's). December 31

	1954	1955	1955	1956	1957	1958	1959	1960	1961
Sales	$1,019	$995	$1,265	$1,478	$1,550	$1,920	$2,380	$2,451	$2,550
Earnings (after tax)	22	(3)	10	40	67	75	110	125	120
Working capital	201	230	225	303	340	328	465	505	490
Net worth	280	300	297	307	331	406	464	545	595

The attainment of a measure of success and security was followed by a change and a broadening of the owners' motivations and interests. One believed that the company should diversify into less seasonal products, the second became active on the local town council, and Carl Lennert, then 55, became concerned about having all his funds tied up in the company. In addition he lost his previous enthusiasm for new product development and was less interested in working long hours.

The changes in the owners' attitudes took place at the same time that the company's once bright future prospects were noticeably dimming. Despite the warning signs the owners found it increasingly difficult to reach any agreement among themselves as to the company's future operations.

By 1962 the company was still able to generate satisfactory profits, but faced the following adverse trends:

1. In 1958 two large U.S. manufacturers entered the Canadian power lawn-mower and power garden equipment market. The impact of their consumer advertising and aggressive merchandising was beginning to be felt.
2. Private brand business had grown from 41% of sales in 1958 to 69% in 1962. The two largest private brand customers, a department store and an automotive supply chain accounting for 35% and 22% of the company sales respectively, were pressing for price reductions.
3. At the same time, consumers were switching their preference to cheaper private brands, from the premium-priced brand names.
4. The May 1962 dollar devaluation and import surcharge had abruptly stopped all imports of a popular gasoline-powered garden tiller that Lennert merchandised under its own name. The garden tiller was an integral part of the product line although sales volume was too low to warrant manufacture and assembly by Lennert.
5. Industry annual sales of power lawn-mowers were expected to decline slightly in the next five years as the market in existing homes became saturated and the rate of new home formations declined.

On June 27, 1962, the three owners completed negotiations for the sale of the company to Glen Hayes. Hayes had spent the previous two months inquiring into the problems of the company, after being introduced to one of the co-owners. The reasons for his growing interest in the situation, as he studied the company, became clearer with a better understanding of his background and motivations.

Glen Hayes was born in 1931, into a middle-class Hamilton, Ontario, family. He showed great promise and intelligence by ranking at or near the head of most of his classes in public school, private preparatory school, and engineering at McGill University. Following graduation from McGill and two years working for a large oil company, he enrolled in the MBA program of a well-known western U.S. business school. His pattern of behavior at the business school was noticeably different from McGill, where he participated in extracurricular activities. Although an excellent athlete, and previously active in student affairs, he was just "too busy" to spend time on these extracurricular activities. To his classmates he appeared aloof and reserved. In class he was regarded as a skeptic, one who constantly challenged many of the basic ideas and concepts that most others readily accepted.

During the time in the MBA program, his ambitions, while complex, crystallized to the point where one stood out to his intimate friends "to make a million dollars before I'm 30." To help achieve this objective he spent the two years following his graduation working for a well-known corporation lawyer in New York City. The lawyer, who was mainly involved in "setting up companies," had a widely known reputation as a sharp financial manipulator. Hayes had an opportunity to learn the lawyer's methods from close personal observations as he appraised various investment opportunities, planned company reorganizations, and worked on the broad problems of defining corporate strategies and structures under the supervision of the lawyer.

Hayes left the lawyer's firm following a fundamental disagreement about the prospects of a proposed speculative electronic apparatus manufacturer. To back up his conviction about the bright future of this company he borrowed heavily and bought enough common shares to gain a controlling interest in this company. He was 28 at this time. Three months after his 30th birthday his controlling interest in the company was acquired for a $1,500,000 cash payment by a large electronics company.

Following this success, he and his Canadian wife decided to return to Canada, primarily because he saw Canada as an interesting geographical area for "creative strategic opportunities." A big advantage, in his view, was the much debated lack of initiative or entrepreneurial drive of Canadians, and the consequent lack of domestic risk capital. The four months following his return to Canada were spent intensively studying a number of "potential investment" opportunities. On June 27, 1962, he purchased the Lennert Company Limited.

Take-over by Glen Hayes

Hayes found all three owners very receptive to his offer to purchase their interest in the company. Since both parties were well aware of the company's clouded and difficult future, the price of $500,000, based on a compromise between the capitalized earnings and adjusted net worth was reached after a short, uninvolved period of negotiations. Before the negotiations were started the owners had separately expressed their concern over the lack of adequate estate provisions for their families and the problems that the death of one of the top management trio would create.

The agreement called for an immediate cash down payment of $20,000 which amounted to an option-to-purchase, and a lump sum payment of $480,000, before the end of October 1962. Hayes' intent was to pay the balance owing with the proceeds from a large stock placement. The placement was to be made in the name of a newly-formed holding company, Lennert (1962) Limited, with an authorized share structure of 100,000 common. The first asset of the company was the option-to-purchase, which Hayes assigned to the company in exchange for 15,000 shares of Lennert (1962) Ltd.

After the holding company was established, Hayes worked out an arrangement with an investment broker who had a reputation for specializing in "risk situations," and who would arrange an over-the-counter placement for about 10% of the proceeds. It was agreed that 56,000 shares, priced at $10.00 per share would find a ready market among the investment broker's "lists and customers." The necessary legal and accounting arrangements were handled by a lawyer, who settled for 2% of the proceeds, and a chartered accountant, who agreed to a fee of $9,000, which was about 2% of the proceeds.

To pave the way for the stock issue, planned for September 1962, Hayes retained a well-known firm of public relations consultants. Their job was to publicize the change in management, the proposed product changes and innovations, and the impetus that the transfusion of capital would provide. A series of brochures and bulletins were planned to constantly publicize the company's "enlarged prospects and bright future." For further help in creating "a dynamic and successful image" he approached a good friend, Harry Fielding, a graduate of the University of Western Ontario MBA program, with a reputation as a shrewd and resourceful marketing man. His work with Kelly Foods Co. had been publicized on a number of occasions.

Hayes's offer to Fielding

The substance of Hayes's comments during his dinner meeting with Fielding was: "This operation is going to be too big for me. Only one of the previous management group is remaining with the company, and I don't have too much confidence in him. I want someone in here with me who thinks as I do. Besides the big problems are all in the marketing area where you can really exercise your skills . . . If you come aboard you'll have your present salary plus 2,500 common shares of Lennert (1962) Limited that I will give you in exchange for a contract to stay with the company for two years.

"As I see it, we'll either make or break it within the next two years. But, regardless of what happens you'll be able to sell your common for a big gain. This offer doesn't mean that you have a long-term commitment to me—you can be on your own in two years if you wish."

Harry Fielding spent most of his time during the next week pondering the offer. He realized that the offer was an unparalleled opportunity, which might not present itself again, to learn the pattern on which many business fortunes were made. He recalled that many times in bull sessions back at school he and his classmates had agreed, "You'll never make money on a salary. You've got to get into a small company, own a piece of the action and go for capital gains." He couldn't help but consider, at the same time, a situation with which he was personally familiar. A friend, and the owner of a successful medium-sized company, was 64 years old and seriously concerned about the condition of his estate. In Fielding's estimation, the situation would be "ripe for a change" in about three years time, and if properly handled could be highly profitable.

The offer meant facing up to some basic personal questions that he had never before considered. The attraction of the stimulating kind of life that Hayes led, and the assurance of large financial gains, overcame his uncertainty about substituting a secure job in a large corporation for what was admittedly a risky situation.

Activities—September 1962 to July 1963

The broker encountered some resistance to the issue of Lennert (1962) Ltd. common, despite the favorable publicity received during the summer. The poor response was blamed on the continuing lack of confidence of the small investor in common stocks of any kind, following the sharp price decline in the spring. Nevertheless, by October 12, 1962, the 57,000 common shares were sold at a price very close to $10.00 per share and the purchase was completed.

During October and November the stock market rose strongly from the summer's low point. The general price rise, combined with the continuing stream of publicity pushed the price of Lennert (1962) Ltd. stock to $14.00 per share in December. Both Hayes and Fielding instructed their broker to feed as many of their own shares into the market as could be absorbed without causing a price break. By May 1963 each man had disposed of over 70% of his personal holdings at a net capital gain (after brokerage fees) of $14.00 per share.

During this time, both men devoted the majority of their time to the problems of the business. Despite their efforts the adverse market and competitive influences were only partially countered. The December 31 statement for 1962, made public on June 20, 1963, after a deliberate two months delay, showed that the past sales levels were maintained only at the cost of a reduction in after-tax earnings to $47,000. Two days after the news was released, the common stock price dropped to $8.50 per share, despite carefully planned publicity that explained the temporary nature of the reverse. Hayes asked Fielding to sit down with him later in the week, to appraise their current position and prospects.

Case 5

J. R. Sanford Corporation (A)

In August, 1958, Richard Trent, a member of the small business consulting firm of Baker and Trent, Inc., was wondering whether to make an offer to purchase the J. R. Sanford Corporation. The Sanford company was a leading producer of certain kinds of automatic paper-handling equipment for use in offices and printing shops; net sales were about $400,000 in 1957. However, the company was near bankruptcy, and Mr. Trent had been asked if he wished to make a purchase offer.

Mr. Trent's background

After graduation from high school in 1936, Mr. Trent spent the next six years with a Boston utility company, working his way up from office boy to assistant to the vice-president. From 1942 to 1945, he served in the army. He then completed the undergraduate course at Harvard in three years and followed that by attending the Harvard Business School. From 1950 to 1952, he was in the planning department of a large West Coast aircraft manufacturer, and from 1952 to 1955 he served on special assignments with National Metals, Inc., a small manufacturing firm. He left the company in 1955 to establish a business consulting firm with Arthur Baker, who had formerly held administrative positions in several small firms. During the next three years, Baker and Trent provided business consulting services for many small businesses and also acted as brokers in finding buyers for certain firms.

Although Mr. Trent had earned a living from consulting, he had found the experience to be frustrating. One problem was the difficulty in getting businessmen to recognize problems and to take corrective action. He said,

Source: This case was prepared by A. C. Cooper and R. B. Wood under the direction of Professor W. A. Hosmer, Harvard University, Graduate School of Business Administration, as the basis for class discussion rather than to illustrate either effective or ineffective administration. Copyright © 1960 by the President and Fellows of Harvard College. Reproduced by permission.

"Many men acquire or found a business for noneconomic reasons, related more to a way of life than making a profit. They do not think in terms of improving their return on investment, but rather in terms of maintaining a comfortable existence. If the consultant makes a suggestion, such as the development of specific accounting data bearing on one of the firm's problems, the manager may reject the advice, more because he dislikes working with figures than because he has thought through the suggestion.

"Another problem is that many managers of small businesses think a consulting firm is a nonprofit institution. Consulting is like medicine in that the patient may decide in retrospect that his recovery was so easy the doctor or consultant couldn't have done much and wasn't worth the fee. They have an emotional resistance to paying fees of $100 per day, which are needed to ensure the consultant a reasonable return after providing for business expenses. A consultant cannot afford to get a reputation as a man who has to sue to collect, so he is foredoomed to failure." Because of these difficulties, Mr. Trent was considering leaving the consulting field when, in November, 1957, Baker and Trent was asked to advise the J. R. Sanford company, located in Middletown, Massachusetts.

History of the Sanford company

The company was founded by J. R. Sanford, in Middletown, Massachusetts, in 1949. Mr. Sanford, an engineer, designed the paper-handling equipment which the company had been selling since that time.

The company's products included collating machines and machines making carbon snap-out forms. Collating machines arranged sheets of paper in a designated order as part of the process of making booklets or of assembling office papers. With a folding device attached, the collator could assemble flat sheets of paper into complete booklets of up to 64 pages. The Sanford machines were automatic and, depending on the size, could collate from 18,000 to 72,000 sheets per hour. The price of these machines ranged from $4,000 to $16,000 apiece. Forms-making machines were used to glue sheets of paper together along one edge with little spots of glue. Carbon interleaved business forms were a typical product of this process. The price of these machines ranged from $1,100 to $2,800.

There were two principal competitors in the collating machine market. One was the Thompson Equipment Company, a manufacturer of printing equipment and supplies. Thompson Equipment sales totaled $35 million in 1956, which was the last year for which data were available at the time Mr. Trent came to consult with Sanford in 1957. The other principal competitor, American Office Equipment, Inc., specialized in office supplies and equipment, and had sales of $70 million in 1956. For both companies, sales of collating machines were only a small percentage of total company sales. Competition in the forms-making machine market came from several very small companies, each of which accounted for only a small fraction of industry sales.

Industry sales of automatic forms-making machines were estimated at $300,000 for 1956, of which Sanford accounted for about 80 percent. Sanford sales of collating machines totaled about $160,000 in 1956, which was about 20 percent of the industry total. Both markets were expected to grow with the increased tendency toward automated office procedures; it was expected that the collating market would grow more rapidly.

Net sales of the Sanford company climbed from $205,000 in 1949 to $535,000 by 1951. The Sanford management believed its machines to be more economical, more compact, and faster than competitive machines. Comparative performance data for collators as prepared by the Sanford management in 1957 are given in Exhibit 5-1. However, sales dropped after 1951, and were $403,000 in 1956. Losses occurred in all years after 1953. Available financial data for the years 1949 through 1956 are given in Exhibits 5-2 and 5-3.

Exhibit 5-1 Comparative performance data for collators[a] as determined by Sanford management

Company	Price[b]	Speed (sheets per hour)	Size (floor space in sq. ft.)
American Office Equipment	$5,700	5,000	12.4
Thompson Equipment[a]	$4,700 to $6,900	16,000	25.0
Sanford[a]	$3,800 to $4,500	18,000	4.9

[a]Four-station machine without folding attachment.
[b]Depends upon the sheet sizes.
Source: Dealer bulletin prepared by the Sanford company in 1957.

The situation

In attempting to assist the Sanford company, Mr. Trent investigated various company activities. He found that all products were marketed through a network of 140 United States dealers and through two company-owned sales offices in Chicago and New York. The dealers received a 25 percent discount from list price, and were expected to install and service the machines as well as train the operators. All dealers also handled other items of printing and office equipment. Dealerships were not exclusive; for example, in Los Angeles there were seven dealers.

Mr. Sanford also personally arranged direct sales to any customers who answered the company's advertisements in trade magazines; dealers were not given a commission on these sales. In 1957, about 50 percent of total sales were made in this way. This created a problem in that dealers were reluctant to service machines they had not sold. In Mr. Trent's opinion, this practice was disrupting the morale of the dealers and converting them into mere order takers.

The company was housed in a modern building containing 20,000 square feet of floor space, which was being used at about 50 percent of capacity in 1957. The building was owned by a separate corporation which

	1949	195...
Gross sales	$220,760	
Less: dealer and cash discounts	15,744	
Net sales	$204,986	
Beginning inventory[a]	$ 33,672	
Purchases	66,982	
Direct labor	n.a.	
Manufacturing overhead	n.a.	
Total	$100,654	
Less: ending inventory[a]	10,989	
Cost of goods sold	$ 89,665	
Gross margin	$115,321	
General and administrative expenses	n.a.	
Selling and shipping expenses	n.a.	
Total	$ 70,775	
Net operating profit	$ 44,546	
Other income	—	
	$ 44,546	
Less: interest	n.a.	
Net profit (loss) before taxes	$ 44,546	
Less: taxes	14,116	
Net profit (loss) after taxes	$ 30,430	

[a]Inventories include only material and direct labor.
Note: These income statements were available to Mr. Trent at the time he was asked to advise the Sanford company in November 1957.
n.a. = not available.

Assets	1949	1950
Cash		$ 16,204
Accounts receivable		102,698
Inventory[a]		17,538
Total		$136,450
Machinery and equipment (net)		n.a.
Furniture and fixtures (net)		n.a.
Total		$ 14,765
Reserve (finance company)		—
Deposits		$ 9,656
Other	MISSING	—
Total		$ 9,656
Total assets		$160,861
Liabilities and capital		
Accounts payable		$ 22,523
Notes payable		—
Accrued payroll and expense		—
Withholding taxes payable		736
Customers' deposits		—
Taxes accrued		47,792
Total		$ 71,051
Long-term note		—
Capital stock outstanding		$ 46,390
Retained earnings		43,419
Total		$ 89,809
Total liabilities and capital		$160,861

[a]Inventories include only materials and direct labor.
[b]Included in taxes accrued.
Note: These balance sheets were available to Mr. Trent in November 1957.
n.a. = not available.

1951	1952	1953	1954	1955	1956
608,111		$515,438	n.a.	n.a.	$453,418
73,023		55,128	n.a.	n.a.	49,565
535,088		$460,310	$365,667	$415,993	$403,853
n.a.		$ 69,626	n.a.	n.a.	$ 87,170
n.a.		139,397	n.a.	n.a.	123,502
n.a.		33,983	n.a.	n.a.	43,118
n.a.		77,361	n.a.	n.a.	131,301
n.a.	M	$320,367	n.a.	n.a.	$385,089
n.a.	I	72,089	n.a.	n.a.	97,737
247,086	S	$248,278	$240,837	$312,562	$287,352
288,002	S	$212,032	$124,850	$103,431	$116,501
n.a.	I	n.a.	n.a.	n.a.	$102,641
n.a.	N	n.a.	n.a.	n.a.	38,103
255,706	G	$159,649	$160,102	$131,023	$140,744
32,296		$ 52,383	$ (35,253)	$ (27,593)	$ (24,243)
7,685		—	495	—	314
39,981		$ 52,383	$ (34,758)	$ (27,593)	$ (23,929)
n.a.		n.a.	n.a.	n.a.	2,299
39,981		$ 52,383	$ (34,758)	$ (27,593)	$ (26,228)
12,755		20,597	(9,255)	(9,627)	n.a.
27,226		$ 31,786	$ (25,503)	$ (17,965)	$ (26,228)

Exhibit 5-2 Income statements for years ending December 31, 1949–1956

1951	1952	1953	1954	1955	1956
1,353		$ 8,103	$ 2,719	$ 1,128	$ 2,390
43,193		79,384	42,205	55,574	38,667
54,629		72,089	76,937	87,170	97,737
99,175		$159,576	$121,861	$143,872	$138,794
n.a.		n.a.	n.a.	n.a.	n.a.
n.a.		n.a.	n.a.	n.a.	n.a.
46,500		$ 53,516	$ 64,194	$ 65,134	$ 61,292
—		—	—	$ 1,795	$ 4,328
9,918		$ 4,860	—	4,346	—
—		2,719	$ 34,423	24,715	5,303
9,918	M	$ 7,579	$ 34,423	$ 30,856	$ 9,631
155,593	I	$220,671	$220,478	239,861	$209,717
	S				
21,164	S	$ 37,714	$ 52,923	$ 85,159	$ 85,380
—	I	—	6,144	18,706	8,184
—	N	1,200	6,221 b	4,887 b	6,678 b
1,012	G	3,526			
—		—	4,466	13,293	10,815
16,380		25,508	23,504	6,075	15,228
38,556		$ 67,948	$ 93,258	$128,120	$126,285
—		—		$ 2,486	$ 408
46,390		$ 46,390	$ 46,390	$ 46,390	$ 46,390
70,646		106,333	80,829	62,864	36,635
117,036		$152,723	$127,219	$109,255	$ 83,025
155,592		$220,671	$220,478	$239,861	$209,717

Exhibit 5-3 Balance sheets as of December 31, 1949–1956

was wholly owned by Mr. Sanford; rent was $1,100 per month and did not include heat, taxes, or insurance. In November, 1957, there were 25 employees in the Middletown plant, two of whom, in addition to Mr. Sanford, served in an executive capacity. However, it appeared to Mr. Trent that most decisions in all areas of company activity were being made by Mr. Sanford.

There were also eight engineers in a research and development laboratory located in Chicago; the cost of maintaining this laboratory was approximately $50,000 per year. In the income statement, this was charged in part to manufacturing overhead. Few improvements or developments had come out of this laboratory, apparently due in part to a rapid turnover in technical personnel. Mr. Trent thought this turnover was due to personal differences between Mr. Sanford and the technical men involved.

Production involved machining of certain parts, assembling, painting, and buffing. The operations performed were typical of many machine shops and, in Mr. Trent's opinion, did not require any special skills. The equipment included lathes, drill presses, and assembly benches—all in excellent condition. Mr. Trent thought there was enough equipment to produce for annual sales of about $1 million.

Mr. Sanford owned 90 percent of the stock. The remaining 10 percent of the stock was owned by Ralph Beller, who did general administrative work. Although records were incomplete, it appeared that Mr. Sanford was drawing a salary of about $50,000 per year and was also charging about $50,000 per year in personal expenses to the company. Loans on accounts receivable and equipment totaling about $13,000 had been obtained from a local finance company at interest rates of 18 percent per year.

Apparently, records were not kept in a consistent manner, and some transactions were not even recorded. There was no knowledge of product costs, and it appeared that the financial statements had not been prepared with sufficient care to be reliable. Such records as had been prepared had not been preserved systematically, so that, as can be seen in Exhibits 5-2 to 5-5, some of the balance sheets and income statements were missing entirely.

After his investigation, Mr. Trent made a number of suggestions designed to improve the management of the company. However, Mr. Sanford did not follow the suggestions; Baker and Trent therefore broke off the association. Eight months later, in late July, 1958, Mr. Trent received a distress telephone call from Mr. Sanford.

Mr. Trent arrived to discover that the company's position had deteriorated considerably. Records indicated there had been a net loss of $38,000 for 1957. Financial data for 1957 and the first six months of 1958 are given in Exhibits 5-4 and 5-5. From a consideration of liabilities and assets, Mr. Trent estimated that the company would have a negative net worth of $30,000 if liquidated at that time. Two signatures were already on a bankruptcy petition. Back payroll taxes had not been paid for two years. It appeared that Mr. Sanford might be liable personally for certain of the company's debts, in which case he might lose his home, his car, and the building.

Exhibit 5-4 Income statements for year ending December 31, 1957, and for six months ending July 30, 1958

	1957	1958 (unaudited)
Gross sales	$453,041	$199,076
Less: dealer and cash discounts	49,468	29,338
Net sales	$403,573	$169,738
Beginning inventory[a]	$ 97,737	$ 81,586
Purchases	127,954	38,088
Direct labor	32,356	12,752
Manufacturing overhead	122,752	44,784
Total	$380,799	$177,210
Less: ending inventory[a]	81,586	59,124
Costs of goods sold	$299,213	$118,086
Gross margin	$104,360	$ 51,652
General and administrative expense	$113,092	$ 67,710
Selling and shipping expense	29,770	9,440
Research and development	—	2,082
Total	$142,862	$ 79,232
Net operating profit	$ (38,502)	$ (27,580)
Other income	1,469	—
Total	$ (37,033)	$ (27,580)
Less: interest	1,847	2,647
Net profit (loss) before taxes	$ (38,880)	$ (30,227)
Less: taxes	—	—
Net profit (loss) after taxes	$ (38,880)	$ (30,227)

[a]Inventories include only material and direct labor.

Note: In addition to earlier financial statements, these were available to Mr. Trent in July 1958.

Mr. Trent told him that he could have aided him eight months or even six months before, but that it was now too late. Mr. Sanford replied by offering to sell his share of the company to Mr. Trent. He pointed out that since the financial situation was so urgent, a decision would have to be made within 24 hours.

The decision

Mr. Trent did not have time to secure an audit of the company's records. He was aware that errors or misrepresentations might exist in the records. He made a personal examination of the inventory and decided that it was undervalued and was probably worth at least twice the $59,000 listed on the balance sheet. Although his previous association with the company as a consultant had been brief, he was aware that a number of improvements could be made in the management of the company. It also appeared to him that the company's products were well designed and superior to competitive products.

Although Mr. Trent had no personal funds that he could invest, he knew of a friend from whom he could secure a long-term loan for $10,000. He had about decided that consulting with small businesses was a dead-end street. He had seen the poor management practices of many managers of small enterprises, including a lack of knowledge of costs and an inability to think in economic terms. It might be easier, he thought, to compete against small businessmen than to advise them.

Mr. Trent realized that, except for his judgment based upon inspection of the inventory, he had little evidence of assets. He was not at all sure the financial statement showed all the liabilities. He was not so familiar as he would wish to be with customer relations and with attitudes of customers and dealers toward the company. Nevertheless, he realized that he would have to give Mr. Sanford an answer the next day.

Exhibit 5-5 Balance sheets as of December 31, 1957, and July 30, 1958

	1957	1958 (unaudited)
Assets		
Cash	$ 576	$ 2,094
Accounts receivable	38,628	38,523
Inventory[a]	81,586	59,124
Total	$120,790	$ 99,741
Machinery and equipment (net)	n.a.	n.a.
Furniture and fixtures (net)	n.a.	n.a.
Total	$ 58,143	$ 48,321
Reserve (finance company)	$ 6,425	$ 5,923
Deposits	—	825
Other	6,557	13,932
Total	$ 12,982	$ 20,680
Total assets	$191,915	$168,742
Liabilities and capital		
Accounts payable	$ 89,471	$ 72,821
Notes payable	11,981	23,093
Accrued payroll and expenses	4,080	3,749
Customers' deposits	10,192	4,664
Taxes accrued	20,772	9,867
Total	$136,496	$114,194
Long-term note	$ 1,275	$ 7,297
Capital stock outstanding	$ 46,390	$ 46,390
Donated surplus	10,000	33,333
Retained earnings	(2,246)	(32,472)
Total	$ 55,419	$ 54,548
Total liabilities and capital	$191,915	$168,742

[a]Inventories include only material and direct labor.
Note: In addition to earlier financial statements, these were available to Mr. Trent in July 1958.
n.a. = not available.

Index

A

Abramson, Adolph G. 88
Abt Associates 548–549
Acceptance theory 142–144
Accountability 175
Accounting
budgets and 472
decentralization in 184–185
external auditing and 486–487
human-assets 548–550
staff 195–196
Achievement motivation 406
Actuating *see* Influencing
Adult life cycle 321–322
Affirmative action programs 333–334
Agarwala-Rogers, Rekha 521–522
Aims *see* Objectives
Allen, Louis A. 219
Allport, Gordon W. 384
American Institute of Management 544–545
American Management Association (AMA) 79, 80, 92, 242, 329
American Society of Mechanical Engineers (ASME) 24–26
American Telephone and Telegraph (AT&T) 312, 314, 334
Animal Farm **(Orwell)** 71
Antitrust policy 82

Appealed policy 62
Appraisal of employees 304–324
assessment center 312
difficulties in 311–312
of executives 323–324
by MBO 315–319
process of 307–310
system of 304–307
Apprenticeship training 426
Argyris, Chris 417, 473
ASME 24–26
Assessment center 312
Assigning duties 171–172
Assistant-to positions 201–202, 327, 339–340
AT&T 312, 314, 334
Attitudes
bureaucracy's effect on 231–232
human 385–388
motivation and 404–405
Audits
by American Institute of Management 544–545
external 486–487
internal 483–484
by management 544–545
by outside consultants 545
self- 544
social 548–550
Authority 139–151, 168–197, 372–377
acceptance theory of 142–144

Authority (cont.)
bases of   145, 372–373
centralization and   254
charismatic   145, 373
compliance with   373–374
concept of   139–151
decentralization of   176–187
definitions of   139, 143
delegation of   168–176
formal   140–141
functional   147–148, 193–197, 373
granting of   172–174
influencing by   372–377
legal-rational   145, 373
limited   193
line   192–193
nature of   139–140
organizational character of   144–149
organizing and   130–131
personal   148, 373
positional   147, 373
power and   375–377
scalar chain of   32, 169–170, 188
source of   139–140
staff   192–197
traditional   145, 373
types of   147–148, 372
unity of command and   170–171
Autocratic leadership   414
Automobile industry   153

B

Babbage, Charles   24
Balance sheet, budgeted   466
Bank of America   138–139
Bar chart   104–107
Barnard, Chester I.   13, 32–33, 142–143, 176, 219
Barriers to communication   see Communication barriers
Barry Corporation   550
Baughman, James P.   113
Bavelas, Alex   533
Bayesian procedure   507

Behavior
attitudes and   385–388
bureaucracy's effect on   232
control and   450–451
as goal directed   404–406
group influence on   399–400
needs and   388–390
in the organization   380–390
perception and   380–385
values   385–388
Behavioral sciences
applied to management   31, 41–42
influencing and   370–371
Bell, Cecil H., Jr.   427
Bell, Daniel   77
Benefit-audit statement   356
Benge, Eugene   99
Bennis, Warren G.   418
Bierstedt, Robert   144
Blomstrom, Robert L.   548
Boards of directors   228, 464
Boeing, William   38
Bonus systems   349–351
"Bottom-up" management   178
Bounded rationality   512–513
Boush, Andrew C.   114
Bray, Douglas W.   323–324
Break-even analysis   477–479
Bross, Irwin   509
Brown, Alvin   220, 226
Budgetary control, defined   461
Budget committee   463–464
Budgeted balance sheet   466
Budgeted income statements   465–466
Budgets   460–475
administration of   464–468
alternative   469
capital expenditure   467–468
cash   468
comprehensive   461
continuous   469
control over   460–461
finished-goods   466
flexibility of   468–471
as forecasts   102–103
materials   466–467

numerical terms of 461
operations 465–466
other management activities and 471–474
partial 461
periodic 469
personnel 467
plans as basis for 102–103
preparation of 462–464
production of 466
review of 470–471
sales 465
supplemental monthly 470
variable expense 470
Bureaucratic problems 231–237
delegation as 234–236
for the organization 232–237
for people 231–232
rules as 233–235
Burnham, James 33
Burns, Tom 256–257
Business climate, and planning 81
Business objectives see Objectives

C

Capital expenditure budget 467–468
Capital funds 181
Capital generation 46–47
Capital standards 455
Career planning 318
Carroll, Lewis 508
Carson, Rachel 47
Cash budget 468
Cash forecast 101–102
Centralization
extent of 176
organizational design and 254, 258–259
in small organizations 177
See also Decentralization
Certainty, in decision theory 503–504
Chairperson, for committees 248–249

Change
executive development and 321–331
organizational climate and 418
organizational design and 421
in organizations 425–428
resistance to 532
Channels of communication see Communication channels
Charismatic authority 145, 373
Charts see Organization charts
Chief executive
salary of 346
staffing responsibility of 286
See also Executives
Choice process 409
Chrysler Corporation 158
CH2M-Hill 263–266
Cicero 153
Circular organization charts 211–212
Clark, C. Spencer 45–46
Classical management 28–32
Climate, organizational 417–422
Closed-loop control systems 447–448
Coaching 327–328
Coch, Lester 426
College recruitment 332–333
College training programs 329
Committees 238–251
assets of 240–242
chairperson for 248–249
effective operation of 245–249
faculty-student 250
groupthink by 244
liabilities of 242–245
line 239
staff 239
standing 240
temporary 239–240
training by service on 342
types of 239–240
Communication
by actions 534–535
barriers to 529–535
channels of 523–527

Communication (cont.)
defined 10, 521
effectiveness in 532–535
by experts 535
feedback as 533–534
government policy on 83
as linking process 14, 521–536
listening's role in 534
media for 527–528
modern technology of 44
nature of 523
oral 528
of plans 74–75
of policy 62–63
relationships in 523, 535
sensitivity in 534
in small groups 395
written 528

Communication barriers 529–535
language as 530–532
listening and 534
methods for overcoming 532–535
organizational structure and 529
position and 529–530
resistance to change and 532
status and 529–530

Communication channels 523–527
diagonal 524–525
downward 524–525
formal 524–525
grapevine 525–527
informal 525–527
lateral 524–525
upward 524–525

Compensation 345–358
benefit-audit statement of 356
deferred 353–354
direct financial 346–355
external competition's effect on 347–349
incentive bonuses as 349–351
indirect financial 355
internal consistency on 347–348
merit 317–318
pension plans as 353–355
perquisites as 355

profit sharing as 353
salaries as 346–349
stock options as 351–352

Competency theory 406
Competition, and executive salaries 347–349
Complexity in organizations 543–544
Complex organizations 2, 40–41
Computers
effect on decentralization 187
management control and 476
Consultants
audit by 545
use in development programs 329–330
Content, latent vs. manifest 534
Contingency approach
effectiveness and 538–552
forecasting as 92
to management 6–7, 37–38
to objectives 52
Contingency model of leadership 413
Continuous budgeting 469
Controller 468
Controlling 443–498
after-the-fact 444
basic steps in 453–454
by budget 460–475
cases on 490–498
coordination in 227
decentralization and 182
definition of 446
as management function 12
models of 447–449
of overall performance 476–488
planning and 70, 80–81
process of 446–459
standards for 454–455
See also Control systems; Control techniques
Control systems 447–459
checking on performance by 456–457
design of 451–453

feedback in   447—448
human aspects of   449—451
models of   447—449
standards for   454—455
steps in control process   453—459
strategic control points   455—456
taking corrective action with   457
See also Controlling
Control techniques   476—488
break-even analysis   477—479
control unit   484—486
external auditing   486—487
internal auditing   483—484
profit-and-loss   479—482
as return on investment   480—483
Cooke, Morris L.   24, 28
Cooperation
committee as aid to   240
as distinct from coordination   219—220
Cooperative system   32—33
Coordination   217—230
budgeting and   472—473
committee as aid to   240
cooperation as distinct from   219—220
definitions of   218—219, 226—227
diagonal   224
difficulties of   220—221
division of labor and   217—218
in effective organizations   226—227
of external relationships   229
horizontal   222—223
by liaison people   227
managerial functions and   225—226
methods of   221—222
by mutual adjustment   222
by plan   221—222
self-   220
by standardization   221
types of   222—224
vertical   222—223
Cordiner, Ralph J.   181
Correlation analysis   90
Cosmopolitans   257—258

Costs
fixed   478
standards for   454
variable   478
Counseling   327—328
CPAs, auditing by   486—487
Critical path method (CPM)   104, 109—110
Crossen, William   203
Cross-relationships   134—135
Cultural environment   4—5
Customer, departmentalization based on   162—163

D
Dale, Ernest   176
Davis, Keith   545—546, 548
Davis, Ralph C.   30, 219
Decentralization   176—187
in accounting   184—185
advantages of   179
amount of   179—183
bottom-up   178
centralization and   176—177, 254, 258—259
computer systems and   187
coordination and   217—218
disadvantages of   179
in finance   183—184
limited   177
in marketing   184
in personnel   186
in production   183
profit-center   185—186
progressive   178
in purchasing   186
timing of   178
trend toward   186—188
Decision making   501—520
under certainty   503—504
conditions for   503—511
definitions of   10, 503
game theory and   518
group   514—515
linear programming and   519
as linking process   13—14
operations research and   515—519

Decision making (cont.)
organizational design and 513–514
prediction systems and 509–510
probability and 505, 518
process of 502–503, 508
programmed 513
queuing theory and 518
rationality and 510–513
rational model of 503–504
under risk 504–506
roles in 426–427
rules for 514
stages in 506
states of nature and 505–506
under uncertainty 507–511
Defense policy 83
Deferred compensation 353–354
Delegation 168–176
assigning duties by 171–172
in a bureaucracy 234–236
creating responsibility by 175–176
defined 254
granting authority by 172–174
scalar chain of 169–170
unity of command and 170–171
Delphi method of forecasting 85
Demand for executives 292–297
Democratic leadership 414
Dent, James K. 9, 52–54
Departmentalization 154–166
composite 164–165
by customer 162–163
differentiation and 252–253
by equipment 163
functional 155–158
geographical 161–162
by process 163
by product 158–161, 178
by time 163–164
Department of Defense 473
Design, organizational 252–268
centralization and 254
characteristics of 252–254
constraints on 255–258
differentiation in 252–253
effectiveness and 542–543
environmental effects on 256–257
examples of 258–260
formalization of 253
goals and 255
matrix 260–266
technology's effect on 257
Development of executives see Executive development
Diagonal coordination 224
Dickson, William J. 30
Differential rate 25
Differentiation 252–253, 258–260
Directing see Influencing
Directorates, interlocking 228
Discrimination, and recruitment 333–334
Dissatisfiers 407–408
Divided responsibility 243
Division of labor
coordination and 217–218
by delegation 168–176
by departmentalization 154–166
differentiation in 252–253
evolution of 152–155
horizontal 154–166
line and staff 189–204
specialization in 153
steps in 154
vertical 154–155, 168
See also Decentralization
Drucker, Peter F. 8, 315
duPont Corporation 214, 239, 480–482
Duties, assigning of 171–172
Dynamic environments 256

E

Economic conditions
demand for executives and 294–295

government policies' effect on 81–83
information on 86–87
Effective influence 414–415
Effectiveness 538–555
complexity and 543–544
as contingency problem 538–550
criteria for 541
efficiency rules for 542
equation for 541
management audits of 544–545
measures of 538–545
organizational design and 542–543
social responsibility and 545–550
Efficiency principles 28
Efficiency rules 542
Eisenhower, Dwight D. 131
Emerging issues 45–48
capital generation 46–47
energy 45–46
environment 47–48
Emerson, Harrington 24, 26n, 28
Emotive roles 411
Emotive satisfactions 393
Employee participation 426–427
Employee performance 304–320
Employment
changes in work force 39–40
equal 293–296, 313, 333–334
hiring policies and 360–367
Energy shortages 45–46
England, George W. 54
Environment
constraints imposed by 99
dynamic 256
of management 4–6
organizational design and 256–257
as organizational variable 7
societal/cultural 4–5
static 256
task 4–5

Equal employment opportunity
appraisals as discriminatory 313
executive demand and 293–296
recruitment and 333–334
Etzioni, Amitai 1
Evaluation see Performance appraisal
Ewing, David W. 73
Exception principle 173, 458
Exchange theory 409
Executive development 321–331
through assistants-to 327
coaching and counseling for 327
committees as training grounds for 240–241
executive obsolescence and 322–323
in-organization 324–328
by lateral transfers 325–326
out-organization 328–330
progression systems of 324–325
special projects and 326
temporary assignments and 326
Executives
attitudes on social responsibility 546
compensation for 345–358
demand for 292–297
development programs for 321–331
forecasting need for 292–303
inventories of 300–302
middle-age changes in 321–322
obsolescent 322–323
perquisites of 355
personnel program for 285–286
promotion from within 286–287
replacement tables for 300–302
rotation of 324–325, 341
skills of 299
spans of management for 132–139
staff use by 190–199
titles for 214–216
types needed 297–299
See also Managers

Expectancy theory 409
Expense forecast 101
Experts, communication by 535
External environment
organizational design and 256
See also Environment
External planning premises
  81–88
External relationships 228–229
External variables 6–7

F

Faculty-student committees 250
Fayol, Henri 28–30, 68,
  139–140, 218–219, 446
Federal Reserve Board 82
Federal Reserve Bulletin 87
Feedback
in communication 533
control and 448
from controlling process 70
Fiedler, Fred E. 413
Filley, Alan C. 200
Finance, decentralization of
  183–184
Financial capital 46–47
Finished-goods budget 466
Fiscal policy 81–82
Fixed costs 478
Follett, Mary Parker 32,
  142–143, 224–225
Follower theory 412–413
Ford Motor Company 351
Forecasting
cash 101–102
as a contingency process 92
economic variables and 78
of executive needs 292–303
expense of 94, 101
external premises and 81–88
internal premises and 88–93
organizational use of 77–79
planning premises and 79–93
prediction systems and 509–510
revenue and 101
role of 77–78
of sales 88–93

shortcomings of 93–94
techniques for 88
technological 85–86
Forecasting in Industry 89
Formal authority 140–141
Formalization
defined 173
organizational design and 253,
  258–260
Formal organization,
  defined 128
Frame of reference 381–383
Frankenhoff, William P. 113
Free rein leadership 414
French, John 426–427
French, Wendell L. 427
French bureaucracy 233–234
Friedman, Milton 57
Fuel supplies 45–46
Functional authority 147–148,
  193–197, 373
Functional decentralization
  183–185
Functional departmentalization
  155–158
Functional principle 32
Functional staff 25
Functions of management 2,
  11–12, 69

G

Galbraith, John Kenneth 39
Game theory 518
Gantt, Henry Lawrence 24,
  27, 104
Gantt chart 104
*General and Industrial
  Management* (Fayol) 29
General Electric Company 79,
  181, 328
General Motors (GM) 158, 160,
  182, 185–186, 334, 350
Geographical departmentalization
  161–162
Gielgold, William C. 318
Gilbreth, Frank Bunker 24,
  27–28

Gilbreth, Lillian Moller 24, 27–28
Given, William B., Jr. 178
GM *see* General Motors
GNP 82, 83, 85
Goal displacement 397
Goals
motivation and 404–406
organizational vs. individual 417–418
See also Objectives
Government policies
antitrust 82
communication 83
defense 83
effect on economy 81–83
fiscal 81–82
monetary 82
space 83
Graicunas, V. A. 32, 134–135
Grapevine 525–527
Graphical charting 85
Gross national product (GNP) 82, 83, 85
Groups, small 42, 391, 397
Groupthink 244
Gulick, Luther 32
Gutoff, Reuben 113

H

Halo effect 308, 384
Hamilton, Ian 131
Hawthorne Studies 30–31
Hennessy, J. H., Jr. 471
Herzberg, Frederick 406–408
Hierarchy of needs 388–390, 406–407
Hiring policies 360–367
History of management 20–34
classical period 28–32
Industrial Revolution 23–24
in preindustrial times 20–23
scientific management 24–28
transition period 32–33
Hollander, James 333
Holmes, Sandra L. 546

Horizontal coordination 222–223
Horizontal division of labor 154–166
Horizontal organization charts 210–211
Hudson Institute 77
Human aspects of managing 386–390
attitudes 385–388
needs 388–390
perception 380–385
values 385–388
Human-assets accounting 548–550
Human relations movement 30–31
Human resource system 283–285, 305
"Hygiene factors" 408

I

IBM 138, 190, 314
Implied policies 63
Imposed policy 62
Incentive systems 25, 349–351
Income tax, for executives 346–347, 351–355
Individual behavior *see* Behavior
Industrial Organization and Management (Davis) 30
Industrial Revolution 23–24
Influence gap 375–376
Influencing 369–441
by authority 372–377
behavioral analysis of 370–371
cases on 432–441
contingency factors in 377–378
human aspects of 380–390
informal relationships and 391–403
leadership and 410–416
as management function 12
motivation and 404–416
organizational climate and 417–429
other names for 370

Influencing (cont.)
by power 374–377
process of 372–379
Informal relationships 391–403
network of 397–401
small-group 391–397
working 401
Information
availability of 86–87
communication of 521–536
control techniques and 476–477
effect on objectives 59–60
electronic technology of 44
forecasting 77–95
for planning 77–95
In-organization programs 324–328
assistant-to positions 327
coaching and counseling 327–328
lateral transfers 325–326
progression systems 324–325
special projects 326
temporary assignments 326
Inputs, in systems theory 4
Interlocking directorates 228
Internal audit 483–484
Internal planning premises 88–93
Internal Revenue Service (IRS) 314, 351–352
Internal variables 6–7
International Business Machines (IBM) 138, 190, 314
Interviews, recruitment 336
Inventories, executive 300–302
IRS 314, 351–352
Issues see Emerging issues

J–K
Janis, Irving L. 244
Job change 425–426
Job descriptions 213–215
Job enlargement 425
Job enrichment 425–426
Job evaluation 348
Job satisfaction 407, 424–425
Job specification 214
Johnson, Lyndon 204
Joint ventures 228
Junior boards 342
Junior executives 341
Jury of executive opinion 89
Justice Department, Anti-Trust Division 82
Kast, Fremont E. 38
Katz, Robert L. 299
Klopfer, F. J. 515
Koontz, Harold 36
Koppers Company 485–486

L
Labor
changes in work force 39–40
delegation of 168–176
departmentalization of 154–166
division of 152–176
line and staff 189–204
Language, role of in communication 530–532
Lateral transfers 325–326
Lawrence, Paul R. 226–227, 256–257
Leadership 410–417
autocratic 414
contingency model of 413
defined 410
democratic 414
effective influence of 414–415
emotive roles and 411
follower theory of 412–413
free rein 414
informal 400
style 413–415
task roles 410
theories of 411–413
Learning principles 338
Leavitt, Harold 311
Leeper, Robert W. 385
Legal-rational authority 145, 373
Levinson, Harry 321
Liaison staff 202, 227

Life cycle
of adults 321—322
of a product 92
Likert, Rensis 420, 548
Line 189—204
authority of 192—193
budget preparation by 462—463
committees 239
defined 189
relation to staff 32, 197—204
staffing responsibilities of 285—286
Linear programming 519
Linking processes
communicating 14, 521—536
decision making 13—14, 501—520
Listening, effective 534
Locals 258
Long-range planning 97—100
Long-Range Planning for Management (Ewing) 73
Lorsch, Jay W. 226—227, 256—257

M

McClelland, David 406
McCormick, Charles P. 241
McGregor, Douglas 307, 418—420
Mack, Russell H. 88
McKinsey, James O. 544
Mahoney, Thomas A. 540—541
Management
aims of 52—54
as art vs. science 13
budgeting and 462—464, 471—474
controlling by 443—498
defined 2
effectiveness of 538—555
emerging issues in 45—48
environment of 4—6
functions of 11—12
history of 20—34
influencing by 369—441
linking by 499—536
modern 35—48
objectives of 51—60
organizing by 127—279
perspective of 17—48
planning by 49—126
policies of 60—64
process of 9—11
rationality of 9
science's contributions to 41—44
scientific 24—28
span of 130—139
staffing by 281—367
theories of 35—38
See also Managers; Managing
Management by objectives (MBO) 174, 315—319
Management information systems (MIS) 476
"Managerialism" 33
Managers
coordination by 217—230
decision making by 501—502, 513—514
mobility of 3
motivation by 410—417
overview of 3
performance appraisal of 304—320
as planners 70—71
recruitment of 332—336
selection of 332—336
sensitivity of 534
skills of 10—11
social background of 3
social responsibility of 545—550
training of 336—344
See also Executives; Management; Managing
Managing
by authority 167—188
contingency approach to 6—7
defined 2
described 8—9
of external relationships 228
functions of 2
history of 20—34

Managing (cont.)
human values in 8
modern methods of 35–48
of organizational effectiveness 538–552
overview of 1–16
process of 9–11
purpose of 14–15
responsibility of 8–9
systems approach to 3–6
See also Management; Managers
Manuals, organization 213–216
March, James G. 222, 510
Marketing decentralization 184
Maslow, Abraham H. 388, 406, 408
Materials budget 466–467
Matheson, James E. 113
Matrix forecasting 85–86
Matrix organization 260–266
"Maximization criteria" 54
Maximizing 503–504, 507
Mayo, Elton 30
MBO (management by objectives) 174, 315–319
Mechanistic organizations 256, 445
Media, communications 527
Mental revolution 26–27
Mergers 228
Merit compensation 317–318
Methods, relationship to policies and procedures 65–66
Middle age 321–322
Miles, R. E. 448
Milestone chart 104–107
Miller, Donald 114
Minimax 507
MIS (management information systems) 476
Mitchell, J. E. 113
Models, use in operations research 517–518
Monetary policy 82
Mooney, James D. 169, 170, 219

Morale 422–425
components of 422
contingencies 423–424
decentralization and 182
productivity and 424–425
satisfaction and 422–425
Moses 131
Motivating *see* Influencing
Motivation 404–416
choice process 409
classification of 406–409
leadership process 410–417
models of 405–409
satisfactions and 406–409
Mott, Paul E. 539

N–O

Napoleon 22–23
National Industrial Conference Board 89, 90
Neale, Gary L. 113
Needs, human 388–390, 406
Nisbet, Robert 376
Nonstandardized positions 289–290
Norms 392
NTL Institute 328, 329
Objectives 51–67
balancing 59
changing 59–60
implementing 60–67
management by (MBO) 174, 315–319
of managers 52–54
model for examining 52–55
operational 58
organizational design and 255
profit 56–57
research on 52–54
social responsibility and 56–57
strategy for 55–58
Observation assignments 340
Obsolescence, executive 322–323
OD (organizational development) 427–428
Odiorne, George S. 315

Oil embargo 45–46
***Onward Industry!* (Mooney and Reiley)** 170
Open systems 4
Operating budget 464–466
Operations research 43–44, 515–519
defined 43
described 43–44
game theory and 518
linear programming and 519
mathematical models for 517–518
methods of 515–516
probability theory and 518
queuing theory and 518
techniques of 518–519
uses of 44
Oral communication 528
Organic organizations 256, 445
Organization
budgets and 472
change in 421
climate of 417–422
complex 2, 40–41
complexity of 543–544
decision making by 513–514
design of 252–268, 542–543
effectiveness of 14, 538–552
formal 128
interacting 2
interdependence in 41
levels 132–134
mechanistic 256
organic 256, 445
overview of 1–2
rationality in 9
relationships in 134–135
structure of 152–166
systems view of 3–6
theory 31–32
variables in 6–7
Organizational development (OD) 427–428
Organization charts 206–213
advantages of 207
circular 211–212
horizontal 210–211
responsibility for 207–208
types of 208–213
vertical 208–211
Organization manuals 213–216
Organizing 127–279
by authority 139–150, 167–188
cases on 270–279
committees and 238–251
coordinating and 217–230
departmentalization and 152–166
introduction to 130–151
line and staff 189–204
as management function 12
problems with traditional methods of 231–237
span of management and 130–139
Originated policy 61–62
Orwell, George 71
Out-organization development programs 328–331
Outputs, in systems theory 4
Outside consultants 545
Overall performance control 476–488

P

***Papers in the Science of Administration* (Gulick and Urwick)** 32, 169
Participation by employees 426–427
Patton, Arch 346–348
Patz, Alan L. 307
Pawelski, Erwin 521–522
Pay *see* Compensation
Peabody, Robert L. 146, 373
Pension plans 349, 353–355
People
adult life cycle of 321–322
attitudes of 385–388
cosmopolitan 257–258
local 258
needs of 388–390
as organizational design factor 257–258

People (cont.)
perception by 380–385
values of 385–388
Perception 380–385
group effect 394–395
halo effect 384
perceptual defense 384–385
of reality 380–383
stereotyping in 383–384
Performance
checking on 456–457
control of 476–488
criteria for 539–540
measuring 304–320, 538–545
Performance appraisal
assessment center approach to 312
difficulties in 311–312
MBO approach to 315–319
process of 307–310
system of 304–307
Periodic budgeting 469
Perquisites, executive 355
Personal authority 148, 373
Personnel
budget for 467
decentralization in 186
executive program for 285–286
movement of, as strategy 228
staff 195, 197–198
staffing and 282
See also Staffing
PERT 103–110
bar charts 106–107
critical path 109–110
limitations of 108
network design 109–110
network development 104–108
uses of 109
Physical environment 47–48
Physical standards 454
Piecework system 25
Planning 49–126
action phase of 96–115
budgeting and 471–472
cases on 118–126
characteristics of 71–72, 74
controlling and 70
coordination of 225
definition of 49
dissemination of 74–75
for executive needs 292–303
forecasting and 77–95
the good plan 74
hints on 112–114
information for 77–95
as intellectual process 69
limitations of 110–112
long-range 73–74, 97–100
as management function 12
by managers 70–71
nature of 68–76
objectives and 51–60
participation in 71
period of 72–73
by PERT 103–110
policies 60–64
procedures 64–66
short-range 74, 101–103
steps in 99
strategy and 97–103
Planning premises 79–93
controllable 80
external 81–88
government policies' effect on 81–83
internal 88–93
noncontrollable 80–81
sales forecasts as 88–93
semicontrollable 80
Planning-Programming-Budgeting System (PPBS) 473
Platt, John 8
Plural executive committee 239
Policies 60–65
appealed 62
communication of 62–63
formulation of 61–62
implied 63
imposed 62
originated 61
relationship of to procedure 64–65
review of 63–64

written 62–63
Political activity, as management strategy 228
Political rationality 9
Population trends 83–84
Position
as communication barrier 529–530
See also Authority
Positional authority 147, 373
Position descriptions 297–298
Power
authority and 375–377
influencing by 374–377
Powers, James T. 483
PPBS 473
Prediction systems 509–510.
See also Forecasting
Prepotency 406
Presupervisory work 338–339
Price, James L. 450
Principle of unity of action 31
Principles approach 35–36
Pro forma statements 102
Probability 505–507
Probability theory 518
Problem solving, small-group 396–397
Procedures 64–66
Process departmentalization 163
Product departmentalization 158–161, 173
Production
budget for 466
decentralization 183
and morale 424–425
Profit, as business objective 54, 56–57
Profitability 54
Profit-and-loss control 479–482
Profit center 185–186
Profit sharing 349, 353
Program Evaluation and Review Technique see PERT
Programming, linear 519

Progression systems 324–325
Promotion from within 286–287
Pronsky, John 357
Psychology, and management theory 42–43
Public policy, and recruitment 333–334
Purchasing decentralization 186

Q–R
Quantitative methods 43–44
Queuing theory 518
Rand Corporation 85
Rationality
in decision theory 512–513
of management 9
Reality, perception of 380–385
Receiver, in communicating 523, 535
Recruitment 332–336
Regulation, federal 228
Reiley, Alan C. 31–32, 169, 170
Relationships
informal 391–403
organizational 134–135
small-group 391–397
working 401
Replacement tables 300–302
Responsibility
accountability 175
delegation of authority and 175
divided by committees 243
executive pay and 347
social 8–9, 56–57, 545–550
Retirement plans 349, 353–355
Return on investment 480–483
Revenue forecast 101
Revenue standards 454–455
R. G. Barry Corporation 550
Risk analysis 506
Roche, Gerald R. 350
Roethlisberger, F. J. 30
Rogers, Everett M. 521–522

Rosenzweig, James E. 38
Rotation of executives 324–325, 341
Rules, defined 66
Rundell, C. A. 113

S

Sachs, Brice A. 114
Salary
for executives 346–347
See also Compensation
Sales budget 465
Sales forecasts 88–93
accuracy of 92–93
by jury of executive opinion 89
methods for 89–91
by sales force 89–90
statistical 90
time span of 91–92
by trend-and-cycle analysis 91
by users' expectations 90
Satisfaction
classifications of 406–408
morale and 422–425
small-group participation and 391–393
Satisficing 510–511
Satisfiers 407–408
Scalar chain 32, 169–172, 188
Schedules, coordination by 221–222
Schleh, Edward C. 174
Science, contributions of to management 41–44
Scientific management 24–28
Screening process 334
Sears, Roebuck Company 138–139, 353
Selection of managers 332–336
Self-audit 544
Self-coordination 220
Sellers, William 24
Semantics 530
Sender-receiver relationship 523, 535
Short-range planning 74, 101–103

Silent Spring (Carson) 47
Simon, Herbert A. 142, 220, 222, 267, 375, 510
Skills
conceptual 337
content 337
executive 299
interpersonal 337
of managers 10–11
Small groups 42, 391–397
Smith, Adam 153
Smith, George 184, 187
Social audit 548–550
Social background of managers 3
Social psychology 43
Social responsibility
arena of 546–548
as effectiveness contingency 545–550
of managers 8–9, 545–550
profit and 56–57
Societal/cultural environment 4–5
Sociology 42–43
Sohio 314
Space policy 83
Span of management 130–139
determination of 134–136
examples of 138–139
organizational levels and 132–134
wide 137–139
Specialization 153
Special projects 326
Staff 189–204
accounting 195–196
assistant-to as 201–202
authority of 192–197
committees 239
companywide service by 197–198
corporate 198–199
defined 189
divisional 198–199
evolution of 190–192
growth of 200
liaison 202

line and   197–204
personnel   195, 197–198
planning by   100
role of in contemporary organizations   190–193
See also Staffing
Staffing   281–367
cases on   360–367
as chief executive's responsibility   286
executive compensation and   345–358
executive development programs for   321–331
forecasting executive needs for   292–303
as management function   12
performance appraisal and   304–320
policies on   286–287
problems of   289–290
process described   283–290
selection of managers and   332–336
steps in   288–289
training of managers and   336–344
Stalker, G. W.   256–257
Standardization
coordination by   221
as lacking in staffing   289–290
Standards   454–455
defined   454
intangible   455
tangible   454–455
Standing committees   240
States of nature   505–507
Static environments   256
Status
as communication barrier   529–531
See also Authority
Steers, Richard M.   539–540
Steiner, George A.   100
Stereotyping   383–384
Stock options   349, 351–352
Strategy
ancient Chinese example   96–97

defined   57–58, 97
long-range   97–100
objectives and   55–58
short-range   101–103
tactics compared with   97, 98
Structure, organizational
as communication barrier   529
decentralization of   176–187
departmentalization of   152–166
Student committees   250
Subsystems, management   6
Sun Tzu   96–97
Supervision levels   134
Survey of Current Business   87
Systems
approach to management   37, 97–98
closed   4
described   3–6
and long-range planning   97–98
MBO   316–319
open   4
theory of   3–6

T

Tactics, compared with strategy   97–98
Tannenbaum, Robert   142
Task achievement   392
Task environment   4–5
Task roles   410
Taxation, and compensation   346–347, 351–355
Taylor, Frederick W.   13, 20, 24–28, 458
Tead, Ordway   219
Teague, Burton W.   353
Technical core   5–6
Technical rationality   9
Technological advancement   38
Technological displacement   148
Technological forecasting   85–86
Technology
changes caused by   38–39
defined   257
organizational design and   257
Temporary assignments   326

Temporary committees 239–240
Territorial departmentalization 161–162
Theories of management 35–38
contingency approach 37–38
systems approach 37
traditional 35–36
Theory X and Theory Y 418–420
Thompson, Paul 357
Titles, executive 214–216
Towne, Henry R. 24
Traditional management theory 35–36
Traditional structures, problems with 231–237
Training of managers 336–344
assistants-to 339–340
committee service 342
evaluation of 343
junior boards 342
learning principles and 338
objectives of 337
observation assignments 340
presupervisory work 338–339
programs for 338–343
Trait theory of leadership 410–411
Transactions 24, 26
Transfers, lateral 325–326
Trend-and-cycle analysis 91
Turnover, and return on investment 480–481

U–V
Uncertainty, in decision theory 507–511
Unity of action 31
Unity of command
functional authority and 193
principle described 170–171
Universal Oil Products 314
University training programs 329
Ure, Andrew 24

Urwick, Lyndall F. 29–32, 78, 136–138, 169, 176
User expectations 90
Values
of business management 50
in decision making 510
human 385–388
managing and 8
objectives as value premises 51
Variable costs 478
Variable expense budget 470
Variance analysis 471
Vergin, R. C. 449
Vertical coordination 222–223
Vertical division of labor 168–176
Vertical organization charts 208–211
Vroom, Victor 424–425

W–Z
Waiting-line theory 518
The Wealth of Nations (Smith) 153
Webber, Ross A. 68
Weber, Max 139, 140, 145–146, 202, 372–373
Weitzel, William 540–541
Westmoreland, William 203–204
White-collar workers 39–40
Wommack, William W. 113
Woodside, William S. 113
Woodward, Joan 36, 37
Word use 530–532
Work force
changes in 39–40
demand for executives and 293
increase in white-collar workers 39–40
See also Labor
Written communication 528
Written policy 62–63
The Year 2000 (Kahn and Wiener) 77
Zone of acceptance 143–144